Adobe® DREAMWEAVER® CS5

COMPREHENSIVE

Gary B. Shelly
Dolores J. Wells
Jennifer T. Campbell

COURSE TECHNOLOGY
CENGAGE Learning™

SHELLY
CASHMAN
SERIES®

Australia • Canada • Denmark • Japan • Mexico • New Zealand • Philippines • Puerto Rico • Singapore • South Africa • Spain • United Kingdom • United States

COURSE TECHNOLOGY
CENGAGE Learning™

Adobe® Dreamweaver® CS5 Comprehensive
Gary B. Shelly, Dolores J. Wells, Jennifer T. Campbell

Vice President, Publisher: Nicole Pinard

Executive Editor: Kathleen McMahon

Product Manager: Jon Farnham

Associate Product Manager: Aimee Poirier

Editorial Assistant: Angela Giannopoulos

Director of Marketing: Cheryl Costantini

Marketing Manager: Tristen Kendall

Marketing Coordinator: Adrienne Fung

Print Buyer: Julio Esperas

Director of Production: Patty Stephan

Content Project Manager: Matthew Hutchinson

Development Editor: Lisa Ruffolo

Copyeditor: Harry Johnson

Proofreader: Foxxe Editorial

Indexer: Rich Carlson

QA Manuscript Reviewers: Jeffrey Schwartz, Serge Palladino, Danielle Shaw, Susan Whalen

Art Director: Marissa Falco

Cover Designer: Lisa Kuhn, Curio Press, LLC

Cover Photo: Tom Kates Photography

Text Design: Joel Sadagursky

Compositor: Bill Smith Group

Adobe, the Adobe logos, and Dreamweaver are either registered trademarks or trademarks of Adobe Systems Incorporated in the United States and/or other countries. THIS PRODUCT IS NOT ENDORSED OR SPONSORED BY ADOBE SYSTEMS INCORPORATED, PUBLISHER OF DREAMWEAVER.

Library of Congress Control Number: 2010936758

ISBN-13: 978-0-538-47394-1
ISBN-10: 0-538-47394-0

Course Technology
20 Channel Center Street
Boston, MA 02210
USA

Cengage Learning is a leading provider of customized learning solutions with office locations around the globe, including Singapore, the United Kingdom, Australia, Mexico, Brazil, and Japan. Locate your local office at: **international.cengage.com/region**

Cengage Learning products are represented in Canada by Nelson Education, Ltd.

For your course and learning solutions, visit **www.cengage.com**

To learn more about Course Technology, visit **www.cengage.com/coursetechnology**

Purchase any of our products at your local college bookstore or at our preferred online store at **www.CengageBrain.com**

Printed in the United States of America
1 2 3 4 5 6 7 14 13 12 11

Adobe® DREAMWEAVER® CS5
COMPREHENSIVE

Contents

Appendices

Preface

The Shelly Cashman Series® offers the finest textbooks in computer education. We are proud of the fact that our previous Dreamweaver books have been so well received. With each new edition of our Dreamweaver books, we make significant improvements based on the software and comments made by instructors and students. For this Adobe Dreamweaver CS5 text, the Shelly Cashman Series development team carefully reviewed our pedagogy and analyzed its effectiveness in teaching today's Dreamweaver student. Students today read less, but need to retain more. They need not only to be able to perform skills, but to retain those skills and know how to apply them to different settings. Today's students need to be continually engaged and challenged to retain what they're learning.

With this Adobe Dreamweaver CS5 text, we continue our commitment to focusing on the user and how they learn best.

The Shelly Cashman Approach

A Proven Pedagogy with an Emphasis on Project Planning

Each chapter presents a practical problem to be solved, within a project planning framework. The project orientation is strengthened by the use of Plan Ahead boxes, which encourage critical thinking about how to proceed at various points in the project. Step-by-step instructions with supporting screens guide students through the steps. Instructional steps are supported by the Q&A, Experimental Step, and BTW features.

A Visually Engaging Book that Maintains Student Interest

The step-by-step tasks, with supporting figures, provide a rich visual experience for the student. Call-outs on the screens that present both explanatory and navigational information provide students with information they need when they need to know it.

Supporting Reference Materials (Appendices and Quick Reference)

The appendices provide additional information about the Application at hand and include such topics as the Help Feature and customizing the application. With the Quick Reference, students can quickly look up information about a single task, such as creating a site, and find page references of where in the book the task is illustrated.

Objectives of This Textbook

Adobe Dreamweaver CS5: Comprehensive is intended for a ten- to fifteen-week period in a course that teaches Dreamweaver CS5 as the primary component. No experience with a computer is assumed, and no mathematics beyond the high school freshman level is required. The objectives of this book are:

- To offer a comprehensive presentation of Dreamweaver CS5
- To expose students to proper Web site design and management techniques
- To acquaint students with the proper procedures to create Web sites suitable for coursework, professional purposes, and personal use
- To develop an exercise-oriented approach that allows learning by doing
- To introduce students to new input technologies
- To encourage independent study and provide help for those who are working independently

Integration of the World Wide Web

The World Wide Web is integrated into the Dreamweaver CS5 learning experience by (1) BTW annotations; (2) BTW, Q&A, and Quick Reference Summary Web pages; and (3) the Learn It Online section for each chapter.

End-of-Chapter Student Activities

Extensive end-of-chapter activities provide a variety of reinforcement opportunities for students where they can apply and expand their skills.

Instructor Resources

The Instructor Resources include both teaching and testing aids and can be accessed via CD-ROM or at **login.cengage.com**.

INSTRUCTOR'S MANUAL Includes lecture notes summarizing the chapter sections, figures and boxed elements found in every chapter, teacher tips, classroom activities, lab activities, and quick quizzes in Microsoft Word files.

SYLLABUS Easily customizable sample syllabi that cover policies, assignments, exams, and other course information.

FIGURE FILES Illustrations for every figure in the textbook in electronic form.

POWERPOINT PRESENTATIONS A multimedia lecture presentation system that provides slides for each chapter. Presentations are based on chapter objectives.

SOLUTIONS TO EXERCISES Includes solutions for all end-of-chapter and chapter reinforcement exercises.

TEST BANK & TEST ENGINE Test Banks include 112 questions for every chapter, featuring objective-based and critical thinking question types, and including page number references and figure references, when appropriate. Also included is the test engine, ExamView, the ultimate tool for your objective-based testing needs.

DATA FILES FOR STUDENTS Includes all the files that are required by students to complete the exercises.

Book Resources

- Instructor's Manual
- PowerPoint Presentations
- Solutions to Exercises (Windows)
- Syllabus
- Test Bank and Test Engine

Additional Student Files

Data Files for Students (Windows)

ADDITIONAL ACTIVITIES FOR STUDENTS Consists of Chapter Reinforcement Exercises, which are true/false, multiple-choice, and short answer questions that help students gain confidence in the material learned.

Content for Online Learning

Course Technology has partnered with the leading distance learning solution providers and class-management platforms today. To access this material, instructors will visit our password-protected instructor resources available at login.cengage.com. Instructor resources include the test banks in Blackboard- and Web CT-compatible formats. For additional information or for an instructor user name and password, please contact your sales representative.

CourseNotes

Course Technology's CourseNotes are six-panel quick reference cards that reinforce the most important and widely used features of a software application in a visual and user-friendly format. CourseNotes serve as a great

reference tool during and after the student completes the course. CourseNotes are available for software applications such as Adobe Dreamweaver CS5, Photoshop CS5, Microsoft Office 2010, and Windows 7. Topic-based CourseNotes are available for Best Practices in Social Networking, Hot Topics in Technology, and Web 2.0. Visit www. cengagebrain.com to learn more!

A Guided Tour

Add excitement and interactivity to your classroom with "*A Guided Tour*" product line. Play one of the brief mini-movies to spice up your lecture and spark classroom discussion. Or, assign a movie for homework and ask students to complete the correlated assignment that accompanies each topic. "*A Guided Tour*" product line takes the prep work out of providing your students with information about new technologies and applications and helps keep students engaged with content relevant to their lives; all in under an hour!

About Our Covers

The Shelly Cashman Series is continually updating our approach and content to reflect the way today's students learn and experience new technology. This focus on student success is reflected on our covers, which feature real students from Bryant University using the Shelly Cashman Series in their courses, and reflect the varied ages and backgrounds of the students learning with our books. When you use the Shelly Cashman Series, you can be assured that you are learning computer skills using the most effective courseware available.

Textbook Walk-Through

The Shelly Cashman Series Pedagogy: Project-Based — Step-by-Step — Variety of Assessments

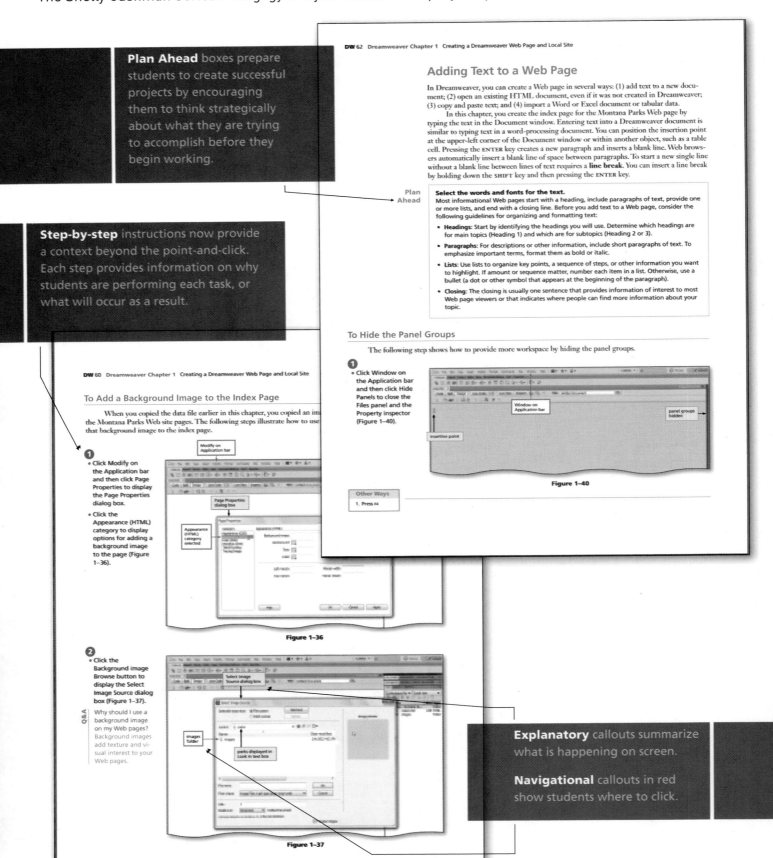

Plan Ahead boxes prepare students to create successful projects by encouraging them to think strategically about what they are trying to accomplish before they begin working.

Step-by-step instructions now provide a context beyond the point-and-click. Each step provides information on why students are performing each task, or what will occur as a result.

Explanatory callouts summarize what is happening on screen.

Navigational callouts in red show students where to click.

DW 62 Dreamweaver Chapter 1 Creating a Dreamweaver Web Page and Local Site

Adding Text to a Web Page

In Dreamweaver, you can create a Web page in several ways: (1) add text to a new document; (2) open an existing HTML document, even if it was not created in Dreamweaver; (3) copy and paste text; and (4) import a Word or Excel document or tabular data.

In this chapter, you create the index page for the Montana Parks Web page by typing the text in the Document window. Entering text into a Dreamweaver document is similar to typing text in a word-processing document. You can position the insertion point at the upper-left corner of the Document window or within another object, such as a table cell. Pressing the ENTER key creates a new paragraph and inserts a blank line. Web browsers automatically insert a blank line of space between paragraphs. To start a new single line without a blank line between lines of text requires a **line break**. You can insert a line break by holding down the SHIFT key and then pressing the ENTER key.

Plan Ahead

Select the words and fonts for the text.
Most informational Web pages start with a heading, include paragraphs of text, provide one or more lists, and end with a closing line. Before you add text to a Web page, consider the following guidelines for organizing and formatting text:

- **Headings:** Start by identifying the headings you will use. Determine which headings are for main topics (Heading 1) and which are for subtopics (Heading 2 or 3).
- **Paragraphs:** For descriptions or other information, include short paragraphs of text. To emphasize important terms, format them as bold or italic.
- **Lists:** Use lists to organize key points, a sequence of steps, or other information you want to highlight. If amount or sequence matter, number each item in a list. Otherwise, use a bullet (a dot or other symbol that appears at the beginning of the paragraph).
- **Closing:** The closing is usually one sentence that provides information of interest to most Web page viewers or that indicates where people can find more information about your topic.

To Hide the Panel Groups

The following step shows how to provide more workspace by hiding the panel groups.

1
- Click Window on the Application bar and then click Hide Panels to close the Files panel and the Property inspector (Figure 1–40).

Window on Application bar

panel groups hidden

insertion point

Figure 1–40

Other Ways
1. Press F4

DW 60 Dreamweaver Chapter 1 Creating a Dreamweaver Web Page and Local Site

To Add a Background Image to the Index Page

When you copied the data file earlier in this chapter, you copied an image the Montana Parks Web site pages. The following steps illustrate how to use that background image to the index page.

1
- Click Modify on the Application bar and then click Page Properties to display the Page Properties dialog box.
- Click the Appearance (HTML) category to display options for adding a background image to the page (Figure 1–36).

Modify on Application bar

Page Properties dialog box

Appearance (HTML) category selected

Figure 1–36

2
- Click the Background image Browse button to display the Select Image Source dialog box (Figure 1–37).

Q&A
Why should I use a background image on my Web pages? Background images add texture and visual interest to your Web pages.

Select Image Source dialog box

images folder

parks displayed in (Look in text box)

Figure 1–37

Textbook Walk-Through

Q&A boxes offer questions students may have when working through the steps and provide additional information about what they are doing right where they need it.

Experiment Steps within our step-by-step instructions, encourage students to explore, experiment, and take advantage of the features of the Dreamweaver CS5 user interface. These steps are not necessary to complete the projects, but are designed to increase the confidence with the software and build problem-solving skills.

DW 48 Dreamweaver Chapter 1 Creating a Dreamweaver Web Page and Local Site

3

- Type `Montana Parks` in the Site name text box to name the site (Figure 1–15).

Q&A Is the site name necessary?
This name is required, but it is for reference only. It is not part of the path and is not visible to viewers of your site.

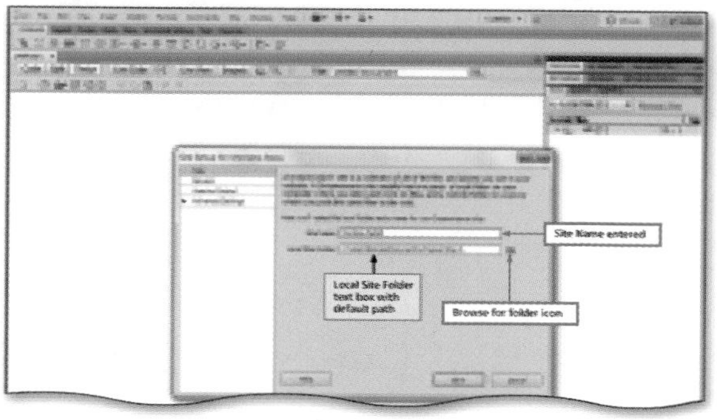

Figure 1–15

4

- Click the Browse for folder icon to display the Choose Root Folder dialog box.
- Navigate to where you will store your Web site files (Figure 1–16).

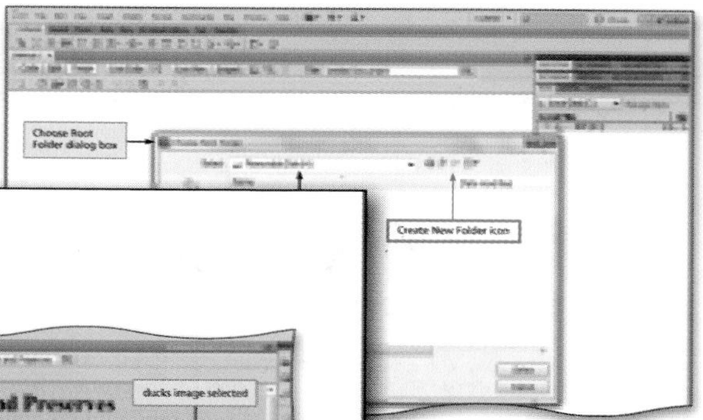

-16

instructor to
e. Other options

letter from
at the device

DW 144 Dreamweaver Chapter 2 Adding Web Pages, Links, and Images

4

- Click the Brightness and Contrast tool in the Property inspector to display the Brightness/Contrast dialog box (Figure 2–53).

Q&A What should I do if a Dreamweaver dialog box is displayed warning that adjusting the brightness and contrast permanently alters the image?
Click the 'Don't show me this message again' check box, and then click the OK button.

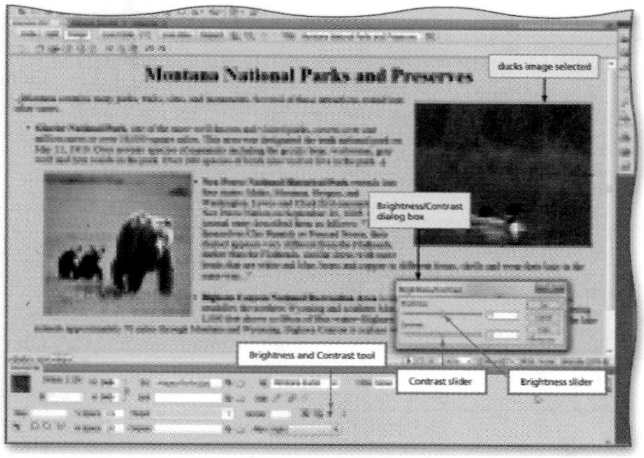

Figure 2–53

5

Experiment

- Drag the Brightness slider and the Contrast slider so you can see how changing the value of each affects the ducks image.
- Drag the Brightness slider to the left and adjust the setting to −10 to change the brightness level.
- Drag the Contrast slider to the right and adjust the setting to 20 to change the contrast level (Figure 2–54).

Q&A What are the ranges for the Brightness and Contrast settings?
The values for the Brightness and Contrast settings range from −100 to 100.

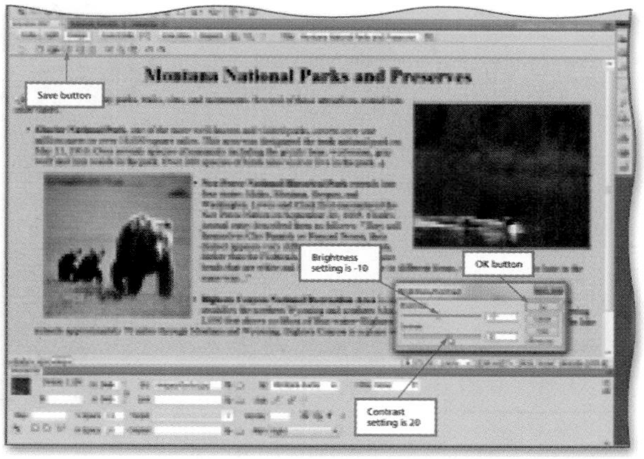

Figure 2–54

Chapter Summary A concluding paragraph, followed by a listing of the tasks completed within a chapter together with the pages on which the step-by-step, screen-by-screen explanations appear.

Quick Reference
For a table that lists how to complete tasks covered in this book using the keyboard, see the Quick Reference at the end of this book.

Quitting Dreamweaver

After you add pages to your Web site, including images and links, and then view your pages in a browser, Chapter 2 is complete.

To Close the Web Site and Quit Dreamweaver

The following steps show how to close the Web site, quit Dreamweaver, and return control to Windows.

1 Click the Close button on the right corner of the Dreamweaver title bar to close the Dreamweaver window, the Document window, and the Montana Parks Web site.

2 Click the Yes button if a prompt is displayed indicating that you need to save changes.

Chapter Summary

Chapter 2 introduced you to images and links, and discussed how to view source code and use Live view. You began the chapter by copying data files to the local site. You added two new pages, one for Lewis and Clark National Historical Trail and one for Montana National Parks and Preserves, to the Web site you started in Chapter 1. Next, you added images to the index page. Following that, you added a background image and page images to the two new pages. Then, you added relative links to all three pages. You added an e-mail link to the index page and absolute links to the Montana National Parks and Preserves and Lewis and Clark National Historical Trail pages. Finally, you learned how to view source code. The items listed below include all the new Dreamweaver skills you have

Preserves
storical
urn on

le (DW 123)
W 124)

l Space

est of an

11. Add Text for Relative Links (DW 147)
12. Create a Relative Link Using Point to File (DW 148)
13. Create a Relative Link Using the Context Menu (DW 150)
14. Create a Relative Link to the Home Page (DW 153)
15. Create Absolute Links (DW 155)
16. Add an E-Mail Link (DW 156)
17. Use Design View and Code View Simultaneously (DW 160)
18. Use Live View (DW 161)

Learn It Online

Test your knowledge of chapter content and key terms.

Instructions: To complete the Learn It Online exercises, start your browser, click the Address bar, and then enter the Web address **scsite.com/dwCS5/learn**. When the Dreamweaver CS5 Learn It Online page is displayed, click the link for the exercise you want to complete and then read the instructions.

Chapter Reinforcement TF, MC, and SA
A series of true/false, multiple choice, and short answer questions that test your knowledge of the chapter content.

Flash Cards
An interactive learning environment where you identify chapter key terms associated with displayed definitions.

Practice Test
A series of multiple choice questions that test your knowledge of chapter content and key terms.

Who Wants To Be a Computer Genius?
An interactive game that challenges your knowledge of chapter content in the style of a television quiz show.

Wheel of Terms
An interactive game that challenges your knowledge of chapter key terms in the style of the television show *Wheel of Fortune*.

Crossword Puzzle Challenge
A crossword puzzle that challenges your knowledge of key terms presented in the chapter.

Apply Your Knowledge

Reinforce the skills and apply the concepts you learned in this chapter.

Adding Text and Formatting a Web Page
Instructions: In this activity, you modify a Web page by adding a background image, changing the heading style, adding bullets, and centering text (Figure 1–69 on the next page). To use Dreamweaver effectively, it is necessary to create a new site for the Apply Your Knowledge exercises in this book. Make sure you have downloaded the data files for Chapter01\apply, which are available in the Data Files for Students folder. See the inside back cover of this book for instructions on downloading the Data Files for Students, or contact your instructor for information about accessing the required files.

Learn it Online Every chapter features a Learn It Online section that is comprised of six exercises. These exercises include True/False, Multiple Choice, Short Answer, Flash Cards, Practice Test, and Learning Games.

Apply Your Knowledge This exercise usually requires students to open and manipulate a file from the Data Files that parallels the activities learned in the chapter. To obtain a copy of the Data Files for Students, follow the instructions on the inside back cover of this text.

Textbook Walk-Through

Extend Your Knowledge

Extend the skills you learned in this chapter and experiment with new skills. You may need to use Help to complete the assignment.

Adding Text and Formatting a Web Page

Instructions: In this activity, you modify a Web page by adding a background image, inserting line breaks, and centering text (Figure 1–70). To use Dreamweaver effectively, it is necessary to create a new site for the Extend Your Knowledge exercises in this book. Make sure you have downloaded the data files for Chapter01\extend, which are available in the Data Files for Students folder. See the inside back cover of this book for instructions on downloading the Data Files for Students, or contact your instructor for information about accessing the required files.

Figure 1–70

Perform the following tasks:

1. Start Dreamweaver. Use the Site Setup dialog box to define a local site. Enter **Extend Exercises** as the name of the new site.
2. Using the Browse for folder icon next to the Local Site Folder text box, in the *your name* folder. Enter **extend** as the name of the subfolder. select it as the local site folder.
3. In the Advanced Settings category of the Site Setup for Extend Exercises, Browse for folder icon next to the Default Images folder text box. In the folder named images. Open the images folder, and then select it as the
4. Make sure the path in the Default Images folder text box ends with *your* Click the Site category and make sure the path in the Local site folder *name*\extend. Click the Save button in the Site Setup for Extend Exercises settings for the new site.
5. Using Windows Explorer or the Windows Computer tool, copy the ex Chapter01\extend folder into the *your name*\extend folder for the Exten the extend_bkg.jpg from the Chapter01\extend\images data files folder images folder for the Extend Exercises Web site.

Extend Your Knowledge projects at the end of each chapter allow students to extend and expand on the skills learned within the chapter. Students use critical thinking to experiment with new skills to complete each project.

---

6. Open the extend.htm page. If necessary, expand the Property inspector. Verify that the HTML button on the left side of the Property inspector is selected.
7. Click the Page Properties button in the Property inspector and apply the extend_bkg background image to the Web page.
8. Type your name and the current date where indicated.
9. Apply the Heading 2 style to the first three lines.
10. On the Format menu, use the Underline command on the Style submenu to underline the third line.
11. Select the next four lines containing the names of flowers and bullet the text. Press SHIFT+ENTER at the end of the first bulleted item, and then press SHIFT+ENTER again to insert a blank, unbulleted line. Do the same to insert a blank line between each of the remaining bulleted items.
12. Center all of the text. Bold the bulleted list, your name, and the date.
13. Enter **Mary's Flower Shoppe** as the title of the document.
14. Save your document and then view it in your browser, comparing your Web page to Figure 1–70. Submit your work in the format specified by your instructor.

Make It Right

In this activity, you analyze a Web page, correct all errors, and/or improve the design.

Adding Text and Formatting a Web Page

Instructions: In this activity, you modify an existing Web page by formatting and adjusting text and adding data (Figure 1–71). To use Dreamweaver effectively, it is necessary to create a new site for the Make It Right exercises in this book. Make sure you have downloaded the data files for Chapter01\ right, which are available in the Data Files for Students folder. See the inside back cover of this book for instructions on downloading the Data Files for Students, or contact your instructor for information about accessing the required files.

Figure 1–71

Make It Right projects call on students to analyze a file, discover errors in it, and fix them using the skills they learned in the chapter.

In the Lab

Create a document using the guidelines, concepts, and skills presented in this chapter. Labs are listed in order of increasing difficulty.

Lab 1: Modifying the Computer Repair Services Web Site

Problem: Now that Bryan has a basic Web page for his Computer Repair Services Web site, he wants to make the page more appealing to visitors. He asks you to help him add images of computers to his Web page.

Image files for the Bryan's Computer Repair Services Web site are included with the data files. See the inside back cover of this book for instructions for downloading the data files or see your instructor for information on accessing the files in this book.

You need to add two new pages to the Bryan's Computer Repair Services Web site: a services page and a references page. In this exercise, you will add relative and absolute links to each page. You also will add a background image to the new pages. Next, you will insert images on all three pages and use the settings in Table 2–4 to align the images and enter the alternate text. You then will add an e-mail link to the home page and relative links from the two new pages to the home page. The pages for the Web site are shown in Figures 2–77a, 2–77b, and 2–77c. (Software and hardware settings determine how a Web page is displayed in a browser. Your Web pages may be displayed differently in your browser from the pages shown in the figures.)

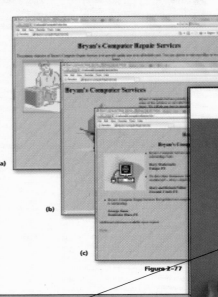

(a)

(b)

(c)

Figure 2–77

In the Lab Three all new in-depth assignments per chapter require students to utilize the chapter concepts and techniques to solve problems on a computer.

---

12. Create an absolute link from the Fair Credit Billing Act text in the answer to question 3. In this link, use the following as the URL: http://www.ftc.gov/bcp/edu/pubs/consumer/credit/cre16.shtm. Save the questions page (Figure 2–79c).

13. View the Web site in your browser and verify that your external and relative links work. *Hint:* Remember to check the link for the image on the theft.htm page. Submit the documents in the format specified by your instructor.

Cases and Places

Apply your creative thinking and problem solving skills to design and implement a solution.

● EASIER ●●MORE DIFFICULT

● 1: Modify the Favorite Sports Web Site

In Chapter 1, you created a Web site named Favorite Sports with a Web page listing your favorite sports and teams. Now, you want to add another page to the site. Create and format the new page, which should include general information about a selected sport. Create a relative link from the home page to the new page and from the new page to the home page. Add a background image to the new page and insert an image on one of the pages. Include an appropriate title for the page. Save the page in the sports subfolder. For a selection of images and backgrounds, visit the Dreamweaver CS5 Media Web page (scsite.com/dwcs5/media).

● 2: Modify the Hobbies Web Site

Several of your friends were impressed with the Web page and Web site you created about your favorite hobby in Chapter 1. They have given you some topics they think you should include on the site. You decide to create an additional page that will consist of details about your hobby and the topics your friends suggested. Format the page. Add an absolute link to a related Web site and a relative link from the home page to the new page and from the new page to the home page. Add a background image to the new page. Create an e-mail link on the index page. Title the page with the name of the selected hobby. Save the page in the hobby subfolder. For a selection of images and backgrounds, visit the Dreamweaver CS5 Media Web page (scsite.com/dwcs5/media).

●● 3: Modify the Politics Web Site

In Chapter 1, you created a Web site and a Web page to publicize your campaign for public office. Develop two additional pages to add to the site. Apply a background image to the new pages. Apply appropriate formatting to the two new pages. Scan a picture of yourself or take a picture with a digital camera and include the picture on the index page. Add a second image illustrating one of your campaign promises. Include at least two images on one of the new pages and one image on the other new page. Add alternate text for all images, and then add appropriate H Space and V Space property features to position the images. Create e-mail links on all three pages and create relative links from the home page to both pages and from each of the pages to the home page. Create an absolute link to a related site on one of the pages. Give each page a meaningful title and then save the pages in the government subfolder. For a selection of images and backgrounds, visit the Dreamweaver CS5 Media Web page (scsite.com/dwcs5/media).

Cases & Places exercises call on students to create open-ended projects that reflect academic, personal, and business settings.

Web Site Development and Adobe Dreamweaver CS5

Objectives

You will have mastered the material in this chapter when you can:

- Describe the Internet, the Web, and their associated terms

- Specify the difference between a Web page and a Web site

- Define Web browsers and identify their main features

- Identify the 13 types of Web sites

- Discuss how to plan, design, develop, test, publish, and maintain a Web site

- Identify the methods and tools for creating a Web page and Web site

- Recognize the basic elements within HTML/XHTML

- Discuss the advantages of using Web page authoring programs such as Dreamweaver

Web Site Development and Adobe Dreamweaver CS5

The Internet

The **Internet**, sometimes simply called the **Net**, is a global network connecting millions of computers. Within this network, a user who has permission at any one computer can access and obtain information from any other computer within the network. A **network** is a group of computers and associated devices that are connected by communications facilities. A network can span a global area and involve permanent connections, such as cables, or temporary connections made through telephone or other communications links. Local, regional, national, and international networks constitute a global network. Each of these networks provides communications, services, and access to information.

No one person or organization is responsible for the birth of the Internet. Its origin, however, can be traced to the early 1960s when the Advanced Research Projects Agency (ARPA), working under the U.S. Department of Defense, began a networking project. The purpose of the project was to create a network that would allow scientists at different locations to share military and scientific information. Today, the Internet is a public, cooperative, and self-sustaining facility that hundreds of millions of people worldwide access.

The World Wide Web and Web Browsers

The World Wide Web (WWW), also called the Web, is one of the more popular services on the Internet. The Web consists of a system of global network servers, also known as Web servers, that support specially formatted documents and provide a means for sharing these resources with many people at the same time. A network server is known as the host computer, and your computer, from which you access the information, is called the client. Hypertext Transfer Protocol (HTTP) enables the transfer of data from the host computer to the client.

Accessing the Web

Users access Web resources, such as text, graphics, sound, video, and multimedia, through a Web page. A unique address, or Uniform Resource Locator (URL), identifies every Web page. The URL provides the global address of the location of the Web page. URLs are discussed later in this Introduction. Viewing data contained on a Web page requires a Web browser, a software program that requests a Web page, interprets the code contained within the page, and then displays the contents of the Web page on your computer display device.

Web Browsers

Web browsers contain special buttons and other features to help you navigate through Web sites. The more popular Web browser programs are **Microsoft Internet Explorer, Mozilla Firefox, Google Chrome, Safari,** and **Opera**. This book uses Internet Explorer as the primary browser. When you start Internet Explorer, it opens a Web page that has been set as the start, or home, page (Figure I–1). Using the browser's Tools menu, the user can designate any page on the Web as the home page or start with a blank page. Important features of Internet Explorer are summarized in Table I–1.

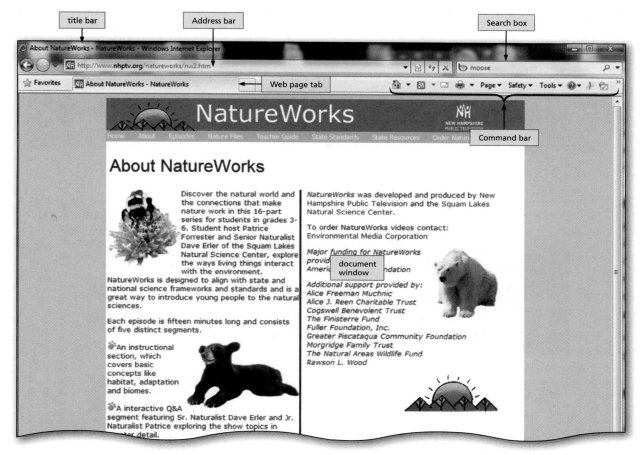

Figure I–1

Table I–1 Internet Explorer Features

Feature	Definition
Title bar	Displays the name of the Web page you are viewing
Search box	Allows Web searches using your favorite search provider
Command bar	Contains buttons, boxes, and menus that allow you to perform tasks quickly
Address bar	Displays the Web site address, or URL, of the Web page you are viewing
Document window	Contains the Web page content
Web page tab	Provides the option to use tabs to switch from one site to another in a single browser window

Nearly all Web pages have unique characteristics, but most share the same basic elements. On most Web pages, you will find headings or titles, text, pictures or images, background enhancements, and hyperlinks. A **hyperlink**, or **link**, can connect to another place in the same Web page or site — or to an entirely different Web page on a server in another city or country. Normally, you click the hyperlink to follow the connected pathway. Figure I–2 contains a variety of link types. Clicking a link causes the Web page associated with the link to be displayed in a browser window. Linked pages can appear in the same browser window, in a new tab, or in a separate browser window, depending on the HTML or XHTML code associated with the link. HTML and XHTML are discussed later in this Introduction.

Figure I–2

Most Web pages are part of a **Web site**, which is a group of related Web pages that are linked together. Most Web sites contain a home page, which generally is the first Web page visitors see when they enter the site. A **home page** (also called an **index page**) typically provides information about the Web site's purpose and content. Most Web sites also contain additional content and pages. An individual, a company, or an organization owns and manages each Web site.

Accessing the Web requires a connection through a regional or national Internet service provider (ISP), an online service provider (OSP), or a wireless service provider (WSP). Figure I–3 illustrates ways to access the Internet using these service providers.

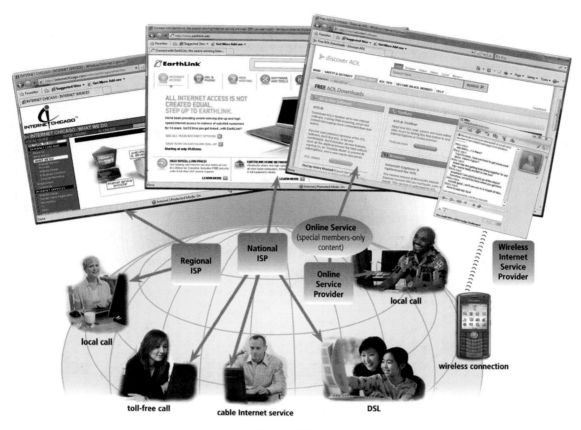

Figure I–3

An **Internet service provider** (**ISP**) provides temporary connections to individuals or businesses through its permanent Internet connection. Similar to an ISP, an **online service provider** (**OSP**) provides additional member-only services such as financial data and travel information. America Online and CompuServe are examples of OSPs. A **wireless service provider** (**WSP**) provides Internet access to users with Web-enabled devices or wireless modems. Generally, all of these providers charge a fee for their services.

Types of Web Sites

Web sites are classified as 13 basic types: portal, news, informational, business/marketing, blog, wiki, social networks, educational, entertainment, advocacy, Web application, content aggregator, and personal, all shown in Figure I-4 on the next page. A **portal** Web site (Figure I–4a) provides a variety of Internet services from a single, convenient location. Most portals offer free services such as search engines; local, national, and worldwide news; sports; weather; reference tools; maps; stock quotes; newsgroups; chat rooms; and calendars. A **news** Web site (Figure I–4b) contains news articles relating to current events. An **informational** Web site (Figure I–4c) contains factual information, such as research and statistics. Governmental agencies and nonprofit organizations are the primary providers of informational Web pages. A **business/marketing** Web site (Figure I–4d) contains content that promotes or sells products or services. A **blog** (Figure I–4e), short for Weblog, uses a regularly updated journal format to reflect the interests, opinions, and personality of the author and sometimes of site visitors. A **wiki** (Figure I–4f) is a collaborative Web site that allows users to create, add to, modify, or delete the Web site content via their Web browser. Most wikis are open to modification by the general public. An **online social network** (Figure I–4g) is an online community that encourages members to share their interests, stories, photos, music, and videos with other members.

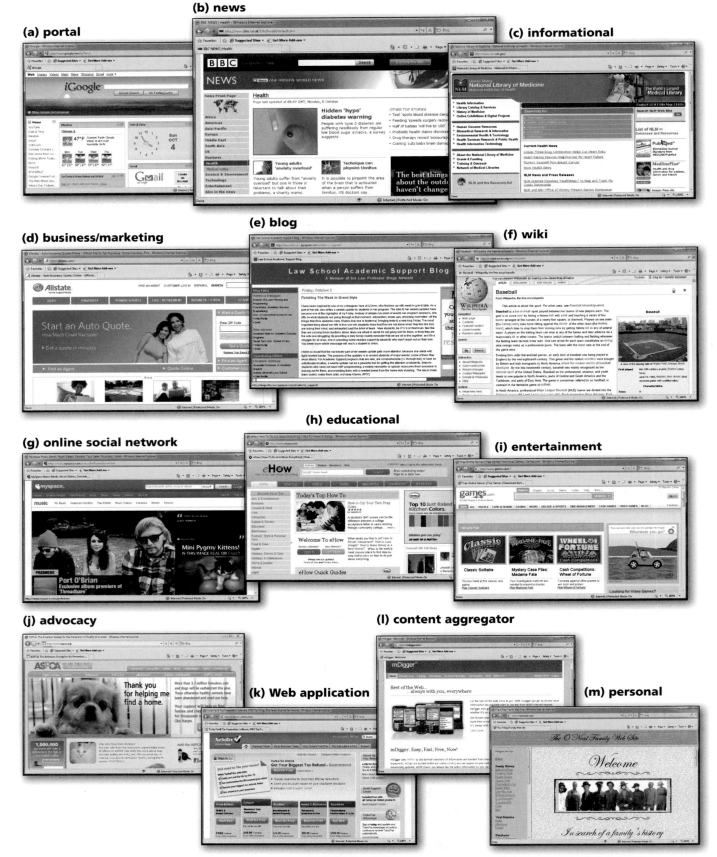

Figure I–4

An **educational** Web site (Figure I–4h) provides exciting, challenging avenues for formal and informal teaching and learning. An **entertainment** Web site (Figure I–4i) offers an interactive and engaging environment and contains music, video, sports, games, and other similar features. Within an **advocacy** Web site (Figure I–4j), you will find content that describes a cause, opinion, question, or idea. A **Web application** (Figure I-4k) uses a browser that allows users to access and interact with software that is connected to the Internet. A **content aggregator** (Figure I–4l) is a business that gathers and organizes Web content and then distributes the content to subscribers free or for a fee. **RSS** 2.0 (**Really Simple Syndication**) is used to distribute content to subscribers. A **personal** Web site (Figure I–4m) is published by an individual or family and generally is not associated with any organization. As you progress through this book, you will have an opportunity to learn more about different types of Web pages.

Planning a Web Site

Thousands of individuals create and publish Web pages every day, some using word processing software or markup languages, such as HTML and XHTML, to create their pages. Others use professional design and management editors such as Dreamweaver. Although publishing a Web page or a Web site is easy, advanced planning is paramount in ensuring a successful Web site. Publishing a Web site, which makes it available on the Internet, is discussed later in this Introduction.

Planning Basics — Purpose

Those who rush into the publishing process without proper planning tend to design Web sites that are unorganized and difficult to navigate. Visitors to this type of Web site often lose interest quickly and do not return. As you begin planning your Web site, consider the following guidelines to ensure that you set and attain realistic goals.

Purpose and Goal Determine the purpose and goal of your Web site. Create a focus by developing a purpose statement, which communicates the intention of the Web site. Consider the 13 basic types of Web sites mentioned previously. Will your Web site consist of just one basic type or a combination of two or more types?

Target Audience Identify your audience. The people who visit your Web site will determine the success of your site. Although you welcome all visitors, you need to know as much as possible about the primary group of people you wish to reach — your target audience. To learn more about the visitors to your Web site, determine whether you want to attract people with similar interests, and consider the gender, education, age range, income, profession/job field, and computer proficiency of your target audience.

Web Technologies Evaluate whether your potential visitors have access to high-speed broadband media or to baseband media, and use this information to determine what elements to include in your Web site. **Broadband** can transmit many moving images or a vast quantity of data at a high speed. Media and hardware such as **T1 lines, DSL (digital subscriber lines), ISDN (Integrated Services Digital Network), fiber optics**, and **cable modems** work with broadband. **Baseband** transmits one signal at a time over a telephone line and includes media and hardware such as 56K modems. Baseband works well with a Web site composed mostly of text and small images. Web sites that contain many images or multimedia, such as video and animations, generally require broadband connections. Increasingly, people are using **mobile Web technologies** to access the Internet using a smartphone or other handheld device connected to a wireless network.

Web Site Comparison   Visit other Web sites that are similar to your proposed site. What do you like about these sites? What do you dislike? Look for inspirational ideas. How can you make your Web site better?

Planning Basics — Content

To ensure a successful Web experience for your visitors, consider the following guidelines to provide appropriate content and other valuable Web page elements.

Value-added Content   Consider the different types of content you can include within your Web site. Use the following questions as guidelines:

- What topics or concepts do you want to cover?
- How much information will you present about each topic and how will you present it?
- What will attract your target audience to your Web site?
- What methods will you use to keep your audience returning to your site?
- What changes will you have to make to keep your site updated?

Text   Text accounts for the bulk of content on most Web pages, so be brief and incorporate lists whenever possible. Statistical studies indicate that most people tend to scan the page, picking out individual words and sentences. Use common words and simple language, and check your spelling and grammar. Create your textual content to accomplish your goals effectively by highlighting key words, using bulleted lists, maintaining one idea per paragraph, and including meaningful subheadings.

Images   After text, images constitute the next most commonly included content. Ask yourself these questions with respect to your use of images:

- Will you have a common logo or theme on all of your Web pages?
- Are these images readily available?
- What images will you have to locate?
- What images will you have to create?
- How many images per page will you have?

Color Palette   The color palette you select for your Web site can enhance or detract from your message or goal. Instead of thinking in terms of your favorite colors, consider how color can support your goal. Ask yourself the following questions:

- Do your selected colors work well with your goal?
- Did you use a color palette generator to select a well-balanced set of colors?
- Did you limit the number of colors to a selected few?

Multimedia   Multimedia adds interactivity and action to your Web pages. Animation, audio, and video are types of **multimedia**. If you plan to add multimedia, determine whether the visitor will require plug-ins. A **plug-in** extends the capability of a Web browser. Some of the more commonly used plug-ins are Shockwave Player, Adobe Flash, and Windows Media Player. Most plug-ins are free and can be downloaded from the Web.

Web Site Navigation

Predicting how a visitor will access a Web site or at what point the visitor will enter the Web site structure is not possible. The importance of a navigation structure, however, cannot be overemphasized. Visitors can arrive at any page within a Web site by a variety of ways: a hyperlink, a search engine, a directory, typing a Web address directly, and so on. On every page of your Web site, you must provide clear answers to the three basic questions your visitors will ask: Where am I? Where do I go from here? How do I get to the home page? A well-organized Web site provides the answers to these questions. Once the visitor arrives at a Web site, **navigation**, the pathway through your site, must be obvious and intuitive. Individual Web pages cannot be isolated from the rest of the site if you want it to be successful. At all times and on all pages in your site, you must give the visitor a sense of place, of context within the site. Most Web designers use a navigation map to help the user visualize the navigation pathway.

Design Basics — Navigation Map

A site map is essential, even for a modestly sized site. A site map, or **navigation map**, outlines the structure of the entire Web site, showing all pages within the site and the connections from one page to the others. The navigation map acts as a road map through the Web site, but does not provide details of the content of the individual pages. Web site navigation should be consistent from page to page, so your visitors do not have to guess where they are within the site each time they encounter a new page. All pages in the site should contain a link to the home page. Consider the types of structures in Figure I-5 for site navigation:

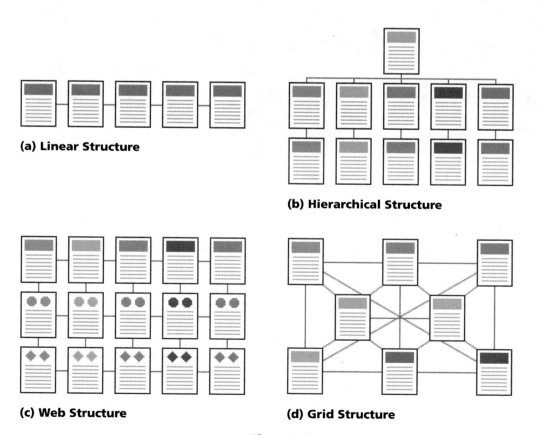

(a) **Linear Structure**

(b) **Hierarchical Structure**

(c) **Web Structure**

(d) **Grid Structure**

Figure I–5

Structure The goal and the type of Web site often determine the structure selected for a specific Web site. Create a navigation map to serve as a blueprint for your navigational structure. Consider the following navigational structures and determine which one best meets your needs.

Figure I–6

- In a **linear structure** (Figure I–5a on the previous page) the user navigates sequentially, moving from one page to the next. Information that flows as a narrative, as a timeline, or in logical order is ideal for sequential treatment. Simple sequential organization, however, usually works only for smaller sites. Many online tutorials use a linear structure.

- A **hierarchical structure** (Figure I–5b on the previous page) is one of the better ways to organize complex bodies of information efficiently. Because many visitors are familiar with hierarchical charts, many Web sites employ this structure. Be aware that effective hierarchical structures require thorough organization of the content.

- A **Web structure** (Figure I–5c on the previous page), which also is called a **random structure**, places few restrictions on organizational patterns. This type of structure is associated with the free flow of ideas and can be confusing to a user. A random structure is better suited for experienced users looking for further education or enrichment and is not recommended if your goal is to provide a basic understanding of a particular topic. If a Web site is relatively small, however, a random structure could work well.

- Use a **grid structure** if your Web site consists of a number of topics of equal importance (Figure I–5d on page DW 9). Procedural manuals, events, and item lists work well in a grid structure.

- Large Web sites frequently use a **hybrid structure**, a combination of the previous listed structures, to organize information. See Figure I–6.

Tools   Determine the tool necessary to create the navigation map (Figure I–7). For small Web sites, you might want to consider using the organizational chart included in the Microsoft PowerPoint application.

For larger, more diverse Web sites, you can chart and organize your content using Visio Professional, Flow Charting PDQ, FlowCharter Professional, and SmartDraw.

Navigation Elements   The more common types of navigation elements include text, buttons, images, image maps, a site index, a menu, a search feature, and navigation bars. Depending on the complexity of your Web site, you may want to include some or all of these elements.

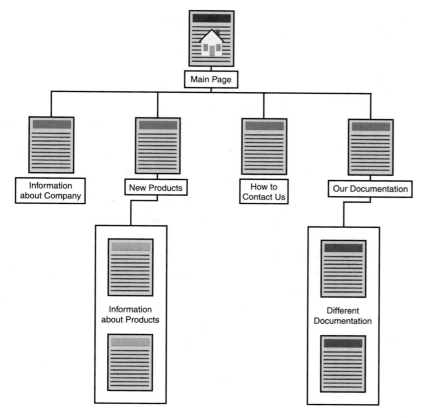

Figure I–7

Developing a Web Site

Once you have established a structure for your Web site, you can begin developing the site. Make text and images the main focus because they are the more common elements. Then consider page layout and color.

Development Basics — Typography, Images, Page Layout, and Color

Typography, images, page layout, and color are the key design elements that will make up your finished Web site. Correct use of these elements plays an important part in the development process. Consider the following guidelines:

Typography   As in all media, good **typography**, the appearance and arrangement of the characters that make up your text, is vital to the success of your Web page. A font consists of all the characters available in a particular style and weight for a specific design. Text always should be easy to read, whether in a book, magazine, Web page, or billboard. Keep readability in mind as you select fonts, especially when you consider that some of your visitors might only be viewing them on screen, and others might print them.

When selecting a font, determine its purpose on your Web page. Is it to be used for a title? For on-screen reading? Is it likely to be printed? Will the font fit in with the theme of the Web site? Is it a Web-safe font, such as Times New Roman, Courier, or Arial? **Web-safe fonts** are the more popular fonts and the ones that most visitors are likely to have installed on their computers. Also, while visitors to your Web page may never consciously notice the design of the text characters, or the **typeface**, it often subconsciously affects their reaction to the page.

Images   Images can enhance almost any Web page if used appropriately. Without the visual impact of shape, color, and contrast, Web pages can be visually uninteresting and will not motivate the visitor to investigate their contents. Consider the balance between the number of images and page performance as you develop your site. When adding images, consider your potential audience and the technology they have available. Remember that a background image or a graphical menu increases visitor download time. You may lose visitors who do not have broadband access if your Web page contains an excessive number of graphical items.

BTW

Keep the Page Simple
Some Web pages take a long time to download or view if they contain multiple elements and appear very "busy." Simple pages download faster and make an immediate impression on the reader.

Page Layout   The importance of proper page layout cannot be overemphasized. A suitable design draws visitors to your Web site. Although no single design system is appropriate for all Web pages, establish a consistent, logical layout that allows you to add text and images easily. The Web page layouts shown in Figure I–8 illustrate two different layouts. The layout on the left (Figure I–8a) shows a page with centered headings and other centered elements, which break up the page and can be difficult to read. The page layout on the right (Figure I–8b) presents strong visual contrast by organizing headings and some types of graphics on the left, while displaying other types of graphics on the right.

(a)   **(b)**

Figure I–8

Maintaining consistency and updating changes throughout a site are two of the biggest challenges facing Web designers. A **template,** a special type of document, can help with these challenges. Dreamweaver provides several page layout templates that can be modified easily. In laying out your Web pages, consider the following guidelines to ensure that visitors have the best viewing experience:

- Include only one topic per page.
- Control the vertical and horizontal size of the page.
- Start text on the left to match the way most people read text.
- Use concise statements and bulleted points to get your point across; studies indicate most people scan the text.

Color   When creating a Web page, use color to add interest and vitality to your site. Include color in tables, as backgrounds, and with fonts. Use the right combination of colors to decorate the layout and tie the Web site pages together.

Reviewing and Testing a Web Site

Some Web site developers argue that reviewing and testing should take place throughout the developmental process. While this may be true, it also is important to review and test the final product. This ongoing process ensures that you identify and correct any problems before publishing to the Web. When reviewing and testing your Web site, ask the following questions:

- Is the Web site free of spelling and grammatical errors?
- Is the page layout consistent, and does it generate a sense of balance and order?
- Are any links broken?
- Do multimedia interactivity and forms function correctly?
- Do the more widely used browsers display the Web site properly?
- Does the Web site function properly in different browsers, including older browser versions?
- Have you initiated a **group test**, in which you have asked other individuals to test your Web site and provide feedback?

Publishing a Web Site

After your Web site has been tested thoroughly, it can be published. **Publishing** a Web site, making it available to your visitors, involves the actual uploading of the Web site to a server. After you complete the uploading process, all pages within the Web site should be tested again.

Publishing Basics — Domain Name, Server Space, and Uploading

With your Web site thoroughly tested and any problems corrected, you must make the site available to your audience by obtaining a domain name, acquiring server space, and uploading the site. Consider the following to ensure site availability:

Obtain a Domain Name   To allow visitors to access your Web site, you must obtain a domain name. Visitors access Web sites by an IP address or a domain name. An **IP address (Internet Protocol address)** is a number that uniquely identifies each computer or device connected to the Internet. A **domain name** is the text version of an IP address. The **Domain Name System (DNS)**, an Internet service, translates domain names into their corresponding IP addresses. The **Uniform Resource Locator (URL)**, also called a Web address, tells the browser on which server the Web page is located. A URL consists of a communications protocol, such as **Hypertext Transfer Protocol (HTTP)**, the domain name, and sometimes the path to a specific Web page (Figure I–9).

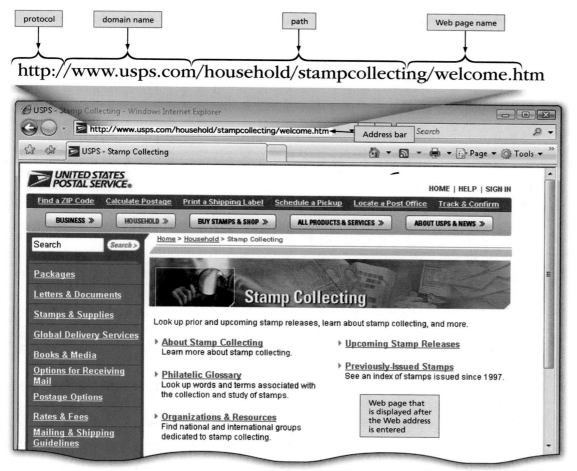

Figure I–9

Domain names are unique and must be registered. The **Accredited Registrar Directory** provides a listing of **Internet Corporation for Assigned Names and Numbers (ICANN)** accredited domain name registrars. Your most difficult task likely will be to find a name that is not registered. You can locate a name by using a specialized search engine at one of the many accredited domain name registrars listed on the ICANN Web site (*icann.org/registrars/accredited-list.html*). In addition to registering your business name as a domain name, you may want to register the names of your products, services, or other related names. Expect to pay approximately $10 to $35 per year for a domain name.

Consider the following guidelines when selecting a domain name:

- Select a name that is easy to pronounce, spell, and remember.
- Select a name that relates to the Web site content and suggests the nature of your product or service.
- If the Web site is a business, use the business name whenever possible.
- Select a name that is free and clear of trademark issues.
- Purchase variations and the .org, .net, and .mobi versions of your domain name.
- Some ISPs will obtain a domain name for you if you use their service to host your Web site.

Acquire Server Space Locate an ISP that will host your Web site. Recall that an ISP is a business that has a permanent Internet connection. ISPs offer connections to individuals and companies free or for a fee.

If you select an ISP that provides free server space, most likely your visitors will be subjected to advertisements and pop-up windows. Other options to explore for free or inexpensive server space include the provider from which you obtain your Internet connection; online communities, such as Bravenet (*bravenet.com*), Tripod (*www.tripod.lycos.com*), and webs.com (*www.webs.com*); and your educational institution's Web server. If the purpose of your Web site is to sell a product or service or to promote a professional organization, you should consider a fee-based ISP. Use a search engine such as Google (*google.com*) and search for Web site hosting, or visit the Web Site Host Directory (*www.websitehostdirectory.com*), where you will find lists of Web hosting plans, as well as reviews and ratings of Web hosting providers. Selecting a reliable provider requires investigation on your part. Many providers offer multiple hosting plans. When selecting an ISP, consider the following questions and how they apply to your particular situation and Web site:

1. What is the monthly fee? Is a discount available for a year-long subscription? Are setup fees charged?
2. How much server space is provided for the monthly fee? Can you purchase additional space? If so, how much does it cost?
3. What is the average server uptime on a monthly basis? What is the average server downtime?
4. What are the server specifications? Can the server handle many users? Does it have battery backup power?
5. Are **server logs**, which keep track of the number of accesses, available?
6. What is the ISP's form of connectivity — that is, how does it connect to the Internet: dial up, DSL, wireless, cable, ISDN, T1, T3, or some other way?
7. Is a money-back guarantee offered?
8. What technical support does the ISP provide, and when is it available? Does it have an online knowledge base?
9. Does the server on which the Web site will reside have CGI scripting capabilities and Active Server Page (ASP) support?
10. Does the server on which the Web site will reside support e-commerce, multimedia, and **Secure Sockets Layer** (**SSL**) for encrypting confidential data such as credit card numbers? Are additional fees required for these capabilities?
11. Does the ISP support Dreamweaver and other Web site development software programs?
12. Are mailboxes included in the package? If so, how many?

Publish the Web Site You must publish, or upload, the files from your computer to a server where your Web site then will be accessible to anyone on the Internet. Publishing, or uploading, is the process of transmitting all the files that make up your Web site from your computer to the selected server or host computer. The files that make up your Web site can include Web pages, PDF documents, images, audio, video, animation, and others.

A variety of tools and methods exist to manage the upload task. Some of the more popular of these are FTP (file transfer programs), Windows Web Publishing Wizard, Web Folders, and Web authoring programs such as Dreamweaver. These tools allow you to link to a remote server, enter a password, and then upload your files. Dreamweaver contains a built-in function similar to independent FTP programs. The Dreamweaver FTP function to upload your Web site is covered in Appendix C.

Maintaining a Web Site

Most Web sites require maintenance and updating. Some types of ongoing Web maintenance include the following:

- Changing content, either by adding new text and images or by deleting obsolete material
- Checking for broken links and adding new links
- Documenting the last change date (even when no revisions have been made)

Use the information from the server logs provided by your ISP to determine what needs to be updated or changed. Statistics contained within these logs generally include the number of visitors trying to access your site at one time, what resources they request, how long they stay at the site, at what point they enter the site, what pages they view, and what errors they encounter. Learning to use and apply the information contained within the server log will help you to make your Web site successful.

After you make updates or changes to the site, notify your viewers with a What's New announcement.

Methods and Tools Used to Create Web Sites

Web developers have several options for creating Web pages: a text editor, an HTML or XHTML editor, software applications, or a WYSIWYG text editor (discussed in detail on page DW 20). Microsoft Notepad and WordPad are each examples of a **text editor**. These simple, easy-to-use programs allow you to enter, edit, save, and print text. An **HTML** or **XHTML editor** is a more sophisticated version of a text editor. In addition to basic text-editing functions, these programs include advanced features such as syntax highlighting, color coding, and spell checking. Software applications such as Microsoft Word, Microsoft Excel, and Adobe Publisher provide a Save as Web Page or Save as HTML command. This feature converts the application document into a file Web browsers can display. Examples of a WYSIWYG text editor are programs such as Microsoft Expression Web and Adobe Dreamweaver. These programs provide an integrated text editor with a graphical user interface that allows you to view the code and the document as you create it.

A Web developer can use any of these options to create Web pages. Regardless of the option selected, however, it still is important to understand the specifics of HTML and XHTML.

Web Site Languages

Web pages are written in plain text and saved in the **American Standard Code for Information Interchange**, or **ASCII** (pronounced ASK-ee), format — the most widely used coding system to represent data. Using the ASCII format makes Web pages universally readable by different Web browsers regardless of the computer platform on which they reside.

The language of the Web is not static; it evolves just like most other languages. HTML (Hypertext Markup Language) has been the primary language of the Web and most likely will continue to be so for at least the near future. HTML is useful for creating headings, paragraphs, lists, and so on, but is limited to these general types of formatting. XHTML is a rewritten version of HTML using XML (Extensible Markup Language).

Unlike HTML, **Extensible Hypertext Markup Language** (**XHTML**) is an authoring language that defines the structure and layout of a document so that it displays as a Web page and is compatible with Web browsers such as Microsoft Internet Explorer,

BTW

W3C
The World Wide Web Consortium (W3C) develops and updates Web protocols. For example, they specified the most recent changes to XHTML, and are directing an effort to make it easier for people to browse the Web on mobile devices.

BTW

Test Web Pages
To test a Web page, you can use the Adobe Browser Lab at *https://browserlab.adobe.com* to see how your pages are displayed in a variety of browsers and versions of browsers.

Mozilla Firefox, Safari, or Google Chrome. Browser rules for interpreting HTML are flexible. XHTML, however, requires Web designers to adhere strictly to its markup language rules.

Two components constitute a Web page: source code and document content. The **source code**, which contains elements, acts as the program instructions. The **elements** within the source code control the appearance of the document content. Browsers display the **document content**, or the text and images. The browser interprets the elements contained within the code, and the code instructs the browser how to display the Web page. For instance, if you define a line of text on your Web page as a heading, the browser knows to display this line formatted as a heading.

All XHTML element formats and HTML tags start with a left angle bracket (< or less than symbol), are followed by the name of the element, and end with a right angle bracket (> or greater than symbol). Most elements have a start and an end element and are called **two-sided elements**. End elements are the same as start elements except they are preceded by a forward slash (/). Some XHTML elements, such as the one used to indicate a line break <br />, do not have an end element. Instead, the right angle bracket is preceded by a space and forward slash. These are known as **one-sided elements**, or **self-closing elements**. In some browsers, the end element can be omitted from certain elements, such as the end element for a new paragraph, </p>. Unlike HTML, however, XHTML standards require you to include both the start and end elements for all two-sided elements.

Some elements can contain an **attribute**, or **property**, which is additional information placed within the angle brackets. Attributes are not repeated or contained in the end element. Some attributes are used individually, while other attributes can include a value modifier. A **value modifier** specifies conditions within the element, and should always be enclosed in double quotation marks. For example, you can use a value modifier to specify the font type or size or the placement of text on the page. To create and display a centered heading, for instance, you would use the following code:

```
<h1 style="text-align:center">This is the largest header
element and the text will be centered</h1>
```

In this example, h1 is the XHTML element, text-align is the attribute, and center is the value modifier. Notice that the attribute does not appear as part of the end element, </h1>.

You can use the Dreamweaver Code window and Microsoft Notepad or WordPad (text editors) to create XHTML documents. Place each element in a pair around the text or section that you want to define (**mark up**) with that element. Use lowercase characters when typing XHTML elements.

XHTML elements also format the hyperlinks that connect information on the World Wide Web. While XHTML elements number in the hundreds, some are used more than others. All documents, however, require four basic elements. Figure I–10 illustrates the basic elements required for all XHTML documents. Table I–2 summarizes the more commonly used XHTML elements.

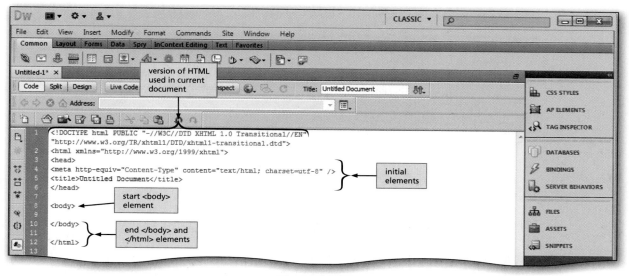

Figure I–10

Table I–2 Commonly Used XHTML Elements

Element (tags)	Structure
<html>...</html>	Encloses the entire XHTML document
<head>...</head>	Encloses the head of the XHTML document
<body>...</body>	Encloses the body of the XHTML document

Element (tags)	Title and Headings
<title>...</title>	Indicates the title of the document
<h1>...</h1>	Heading level 1
<h2>...</h2>	Heading level 2
<h3>...</h3>	Heading level 3
<h4>...</h4>	Heading level 4
<h5>...</h5>	Heading level 5
<h6>...</h6>	Heading level 6

Element (tags)	Paragraphs, Breaks, and Separators
<p>...</p>	Paragraph
 	Line break
<hr />	Horizontal rule
<ol>...</ol>	Ordered, numbered list
<ul>...</ul>	Unordered, bulleted list
<li>...</li>	List item, used with <ol>, <ul>, <menu>, and <dir>
<dl>...</dl>	Definition of glossary list
<dt>...</dt>	Definition term; part of a definition list
<dd>...</dd>	Definition corresponding to a definition term

Element (tags)	Character Formatting
...	Bold text
<u>...</u>	Underlined text
<i>...</i>	Italic text

Table I–2 Commonly Used XHTML Elements *(continued)*

Element (tags)	Links
<a>...</a>	Combined with the href attribute, creates a link to another document or anchor
<a>...</a>	Combined with the name attribute, creates an anchor to which elements can be linked

Element (tags)	Image
<img />	Inserts an image into the document

Web Page Authoring Programs

Many of today's Web page authoring programs, including Dreamweaver, are What You See Is What You Get (WYSIWYG) text editors. As mentioned earlier, a **WYSIWYG text editor** allows a user to view a document as it will appear in the final product and to edit the text, images, or other elements directly within that view. Before programs such as Dreamweaver existed, Web page designers were required to type, or hand-code, Web pages. Educators and Web designers still debate the issue surrounding the necessity of knowing HTML and XHTML. Technically, you do not need to know either HTML or XHTML to create Web pages in Dreamweaver; however, an understanding of HTML and XHTML will help you if you need to alter Dreamweaver-generated code. If you know HTML and XHTML, then you can make changes to the code and Dreamweaver will accept the changes.

Adobe Dreamweaver CS5

The standard in visual authoring, Adobe Dreamweaver CS5 is part of the Adobe Creative Suite, which includes Adobe Flash, Fireworks, Photoshop, Illustrator, InDesign, Acrobat, and other programs depending on the particular suite. Dreamweaver provides features that access these separate products. Some of the new Dreamweaver CS5 features include the following:

- Integrated content management system (CMS) support
- New rendering mode that displays the design like a standard-based browser
- CSS inspection
- Integration with Adobe BrowserLab, PHP custom class code hinting, and Business Catalyst
- Enhanced CSS starter page

Dreamweaver makes it easy to get started and provides you with helpful tools to enhance your Web design and development experience. Working in a single environment, you create, build, and manage Web sites and Internet applications. In Dreamweaver, you can customize the workspace environment to fit your particular needs.

Dreamweaver contains coding tools and features that include references for HTML, XHTML, XML, CSS, and JavaScript as well as code editors that allow you to edit the code directly. Using **Adobe Roundtrip technology**, Dreamweaver can import Microsoft Office or other software Web pages and delete the unused code. Downloadable extensions from the Adobe Web site make it easy to add functionality to any Web site. Examples of these extensions include shopping carts and online payment features.

Instead of writing individual files for every page, you can use a database to store content and then retrieve the content dynamically in response to a user's request. Implementing and using this feature, you can update the information once, in one place, instead of manually editing many pages. Another key feature is **Cascading Style Sheets styles** (**CSS styles**). CSS styles are collections of formatting definitions that affect the appearance of Web page elements. You can use CSS styles to format text, images, headings, tables, and so forth. Implementing and applying this feature, you can update the formatting one time across many Web pages.

Dreamweaver provides the tools that help you author accessible content. These accessible pages comply with government guidelines and Section 508 of the Federal Rehabilitation Act. Accessibility is discussed in more detail as you progress through the book.

Dreamweaver allows you to publish Web sites with relative ease to a local area network, which connects computers in a limited geographical area, or to the Web, so that anyone with Internet access can see them. The concepts and techniques presented in this book provide the tools you need to plan, develop, and publish professional Web sites, such as those shown in Figure I–11 and Figure I–12.

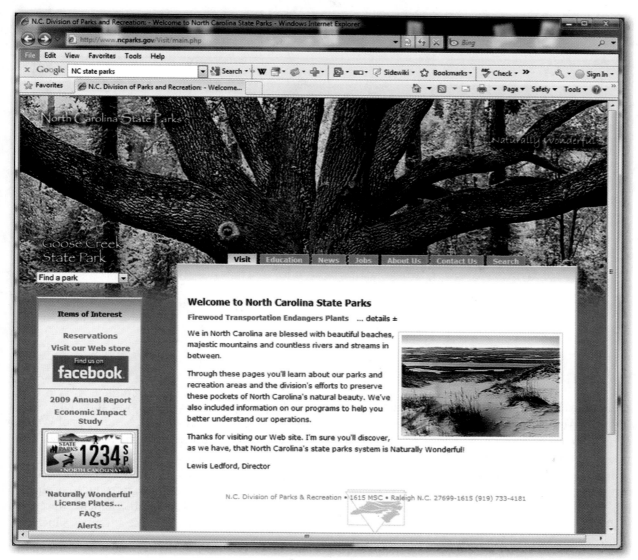

Figure I–11

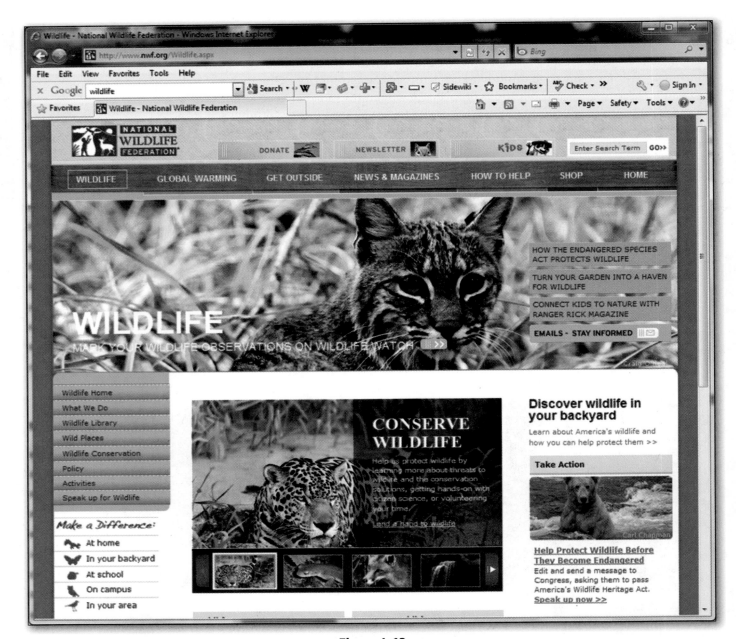

Figure I–12

Chapter Summary

The Introduction to Web Site Development and Adobe Dreamweaver CS5 provided an overview of the Internet and the World Wide Web and the key terms associated with those technologies. An overview of the basic types of Web pages also was presented. The Introduction furnished information on developing a Web site, including planning basics. The process of designing a Web site and each phase within this process were discussed. Information about testing, publishing, and maintaining a Web site also was presented, including an overview of obtaining a domain name, acquiring server space, and uploading a Web site. Methods and tools used to create Web pages were introduced. A short overview of HTML and XHTML and some of the more commonly used HTML tags and XHTML elements were presented. Finally, the advantages of using Dreamweaver in Web development were discussed. These advantages include a WYSIWYG text editor; a visual, customizable development environment; accessibility compliance; downloadable extensions; database access capabilities; and Cascading Style Sheets.

Learn It Online

Test your knowledge of chapter content and key terms.

Instructions: To complete the Learn It Online exercises, start your browser, click the Address bar, and then enter the Web address `scsite.com/dwcs5/learn`. When the Dreamweaver CS5 Learn It Online page is displayed, click the link for the exercise you want to complete and then read the instructions.

Chapter Reinforcement TF, MC, and SA
A series of true/false, multiple choice, and short answer questions that test your knowledge of the chapter content.

Flash Cards
An interactive learning environment where you identify chapter key terms associated with displayed definitions.

Practice Test
A series of multiple choice questions that test your knowledge of chapter content and key terms.

Who Wants To Be a Computer Genius?
An interactive game that challenges your knowledge of chapter content in the style of a television quiz show.

Wheel of Terms
An interactive game that challenges your knowledge of chapter key terms in the style of the television show *Wheel of Fortune*.

Crossword Puzzle Challenge
A crossword puzzle that challenges your knowledge of key terms presented in the chapter.

Apply Your Knowledge

Reinforce the skills and apply the concepts you learned in this chapter.

Creating a Web Site
Instructions: As discussed in this Introduction, creating a Web site involves planning, designing, developing, reviewing and testing, publishing, and maintaining the site. Use the information contained in Table I-3 to develop a plan for creating a Web site.

Table I-3 Creating a Web Site	
Planning	
Web site name	What is your Web site name?
Web site type	What is the Web site type: portal, news, informational, business/marketing, educational, entertainment, advocacy, blog, wiki, social network, content aggregator, Web application, or personal?
Web site purpose	What is the purpose of your Web site?
Target audience	How can you identify your target audience?
Web technologies to be used	Will you design for broadband, baseband, or mobile? Explain your selection.
Content	What topics will you cover? How much information will you present on each topic? How will you attract your audience? What will you do to entice your audience to return to your Web site? How will you keep the Web site updated?
Text, images, and multimedia	Will your site contain text only? What type of images will you include? Where will you obtain your images? Will you have a common logo? Will plug-ins be required?
Designing	
Navigation map	What type of structure will you use? What tools will you use to design your navigation map?
Navigational elements	What navigational elements will you include?

Apply Your Knowledge *continued*

Table I–3 Creating a Web Site *(continued)*

Developing

Typography	What font will you use? How many different fonts will you use on your site?
Images	How will you use images to enhance your site? Will you use a background image?
Page layout	What type of layout will you use? How many topics per page? How will text be presented: bulleted or paragraph style? Will the audience need to scroll the page?
Color	What color combinations will you use for your site? To what elements will you apply the color(s) — fonts, background, tables, other elements?

Reviewing and Testing

Review	What elements will you review? Will you use a group review?
Testing	What elements will you test? Will you use group testing?

Publishing

Domain name	What is your domain name? Have you registered your domain name? What ISP will host your Web site? What criteria did you use to select the ISP?

Maintaining

Ongoing maintenance	How often will you update your Web site? What elements will you update? Will you add additional features? Does your ISP provide server logs? Will you use the server logs for maintenance purposes?

Perform the following tasks:

1. Download and then use your word processing program to open the Apply I-1 Web Site Creation file. With the Apply I-1 Web Site Creation file open in your word processing program, select a name for your Web site.

2. Use a specialized search engine at one of the many accredited domain name registrars to verify that your selected Web site name is available.

3. Answer each question in the Planning table. Use complete sentences to answer the questions. Type your answers in column 3.

4. Save the document with the file name Apply I-1_your initials. Submit the document in the format specified by your instructor.

Extend Your Knowledge

Extend the skills you learned in this chapter and experiment with new skills. You may need to use Help to complete the assignment.

Identifying Web Site Types

Instructions: As you learned in this Introduction, Web sites can be classified into 13 basic types. Use a browser such as Internet Explorer to identify Web site types.

Perform the following tasks:

Part 1: Web Site Types
1. Review the different types of Web sites described on pages DW 5-6.
2. Select three of the Web site types.

Part 2: Search for Web Sites
1. Start your word processing program.
2. Start your browser and search for each of your three selected Web site types. Locate at least two examples of each type.
3. Copy and paste the Web site address for each example, and then compose a short paragraph explaining how each Web site meets the selected criteria.

Make It Right

Analyze a Web site structure and suggest how to improve the organization or design.

Improving Navigation Structures

Instructions: Start your Web browser. Select and analyze a Web site and determine the navigation structure used within the Web site.

Figure I–5 (a) through (d) on page DW 9 contains examples of four types of navigation structures. This figure is reproduced as Figure I–13 on page DW 26. Select a Web site and review the structure of the Web site. Start your word processing program. Describe the structure used in your selected Web site. Include any suggestions you may have on how this structure could be improved. If you are using Microsoft Office Word 2007 or Word 2010, click the Insert tab on the Ribbon. In the Illustrations group, use the Shapes or SmartArt options to create an image of the structure. Save your document and submit it in the format specified by your instructor.

Make It Right *continued*

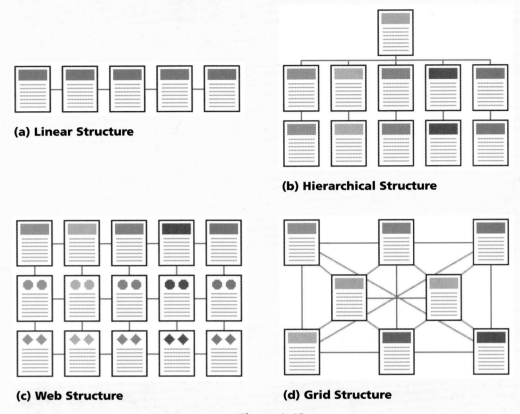

(a) Linear Structure

(b) Hierarchical Structure

(c) Web Structure

(d) Grid Structure

Figure I–13

In the Lab

Design and/or create a document using the guidelines, concepts, and skills presented in this chapter. Labs are listed in order of increasing difficulty.

Lab 1: Using Internet Explorer

Problem: Microsoft Internet Explorer (IE) has many features that can make your work on the Internet more efficient. Using the Accelerators feature, for example, you can quickly display driving directions, translate and define words, or e-mail content to others without navigating to other Web sites. IE also includes other enhancements. Visit the Internet Explorer 8: Features Web page (Figure I–14 on page DW 27) and select three articles concerning topics with which you are not familiar. Read the articles and then create a word processing document detailing what you learned.

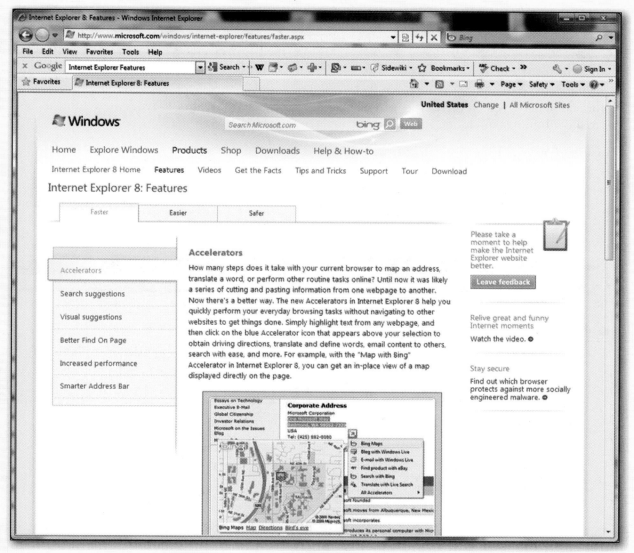

Figure I–14

Perform the following tasks:

1. Start your browser. Open the Internet Explorer 8: Features Web page (*www.microsoft.com/windows/ internet-explorer/features/faster.aspx*).

2. Scroll down the page, click a tab such as the Easier tab, and then scroll to display all the information on that tab.

3. Select three features with which you are not familiar.

4. Click the link for each article and read the article.

5. Start your word processing program.

6. List three important points that you learned from this Web site.

7. Write a summary of what you learned from each article. Include within your summary your opinion of the article and if you will apply what you learned or use it with your Web browser.

8. Save the document on a USB flash drive using the file name Lab I-1 IE Features.

9. Submit the document in the format specified by your instructor.

In the Lab

Lab 2: Identifying Types of Web Sites

Problem: A Web designer should be familiar with different types of Web pages and the sort of information displayed on these types of Web pages. This chapter describes 13 types of Web sites. Search the Internet and locate at least one example of each type of Web site.

Perform the following tasks:

1. Start your browser. Open the Google (google.com) search engine Web page (Figure I–15) and search for an example of each of the following types of Web sites: portal, news, informational, business/marketing, blog, wiki, social networks, educational, entertainment, advocacy, Web application, content aggregator, and personal.

Figure I–15

2. Start your word processing program.
3. Copy and paste the link for each of these Web page types into your word processing document.
4. Identify the type of Web page for each link.
5. Explain why you selected this Web page and how it fits the definition of the specific type.
6. Save the document with the file name Lab I-2 Web Page Types.
7. Submit the document in the format specified by your instructor.

In the Lab

Lab 3: Hosting a Web Site

Problem: Selecting the correct host or ISP for your Web site can be a confusing process. Many Web sites offer this service, but determining the best one for your particular needs can be somewhat complicated. Assume your Web site will sell a product. Compare several ISPs and select the one that will best meet your needs.

Perform the following tasks:

1. Review the information and questions on page DW 16 discussing the guidelines for acquiring active server space to host your Web site.

Figure I–16

2. Start your browser. Open Web page shown in Figure I–16 (*www.the10besthosts.com*).

3. Click one of the host server links and review the information relating to the services offered by your selected ISP.

4. Start your word processing program.

5. Read and answer the questions on page DW 16. Use the information provided in the list of services offered by your selected ISP.

6. Use your word processing program to write a short summary explaining why you would or would not select this ISP to host your Web site.

7. Save the document with the file name Lab I-3 Web Site Hosting. Submit the document in the format specified by your instructor.

Cases and Places

Apply your creative thinking and problem solving skills to design and implement a solution.

• Easier •• More Difficult

• 1: Research Web Site Planning

You are working as an assistant to the manager of Upscale Renovations, a firm that specializes in lawn and garden renovations. The marketing director is considering whether to create a Web site for Upscale Renovations, and asks you to conduct some research. Use a search engine such as Google (google.com) and research information about planning a Web site. Use your word processing program and write a two-page summary of what you learned. Save the document as Case I-1 Web Site Research. Check the spelling and grammar of the finished paper. Submit the document in the format specified by your instructor.

• 2: Explore Typography

Typography within a Web page is one of its more important elements. Start your browser and search for examples of Web sites that include what you consider appropriate typography and Web sites with inappropriate typography. Use your word processing program to define typography and to write a short summary of why you consider the Web sites to be appropriate and inappropriate. Copy and paste the Web site addresses into your document. Check the spelling and grammar of the finished paper. Save the document as Case I-2 Typography. Submit the document in the format specified by your instructor.

•• 3: Research Web Site Plug-ins

You are working as an intern in an animal shelter, helping the director design a Web site. He wants to show a video of the animals at the shelter on the site, and has heard that viewers might need a plug-in to view videos. He asks you to research the topic. Start your browser and search the Web for plug-ins. Prepare a list of and a short description of the plug-ins you found. Use your word processing program to create a summary statement describing how and why you could use each plug-in in a Web site. Include the link where you can download each of the plug-ins. Check the spelling and grammar of the finished paper. Save the document as Case I-3 Web Site Plug-ins. Submit the document in the format specified by your instructor.

•• **4: Create a Web Site Navigation Map**

Make It Personal

In preparation for an upcoming wedding, the bride is asking members of the bridal party to create a personal Web site. Working with two or three members of your class, use a software program of your choice to create a navigation map for your proposed Web site. Show the link(s) from the home page to the other two pages. Use your word processing program and write a sentence or two describing the type of structure your group created and why you selected that structure. Check the spelling and grammar of the finished paper. Save the document as Case I-4 Navigation Map. Submit the document in the format specified by your instructor.

•• **5: Create Web Site Structures**

Working Together

Each team member is to search the Internet for Web sites illustrating each of the Web site structures on page DW 9. Each team member then will use word processing software to write a minimum of 100 words describing the Web sites and explaining why he or she thinks the structure used is appropriate or inappropriate for that particular Web site. Check the spelling and grammar of the finished paper. Save the document as Case I-5 Web Site Structures. Submit the document in the format specified by your instructor.

1 Creating a Dreamweaver Web Page and Local Site

Objectives

You will have mastered the material in this chapter when you can:

- Describe Dreamweaver and identify its key features
- Start and quit Dreamweaver
- Describe the Dreamweaver window
- Define a local site
- Create and save a Web page
- Add a background image
- Open and close panels

- Display the Property inspector
- Format and modify text elements
- Define and insert a line break
- Change a Web page title and check spelling
- Preview and print a Web page
- Open a new Web page

1 | Creating a Dreamweaver Web Page and Local Site

What Is Adobe Dreamweaver CS5?

Adobe Dreamweaver CS5 is a powerful Web page authoring and Web site management software program with an HTML editor that is used to design, code, and create professional-looking Web pages, Web sites, and Web applications. The visual-editing features of Dreamweaver allow you to create pages without writing a line of code. Dreamweaver provides many tools and features, including the following:

- **Automatic Web page creation:** Dreamweaver provides tools you can use to develop Web pages without having to spend hours writing HTML code. Dreamweaver automatically generates the HTML code necessary to publish your Web pages.

- **Web site management:** Dreamweaver enables you to view a site, including all local and remote files associated with the selected site. You can perform standard maintenance tasks such as viewing, opening, and moving files and transferring files between local and remote sites.

- **Standard Adobe Web authoring tools:** Dreamweaver includes a user interface that is consistent across all Adobe authoring tools. This consistency enables easy integration with other Adobe Web-related programs such as Adobe Flash, Director, Shockwave, and ColdFusion.

Other key features include the integrated user interface, the integrated file explorer, panel management, database integration, and standards and accessibility support. Dreamweaver CS5 is customizable and runs on many operating systems including Windows 7, Windows Vista, Windows XP, Mac OS X, and others.

Project Planning Guidelines

The process of developing a Web site that communicates specific information requires careful analysis and planning. As a starting point, determine the type of and purpose of the Web site. Once the type and purpose are determined, decide on the content to be included. Design basics and Web site navigation then should be considered. Finally, creating a navigation map or flowchart will help determine the design that will be most helpful in delivering the Web site content. With the structure in place, the Web site is ready to be developed. Details of these guidelines are provided in the Introduction. In addition, each project in this book provides practical applications of these planning considerations.

Project — Montana Parks Web Site Home Page

To create documents similar to those you will encounter on the Web and in academic, business, and personal environments, you can use Dreamweaver to produce Web pages such as the Montana Parks and Recreation Areas Web page shown in Figure 1–1. This Web page is the index, or home, page for the Montana Parks Web site and provides interesting facts about three of Montana's parks and recreational areas. The page begins with a centered main heading, followed by two short informational paragraphs, and then an introductory sentence for a bulleted list. The list contains three bulleted items. A concluding sentence, the author's name, and current date end the page. A background image is applied to the page.

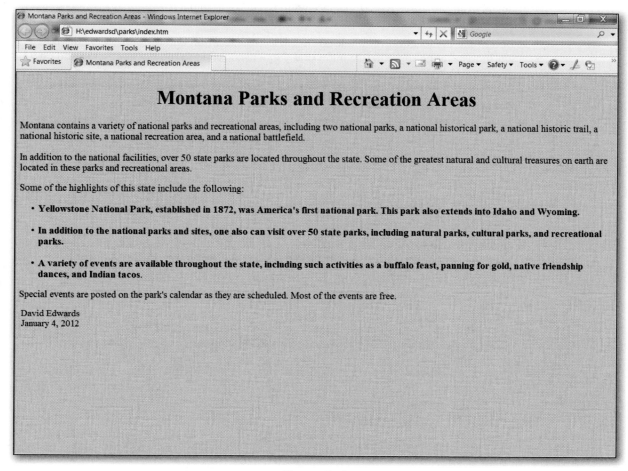

Figure 1–1

Overview

As you read this chapter, you will learn how to create the Web page shown in Figure 1–1 by performing these general tasks:

- Enter text in the document.
- Save the document.
- Add a background image.
- Format the text in the document.
- Insert a line break.
- Check spelling.
- Preview the Web page in a browser.
- Save and print the Web page.

Plan Ahead

General Project Guidelines

When creating a Dreamweaver Web site, the actions you perform and decisions you make will affect the appearance and characteristics of the entire Web site. As you create the home page, such as the page shown in Figure 1–1 on the previous page, you should follow these general guidelines:

1. **Review the Dreamweaver workspace window.** Become familiar with the various layouts and available panels.

2. **Determine the location for the local site.** Select the location and the storage media on which to save the site. Keep in mind that you will continue to modify pages and add new pages to the site as you progress through this book. Storage media can be a hard disk, USB flash drive, or read/write CD. If you are using a flash drive and intend to complete all exercises, the media storage capacity should be a minimum of 25 MB.

3. **Define the local site.** Create the local site using Dreamweaver's Site Setup dialog box.

4. **Add a background for the Web page.** Adding a background color or background image adds interest and vitality to a Web site.

5. **Select the words and fonts for the text.** Text accounts for the bulk of the content on most Web pages, but Web site visitors often avoid reading long blocks of text. It is best to be brief. Include headings to organize the text into sections. Use lists whenever possible. Use common words and simple language.

6. **Identify how to format various elements of the text.** Determine which text will be headings and subheadings, paragraphs, and bulleted and numbered lists on the Web page.

7. **Review final tasks.** Prepare to display a Web page to others by adding professional finishing touches such as a Web page title and by checking the spelling of the text.

When necessary, more specific details concerning the above guidelines are presented at appropriate points in the chapter. The chapter also will identify the actions performed and decisions made regarding these guidelines during the creation of the Web site home page shown in Figure 1–1.

Starting Dreamweaver

If you are using a computer to step through the project in this chapter and you want your screen to match the figures in this book, you should change your screen's resolution to 1024 x 768. The browser used to display the Web page figures is Internet Explorer 8. The browser text size is set to Medium.

To Start Dreamweaver

Getting started in Dreamweaver is as easy as opening an existing HTML document or creating a new document. The following steps show how to start Dreamweaver based on a typical installation. You may need to ask your instructor how to start Dreamweaver for your computer.

- Click the Start button on the Windows 7 taskbar to display the Start menu (Figure 1–2).

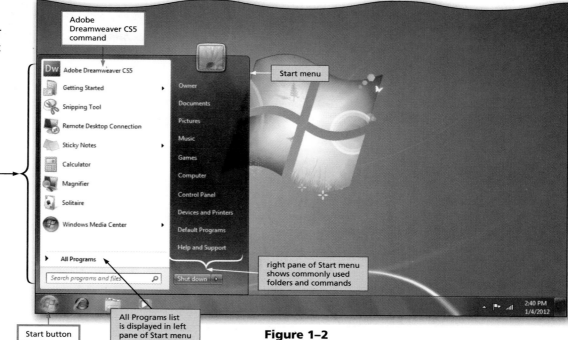

Figure 1–2

2

- Click Adobe Dreamweaver CS5 on the Start menu or point to All Programs on the Start menu and then click Adobe Dreamweaver CS5 on the All Programs list to start Dreamweaver and display the Welcome screen.

- If necessary, click the Workspace switcher arrow on the Application bar, and then click Classic to switch to the Classic workspace (Figure 1–3).

Q&A What is the Classic workspace?
The Classic workspace provides all the tools a beginning Web designer needs, and omits features for advanced designers and programmers.

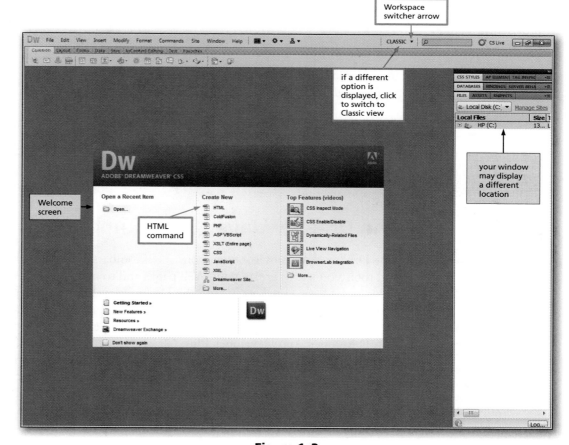

Figure 1–3

3

- Click HTML in the Create New column to close the Welcome screen and display the Dreamweaver workspace.

- If necessary, click the Maximize button to maximize the Dreamweaver window.

- If necessary, click the Design button on the Document toolbar to switch to Design view.

- If the Browser Navigation toolbar is displayed, right-click a blank spot on the Document toolbar, point to Toolbars, and then click Browser Navigation to remove the check mark so the Browser Navigation toolbar is not displayed in the Dreamweaver window.

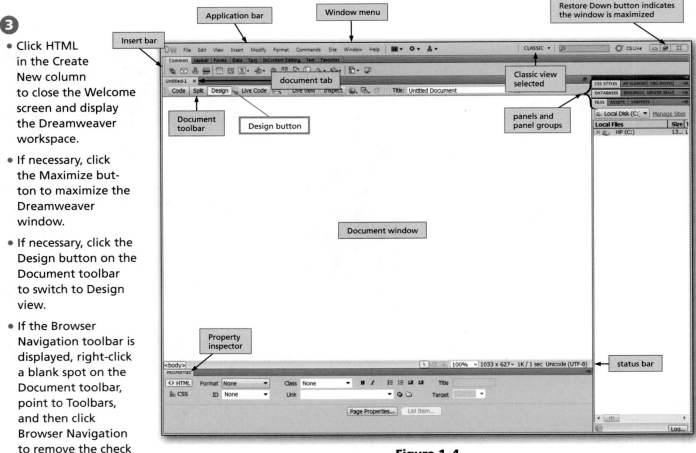

Figure 1–4

- If the Insert bar is not displayed, click Window on the Application bar and then click Insert (Figure 1–4).

Q&A

What if a message is displayed regarding default file types?

If a message is displayed, click the Close button.

Other Ways

1. Double-click Dreamweaver icon on desktop

BTW

The Dreamweaver Window
The screen in Figure 1–4 shows how the Dreamweaver window looks the first time you start Dreamweaver after installation on most computers. Your screen might look different depending on your Dreamweaver and computer settings.

The Dreamweaver Environment and Workspace

The Dreamweaver environment consists of toolbars, windows, objects, panels, inspectors, and tools you use to create your Web pages and to manage your Web site. It is important to learn the basic concepts behind the Dreamweaver workspace and to understand how to choose options, use inspectors and panels, and set preferences that best fit your work style.

Dreamweaver provides the Web site developer with eight preset workspace layouts: App Developer, App Developer Plus, Classic, Coder, Coder Plus, Designer, Designer Compact, and Dual Screen. Programmers who work primarily with HTML and other languages generally select the Coder or App Developer workspace. The Dual Screen option requires two monitors. In this layout, the Document window and Property inspector are displayed on one monitor and the panels are displayed on a secondary monitor. The Classic workspace contains a visually integrated workspace and is ideal for beginners and nonprogrammers. The projects and exercises in this book use the Classic workspace.

The settings on your computer determine what is displayed when the Dreamweaver CS5 program starts. By default, the Welcome screen is displayed each time you start

Dreamweaver. The Welcome screen's visual representation is a good tool for beginners, but more proficient Dreamweaver users generally disable this feature. You will disable the Welcome screen at the end of this chapter. If you are opening Dreamweaver from a computer at your school or other location, most likely the program is set up and ready to use.

The screen in Figure 1–4 shows a typical Dreamweaver workspace, with some of the more commonly used components displayed. The **Dreamweaver workspace** is an integrated environment in which the Document window and panels are incorporated into one larger application window. The panel groups are docked, or attached, on the right. The Insert bar (also called the Insert panel) is located at the top of the Document window, and the Property inspector is located at the bottom of the Document window. You can move, resize, close, or collapse the panels to accommodate your individual preferences.

The next section discusses the following components of the Dreamweaver workspace: title bar, Document window, panels and panel groups, status bar, Application bar, and toolbars.

As you learn to use each of these tools, you will discover some redundancy. For example, to apply a font tag, you can access the command through the CSS Property inspector, the Format menu, or the Text category on the Insert bar. The different options accommodate various user preferences. The chapters in this book present the more commonly used methods. The Other Ways boxes describe additional methods to accomplish a task when they are available. As you become proficient working in the Dreamweaver environment, you will develop techniques for using the tools that best suit your personal preferences.

Document Tab

The **document tab** displays the Web page name, which is Untitled-1 for the first Web page you create in a Dreamweaver session, as shown in Figure 1–4. (The "X" is the Close button for the document tab.) After you save and name the Web page, the document tab reflects the changes by displaying the document name. When you make changes to the document, Dreamweaver includes an asterisk following the file name. The asterisk is removed after the document is saved, and the file path leading to the document's location is displayed to the right of the document tab.

Document Window

The **Document window** displays the current document, or Web page, including text, tables, graphics, and other items. In Figure 1–4, the Document window is blank. You work in the Document window in one of the following views: **Design view**, the design environment where you assemble your Web page elements and design your page (Figure 1–4 displays Design view); **Code view**, which is a hand-coding environment for writing and editing code; **Split view**, which allows you to see both Code view and Design view for the same document in a single window; **Live View**, which shows the page such as it would appear in a browser; **Live Code**, which displays any HTML code produced by JavaScript or server-side programming; or **Inspect Mode**, which evaluates the code. When you open a new document in Dreamweaver, the default view is Design view. These views are discussed in detail in Chapter 2.

Panels and Panel Groups

Panel groups are sets of related panels docked together below one heading. Panels provide control over a wide range of Dreamweaver commands and functions. Each panel group can be expanded or collapsed, and can be undocked or docked with other panel

BTW

Change the Insert Bar to a Menu
Right-click any category name on the Insert bar and then click Show as Menu to change the horizontal tabs on the Insert bar to a vertical menu.

groups. Panel groups also can be docked to the integrated Document window. This makes it easy to access the panels you need without cluttering your workspace. Panels within a panel group are displayed as tabs. Each panel is explained in detail as it is used in the chapters throughout the book. Some panels, such as the Insert bar and Property inspector, are stand-alone panels.

The **Insert bar** allows quick access to frequently used commands. It contains buttons for creating and inserting various types of objects — such as images, tables, links, dates, and so on — into a document. As you insert each object, a dialog box allows you to set and manipulate various attributes. The buttons on the Insert bar are organized into several categories, such as Common and Layout, which you can access through tabs. Some categories also have buttons with pop-up menus. When you select an option from a pop-up menu, it becomes the default action for the button. When you start Dreamweaver, the category in which you last were working is displayed.

The **Property inspector** displays settings for the selected object's properties or attributes. This panel is context sensitive, meaning it changes based on the selected object, which can include text, tables, images, and other objects. When Dreamweaver starts, the Property inspector is positioned at the bottom of the Document window and displays text properties if a Document window is open. Otherwise, the Property inspector is blank.

Status Bar

The **status bar** located below the Document window (Figure 1–5) provides additional information about the document you are creating.

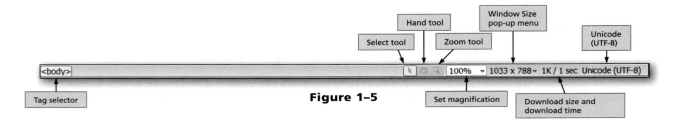

Figure 1–5

The status bar presents the following options:

- **Tag selector**: Click any tag in the hierarchy to select that tag and all its contents.
- **Select tool**: Use the Select tool to return to default editing after using the Zoom or Hand tool.
- **Hand tool**: To pan a page after zooming, use the Hand tool to drag the page.
- **Zoom tool**: Available in Design view or Split view, the Zoom tool can be used to check the pixel accuracy of graphics or to better view the page.
- **Set magnification**: Use the Set magnification pop-up menu to change the view from 6% to 6400%; default is 100%.
- **Window size**: Displays the Window size value, which includes the window's current dimensions (in pixels) and the Window size pop-up menu.
- **Download size and download time**: Displays the size and estimated download time of the current page. Dreamweaver CS5 calculates the size based on the entire contents of the page, including all linked objects such as images and plug-ins.
- **Unicode (UTF-8)**: An industry standard that allows computers to consistently represent and manipulate text expressed in most of the world's writing systems.

Vertical/Horizontal Bars

A vertical bar separates the panel groups from the Document window, and a horizontal bar separates the Property inspector from the Document window. Double-clicking the Property inspector bar hides or displays the Property inspector. The panel groups contain a Collapse to Icons/Expand Panels button (Figure 1–6). If your screen resolution is set to 800 × 600, a portion of the Property inspector may not be displayed when the panel groups are expanded.

Application Bar

The **Application bar** displays the Dreamweaver menu names (Figure 1–6). Each menu contains a list of commands you can use to perform tasks such as opening, saving, modifying, previewing, and inserting data into your Web page. When you point to a menu name on the Application bar, the area of the Application bar containing the name is selected.

To display a menu, such as the Edit menu (Figure 1–6), click the menu name on the Application bar. If you point to a menu command that has an arrow at its right edge, a submenu displays another list of commands. Many menus display some commands that appear gray, or dimmed, instead of black, which indicates they are not available for the current selection.

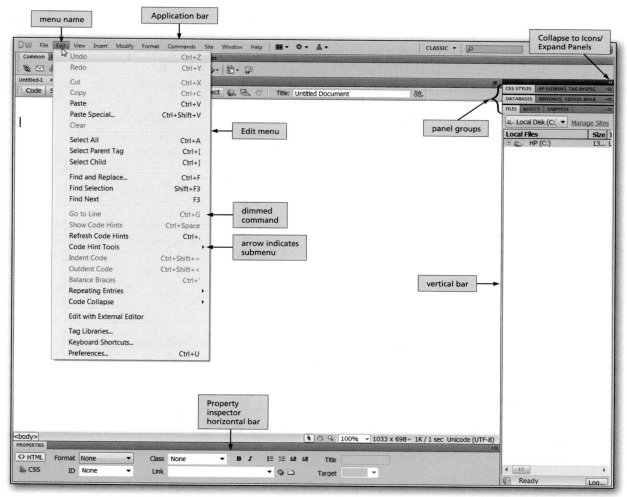

Figure 1–6

Toolbars

In the Classic workspace, or view, Dreamweaver can display four toolbars: Document, Standard, Style Rendering, and Browser Navigation. You can choose to display or hide the toolbars by clicking View on the Application bar and then pointing to Toolbars. If a toolbar name has a check mark next to it, it is displayed in the window. To hide the toolbar, click the name of the toolbar with the check mark, and it no longer is displayed. The Insert bar is considered a panel and was discussed previously in this chapter.

The **Document toolbar** (Figure 1–7) is the default toolbar displayed in the Document window. It contains buttons that provide different views of the Document window (e.g., Code, Split, and Design), the Document title, and some common operations, such as Preview/Debug in Browser, Refresh Design View, View Options, Visual Aids, and Check Browser Compatibility.

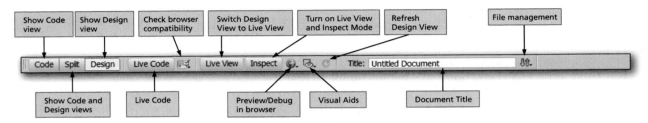

Figure 1–7

The **Standard toolbar** (Figure 1–8) contains buttons for common operations from the File and Edit menus: New, Open, Browse in Bridge, Save, Save All, Print Code, Cut, Copy, Paste, Undo, and Redo. The Standard toolbar is not displayed by default in the Dreamweaver Document window when you first start Dreamweaver. You can display the Standard toolbar through the Toolbars command on the View menu, or by right-clicking a blank area on the Document toolbar and then clicking Standard on the context menu. As with other toolbars and panels, you can dock or undock and move the Standard toolbar, so it might be displayed in a different location on your screen.

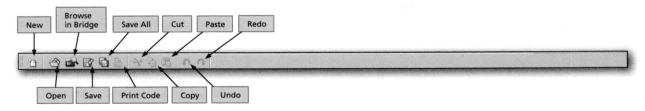

Figure 1–8

The **Style Rendering toolbar** (not shown by default) provides options for designing for different media types, such as screen, print, handheld, projection, TTY (teletype), television, CSS Styles, and Style Sheets. The CSS (Cascading Style Sheets) Styles button works independently of the other seven buttons and provides the option to disable or enable the display of CSS styles.

The **Browser Navigation toolbar** (also not shown by default) provides feedback regarding browser capability.

Opening and Closing Panels

The Dreamweaver workspace accommodates different work styles and levels of expertise. Through the workspace, you can open and close the panel groups and display or hide other Dreamweaver features as needed. To open a panel group, select and then click the name of a panel on the Window menu. Closing unused panels provides an uncluttered workspace in the Document window. To close an individual panel group, click Close Tab Group on the context menu accessed through the panel group's title bar (Figure 1–9) or click the Window menu and then click the panel name. To expand/collapse a panel, click the Expand Panels/Collapse to Icons button above the panel groups.

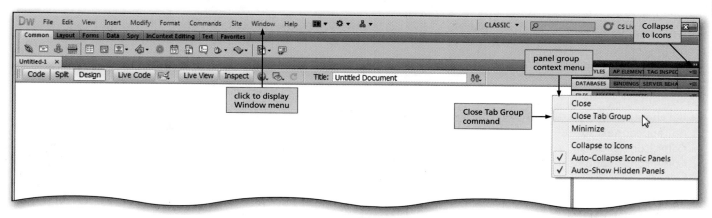

Figure 1–9

To Display the Standard Toolbar, Change the Icon Colors, and Close and Open Panels

The following steps illustrate how to display the Standard toolbar, change the icon colors, and close and open the panels.

- Click View on the Application bar to display the View menu.

- If necessary, click the down-pointing arrow at the bottom of the View menu to scroll the menu.

- Point to Toolbars, and then point to Standard on the Toolbars submenu to highlight Standard on the Toolbars submenu (Figure 1–10).

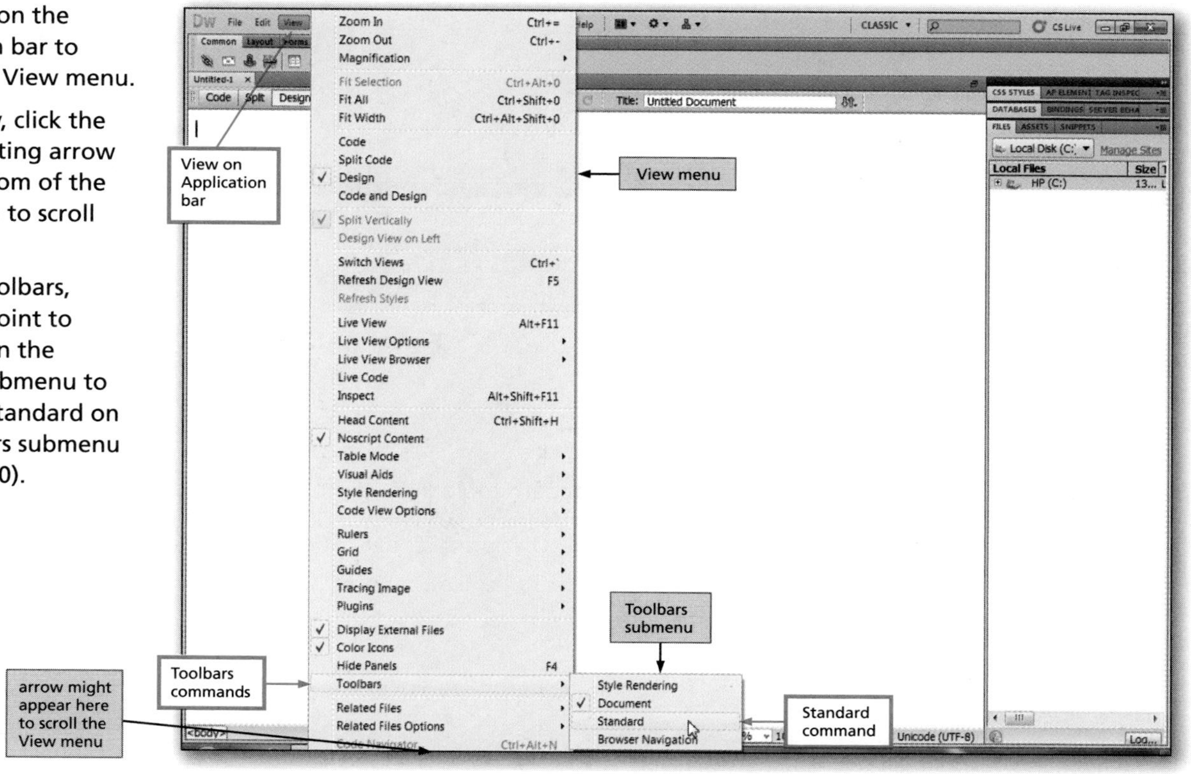

Figure 1–10

2

- Click Standard to display the Standard toolbar.

- If your Dreamweaver window does not display icons in color, right-click a blank spot on the Insert bar to display the context menu.

- Point to Color Icons on the context menu to highlight the command (Figure 1–11).

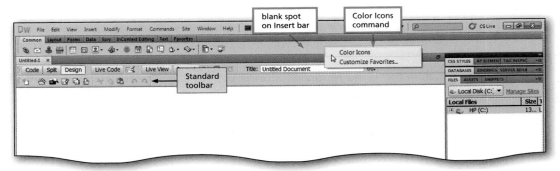

Figure 1–11

3

- If a check mark does not appear next to Color Icons, click Color Icons to add color to the icons.

- Press the F4 key to close all open panels and inspectors and to maximize the workspace available in the Document window.

- Press the F4 key again to redisplay the panels (Figure 1–12).

Q&A What is the fastest way to open and close panels?

The fastest way to open and close panels in Dreamweaver is to use the F4 key, which opens or closes all panels and inspectors at one time.

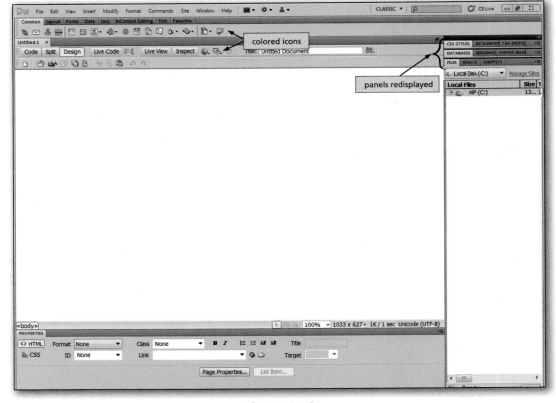

Figure 1–12

Q&A Can the location of the Standard toolbar change?

Yes. Previous settings determine the location of the Standard toolbar. It might be displayed below the Document toolbar or in another location in the Dreamweaver window.

Other Ways

1. Right-click blank area on toolbar, click Standard

2. Click View on Application bar, click Color Icons

Defining a Local Site

Web design and Web site management are two important skills that a builder of Web sites must understand and apply. Dreamweaver CS5 is a site creation and management tool. To use Dreamweaver efficiently, you first must define the local site. After defining the local site, you then publish to a remote site. Publishing to a remote site is discussed in Chapter 3 and Appendix C.

The general definition of a **site**, or Web site, is a set of linked documents with shared attributes, such as related topics, a similar design, or a shared purpose. In Dreamweaver, however, the term site can refer to any of the following:

- **Web site**: A set of pages on a server that are viewed through a Web browser by a visitor to the site.

- **Remote site**: Files on the server that make up a Web site, from the author's point of view rather than a visitor's point of view.

- **Local site**: Files on your computer that correspond to the files on the remote site. You edit the files on your computer, and then upload them to the remote site.

- **Dreamweaver site definition**: Set of defining characteristics for a local site, plus information on how the local site corresponds to a remote site.

All Dreamweaver Web sites begin with a local root folder. As you become familiar with Dreamweaver and complete the chapters in this book, you will find references to a **local site folder, local root folder, root folder**, and **root**. These terms are interchangeable. This folder is no different from any other folder on your computer's hard drive or other storage media, except for the way in which Dreamweaver views it. When Dreamweaver looks for Web pages, links, images, and other files, it looks in the designated root folder by default. Any media within the Web site that are outside of the root folder are not displayed when the Web site is previewed in a Web browser. Within the root folder, you can create additional folders and subfolders to organize images and other objects. A **subfolder** (also called a **nested folder**) is a folder inside another folder.

Dreamweaver provides two options to define a site and create the hierarchy: You can create the root folder and any subfolders, or create the pages and then create the folders when saving the files. In this book, you create the root folder and subfolders and then create the Web pages.

Determine the location for the local site.

Before you create a Web site, you need to determine where you will save the site and its files.

- If you plan to work on your Web site in various locations or on more than one computer, you should create your site on removable media, such as a USB flash drive. The Web sites in this book use a USB flash drive because these drives are portable and can store a lot of data.

- If you always work on the same computer, you probably can create your site on the computer's hard drive. However, if you are working in a computer lab, your instructor or the lab supervisor might instruct you to save your site in a particular location on the hard drive or on removable media such as a USB flash drive.

Plan Ahead

Creating the Local Root Folder and Subfolders

Several options are available to create and manage your local root folder and subfolders: Dreamweaver's Files panel, Dreamweaver's Site Setup feature, or Windows file management. In this book, you use Dreamweaver's Site Setup feature to create the local root folder and subfolders, the Files panel to manage and edit your files and folders, and Windows file management to download and copy the data files.

To organize and create a Web site and understand how you access Web documents, you need to understand paths and folders. The term path sometimes is confusing for new users of the Web. It is, however, a simple concept: A **path** is the succession of folders that must be navigated to get from one folder to another. Folders sometimes are referred to as **directories**. These two terms often are used interchangeably.

A typical path structure has a **master folder**, usually called the root and designated by the symbol "\". This root folder contains within it all of the other subfolders or nested folders. Further, each subfolder may contain additional subfolders or nested folders. These folders contain the Web site files. Most sites include a subfolder for images.

For this book, you first create a local root folder using your last name and first initial. Examples in this book use David Edwards as the Web site author. Thus, David's local root folder is edwardsd and is located on drive H (a removable disk). Next, for this chapter, you create a subfolder for the Montana Parks site and name it parks. Finally, you create another subfolder within parks and name it images. All Montana parks-related files and subfolders are stored within the parks folder. When you navigate through this folder hierarchy, you are navigating along the path. The path to the Montana Parks Web site is H:\edwardsd\parks\. The path to the images folder is H:\edwardsd\parks\images\. In all references to H:\edwardsd, substitute your last name and first initial and your drive location.

Using Site Setup to Create a Local Site

You create a local site using Dreamweaver's Site Setup dialog box. You work with two categories of settings:

- **Site category**: Enter the name of your site and the path to the local site folder. For example, you will use Montana Parks as the site name and H:\edwardsd\parks as the path to the local site. You can select the location of the local site folder instead of entering its path.

- **Advanced Settings category**: Enter Local Info settings, which include the path to the default images folder. For example, you will use H:\edwardsd\parks\images as the path to the folder containing the Web site images. You can select the location of the images folder instead of entering its path.

  Local Info settings also include options for specifying the types of links you will create in your site (relative to the document or to the site), and entering the URL of your Web site if you are using site-relative links. You also can check links for case-sensitivity (useful if you are publishing your site on a UNIX server) and enable caching to store frequently used site data.

  Note that the paths you enter to the local site folder and the images folder are included as part of the Web site. If you use removable media to store your files and move to another computer, you must recreate the local site setup on that computer.

  After you have completed the site definition, the hierarchy structure is displayed in the Dreamweaver **Local Files** list in the Files panel. This hierarchy structure is similar to the Windows file organization. The Local Files list provides a view of the devices and folders on your computer and shows how these devices and folders are organized.

To Use Site Setup to Create a Local Web Site

You define a local site by telling Dreamweaver where you plan to store local files. Use the Site Setup dialog box and the following steps to create a local Web site. A USB drive is used for all exercises in this book. If you are saving your sites at another location or on removable media, substitute that location for Removable Disk (H:).

- Click Site on the Application bar to display the Site menu, and then point to New Site to highlight that command (Figure 1–13).

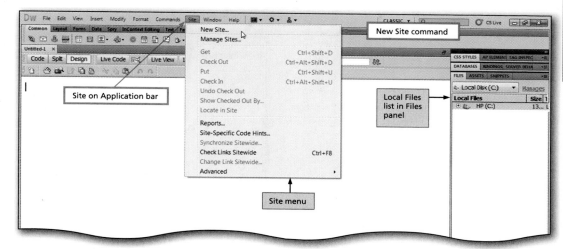

Figure 1–13

- Click New Site to display the Site Setup dialog box (Figure 1–14).

Q&A Should the name that appears in the Site Name text box be Unnamed Site 2?

Not necessarily. Your site number may be different.

Q&A What is the difference between the Local folder and the Remote folder?

The Local folder contains information about a Web site that you create on your computer, which is the way you develop a site. The Remote folder contains information about settings on a remote computer, such as a Web server, which is where you publish a site.

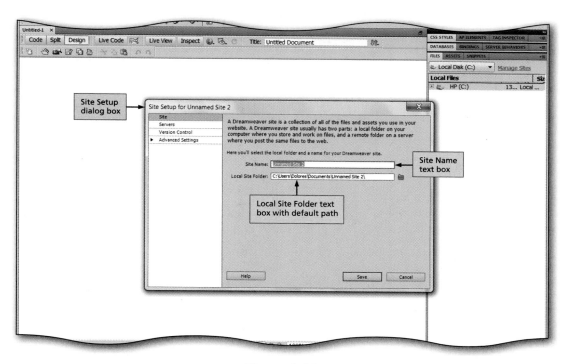

Figure 1–14

- Type **Montana Parks** in the Site name text box to name the site (Figure 1–15).

Q&A

Is the site name necessary?

This name is required, but it is for reference only. It is not part of the path and is not visible to viewers of your site.

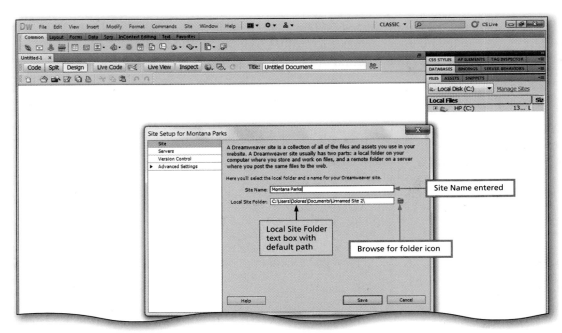

Figure 1–15

- Click the Browse for folder icon to display the Choose Root Folder dialog box.

- Navigate to where you will store your Web site files (Figure 1–16).

Q&A

On what drive should I store the Web site files?

Because most Web sites require many files, you should create the projects using a hard drive or removable drive with plenty of space — not the floppy drive (A:), if you have one. Steps in this chapter assume you are creating the local site on a USB drive. Check with your instructor to verify the location and path you will use to create and save your local Web site. Other options may include a CD-RW disc or a network drive.

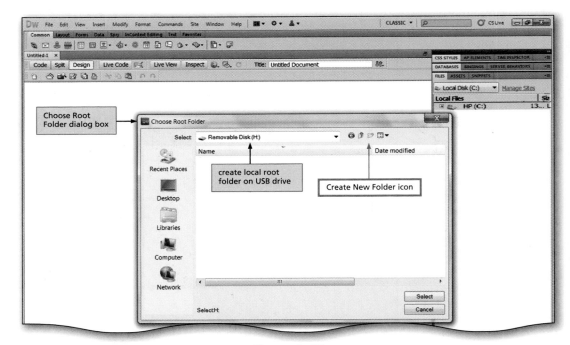

Figure 1–16

Q&A

What if my USB flash drive has a different name or letter?

It is very likely that your USB flash drive will have a different name and drive letter from the one shown in Figure 1–16 and be connected to a different port. Verify that the device displayed in the Select text box is correct.

5

- Click the Create New Folder icon to create a folder for your local site (Figure 1–17).

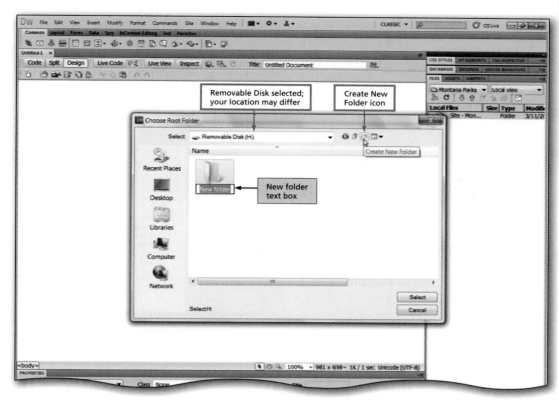

Figure 1–17

6

- For the root folder name, type your last name and first initial (with no spaces between your last name and initial) in the New folder text box. For example, type edwardsd. Press the ENTER key to rename the new folder, and then click the Open button to open the root folder (Figure 1–18).

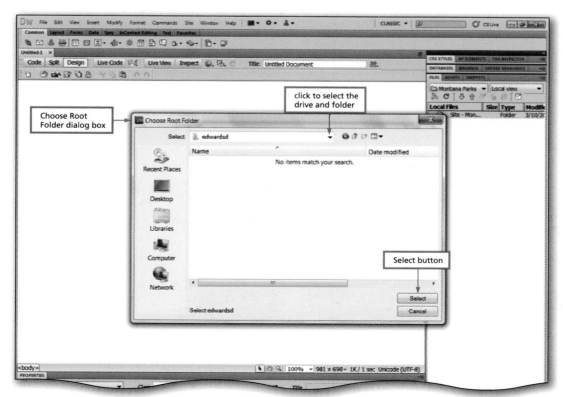

Figure 1–18

7

- Click the Create New Folder icon to create a folder for the Montana Parks Web site.

- Type **parks** as the name of the new folder, press the ENTER key, and then click the Open button to create the parks subfolder and open it.

- Click the Select button to display the Site Setup dialog box (Figure 1–19).

Q&A Why should I create a folder on the drive for my Web site?

Organizing your Web site folders now will save you time and prevent problems later.

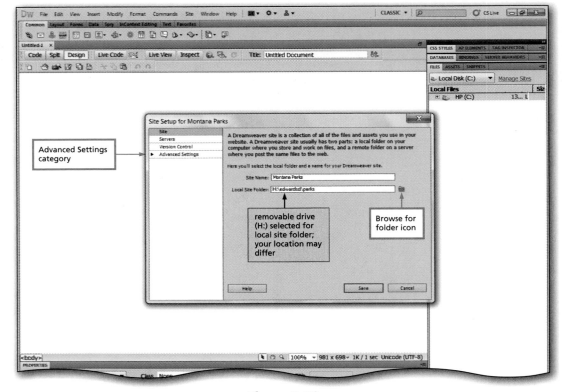

Figure 1–19

Create a main folder such as edwardsd for the sites in this book. (Substitute your last name and first initial for "edwardsd.") Create a subfolder in that main folder for the Montana Parks Web site. Finally, create a subfolder in the Montana Parks Web site folder for images.

Q&A Which files will I store in the parks folder?

The parks folder will contain all the files for the Montana Parks Web site. In other words, the parks folder is the local root folder for the Montana Parks Web site.

Q&A Am I finished defining the new Web site?

Not yet. Nearly every Web site displays graphics, photos, and other images, and you need to create a subfolder for these images.

8

- Click Advanced Settings in the category list to display the option for selecting the default images folder.

- Click the Browse for folder icon to specify the folder for the images.

- Navigate to the *your name*\parks folder.

- Click the Create New Folder icon to create a subfolder for images.

- Type **images** and then press the ENTER key to enter the name of the images subfolder.

- Click the Select button to select the images folder as the default folder for images and to display the Site Setup for Montana Parks dialog box (Figure 1–20).

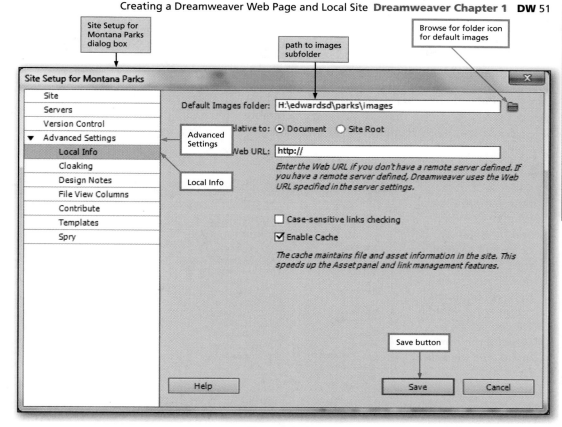

Figure 1–20

9

- Click the Save button to save the site settings and display the Dreamweaver workspace. The Montana Parks Web site hierarchy is displayed in the Files panel (Figure 1–21).

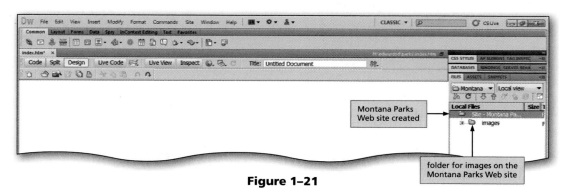

Figure 1–21

Q&A

What do the icons in the Files panel mean?

A small device icon or folder icon is displayed next to each object listed in the Files panel. The device icon represents a device such as the Desktop or a disk drive, and the folder icon represents a folder. Many of these icons have a plus or minus sign next to them, which indicates whether the device or folder contains additional folders. The plus and minus signs are controls that you can click to expand or collapse the view of the file hierarchy. In the Files panel, the site folders and files appear in a different color than non-site folders and files so that you easily can distinguish between the two.

Q&A

What else does the Local Files list in the Files panel display?

The Local Files list displays a site, including local, remote, and testing server files associated with a selected site. In this chapter, you view only the local site.

Other Ways

1. Click Site button in Files panel, click Manage Sites, click New

To Copy Data Files to the Local Web Site

Your data files contain background images and text files for the Chapter 1 project and exercises. You can copy the data files one by one through the Dreamweaver Files panel as you progress through this chapter. Alternatively, using the Windows Computer tool, you can establish the basic framework for the parks Web site by copying all the files and images at one time. The following steps illustrate how to copy data files to the local Web site.

- Click the Start button on the Windows taskbar and then click Computer to display the Computer window. If necessary, right-click the background of the folder window, point to View on the context menu, and then click List.

- Navigate to the location of the data files for this book to display the files in the Computer window (Figure 1–22).

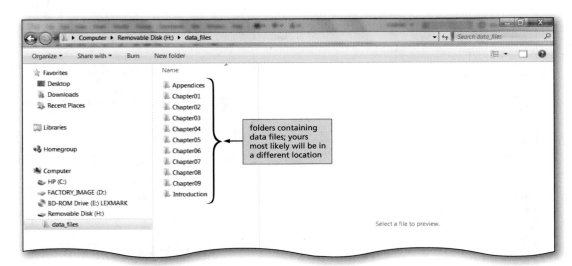

Figure 1–22

Q&A

What if my data files are located on a different drive or folder?

In Figure 1–22, the location is Removable Disk (H:), a USB drive. Most likely your data files are stored in a different location. Your data files also could be stored in a folder with a name other than "data_files."

- Double-click the Chapter01 folder to open it (Figure 1–23).

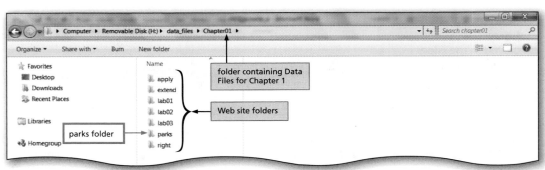

Figure 1–23

- Double-click the parks folder to open it (Figure 1–24).

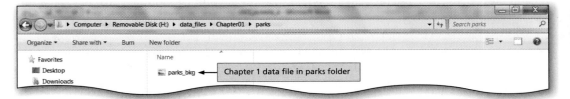

Figure 1–24

4

- Right-click the parks_bkg image file to display a context menu.
- Point to the Copy command on the context menu to highlight the command (Figure 1–25).

 My context menu contains different commands. Is that a problem?

No. A file's context menu often changes depending on the programs on your computer. The Copy command, however, always appears on this menu.

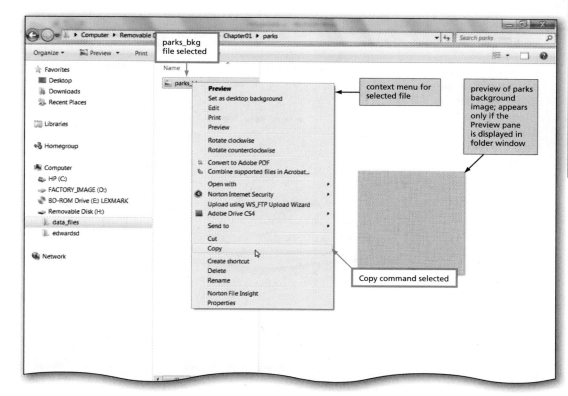

Figure 1–25

5

- Click Copy and then click the Back button the number of times necessary to navigate to the Computer window.
- Navigate to the drive containing the *your name* folder.
- Double-click the *your name* folder, double-click the parks folder, and then double-click the images folder to open the images folder for your Web site.
- Right-click anywhere in the open window to display the context menu.
- Point to the Paste command to highlight it (Figure 1–26).

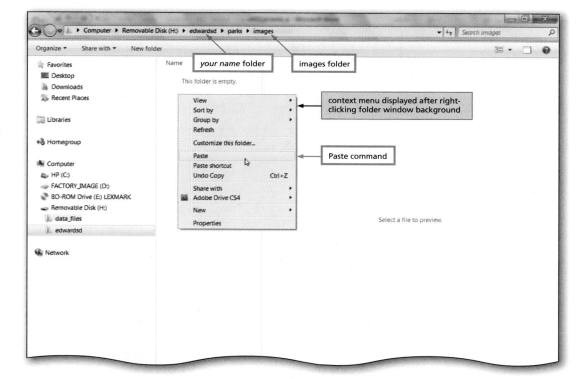

Figure 1–26

• Click the Paste command to paste the parks_bkg image into the *your name*\parks\images folder, which is the images folder for the Montana Parks Web site (Figure 1–27).

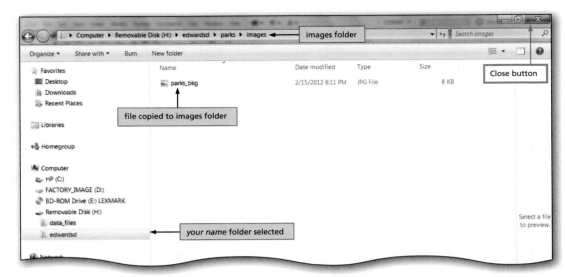

Figure 1–27

• Click the images window's Close button to close the images folder window.

• Double-click the images folder in the Dreamweaver Files panel to open the images folder (Figure 1–28).

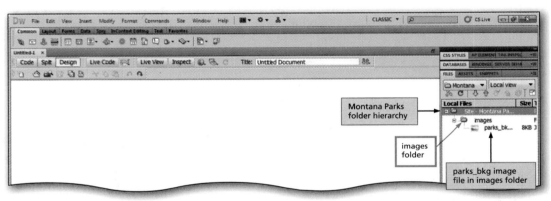

Figure 1–28

Other Ways

1. Open data files folder, open images folder for Web site, select data files, hold down CTRL and drag to images folder

Removing or Editing a Web Site

On occasion, you may need to remove or edit a Web site. To remove or edit a Web site, click Site on the Application bar and then click the Manage Sites command. This displays the Manage Sites dialog box. Select the site name and then click the Remove button to remove the site. Dreamweaver displays a caution box providing you with an opportunity to cancel. Click the No button to cancel. Otherwise, click the Yes button, and Dreamweaver removes the site. Removing a site in Dreamweaver removes the settings for the site. The files and folders remain and must be deleted separately.

To edit a site, click the site name and then click the Edit button. Dreamweaver displays the Site Setup dialog box; from there, you can change any of the options you selected when you first created the site.

Preparing Your Workspace and Saving a Web Page

With the Montana Parks site defined and the data file copied to the site, the next step is to save the untitled Dreamweaver document. When you defined the site, you designated the local root folder (*your name*\parks). You can copy and paste files into this folder using Windows, or you can use Dreamweaver's file management tools to copy and paste. You also can save a Dreamweaver document into this folder. Dreamweaver treats any item placed in the folder as part of the site.

When a document is saved as a Web page, the Web page also remains in the computer's memory and is displayed in the Document window. It is a good practice to save when you first open the document and then save regularly while you are working in Dreamweaver. By doing so, you protect yourself from losing all the work you have done since the last time you saved.

Rulers

Rulers help you measure, organize, and plan your layout. They are turned off by default in the Classic workspace. When rulers are turned on, they appear on the left and top borders of the page, marked in pixels, inches, or centimeters. They especially are helpful when working with tables or layers. Rulers, however, sometimes can be distracting when first learning how to use Dreamweaver, so you will make sure they are turned off shortly.

The Index Page

The **home page** is the starting point for the rest of your Web site. For most Web sites, the home page is named index. This name has special significance because most Web servers recognize index.htm (or index.html) as the default home page.

Dreamweaver comes with a number of default commands. These defaults are stored in different categories in Dreamweaver's Preferences dialog box. Dreamweaver's default extension for new documents is .html. Although there is some debate about which extension to use — .htm or .html — most Web sites use .htm. You change the default through the Preferences dialog box. Therefore, when you save your document, Dreamweaver automatically adds the extension .htm to the file name. Documents with the .htm extension are displayed in Web browsers.

BTW

Best Practices for Naming Web Pages
To make sure your Web pages work well with most servers and browsers, name Web site files and folders using all lowercase characters, do not use spaces (use an underscore instead, as in file_name), do not use special characters such as @ or slashes, and keep the names short (up to eight characters).

To Hide the Rulers, Change the .html Default, and Save a Document as a Web Page

The home page for your Montana Parks Web site is named index.htm. The following steps show how to prepare your workspace by turning off the rulers, if necessary, and changing the .html default extension to .htm. You then save the untitled document as index.htm in the parks local root folder. If the Rulers are not displayed in your Document window, omit Steps 1 and 2.

1

- If Rulers are turned on, click View on the Application bar, point to Rulers, and then point to Show on the Rulers submenu to highlight the command (Figure 1–29).

Q&A

What should I do if rulers are not displayed in my Document window?

Skip Steps 1 and 2 and start with Step 3 to change the default file name extension.

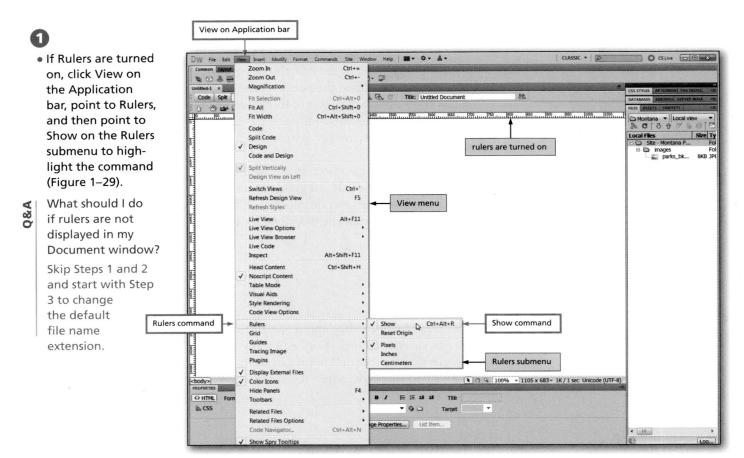

Figure 1–29

2

- Click Show to turn off the rulers (Figure 1–30).

Q&A

How can I display the rulers again later?

Perform Steps 1 and 2 again: click View on the Application bar, point to Rulers, and then click Show.

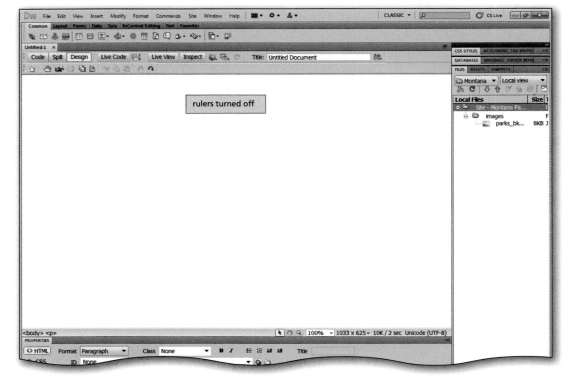

Figure 1–30

3

- Click Edit on the Application bar, and then click Preferences to display the Preferences dialog box (Figure 1–31).

Q&A

What if the Preferences dialog box displays a category of options different from the one shown in Figure 1–31?

The Preferences dialog box displays the last category of options used on your computer. You'll select the category for changing the default extension in the next step.

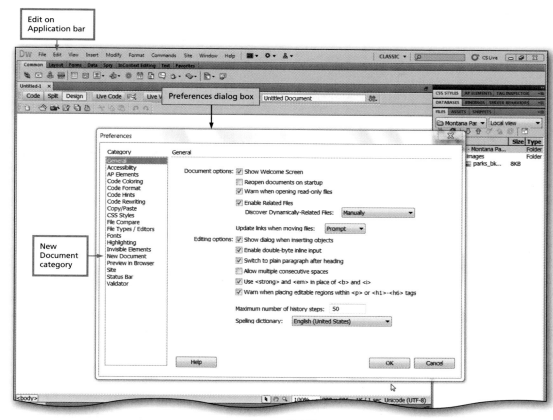

Figure 1–31

4

- Click the New Document category, if necessary, delete .html as the Default extension, and then type **.htm** to change the Default extension (Figure 1–32).

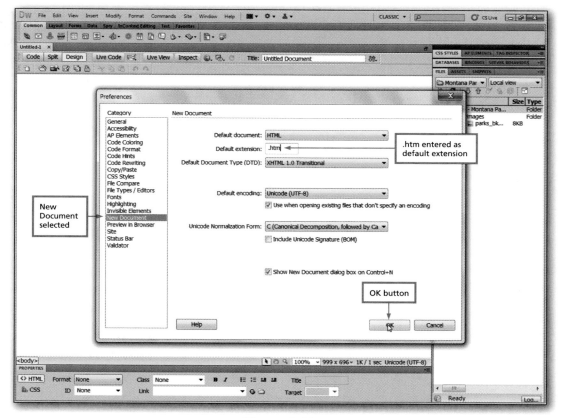

Figure 1–32

5

- Click the OK button in the Preferences dialog box to accept the setting and display the Document window.

- Click the Save button on the Standard toolbar to display the Save As dialog box (Figure 1–33).

Figure 1–33

6

- Type **index** as the file name of the new document (Figure 1–34).

Why is the file name specified in all lowercase characters?

Some Web servers are case sensitive, which means that they consider a file named "index" different from one named "Index." It's common practice among Web designers to use only lowercase characters for the names of all Web site files, including documents and images.

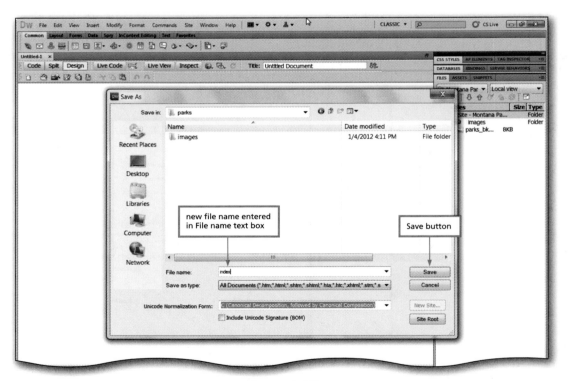

Figure 1–34

7

- Click the Save button to save the index.htm file in the Files panel under Local Files.

- Click the collapse icon next to the images folder to display only the images folder and the index.htm file in the Local Files list (Figure 1–35).

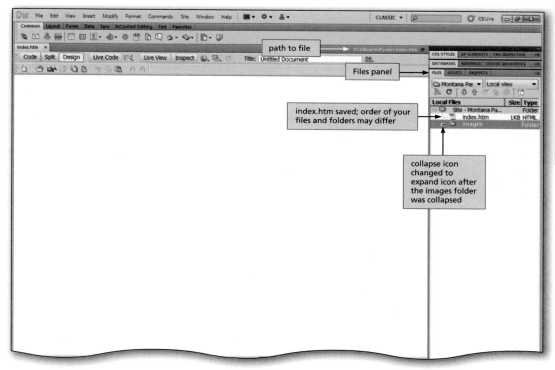

Figure 1–35

Web Page Backgrounds

Each new Web page you create is displayed with a default white or gray background and other default properties. You can modify these default properties using the **Page Properties** dialog box. The Page Properties dialog box lets you specify appearance, links, and many other aspects of page design. You can assign new page properties for each new page you create, and modify properties for existing pages. The page properties you select apply only to the active document.

Plan Ahead

Add a background for the Web page.

As you design and plan a Web page, consider the following guidelines for applying color and images to the background:

- You can change the default background and enhance your Web page by adding a background image or background color. If you use both a background image and a background color, the color appears while the image downloads, and then the image covers the color.

- Use a background image to add texture and interesting color to a Web page. You can find copyright-free background images on the Web or you can design them yourself.

- Be cautious when selecting or designing background images. Web page images displayed on top of a busy background image may not mix well, and text may be difficult to read. Images and image formats are discussed in more detail in Chapter 2.

To Add a Background Image to the Index Page

When you copied the data file earlier in this chapter, you copied an image file that will be the background for the Montana Parks Web site pages. The following steps illustrate how to use the Page Properties dialog box to add that background image to the index page.

1
- Click Modify on the Application bar and then click Page Properties to display the Page Properties dialog box.
- Click the Appearance (HTML) category to display options for adding a background image to the page (Figure 1–36).

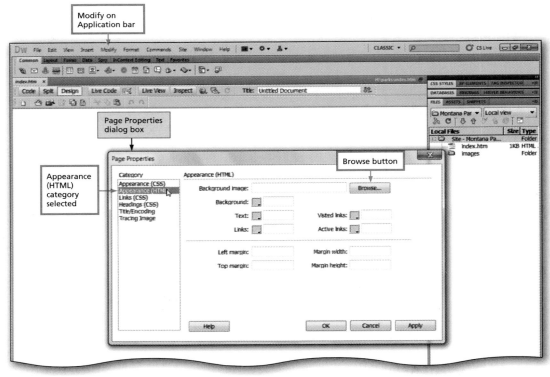

Figure 1–36

2
- Click the Background image Browse button to display the Select Image Source dialog box (Figure 1–37).

Q&A

Why should I use a background image on my Web pages? Background images add texture and visual interest to your Web pages.

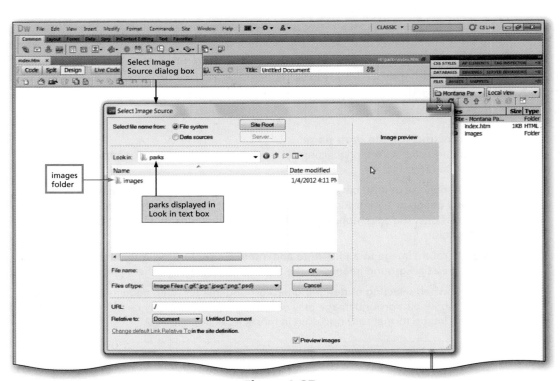

Figure 1–37

3

- Double-click the images folder to display the images file list.

- If necessary, click the View Menu button and then click Details to display the file list in Details view.

- Click the parks_bkg file to select the file (Figure 1–38).

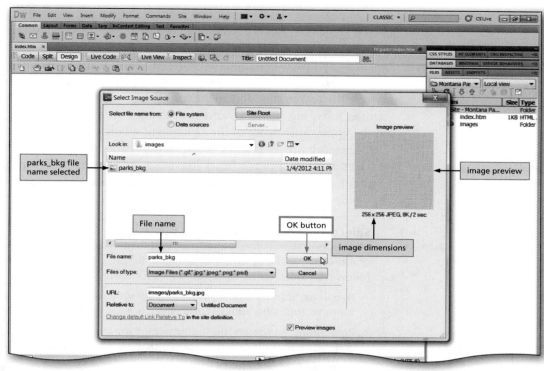

Figure 1–38

4

- Click the OK button to accept the background image and close the Select Image Source dialog box.

- Click the OK button to apply the image to the page.

- Click the Save button on the Standard toolbar to save the document (Figure 1–39).

Q&A

How do I know the document is saved?

When the document is saved, the Save button on the Standard toolbar is dimmed.

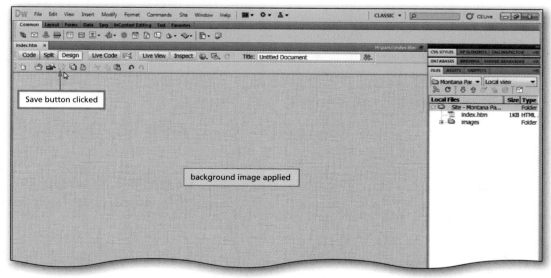

Figure 1–39

Other Ways

1. Right-click Document window, click Page Properties on context menu
2. Click Page Properties button in Property inspector
3. Press CTRL+J

Adding Text to a Web Page

In Dreamweaver, you can create a Web page in several ways: (1) add text to a new document; (2) open an existing HTML document, even if it was not created in Dreamweaver; (3) copy and paste text; and (4) import a Word or Excel document or tabular data.

In this chapter, you create the index page for the Montana Parks Web page by typing the text in the Document window. Entering text into a Dreamweaver document is similar to typing text in a word-processing document. You can position the insertion point at the upper-left corner of the Document window or within another object, such as a table cell. Pressing the ENTER key creates a new paragraph and inserts a blank line. Web browsers automatically insert a blank line of space between paragraphs. To start a new single line without a blank line between lines of text requires a **line break**. You can insert a line break by holding down the SHIFT key and then pressing the ENTER key.

Plan Ahead

Select the words and fonts for the text.

Most informational Web pages start with a heading, include paragraphs of text, provide one or more lists, and end with a closing line. Before you add text to a Web page, consider the following guidelines for organizing and formatting text:

- **Headings**: Start by identifying the headings you will use. Determine which headings are for main topics (Heading 1) and which are for subtopics (Heading 2 or 3).

- **Paragraphs**: For descriptions or other information, include short paragraphs of text. To emphasize important terms, format them as bold or italic.

- **Lists**: Use lists to organize key points, a sequence of steps, or other information you want to highlight. If amount or sequence matter, number each item in a list. Otherwise, use a bullet (a dot or other symbol that appears at the beginning of the paragraph).

- **Closing**: The closing is usually one sentence that provides information of interest to most Web page viewers or that indicates where people can find more information about your topic.

To Hide the Panel Groups

The following step shows how to provide more workspace by hiding the panel groups.

1

- Click Window on the Application bar and then click Hide Panels to close the Files panel and the Property inspector (Figure 1–40).

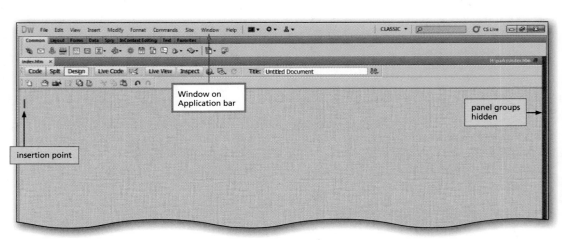

Figure 1–40

Other Ways
1. Press F4

Adding Text

Table 1–1 includes the text for the Montana Parks and Recreation Areas Web page. After typing each section of the document, you press the ENTER key to insert a blank line.

Table 1–1 Montana Parks and Recreation Areas Web Page Text	
Section	**Heading, Part 1, and Part 2 Text**
Heading	Montana Parks and Recreation Areas
Part 1 – first paragraph	Montana contains a variety of national parks and recreational areas, including two national parks, a national historical park, a national historic trail, a national historic site, a national recreation area, and a national battlefield.
Part 2 – second paragraph	In addition to the national facilities, over 50 state parks are located throughout the state. Some of the greatest natural and cultural treasures on earth are located in these parks and recreational areas.
Part 3 – bulleted list	Some of the highlights of this state include the following: Yellowstone National Park, established in 1872, was America's first national park. This park also extends into Idaho and Wyoming. In addition to the national parks and sites, you also can visit over 50 state parks, including natural parks, cultural parks, and recreational parks. A variety of events are available throughout the state, including such activities as a buffalo feast, panning for gold, native friendship dances, and Indian tacos.
Part 4 – closing paragraph	Special events are posted on the park's calendar as they are scheduled. Most of the events are free.

To Add a Heading and Introductory Paragraph Text

The following steps show how to add text to the Document window and insert blank lines between sections of text.

1
- Click in the Document window, type the heading **Montana Parks and Recreation Areas** as shown in Table 1–1, and then press the ENTER key to enter the heading for the Web page.

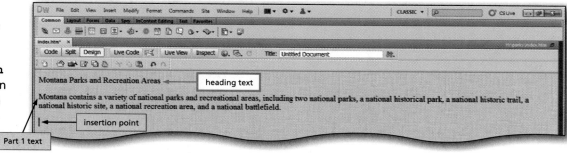

Figure 1–41

- Type the text of Part 1 as shown in Table 1–1, and then press the ENTER key (Figure 1–41).

Q&A What should I do if I make a typing error?

Press the BACKSPACE key to delete text you typed, or select the text and then press the DELETE key. Correct your typing mistakes the way you would in a word-processing program.

2

- Type the text of Part 2 as shown in Table 1–1 on the previous page, and then press the ENTER key to insert a blank line (Figure 1–42).

Q&A

Why does my text wrap at different locations from those shown in Figure 1–42?

Where your text wraps depends on whether your Dreamweaver window is maximized, the screen resolution (which is 1024 x 768 in the figures in this book), and whether your computer has a standard or wide-screen monitor.

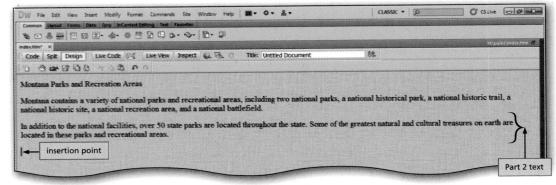

Figure 1–42

3

- Type the first line of the Part 3 text shown in Table 1–1, and then press the ENTER key to insert a blank line (Figure 1–43).

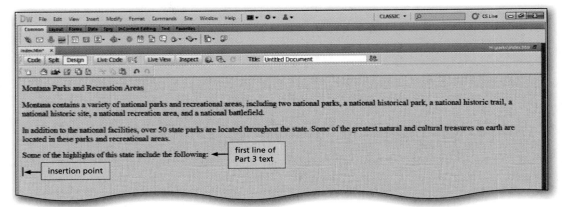

Figure 1–43

4

- Type the three items for the bulleted list as shown in Table 1–1. Press the ENTER key after each entry to insert space between the lines (Figure 1–44).

Q&A

When do I add bullets to the list? You will add bullets when you format the text in the next section of this chapter.

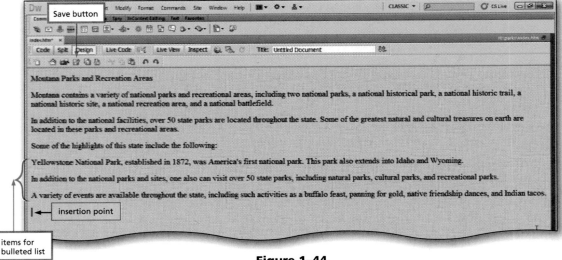

Figure 1–44

5
• Type the closing paragraph shown in Table 1–1, and then press the ENTER key to insert a blank line.

• Click the Save button on the Standard toolbar to save your work (Figure 1–45).

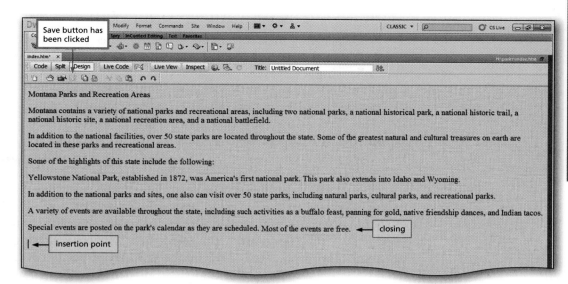

Figure 1–45

Deleting Web Pages

If you need to start over for any reason, you can delete a Web page file. Close the page, display the panel groups if necessary, right-click the name of the page you want to delete, point to Edit on the context menu, and then click Delete. You also can select a file and press the DELETE key. Dreamweaver will display a warning dialog box. If files are linked to other files, information will be displayed indicating how to update the links. To delete the file, click Yes in the dialog warning box or click No to cancel.

Formatting Features

The next step is to format the text on your Web page. **Formatting** means to change heading styles, insert special characters, and insert or modify other elements that enhance the appearance of the Web page. Dreamweaver provides three options for formatting text: the Format menu on the Application bar, the Insert bar Text category, and the Property inspector. To format the text for the Montana Parks index page, you use the text-related features of the Property inspector.

The Property inspector is one of the panels you use most often when creating and formatting Web pages. It displays the properties, or characteristics, of the selected object. The object can be a table, text, image, or some other item. The Property inspector is context sensitive, so its options change relative to the selected object.

Property Inspector Features

Divided into two sections, the HTML Property inspector lets you see the current properties of the selected object and alter or edit them. When the panel groups are closed, you can click the expander arrow in the lower-right corner of the Property inspector to collapse the Property inspector to show only the more commonly used properties for the selected element or to expand the Property inspector to show more options.

Collapsing/Hiding the Property Inspector

Displaying panels such as the Property inspector requires considerable window space. If you are finished working with a panel, it generally is better to collapse it or close it. **Collapsing** it leaves the title bar in the window. Double-clicking the horizontal bar collapses and expands the Property inspector. Pressing CTRL+F3 also collapses/expands the Property inspector. **Closing** the Property inspector removes it from the Document window. To close the Property inspector, display its context menu by right-clicking the Properties title bar and then selecting the Close Tab Group command. (You also can click the Options button on the Property inspector and then select Close Tab Group.) To open the Property inspector, click the Window menu and then click Properties.

By default, the Property inspector displays the properties for text in a blank document. Most changes you make to properties are applied immediately in the Document window. For some properties, however, you must apply changes by clicking outside a text box in the Properties inspector, pressing the ENTER key, or pressing the TAB key to switch to another property. The left side of the Property inspector contains two buttons: HTML and CSS. Most CSS options are discussed in detail in Chapter 5 of the Complete edition of this book. The following section describes the HTML-related features of the Property inspector (Figure 1–46).

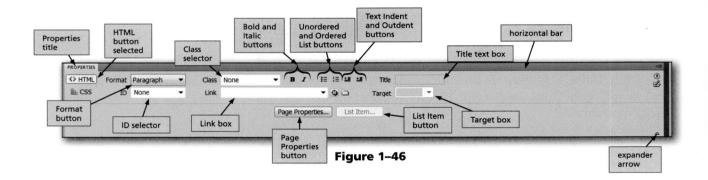

Figure 1–46

Format The **Format button** allows you to apply a Paragraph, Heading, or Preformatted style to the text. Clicking the Format button displays a pop-up menu from which you can select a style.

The **Paragraph style** is the normal default style for text on a Web page. **Paragraph formatting** is the process of changing the appearance of text. **Heading styles** are used to create divisions and separate one segment of text from another. These formats are displayed based on how different browsers interpret the tags, offering little consistency and control over layout and appearance. When you apply a heading tag to text, Dreamweaver automatically adds the next line of text as a standard paragraph. You can use the **Preformatted style** when you do not want a Web browser to change the line of text in any way.

Class Class displays the style that currently is applied to the selected text. If no styles have been applied to the selection, the Class text box shows None. If multiple styles have been applied to the selection, the text box is blank.

Bold and Italic The **Bold button** and the **Italic button** allow you to format text using these two common font styles. Dreamweaver also supports a variety of other font styles, which are available through the Format menu Style command. To view these styles, click Format on the Application bar and then point to Style. The Style submenu contains a list of additional styles, such as Underline, Strikethrough, and Teletype.

Unordered List Web developers often use a list to structure a page. An unordered list turns the selected paragraph or heading into an item in a bulleted list. If no text is selected before the **Unordered List button** is clicked, a new bulleted list is started. This command is also available through the HTML Property inspector and through the Application bar Format menu List command.

Ordered List An ordered list is similar to an unordered list. This type of list, however, turns the selected paragraph or heading into an item in a numbered list. If no text is selected before the **Ordered List button** is clicked, a new numbered list is started. This command also is available through the HTML Property inspector and through the Application bar Format menu List command.

Definition List A definition list is composed of items followed by an indented description, such as a glossary list. This command is available through the Application bar Format menu List command.

Indent and Outdent To set off a block quote, you can use the Indent feature. The **Text Indent button** will indent a line or a paragraph from both margins. In XHTML and HTML, this is the blockquote tag. The **Text Outdent button** removes the indentation from the selected text by removing the blockquote tag. In a list, indenting creates a nested list, and removing the indentation removes the nesting from the list. A **nested list** is one list inside another list and is not the same as the block quote created by the Indent feature.

Title Specifies the ScreenTip text for a hypertext link.

ID Identifies the content of an element with a unique name; used to select an ID from any linked or external CSS style sheet. CSS style sheets are covered in Chapter 5.

Link The **Link (Hyperlink) box** allows you to make selected text or other objects a hyperlink to a specified URL or Web page. To use the Property inspector to select the URL or Web page, you can (a) click the Point to File or Browse for File icon to the right of the Link box to browse to a page in your Web site and select the file name, (b) type the URL, or (c) drag a file from the Files panel into the Link box. Links are covered in detail in Chapter 2. The Insert menu on the Application bar also contains a Hyperlink option.

Page Properties Clicking the Page Properties button on the Property inspector or the Properties command on the Modify menu opens the Page Properties dialog box.

List Item If the selected text is part of a list, click the List Item button to set list properties for the text, such as the type of bullet or the starting number.

Target In the **Target text box**, you specify the frame or window in which the linked page should load. If you are using frames, the names of all the frames in the current document are displayed in the list. If the specified frame does not exist when the current document is opened in a browser, the linked page loads in a new window with the name you specified. Once this window exists, other files can be targeted to it.

BTW

Understanding Fonts
The default font used for new Web pages is 12-pt Times New Roman. You can change the font of selected text using the Font submenu on the Format menu. Select Default to remove previously applied fonts. For HTML text, selecting Default displays the text in the browser's default font.

Applying Text-Related Features

The text for your Web page is displayed in the Document window. The next step in creating your Web page is to format this text. You use commands from the Property inspector and the Format menu on the Application bar to format the text.

Within Dreamweaver, you can format text before you type, or you can apply new formats after you type. If you have used word-processing software, you will find many of the Dreamweaver formatting commands similar to the commands within a word-processing program. At this point, your Web page contains only text, so the Property inspector displays attributes related to text.

To set block formatting, such as formatting a heading or an unordered list, position the insertion point in the line or paragraph and then format the text.

Text Headings

Just as in a word-processing document, designers use the heading structure in a Web page to set apart document or section titles. The six levels of HTML headings are Heading 1 through Heading 6. **Heading 1 <h1>** produces the largest text and **Heading 6 <h6>** the smallest. By default, browsers will display the six heading levels in the same font, with the point size decreasing as the importance of the heading decreases.

To Format Text with the Heading 1 Style

The following steps show how to format a heading.

1

- Click Window on the Application bar, and then click Properties to display the Property inspector.

- If necessary, scroll up and then position the insertion point anywhere in the heading text, Montana Parks and Recreation Areas to prepare for applying the Heading 1 format to that text (Figure 1–47).

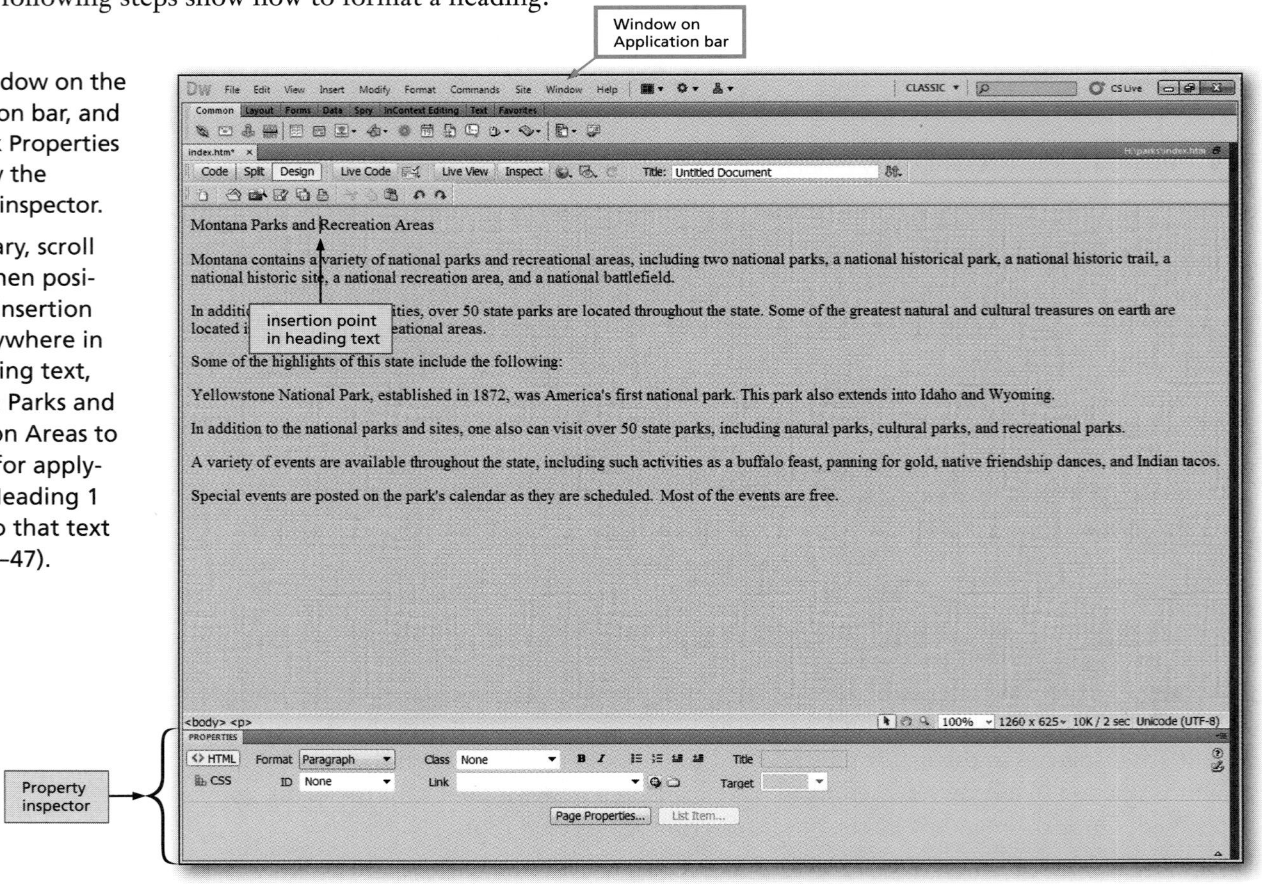

Figure 1–47

2

- Click the Format button in the Property inspector, and then point to Heading 1 to highlight the command (Figure 1–48).

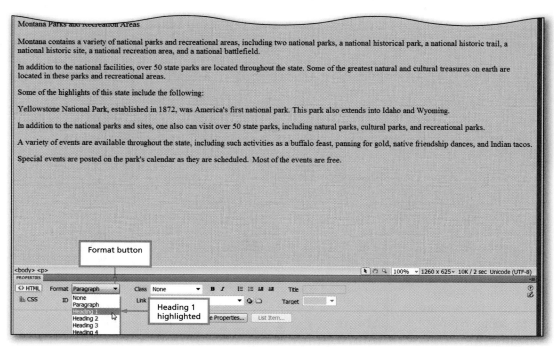

Figure 1–48

3

- Click Heading 1 to apply the Heading 1 style to the Montana Parks and Recreation Areas text (Figure 1–49).

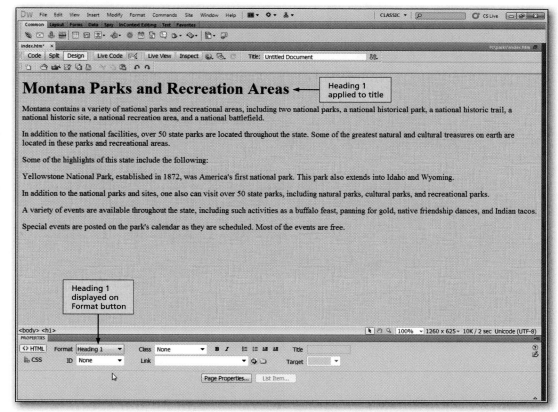

Figure 1–49

Other Ways

1. On Format menu, point to Paragraph Format, click Heading 1

2. Right-click selected text, point to Paragraph Format, click Heading 1

Centering Text

Using the Center command on the Align submenu on the Format menu allows you to center text. This command is very similar to the Center command or button in a word-processing program. To center a single line or a paragraph, position the mouse pointer anywhere in the line or paragraph, and then click the Format menu on the Application bar, point to Align, and then click Center to center the text. You do not need to select a single line or single paragraph to center it. To center more than one paragraph at a time, however, you must select all paragraphs.

To Center the Web Page Heading

The following steps illustrate how to center a heading.

1

- If necessary, click anywhere in the Montana Parks and Recreation Areas heading to prepare for centering that text.

- Click Format on the Application bar, point to Align, and then point to Center to highlight that command (Figure 1–50).

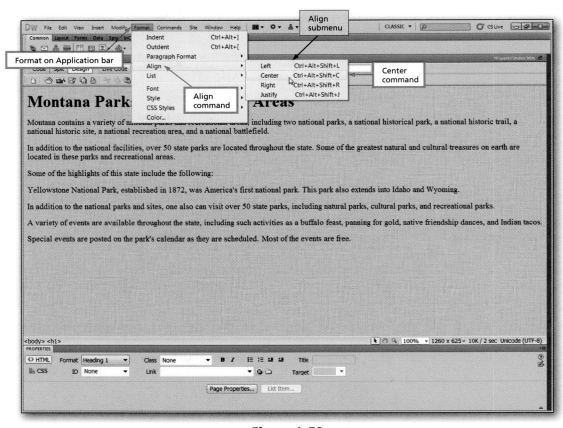

Figure 1–50

2

- Click Center on the Align submenu to center the heading (Figure 1–51).

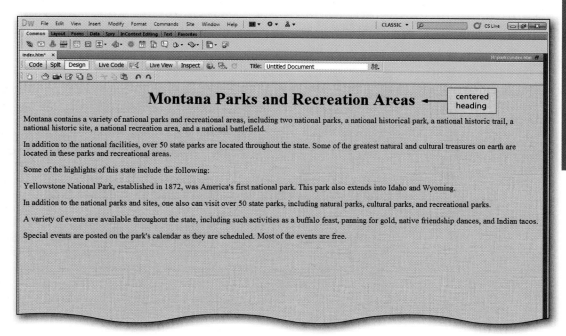

Figure 1–51

Types of Lists

One way to group and organize information is by using lists. Web pages can have three types of lists: ordered (numbered), unordered (bulleted), and definition. Ordered **lists** contain text preceded by numbered steps. Unordered lists contain text preceded by bullets (dots or other symbols) or image bullets. You use an unordered list if the items need not be listed in any particular order. **Definition lists** do not use leading characters such as bullet points or numbers. Glossaries and descriptions often use this type of list.

The Unordered List and Ordered List buttons are available in the Property inspector. You can access the Definition List command through the Application bar List command submenu. Through the List Properties dialog box, you can set the number style, reset the count, or set the bullet style options for individual list items or for the entire list. To access the List Properties dialog box, click anywhere in the list, and then click the List Item button in the Property inspector.

You can create a new list or you can create a list using existing text. When you select existing text and add bullets, the blank lines between the list items are deleted. Later in this chapter, you add line breaks to reinsert a blank line between each list item.

BTW

Lists
You can remove the bullets or numbers from a formatted list just as easily as you added them. Select the formatted list, and then click the button in the Property inspector that you originally used to apply the formatting.

To Create an Unordered List

The following steps show how to create an unordered (bulleted) list using existing text.

1
- Click to the left of the line that begins with "Yellowstone National Park".
- Drag to select the Yellowstone National Park paragraph and the next two paragraphs (Figure 1–52).

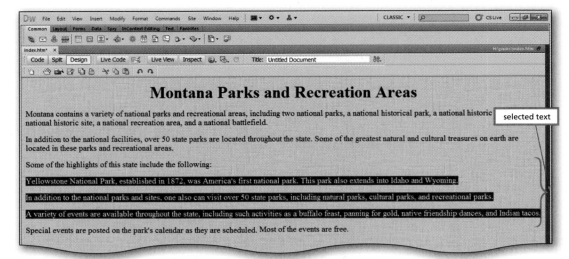

Figure 1–52

2
- In the Property inspector, click the Unordered List button to indent the text and add a bullet to each line (Figure 1–53).

  How do I start a list with a different number or letter?

  In the Document window, click the list item you want to change, click the Format menu, point to List, and then click Properties. In the List Properties dialog box, select the options you want to define.

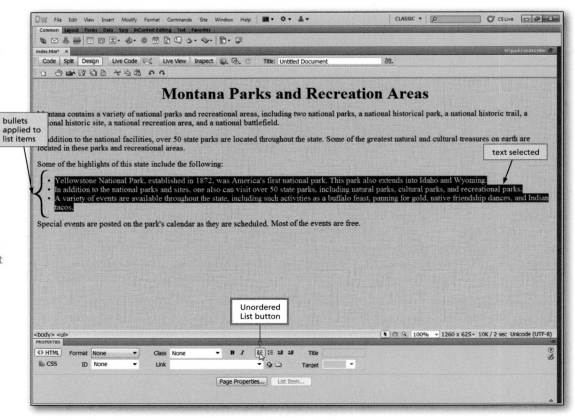

Figure 1–53

Other Ways
1. On Format menu point to List, click Unordered List
2. Select text, right-click, point to List, click Unordered List

Bold Formatting

Other text formatting options are applying bold or italic styles to text. **Bold** characters are displayed somewhat thicker and darker than those that are not bold. **Italic** characters slant to the right. The Property inspector contains buttons for both bold and italic font styles. To bold text within Dreamweaver is a simple procedure. If you have used word-processing software, you are familiar with this process. You italicize text in a similar way.

To Bold Text

The following steps illustrate how to emphasize the bulleted items by applying bold formatting.

1

- If necessary, drag to select all of the lines of the bulleted points to prepare for formatting the lines.

2

- Click the Bold button in the Property inspector to bold the selected text.

- Click anywhere in the Document window to deselect the text (Figure 1–54).

Q&A

What other types of formatting can I apply to text?

To select fonts, apply underlining, colors, and other attributes to text, you can use the commands and submenus on the Format menu. Chapter 5 also explains how to use CSS to format text.

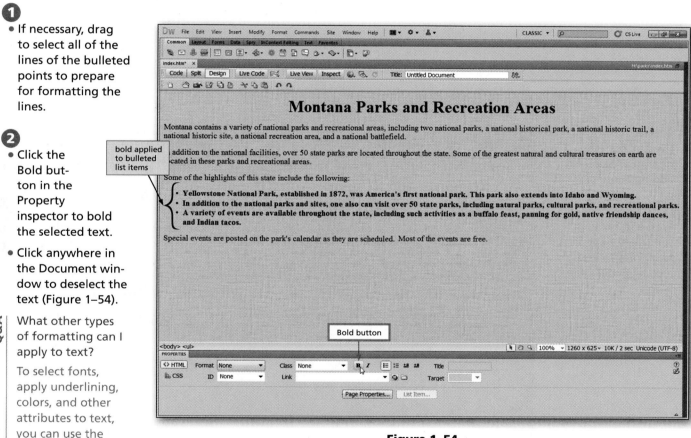

Figure 1–54

Other Ways

1. Click Format on Application bar, point to Style, click Bold
2. Press CTRL+B

Understanding Line Breaks

When you added bullets to the items list earlier in this chapter, the blank line between each item was removed. Removing the blank line between items is a result of how Dreamweaver interprets the HTML code. A blank line between the bulleted items, however, will provide better spacing and readability when viewing the Web page in a browser. You can add blank lines in several ways. You might assume that pressing the ENTER key at the end of each line would be the quickest way to accomplish this. Pressing the ENTER key, however, adds another bullet. The easiest way to accomplish the task of adding blank lines is to insert line breaks. Recall that the line break starts a new single line without inserting a blank line between lines of text. Inserting two line breaks, however, adds a single blank line.

Dreamweaver provides a Line Break command through the Insert HTML Special Characters submenu. It is easier, however, to use the SHIFT+ENTER keyboard shortcut.

To Add a Line Break

The following steps show how to add a blank line between each of the bulleted items.

1
- Click at the end of the first bulleted item to prepare for adding a line break.

2
- Press the SHIFT+ENTER keys two times to insert a blank line (Figure 1–55).

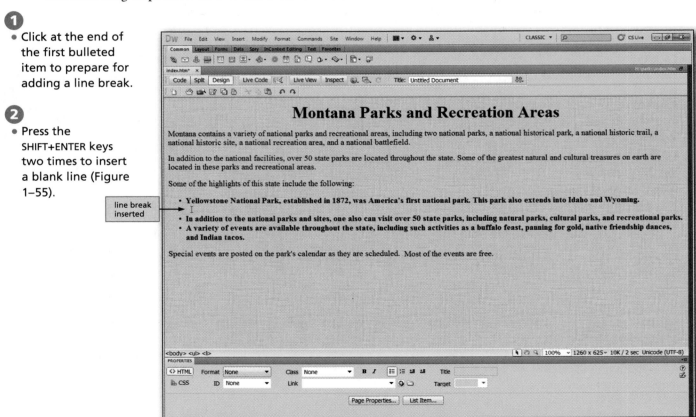

line break inserted

Figure 1–55

3

- Press the SHIFT+ENTER keys two times at the end of the second bulleted item to insert a blank line between the second and third bulleted list items (Figure 1–56).

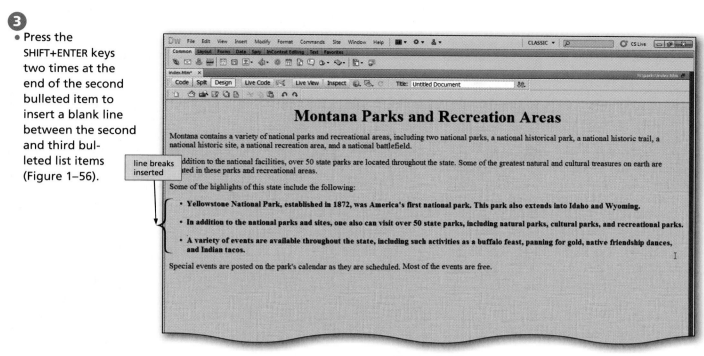

Figure 1–56

To Add Your Name and Date

When creating a Web document, it is a good idea to add your name and date to the document. Insert a single line break between your name and the date. The following steps show how to add this information to the page.

1

- If necessary, scroll down to display the closing paragraph.

- Click at the end of the closing paragraph to prepare for adding your name to the document.

- If necessary, press the ENTER key to move the insertion point to the next paragraph (Figure 1–57).

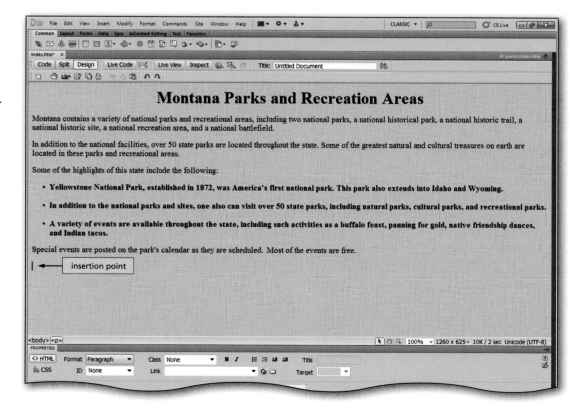

Figure 1–57

2
- Type your name and then press the SHIFT+ENTER keys to insert a line break.
- Type the current date and then press the ENTER key to add your name and the current date to the Web page (Figure 1–58).

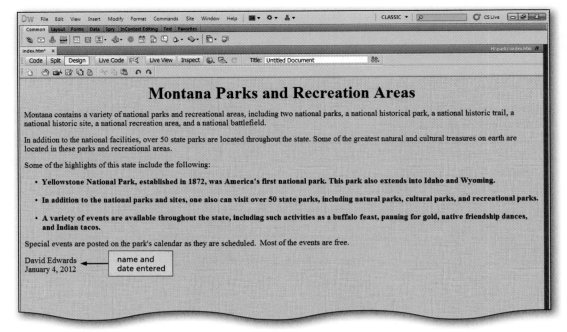

Figure 1–58

Plan Ahead

Review final tasks.
Before completing a Web page, perform the following tasks to make sure it is ready for others to view:

- Give your Web page a title.
- Consider enhancements such as special characters to make the page look professional.
- Check the spelling and proofread the text.
- Preview the page in one or more browsers to see how it looks when others open it.

BTW

Keep Data Confidential
Web pages reach a global audience. Therefore, to limit access to certain kinds of information, avoid including any confidential data on your Web pages. In particular, do not include your home address, telephone number, or other personal information.

Web Page Titles

A **Web page title** helps Web site visitors keep track of what they are viewing as they browse. It is important to give your Web page an appropriate title. When visitors to your Web page create bookmarks or add the Web page to their Favorites lists, they use the title for reference. If you do not title a page, the browser displays the page in the browser window, Favorites lists, and history lists as Untitled Document. Because many search engines use the Web page title, use a descriptive and meaningful name. Giving the document a file name when saving it is not the same as giving the page a title.

To Change the Web Page Title

The following steps show how to change the name of the Web page to Montana Parks and Recreation Areas.

- Drag to select the text, Untitled Document, in the Title text box on the Document toolbar to prepare for replacing the text.

- Type **Montana Parks and Recreation Areas** in the Title text box and then press the ENTER key to enter a descriptive title for the Web page (Figure 1–59).

- Click the Save button on the Standard toolbar to save the document.

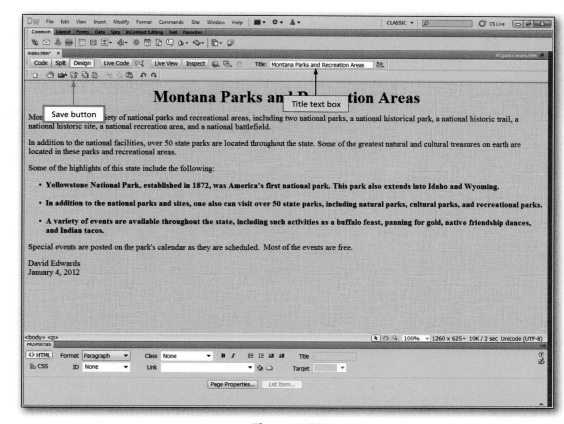

Figure 1–59

Other Web Page Enhancements

Dreamweaver includes many other features that you can use to enhance your Web page. Some of the more commonly used enhancements that you may want to apply to a Web page are special characters.

Special Characters

Sometimes you need to enter special characters such as quotation marks and ampersands as well as non-keyboard symbols like trademarks and registrations into a Web page. To have the browser display these special characters requires a character code. **Character entities**, another name for character codes, allow a browser to show special characters. HTML represents these codes by a name (named entity) or a number (numbered entity). Both types of entities begin with an ampersand (&) and end with a semicolon (;). HTML includes entity names for characters such as the copyright symbol (©), the ampersand (&), and the registered trademark symbol (®). Some entities, such as the left and right quotation marks, include a number sign (#) and a numeric equivalent (such as —). Table 1–2 lists the HTML entities that Dreamweaver supports. To add an entity to your Web page, you click Insert on the Application bar, point to HTML, point to Special Characters on the HTML submenu, and then click the entity name on the Special Characters submenu.

Table 1–2 Character Entities		
Name	**Description**	**HTML Tags and Character Entities**
Nonbreaking Space	Places a nonbreaking space at the insertion point	&#nbsp;
Left Quote	Places an opening, curved double quotation mark at the insertion point	$#147;
Right Quote	Places a closing, curved double quotation mark at the insertion point	$#148;
Em Dash	Places an em dash at the insertion point	$#151;
Pound	Places a pound (currency) symbol at the insertion point	&pound;
Euro	Places a euro (currency) symbol at the insertion point	&euro;
Yen	Places a yen (currency) symbol at the insertion point	&yen;
Copyright	Places a copyright symbol at the insertion point	&copy;
Registered Trademark	Places a registered trademark symbol at the insertion point	&reg;
Trademark	Places a trademark symbol at the insertion point	&#153;
Other Characters	Provides a set of special characters from which to select	Other ASCII characters

Check Spelling

After you create a Web page, you should check it visually for spelling errors. In addition, you can use Dreamweaver's Check Spelling command to identify possible misspellings. The Check Spelling command ignores HTML tags and attributes. Recall from the Introduction that attributes are additional information contained within an HTML tag.

To Check Spelling

The following steps show how to use the Check Spelling command to spell check your entire document. Your Web page may contain different misspelled words depending on the accuracy of your typing.

1

- In the second bullet, select the word-92cultural, and then type `cultral` to insert a deliberately misspelled word in the document.

- Click at the beginning of the document to position the insertion point.

- Click Commands on the Application bar and then point to Check Spelling to highlight the command (Figure 1–60).

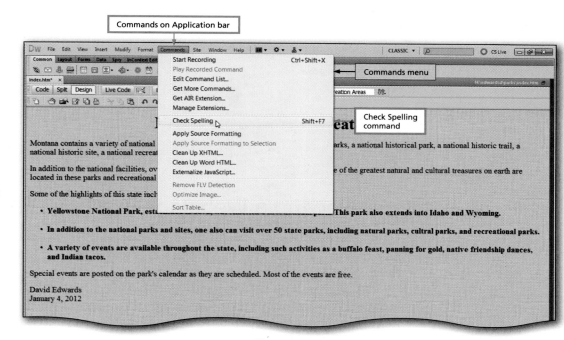

Figure 1–60

2

- Click Check Spelling to display the Check Spelling dialog box (Figure 1–61).

What does the information in the Check Spelling dialog box mean?

The Dreamweaver Check Spelling dialog box displays the word cultral in the 'Word not found in dictionary' text box. Suggestions for the correct spelling are displayed in the Suggestions list.

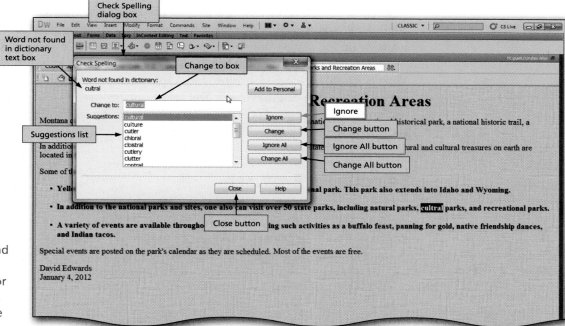

Figure 1–61

Does Dreamweaver contain a dictionary with American/British spelling options?

Yes. Dreamweaver contains 15 different spelling option dictionaries, including English (British) and English (Canadian). Access the dictionaries by clicking the Preferences command on the Edit menu, selecting the General category, and then clicking the Spelling dictionary pop-up menu arrow.

❸

- The word displayed in the Change to text box shows the correct spelling of the word, so click the Change button to change cultral to cultural and continue with the spell checking.
- Continue to check the spelling and, as necessary, correct any misspelled word by accepting the suggested replacement, by clicking the Change or Change All buttons, or by typing the correct word in the Change to text box. Click Ignore if proper names are displayed as errors.
- Click the OK button to close the Check Spelling dialog box.
- Press the CTRL+S keys to save any changes.

Other Ways
1. Press SHIFT+F7

Previewing a Web Page in a Browser

After you have created a Web page, it is a good practice to test your Web page by previewing it in Web browsers to ensure that it is displayed correctly. Using this strategy helps you catch errors so you will not copy or repeat them.

As you create your Web page, you should be aware of the variety of available Web browsers. More than 25 Web browsers are in use, most of which have been released in more than one version. Each browser might display text, images, and other Web page elements differently. For this reason, you want to preview your Web pages in more than one browser to make sure it displays your Web pages as you designed them. Most Web developers target recent versions of Microsoft Internet Explorer and Mozilla Firefox, which the majority of Web visitors use. You also should know that visitors viewing your Web page might have earlier versions of these browsers. Free browser compatibility checkers also are available online (*http://browsershots.org* and *https://browserlab.adobe.com*).

You can define up to 20 browsers for previewing, including Internet Explorer, Mozilla Firefox, Google Chrome, and Apple Safari. A browser must be installed on your system before you can preview it. You select one browser as the primary browser. When you press the F12 key to preview a Web page, Dreamweaver displays the page in the primary browser.

Selecting a Browser

BTW

Remove a Browser
Just as you can specify a primary and secondary browser, you can remove a browser from the list of target browsers. Click Edit on the Application bar, click Preferences, and then click the Preview in Browser category. Select the name of the browser you want to remove, and then click the minus (–) button.

You select browser preferences in the Preferences dialog box. This dialog box provides options to select and define the settings for a primary and a secondary browser. Additionally, a Preview using temporary file option is available. Select the check box for this option to preview a page without saving it. Although it is a good practice to save before previewing in a browser, you might want to view a page quickly before saving it.

To Select Primary and Secondary Target Browsers

The following steps show how to select your target browsers — Internet Explorer and Firefox. To complete these steps requires that you have both Internet Explorer and Firefox installed on your computer. Note, however, that it is not necessary to install a secondary browser. If your choice is to use just one browser, you can choose to install only the one you would like to use. Or, you can choose to install additional browsers as well.

1

• Click Edit on the Application bar and then click Preferences to open the Preferences dialog box.

• If necessary, click the Preview in Browser category in the Preferences dialog box to select the Preview in Browser category (Figure 1–62).

Q&A What is the primary browser?

The primary browser was selected when Dreamweaver was installed on your computer. In this book, the primary browser is Internet Explorer. The browser name, IExplore, was selected automatically during the Dreamweaver installation. The browser name on your computer may be different.

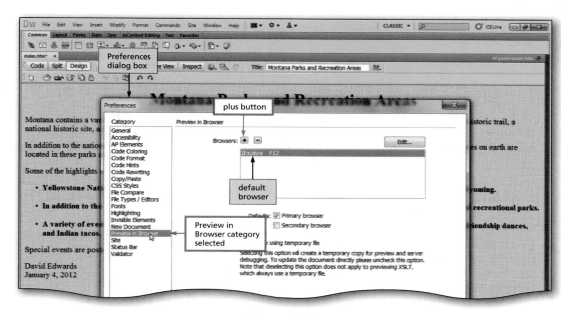

Figure 1–62

2

• Click the plus (+) button in the Preview in Browser area to display the Add Browser dialog box (Figure 1–63).

Q&A What should I do if the Preview in Browser dialog box already lists Firefox and IExplore?

Skip Steps 2 through 5. Click Firefox in the Preview in Browser dialog box, and then click the Secondary browser check box. Click IExplore in the Preview in Browser dialog box, and then click the Primary browser check box. Then click the OK button.

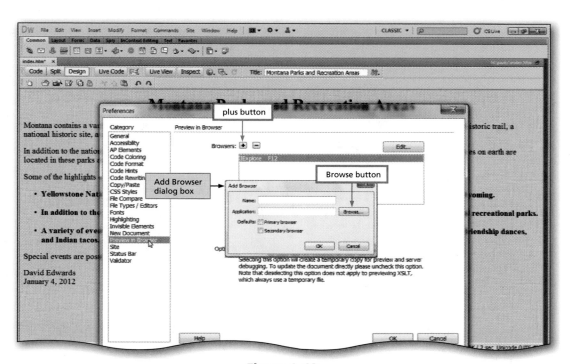

Figure 1–63

3

- Click the Browse button and then locate and click the Firefox program file to select the file.

Q&A

Where can I find the Firefox program file?

Most likely this file is located on Local Drive (C:). Use the following path to locate the file: C:\Program Files\ Mozilla Firefox\ firefox. The path and file name on your computer may be different.

- Click the Open button to add the browser name and path to the Add Browser dialog box (Figure 1–64).

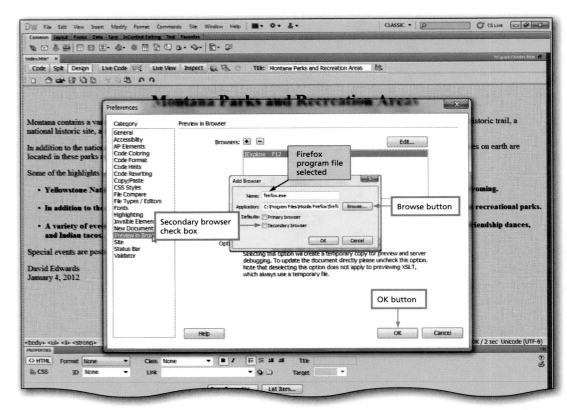

Figure 1–64

4

- If necessary, click the Secondary browser check box to select it.

Q&A

What does the information in the Add Browser dialog box mean?

The Name text box displays firefox. exe, the name of the Firefox program file. The Application text box displays the path and file name. The path and spelling of Firefox on your computer may be different from those shown in Figure 1–64.

- Click the OK button to add Firefox as the secondary browser.

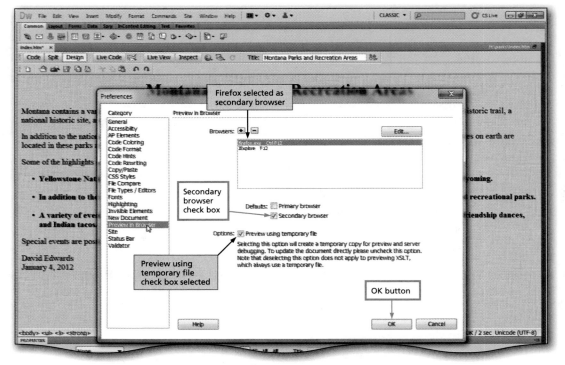

Figure 1–65

- If necessary, click the 'Preview using temporary file' check box to select it (Figure 1–65).

- Click the OK button to select Internet Explorer and Firefox as the preview browsers.
- If a Dreamweaver CS5 dialog box appears, click the OK button to confirm your selections and close the dialog box.
- Click the Save button on the Standard toolbar to save your work.

To Preview the Web Page

With the target browsers set up, you are ready to preview a Web page. To select the browser you want to use for the preview, you use the Preview in Browser command on the File menu. The following steps illustrate how to preview the Montana Parks and Recreation Areas Web page using Internet Explorer and Firefox.

1

- Click File on the Application bar, point to Preview in Browser, and then click IExplore to display the Montana Parks and Recreation Areas Web page in the Internet Explorer browser.
- If necessary, maximize your browser window to display the entire Web page (Figure 1–66).

2

- Click the Internet Explorer Close button to close the browser.
- Click File on the Application bar and then point to Preview in Browser to prepare for changing browsers.

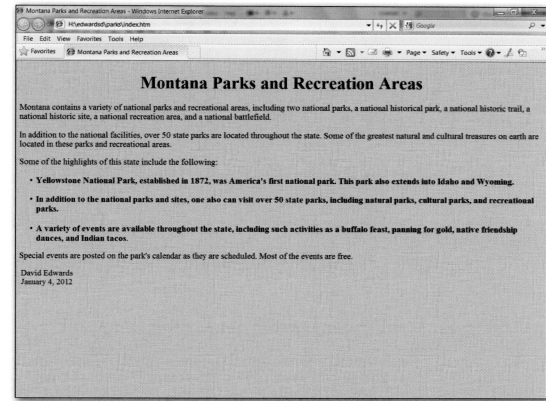

Figure 1–66

- Click Firefox.exe on the Preview in Browser submenu to display the Web page in the Firefox browser.
- Click the Firefox Close button to close the browser.

Other Ways

1. Press F12 to display primary browser
2. Press CTRL+F12 to display secondary browser

Printing a Web Page

You may want to print a Web page for a variety of reasons. Dreamweaver provides an option to print code, but does not provide an option to print Design view. To print a Web page, you first must preview it in a browser. Printing a page from your browser is similar to printing a word-processing document.

To Print a Web Page

The following steps illustrate how to print a Web page in a browser.

1
- Press the F12 key to display the page in your primary browser.
- Click the Print button arrow on the Internet Explorer toolbar to display the Print commands (Figure 1–67).

2
- Click Print to display the Print dialog box.
- Select an appropriate printer and click the Print button to send your Web page to the printer.
- Retrieve your printout.
- Close Internet Explorer.

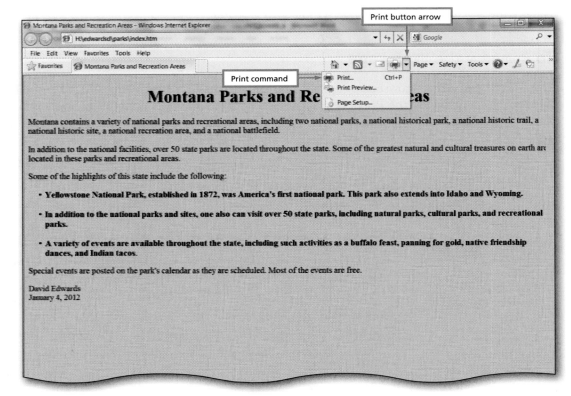

Figure 1–67

Dreamweaver Help System

Reference materials and other forms of assistance are available using the Dreamweaver Help system. You can display these documents, print them, or download them as a PDF file. All of the Dreamweaver CS5 Help is available online. Click Help on the Application bar, and then select one of the commands listed in Table 1–3, or press the F1 key. The main Help page opens connected to the Adobe Web site. Appendix A provides detailed instructions on using Dreamweaver Help.

Table 1–3 Dreamweaver Help System	
Command	**Description**
Dreamweaver Help	Displays the Dreamweaver online help system, which is connected to the Adobe Web site by default. You can search for help or download a PDF file containing the program's documentation.
Reference	Opens the Reference panel, a searchable guide to HTML tags, Cascading Style Sheets, and JavaScript commands.
Dreamweaver Support Center	Opens the online Dreamweaver Help and Support Web page. This page is part of the Adobe Web site and offers links to tutorials and the Dreamweaver Help system, troubleshooting suggestions, videos showing how to perform typical tasks, and access to online forums.

Disabling the Welcome Screen and Quitting Dreamweaver

After you create, save, preview, and print the Montana Parks and Recreation Areas Web page and review how to use Help, your work in Chapter 1 is complete.

To Disable the Welcome Screen, Close the Web Site, and Quit Dreamweaver

The following steps show how to disable the Welcome screen, close the Web page, quit Dreamweaver CS5, and return control to Windows.

- Click Edit on the Application bar and then click Preferences to display the Preferences dialog box.

- If necessary, click General in the Category column to display the General options.

- In the Document options section, click the Show Welcome Screen check box to deselect it (Figure 1-68).

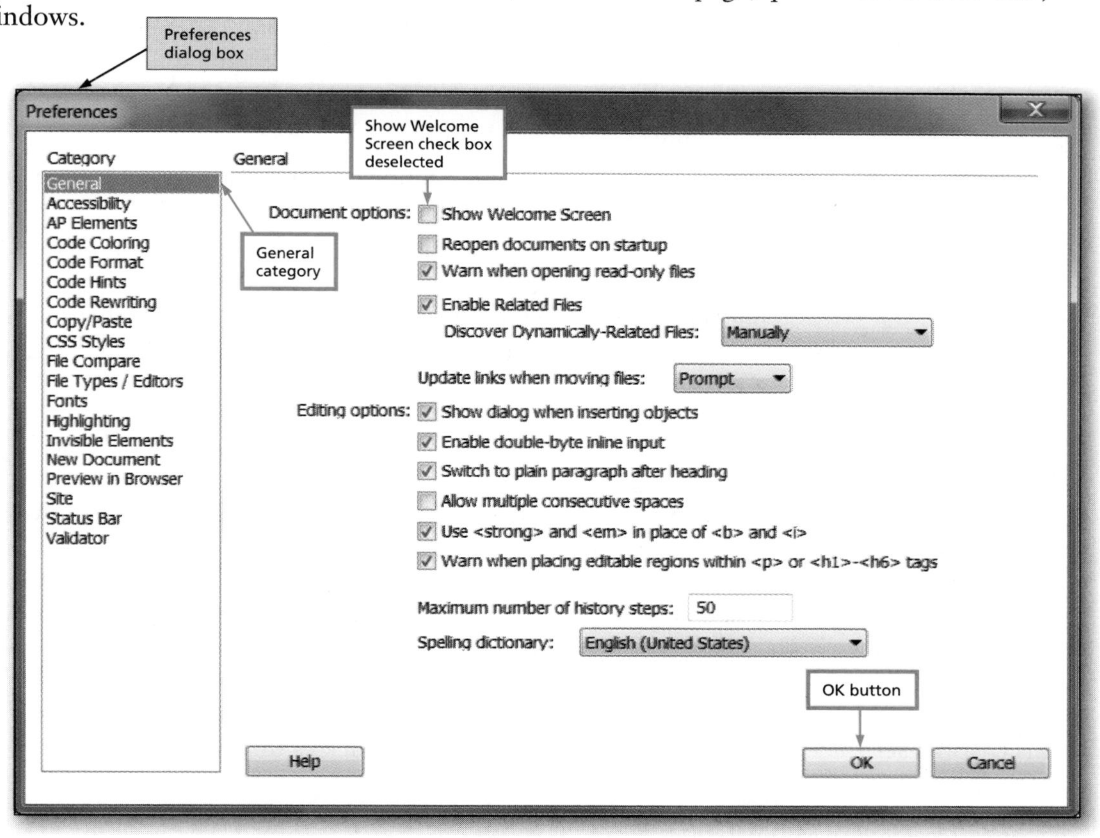

2

- Click the OK button to accept the setting change.

- Click the Close button in the upper-right corner of the Dreamweaver window to close Dreamweaver.

Figure 1–68

Other Ways

1. On File menu, click Exit
2. Press CTRL+Q

Starting Dreamweaver and Opening a Web Page

Opening an existing Web page in Dreamweaver is much the same as opening an existing document in most other software applications: that is, you use the File menu and Open command. In addition to this common method to open a Web page, Dreamweaver provides other options. The Dreamweaver File menu also contains the Open Recent command. Pointing to this command displays the Open Recent submenu, which contains a list of the 10 most recently opened files. Additionally, if you want to display the page on which you currently are working when you next open Dreamweaver, you can select the Reopen Documents on Startup command from the Open Recent submenu.

If the page you want to open is part of a Dreamweaver Web site, you can open the file from the Files panel. To open a Web page from the Files panel, you first must select the appropriate Web site. The Sites pop-up menu button in the Files panel lists sites you have defined. When you open the site, a list of the pages and subfolders within the site is displayed. To open the page you want, double-click the file name. After opening the page, you can modify text, images, tables, and any other elements.

Because you disabled the Welcome screen, the next time you open Dreamweaver, the Welcome screen will not be displayed. Instead, a blank window is displayed, requiring that you open an existing document or open a new document. Dreamweaver provides four options to open a new Document window:

- Click File on the Application bar, click New, and then select Blank Page
- Press CTRL+N and then select Blank Page
- Right-click the site's root folder in the Files panel, and then click New File on the context menu
- Click the Files panel Options menu button, point to File on the pop-up menu, and then click the New File command

The first two options display the New Document dialog box. From this dialog box, you select the Blank Page category and the HTML page type and then click the Create button. When you create a new page by right-clicking the root folder in the Files panel or by using the Options menu button, a default untitled file is created in the Files panel.

BTW

Quick Reference
For a table that lists how to complete tasks covered in this book using the keyboard, see the Quick Reference at the end of this book.

Chapter Summary

Chapter 1 introduced you to starting Dreamweaver, defining a Web site, and creating a Web page. You added an image background and used Dreamweaver's Property inspector to format text. You also learned how to use an unordered list to organize information. You added line breaks and learned about special characters. Once your Web page was completed, you learned how to save the Web page and preview it in a browser. You also learned how to print using the browser. To enhance your knowledge of Dreamweaver further, you learned the basics about the Dreamweaver Help system. The following tasks are all the new Dreamweaver skills you learned in this chapter, listed in the same order they were presented in the chapter. For a list of keyboard commands for topics introduced in this chapter, see the Quick Reference for Windows at the back of this book.

1. Start Dreamweaver (DW 36)
2. Display the Standard Toolbar, Change the Icon Colors, and Close and Open Panels (DW 43)
3. Use Site Setup to Create a Local Web Site (DW 47)
4. Copy Data Files to the Local Web Site (DW 52)
5. Hide the Rulers, Change the .html Default, and Save a Document as a Web Page (DW 55)
6. Add a Background Image to the Index Page (DW 60)
7. Hide the Panel Groups (DW 62)
8. Add a Heading and Introductory Paragraph Text (DW 63)
9. Format Text with the Heading 1 Style (DW 68)
10. Center the Web Page Heading (DW 70)
11. Create an Unordered List (DW 72)
12. Bold Text (DW 73)
13. Add a Line Break (DW 74)
14. Add Your Name and Date (DW 75)
15. Change the Web Page Title (DW 77)
16. Check Spelling (DW 78)
17. Select Primary and Secondary Target Browsers (DW 81)
18. Preview the Web Page (DW 83)
19. Print a Web Page (DW 84)
20. Disable the Welcome Screen, Close the Web Site, and Quit Dreamweaver (DW 85)

Learn It Online

Test your knowledge of chapter content and key terms.

Instructions: To complete the Learn It Online exercises, start your browser, click the Address bar, and then enter the Web address `scsite.com/dwCS5/learn`. When the Dreamweaver CS5 Learn It Online page is displayed, click the link for the exercise you want to complete and then read the instructions.

Chapter Reinforcement TF, MC, and SA

A series of true/false, multiple choice, and short answer questions that test your knowledge of the chapter content.

Flash Cards

An interactive learning environment where you identify chapter key terms associated with displayed definitions.

Practice Test

A series of multiple choice questions that test your knowledge of chapter content and key terms.

Who Wants To Be a Computer Genius?

An interactive game that challenges your knowledge of chapter content in the style of a television quiz show.

Wheel of Terms

An interactive game that challenges your knowledge of chapter key terms in the style of the television show *Wheel of Fortune.*

Crossword Puzzle Challenge

A crossword puzzle that challenges your knowledge of key terms presented in the chapter.

Apply Your Knowledge

Reinforce the skills and apply the concepts you learned in this chapter.

Adding Text and Formatting a Web Page

Instructions: In this activity, you modify a Web page by adding a background image, changing the heading style, adding bullets, and centering text (Figure 1–69 on the next page). To use Dreamweaver effectively, it is necessary to create a new site for the Apply Your Knowledge exercises in this book. Make sure you have downloaded the data files for Chapter01\apply, which are available in the Data Files for Students folder. See the inside back cover of this book for instructions on downloading the Data Files for Students, or contact your instructor for information about accessing the required files.

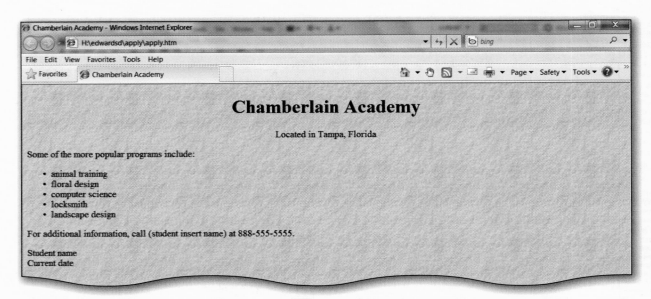

Figure 1–69

Perform the following tasks:

1. Start Dreamweaver. Use the Site Setup dialog box to define a local site in the *your name* folder. Enter **Apply Exercises** as the name of the new site.

2. Using the Browse for folder icon next to the Local Site Folder text box, create a new subfolder in the *your name* folder. Enter **apply** as the name of the subfolder. Open the folder and then select it as the local site folder.

3. In the Advanced Settings category of the Site Setup for Apply Exercises dialog box, click the Browse for folder icon next to the Default Images folder text box. In the apply folder, create a subfolder named images. Open the images folder, and then select it as the default folder for images.

4. Make sure the path in the Default Images folder text box ends with *your name*\apply\images. Click the Site category and make sure the path in the Local site folder text box ends with *your name*\apply. Click the Save button in the Site Setup for Apply Exercises dialog box to save the settings for the new site.

5. Using Windows Explorer or the Windows Computer tool, copy the apply.htm data file from the Chapter01\apply data files folder into the *your name*\apply folder for the Apply Exercises Web site. Copy the apply_bkg.jpg from the Chapter01\apply\images data files folder into the *your name*\apply\images folder for the Apply Exercises Web site.

6. In the Local Files list of the Files panel, double-click apply.htm to open the apply.htm page. If necessary, expand the Property inspector. Verify that the HTML button is selected on the left side of the Property inspector.

7. Click the Page Properties button in the Property inspector and apply the apply_bkg background image to the Web page.

8. Apply the Heading 1 style to the first line of text.

9. Select the first two lines. Use the Align command on the Format menu to center the lines.

10. Select the list of items (beginning with animal training and ending with landscape design) and create an unordered list by applying bullets.

11. Click at the end of the last line and press ENTER.

12. Add your name, press SHIFT+ENTER to insert a line break, and then add the current date. Title the document **Chamberlain Academy**.

13. Save your document and then view it in your browser, comparing your Web page to Figure 1–69. Make any changes as necessary, save your changes, and then submit your work in the format specified by your instructor.

Extend Your Knowledge

Extend the skills you learned in this chapter and experiment with new skills. You may need to use Help to complete the assignment.

Adding Text and Formatting a Web Page

Instructions: In this activity, you modify a Web page by adding a background image, inserting line breaks, and centering text (Figure 1–70). To use Dreamweaver effectively, it is necessary to create a new site for the Extend Your Knowledge exercises in this book. Make sure you have downloaded the data files for Chapter01\extend, which are available in the Data Files for Students folder. See the inside back cover of this book for instructions on downloading the Data Files for Students, or contact your instructor for information about accessing the required files.

Figure 1–70

Perform the following tasks:

1. Start Dreamweaver. Use the Site Setup dialog box to define a local site in the *your name* folder. Enter **Extend Exercises** as the name of the new site.

2. Using the Browse for folder icon next to the Local Site Folder text box, create a new subfolder in the *your name* folder. Enter **extend** as the name of the subfolder. Open the folder, and then select it as the local site folder.

3. In the Advanced Settings category of the Site Setup for Extend Exercises dialog box, click the Browse for folder icon next to the Default Images folder text box. In the extend folder, create a sub-folder named images. Open the images folder, and then select it as the default folder for images.

4. Make sure the path in the Default Images folder text box ends with *your name*\extend\images. Click the Site category and make sure the path in the Local site folder text box ends with *your name*\extend. Click the Save button in the Site Setup for Extend Exercises dialog box to save the settings for the new site.

5. Using Windows Explorer or the Windows Computer tool, copy the extend.htm data file from the Chapter01\extend folder into the *your name*\extend folder for the Extend Exercises Web site. Copy the extend_bkg.jpg from the Chapter01\extend\images data files folder into the *your name*\extend\images folder for the Extend Exercises Web site.

6. Open the extend.htm page. If necessary, expand the Property inspector. Verify that the HTML button on the left side of the Property inspector is selected.

7. Click the Page Properties button in the Property inspector and apply the extend_bkg background image to the Web page.

8. Type your name and the current date where indicated.

9. Apply the Heading 2 style to the first three lines.

10. On the Format menu, use the Underline command on the Style submenu to underline the third line.

11. Select the next four lines containing the names of flowers and bullet the text. Press SHIFT+ENTER at the end of the first bulleted item, and then press SHIFT+ENTER again to insert a blank, unbulleted line. Do the same to insert a blank line between each of the remaining bulleted items.

12. Center all of the text. Bold the bulleted list, your name, and the date.

13. Enter **Mary's Flower Shoppe** as the title of the document.

14. Save your document and then view it in your browser, comparing your Web page to Figure 1–70. Submit your work in the format specified by your instructor.

Make It Right

In this activity, you analyze a Web page, correct all errors, and/or improve the design.

Adding Text and Formatting a Web Page

Instructions: In this activity, you modify an existing Web page by formatting and adjusting text and adding data (Figure 1–71). To use Dreamweaver effectively, it is necessary to create a new site for the Make It Right exercises in this book. Make sure you have downloaded the data files for Chapter01\ right, which are available in the Data Files for Students folder. See the inside back cover of this book for instructions on downloading the Data Files for Students, or contact your instructor for information about accessing the required files.

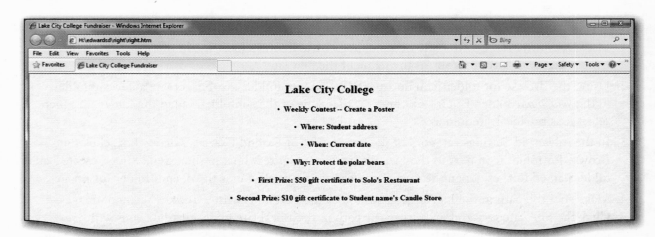

Figure 1–71

Perform the following tasks:

1. Start Dreamweaver. Use Site Setup dialog box to define a local site in the *your name* folder. Enter **Right Exercises** as the name of the new site.

2. Using the Browse for folder icon next to the Local Site Folder text box, create a new subfolder in the *your name* folder. Enter **right** as the name of the subfolder. Open the folder, and then select it as the local site folder.

3. In the Advanced Settings category of the Site Setup for Right Exercises dialog box, click the Browse for folder icon next to the Default Images folder text box. In the right folder, create a subfolder named images. Open the images folder, and then select it as the default folder for images.

4. Make sure the path in the Local Site Folder text box ends with *your name*\right and the path in the Default Images folder text box ends with *your name*\right\images, and then click the Save button in the Site Setup for Right Exercises dialog box to save the settings for the new site.

5. Using Windows Explorer or the Windows Computer tool, copy the right.htm data file from the Chapter01\right folder into the *your name*\right folder for the Right Exercises Web site. Copy the right_bkg.jpg from the Chapter01\right\images data files folder into the *your name*\right\images folder for the Right Exercises Web site.

6. Open the right.htm page. If necessary, expand the Property inspector. Verify that HTML is selected in the Property inspector.

7. Apply the right_bkg background image to the Web page. Select and center the title. Apply the Heading 2 format.

8. Select the rest of the text and add bullets. Bold the bulleted text. Center the text and add a blank, unbulleted line break between each item.

9. Insert your school's address and a date where indicated. Replace "Carole" with your name.

10. Enter **Lake City College Fundraiser** as the document title.

11. Save your document and then view it in your browser, comparing your Web page to Figure 1–71. Submit your work in the format specified by your instructor.

In the Lab

Create a Web page using the guidelines, concepts, and skills presented in this chapter. Labs are listed in order of increasing difficulty.

Lab 1: Creating a Computer Repair Services Web Site

Problem: After watching his computer repair service grow, Bryan asks for your help creating a Web page describing his services. He asks you to assist him in preparing a Web site to list his activities and promote his mission statement.

Define a Web site and create and format a Web page for Bryan's Computer Repair Services. The Web page as it is displayed in a browser is shown in Figure 1–72 on the next page. The text for the Web site is shown in Table 1–4 on the next page.

Software and hardware settings determine how a Web page is displayed in a browser. Your Web pages may be displayed differently in your browser than the pages shown in the figure.

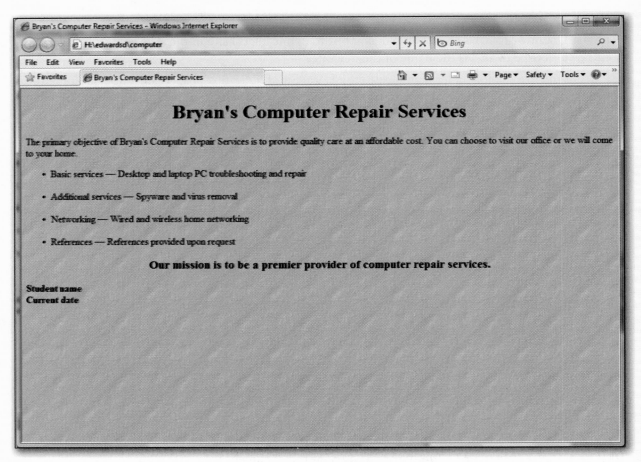

Figure 1–72

Table 1–4 Bryan's Computer Repair Services	
Section	**Text**
Heading	Bryan's Computer Repair Services
Introductory paragraph	The primary objective of Bryan's Computer Repair Services is to provide quality care at an affordable cost. You can choose to visit our office or we will come to your home.
List item 1	Basic services — Desktop and laptop PC troubleshooting and repair
List Item 2	Additional services — Spyware and virus removal
List Item 3	Networking — Wired and wireless home networking
List Item 4	References — References provided upon request
Closing	Our mission is to be a premier provider of computer repair services.

Perform the following tasks:

1. In Dreamweaver, click Site on the Application bar, click New Site, and then use the Site Setup dialog box to create a local Web site in the *your name* folder. In the Site Name text box, enter **Computer Repair Services** as the name of the site.

2. Using the Browse for folder icon next to the Local Site Folder text box, create a new subfolder in the *your name* folder. Enter **computers** as the name of the subfolder. Open the folder, and then select it as the local site folder. The path will be H:*your name*\computers (substitute your name and the drive letter of the drive on which you are saving your files).

3. In the Advanced Settings category of the Site Setup for Computer Repair Services dialog box, click the Browse for folder icon next to the Default Images folder text box. In the computers folder, create a new subfolder. Enter **images** as the name of the subfolder. Open the images folder, and then select it as the default images folder. The path will be H:*your name*\computers\images.

4. Click the Save button in the Site Setup for Computer Repair Services dialog box to save the settings for the new site.

5. Using Windows Explorer or the Windows Computer tool, copy the repair_bkg.jpg from the Chapter01\lab01\images data files folder into the *your name*\computer\images folder for the Computer Repair Services Web site.

6. Click File on the Application bar and then click New. Click Blank Page and HTML, verify that <none> is selected under Layout, and then click Create. Use the Save As command on the File menu to save the page with the name index.

7. Click Modify on the Application bar, and then click Page Properties. Apply the repair_bkg background image (located in the images folder) to the index page.

8. Type the Web page text shown in Table 1–4 on the previous page. Press the ENTER key after typing the text in each section and after each one of the list items in the table. The em dash, used in the four list items, is an HTML object. To insert the em dash, click the Insert menu, point to HTML, point to Special Characters, and then click Em-Dash.

9. Select the heading text and then apply the Heading 1 format. Use the Format menu to center the heading.

10. Select the four list items. Click the Unordered List button in the Property inspector to create a bulleted list with these four items.

11. Click at the end of the first bulleted item. Press the SHIFT+ENTER keys twice to insert a blank line between the first and second items, press the SHIFT+ENTER keys twice to insert a blank line between the second and third items, and then press the SHIFT+ENTER keys twice to insert a blank line between the third and the fourth items.

12. Select the closing paragraph. Center the sentence and then click the Bold button in the Property inspector. When this is complete, do not deselect the sentence.

13. Click the Format button in the Property inspector and apply Heading 3 to the sentence.

14. In the Title text box on the Document toolbar, enter **Bryan's Computer Repair Services** as the title of the Web page.

15. Click at the end of the closing paragraph and then press the ENTER key. Point to Align on the Format menu and then click Left. Type your name, insert a line break, and then type the current date.

16. Select your name and the current date, and then apply bold to the text.

17. Click at the beginning of the document, click Commands on the Application bar, and then click Check Spelling. Spell check your document and correct any errors.

18. Click File on the Application bar and then click Save.

19. Press the F12 key to view the Web page in the primary browser. Compare the Web page to Figure 1–72 on the previous page and make additional changes as necessary. Submit your work in the format specified by your instructor.

In the Lab

Lab 2: Creating a Gift Baskets Web Site

Problem: Putting together gift baskets has long been a hobby of Carole Wells, a friend of yours. She enjoys the hobby so much that she has decided to start her own online business. She has asked you to assist her in preparing a Web site to help her understand how to share her knowledge and her work with others and how to turn her hobby into a business (Figure 1–73). Software and hardware settings determine how a Web page is displayed in a browser. Your Web pages may be displayed differently in your browser than the one shown in the figure.

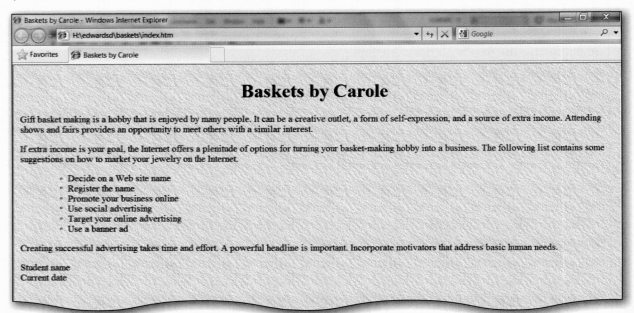

Figure 1–73

Define a Web site and create and format a Web page for Baskets by Carole. The text for the Web page is shown in Table 1–5.

Table 1–5 Baskets by Carole Web Page	
Section	**Web Page Text**
Heading	Baskets by Carole
Introductory paragraph	Gift basket making is a hobby that is enjoyed by many people. It can be a creative outlet, a form of self-expression, and a source of extra income. Attending shows and fairs provides an opportunity to meet others with a similar interest.
Second paragraph	If extra income is your goal, the Internet offers a plenitude of options for turning your basket-making hobby into a business. The following list contains some suggestions on how to market your baskets on the Internet.
List item 1	Decide on a Web site name
List item 2	Register the name
List item 3	Promote your business online
List item 4	Use social advertising
List item 5	Target your online advertising
List item 6	Use a banner ad
Closing	Creating successful advertising takes time and effort. A powerful headline is important. Incorporate motivators that address basic human needs.

Perform the following tasks:

1. In Dreamweaver, use the Site Setup dialog box to create a local Web site in the *your name* folder. Enter `Gift Basket Designs` as the name of the new site.

2. Using the Browse for folder icon next to the Local Site Folder text box, create a new subfolder in the *your name* folder. Enter `baskets` as the name of the subfolder. Open the folder, and then select it as the local site folder.

3. Using the Advanced Settings category of the Site Setup for Gift Basket Designs dialog box, create and then select the *your name*\baskets\images folder as the default folder for images.

4. Make sure the path in the Default Images folder text box ends with *your name*\baskets\images and make sure the path in the Local site folder text box ends with *your name*\baskets. Click the Save button in the Site Setup for Gift Baskets Designs dialog box to save the settings for the new site.

5. Using Windows Explorer or the Windows Computer tool, copy the baskets_bkg.jpg from the Chapter01\lab02\images data files folder into the *your name*\baskets\images folder for the Gift Basket Designs Web site.

6. Click File on the Application bar, and then click New. Click Blank Page, verify that HTML and <none> are selected, and then click Create. Use the Save As command on the File menu to save the page with the name index.

7. Click the Modify menu and then click Page Properties. Apply the baskets_bkg background image to the index page.

8. Click in the Document window and then type the Web page text shown in Table 1–5. Press the ENTER key after typing each section and after each list item in the table.

9. Apply the Heading 1 format to the heading and then center the heading.

10. Create an unordered list for the list items. With these items still selected, click the Indent button in the Property inspector to increase the indent.

11. Enter `Baskets by Carole` as the Web page title.

12. Click at the end of the closing line and then press the ENTER key. Type your name. Insert a line break and then type the current date.

13. Check the spelling of your document and correct any errors.

14. Save your document and then view it in your browser, comparing your Web page to Figure 1–73. Submit your work in the format specified by your instructor.

In the Lab

Lab 3: Creating a Credit Protection Web Site

Problem: Identity theft is a growing issue and one of the major concerns facing people today. Recently, you learned that two fellow employees became victims of identity theft; you have decided to create a Web site (Figure 1–74) that will provide some information on how to prevent becoming a victim.

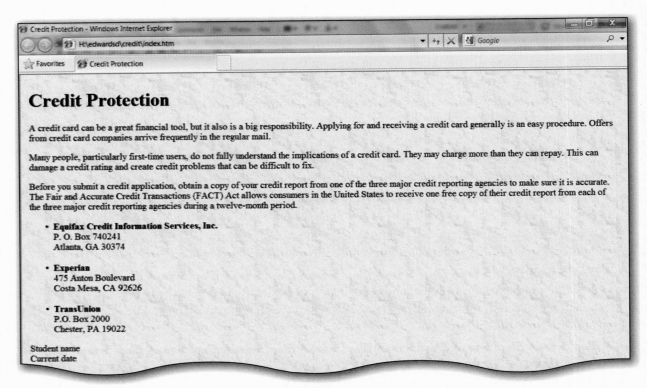

Figure 1–74

Table 1–6 Credit Protection Web Page

Section	Web Page Text
Heading	Credit Protection
Introductory paragraph	A credit card can be a great financial tool, but it also is a big responsibility. Applying for and receiving a credit card generally is an easy procedure. Offers from credit card companies arrive frequently in the regular mail.
Second paragraph	Many people, particularly first-time users, do not fully understand the implications of a credit card. They may charge more than they can repay. This can damage a credit rating and create credit problems that can be difficult to fix.
Third paragraph	Before you submit a credit application, obtain a copy of your credit report from one of the three major credit reporting agencies to make sure it is accurate. The Fair and Accurate Credit Transactions (FACT) Act allows consumers in the United States to receive one free copy of their credit report from each of the three major credit reporting agencies during a twelve-month period.
List item 1	Equifax Credit Information Services, Inc. P. O. Box 740241 Atlanta, GA 30374
List item 2	Experian 475 Anton Boulevard Costa Mesa, CA 92626
List item 3	TransUnion P.O. Box 2000 Chester, PA 19022

Perform the following tasks:

1. In Dreamweaver, define a local Web site in the *your name* folder. Enter **Credit Protection** as the name of the site. Create a new subfolder in the *your name* folder and name the new subfolder **credit.** Select the *your name*\credit folder as the local site folder.

2. Create a subfolder in the credit folder and name it **images.** Select the *your name*\credit\images folder as the default folder for images.

3. Copy the image data file (credit_bkg.jpg) into the *your name*\credit\images folder.

4. Open a new Document window and use the Save As command to save the page with the name index. Apply the background image to the index page.

5. Type the heading and first three paragraphs of the Web page text shown in Table 1–6. Press the ENTER key after typing each section of the text in the table. Insert line breaks where shown in Figure 1–74.

6. Type List item 1 as shown in Table 1–6. Insert a line break after the company name and after the address. Press the ENTER key after the city, state, and zip code. Type List items 2 and 3 in the same fashion.

7. Apply the Heading 1 style to the heading text. Align the heading to the left (to ensure it is displayed properly in the browser).

8. Select the three list items (companies and addresses) and create an unordered list. Insert two line breaks between item 1 and item 2, and between item 2 and item 3.

9. Bold the company name of the first item in the bulleted list (Equifax Credit Information Services, Inc.). Bold the names of the other two companies.

10. Title the Web page Credit Protection.

11. Click at the end of the last line of text and then press the ENTER key. If a bullet is displayed, click the Unordered List button in the Property inspector to remove the bullet. Type your name, add a line break, and then type the current date.

12. Check the spelling of your document and correct any errors.

13. Save your document and then view it in your browser, comparing your Web page to Figure 1–74. Submit your work in the format specified by your instructor.

Cases and Places

Apply your creative thinking and problem-solving skills to design and implement a solution.

● EASIER ●●MORE DIFFICULT

● 1: Create the Favorite Sports Web Site

Define a Web site named Favorite Sports with a local root folder named sports (stored in the *your name* folder). Prepare a Web page listing your favorite sports and favorite teams. Include a title for your Web page. Bold and center the title, and then apply the Heading 1 style. Include a sentence or two explaining why you like the sport and why you like the teams. Bold and italicize the names of the teams and the sports. Give the Web page a meaningful title. Apply a background image to your Web page. Check the spelling in the document. Use the concepts and techniques presented in the chapter to format the text. Save the file in the sports folder. For a selection of images and backgrounds, visit the Dreamweaver CS5 Media Web page (scsite.com/dwcs5/media).

• 2: Create the Hobbies Web Site

Your instructor has asked you to create a Web page about one of your hobbies. Define the Web site using Hobbies for the site name and hobby for the local root folder name. Store the hobby folder in the *your name* folder. Italicize and center the title, and then apply the Heading 1 style. Type a paragraph of three or four sentences explaining why you selected the subject. Select and center the paragraph. Add a list of five items and create an ordered list from the five items. Include line breaks between each numbered item. Title the Web page the name of the hobby you selected. Check the spelling in your document. Use the concepts and techniques presented in the chapter to format the text. For a selection of images and backgrounds, visit the Dreamweaver CS5 Media Web page (scsite.com/dwcs5/media).

•• 3: Create the Politics Web Site

Assume you are running for office in your city's local government. Define a Web site using the name of the city in which you live and a local root folder named government. Include the following information in your Web page: your name, centered, with Heading 1 and a font color of your choice; the name of the office for which you are running, bold and italicized; and a paragraph about the duties of the office. Create a bulleted list within your Web page. Change the title of the Web page from Untitled to your name. Use the concepts and techniques presented in the chapter to format the text. For a selection of images and backgrounds, visit the Dreamweaver CS5 Media Web page (scsite.com/dwcs5/media).

•• 4: Create the Favorite Baseball Player Web Site

Make It Personal

Define a Web site and create a Web page that gives a description and information about your favorite baseball player. Name the Web site Favorite Player and the local root folder player. Apply a background image to the Web page. Include a center-aligned heading formatted with the Heading 1 style. Include a subheading formatted with Heading 3. List four facts about why you selected this baseball player. Include informational facts regarding a) the team for which he plays, b) his position, and c) his batting average. Bold and italicize each of the facts and apply a font color of your choice. Create an ordered list from the three facts. Title the Web page Favorite Player. Use the concepts and techniques presented in the chapter to format the text. Save the file as index in the baseball folder. For a selection of images and backgrounds, visit the Dreamweaver CS5 Media Web page (scsite.com/dwcs5/media).

•• 5: Create the Student Trips Web Site

Working Together

Your school has a budget for student celebrations and dances. Your assignment and that of your teammates is to put together a Web site and Web page that lists various information about these two topics. Save the site in a local root folder named celebrations. Apply an appropriate background image. Include a title, formatted with Heading 1, and a subtitle, formatted with Heading 2. Add a bullet to each item and include information about the location for each item. Title the page Student Celebrations. Use the concepts and techniques presented in the chapter to format the text. For a selection of images and backgrounds, visit the Dreamweaver CS5 Media Web page (scsite.com/dwcs5/media).

2 | Adding Web Pages, Links, and Images

Objectives

You will have mastered the material in this chapter when you can:

- Add pages to a Web site
- Describe Dreamweaver's image accessibility features
- Describe image file formats
- Insert, resize, and align images within a Web page
- Describe the different types of links
- Create relative, absolute, and e-mail links

- Describe how to change the color of links
- Edit and delete links
- Check spelling
- Describe Code view, Split view, and Design view
- Display Code view
- Use Live view

2 | Adding Web Pages, Links, and Images

Introduction

The majority of Web sites consist of several pages with links between the pages. The pages in a site generally are linked and contain shared attributes, such as related topics, a similar design, or a shared purpose. Dreamweaver contains a site structure feature that provides a way to maintain and organize your files within a site. Most Web site developers also enhance a Web site by including images on their Web pages.

Project — Two New Pages, Links, and Images

When creating a Web site, you should follow a standard format or style for all pages contained within the site. The content, which is the information provided on the Web site, should be engaging, relevant, and appropriate to the audience. Accessibility issues should be addressed when developing the site. Experience level of the users, the types of tasks that will be performed on the site, and required connection speeds are important components.

In this chapter, you continue building the Montana Parks Web site. You create two additional Web pages, add image backgrounds to the two new pages, add images to the two new pages and to the index page, add links to and from the index page, and add absolute links to the national preserves and historic sites highlighted in the two new pages.

Each new page contains a link to the home (index) page, and the index page contains links to each new page. This arrangement presents the information to the users in a logical order, making it easy to always return to the home page from any point within the Web site. The two new pages and the home page also follow Web site design guidelines that address accessibility principles (Figures 2–1a, 2–1b, and 2–1c on the next page).

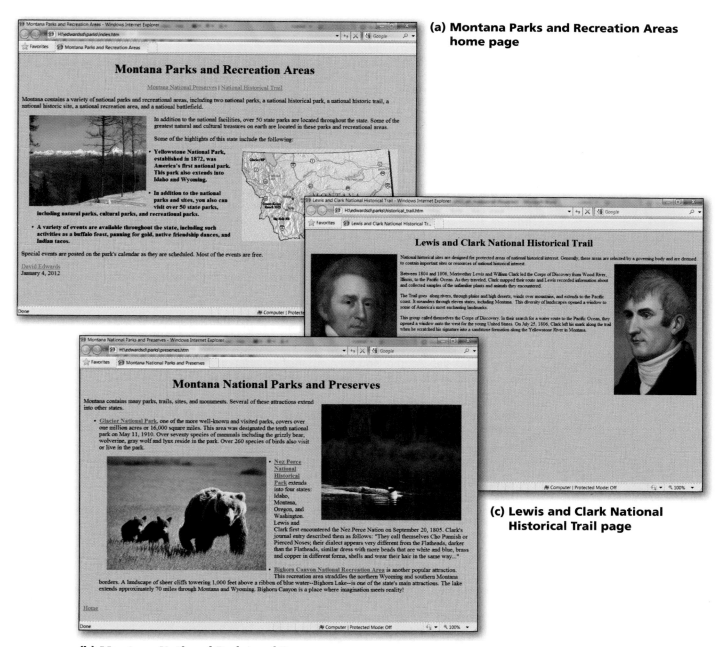

(a) Montana Parks and Recreation Areas home page

(c) Lewis and Clark National Historical Trail page

(b) Montana National Parks and Preserves page

Figure 2–1

Overview

As you read this chapter, you will learn how to add pages to the Montana Parks Web site to create and modify the documents shown in Figure 2–1 and how to use Dreamweaver to perform the following tasks:

- Copy data files to the Web site folder.
- Add pages to a Web site.
- Use Dreamweaver's image accessibility features.
- Insert, resize, and align images within a Web page.

- Create relative, absolute, and e-mail links.
- Edit, change color, and delete links.
- Check spelling.
- Use Live view.
- Display a page in Code view.

**Plan
Ahead**

General Project Guidelines

When creating a Web site, the organization of the site and how different users will approach the site is of paramount importance. Most Web sites have a home page or index page, but that does not necessarily mean that all visitors enter the Web site through the home page. Generally, with most Web sites, considering that the visitor has a Web page address, they can enter the site at any point. As you modify the home page and add the pages shown in Figures 2–1a, b, and c, you should follow these guidelines.

1. **Organize your content.** Create and organize the content for the two new pages.

2. **Identify links.** Consider the content of each new page and how it will link to and from the home page.

3. **Include standard links for navigation.** Visitors to your Web site will use links to navigate the site, and expect to find links to the home page and to main topics. They also expect descriptive links and links for sending e-mail to someone in charge of the Web site.

4. **Prepare images.** Acquire and then organize your images within the Assets panel. Determine which one goes with which Web page.

5. **Consider image placement.** Consider where you will place the images on each of the pages. Determine how much vertical and horizontal space to designate around the image.

6. **Resize images as necessary.** Review each of the images regarding size and determine which ones, if any, need to be resized.

7. **Consider accessibility.** Consider accessibility issues, how they can be addressed, and which ones you need to address within the Web site.

8. **Verify browser viewing.** Use your browser to verify that the page is displayed appropriately and that the links work.

9. **Proofread and check spelling.** Proofread each page and check the spelling.

With a good understanding of the requirements, and an understanding of the necessary decisions and planning process, the next step is to copy the data files to the parks Web site.

Copying Data Files to the Local Web Site

Your data files contain images for Chapter 2. These images are in an images folder. You can use Windows Computer or Windows Explorer to copy the Chapter 2 images to your parks\images folder. See the inside back cover of this book for instructions for downloading the data files, or see your instructor for information about accessing the files required for this book.

The folder containing the data files for this chapter is stored on Removable Disk (H:). The location on your computer may be different. If necessary, verify the location of the data files folder with your instructor.

To Copy Data Files to the Parks Web Site

The following steps show how to copy the files to the parks local root folder using Windows Computer. Before you start enhancing and adding to your Web site, you need to copy the data files into the site's folder hierarchy.

1 Click the Start button on the Windows taskbar and then click Computer to display the Computer window.

2 Navigate to the location of the downloaded data files for Chapter 2, double-click the folder containing your data files, double-click the Chapter02 folder to open it, double-click the parks folder to display the data files, and then double-click the images folder to display the image data files.

3 Click the clark01 image file, or the first file in the list, hold down the SHIFT key, and then click the montana_map image file, or the last file in the list.

4 Right-click the selected files to display the context menu, click the Copy command, and then navigate to the *your name* folder, which contains the folders and files for the Montana Parks Web site.

5 Double-click the *your name* folder, double-click the parks folder, and then double-click the images folder.

6 Right-click anywhere in the open window to display the context menu, and then click the Paste command to copy the images into the Montana Parks Web site images folder. Verify that the folder now contains seven images, including the parks_bkg image (Figure 2–2).

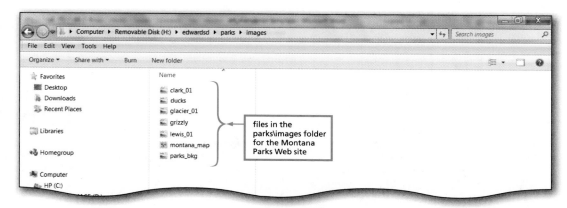

Figure 2–2

Q&A Is it necessary to create a folder for images within the Web site?

The hierarchy of folders and files in a Web site is critical to Web development. Even for the simplest of sites, you should create a separate folder for the images. The folder name can be any name you choose, but it is best to use a descriptive, meaningful name.

Starting Dreamweaver and Opening a Web Site

Each time you start Dreamweaver, it opens to the last site displayed when you closed the program. You might therefore need to open the parks Web site. Clicking the **Site pop-up menu button** on the Files panel lists the sites you have defined. When you open the site, a list of pages and subfolders within the site is displayed.

To Start Dreamweaver and Open the Montana Parks Web Site

The following steps illustrate how to start Dreamweaver and open the Montana Parks Web site.

- Click the Start button on the Windows taskbar.

- Click Adobe Dreamweaver CS5 on the Start menu or point to All Programs on the Start menu, and then click Adobe Dreamweaver CS5 on the All Programs list to start Dreamweaver.

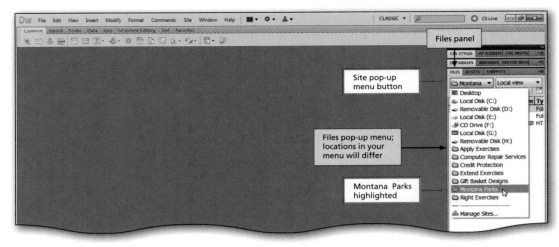

Figure 2–3

- If necessary, display the panel groups.

- If the Montana Parks hierarchy is not displayed, click the Site pop-up menu button in the Files panel to display the drives on your computer and Web sites created with Dreamweaver (Figure 2–3).

Q&A My Dreamweaver window appears in a different size from the one shown in Figure 2–3. Is that a problem?

No. Make sure your Dreamweaver window is maximized. The figures in this book show the Dreamweaver window using a 1024 x 768 resolution. The window might still appear in a different size depending on the type of monitor you are using.

2

- Click Montana Parks to display the Montana Parks Web site hierarchy (Figure 2–4).

Q&A What type of Web structure does this chapter use for the Montana Parks Web pages?

The Introduction chapter illustrates four types of Web

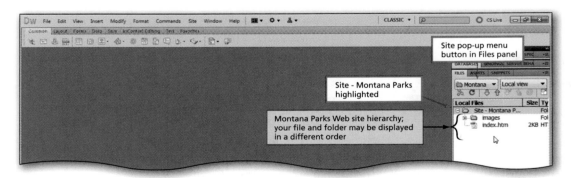

Figure 2–4

structures: linear, hierarchical, web (or random), and grid. This chapter uses a hierarchical structure. The index page is the home page, or entrance to the Web site. From this page, the visitor to this site can link to a page about Montana National Parks and Preserves or to a page about the Lewis and Clark National Historical Trail.

Q&A My Files panel is open, but the Montana Parks files are not displayed. How can I display them?

Refresh the Files panel. To do so, click the Refresh button on the Files panel toolbar or press the F5 key.

Managing a Web Site

Organization is a key element of Web design. Dreamweaver works best with entire sites rather than individual Web pages and has many built-in tools, such as checking links and organizing files, to make site creation easy. You defined the Montana Parks Web site in Chapter 1 and created the index page. You can add pages to your site by creating a new page and saving it as part of the site, or by opening an existing page from another source and saving it as part of the site. In this chapter, you will create two new pages.

Almost all Web sites have a home page. Compare the home page to your front door. Generally, the front door is the first thing guests see when they visit you. The same applies to a Web site's home page. When someone visits a Web site, he or she usually enters through the home page.

The home page normally is named **index.htm** or **index.html**. Recall that this file name has special significance. Most Web servers recognize index.htm (or index.html) as the default home page and automatically display this page without requiring that the user type the full Uniform Resource Locator (URL), or Web address. For example, if you type *nps.gov* into a Web browser's Address box to access the National Park Services Web site, what you see is http://www.nps.gov/index.htm — the actual file name of the site's home page — even though you did not type it that way.

Organizing your Web site and using Dreamweaver's site management features can assure you that the media within your Web page will be displayed correctly. Bringing all of these elements together will start you on your way to becoming a successful Web site developer.

The Files Panel

Organization is one of the keys to a successful Web site. Creating documents without considering where they belong in the folder hierarchy generally creates a difficult-to-manage Web site. The Dreamweaver **Files panel** provides a view of the devices and folders on your computer and shows how these devices and folders are organized. You can create new folders and files for your site through the Files panel, which is similar to organizing files in Windows. You also can use the Files panel to drag or copy and paste files from one folder to another on your computer or from one Web site to another. You cannot, however, copy a file from a Windows folder and paste it into a site in the Dreamweaver Files panel.

In Windows, the main directory of a disk is called the **root directory** or the **top-level directory**. A small device icon or folder icon is displayed next to each object in the list. The **device icon** represents a device such as the desktop or a disk drive, and the **folder icon** represents a folder. Many of these icons have an expand or collapse icon next to them, which indicates whether the device or folder contains additional folders or files. Windows arranges all of these objects — root directory, folders, subfolders, and files — in a hierarchy. The expand and collapse icons are controls that you can click to expand or collapse the view of the file hierarchy. In the Files panel, Dreamweaver uses the same hierarchy arrangement, but site folders and other file icons appear in a different color than non-site folders and files so that you easily can distinguish between the two.

The Home Page

Most Web sites have a starting point, called a home page. In a personal home page within a Web site, for example, you probably would list your name, your e-mail address, some personal information, and links to other information on your Web site. The index page you created in Chapter 1 is the home page for the Montana Parks Web site.

Adding Pages to a Web Site

You copied the data files necessary and pasted them in the parks local root folder in the Files panel. It is time to start building and enhancing your site. You will create two additional pages for the Web site: the Montana National Parks and Preserves page and the Lewis and Clark National Historical Trail page. You will add links and Web page images to the index (or home) page and add links, a background image, and Web page images to the two new pages.

To Open a New Document Window

The first task is to open a new Document window. This will become the Montana National Parks and Preserves Web page. The following steps illustrate how to open a new Document window and save the page as preserves.htm.

1

- Click File on the Application bar and then point to New (Figure 2–5).

Q&A

What are other ways to add a Web page to a site?

If you have already created a document that you can use as a Web page, store it in the root folder for your site, and then use the Open command on the File menu (or the Open button on the Standard toolbar). You can then edit the page in Dreamweaver. You also can insert the contents of a document such as a Microsoft Word or Excel file into a new or existing Web page. To do this, use the Import command on the File menu.

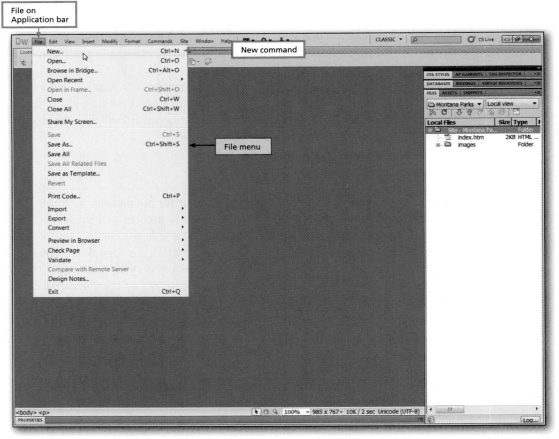

Figure 2–5

2

• Click New to display the New Document dialog box. If necessary, click Blank Page.

• If necessary, click HTML in the Page Type column to specify the type of Web page you are creating.

• If necessary, click <none> in the Layout column to specify no layout. Verify that XHTML 1.0 Transitional is selected on the DocType pop-up menu button (Figure 2–6).

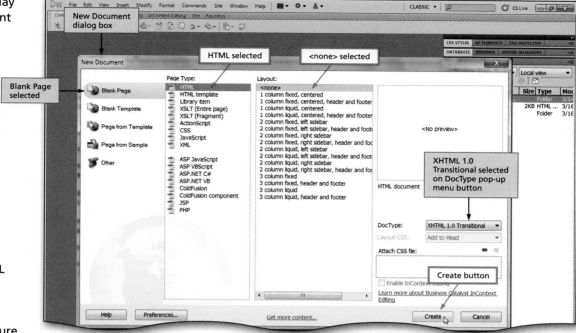

Figure 2–6

Q&A What is XHTML and why is it important?

XHTML is an authoring language that defines the structure and layout of a document so that it is displayed as a Web page and is compatible with most Web browsers.

3

• Click the Create button to create and display a new Untitled-1 document.

• If necessary, click View on the Application bar, point to Toolbars, and then click Standard to display the Standard toolbar (Figure 2–7).

Q&A Is it a problem if my new Web page is named Untitled-2?

No. Dreamweaver increments the number for untitled Web pages. You save the page with a more descriptive name in the next step.

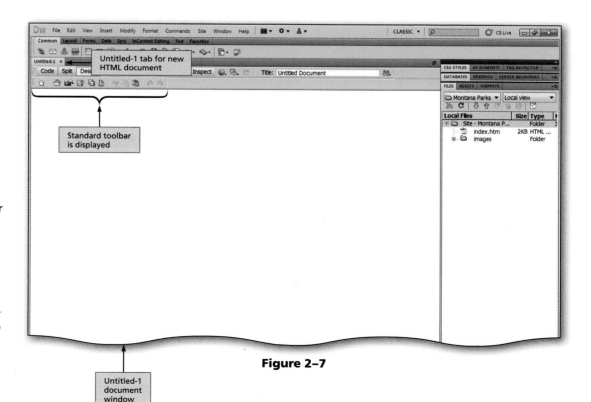

Figure 2–7

- Click the Save button on the Standard toolbar to display the Save As dialog box.

- Type **preserves** in the File name text box to provide a descriptive name for the Web page (Figure 2–8).

Do I need to specify the path or folder for the new Web page?

No. Dreamweaver assumes you want to save the new Web page in the root local folder, which is parks for the preserves page.

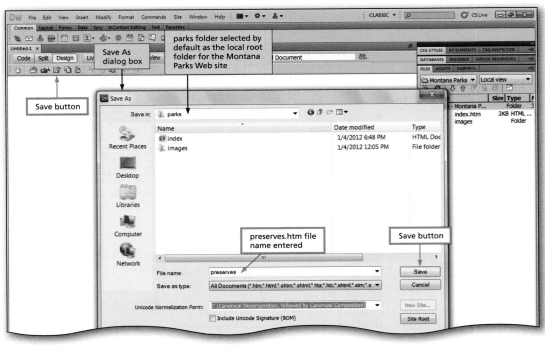

Figure 2–8

- Click the Save button in the Save As dialog box to save the preserves page in the parks local folder (Figure 2–9).

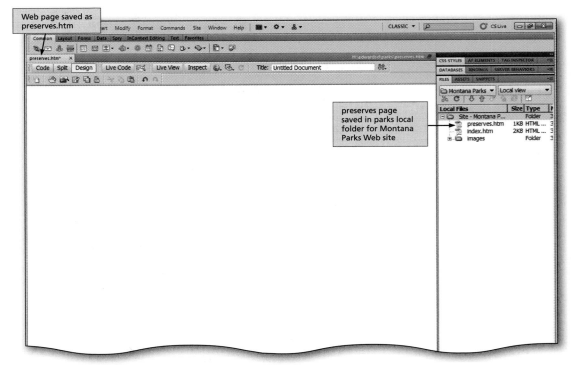

Figure 2–9

Other Ways

1. Click New button on Standard toolbar
2. Press CTRL+N

Creating the Montana National Parks and Preserves Web Page

To create the Montana National Parks and Preserves Web page, you type its text in the Document window. Table 2–1 includes the text for the Montana National Parks and Preserves Web page. Press the ENTER key after typing each section as indicated in Table 2–1.

Table 2–1 Montana National Parks and Preserves Web Page Text	
Section	**Text to Add**
Main heading	Montana National Parks and Preserves < ENTER >
Introduction	Montana contains many parks, trails, sites, and monuments. Several of these attractions extend into other states. < ENTER >
Part 1	Glacier National Park, one of the more well-known and visited parks, covers over one million acres or 16,000 square miles. This area was designated the tenth national park on May 11, 1910. Over seventy species of mammals including the grizzly bear, wolverine, gray wolf and lynx reside in the park. Over 260 species of birds also visit or live in the park.< ENTER >
Part 2	Nez Perce National Historical Park extends into four states: Idaho, Montana, Oregon, and Washington. Lewis and Clark first encountered the Nez Perce Nation on September 20, 1805. Clark's journal entry described them as follows: "They call themselves Cho Punnish or Pierced Noses; their dialect appears very different from the Flatheads, darker than the Flatheads, similar dress with more beads that are white and blue, brass and copper in different forms, shells and wear their hair in the same way..." < ENTER >
Part 3	Bighorn Canyon National Recreation Area is another popular attraction. This recreation area straddles the northern Wyoming and southern Montana borders. A landscape of sheer cliffs towering 1,000 feet above a ribbon of blue water—Bighorn Lake—is one of the state's main attractions. The lake extends approximately 70 miles through Montana and Wyoming. Bighorn Canyon is a place where imagination meets reality! < ENTER >
Closing	Home < ENTER >

To Create the Montana National Parks and Preserves Web Page

The following steps show how to create the first new Web page.

- Type the heading for the Montana National Parks and Preserves Web page as shown in Table 2–1. Press the ENTER key to create a new paragraph.

- Type the rest of the text as shown in Table 2–1. Press the ENTER key as indicated in the table to add blank lines between the paragraphs (Figure 2–10).

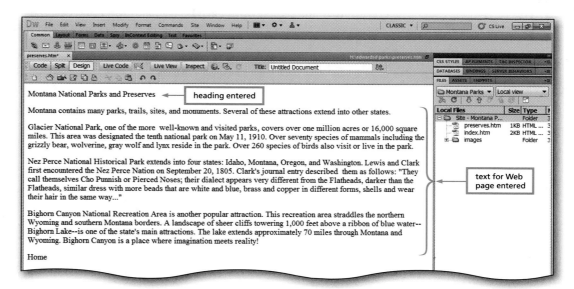

Figure 2–10

To Format the Montana National Parks and Preserves Web Page

In Chapter 1, you formatted the index page by adding headings and bullets and by centering and bolding text. The following steps show how to apply similar formatting to the Montana National Parks and Preserves page.

1 If necessary, scroll up to the top of the Web page, apply Heading 1 to the heading text, and then center the heading.

2 Select and then add bullets to the following three paragraphs that begin: Glacier National Park, Nez Perce National Historical Park, and Bighorn Canyon National Recreation Area (Figure 2–11).

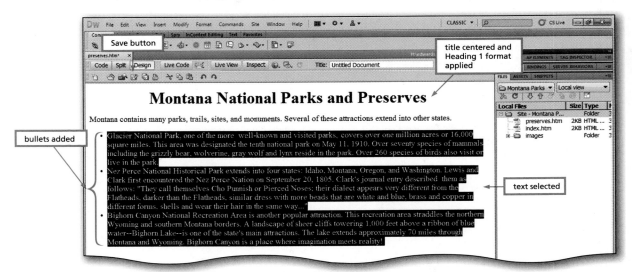

Figure 2–11

3 Click anywhere on the page to deselect the bulleted items.

4 Bold the names of the parks and preserves at the beginning of each of the three paragraphs: Glacier National Park, Nez Perce National Historical Park, and Bighorn Canyon National Recreation Area.

5 Add two line breaks after each bullet paragraph describing the Glacier National Park, Nez Perce National Historical Park, and Bighorn Canyon National Recreation Area.

6 On the Document toolbar, select the text in the Title text box, type `Montana National Parks and Preserves` to enter a descriptive title for the page, and then press ENTER.

7 Click the Save button on the Standard toolbar to save your changes to the preserves.htm Web page (Figure 2–12).

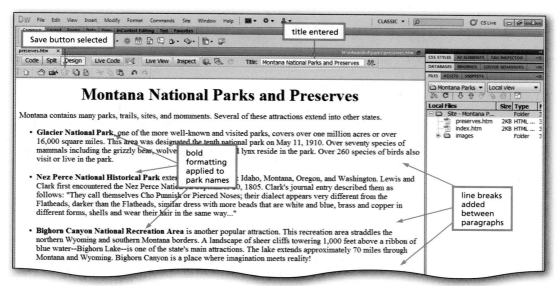

Figure 2–12

Creating the Lewis and Clark National Historical Trail Web Page

You create the Lewis and Clark National Historical Trail Web page by entering text the same way you entered the text for the Montana National Parks and Preserves page. Start by opening a new Document window, add the text, and then format it.

To Open a New Document Window

The following steps show how to open a new Document window for the third Web page for the Montana Parks Web site — the Lewis and Clark National Historical Trail page.

1 Click File on the Application bar, click New, and then, if necessary, click Blank Page.

2 If necessary, click HTML in the Page Type column to select the page type for the Web page.

3 If necessary, click <none> in the Layout column to specify no predefined layout.

4 Click the Create button to create and display the new blank Web page.

5 Save the Web page as historical_trail in the parks folder (Figure 2–13).

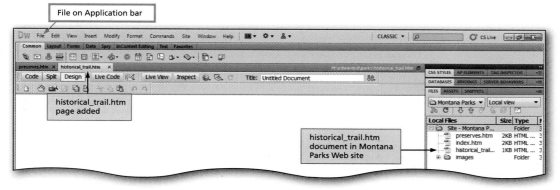

Figure 2–13

Entering Text for the Lewis and Clark National Historical Trail Web Page

Type the text for the Lewis and Clark National Historical Trail Web page using Table 2–2 and the following steps. Press the ENTER key as indicated in the table.

Table 2-2 Lewis and Clark National Historical Trail Web Page Text	
Section	**Text to Add**
Main Heading	Lewis and Clark National Historical Trail < ENTER >
Introduction	National historical sites are designated for protected areas of national historical interest. Generally, these areas are selected by a governing body and are deemed to contain important sites or resources of national historical interest. < ENTER >
Part 1	Between 1804 and 1806, Meriwether Lewis and William Clark led the Corps of Discovery from Wood River, Illinois, to the Pacific Ocean. As they traveled, Clark mapped their route and Lewis recorded information about and collected samples of the unfamiliar plants and animals they encountered. < ENTER >
Part 2	The Trail goes along rivers, through plains and high deserts, winds over mountains, and extends to the Pacific coast. It meanders through eleven states, including Montana. This diversity of landscapes opened a window to some of America's most enchanting landmarks. < ENTER >
Part 3	This group called themselves the Corps of Discovery. In their search for a water route to the Pacific Ocean, they opened a window onto the west for the young United States. On July 25, 1806, Clark left his mark along the trail when he scratched his signature into a sandstone formation along the Yellowstone River in Montana. < ENTER >
Closing	Home < ENTER >

To Create the Lewis and Clark National Historical Trail Web Page

The next task is to add text to the Web page and then format it. The following steps show how to enter and then format text for the Lewis and Clark National Historical Trail Web page.

1 Type the text of the Web page as shown in Table 2–2, and then click the Save button to save your changes (Figure 2–14).

Q&A If I have already entered text in another document, how can I add it to a new Web page?

You can copy and paste the text just as you do in a word processing document. Copy text from another application, switch to Dreamweaver, position the insertion point in the Design view of the Document window, and then press CTRL+V to paste the text.

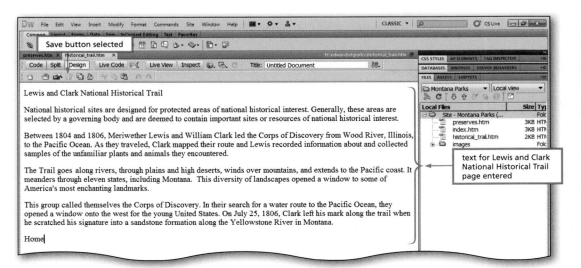

Figure 2–14

2 If necessary, scroll to the top of the Web page, apply Heading 1 to the title, and then center the title.

3 Type `Lewis and Clark National Historical Trail` as the Web page title.

4 Click the Save button on the Standard toolbar to save your work (Figure 2–15).

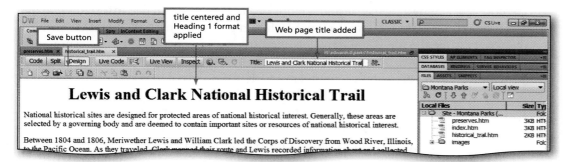

Figure 2–15

Images

You have finished entering and formatting the text for the two new pages and copied the images to the images folder for the Montana Parks Web site. It is time to add other enhancements to your site. In Chapter 1, you added a background image to the index page. In this chapter, you learn more about images. You will add the same background image to the two new pages, and then add images and links to all three pages.

If used correctly and with an understanding of the Web site audience, images add excitement and interest to a Web page. When you are selecting images for a Web site, you should understand that the size and type of image or images used within a Web page affect how fast the Web page downloads and is displayed in the viewer's Web browser. A Web page that downloads too slowly will turn away visitors.

Image File Formats

Graphical images used on the Web are in one of two broad categories: vector and bitmap. **Vector images** are composed of key points and paths, which define shapes and coloring instructions, such as line and fill colors. The vector file contains a mathematical description of the image. The file describes the image to the computer, and the computer draws it. This type of image generally is associated with Adobe Flash or LiveMotion animation programs. One of the benefits of vector images is the small file size, particularly compared to the larger file size of bitmap images.

Bitmap images are the more common type of image file. A bitmap file maps out or plots an image pixel by pixel. A **pixel**, or **picture element**, is the smallest point in a graphical image. Computer monitors display images by dividing the display screen into thousands (or millions) of pixels, arranged in a **grid** of rows and columns. The pixels appear connected because they are so close together. This grid of pixels is a **bitmap**. The **bit-resolution** of an image is the number of bits used to represent each pixel. There are 8-bit images as well as 24- or 32-bit images, where each bit represents a pixel. An 8-bit image supports up to 256 colors, and a 24- or 32-bit image supports up to 16.7 million colors.

Web browsers currently support three bitmap image file types: GIF, JPEG, and PNG.

GIF (.gif) is an acronym for **Graphics Interchange Format**. The GIF format uses 8-bit resolution, supports up to a maximum of 256 colors, and uses combinations of these 256 colors to simulate colors beyond that range. The GIF format is best for displaying images such as logos, icons, buttons, and other images with even colors and tones. GIF images come in two different versions: GIF87 format and GIF89a format. The GIF89a format contains three features not available in the GIF87 or JPEG formats: transparency, interlacing, and animation. Using the **transparency** feature, you can specify a transparency color, which allows the background color or image to appear. The **interlacing** feature lets the browser begin to build a low-resolution version of the full-sized GIF picture on the screen while the file is still downloading, so something is visible to the visitor as the Web page downloads. The **animation** feature allows you to include moving images. Animated GIF images are simply a number of GIF images saved into a single file and looped, or repeated, over and over. A number of shareware GIF editors are available to create animated GIFs. If you do not want to create your own animations, you can find thousands of free animated GIFs on the Internet available for downloading.

JPEG (.jpg) is an acronym for **Joint Photographic Experts Group**. JPEG files are the best format for photographic images because JPEG files can contain up to 16.7 million colors. **Progressive JPEG** is a new variation of the JPEG image format. This image format supports a gradually built display similar to the interlaced GIFs. Older browsers do not support progressive JPEG files.

PNG (.png) stands for **Portable Network Graphics**. PNG, which is the native file format of Adobe Fireworks, is a GIF competitor, and is used mostly for Web site images. Some older browsers do not support this format without a special plug-in. Generally, it still is better to use GIF or JPEG images in your Web pages.

When developing a Web site that consists of many pages, you should maintain a consistent, professional layout and design throughout all of the pages. The pages in a single site, for example, should use similar features such as background colors or images, margins, and headings.

Plan Ahead

Prepare images.
Nearly every Web site displays images such as photographs, drawings, and background textures. Before you add images to a Web site, prepare them using the following guidelines:

- **Acquire the images.** To create your own images, you can take photos with a digital camera and store them in the JPEG format, use a scanner to scan your drawings and photos, or use a graphics editor such as Adobe Photoshop to design images. You also can download images from public domain Web sites, use clip art, or purchase images from stock photo collections. Be sure you have permission to reproduce the images you acquire from Web sites, unless the images are clearly marked as in the public domain.

- **Choose the right format.** Use JPEG files for photographic images and complicated graphics that contain color gradients and shadowing. Use GIF files for basic graphics, especially when you want to take advantage of transparency. You also can use PNG for basic graphics, but not for photos.

- **Keep image file size small.** Images with small file sizes appear in a browser faster than larger images. Use a graphics editor such as Adobe Photoshop to compress image files and reduce their file size without affecting quality. Background images in particular should have a small file size because they often appear on every page.

- **Check the dimensions.** Determine the dimensions of an image file in pixels. You can reduce the dimensions on the Web page by changing the width and height or by cropping the image. Enlarging images generally produces poor results.

Background Colors and Background Images

Many Web pages are displayed with a default white or gray background. Generally, the browser used to display the Web page determines the default background. Recall that you can enhance your Web page by adding a background image or background color.

If you use a background color, be sure to use Web-safe colors. This means the colors will be displayed correctly on the computer screen when someone is viewing your Web page.

Background images add texture and interesting color to a Web page and set the overall appearance of the document. Most browsers support background images. A background image can be a large image, but more frequently it is a smaller image. The image tiles to fill the screen in the Dreamweaver Document window and in the browser window.

To Add a Background Image to the Lewis and Clark National Historical Trail Web Page

In Chapter 1, you added a background image to the index page. Now you use the Page Properties dialog box to add the same image to the Lewis and Clark National Historical Trail Web page and the Montana National Parks and Preserves page. The following steps show how to add a background image to the Lewis and Clark National Historical Trail page.

1 If necessary, click the historical_trail.htm tab to display the page in the Document window.

2 Click Modify on the Application bar and then click Page Properties to open the Page Properties dialog box.

3 Click Appearance (HTML) in the Category column.

4 Click the Browse button to the right of the Background image text box to navigate to the images folder.

5 If necessary, navigate to and then open the images folder.

6 Click parks_bkg and then click the OK button in the Select Image Source dialog box to select the image.

7 Click the OK button in the Page Properties dialog box to apply the background image.

8 Click the Save button on the Standard toolbar to save your work (Figure 2–16 on the next page).

Q&A Is it necessary to add a background image to a Web page?

No, you do not need to add a background image. If you do add a background image to your Web page, however, select an image that does not clash with the text and other content. The background image should not overwhelm the Web page.

Q&A How can I apply a background color instead of a background image?

To apply a background color to a Web page, you can click the Page Properties button in the Property inspector, click the Appearance (HTML) category, and then click the Background icon to display a color picker, which provides a palette of Web-safe colors. Click a color in the palette, and then click the OK button to apply the color to the Web page background.

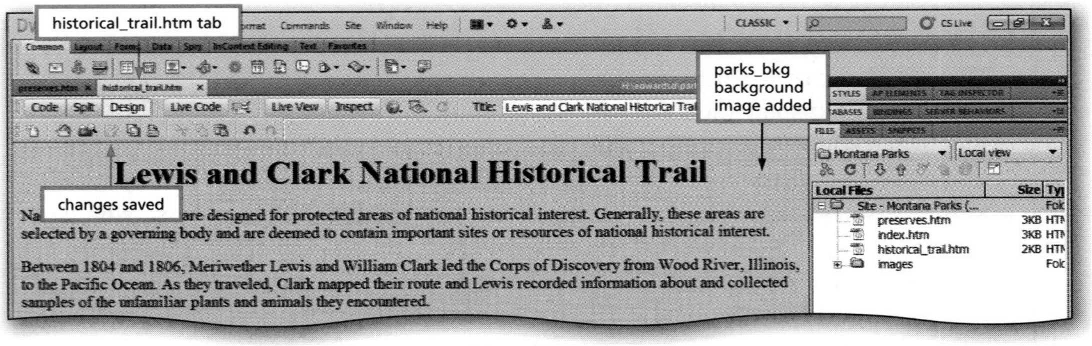

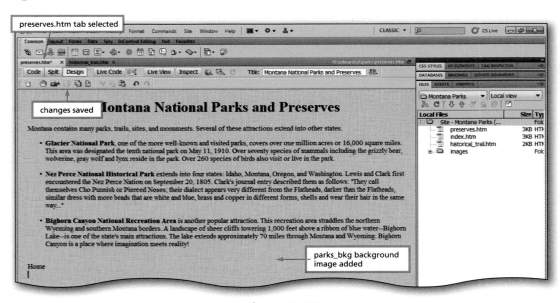

Figure 2–16

To Add a Background Image to the Montana National Parks and Preserves Web Page

The following steps illustrate how to add a background image to the Montana National Parks and Preserves page.

1 Click the preserves.htm tab to display the page in the Document window.

2 Click Modify on the Application bar and then click Page Properties to open the Page Properties dialog box.

3 Click Appearance (HTML) in the Category column.

4 Click the Browse button to the right of the Background image box to navigate to the images folder.

5 Click parks_bkg and then click the OK button in the Select Image Source dialog box.

6 Click the OK button in the Page Properties dialog box to apply the background image.

7 Click the Save button on the Standard toolbar (Figure 2–17).

Figure 2–17

Assets Panel

Besides adding background images, you also can add images such as photos to your Web pages. To enhance your index.htm Web page, you will add two images. One image will be displayed in the upper-left part of the page, and the second image will be displayed to the right of the bulleted list. Dreamweaver has features to assist with placing and enhancing images. The Assets panel provides visual cues for your images, the invisible element feature provides placement control for the images, and the accessibility tools provide information for individuals with disabilities.

Assets are elements, such as images or Flash files, that you use in building a page or a site. The **Assets panel**, which is grouped with the Files panel, helps you manage and organize your Web site's assets (Figure 2–18). This panel contains a list of all the asset types (images, colors, URLs, Flash and Shockwave files, movies, scripts, templates, and library items) within the selected local root folder. The Site option shows the assets in your site. The Favorites list shows only the assets you have selected and added to the list. The Assets panel in Figure 2–18 is resized to show all options.

You can insert most asset types into a document by dragging them into the Document window, using the Insert button at the bottom of the Assets panel, or using the Media command on the Insert menu. Also, you can either insert colors and URLs or apply them to selected text in Design view. Additionally, you can apply URLs to other elements in Design view, such as images. When an image file name is selected, a thumbnail of the image is displayed at the top of the Assets panel. You will use the Assets panel to insert the images into the Montana Parks Web pages.

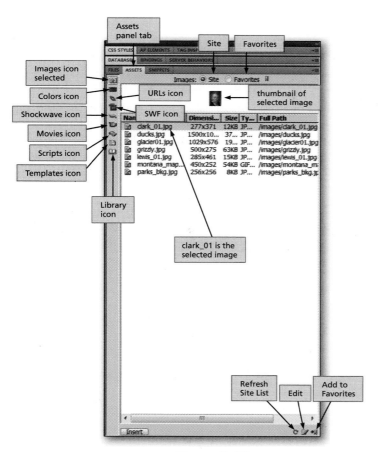

Figure 2–18

Accessibility

When developing a Web page, the Web page developer needs to consider the full spectrum of visitors who might access the site. Dreamweaver provides accessibility tools that allow the Web site developer to create pages to meet the needs of all visitors, including those with disabilities. The four accessibility object tools included in Dreamweaver are form objects, frames, media, and images. This chapter includes accessibility information relative to images. The three other objects are covered in later chapters.

Plan Ahead

> **Consider accessibility.**
> Accessibility features let people with visual, auditory, motor, and other disabilities use Web sites easily. Prepare for providing accessible content on your Web pages by using the following guidelines:
>
> - **Set up the workspace for accessible page design.** Make sure that Dreamweaver reminds you to enter accessibility information for objects such as images. Use the Accessibility category in the Preferences dialog box to select the Show Attributes When Inserting option.
>
> - **Enter accessibility attributes.** When you insert an image, Dreamweaver prompts you to enter accessibility attributes such as text equivalents for the image. Electronic screen readers can then recite the text equivalents. Be sure to enter text that describes the image briefly but thoroughly.

When you insert an image, the Image Tag Accessibility Attributes dialog box is displayed (Figure 2–19). This dialog box contains two text boxes — one for Alternate text and one for Long description. Screen readers translate and recite the information you enter in both text boxes. You should limit your Alternate text entry to 50 characters or less so it is easy to remember. For a more detailed description of the image, create and save a text file and then add it as a link to the file. When the link is activated, the screen reader recites the text for visually impaired visitors. Clicking Cancel removes the dialog box and inserts the image. The Accessibility feature is turned on by default when you install Dreamweaver. To turn off the Accessibility feature, click Edit on the Application bar and then click Preferences. Click Accessibility in the Category column and then deselect the check boxes for the four attributes. Appendix B contains a full overview of Dreamweaver's accessibility features.

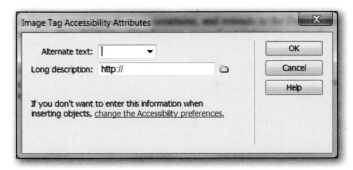

Figure 2–19

Invisible Elements

Dreamweaver's Document window displays basically what you see in a Web browser window. It sometimes is helpful, however, when designing a Web page to see the placement of certain code elements. For example, viewing the Line Break code <br/> provides a visual cue regarding the layout. Dreamweaver lets you control the visibility of 13 different codes, including those for image placement, through the Preferences dialog box.

When you insert and then align an image in a Document window, Dreamweaver can display an **invisible element marker** that shows the location of the inserted image within the HTML code. This visual aid is displayed as a small yellow icon. When you select the icon, you can use it to cut and paste or drag and drop the image. When using invisible elements with images, however, the invisible element marker is not displayed if the image is aligned to the left. Dreamweaver provides the invisible element marker for 12 other elements, including tables, ActiveX objects, plug-ins, and applets. To hide all invisible elements temporarily, select Hide All on the View menu Visual Aids submenu or use CTRL+SHIFT+I.

BTW

Invisible Elements and Precision Layout
Displaying invisible elements can change the layout of a page slightly, so for precision layout, when moving elements by a few pixels might change the entire page, hide the invisible elements.

To Set Invisible Element Preferences and Turn on Visual Aids

The following steps illustrate how to display the invisible element marker for aligned elements such as images and how to turn on invisible elements through the Visual Aids submenu command.

1
- Click Edit on the Application bar and then click Preferences to display the Preferences dialog box (Figure 2–20).

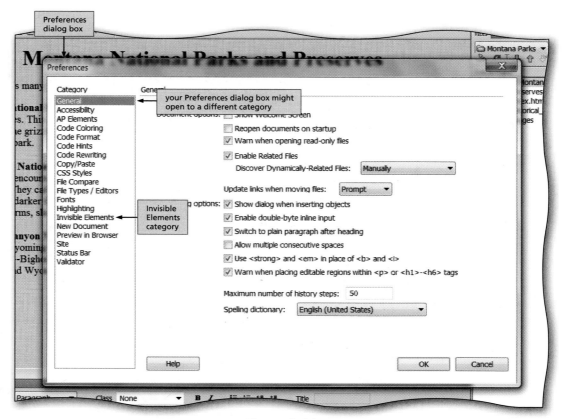

Figure 2–20

2

- Click Invisible Elements in the Category list to display the Invisible Elements options in the Preferences dialog box (Figure 2–21).

Q&A

Is it necessary for me to display the invisible element markers when working with images?

No. You can work with images without displaying the invisible element markers. However, the markers help you locate and work with images on a Web page in Design view.

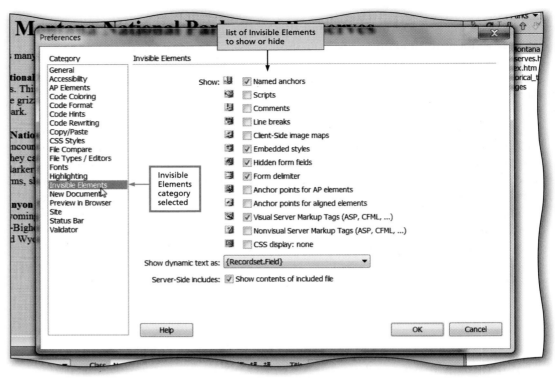

Figure 2–21

3

- Click the Anchor points for aligned elements check box to select this option, which makes it easier to align elements (Figure 2–22).

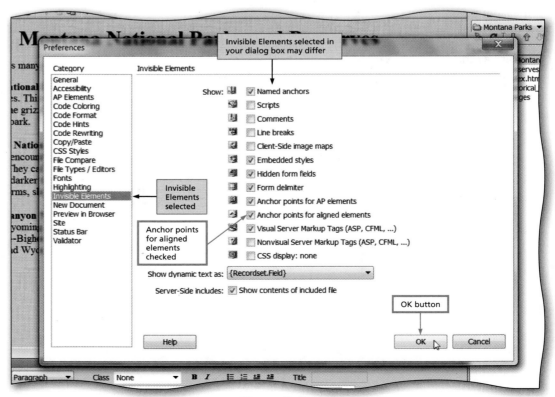

Figure 2–22

4

- Click the OK button in the Preferences dialog box to confirm the new setting and close the Preferences dialog box.

- Click View on the Application bar, point to Visual Aids, and then point to Invisible Elements on the Visual Aids submenu to highlight the command (Figure 2–23).

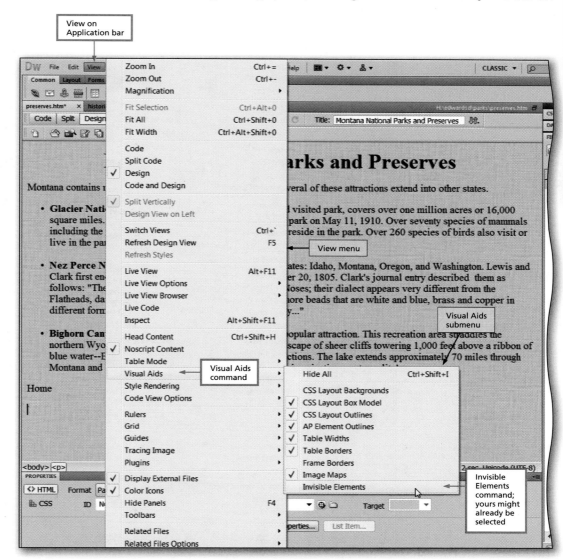

Figure 2–23

5

- If necessary, click Invisible Elements to add a check mark to the Invisible Elements command (Figure 2–24).

What if the Invisible Elements command is already checked?

Do not complete Step 5 — the Invisible Elements command already is selected. Click the Document window to close the View menu.

Should I notice a change in the Document window after displaying the visual aids?

No. No visible changes are displayed in the Document window.

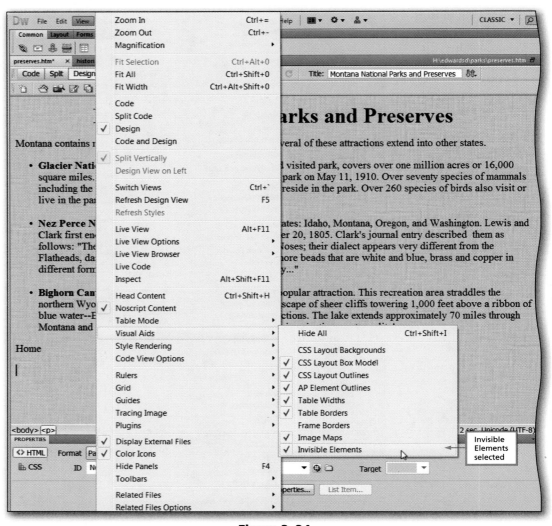

Figure 2–24

Opening a Web Page

Once you have created and saved a Web page or copied a Web page to a Web site, you often need to retrieve it from a disk. Opening an existing Web page in Dreamweaver is much the same as opening an existing document in most other software applications; that is, you use the File menu and Open command or Open Recent command, or you can click the Open button on the Standard toolbar. If, however, the page is part of a Web site created with Dreamweaver, you also can open the file from the Files panel. After opening the page, you can modify text, images, tables, and any other elements.

To Open a Web Page from a Local Web Site

The following step illustrates how to open a Web page from a local site in the Files panel.

1

- Double-click index.htm in the Files panel to open the index page.

- If the Standard toolbar is not displayed, click View on the Application bar, point to Toolbars, and then click Standard to display the Standard toolbar (Figure 2–25).

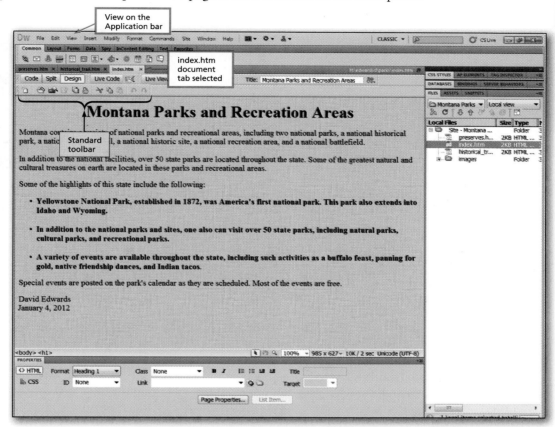

Figure 2–25

Other Ways

1. On File menu, click Open, select file
2. Press CTRL+O, select file

Inserting an Image into a Web Page

Inserting images into your Web page is easy and quick with Dreamweaver — you drag and drop the image from the Files panel or the Assets panel. Image placement, however, can be more complex. When you view the Web page in a browser, the image might be displayed differently than in the Document window. If the images are not displayed correctly, you can select and modify the placement of the images in the Document window by dragging the invisible element marker to move the image.

To Insert an Image into the Index Page

In the following steps, you add an image of a map of Montana to the index.htm Web page.

1

- If necessary, scroll to the top of the page.

- Click the Assets panel tab to display the Assets panel. Verify that the Images icon is selected.

- Click montana_map .gif in the Assets panel to select the image file (Figure 2–26).

Q&A How do I resize the Assets panel?

You resize panels by pointing to the panel's vertical bar until it changes to a two-headed arrow, and then you hold down the mouse button and drag.

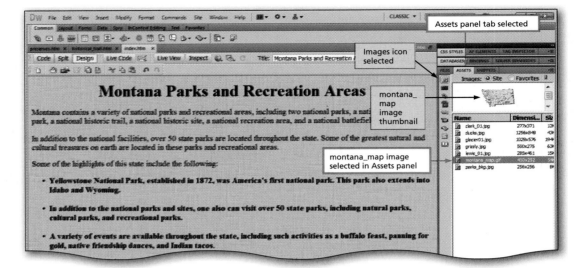

Figure 2–26

Q&A How do I add an asset to the Favorites list?

To add an asset to the Favorites list, select the item in the Site list and then click the Add to Favorites button. Remove an item from the list by selecting the Favorites option button, selecting the item, and then clicking the Remove from Favorites button.

2

- Drag montana_map from the Assets panel to the left of the first bulleted line. The Image Tag Accessibility Attributes dialog box is displayed (Figure 2–27).

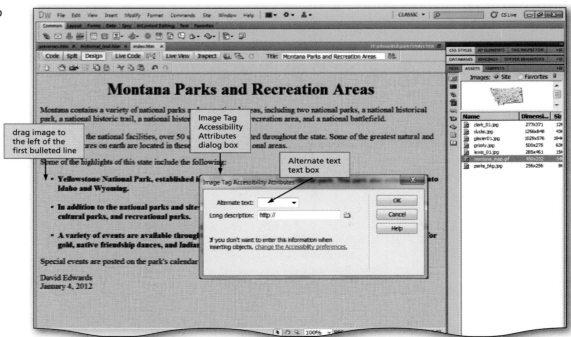

Figure 2–27

3

- Type **Montana map** in the Alternate text text box to provide alternate text for the montana_map image (Figure 2–28).

Q&A

Am I required to enter text in the Alternate text or Long description text box?

No. It is not required that you enter text in either text box. For images in this chapter and other chapters, however, instructions are included to add alternate text.

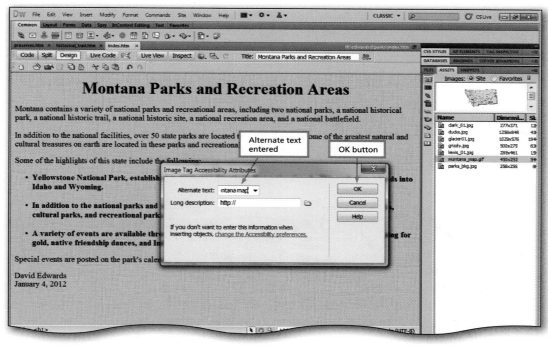

Figure 2–28

4

- Click the OK button in the Image Tag Accessibility Attributes dialog box to display the selected image in the Document window and to view the attribute changes in the Property inspector (Figure 2–29).

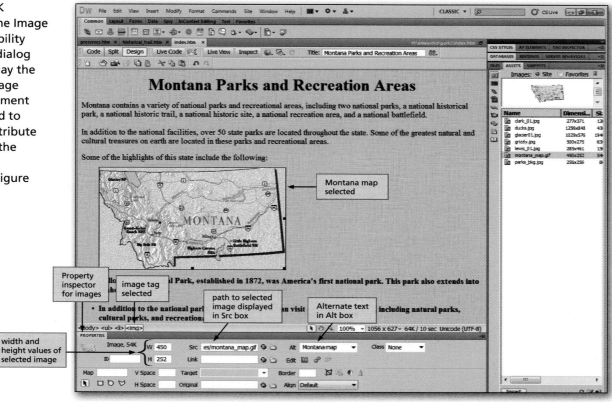

Figure 2–29

Other Ways
1. Drag image from Files panel 3. In Assets panel, right-click image file, click Insert
2. On Insert menu, click Image, select file 4. Press CTRL+ALT+I, select file

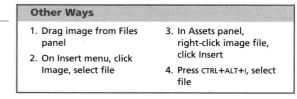

Property Inspector Image Tools

In addition to the visual aid feature, you can use the Property inspector to help with image placement and to add other attributes. When you select an image within the Document window, the Property inspector displays properties specific to that image. The Property inspector is divided into two sections. Clicking the expander arrow in the lower-right corner of the Property inspector expands or collapses the Property inspector. When it is collapsed, it shows only the more commonly used properties for the selected element. The expanded Property inspector shows more advanced options. The Property inspector for images contains several image-related features in the upper and lower sections.

The following section describes the image-related features of the Property inspector (Figure 2–30).

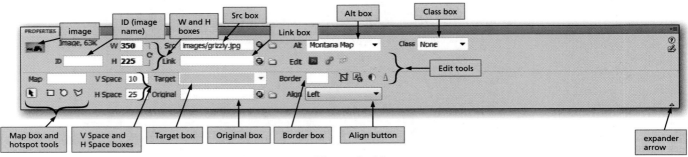

Figure 2–30

Align Set the alignment of an image in relation to other elements in the same paragraph, table, or line with the **Align button**. This property option is discussed in more detail later in this chapter.

Alt Use Alt to specify alternate text for the image. For visually impaired users who use speech synthesizers with text-only browsers, the text is spoken aloud.

Border The **Border** is the width, in pixels, of the image's border. The default is no border.

Edit The **Edit** section contains the following editing option tools: (a) **Edit** opens the computer's default image editor, such as Adobe Fireworks or Photoshop; the Edit icon matches the icon of the default image editor on your computer; (b) **Edit Image Settings** opens the Image Preview dialog box, which contains options to remove colors, add smoothing to the edges, modify colors, and other image formatting choices; (c) update from original; (d) crop (reduce the area of the image); (e) resample (add or subtract pixels from a resized JPEG or GIF image file to match the appearance of the original image as closely as possible); (f) modify the brightness and contrast of pixels in an image; and (g) sharpen (adjust the focus of an image by increasing the contrast of edges found within the image).

ID Specifies the image name that is contained in the source code.

Link The **Link** box allows you to make the selected image a hyperlink to a specified URL or Web page. To create a relative link, you can click the Point to File or Browse for File icons to the right of the Link box to browse to a page in your Web site, or you can drag a file from the Files panel into the Link box. For an external link, you can type the URL directly into the Link box or use copy and paste.

Map and Hotspot Tools Use the **Map** box and the **Hotspot tools** to label and create an image map.

Original The path to an image file stored outside of the current Web site.

Reset Size If you change an image size, the **Reset Size** tool is displayed next to the W and H text boxes after an image size has been changed. Use this tool to reset the W and H values to the original size of the image.

Src The path to an image file stored in the current Web site.

Target Use **Target** to specify the frame or window in which the linked page should load. This option is not available when the image is linked to another file.

V Space and H Space Use V Space and H Space to add space, in pixels, along the sides of the image. **V Space** adds space along the top and bottom of an image. **H Space** adds space along the left and right of an image.

W and H The W and H boxes indicate the width and height of the image, in pixels. Dreamweaver automatically displays the dimensions when an image is inserted into a page. You can specify the image size in the following units: pc (picas), pt (points), in (inches), mm (millimeters), cm (centimeters), and combinations, such as 2in+5mm. Dreamweaver converts the values to pixels in the source code.

Aligning the Image and Adjusting the Image Size

After you insert the image into the Web page and then select it, the Property inspector displays features specific to the image. As discussed earlier, alignment is one of these features. **Alignment** determines where on the page the image is displayed and if and how text wraps around the image.

You also can adjust the image size easily through the W and H text boxes in the Property inspector or by dragging the handles surrounding the image. Additionally, when you insert an image into a Web page that contains text, by default, the text around the image aligns to the right and bottom of the image. The image alignment options on the Align button pop-up menu in the Property inspector let you set the alignment for the image in relation to other page content. Dreamweaver provides 10 alignment options for images. Table 2–3 describes these image alignment options.

Table 2–3 Image Alignment Options	
Alignment Option	**Description**
Default	Aligns the image with the baseline of the text in most browser default settings
Baseline	Aligns the image with the baseline of the text regardless of the browser setting
Top	Aligns the image with the top of the item; an item can be text or another object
Middle	Aligns the image with the baseline of the text or object at the vertical middle of the image
Bottom	Aligns the image with the baseline of the text or the bottom of another image regardless of the browser setting
TextTop	Aligns the image with the top of the tallest character in a line of text
Absolute Middle	Aligns the image with the middle of the current line of text
Absolute Bottom	Aligns the image with the bottom of the current line of text or another object
Left	Aligns the image at the left margin
Right	Aligns the image at the right margin

To Align an Image

The following steps show how to align the Montana map image to the right and wrap text to the left of the image. To have a better overview of how the page will be displayed in a browser, you start by collapsing the panel groups.

- Click the panel groups Collapse to Icons arrow to collapse the panel groups.

- If necessary, click the montana_map image in the Document window to select the image.

- Click the Align button in the Property inspector to display the alignment options.

- Point to Right on the pop-up menu to highlight the Right command (Figure 2–31).

Q&A

What are the most widely used Align options?

The most widely used options are Left and Right.

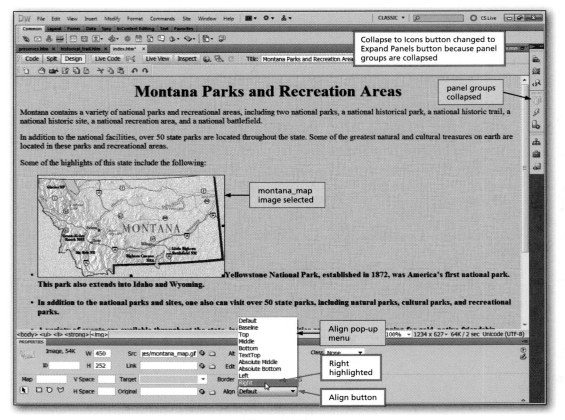

Figure 2–31

2

- Click Right to move the selected image to the right side of the Document window and to display the element marker (Figure 2–32).

Q&A

What should I do if the element marker is not displayed?

First, open the Preferences dialog box, click the Invisible Elements category, and then make sure the Anchor points for aligned elements box is checked. Next, click View on the Application bar, point to Visual Aids, and make sure the Invisible Elements command is checked.

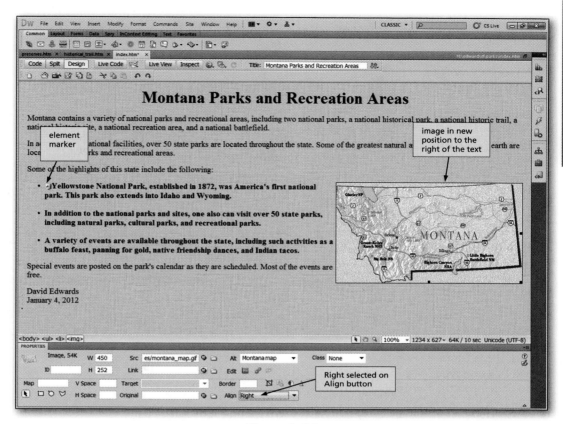

Figure 2–32

Adjusting Space Around Images

When aligning an image, by default, only about three pixels of space are inserted between the image and adjacent text. You can adjust the amount of vertical and horizontal space between the image and text by using the V Space and H Space settings in the Property inspector. The V Space setting controls the vertical space above and below an image. The H Space setting controls the horizontal space to the left and right side of the image.

To Adjust the Image Size and the Horizontal Space

The following steps show how to resize an image and add horizontal space around an image.

- If necessary, click to select the image.

- Double-click the W text box in the Property inspector to select the current width value, and then type **400** to adjust the width of the image.

- Press the TAB key and type **245** in the H text box to adjust the height of the image.

- Press the ENTER key.

- Click the H Space text box and type **25** to adjust the horizontal space between the image and the text.

- Press the TAB key to apply the horizontal space setting to the image (Figure 2–33).

Figure 2–33

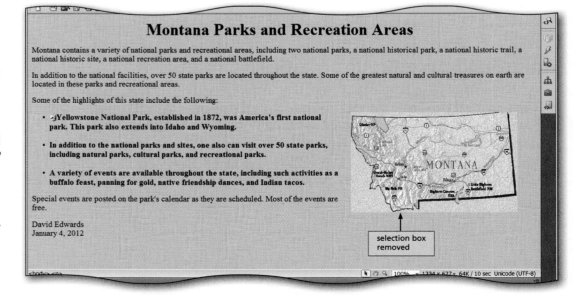

- Click outside the image to remove the selection box and to view the added space and the reduced size (Figure 2–34).

Q&A Why do I need to adjust the width and height of the image?

In many instances, adjusting the image size creates a better balance on the page.

Q&A How do the V Space and H Space settings change the placement of the image?

V Space adds space along the top and bottom of an image. H Space adds space along the left and right of an image.

Montana Parks and Recreation Areas

Montana contains a variety of national parks and recreational areas, including two national parks, a national historical park, a national historic trail, a national historic site, a national recreation area, and a national battlefield.

In addition to the national facilities, over 50 state parks are located throughout the state. Some of the greatest natural and cultural treasures on earth are located in these parks and recreational areas.

Some of the highlights of this state include the following:

- Yellowstone National Park, established in 1872, was America's first national park. This park also extends into Idaho and Wyoming.

- In addition to the national parks and sites, one also can visit over 50 state parks, including natural parks, cultural parks, and recreational parks.

- A variety of events are available throughout the state, including such activities as a buffalo feast, panning for gold, native friendship dances, and Indian tacos.

Special events are posted on the park's calendar as they are scheduled. Most of the events are free.

David Edwards
January 4, 2012

Figure 2–34

Other Ways

1. Select image, drag sizing handle

To Insert the Second Image

To enhance your index Web page further, you will add a second image. This image will appear on the left side of the page, below the first paragraph. The following steps show how to insert a second image on the Montana Parks and Recreation Areas page.

1 If necessary, scroll up and position the insertion point to the left of the second paragraph, which begins "In addition to the national facilities."

2 Expand the panel groups, and then click the Assets tab, if necessary, to display the images in the Assets panel (Figure 2–35).

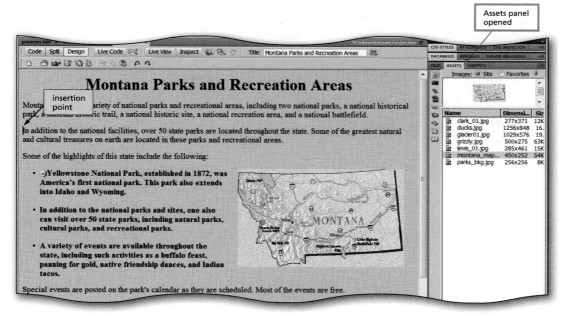

Figure 2–35

3 Drag the glacier01.jpg image from the Assets panel to the insertion point to add the image to the Web page and to display the Image Tag Accessibility Attributes dialog box.

4 Type **Montana glacier** in the Alternate text text box, and then click the OK button to insert the glacier01 image into the Web page (Figure 2–36 on the next page).

Q&A
How does the Alternate text make my Web page more accessible?

For visually impaired users who use speech synthesizers with text-only browsers, the Alternate text is spoken aloud.

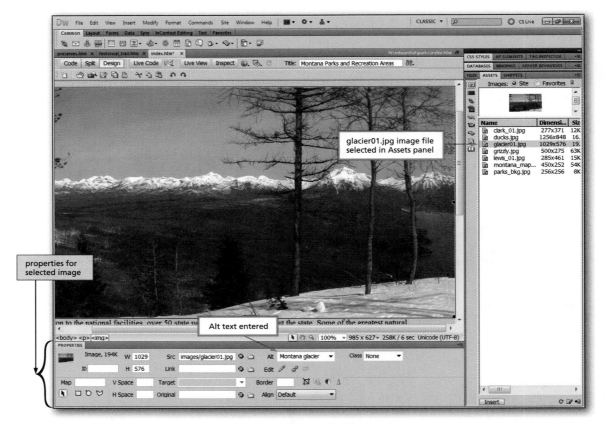

Figure 2–36

5 In the Property inspector, click the Align button, and then click Left in the Align pop-up menu to move the image to the left side of the window (Figure 2–37).

Q&A How can I tell that the image is now left-aligned?

It is difficult to see the alignment of the figure because it is so large. The alignment will be clear when you resize the image in the next step.

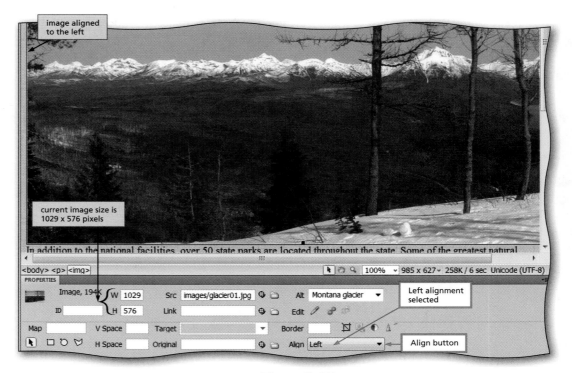

Figure 2–37

6 In the Property inspector, change the W value to 300 and the H value to 240.

7 Click the H Space box, type 2 0 as the horizontal space, and then press the ENTER key to apply the setting changes to the glacier01 image (Figure 2-38).

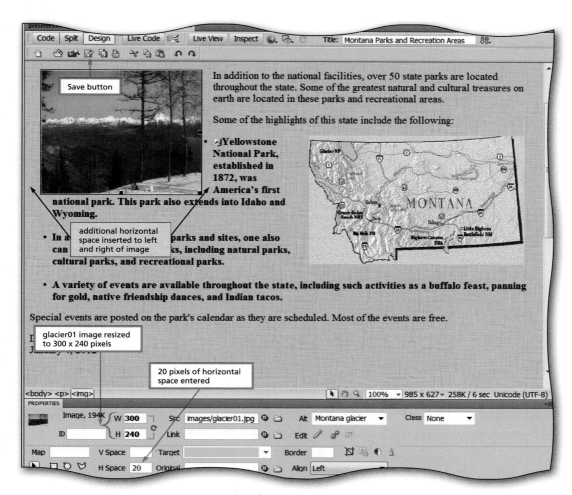

Figure 2–38

8 Click the Save button on the Standard toolbar to save the index.htm page.

9 Press the F12 key to view the Web page in your browser (Figure 2–39).

10 Close the browser to return to Dreamweaver.

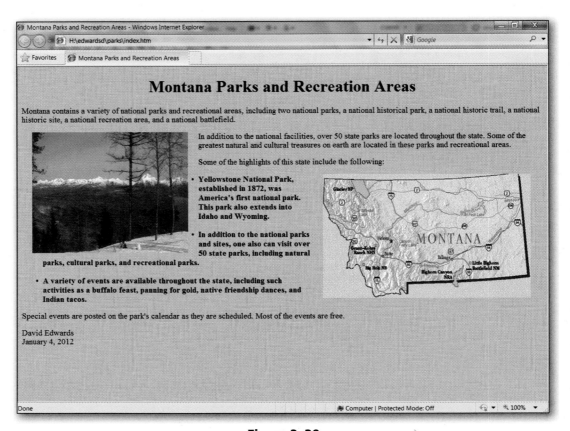

Figure 2–39

To Insert and Align an Image in the Montana National Parks and Preserves Web Page

The next page in your Web site is the Montana National Parks and Preserves page. The following steps show how to further develop this Web page by adding an image to it.

1 Click the preserves.htm document tab to display the page in the Document window.

2 Position the insertion point to the left of the first sentence after the heading, and then drag the ducks.jpg image file from the Assets panel to the insertion point.

3 Type **Montana ducks** in the Alternate text text box and then click the OK button to display the image.

4 Enter **430** in the W box to change the width, enter **360** in the H box to change the height, and then press the ENTER key to display the resized image in the Document window.

5 Enter **15** in the V Space box and **20** in the H Space box to add space around the ducks image.

6 Click the Align button in the Property inspector, and then click Right to align the image to the right side of the window.

7 If necessary, scroll up to display the entire ducks image (Figure 2–40).

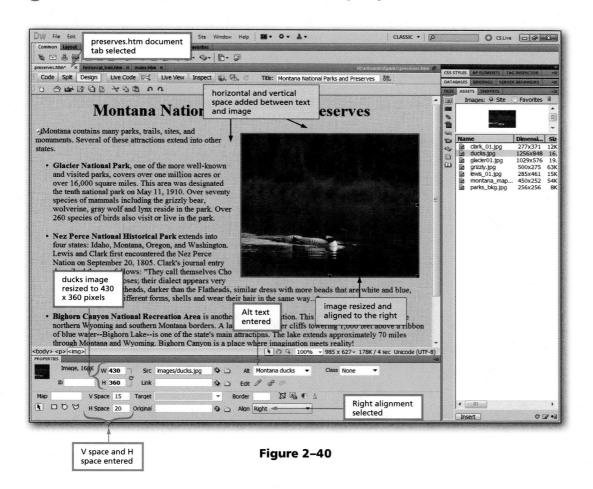

Figure 2–40

To Insert and Align a Second Image in the Montana National Parks and Preserves Web Page

The following steps show how to add a second image to the Montana National Parks and Preserves Web page.

1 Drag the grizzly.jpg image from the Assets panel to the end of the second paragraph (the "Glacier National Park" bullet).

2 Type **Montana Grizzly** in the Alternate text text box and then click the OK button to enter Alt text for this image.

3 Click the Align button in the Property inspector, and then click Left to align the image to the left.

4 Change the width value in the W box to 300 and the height value in the H box to 300.

5 Enter 15 as the vertical space value in the V Space box, enter 20 as the horizontal space value in the H Space box, and then press the ENTER key to add the space around the grizzly image.

6 Click the Save button on the Standard toolbar to save the preserves.htm page with the new image (Figure 2–41).

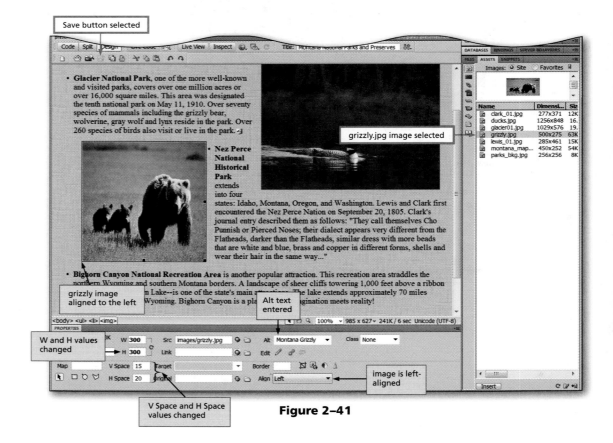

Figure 2–41

7 Press the F12 key to display the Montana National Parks and Preserves page in the browser (Figure 2–42).

8 Close the browser to return to Dreamweaver.

Figure 2–42

To Insert and Align an Image in the Lewis and Clark National Historical Trail Web Page

The third page in your Web site is the Lewis and Clark National Historical Trail page. The following steps illustrate how to add the first of two images to the Lewis and Clark National Historical Trail Web page.

1 Click the historical_trail.htm Web page tab to display that page in the Document window.

2 Click the clark_01.jpg file in the Assets panel, and then position the insertion point to the left of the first sentence (Figure 2–43).

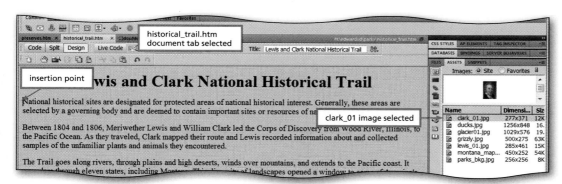

Figure 2–43

3 Drag the clark_01.jpg file from the Assets panel to the insertion point to display the Image Tag Accessibility Attributes dialog box.

4 Type **William Clark** in the Alternate text text box and then click the OK button to enter Alt text for this image and to insert the image in the page.

5 Click the Align button in the Property inspector and then click Left on the Align pop-up menu to align the image to the left side of the page (Figure 2–44).

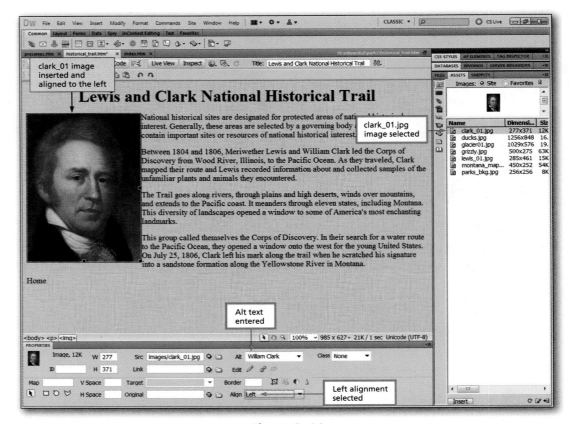

Figure 2–44

6 In Property inspector, click the H Space box, type **10** as the horizontal space, and then press the ENTER key to add the space (Figure 2–45).

Q&A When I add horizontal and vertical space, what are the measurement units?

The measurement units are in pixels, so when you enter 10 in the H Space box, you are specifying 10 pixels of horizontal space around the image.

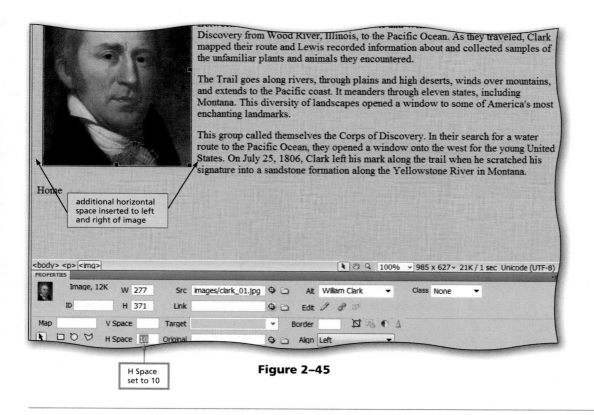

Figure 2–45

To Insert and Align a Second Image in the Lewis and Clark National Historical Trail Web Page

The following steps illustrate how to add the second of two images to the Lewis and Clark National Historical Trail Web page.

1 Position the insertion point to the right of the first paragraph to prepare for adding the second image to the page (Figure 2–46).

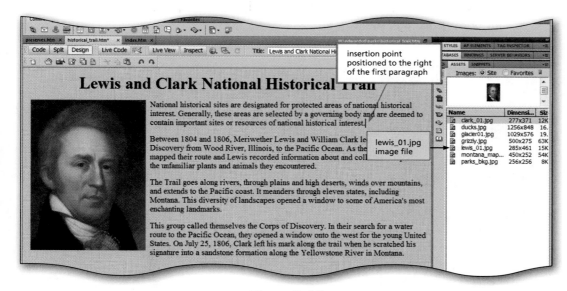

Figure 2–46

2 Drag the lewis01.jpg image from the Assets panel to the insertion point to display the Image Tag Accessibility Attributes dialog box.

3 Type **Meriwether Lewis** in the Alternate text box and then press the ENTER key to enter Alt text for this image and to insert the image in the page. If necessary, scroll down to view the image (Figure 2–47).

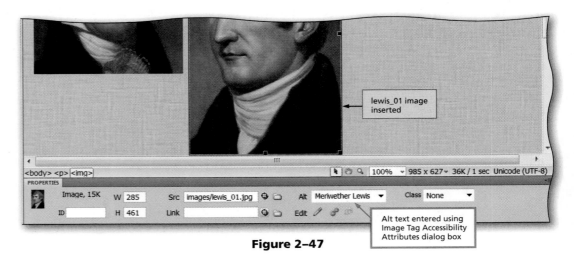

Figure 2–47

4 In the Property inspector, click the Align button and then click Right on the Align pop-up menu to align this image to the right side of the page.

5 Change the width value in the W box to **265** and change the height value in the H box to **435**.

6 In the V Space box, enter **10** as the vertical space, and in the H Space box, enter **10** as the horizontal space.

7 Press the ENTER key to resize and position the image, and then click anywhere on the page to deselect the image.

8 Click the Save button on the Standard toolbar to save the changes to the historical_trail.htm page (Figure 2–48).

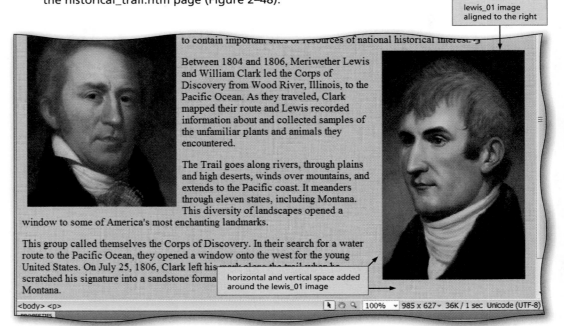

Figure 2–48

9 Press the F12 key to view the Lewis and Clark National Historical Trail page in your browser (Figure 2–49).

10 Close the browser.

Figure 2–49

Image Editing Tools

Dreamweaver provides several basic image editing tools in the Property inspector to modify and enhance an image.

- Use an external image editor: Adobe Photoshop is the default image editor if it is installed on your computer, but you can specify which external editor should start for a specified file type. To select an external editor, click Edit on the Application bar and display the Preferences dialog box. Select File Types/Editors from the Category list to display the Preferences File Types/Editors dialog box. Select the image extension and then browse for the External Code Editor executable file.

- Crop an image: **Cropping** lets you edit an image by reducing the area of the image and allows you to eliminate unwanted portions of the image. When you crop an image and then save the page, the source image file is changed on the disk. Prior to saving, make a backup copy of the image file in case you need to revert to the original image.

- Resample an image: **Resampling** adds or subtracts pixels to or from a resized JPEG or GIF image file to match the appearance of the original image as closely as possible. Resampling an image also reduces an image's file size, resulting in improved download performance. When you resize an image in Dreamweaver, you can resample it to accommodate its new dimensions. To resample a resized image, first resize the image and then click the Resample button in the Property inspector.

BTW

Resizing Images Visually
Besides using the W and H boxes in the Property inspector, you can click an image and then drag a selection handle to visually resize the image. Whether you resize by dragging or by using the Property inspector, you are not changing the size of the original image file, only the appearance of the image on the Web page.

• Adjust brightness and contrast: The **Brightness and Contrast** tool modifies the contrast or brightness of the pixels in an image. Recall that a pixel is the smallest point in a graphical image. Brightness makes the pixels in the image lighter or darker overall, while Contrast either emphasizes or de-emphasizes the difference between lighter and darker regions. This affects the highlights, shadows, and midtones of an image.

• Sharpen an image: **Sharpening** adjusts the focus of an image by increasing the contrast of edges found within the image.

To Crop and Modify the Brightness/Contrast of an Image

The ducks image in the Montana National Parks and Preserves page needs some modification. Cropping the image and emphasizing a better view of the ducks in the image will enhance the page. The following steps show how to crop the image, and then modify the brightness and contrast.

1

• Click the preserves .htm document tab to open the preserves.htm page.

• Select the ducks image to prepare for cropping it.

• Collapse the panel groups so you have more room to work.

• Click the Crop tool in the Property inspector to apply the bounding box (Figure 2–50).

Q&A What should I do if a Dreamweaver dialog box is displayed warning that cropping permanently alters the image?

Click the 'Don't show me this message again' check box, and then click the OK button.

Figure 2–50

Q&A When is cropping an image effective?

Cropping can be very effective for improving the appearance of a photo by highlighting the main point of interest in an image.

2

- Click the crop handle in the lower-right corner of the ducks image and adjust the handles until the bounding box surrounds the area of the image similar to that shown in Figure 2–51. The W value should be approximately 360 and the H value approximately 305.

Figure 2–51

3

- Double-click inside the bounding box to apply the cropping by resizing the image to match the size of the bounding box.

- If necessary, click the ducks image to select it and to verify that the size after cropping is about 360 x 305 pixels (Figure 2–52).

Q&A

How can I make changes after I apply the cropping?

If you need to make changes, click the Undo button on the Standard toolbar and repeat Steps 1 – 3.

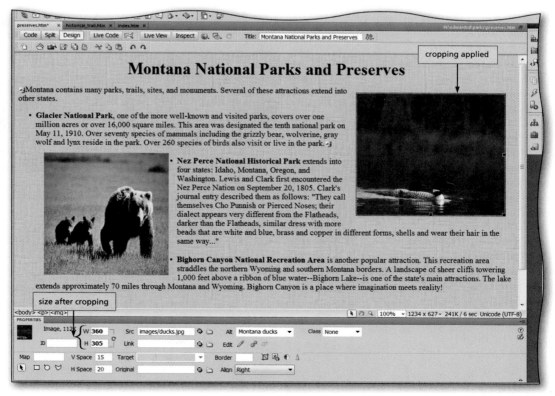

Figure 2–52

4

- Click the Brightness and Contrast tool in the Property inspector to display the Brightness/ Contrast dialog box (Figure 2–53).

Q&A

What should I do if a Dreamweaver dialog box is displayed warning that adjusting the brightness and contrast permanently alters the image?

Click the 'Don't show me this message again' check box, and then click the OK button.

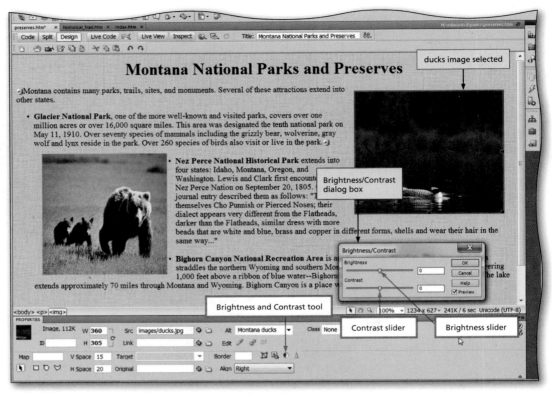

Figure 2–53

5

Experiment

- Drag the Brightness slider and the Contrast slider so you can see how changing the value of each affects the ducks image.

- Drag the Brightness slider to the left and adjust the setting to –10 to change the brightness level.

- Drag the Contrast slider to the right and adjust the setting to 20 to change the contrast level (Figure 2–54).

Q&A

What are the ranges for the Brightness and Contrast settings?

The values for the Brightness and Contrast settings range from –100 to 100.

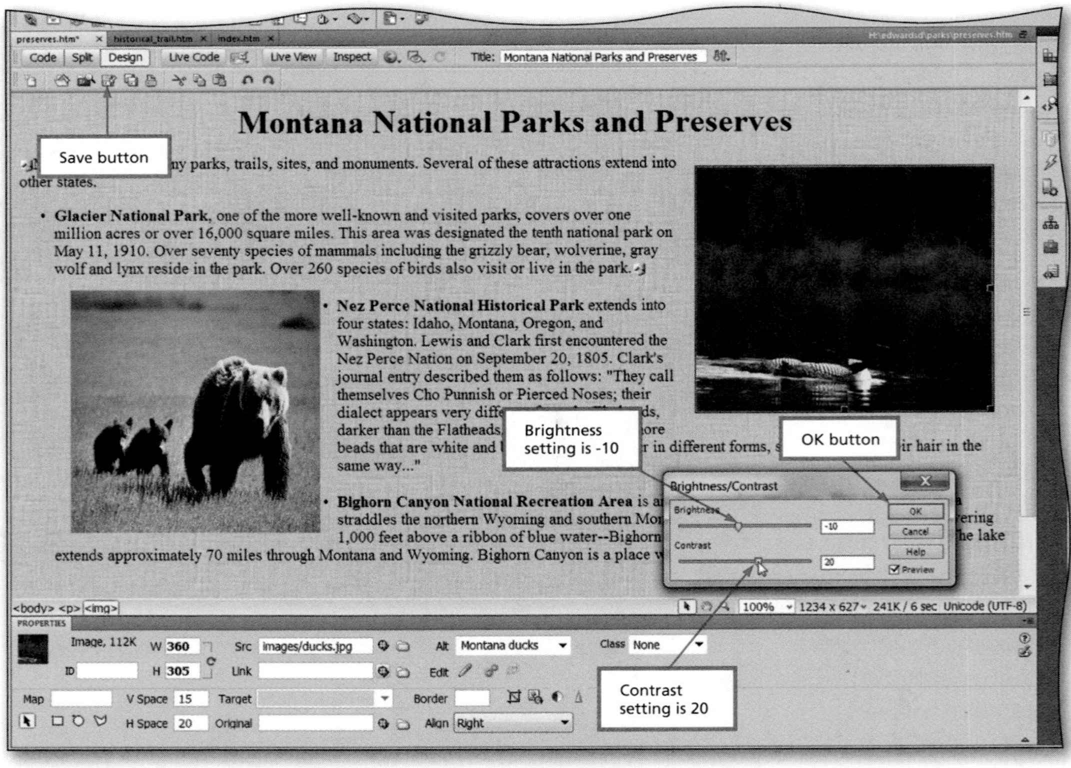

Figure 2–54

6

- Click the OK button to accept the Brightness and Contrast settings.

- Click the Save button on the Standard toolbar to save the changes to the preserves.htm page.

- Press the F12 key to view the preserves .htm page in your browser (Figure 2–55).

7

- Close the browser to return to the Dreamweaver window.

Figure 2–55

Other Ways

1. On Modify menu, point to Image, click Crop
2. On Modify menu, point to Image, click Brightness/Contrast

Understanding Different Types of Links

To connect the pages within the Web site, you create links. Links are the distinguishing feature of the World Wide Web. A link, also referred to as a hyperlink, is the path to another document, to another part of the same document, or to other media such as an image or a movie. Most links are displayed as colored and/or underlined text, although you also can link from an image or other object. Clicking a link accesses the corresponding document, other media, or another place within the same document. If you place the mouse pointer over the link in the browser, the Web address of the link, or path, usually appears at the bottom of the window, on the status bar.

Three types of link paths are available: absolute, relative, and root-relative. An **absolute link** provides the complete URL of the document. This type of link also is referred to as an **external link**. Absolute links generally contain a protocol (such as http://) and primarily are used to link to documents on other servers.

You use **relative links** for local links. This type of link also is referred to as a **document-relative link**, or an **internal link**. If the linked documents are in the same folder, such as those in your parks folder, this is the best type of link to use. You also can use a relative link to link to a document in another folder, such as the images folder. All the files you see in the Files panel in the Local Files list are internal files and are referenced as relative links. You link to a document in another folder on your Web site by specifying the path through the folder hierarchy from the current document to the linked document. Consider the following examples.

- To link to another file in the same folder, specify the file name. Example: preserves.htm.
- To link to a file in a subfolder of the current Web site folder (such as the images folder), the link path would consist of the name of the subfolder, a forward slash (/), and then the file name. Example: images/ducks.jpg.

You use the **root-relative link** primarily when working with a large Web site that requires several servers. Web developers generally use this type of link when they must move HTML files from one folder or server to another folder or server. Root-relative links are beyond the scope of this book.

Two other types of links are named anchor and e-mail. A **named anchor** lets you link to a specific location within a document. To create a named anchor, click the Named Anchor command on the Insert menu. An **e-mail link** creates a blank e-mail message containing the recipient's address. Another type of link is a **null**, or **script**, **link**. This type of link provides for attaching behaviors to an object or executes JavaScript code.

Relative Links

Dreamweaver offers a variety of ways to create a relative link. Three common methods are point to file, drag-and-drop, and browse for file. The point to file and drag-and-drop methods require that the Property inspector and the Files or Assets panels be open. To use the **point to file method**, you drag the Point to File icon to the file or image in the Files or Assets panel. In the **drag-and-drop method**, you drag the file from the Files or Assets panel to the Link text box in the Property inspector. The **browse for file method** is accomplished through the Select File dialog box, which is accessed through the Make Link command on the Modify menu. A fourth method is to use the context menu. To do this, you select the text for the link, right-click to display the context menu, and then select the Make Link command.

Plan Ahead

Identify links.

Before you use links to create connections from one document to another on your Web site or within a document, keep the following guidelines in mind:

- **Prepare for links.** Some Web designers create links first, before creating the associated page. Others prefer to create all the files and pages first, and then create links. Choose a method that suits your work style, but be sure to test all your links before publishing your Web site.

- **Link to text or images.** You can select any text or image on a page to create a link. When you do, visitors to your Web site can click the text or image to open another document or move to another place on the page.

- **Know the path or address.** To create relative links, the files need to be stored in the same root folder or a subfolder in the root folder. To create absolute links, you need to know the URL to the Web page. To create e-mail links, you need to know the e-mail address.

- **Test the links.** Test all the links on a Web page when you preview the page in a browser. Fix any broken links before publishing the page.

To Add Text for Relative Links

To create relative links from the index page, you add text to the index page and use the text to create the links to the other two Web pages in your Web site. You will center the text directly below the Montana National Parks and Recreation Areas heading. The following steps show how to add the text for the links.

1

- Expand the panel groups, and then click the Files tab to display the Files panel.

- Click the index.htm tab in the Document window. If necessary, scroll to the top of the page and then position the insertion point at the end of the title, Montana National Parks and Recreation Areas.

- Press the ENTER key to move the insertion point to the next line. If necessary, click the Align command on the Format menu and select Center to center the insertion point (Figure 2–56).

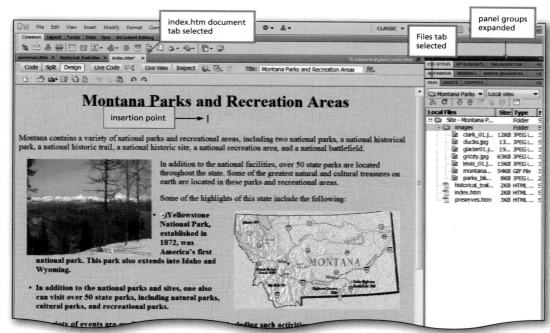

Figure 2–56

2

- Type **Montana National Preserves** and then press the SPACEBAR to enter the text for the first link.

- Hold down the SHIFT key and then press the vertical line key (|) to insert a vertical line.

- Press the SPACEBAR and then type **National Historical Trail** to add the text for the second link (Figure 2–57).

Figure 2–57

To Create a Relative Link Using Point to File

You will use the Montana National Preserves text to create a link to the preserves.htm page and the National Historical Trail text to create a link to the historical_trail.htm page. The following steps illustrate how to use the point to file method to create a relative link from the Montana Parks home page to the Montana National Parks and Preserves Web page.

- Drag to select the text Montana National Preserves (Figure 2–58).

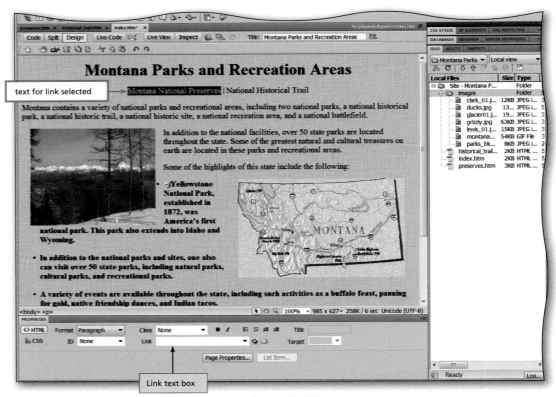

Figure 2–58

2

- Click the Point to File tool next to the Link text box in the Property inspector, and then drag the pointer to the preserves.htm file in the Files panel (Figure 2-59).

3

- When the pointer is over the preserves.htm file in the Files panel, release the mouse button to display the linked text in the Property inspector Link box.

Q&A

Why am I inserting a relative link?

You use relative links when the linked documents are in the same folder, such as those in your parks folder.

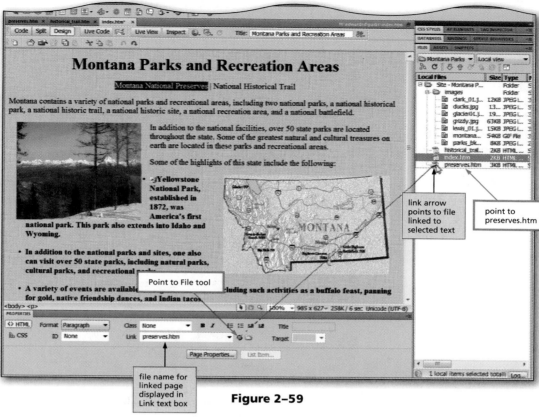

Figure 2–59

Other Ways

1. Hold down SHIFT key, drag to file

To Create a Relative Link Using the Context Menu

The context menu is a second way to create a link. Using this method, you select the file name in the Select File dialog box. The following steps illustrate how to use the context menu to create a link to the Lewis and Clark National Historical Trail page.

1

• Drag to select the text National Historical Trail on the index.htm page, and then right-click the selected text to display the context menu.

• Point to Make Link to highlight the command (Figure 2–60).

Q&A How can I create a link from an image?

Use the same techniques as you do for creating a link from text. Select the image, and then use the context menu to select the Web page file. You can also type or drag the file name into the Property inspector Link box.

Q&A Can I create links on a new page that doesn't contain any text or images yet?

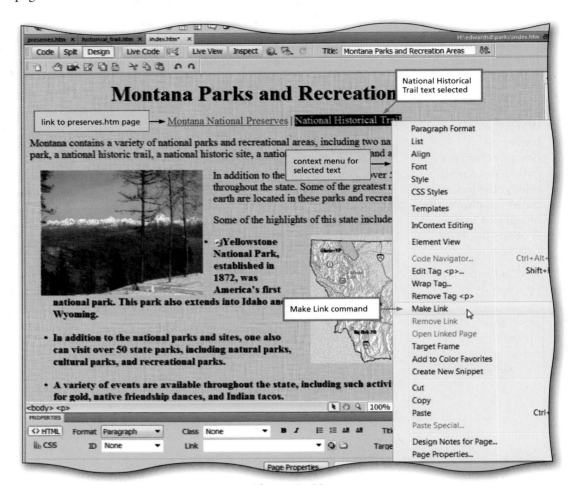

Figure 2–60

No. You must select something on a page that becomes the link to another location, so you need to add text or images before creating links. If you want to create links on a new page, it's a good idea to save the page before making the links.

2

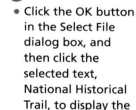

- Click the Make Link command and then click historical_trail in the Select File dialog box to indicate you want to link to the Lewis and Clark National Historical Trail page (Figure 2–61).

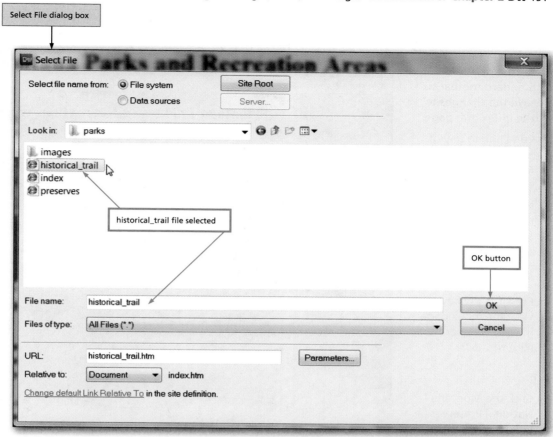

Figure 2–61

3

- Click the OK button in the Select File dialog box, and then click the selected text, National Historical Trail, to display the underlined link (Figure 2–62).

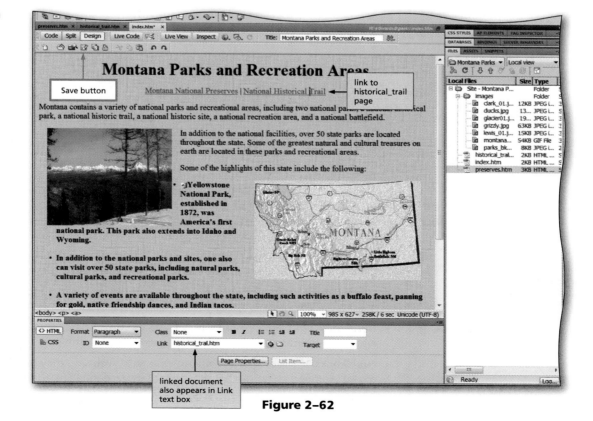

Figure 2–62

- Click the Save button on the Standard toolbar to save the changes to the index.htm page.

Q&A Can I link to any of the files listed in the Files panel?

Yes. All the files you see in the Files panel in the Local Files list are internal files and are referenced as relative links.

- Press the F12 key to view the index page in your browser (Figure 2–63).

- Click the Montana National Preserves link to verify that the link displays the

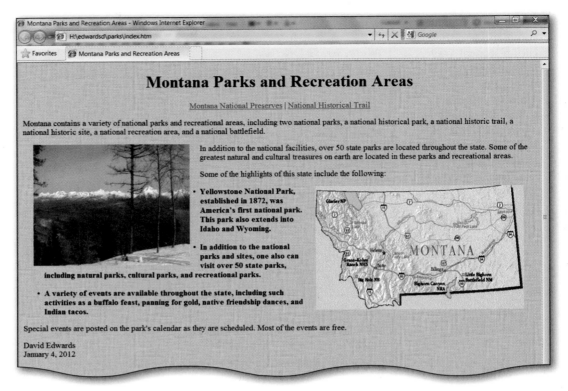

Figure 2–63

preserves.htm page (titled Montana National Parks and Preserves), and then click the browser Back button to return to the index page.

- Click the National Historical Trail link to verify that the link displays the historical_trail.htm page (titled Lewis and Clark National Historical Trail).

- Close the browser.

Other Ways

1. On Insert menu, click Hyperlink, enter link text, enter file name
2. In Common category of Insert panel, click Hyperlink, enter link text, enter file name

Plan Ahead

Include standard links for navigation.
Visitors to your Web site will use links to navigate the site, and expect to find the following types of links:

- **Links to the home page.** If your site is organized around a home page, include a link to the home page on every page in your site so visitors easily can return to it.

- **Links to main topics.** For each Web page that discusses a main topic, include links to other main-topic Web pages.

- **Descriptive links.** For text links, make sure the text is descriptive so that visitors know what kind of information will appear when they click the link.

- **E-mail links.** If visitors have problems with your Web site, they expect to be able to contact someone who can help them. Include an e-mail link to the appropriate person.

To Create a Relative Link to the Home Page

Visitors can enter a Web site at any point, so you should always include a link from each page within the site to the index page. To accomplish this for the Montana Parks Web site, you create a relative link to the index page from the Lewis and Clark National Historical Trail page and from the Montana National Parks and Preserves page, as shown in the following steps.

- Click the preserves .htm tab to display that page in the Document window, and then scroll to the bottom of the page. Drag to select the text Home.

- Drag the index. htm file name from the Files panel to the Link box in the Property inspector, and then click in the Document window to deselect the text.

- Click the Save button on the Standard toolbar to save your changes to the preserves.htm page.

- Press the F12 key to view the Montana National Parks and Preserves page in your browser (Figure 2–64).

Figure 2–64

Q&A

Do I need to specify the complete path to the index.htm page?

No. When you link to another file in the same folder, you only need to specify the file name.

Q&A

Can I make a linked Web page open in a new browser window?

Yes. By default, when you click a link, the linked Web page opens in the current browser window. However, you can specify that a linked Web page opens in a new browser window. To do this, first select the item and create the link. Next, in the Property inspector, click the Target box arrow and then click _blank on the Target pop-up menu. When you view the page in a browser and click the link, it is displayed in a new window.

2

- Click the Home link to display the index page (Figure 2–65).

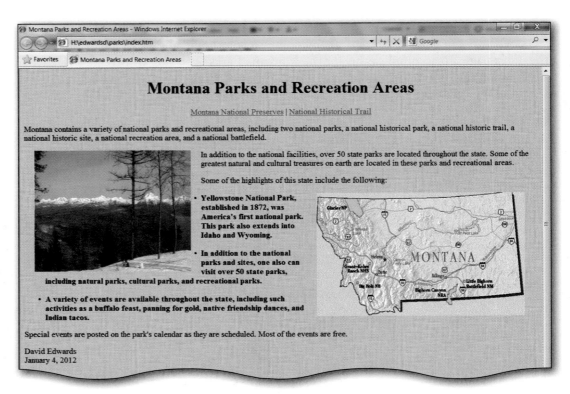

Figure 2–65

3

- Close the browser to redisplay Dreamweaver.

- Click the historical_trail.htm tab to display that page in the Document window. If necessary, scroll to the end of the document and then drag to select the text Home.

- Drag the index .htm file name from the Files panel to the Link box in the Property inspector to create the link, and then click anywhere in the Document window to deselect the text.

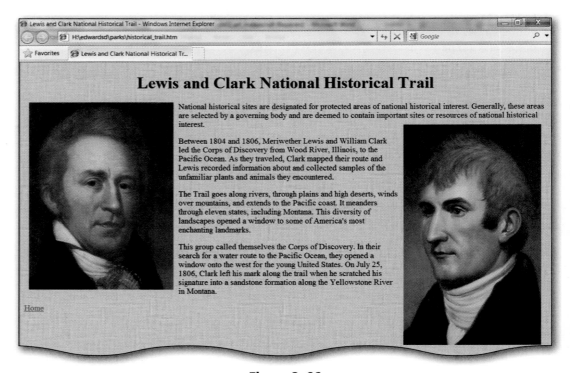

Figure 2–66

- Click the Save button on the Standard toolbar to save your changes to the historical_trail.htm page.

- Press the F12 key to view the Lewis and Clark National Historical Trail page in your browser (Figure 2–66).

- Click the Home link to verify that it works.

- Close the browser.

Other Ways

1. Click Link box, type file name

2. Click Browse icon next to Link box, select file

Creating an Absolute Link

Recall that an absolute link (also called an external link) contains the complete Web site address of a document. You create absolute links the same way you create relative links — select the text and paste or type the Web site address.

To Create Absolute Links

You now will create three absolute links in the Montana National Parks and Preserves page and two absolute links in the Lewis and Clark National Historical Trail page. The links in the Montana National Parks and Preserves page are to Web pages about the selected preserve. In the Lewis and Clark National Historical Trail page, the links are to Web pages about Lewis and Clark. The following steps show how to create these links. Keep in mind that Web site addresses change. If the absolute links do not work, check the Dreamweaver CS5 companion site at *www.scsite.com/dwcs5/* for updates.

1

- Select the Montana National Parks and Preserves page (preserves.htm). Drag to select the text Glacier National Park in the first bulleted item.

- Click the Link box in the Property inspector and then type `http://www.nps.gov/glac/index.htm` as the link. Press the ENTER key.

- Drag to select the text Nez Perce National Historical Park. Click the Link box and then type `http://www.nps.gov/nepe/index.htm` as the link. Press the ENTER key.

Figure 2–67

- Drag to select the text Bighorn Canyon National Recreation Area. Click the Link box and then type `http://www.nps.gov/bica/index.htm` as the link. Press the ENTER key.

- Save the preserves.htm page.

- Press the F12 key and then click each link to verify that they work (Figure 2–67).

Q&A   How do I return to the Montana National Parks and Preserves page after clicking each link?

Click the Back button in your browser.

2

- Close the browser to return to the Dreamweaver window.

Other Ways
1. Start browser, open Web page, select URL, copy URL, close browser, paste in Link box

E-Mail Links

An **e-mail link** is one of the foundation elements of any successful Web site. Visitors must be able to contact you for additional information or to comment on the Web page or Web site. When visitors click an e-mail link, their default e-mail program opens a new e-mail message. The e-mail address you specify is inserted automatically in the To box of the e-mail message header.

To Add an E-Mail Link

The following steps show how to use the Insert menu to create an e-mail link for your home page using your name as the linked text.

 1

- Click the index.htm tab, scroll down to the end of the page, and then drag to select your name.

- Click Insert on the Application bar and then point to Email Link to highlight it (Figure 2–68).

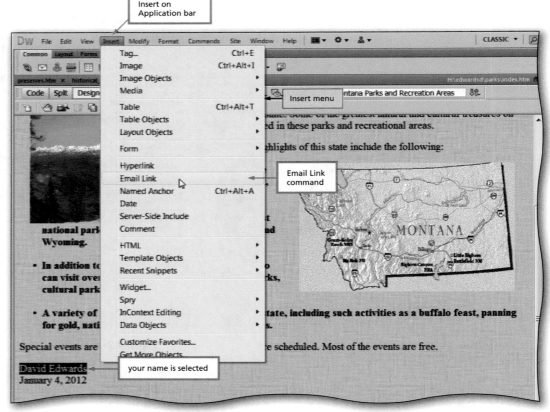

Figure 2–68

2

- Click Email Link to display the Email Link dialog box (Figure 2–69).

Q&A What happens if I change the name in the Text box?

The text that you selected to create the e-mail link is also changed.

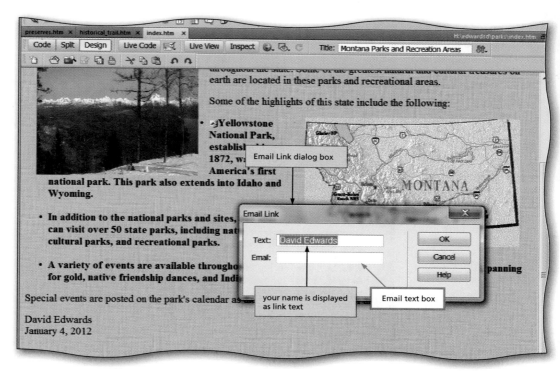

Figure 2–69

3

- Click the Email text box and then type your e-mail address (Figure 2–70).

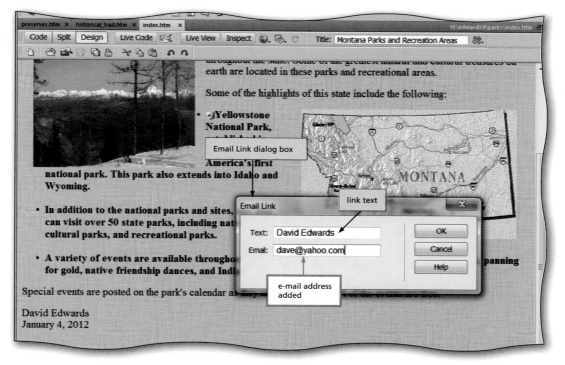

Figure 2–70

• Click the OK button to accept the entries in the Email Link dialog box.

• Click anywhere in the selected text of your name to view your e-mail address in the Property inspector Link box (Figure 2–71).

Q&A

What does mailto mean in the Link box?

This text refers to the Internet protocol used to send electronic mail. E-mail links start with "mailto" to indicate that the Web page should use this protocol when linking to the e-mail address in the Link box.

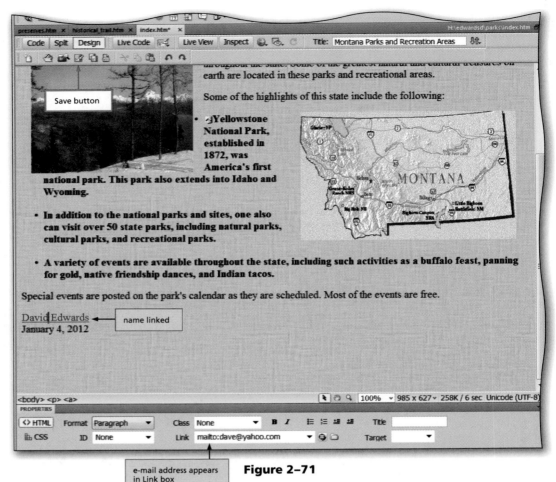

Save button

name linked

e-mail address appears in Link box

Figure 2–71

• Click the Save button on the Standard toolbar to save the changes to the index.htm page.

• Press the F12 key to view the page in your browser.

• Click your name to open your e-mail program.

• Send a message to yourself and one of your classmates.

• Close your e-mail program and then close the browser.

Other Ways

1. In Common category of Insert panel, click Email Link, enter e-mail address

2. Select text or image, type mailto: followed by e-mail address in Link box

Changing the Color of Links

The Page Properties HTML dialog box provides three options for link colors: Link (the link has not been clicked), Active Link (the link changes color when the user clicks it), and Visited Link (the link has been visited). The default color for a link is blue and a visited link is purple. You easily can make changes to these default settings and select colors that complement the background and other colors you are using on your Web pages. This is accomplished through the Page Properties dialog box. You display the Page Properties dialog box by clicking Modify on the Application bar or by clicking the Page Properties button in the Property inspector and then selecting the Appearance (HTML) option. You then can click the box that corresponds to one of the three types of links (Links, Visited links, and Active links) and select a color to match your color scheme.

Editing and Deleting Links

Web development is a never-ending process. At some point, it will be necessary to edit or delete a link. For instance, an e-mail address may change, a URL to an external link may change, or an existing link may contain an error.

Dreamweaver makes it easy to edit or delete a link. First, select the link or click the link you want to change. The linked document name is displayed in the Link box in the Property inspector. To delete the link without deleting the text on the Web page, delete the text from the Link box in the Property inspector. To edit the link, make the change in the Link box.

A second method to edit or delete a link is to use the context menu. Right-click the link you want to change, and then click Remove Link on the context menu to eliminate the link or click Change Link on the context menu to edit the link. Clicking the URLs icon in the Assets panel displays a list of all absolute and e-mail links within the Web site.

Dreamweaver Views

Dreamweaver provides several ways to look at a document: **Design view**, **Code view**, **Split view**, and **Live view**. Thus far, you have been working in Design view. As you create and work with documents, Dreamweaver automatically generates the underlying source code. Recall that the source code defines the structure and layout of a Web document by using a variety of tags and attributes. Even though Dreamweaver generates the code, occasions occur that necessitate the tweaking or modifying of code.

Dreamweaver provides several options for viewing and working with source code. You can use Split view to split the Document window so that it displays both Code view and Design view. You can display only Code view in the Document window, or you can open the Code inspector.

Using Code View and Design View

In Split view, you work in a split-screen environment. You can see the design and the code at the same time. When you make a change in Design view, the HTML code also is changed but is not visible in the Document window. You can set word wrapping, display line numbers for the code, highlight invalid HTML code, set syntax coloring for code elements, and set indenting through the View menu's Code View Options submenu. Viewing the code at this early stage may not seem important, but the more code you learn, the more productive you will become.

BTW

Using the Quick Tag Editor
If you are familiar with HTML, you can use the Dreamweaver Quick Tag Editor to quickly review, insert, and edit HTML tags without leaving Design view. To use the Quick Tag Editor, select the text or image associated with the code you want to view, and then press CTRL+T. The Quick Tag Editor window opens displaying the HTML code, if appropriate, so you can examine or edit the code. If you type invalid HTML in the Quick Tag Editor, Dreamweaver attempts to correct it by inserting quotation marks or angle brackets where needed.

Within the HTML source code, tags can be entered in uppercase, lowercase, or a combination of upper- and lowercase. The case of the tags has no effect on how the browser displays the output.

If the code is XHTML compliant, however, all tags are lowercase. In this book, if you use the instructions provided in Chapter 1 to create a new Web page, then your page is XHTML compliant. XHTML was discussed in the Introduction chapter. Therefore, when describing source code tags, this book uses lowercase letters for tags and attributes to make it easier to differentiate them from the other text and to coordinate with the XHTML standard.

To Use Design View and Code View Simultaneously

The following steps show how to use the Split button to display Code view and Design view at the same time.

1

- Click the preserves .htm tab to display that page in the Document window.

- Collapse the panel groups to provide room for Split view.

- Position the insertion point to the left of the heading, Montana National Parks and Preserves.

- Click the Split button on the Document toolbar to display Code view in the left pane and Design view in the right pane (Figure 2–72).

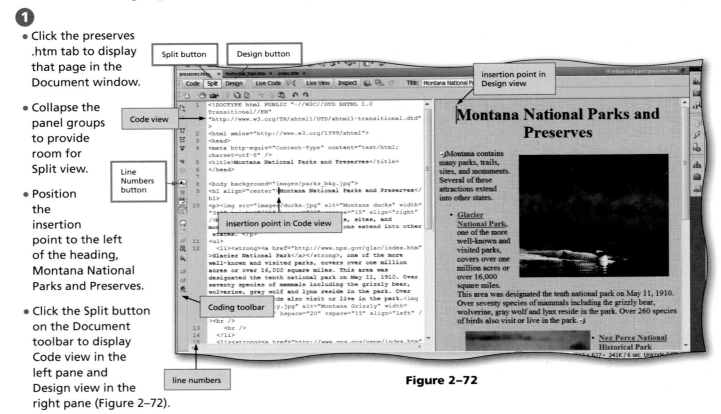

Figure 2–72

Q&A What should I do if line numbers do not appear in the Code view pane?

Click the Line Numbers button on the vertical Coding toolbar to display the line numbers.

Q&A What is the advantage of working in Split view?

Splitting the Document window to view the code makes it easier to view the visual design while you make changes in the source code.

2

- Click the Design button on the Document toolbar to return to Design view.

Other Ways

1. On View menu, click Code and Design

Modifying Source Code

One of the more common problems within Dreamweaver and the source code relates to line breaks and paragraphs. Occasionally, you inadvertently press the ENTER key or insert a line break and need to remove the tag. Or, you may copy and paste or open a text file that contains unneeded paragraphs or line breaks.

Pressing the BACKSPACE key or DELETE key may return you to the previous line, but does not always delete the line break or paragraph tag within the source code. The deletion of these tags is determined by the position of the insertion point when you press the BACKSPACE or DELETE keys. If the insertion point is still inside the source code, pressing the BACKSPACE key will not delete these tags and your page will not be displayed correctly. When this occurs, the best solution is to delete the tag through Code view.

Live View

Generally, to view a Web page in a browser such as Internet Explorer or Firefox requires that you leave Dreamweaver and open the browser in another window. If the Web designer wants to view the source code, an additional window also needs to be opened. Dreamweaver's **Live view** feature, however, allows you to preview how the page will look in a browser without leaving Dreamweaver. If you want to view and modify code, you can do so through a split screen; and the changes to the code are reflected instantly in the rendered display.

To Use Live View

In the following steps, you switch to Live view.

● Click the Live View button on the Document toolbar to view the page as it would appear in the browser and to verify that the line spacing is correct and that the document is properly formatted (Figure 2–73).

Q&A What should I do if an Information bar appears explaining a Flash plug-in was not found?

Click the Close link in the Information bar, and then install the Flash plug-in from the Adobe Web site at *www.adobe.com*.

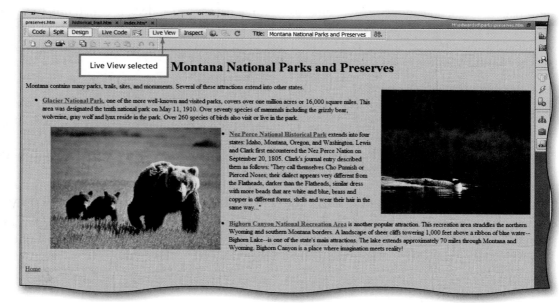

Figure 2–73

❷
● Click the Live View button to return to Design view and make any necessary corrections. If necessary, click the Save button.

BTW

Quick Reference
For a table that lists how to complete tasks covered in this book using the keyboard, see the Quick Reference at the end of this book.

Quitting Dreamweaver

After you add pages to your Web site, including images and links, and then view your pages in a browser, Chapter 2 is complete.

To Close the Web Site and Quit Dreamweaver

The following steps show how to close the Web site, quit Dreamweaver, and return control to Windows.

1 Click the Close button on the right corner of the Dreamweaver title bar to close the Dreamweaver window, the Document window, and the Montana Parks Web site.

2 Click the Yes button if a prompt is displayed indicating that you need to save changes.

Chapter Summary

Chapter 2 introduced you to images and links, and discussed how to view source code and use Live view. You began the chapter by copying data files to the local site. You added two new pages, one for Lewis and Clark National Historical Trail and one for Montana National Parks and Preserves, to the Web site you started in Chapter 1. Next, you added images to the index page. Following that, you added a background image and page images to the two new pages. Then, you added relative links to all three pages. You added an e-mail link to the index page and absolute links to the Montana National Parks and Preserves and Lewis and Clark National Historical Trail pages. Finally, you learned how to view source code. The items listed below include all the new Dreamweaver skills you have learned in this chapter.

1. Create the Montana National Parks and Preserves Web Page (DW 109)
2. Create the Lewis and Clark National Historical Trail Web Page (DW 112)
3. Set Invisible Element Preferences and Turn on Visual Aids (DW 119)
4. Open a Web Page from a Local Web Site (DW 123)
5. Insert an Image into the Index Page (DW 124)
6. Align an Image (DW 128)
7. Adjust the Image Size and the Horizontal Space (DW 130)
8. To Insert the Second Image (DW 131)
10. Crop and Modify the Brightness/Contrast of an Image (DW 142)
11. Add Text for Relative Links (DW 147)
12. Create a Relative Link Using Point to File (DW 148)
13. Create a Relative Link Using the Context Menu (DW 150)
14. Create a Relative Link to the Home Page (DW 153)
15. Create Absolute Links (DW 155)
16. Add an E-Mail Link (DW 156)
17. Use Design View and Code View Simultaneously (DW 160)
18. Use Live View (DW 161)

Learn It Online

Test your knowledge of chapter content and key terms.

Instructions: To complete the Learn It Online exercises, start your browser, click the Address bar, and then enter the Web address `scsite.com/dwCS5/learn`. When the Dreamweaver CS5 Learn It Online page is displayed, click the link for the exercise you want to complete and then read the instructions.

Chapter Reinforcement TF, MC, and SA
A series of true/false, multiple choice, and short answer questions that test your knowledge of the chapter content.

Flash Cards
An interactive learning environment where you identify chapter key terms associated with displayed definitions.

Practice Test
A series of multiple choice questions that test your knowledge of chapter content and key terms.

Who Wants to Be a Computer Genius?
An interactive game that challenges your knowledge of chapter content in the style of a television quiz show.

Wheel of Terms
An interactive game that challenges your knowledge of chapter key terms in the style of the television show *Wheel of Fortune*.

Crossword Puzzle Challenge
A crossword puzzle that challenges your knowledge of key terms presented in the chapter.

Apply Your Knowledge

Reinforce the skills and apply the concepts you learned in this chapter.

Adding, Aligning, and Resizing an Image on a Web Page

Instructions: In this activity, you modify a Web page by adding, aligning, and resizing an image (Figure 2–74). Make sure you have downloaded the data files for Chapter02\apply, which are available in the Data Files for Students folder. See the inside back cover of this book for instructions on downloading the Data Files for Students, or contact your instructor for information about accessing the required files.

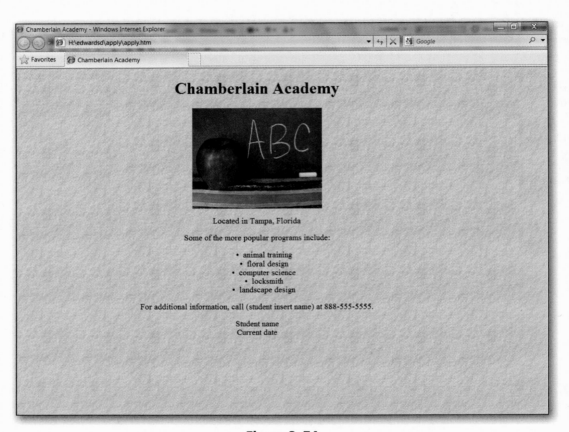

Figure 2–74

Perform the following tasks:

1. Use Windows Computer or Windows Explorer to copy the school_house.jpg image from the Chapter02\apply data files folder into the images folder for your Apply Exercises local Web site. (For example, the images folder might be stored on H:\edwardsd\apply\images.)

2. Start Dreamweaver, and then open the Apply Exercises site.

3. Open the apply.htm file (the page you created for the Apply Your Knowledge exercise in Chapter 1).

4. Insert a new blank line after the "Chamberlain Academy" heading by clicking at the end of the heading and then pressing the ENTER key.

5. Display the Assets panel, and then click the Refresh Site List button at the bottom of the panel, if necessary, to display the images. Select the school_house.jpg image, and then drag it to the insertion point on the new blank line.

6. Type the following text in the Image Tag Accessibility Attributes text box: `school`. Click the OK button.

7. If necessary, select the image. Double-click the W text box and type `250`. Double-click the H text box, type `200`, and then press the ENTER key.

8. Use the Align button to align the image to the middle of the line.

9. Use the Format menu to center all of the text on the page.

10. Save your document and then view it in your browser. Submit it in the format specified by your instructor.

Extend Your Knowledge

Extend the skills you learned in this chapter and experiment with new skills. You may need to use Help to complete the assignment.

Adding, Aligning, and Resizing Images on a Web Page

Instructions: In this activity, you modify a Web page by adding, aligning, and resizing images (Figure 2–75). Make sure you have downloaded the data files for Chapter02\extend, which are available in the Data Files for Students folder. See the inside back cover of this book for instructions on downloading the Data Files for Students, or contact your instructor for information about accessing the required files.

Figure 2–75

Perform the following tasks:

1. Copy the data files from the Chapter02\extend data files folder into the images folder for your Extend Exercises local Web site. (For example, the images folder might be stored on H:\edwardsd\ extend\images.)

2. Start Dreamweaver, and open the Extend Exercises site.

3. Open the extend.htm file (the page you created for the Extend Your Knowledge exercise in Chapter 1).

4. Remove the bold from the bulleted list, your name, and the date.

4. Drag the flower01 image to the top of the page and to the left of the second line, which begins, "Choose from among".

5. Type flower01 in the Alternate text text box.

6. Resize the image width to 165 and the height to 185.

7. Type 25 in both the V Space box and the H Space box.

8. Align the image to the left.

9. Click after the second line (which begins, "Choose from among"). Drag the flower02 image to the insertion point. Type flower02 in the Alternate text text box.

10. Resize the image width to 165 and the height to 185.

11. Enter 25 for both the V Space and the H Space.

12. Align the image to the right.

13. Move the sentence that begins with "Choose from among" after the bulleted list. Make sure you do not move the element marker. Also make sure the sentence remains centered and does not have a bullet. Bold the sentence if it is not already bolded.

14. Save your document and then view it in your browser. Submit it in the format specified by your instructor.

Make It Right

Analyze a document and then correct all errors and/or improve the design.

Adding an Image to a Web Page

Instructions: In this activity, you modify an existing Web page by adding an image (Figure 2–76). Make sure you have downloaded the data files for Chapter02\right, which are available in the Data Files for Students folder. See the inside back cover of this book for instructions on downloading the Data Files for Students, or contact your instructor for information about accessing the required files.

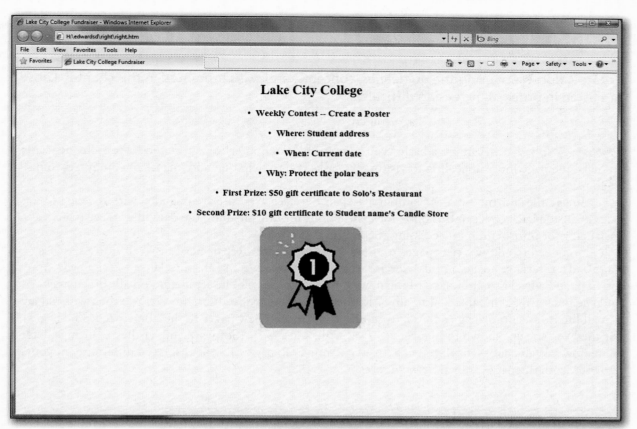

Figure 2–76

Perform the following tasks:

1. Copy the data file from the Chapter02\right data files folder into the images folder for your Right Exercises local Web site. (For example, the images folder might be stored on H:\edwardsd\right\ images.)

2. Start Dreamweaver, open the Right Exercises site, and then open the right.htm page. If necessary, open the Local Files panel and the Property inspector. Verify that HTML is selected.

3. Insert a new line after the last item in the list. If a bullet is displayed, click the Unordered List button in the Property inspector. Center the line, if necessary.

4. Drag the ribbon01 image to the insertion point. Type **ribbon** for the alternate text.

5. Adjust the image width to 177 and the height to 183.

6. Make any other adjustments as necessary to make your Web page match the one shown in Figure 2–76.

7. Save your document and then view it in your browser.

8. Submit your Web page in the format specified by your instructor.

In the Lab

Create a document using the guidelines, concepts, and skills presented in this chapter. Labs are listed in order of increasing difficulty.

Lab 1: Modifying the Computer Repair Services Web Site

Problem: Now that Bryan has a basic Web page for his Computer Repair Services Web site, he wants to make the page more appealing to visitors. He asks you to help him add images of computers to his Web page.

Image files for the Bryan's Computer Repair Services Web site are included with the data files. See the inside back cover of this book for instructions for downloading the data files or see your instructor for information on accessing the files in this book.

You need to add two new pages to the Bryan's Computer Repair Services Web site: a services page and a references page. In this exercise, you will add relative and absolute links to each page. You also will add a background image to the new pages. Next, you will insert images on all three pages and use the settings in Table 2–4 to align the images and enter the alternate text. You then will add an e-mail link to the home page and relative links from the two new pages to the home page. The pages for the Web site are shown in Figures 2–77a, 2–77b, and 2–77c. (Software and hardware settings determine how a Web page is displayed in a browser. Your Web pages may be displayed differently in your browser from the pages shown in the figures.)

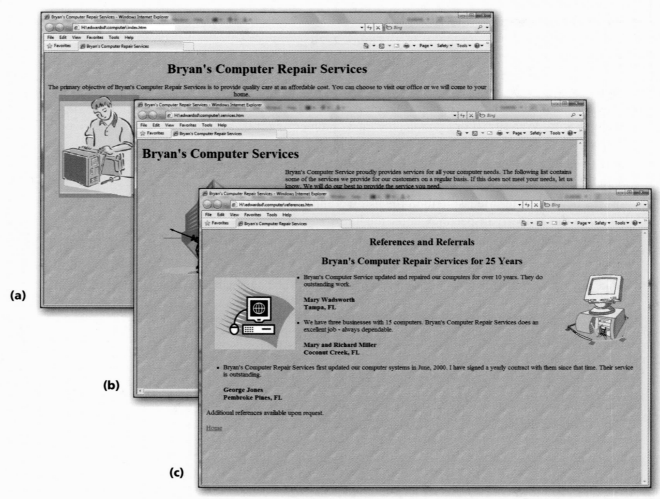

Figure 2–77

Table 2–4 Image Property Settings for the Bryan's Computer Repair Services Web Site						
Image Name	**W**	**H**	**V Space**	**H Space**	**Align**	**Alt**
computer_repair01	191	253	10	25	left	repairs
computer_repair02	239	235	25	50	left	desktop computer
computer_repair03	150	174	20	20	right	disk drive
computer_repair04	190	175	10	20	left	monitor
hard_drive	260	260	20	50	right	hard drive

Perform the following tasks:

1. Copy the services and references data files from the Chapter02\computers data files folder into the root folder for your Computer Repair Services local Web site. (For example, the root folder might be stored on H:\edwardsd\computers.) Copy the image data files from the Chapter02\computers\ images data files folder into the images folder for your Computer Repair Services local Web site. (For example, the images folder might be stored on H:\edwardsd\computers\images.)

2. Start Dreamweaver and display the panel groups. Open the Computer Repair Services site, and then open the index.htm file (which you created in Chapter 1).

3. If necessary, click the expander arrow to expand the Property inspector and display the Standard toolbar.

4. Open the Assets panel to display the contents of the images folder. Position the insertion point at the end of the first sentence. Drag the computer_repair01 image to the insertion point, add the alternate text as indicated in Table 2–4, and then apply the settings shown in Table 2–4 to resize and align the image.

5. Position the insertion point at the end of the first sentence again. Drag the hard_drive image to the insertion point and then apply the settings shown in Table 2–4.

6. Select the text Basic services in the first bulleted item. Click the Files tab in the panels group, and then use the drag-and-drop file method to create a link to the services page. Repeat this process to add a link from the References text to the references page.

7. Select your name. Use the Insert menu to create an e-mail link using your name. Center the first sentence, if necessary. Save the index page (Figure 2–77a).

8. Open the services page. Click Modify on the Application bar and then click Page Properties. Apply the repair_bkg background image (located in the images folder) to the services page.

9. Position the insertion point to the left of the first sentence. Open the Assets panel, drag the computer_repair02 image to the insertion point, and then apply the settings shown in Table 2–4.

10. If necessary, scroll down. Select Home, click the Files tab in the panels group, and then create a relative link to the index page. Save the services page (Figure 2–77b).

11. Open the references page. Apply the repair_bkg background image (located in the images folder) as you did in Step 8 for the services page.

12. Position the insertion point to the right of the second heading and then drag the computer_ repair03 image to the insertion point. Apply the settings shown in Table 2–4 to the image.

13. Insert a blank line before the first bulleted item in the list. Remove the bullet, if necessary. Drag the computer_repair04 image to the insertion point. Apply the settings shown in Table 2–4 to the image.

14. Scroll to the bottom of the page. Select Home and then create a relative link to the index page. Save the references page (Figure 2–77c).

15. View the Web site in your browser. Check each link to verify that it works. Submit the documents in the format specified by your instructor.

In the Lab

Lab 2: Modifying the Baskets Web Site

Problem: Carole Wells, for whom you created the Baskets by Carole Web site and Web page, is very pleased with the response she has received. She asks you to add two images to the index page and to create a second page with links and images. Carole wants the new page to include information about her company's history.

Add a second Web page to the Baskets by Carole Web site. The revised Web site is shown in Figures 2–78a and 2–78b. Table 2–5 includes the settings and alternate text for the images. Software and hardware settings determine how a Web page displays in a browser. Your Web pages may be displayed differently in your browser from those in the figures.

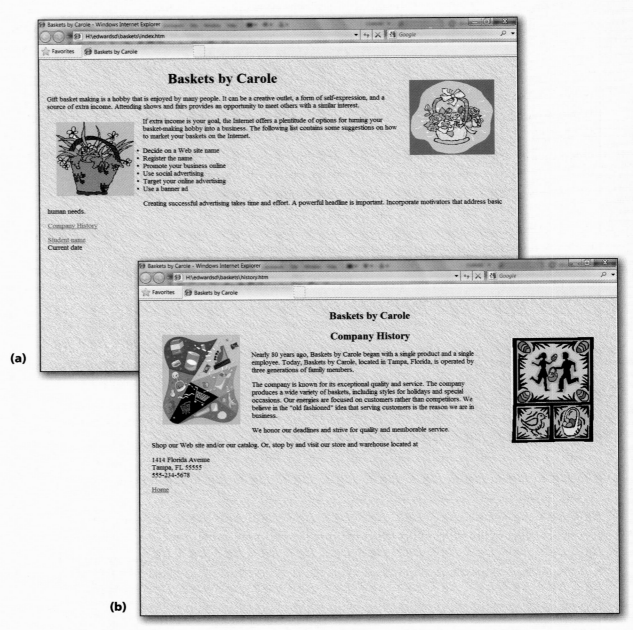

(a)

(b)

Figure 2–78

Table 2–5 Image Property Settings for the Baskets by Carole Web Site

Image Name	W	H	V Space	H Space	Align	Alt
basket01	190	174	25	25	right	rose basket
basket02	174	170	10	20	left	daisy basket
basket03	183	239	20	50	right	baskets
basket04	174	204	10	25	left	shopping

Perform the following tasks:

1. Copy the history data file from the Chapter02\baskets data files folder into the root folder for your Gift Basket Designs local Web site. (For example, the root folder might be stored on H:\edwardsd\ baskets.) Copy the image data files from the Chapter02\baskets\images data files folder into the images folder for your Gift Basket Designs local Web site. (For example, the images folder might be stored on H:\edwardsd\baskets\images.)

2. Start Dreamweaver and display the panel groups. Open the Gift Basket Designs site, and then open the index.htm file (which you created in Chapter 1).

3. If necessary, click the expander arrow to expand the Property inspector and display the Standard toolbar.

4. Position the insertion point to the right of the heading and then drag the basket01 image to the insertion point. Enter the Alt text, and then apply the settings shown in Table 2–5 to resize and align the image.

5. Position the insertion point to the left of the paragraph that begins "If extra income is your goal", and then drag the basket02 image to the insertion point. Apply the settings shown in Table 2–5.

6. Position the insertion point to the right of the last sentence and then press the ENTER key.

7. Type the following text: **Company History**. Select the Company History text and use the drag-and-drop method to create a link to the history page. Select your name. Use the Insert menu to create an e-mail link using your e-mail address. Save the index page.

8. Open the history page. Open the Page Properties dialog box, and then add the background image (baskets_bkg) to the history page.

9. Position the insertion point at the end of subhead, Company History, and then drag the basket03 image to the insertion point. Apply the settings shown in Table 2–5.

10. Position the insertion point at the end of the Company History subhead again. Drag the basket04 image to the insertion point. Apply the settings shown in Table 2–5.

11. Select Home and then create a relative link to the index page. Save the history page.

12. Check the spelling of your document and correct any errors.

13. Save the file.

14. View the Web site in your browser. Check each link to verify that it works. Submit the documents in the format specified by your instructor.

In the Lab

Lab 3: Modifying the Credit Protection Web Site

Problem: Jessica Minnick has received favorable comments about the Web page and site you created on credit information. Her bank wants to use the Web site to provide additional information to its customers. Jessica has asked you and another intern at the bank to work with her to create two more Web pages to add to the site. They want one of the pages to discuss credit protection and the other page to contain information about identity theft.

Revise the Credit Protection Web site. The revised pages for the Web site are shown in Figures 2–79a, 2–79b, and 2–79c. Table 2–6 on the next page includes the settings and Alt text for the images. Software and hardware settings determine how a Web page displays in a browser. Your Web pages may be displayed differently in your browser from those in the figures.

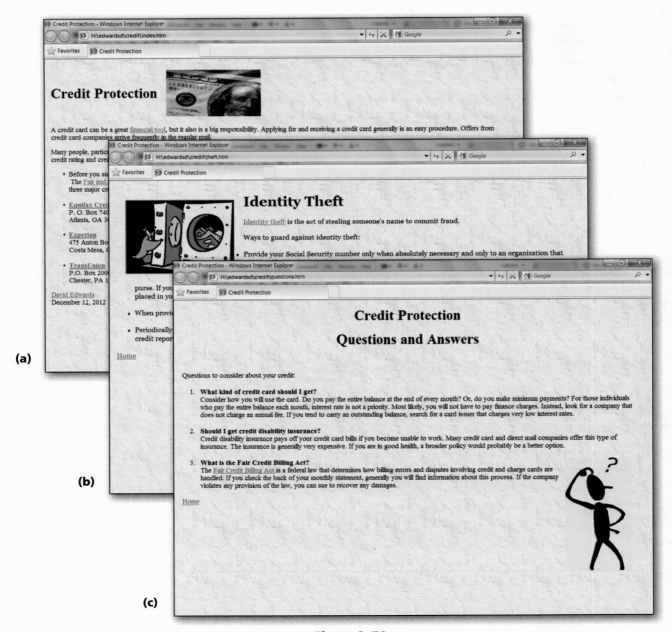

Figure 2–79

Table 2–6 Image Property Settings for the Credit Protection Web Site

Image Name	W	H	V Space	H Space	Align	Alt
money	211	107	none	20	absolute middle	Money
protection	240	170	14	20	left	Identity theft
question	150	300	none	none	right	Questions?
theft	188	193	none	100	right	Protect personal information

Perform the following tasks:

1. Copy the questions and theft data files from the Chapter02\credit data files folder into the root folder for your Credit Protection local Web site. (For example, the root folder might be stored on H:\edwardsd\credit.) Copy the image data files from the Chapter02\credit\images data files folder into the images folder for your Credit Protection local Web site. (For example, the images folder might be stored on H:\edwardsd\credit\images.)

2. Start Dreamweaver and display the panel groups. Open the Credit Protection site, and then open index.htm (which you created in Chapter 1).

3. If necessary, display the Property inspector and the Standard toolbar. Expand the Property inspector.

4. Position the insertion point to the right of the heading and then drag the money image to the insertion point. Apply the settings shown in Table 2–6.

5. Select the text financial tool, located in the first sentence of the first paragraph. Create a relative link from the selected text to the questions page. Select the text Fair and Accurate Credit Transactions (FACT), located in the second sentence of the third paragraph. Create an absolute link to http://www.annualcreditreport.com. Select the name of the company in the first bulleted list item (Equifax Credit Information Services, Inc.) and create an absolute link using http://www .equifax.com. Create absolute links from the other two company names, using http://www.experian .com and http://www.transunion.com, respectively.

6. Position the insertion point at the end of the second paragraph (after the word fix). Press the SPACEBAR. Type the following text: `Credit card and identity theft can be a major issue when applying for credit.` Select the text you just typed and then create a relative link to the theft page. Add an e-mail link to your name. Save the index page (Figure 2–79a on the previous page). Position the insertion point at the end of the second line in the second bulleted point, and then drag the theft image to the insertion point. Apply the settings shown in Table 2–6.

7. Open the theft page and apply the background image (credit_bkg) to the page.

8. Position the insertion point to the left of the second line and then drag the protection image to the insertion point. Apply the settings shown in Table 2–6.

9. Drag to select the text Identity theft at the beginning of the first sentence, and then create an absolute link using http://www.consumer.gov/idtheft as the URL. Create an absolute link from the protection image using the same URL. Select the image and then type the URL in the Link box. Select Home and then create a relative link to the index.htm page. Save the theft page (Figure 2–79b).

10. Open the questions page. Apply the background image that you added to the theft page in Step 7. Use the text, Home, at the bottom of the page to create a relative link to the index page.

11. Position the insertion point to the right of question 3, What is the Fair Credit Billing Act? Drag the question image to the insertion point. Apply the settings in Table 2–6.

12. Create an absolute link from the Fair Credit Billing Act text in the answer to question 3. In this link, use the following as the URL: http://www.ftc.gov/bcp/edu/pubs/consumer/credit/cre16.shtm. Save the questions page (Figure 2–79c).

13. View the Web site in your browser and verify that your external and relative links work. *Hint*: Remember to check the link for the image on the theft.htm page. Submit the documents in the format specified by your instructor.

Cases and Places

Apply your creative thinking and problem solving skills to design and implement a solution.

● EASIER ●●MORE DIFFICULT

● 1: Modify the Favorite Sports Web Site

In Chapter 1, you created a Web site named Favorite Sports with a Web page listing your favorite sports and teams. Now, you want to add another page to the site. Create and format the new page, which should include general information about a selected sport. Create a relative link from the home page to the new page and from the new page to the home page. Add a background image to the new page and insert an image on one of the pages. Include an appropriate title for the page. Save the page in the sports subfolder. For a selection of images and backgrounds, visit the Dreamweaver CS5 Media Web page (scsite.com/dwcs5/media).

● 2: Modify the Hobbies Web Site

Several of your friends were impressed with the Web page and Web site you created about your favorite hobby in Chapter 1. They have given you some topics they think you should include on the site. You decide to create an additional page that will consist of details about your hobby and the topics your friends suggested. Format the page. Add an absolute link to a related Web site and a relative link from the home page to the new page and from the new page to the home page. Add a background image to the new page. Create an e-mail link on the index page. Title the page with the name of the selected hobby. Save the page in the hobby subfolder. For a selection of images and backgrounds, visit the Dreamweaver CS5 Media Web page (scsite.com/dwcs5/media).

●● 3: Modify the Politics Web Site

In Chapter 1, you created a Web site and a Web page to publicize your campaign for public office. Develop two additional pages to add to the site. Apply a background image to the new pages. Apply appropriate formatting to the two new pages. Scan a picture of yourself or take a picture with a digital camera and include the picture on the index page. Add a second image illustrating one of your campaign promises. Include at least two images on one of the new pages and one image on the other new page. Add alternate text for all images, and then add appropriate H Space and V Space property features to position the images. Create e-mail links on all three pages and create relative links from the home page to both pages and from each of the pages to the home page. Create an absolute link to a related site on one of the pages. Give each page a meaningful title and then save the pages in the government subfolder. For a selection of images and backgrounds, visit the Dreamweaver CS5 Media Web page (scsite.com/dwcs5/media).

● ● **4: Modify the Favorite Music Web Site**

Make It Personal

Modify the music Web site you created in Chapter 1 by creating a new page. Format the page. Discuss your favorite artist or band on the new page. Add a background image to the new page. On the index page, add an image and align the image to the right, and on the new page, add a different image and align the image to the left. Add appropriate alternate text for each image. Position each image appropriately on the page by using the H Space and V Space property features. Add an e-mail link on the index page, and add text and a relative link from the new page to the index page. View your Web pages in your browser. Give the page a meaningful title and then save the page in your music subfolder. For a selection of images and backgrounds, visit the Dreamweaver CS5 Media Web page (scsite.com/dwcs5/media).

● ● **5: Create the Student Trips Web Site**

Working Together

The student trips Web site you and your classmates created in Chapter 1 is a success. Everyone loves it. The dean is so impressed that she asks the group to continue with the project. Your team creates and formats three additional Web pages, one for each of three possible locations for the trip. Add a background image to all new pages. Add two images to each of the pages, including the index page. Resize one of the images. Add the Alt text for each image, and then position each image appropriately using the H Space and V Space property features. Create a link from the index page to each of the three new pages and a link from each page to the index page. Create an absolute link to a related informational Web site on each of the three new pages. Add an appropriate title to each page. Preview in a browser to verify the links. Save the pages in your trips subfolder. For a selection of images and backgrounds, visit the Dreamweaver CS5 Media Web page (scsite.com/dwcs5/media).

3 | Tables and Page Layout

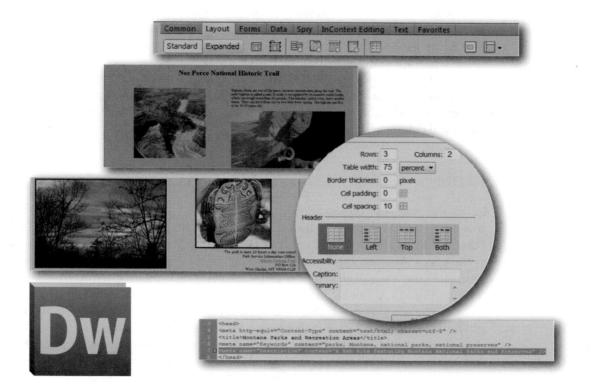

Objectives

You will have mastered the material in this chapter when you can:

- Understand page layout
- Design a Web page using tables
- Create a table structure
- Modify a table structure
- Describe HTML table tags
- Add content to a table

- Add a border to a table
- Format table content
- Format a table
- Add borders to images
- Create head content

3 | Tables and Page Layout

Introduction

Chapter 3 introduces you to using tables for page layout and adding head content elements. Page layout is an important part of Web design because it determines the way your page will be displayed in a browser, which is one of the major challenges for any Web designer.

Dreamweaver's table feature is a great tool for designing a Web page. One reason is that it is very similar to the table feature in word-processing programs such as Microsoft Office Word. A table allows you to add vertical and horizontal structure to a Web page. Using a table, you can put just about anything on your page and have it be displayed in a specific location. Using tables in Dreamweaver, you can create columns of text or navigation bars and lay out tabular data. You can delete, split, and merge rows and columns; modify table, row, or cell properties to add color and adjust alignment; and copy, paste, and delete cells in the table structure.

Project — Formatted Tables with Images

In this chapter, you continue creating the Montana Parks Web site. You use tables to create two new Web pages focusing on two of Montana's more popular parks — Nez Perce National Historic Trail and Glacier National Park. You then add these new pages to the park's Web site and link to them from the index.htm Web page. When you complete your Web page additions, you add keywords and a description as the head content. Figures 3–1a and 3–1b show the two new pages in their final form.

In the second part of this chapter, you learn the value of head content and how to add it to a Web page. When you create a Web page, the underlying source code is organized into two main sections: the head section and the body section. In Chapters 1 and 2, you created Web pages in the body section, which contains the page content that is displayed in the browser. The head section contains a variety of information, including keywords that search engines use. With the exception of the page title, all head content is invisible when viewed in the Dreamweaver Document window or in a browser. Some head content is accessed by other programs, such as search engines, and some content is accessed by the browser. This chapter discusses the head content options and the importance of adding this content to all Web pages.

Figure 3–1a

Figure 3–1b

Overview

As you read this chapter, you learn how to add to your Web site the pages shown in Figures 3–1a and 3–1b by performing these general tasks:

- Insert a table into a Dreamweaver Web page.
- Center the table.
- Change vertical alignment within the table.
- Specify column width.
- Merge cells.
- Add accessibility attributes.
- Add text and images to a table.
- Add links.
- Add borders to tables and images.

General Project Guidelines

When adding pages to a Web site, consider the appearance and characteristics of the completed site. As you create and add the two Web pages to the Montana Parks Web site shown in Figure 3–1a and Figure 3–1b, you should follow these general guidelines:

1. **Plan the Web pages.** Determine how the pages will fit into the Web site.

2. **Determine when to insert tables.** Create and organize the new content for the Web pages on your site. Consider whether you can organize and format some content in tables.

3. **Lay out Web pages with tables.** Insert Web page elements in a specific order — tables, text, and then images — as you create and enhance each page.

4. **Determine when to add borders.** Consider when and where to add borders to tables and images. Determine the number of pixels that should be added for these elements.

5. **Identify cells to merge.** Determine whether cells within the table need to be merged to provide a better layout. If so, determine which cells need to be merged to provide a more attractive Web page.

6. **Plan head content.** Select the keywords and descriptions to add to the head content for each page so that search engines and Web users can find your pages easily.

When necessary, more specific details concerning the above guidelines are presented at appropriate points in the chapter. The chapter also will identify the actions performed and decisions made regarding these guidelines during the creation of the Web pages shown in Figures 3–1a and 3–1b on pages DW 179 and DW 180.

**Plan
Ahead**

Starting Dreamweaver and Opening a Web Site

Each time you start Dreamweaver, it opens to the last site displayed when you closed the program. It therefore may be necessary for you to open the parks Web site.

To Start Dreamweaver and Open the Montana Parks Web Site

With a good understanding of the requirements, the necessary decisions, and the planning process, the next step is to start Dreamweaver and open the Montana Parks Web site.

1 Click the Start button on the Windows taskbar.

2 Click Adobe Dreamweaver CS5 on the Start menu or point to All Programs on the Start menu, click Adobe Design Premium CS5 if necessary, and then click Adobe Dreamweaver CS5 on the All Programs list.

3 If necessary, display the panel groups.

4 If the Montana Parks hierarchy is not displayed, click the Sites pop-up menu button on the Files panel and point to Montana Parks to highlight it (Figure 3–2).

Figure 3–2

Q&A How can I see a list of the sites I have defined in Dreamweaver?

Clicking the **Sites pop-up menu button** in the Files panel lists the sites you have defined. When you open the site, a list of pages and subfolders within the site is displayed.

5 If necessary, click Montana Parks to display the Montana Parks Web site in the Files panel.

Copying Data Files to the Local Web Site

In the following steps, the data files for this chapter are stored on drive H:. The location on your computer may be different. If necessary, verify the location of the data files with your instructor.

To Copy Data Files to the Parks Web Site

Your data files contain images for Chapter 3. In Chapters 1 and 2, you copied the data files using the Windows Computer tool. Now that you are more familiar with the Files panel, you can use it to copy the data files for Chapter 3 into the images folder for your Montana Parks Web site. In the following steps, you copy the data files for Chapter 3 from the Chapter03 folder on a USB drive to the parks\images folder stored in the *your name* folder on the same USB drive.

1 Click the Sites pop-up menu button in the Files panel, and then click the name of the drive containing your data files, such as Removable Disk (H:).

2 If necessary, click the plus sign (+) next to the folder containing your data files to expand that folder, and then click the plus sign (+) next to the Chapter03 folder to expand it.

3 Expand the parks folder to display the data files.

4 Click the first file in the list, which is the arrowheads image file, to select the file.

5 Hold down the SHIFT key and then click the last file in the list, which is the sunset image, to select all the data files.

6 Press CTRL+C to copy the files.

7 If necessary, click the Sites pop-up menu button, and then click the drive containing the Montana Parks Web site. Expand the *your name* folder and the parks folder, and then click the images folder to select it.

8 Press CTRL+V to paste the files in the images folder (Figure 3–3).

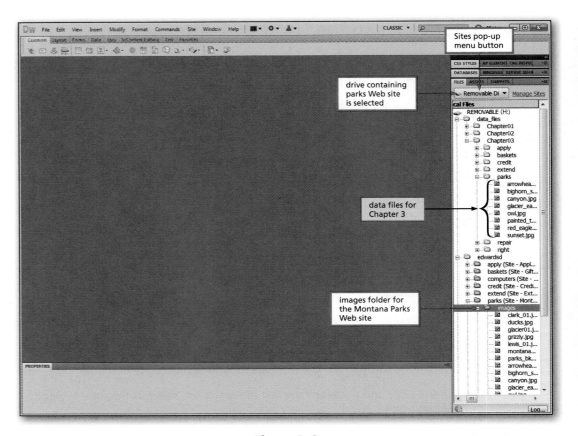

Figure 3–3

Is there another method for copying data files into the Web site folder?

Yes, you can copy the files using Windows Explorer or the Windows Computer tool.

What if my Files panel doesn't match the one in Figure 3–3?

In Figure 3–3, the Files panel displays the contents of the USB drive, Removable Disk (H:), which includes both the data files for Chapter 3 and the *your name* folder for the Web sites you create in this book. If your Montana Parks Web site is stored on a drive other than Removable Disk (H:), the name of the drive appears in the Sites pop-up menu button, and the data files for Chapter 3 are listed on your designated drive.

Adding Pages to a Web Site

You copied the images necessary to begin creating your new Web pages in the Montana Parks local root folder in the Files panel. You will add two pages to the Web site: a page for the Nez Perce National Historic Trail and a page for Glacier National Park. You first create the Nez Perce National Historic Trail Web page. You add the background image and a heading to each new page. Next, you insert a table on each page and add text, images, and links into the cells within the table.

To Open a New Document Window

The following steps illustrate how to open a new Document window, which will become the Nez Perce National Historic Trail page, and then save the page.

1 Click the Sites pop-up menu button on the Files panel, and then click Montana Parks to display the files for the Montana Parks Web site.

2 Click File on the Application bar, and then click New to display the New Document dialog box.

3 If necessary, click Blank Page to indicate you are creating a new page.

4 If necessary, click HTML in the Page Type list to indicate the page is a standard HTML page.

5 If necessary, click <none> in the Layout list to indicate you are not using a predefined layout.

6 Click the Create button to create the page.

7 Click the Save button on the Standard toolbar to display the Save As dialog box.

8 Type `nez_perce` as the file name.

9 Click the Save button in the Save As dialog box to display the new, blank nez_perce.htm page in the Document window (Figure 3–4).

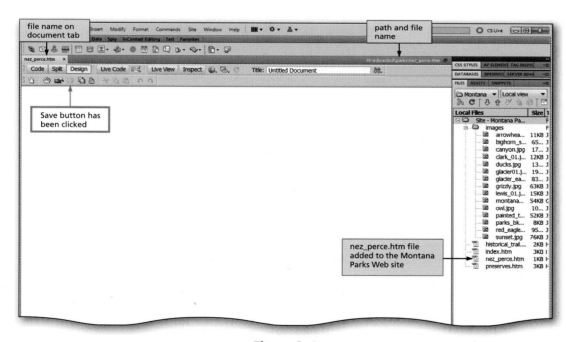

Figure 3–4

Creating the Nez Perce National Historic Trail Web Page

You start creating the Nez Perce National Historic Trail page by applying a background image. This is the same background image you used for the Montana Parks Web site pages in Chapters 1 and 2.

To Add a Background Image to the Nez Perce National Historic Trail Web Page

To provide additional space in the Document window and to create a better overview of the layout, collapse the panel groups. Next, expand the Property inspector to display the additional table options. The following steps also illustrate how to apply the background image.

1 Click the Collapse to Icons button to collapse the panel groups. If necessary, drag the vertical bar between the Document window and the panel groups to resize the panel groups so they display icons only.

2 If necessary, click the Property inspector expander arrow to display both the upper and lower sections of the Property inspector.

3 Click the Page Properties button in the Property inspector to display the Page Properties dialog box.

4 Click Appearance (HTML) in the Category column.

5 Click the Browse button to the right of the Background image box to display the Select Image Source dialog box.

6 If necessary, navigate to and open the parks\images folder.

7 Click parks_bkg and then click the OK button to select the background image.

8 Click the OK button in the Page Properties dialog box to apply the background to the page (Figure 3–5).

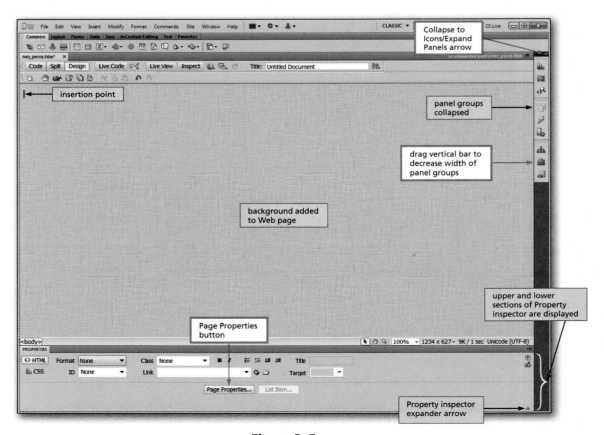

Figure 3–5

To Insert and Format the Heading

Next, you insert and format the heading. You apply the same heading format you applied to the heading in the index page. The following steps show how to add the heading and apply the Heading 1 format.

1 Type **Nez Perce National Historic Trail** as the page heading.

2 Click the Format button in the Property inspector, and then click Heading 1 to apply Heading 1 to the text.

3 Click Format on the Application bar, point to Align, and then click Center to center the heading.

4 Select the text in the Title box on the Document toolbar, and then type **Nez Perce National Historic Trail** as the page title.

5 Click at the end of the heading in the Document window, and then press the ENTER key to move the insertion point to the next line.

6 Click the Save button on the Standard toolbar to save the page with the centered and formatted heading (Figure 3–6).

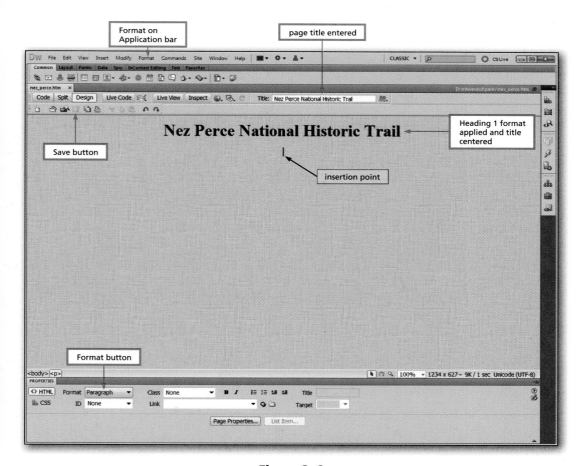

Figure 3–6

Understanding Tables and Page Layout

Tables have many uses in HTML design. The most obvious is a table of data, but, as already mentioned, tables also are used for page layout, such as placing text and graphics on a page at just the right location. **Tables** also provide Web designers with a method to add vertical and horizontal structure to a page. ClassicA table consists of three basic components: rows, columns, and cells. A **row** is a horizontal collection of cells and a **column** is a vertical collection of cells. A **cell** is the container created when the row and column intersect. Each cell within the table can contain any standard element you use on a Web page. This includes text, images, and other objects.

Page layout is the process of arranging the text, images, and other elements on the page. The basic rules of page layout are that your site should be easy to navigate, easy to read, and quick to download. Studies indicate that visitors lose interest in your Web site if the majority of a page does not download within 15 seconds. One popular design element that downloads quickly is tables.

Tables download quickly because they are created with HTML code. They can be used anywhere — for the home page, menus, images, navigation bars, frames, and so on. Tables originally were intended for presenting data arranged by rows and columns, such as tabular data within a spreadsheet. Web designers, however, quickly seized upon the use of tables to produce specific layout effects. You can produce good designs by using tables creatively. Tables allow you to position elements on a Web page with much greater accuracy. Using tables for layout provides the Web page author with endless design possibilities.

Plan Ahead

> **Determine when to insert tables.**
> A typical Web page is composed of three sections: the header, the body, and the footer.
>
> - The **header**, generally located at the top of the page, can contain logos, images, or text that identifies the Web site. The header also can contain hyperlinks to other pages within the Web site.
>
> - The **body** of the Web page contains information about your site. This content may be in the form of text, graphics, animation, video, and audio, or a combination of any of these elements.
>
> - The **footer** provides hyperlinks for contact information and navigational controls.
>
> The controls in the footer might be in addition to the navigation controls in the header. Other common items contained in a footer are the name and e-mail address of the author or the Webmaster. Sometimes, hyperlinks to other resources or to Help information are part of the footer.
>
> Tables make it easy to create this header/body/footer structure or to create any other layout structure that meets your specific Web page needs. The entire structure can be contained within one table or a combination of multiple and nested tables. A nested table is a table inside another table. You will use tables to create the two new pages for the Montana Parks Web site.

To insert a table, you can use the Table button on the Insert bar or the Table command on the Insert menu. Both the Common category and the Layout category on the Insert bar contain a Table button that works the same way in either category. However, the Layout category includes the Standard and Expanded Tables mode buttons. In Expanded Tables mode, Dreamweaver temporarily adds cell padding and spacing to all the tables in a document and expands the tables' borders to make detailed editing easier. Some operations, such as resizing tables and images, work unpredictably in Expanded

Tables mode and are better performed in Standard mode. In this chapter, you work in Standard mode only because you do not need to perform the types of precise selections that Expanded Tables mode makes possible.

If you have a table created in another application, such as Microsoft Word or Excel, you can import the data. To do so, click File on the Application bar, point to Import, and then click Tabular Data. (You also can click Insert on the Application bar, point to Table Objects, and then click Import Tabular Data.) Select the file you want to import, specify settings such as table width, border, cell padding, and cell spacing, and then click OK.

Inserting a Table into the Nez Perce National Historic Trail Page

You will add two tables to the Nez Perce National Historic Trail page and then add text and images to the cells within the tables. The first table will consist of three rows and two columns, with a cell padding of 5 and cell spacing of 10. **Cell padding** is the amount of space between the edge of a cell and its contents, whereas **cell spacing** is the amount of space between cells. The border will be set to 0, which is the default. When the table is displayed in Dreamweaver, a border outline appears around the table. When the table's border is set to 0 and the table is viewed in a browser; however, this outline is not displayed.

The table width is 90 percent. When specifying the width, you can select percent or pixels. A table with the width specified as a **percent** expands with the width of the window and the monitor size in which it is being viewed. A table with the width specified as **pixels** will remain the same size regardless of the window and monitor size. If you select percent and an image is larger than the selected percentage, the cell and table will expand to accommodate the image. Likewise, if the **No wrap** property is enabled and the text will not fit within the cell, the cell and table will expand to accommodate the text. It is not necessary to declare a table width. When no value is specified, the table is displayed as small as possible and then expands as content is added. If modifications are necessary to the original specified table values, you can change these values in the Property inspector.

The second table for the Nez Perce National Historic Trail page is a one-cell table, consisting of one row and one column. This table will contain links to the Home page and to other pages in the Web site. You use the Layout category on the Insert bar and the Property inspector to control and format the tables.

Using the Insert Bar

By default, the Classic workspace shows the Insert bar at the top of the window below the Application bar. This toolbar contains several categories, or tabs, and is fully customizable through the Favorites tab. The Insert bar contains buttons for creating and inserting objects such as tables and advanced elements such as div tags, frames, the Spry Menu Bar, and other Spry options.

You can hide, customize, or display the Insert bar as necessary. All selections within the categories also are available through the Application bar and many of the selections also are available through the Property inspectors. The Table button command also can be accessed through the Insert menu on the Application bar.

BTW

Inserting Content with the Insert Bar
Besides inserting tables, you can insert other types of content using the Insert bar, including images, video, and widgets such as calendars and tabbed panels.

To Display the Insert Bar and Select the Layout Tab

You use the Table buttons on the Layout tab of the Insert bar to assist with page design. The following steps illustrate how to display the Insert bar if necessary and select the Layout tab.

1

- If necessary, click Window on the Application bar and then click Insert to display the Insert bar.

Q&A

What should I do if the Insert bar is displayed as a pane instead of a bar?

Drag the title bar of the Insert pane below the Application bar to display it as a bar.

- Point to the Layout tab on the Insert bar (Figure 3–7).

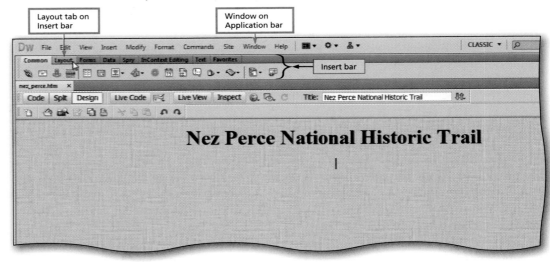

Figure 3–7

2

- Click the Layout tab to display the Insert bar Layout category (Figure 3–8).

Q&A

What kinds of options are available on the Layout tab of the Insert bar?

The Layout tab contains options for working with tables, div tags, and panels.

Q&A

What are the dimmed buttons to the right of the Table button?

When any part of a table is selected, the four dimmed buttons are displayed so you can format the table.

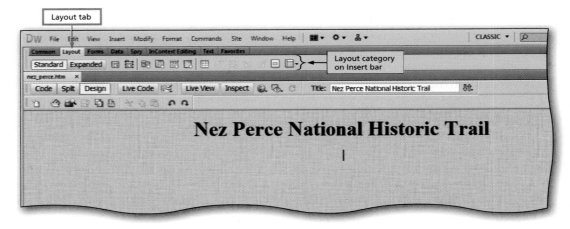

Figure 3–8

Layout Tab

You use the Layout tab (Figure 3–9 on the next page) to work with tables and table features. Dreamweaver provides two modes, or ways, to use the table feature: Standard mode and Expanded Tables mode. Standard mode uses the Table dialog box. When you create a table, the Table dialog box opens in Standard mode by default so you can set the basic structure of the table. It then is displayed as a grid and expands as you add text and images.

As mentioned earlier, you use the Expanded button on the Layout tab to switch to Expanded Tables mode. This mode temporarily enlarges your view of the cells so you can select items easily and place the insertion point precisely. Use this mode as a temporary visual aid for selection and insertion point placement. After placing the insertion point, return to Standard mode to make your edits and to provide a better visualization of your changes. Other buttons on the Layout tab are for working with Spry objects, which don't apply to tables.

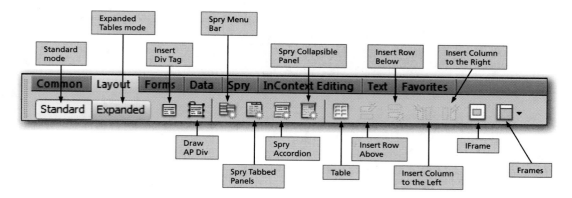

Figure 3–9

Table 3–1 lists the button names and descriptions available in the Insert bar Layout category.

Table 3–1 Buttons on the Layout tab of the Insert Bar	
Button Name	**Description**
Standard mode	Displays a table as a grid of lines
Expanded Tables mode	Temporarily adds cell padding and spacing
Insert Div Tag	Inserts a <div> tag
Draw AP Div	Inserts a <div> tag at a fixed absolute point within a Web document
Spry Tabbed Panels	Inserts a tabbed panel widget directly into the Web page
Spry Menu Bar	Inserts an AJAX predefined control
Spry Accordion	Creates horizontal regions on a Web page that can be expanded or collapsed
Spry Collapsible Panel	Displays collapsible panels that have a clickable tab
Table	Places a table at the insertion point
Insert Row Above	Inserts a row above the selected row
Insert Row Below	Inserts a row below the selected row
Insert Column to the Left	Inserts a column to the left of the selected column
Insert Column to the Right	Inserts a column to the right of the selected column
IFrame	Displays data (text and image) that is stored in a separate page
Frames	Displays Frames pop-up menu

Table Defaults and Accessibility

When you insert a table, the Table dialog box is displayed and contains default settings for each of the table attributes (Figure 3–10 on the next page). After you create a table and change these defaults, the settings that are displayed remain until you change them for the next table. Table 3–2 lists and describes the defaults for each table attribute.

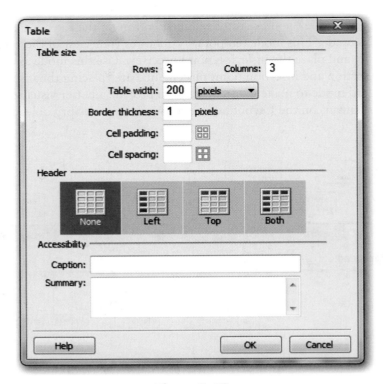

Figure 3–10

Table 3–2 Table Dialog Box Default Values		
Attribute	**Default**	**Description**
Rows	3	Determines the number of rows in the table
Columns	3	Determines the number of columns in the table
Table width	200 pixels	Specifies the width of the table in pixels or as a percentage of the browser window's width
Border thickness	1	Specifies the border width in pixels
Cell padding	None	Specifies the number of pixels between a cell's border and its contents
Cell spacing	None	Specifies the number of pixels between adjacent table cells
Header	None	Specifies whether the top row and/or column is designated as a header cell
Caption	None	Provides a table heading
Summary	None	Provides a table description; used by screen readers

It is advisable to use headers for tables when the table presents tabular information. Screen readers scan table headings and help screen-reader users keep track of table information. Additionally, the Caption option provides a table title that is displayed outside of the table. If a Caption is specified, the Align Caption option indicates where the table caption appears in relation to the table. The Summary option provides a table description. Summary text is similar to the Alt text you added for images in Chapter 2. You add Summary text to the tables you create in this chapter. Screen readers read the summary text, but the text does not appear in the user's browser.

Table Layout

As indicated previously, the Header and Caption options are important when a table displays tabular data. When using a table for layout, however, other options apply. Structurally and graphically, the elements in a table used for layout should be invisible in the browser. For instance, when using a table for layout, use the None option for Headers. The None option prevents the header tags <th> and </th> from being added to the table. Because the table does not contain tabular data, a header would be of no benefit to the screen-reader user. Screen readers, however, read table content from left to right and top to bottom. Therefore, it is important to structure the table content in a linear arrangement.

Lay out Web pages with tables.

Tables help you lay out Web pages that contain text and images. After creating a Web page and setting its properties, add tables, text, and images in the following order:

1. **Table:** Insert a table before entering any text other than the page heading. Set table properties such as size, cell padding, and cell spacing.

2. **Text:** Add text to the table cells. You can apply formats to the text such as Heading 1 and bold text to emphasize it, for example.

3. **Images:** Insert images after you enter text to balance the images and the rest of the table content. Then you can resize each image, align it, and set other image properties.

Plan Ahead

To Insert a Table

The following steps illustrate how to insert a table with three rows and two columns into the Nez Perce National Historic Trail Web page.

1

- Click the Table button on the Layout tab to display the Table dialog box (Figure 3–11).

Q&A

Should the settings in my Table dialog box match those in the figure?

The settings displayed are the settings from the last table created, so your dialog box might contain different values.

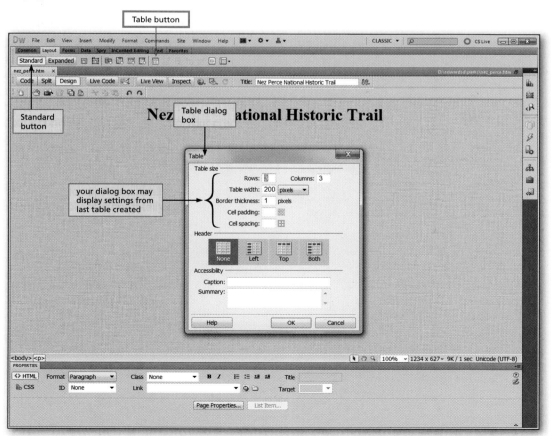

Figure 3–11

2

- If necessary, type **3** in the Rows box to create a table with three rows, and then press the TAB key to move to the Columns box.

- Type **2** to create a table with two columns, and then press the TAB key to move to the Table width box.

- Type **90** to set the table width, and then click the Table width button to display the Table width options.

- Click percent to specify the table width as a percentage, and then press the TAB key to move to the Border thickness box.

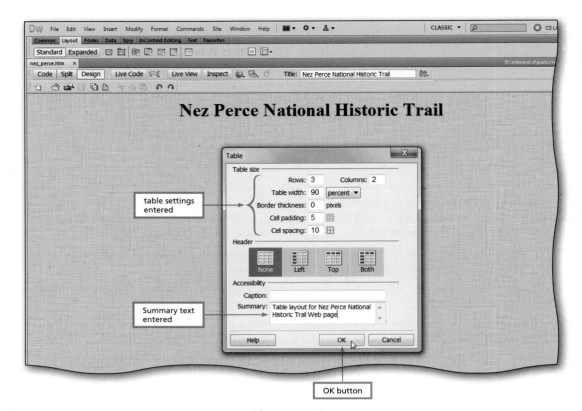

Figure 3–12

- Type **0** to set the border thickness, and then press the TAB key to move to the Cell padding box.

- Type **5** to add 5 pixels of cell padding, and then press the TAB key to move to the Cell spacing box.

- Type **10** to add 10 pixels of space between adjacent table cells.

- Click the Summary text box and type `Table layout for Nez Perce National Historic Trail Web page` (Figure 3–12).

3

- Click the OK button to insert the table into the Document window (Figure 3–13).

Why does a border appear around the table if the Border thickness is set to 0?

Although the border thickness is set to 0, it appears as an outline in the Document window. The border will not appear when displayed in the browser.

Can I add rows after I create a table?

Yes. Right-click a row to display the context menu, point to Table, and then click Insert Row to add a row after the current one.

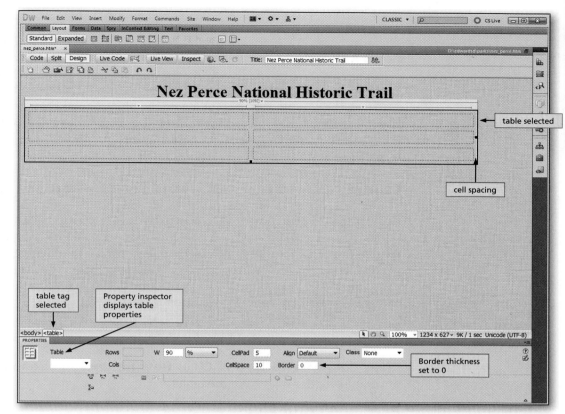

Figure 3–13

Property Inspector Table Features

As you have seen, the Property inspector options change depending on the selected object. You use the Property inspector to modify and add table attributes. When a table is selected, the Property inspector displays table properties in both panels. When another table element — a row, column, or cell — is selected, the displayed properties change and are determined by the selected element. The following section describes the table-related features of the Property inspector shown in Figure 3–14.

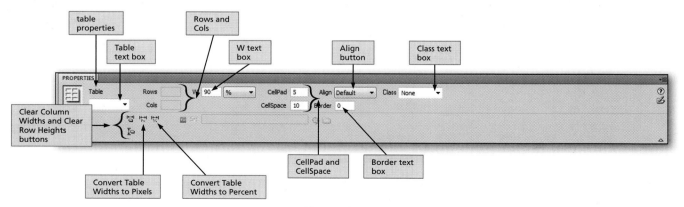

Figure 3–14

Table Specifies the table ID, an identifier used for Cascading Style Sheets, scripting, and accessibility. A table ID is not required; however, it is a good idea always to add this identifier.

Rows and Cols The number of rows and columns in the table.

W Specifies the minimum width of the table in either pixels or percent. If a size is not specified, the size can vary depending on the monitor and browser settings. A table width specified in pixels is displayed as the same size in all browsers. A table width specified in percent is altered in appearance based on the user's monitor resolution and browser window size.

CellPad The number of pixels between the cell border and the cell content.

CellSpace The number of pixels between adjacent table cells.

Align Determines where the table appears, relative to other elements in the same paragraph such as text or images. The default alignment is to the left.

Class An attribute used with Cascading Style Sheets.

Border Specifies the border width in pixels.

Clear Column Widths and Clear Row Heights Deletes all specified row height or column width values from the table.

Convert Table Widths to Pixels Sets the width of each column in the table to its current width expressed as pixels.

Convert Table Widths to Percent Sets the width of the table and each column in the table to their current widths expressed as percentages of the Document window's width.

Cell, Row, and Column Properties

When a cell, row, or column is selected, the properties in the upper pane of the Property inspector are the same as the standard properties for text. You can use these properties to include standard HTML formatting tags within a cell, row, or column. The part of the table selected determines which properties are displayed in the lower pane of the Property inspector. The properties for cells, rows, and columns are the same, except for one element — the icon displayed in the lower-left pane of the Property inspector. The following section describes the row-related features (Figure 3–15), cell-related features (Figure 3–16 on the next page), and column-related features (Figure 3–17 on the next page) of the Property inspector.

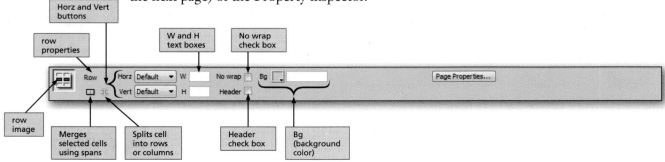

Figure 3–15

Figure 3–16

Figure 3–17

Horz　Specifies the horizontal alignment of the contents of a cell, row, or column. The contents can be aligned to the left, right, or center of the cells.

Vert　Specifies the vertical alignment of the contents of a cell, row, or column. The contents can be aligned to the top, middle, bottom, or baseline of the cells.

W and H　Specifies the width and height of selected cells in pixels or as a percentage of the entire table's width or height.

No wrap　Prevents line wrapping, keeping all text in a given cell on a single line. If No Wrap is enabled, cells widen to accommodate all data as it is typed or pasted into a cell.

Bg (background color)　Sets the background color of a cell, row, or column selected from the color picker (use the Bg icon) or specified as a hexadecimal number (use the Bg text box).

Header　Formats the selected cells as table header cells. The contents of table header cells are bold and centered by default.

Merges selected cells using spans　Combines selected cells, rows, or columns into one cell (available when two or more cells, rows, or columns are selected).

Splits cell into rows or columns　Divides a cell, creating two or more cells (available when a single cell is selected).

Table Formatting Conflicts

　　　When formatting tables in Standard mode, you can set properties for the entire table or for selected rows, columns, or cells in the table. Applying these properties, however, introduces a potential for conflict. To prevent conflicts, HTML assigns levels of precedence. The order of precedence for table formatting is cells, rows, and table. When a property, such as background color or alignment, is set to one value for the whole table and another value for individual cells, cell formatting takes precedence over row formatting, which in turn takes precedence over table formatting.

For example, if you set the background color for a single cell to green, and then set the background color of the entire table to red, the green cell does not change to red, because cell formatting takes precedence over table formatting. Dreamweaver, however, does not always follow the precedence. The program will override the settings for a cell if you change the settings for the row that contains the cell. To eliminate this problem, you should change the cell settings last.

Understanding HTML Structure in a Table

As you work with and become more familiar with tables, it is helpful to have a basic understanding of the HTML structure within a table. Suppose, for example, you have a table with two rows and two columns, displaying a total of four cells, such as the following:

First cell	Second cell
Third cell	Fourth cell

The general syntax of the table is:
```
<table>
<tr>
 <td> First cell </td>
 <td> Second cell </td>
</tr>
<tr>
 <td> Third cell </td>
 <td> Fourth cell </td>
</tr>
</table>
```
In Dreamweaver, the tag selector displays the <table>, <td>, and <tr> tags. The <table> tag indicates the whole table. Clicking the <table> tag in the tag selector selects the whole table. The <td> tag indicates table data. Clicking the <td> tag in the tag selector selects the cell containing the insertion point. The <tr> tag indicates table row. Clicking the <tr> tag in the tag selector selects the row containing the insertion point.

Selecting the Table and Selecting Cells

The Property inspector displays table attributes only if the entire table is selected. To select the entire table, click the upper-left corner of the table, click anywhere on the top or bottom edge of the table, or click in a cell and then click <table> in the tag selector. When selected, the table is displayed with a dark border and selection handles on the table's lower and right edges (Figure 3–18 on the next page).

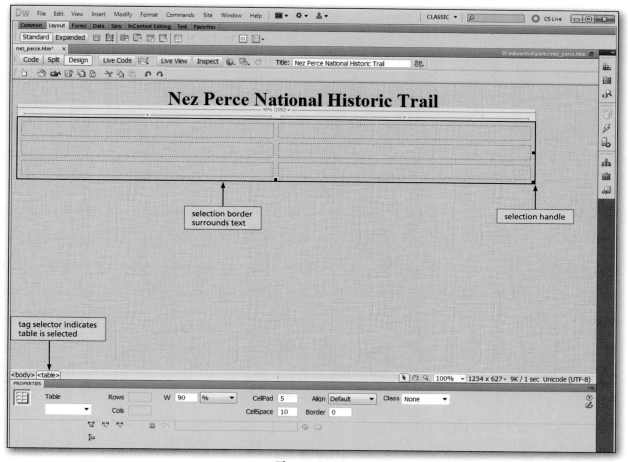

Figure 3–18

Selecting a cell, row, or column is easier than selecting the entire table. When a cell, row, or column is selected, the selected item has a dark border. To select a cell, click inside the cell. When you click inside the cell, the <td> tag is displayed as selected on the status bar. To select a row or column, click inside one of the cells in the row or column and drag to select the other cells. When you select a row, the <tr> tag is displayed on the status bar. In Figure 3–19 on the next page, a row is selected.

A second method for selecting a row or column is to point to the left edge of a row or the top edge of a column. When the pointer changes to a selection arrow, click to select the row or column. In Figure 3–20 on the next page, a column is selected.

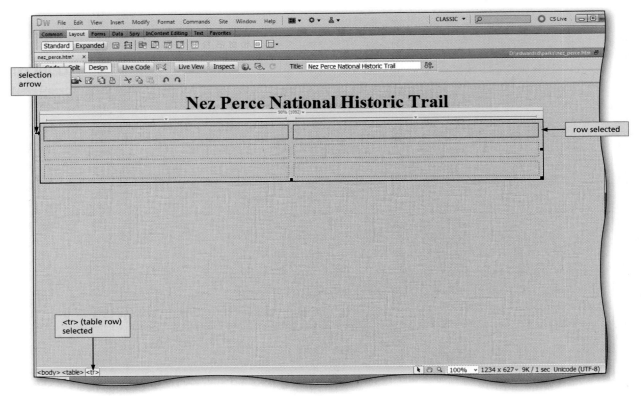

Figure 3–19

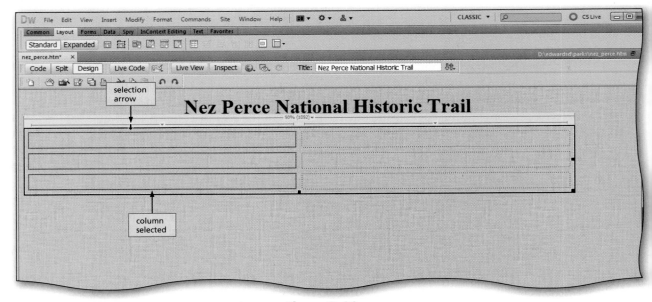

Figure 3–20

Centering a Table

When a table is inserted into the Document window with a specified width, it aligns to the left by default. Using the Property inspector, you can center the table by selecting it and then applying the Center command.

To Select and Center a Table

The following steps illustrate how to select and center the table using the Property inspector.

1
- Click in row 1, column 1 to place the insertion point in the first cell of the table (Figure 3–21).

2
- Click <table> in the tag selector to select the table and to display handles on the lower and right borders of the table.

Figure 3–21

- Click the Align button in the Property inspector and then point to Center (Figure 3–22).

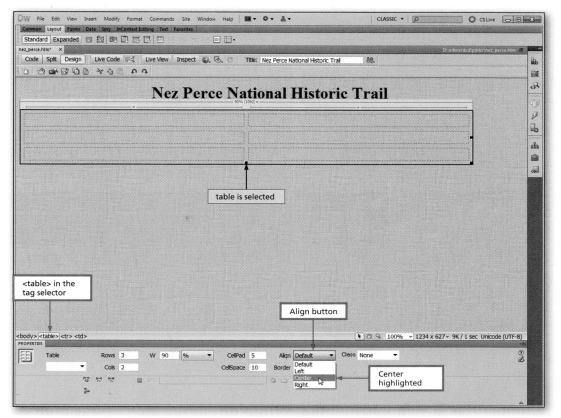

Figure 3–22

- Click Center to center the table on the page (Figure 3–23).

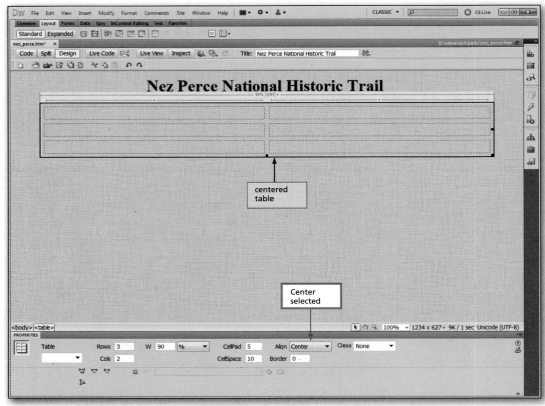

Figure 3–23

Changing the Default Cell Alignment for Text

The default horizontal cell alignment for text is left. When you enter text in a cell, it defaults to the left margin of the cell. You can change the horizontal alignment through the Property inspector Align button pop-up menu by clicking the cell and then changing the default to Center or Right. The default vertical cell alignment is Middle, which aligns the cell content in the middle of the cell. Table 3–3 describes the cell alignment options.

Table 3–3 Cell Alignment Options	
Alignment	**Description**
Default	Specifies a baseline alignment; default may vary depending on the user's browser
Baseline	Aligns the cell content at the bottom of the cell (same as Bottom)
Top	Aligns the cell content at the top of the cell
Bottom	Aligns the cell content at the bottom of the cell
TextTop	Aligns the top of the image with the top of the tallest character in the text line
Absolute Middle	Aligns the middle of the image with the middle of the text in the current line
Absolute Bottom	Aligns the bottom of the image with the bottom of the line of text

Table 3–3 Cell Alignment Options (*continued*)	
Alignment	**Description**
Left	Places the selected image on the left margin, wrapping text around it to the right; if left-aligned text precedes the object on the line, it generally forces left-aligned objects to wrap to a new line
Middle	Aligns the middle of the image with the baseline of the current line
Right	Places the image on the right margin, wrapping text around the object to the left; if right-aligned text precedes the object on the line, it generally forces right-aligned objects to wrap to a new line

You can change the alignment using the Align button in the Property inspector by clicking the cell and then selecting another alignment option. These properties can be applied to a single cell, to multiple cells, or to the entire table.

To Change Vertical Alignment from Middle to Top

The following steps show how to select all of the cells and change the default alignment from middle to top.

1

- Click in row 1, column 1 and then drag to the right and down to select the three rows and two columns in the table.

- Click the Vert button in the Property inspector to display the Vert pop-up menu and then point to Top (Figure 3–24).

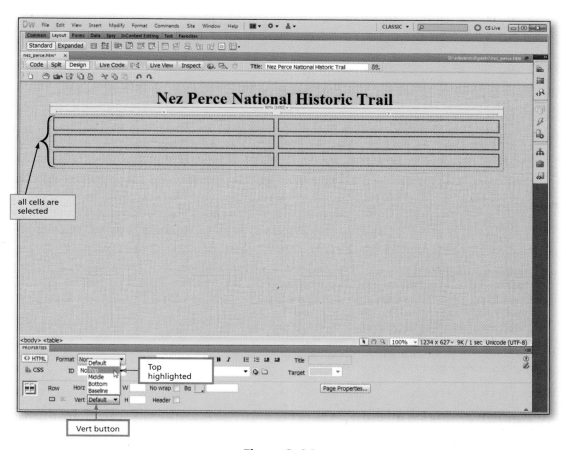

Figure 3–24

2

- Click Top to change the vertical alignment from Middle to Top (Figure 3–25).

Q&A

Should the appearance of the table change after applying a new vertical alignment? The change is not visible in the Document window yet — the new alignment is noticeable when the cells contain text or images.

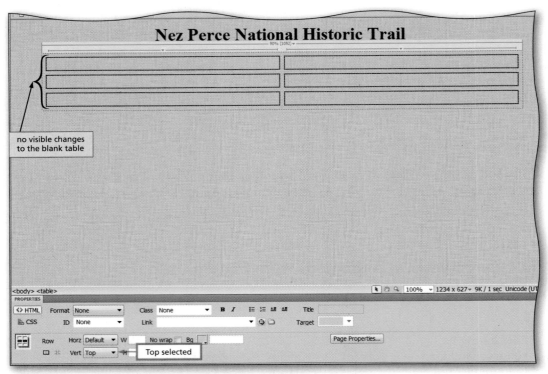

Figure 3–25

Specifying Column Width

When a table width is specified as a percentage, each column's width expands to accommodate the text or image. When you add content to the table, this expansion can distort the table appearance and make it difficult to visualize how the final page will be displayed. You can control this expansion by setting the column width.

Changing Column Width
In addition to using the Property inspector to change the width or height of a column, you can drag the right border of a column to resize it. To change a column width without affecting other columns in the table, hold down the SHIFT key as you drag. If you are familiar with HTML, you can change cell widths and heights directly in the HTML code.

Clearing Column Widths and Row Heights
To clear all the column widths you set in a table, select the table, and then click the Clear Column Widths button in the Property inspector. To clear all the row heights you set, select the table, and then click the Clear Row Heights button.

To Specify Column Width

The objective for the Nez Perce National Historic Trail page is to display the page in two columns — column 1 at 45% and column 2 at 35%. The following steps show how to specify column width.

- Click the cell in row 1, column 1 and then drag to select all cells in column 1.

- Click the W box in the Property inspector, type **45%**, and then press the ENTER key to set the width for column 1 at 45%.

- Click the cell in row 1, column 2 and then drag to select all cells in column 2.

- Click the W box in the Property inspector, type **35%**, then press the ENTER key to set the width for column 2 at 35% (Figure 3–26).

2

- Click anywhere in the table to deselect the column.

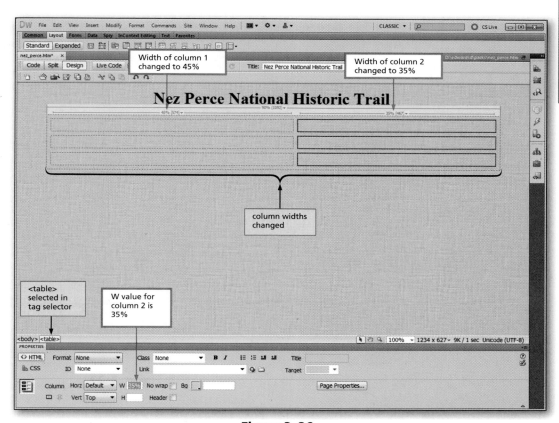

Figure 3–26

Adding an ID

Tables, images, and other Web site elements can be assigned a name through the Table field located in the Property inspector. This ID identifies the content of an object within the HTML code. Spaces and characters cannot be used except for the dash or underscore.

To Add a Table ID to the Nez Perce National Historic Trail Table

The following step illustrates how to select the table and add a table ID to the Nez Perce National Historic Trail feature table.

- Click <table> in the tag selector to select the table.

- Click the Table text box and then type **nez_perce** as the ID text.

- Press the ENTER key to add the table ID (Figure 3–27).

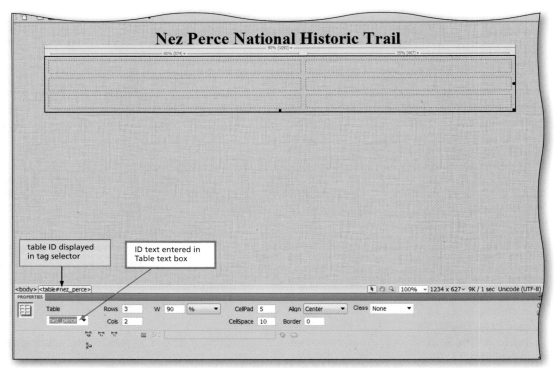

Figure 3–27

Adding Text to the Nez Perce National Historic Trail Web Page

Next, you enter and format the text for the Nez Perce National Historic Trail Web page. Table 3–4 on the next page includes the text for the first table. The text is entered into the table cells. If you have not set the width and height of a cell, when you begin to enter text into a table cell, the cell expands to accommodate the text. The other cells may appear to shrink, but they also will expand when you type in the cells or add an image to the cells.

Table 3–4 Nez Perce National Historic Trail Text	
Section	**Text**
Part 1	Nez Perce National Historic Trail is more than 415 square miles and has 114 named peaks over 10,000 feet. One of the more popular hiking trails is the Keyhole Route on Longs' Peak. At 14,255 feet, Longs' Peak is the highest peak in the Nez Perce National Historic Trail and the fifteenth tallest in Montana. <ENTER> The park contains three distinct ecosystems which correspond to elevation: the montane, which is 7,000 to 9,000 feet above sea level; the subalpine ecosystem, which is 9,000 to 11,500 feet and spans the tree line; and the alpine tundra, at the top, which is over 11,500 feet.
Part 2	Birds and animals add color and interest to the landscape. The park contains 65 species of mammals, 260 species of birds, and 900 species of plants. Black bears, mountain lions, and bobcats live in the park, but seldom are seen. Moose and mule deer are more visible. In autumn, herds of American elk roam the park and frequently are visible, even at the lower elevations. <ENTER> Interesting facts: a) In the summer of 2005, a dinosaur footprint was found. The print was identified as belonging to a three-toed foot of a Cretaceous Theropod. b) The park contains over 650 species of flowering plants as well as many species of mosses, lichens, fungi, algae, and other plant life.
Part 3	The park is open 24 hours a day year round.< br /> Park Service Information Office: Nez Perce National Historic Trail 12730 Highway 12 Orofino, ID 83544<ENTER> E-mail: nez_perce_trail@fs.fed.us
Bighorn sheep text	Bighorn sheep are one of the more common animals seen along the trail. The male bighorn is called a ram. It easily is recognized by its massive curled horns, which can weigh more than 30 pounds. The females, called ewes, have smaller horns. They can have from one to two kids every spring. The bighorn can live to be 10–15 years old.

To Add Text to the Nez Perce National Historic Trail Web Page

The following steps show how to add text to the Nez Perce National Historic Trail page. Press the ENTER key when indicated or press SHIFT+ENTER to insert a line break, <br />, as specified in Table 3–4 on the previous page. Press the TAB key to move from cell to cell.

1

- Type the two paragraphs of Part 1 in Table 3–4 in row 1, column 1 of the table in the Document window, pressing the ENTER key as indicated in the table (Figure 3–28).

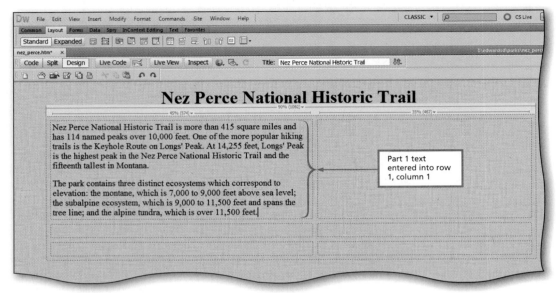

Figure 3–28

2

- Type the two paragraphs of Part 2, as shown in Table 3–4, into row 2, column 2 of the table.

- Type the text of Part 3, as shown in Table 3–4, into row 3, column 1 of the Document window (Figure 3–29).

Q&A How do I enter the line breaks?

Press SHIFT+ENTER to insert the line breaks.

Q&A Where is the insertion point after I insert a line break?

The insertion point is within the cell below the last line and may not be visible.

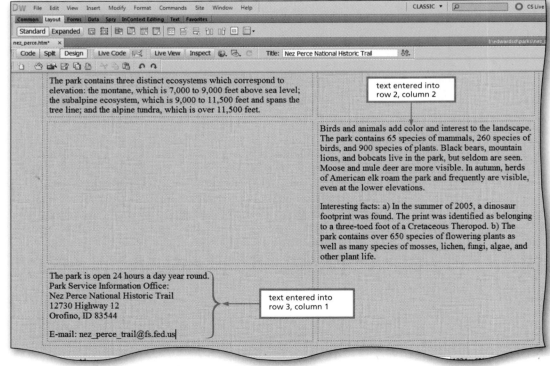

Figure 3–29

- Select the text in row 3, column 1 to prepare for aligning the text.

- Click the Horz button in the Property inspector, and then click Right to align the text to the right.

- Click anywhere on the page to deselect the text (Figure 3–30).

- Click the Save button to save the page.

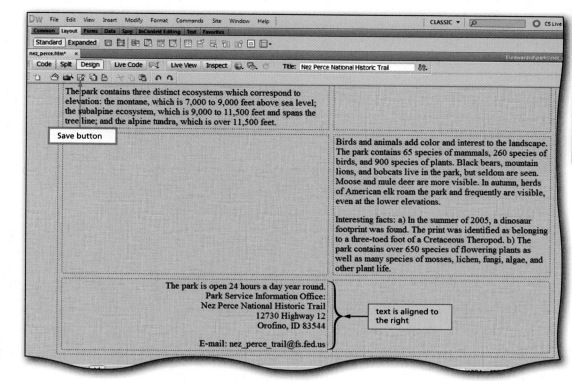

Figure 3–30

Other Ways
1. Right-click selected text, point to Align, click Right

Adding a Second Table to the Nez Perce National Historic Trail Web Page

Next, you add a second table to the Nez Perce National Historic Trail Web page. This table will contain one row and one column and will serve as the footer for your Web page.

To Add a Second Table to the Nez Perce National Historic Trail Web Page

The text for the footer should be centered in the cell and contain links to the home page and to the other pages within the Web site. When you create the page for the Nez Perce National Historic Trail, you can copy and paste these links into that page. The following steps show how to add the second table using the Layout tab on the Insert bar.

- Click outside the right border of the existing table to position the insertion point outside the table (Figure 3–31).

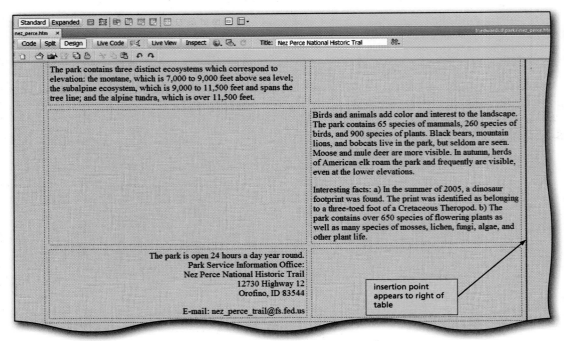

Figure 3–31

- Press the ENTER key to move the insertion point below the table.

- Click the Table button on the Layout tab on the Insert bar to display the Table dialog box (Figure 3–32).

Q&A

Should the settings in my Table dialog box match those in Figure 3–32?

Not necessarily. The dialog box on your computer may show different settings.

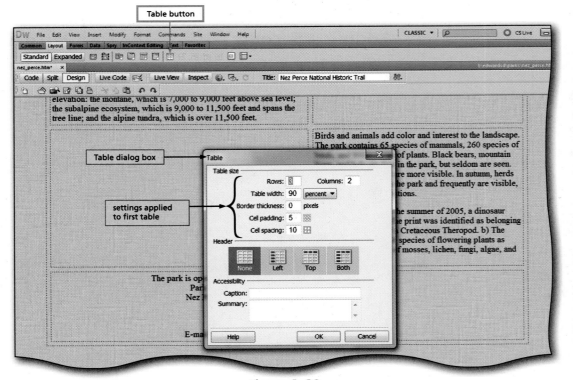

Figure 3–32

3

- Change the number of rows to 1, the number of columns to 1, the width to 75 percent, the border thickness to 0, the cell padding to 0, and the cell spacing to 10 to set the properties for the table.

- Type **Footer table for links** in the Summary text box to add the table description.

- If necessary, change other settings to match the settings shown in Figure 3–33.

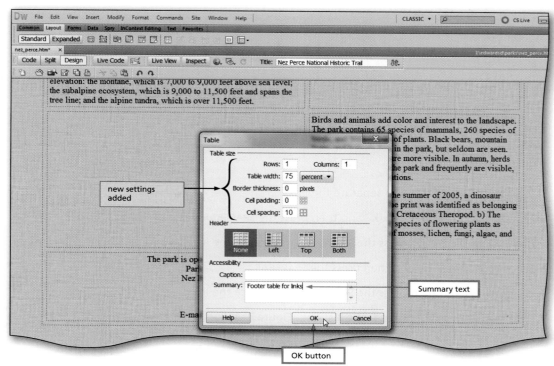

Figure 3–33

4

- Click the OK button to insert the one-cell table.

- Click the Align button and then click Center to center the one-cell table (Figure 3–34).

Why does the table have a dark border and handles?

The dark border and handles indicate that the table is selected.

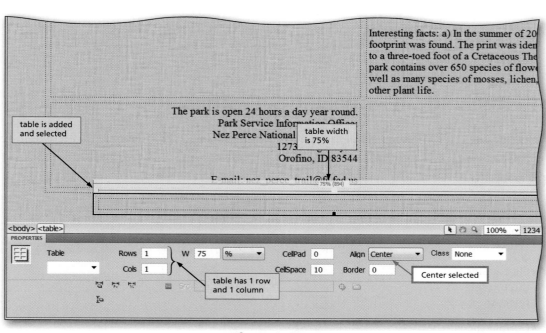

Figure 3–34

5

- Click the cell in the table. Type **Home** and then press the SPACEBAR to enter the first link.

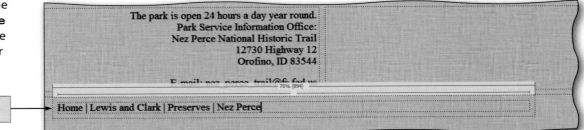

links text added to table

Figure 3–35

- Press SHIFT+| (vertical bar) and then press the SPACEBAR to separate the links.

- Type **Lewis and Clark** and then press the SPACEBAR to enter the next link.

- Press SHIFT+| and then press the SPACEBAR to separate the links.

- Type **Preserves** and then press the SPACEBAR.

- Press SHIFT+| and then press the SPACEBAR to separate the links.

- Type **Nez Perce** to enter the last link (Figure 3–35).

BTW

Hiding the Table Width Bar
You can hide the bar that shows the column and table widths by clicking the down-pointing arrow next to the table width indicator and then clicking Hide Table Widths.

Adjusting the Table Width

If you overestimate or underestimate the table width when first inserting a table into the Document window, it is easy to make adjustments to the table width through the Property inspector.

To Adjust the Table Width, Center the Text, and Add the Table ID

The links table is too wide for the text it contains and needs to be adjusted. You adjust the table width by selecting the table and then changing the width in the Property inspector. The following steps illustrate how to adjust the width and add the table ID to the links table.

1

- If necessary, click in the cell in the links table to make it the active table.

- Click <table> in the tag selector to select the table.

- Double-click the W box in the Property inspector to select the width value.

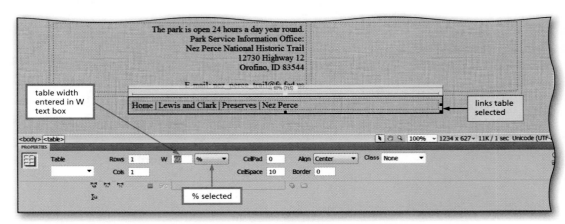

table width entered in W text box

links table selected

% selected

Figure 3–36

- Type **60** and then press the ENTER key to decrease the table width.

- If necessary, click the W button arrow and select % (the percent sign) (Figure 3–36).

- Click the cell in the table to select the cell.

- Click the Horz button, and then click Center to center the text.

- Click <table> in the tag selector to select the table.

- Click the Table text box, type **Montana_ parks_links**, and then press the ENTER key to name the table (Figure 3–37).

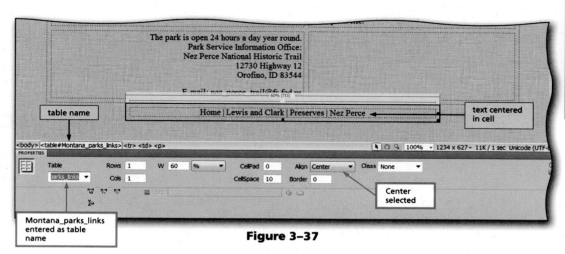

Figure 3–37

- Click anywhere in the Document window to deselect the table.

To Add Links to the Nez Perce National Historic Trail Web Page

Next, you add absolute, e-mail, and relative links to the Nez Perce National Historic Trail page. The following steps show how to add the links. You add relative links to the index, historical_trail, preserves, and nez_perce pages. You include a link to the nez_perce page so you can copy all the links to other pages for consistency.

1 Select the first instance of Nez Perce National Historic Trail located in the first table in row 1, column 1. In the Link box, type **http://www.nps.gov/nepe/index.htm** and then press ENTER to create an absolute link.

2 Select nez_perce_trail@fs.fed.us located in the first table in row 3, column 1. Click Insert on the Application bar and then click Email Link to display the Email Link dialog box.

3 Make sure the Email text box contains nez_perce_trail@fs.fed.us as the e-mail address, and then click the OK button to enter the e-mail link.

4 Select Home in the second table, click the Link box, type **index.htm,** and then press ENTER to enter a relative link to the home page for the Montana Parks Web site.

5 Select Lewis and Clark in the second table, click the Link box, type **historical_ trail.htm,** and then press ENTER to create the relative link to the Lewis and Clark Web page.

6 Select Preserves in the second table, click the Link box, type **preserves.htm,** and then press ENTER to create the relative link to the Montana National Parks and Preserves page.

7 Select Nez Perce in the second table, click the Link box, type `nez_perce.htm,` and then press ENTER to create the relative link to the Nez Perce National Historic Trail page.

Q&A Why are we creating a link to the current page?

The links table serves as the footer, and will be repeated on each page in the site.

8 Click the Save button on the Standard toolbar.

9 Press the F12 key to view the Web page, and then scroll as necessary to view the links (Figure 3–38).

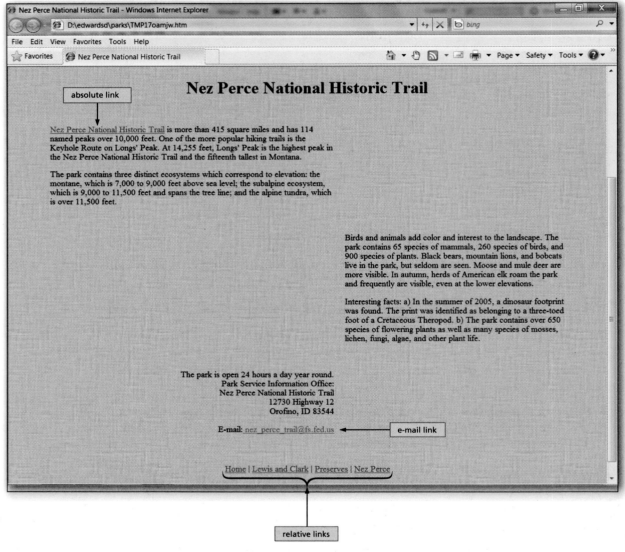

Figure 3–38

10 Click the Home link to display the index.htm page, and then click the browser Back button and test each of the links, including the e-mail link.

11 Close the browser and return to the Dreamweaver window.

Editing and Modifying Table Structure

Thus far, you have created two tables and made adjustments in Dreamweaver for the Nez Perce National Historic Trail Web page. For various reasons, as you create and develop Web sites, you will need to edit and modify a table, change the dimensions of a table, add rows and columns, or delete the table and start over. The following section describes how to edit, modify, and delete table elements within the structure. Several options are available to accomplish the same task.

Delete a Row or Column   Select a row or column and then press the DELETE key. You also can delete a row or column by clicking a cell within the row or column, clicking Modify on the Application bar, pointing to Table, and then clicking Delete Row or Delete Column on the submenu. Or click a cell within a row or column, right-click to display the context menu, point to Table, and then click Delete Row or Delete Column.

Insert a Row or Column   Click in a cell. Right-click to display the context menu, point to Table, and then click Insert Row or Insert Column on the Table submenu. Click Modify on the Application bar, point to Table, and then click Insert Row or Insert Column on the submenu. To insert more than one row or column and to control the row or column insertion point, click in a cell, right-click to display the context menu, point to Table, and then click Insert Rows or Columns on the Table submenu to display the Insert Rows or Columns dialog box (Figure 3–39). Make your selection and then click the OK button. To add a row automatically, press the TAB key in the last cell of a table.

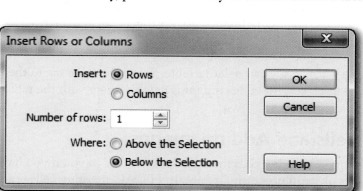

Figure 3–39

Merge and Split Cells   By merging and splitting cells, you can set alignments that are more complex than straight rows and columns. To merge two or more cells, select the cells and then click Merge Cells in the Property inspector. The selected cells must be contiguous and in the shape of a line or a rectangle. You can merge any number of adjacent cells as long as the entire selection is a line or a rectangle. To split a cell, click the cell and then click Split Cells in the Property inspector to display the Split Cell dialog box (Figure 3–40 on the next page). In the Split Cell dialog box, specify how to split the cell and then click the OK button. You can split a cell into any number of rows or columns, regardless of whether it was merged previously. When you split a cell into two rows, the other cells in the same row as the split cell are not split. If you split a cell into two or more columns, the other cells in the same column are not split. To select a cell quickly, click in the cell and then click the <td> tag on the tag selector.

BTW

Deleting Cells
If you delete a cell, the content also is deleted. Dreamweaver does not caution you that this will occur. If you accidentally remove content, click the Undo button on the Standard toolbar, or, on the Edit menu, click the Undo command.

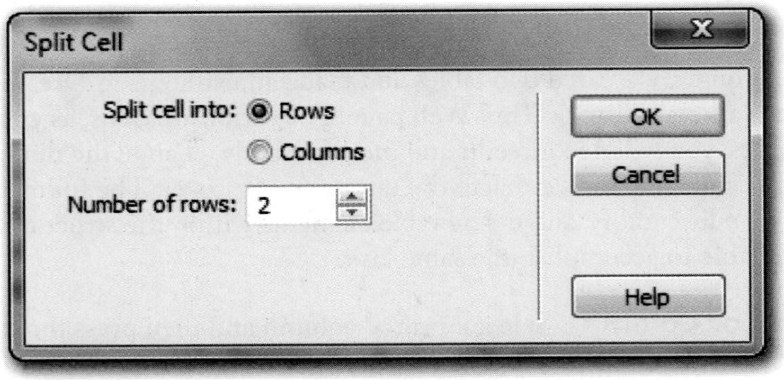

Figure 3–40

Resize a Table, Columns, and Rows   You can resize an entire table or resize individual rows and columns. To resize the table, select the table and change the W (width) in the Property inspector. A second method is to select the table and then drag one of the table selection handles. When you resize an entire table, all of the cells in the table change size proportionately. If you have assigned explicit widths or heights to a cell or cells within the table, resizing the table changes the visual size of the cells in the Document window but does not change the specified widths and heights of the cells. To resize a column or row, select the column or row and change the W or H numbers in the Property inspector. A second method to resize a column is to click the column border and then drag the border right or left. A second method to resize a row is to click the row border and then drag up or down.

Delete a Table   You easily can delete a table. Select the table tag in the tag selector and then press the DELETE key. All table content is deleted along with the table.

BTW

Splitting and Merging Cells
An alternative approach to merging and splitting cells is to increase or decrease the number of rows or columns spanned by a cell.

Merging Cells and Adding Images

The concept of merging cells most likely is familiar to you if you have worked with spreadsheets or word processing tables. In HTML, merging cells is a more complicated process. Dreamweaver, however, simplifies merging cells by hiding some complex HTML table restructuring code behind an easy-to-use interface in the Property inspector. Dreamweaver also makes it easy to add images to a table. When you add and then select an image in a table cell, the Property inspector displays the same properties as were displayed when you added and selected an image in the Document window in Chapter 2. When the image in the cell is not selected, the Property inspector displays the same properties as it does for any cell. These properties were described earlier in this chapter.

To Merge Two Cells in a Table

You will merge two cells (rows 1 and 2, column 1) so you can add four images to the Nez Perce National Historic Trail page. The following steps show how to merge two cells.

1

• If necessary, scroll up and then click in row 1, column 1 in the first table.

• Drag to select the cells in rows 1 and 2 in column 1 (Figure 3–41).

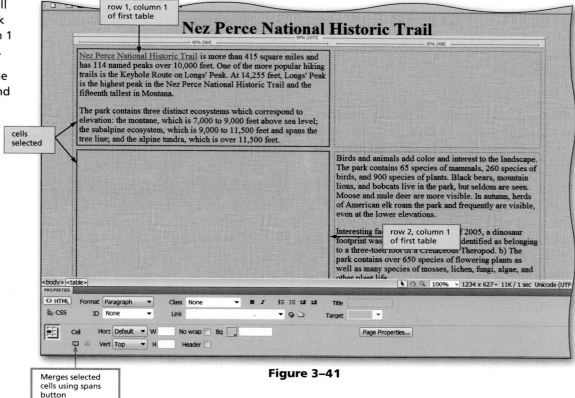

Figure 3–41

2

• Click the 'Merges selected cells using spans' button to merge the cells (Figure 3–42).

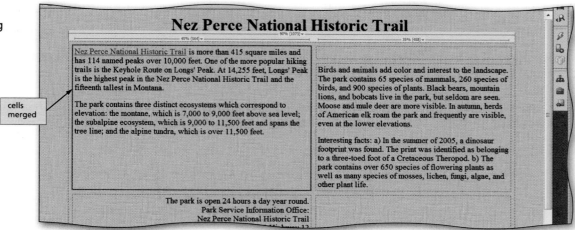

Figure 3–42

To Disable the Image Tag Accessibility Attributes Dialog Box

Recall from Chapter 2 that when you inserted an image, the default Image Tag Accessibility Attributes dialog box was displayed. In this dialog box, you can add Alternate text or create a link to a text file with a long description. For images in this chapter and the other chapters in this book, you insert alternate text using the Property inspector. Therefore, you can disable the Image Tag Accessibility Attributes dialog box now. The following steps show how to disable the Image Tag Accessibility Attributes dialog box.

1

- Click Edit on the Application bar, and then click Preferences to display the Preferences dialog box.

- Click Accessibility in the Category list to display the accessibility options.

Where can I find more information on accessibility?

For additional information on making Web content accessible for people with disabilities, search for *Accessibility* using the Dreamweaver CS5 Help system.

- If necessary, click the check boxes to deselect Form objects, Frames, Media, and Images, which disables the Image Tag Accessibility Attributes dialog box (Figure 3–43).

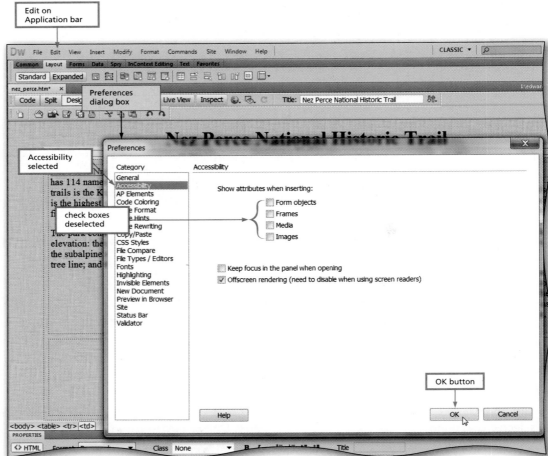

Figure 3–43

2

- Click the OK button.

To Add Images to a Table

Next, you add four images to the table. You then align the four images within the table cells and modify the size of the images. The following steps illustrate how to display the images in the Assets panel and then add, align, and modify images in a table using Standard mode.

1

- Click the Expand Panels button to expand the panel groups, and then click the Assets tab to display the assets for this Web site.

- If necessary, click the Images button and the Site option button in the Assets panel to display the images for this Web site.

Q&A

What should I do if the Assets panel does not display all my images?

Click the Refresh Site List button to view the images.

- Click at the beginning of row 1, column 1 in the first table, and then press the ENTER key to insert a blank line.

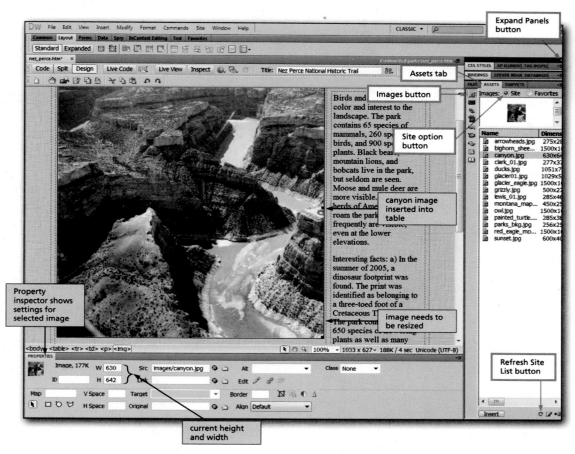

Figure 3–44

- Click the new blank line in row 1, column 1.

- Drag the canyon.jpg image from the Assets panel to the insertion point in the merged cell (Figure 3–44).

2

- With the image still selected, double-click the W box and change the width to 315.

- Double-click the H box, change the height to 320, and then press the ENTER key (Figure 3–45).

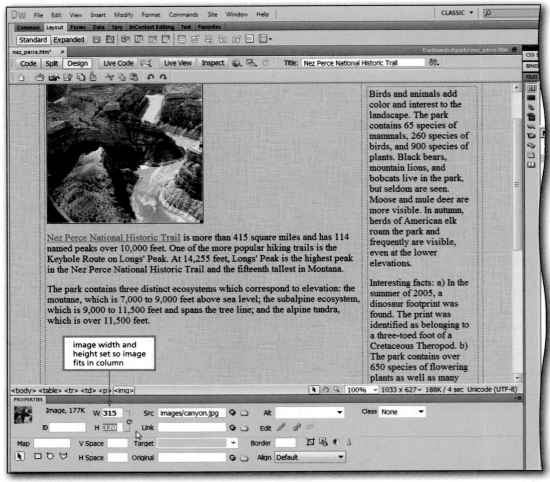

Figure 3–45

3

- Click the ID text box in the Property inspector and type `nez_perce` as the image ID.

- Click the Alt box, type **Nez Perce Canyon**, and then press the ENTER key to add the Alt text.

- Scroll as necessary to display the completed image (Figure 3–46).

Q&A

The left column of the table is still widened, even after resizing the image. What should I do?

If the table column isn't resized when you resize the image, move the insertion point above the column, and then click to select the column, click anywhere outside the cell containing the image, or press the F5 key to refresh the page.

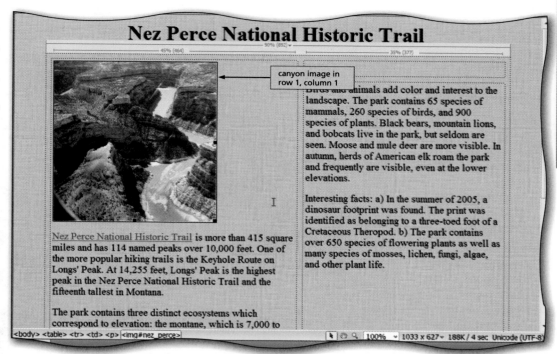

Figure 3–46

4

- Click to the right of the image to deselect the canyon image.

- Press the ENTER key to insert a blank line after the canyon image (Figure 3–47).

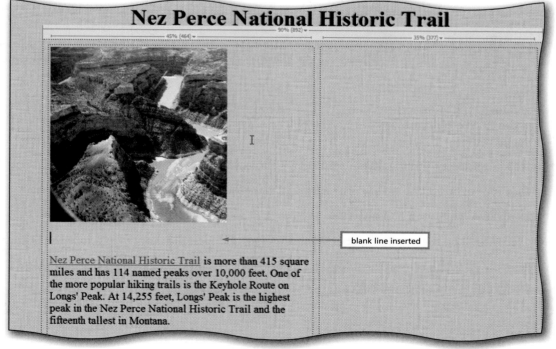

Figure 3–47

5

- Click the canyon image, click the Align button in the Property inspector, and then click Middle to align the image in the middle of the line.

- Click row 1, column 2 and then type the Bighorn sheep text as indicated in Table 3–4 on page DW 207.

- Press the ENTER key, and then drag the bighorn_sheep image from the Assets panel to the insertion point to insert the image in the table.

- Verify that the bighorn_sheep image is selected, click the ID box in the Property inspector, and then type **bighorn** to name the image.

- Press the TAB key and then type **500** in the W box to set the image width.

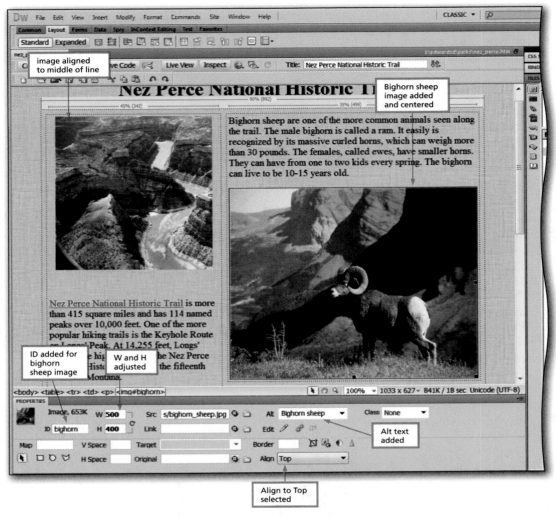

Figure 3–48

- Press the TAB key and then type **400** in the H box to set the image height.

- Click the Alt box, type **Bighorn sheep** as the Alt text, and then press the ENTER key.

- Click the Align button and select Top to align the top of the image at the top of the line.

- Click Format on the Application bar, point to Align, and then click Center to center the resized image in the cell.

- Press the F5 key to refresh the page, and then scroll as necessary to display the sheep image (Figure 3–48).

Q&A The width of the table and its columns changed after resizing the image. What should I do?

Press the F5 key to refresh the page.

Q&A How are the alignment options in the Property inspector different from those on the Format menu?

When you are working with images, you use the options on the Align pop-up menu in the Property inspector to align the image in relation to other objects, such as the current line or table cell. You use the options on the Align submenu on the Format menu to align text or objects in relation to the page. However, when you're working in a table, the options in the Align submenu align text or objects with a column.

6

- Click at the end of row 1, column 1 and then press the ENTER key.

- Drag the owl image to the insertion point to insert the image in the table.

- Click the ID text box in the Property inspector and then type **owl** as the image ID.

- Press the TAB key and then type **500** in the W box as the image width.

- Press the TAB key and then type **315** as the image height.

- Click the Alt box, type **Nez Perce owl** as the Alt text, and then press the ENTER key.

- Click Format on the Application bar, point to Align, and then click Center to center the resized image. Scroll as necessary to display the owl image.

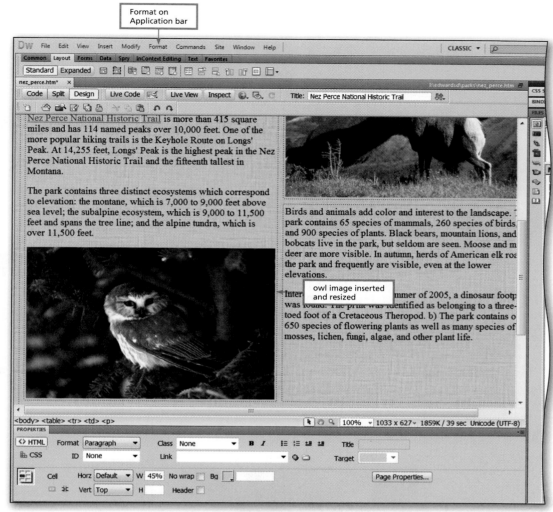

Figure 3–49

- Click the Align button in the Property inspector and then click Top.

- Click anywhere on the page to deselect the image, and then press the F5 key to refresh the page (Figure 3–49).

7

- Click row 3, column 2, type **The Nez Perce National Historic Trail is managed by the U.S. Forestry Service** and then press the ENTER key (Figure 3–50).

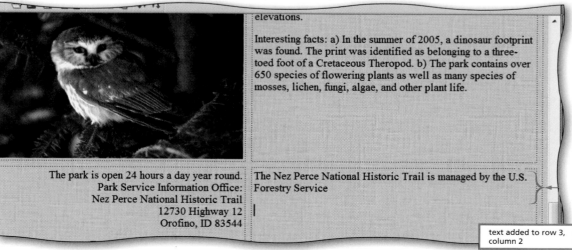

Figure 3–50

8

- Select the text, click Format on the Application bar, point to Align, and then click Right to align the text to the right (Figure 3–51).

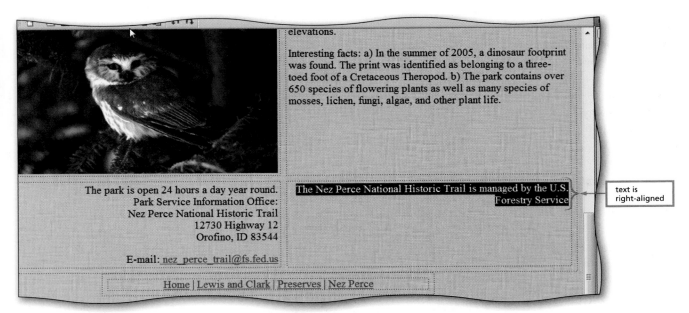

Figure 3–51

9

- Click below the text you just entered.

- Drag the arrowheads.jpg image from the Assets panel to the insertion point.

- Click the Align button in the Property inspector, and then click Right to right-align the image.

- Change the W value in the Property inspector to 125 to change the image width, and change the H value to 131 to change the image height (Figure 3–52).

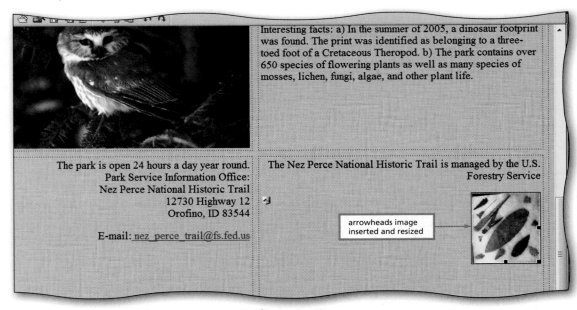

Figure 3–52

10

- Click the Save button on the Standard toolbar to save your work.

- Press the F12 key to view the page in your browser (Figure 3–53).

11

- Close the browser window to redisplay Dreamweaver.

- Close the Nez Perce National Historic Trail page.

Figure 3–53

Creating the Glacier National Park Web Page

To create the Glacier National Park Web page, you open a new document. You start by applying the background image.

To Open a New Document and Add a Background Image to the Glacier National Park Web Page

The following steps illustrate how to open a new document and apply a background image.

1 Click File on the Application bar and then click New to begin creating a new Web page. If necessary, click Blank Page, click HTML in the Page Type list, and then click <none> in the Layout list.

2 Click the Create button to create the page.

3 Click the Save button on the Standard toolbar to name the file, and then type `glacier` as the file name. Save the Web page in the parks folder.

4 If necessary, display the Property inspector and then click the Page Properties button to prepare for applying the background image.

5 Click Appearance (HTML) in the Category list to display the Appearance options.

6 Click the Browse button to the right of the Background image box to find the background image.

7 If necessary, navigate to and open the parks\images folder. Click parks_bkg.jpg and then click the OK button to select the background image.

8 Click the OK button in the Page Properties dialog box to apply the background image (Figure 3–54).

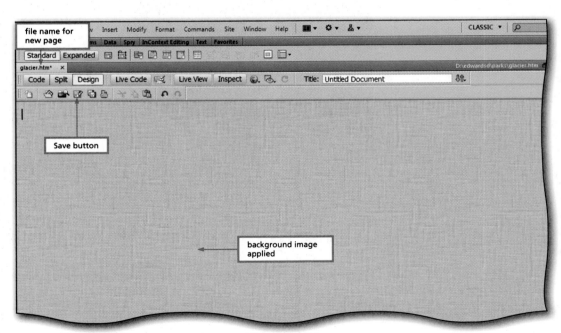

Figure 3–54

To Insert and Center a Table

Next, you enter a title, and then insert and center a four-row, two-column table. You use the table to create the Glacier National Park page by adding text and four images. You modify image placement and image size. You also add an absolute link and e-mail addresses for the park. Then you copy and paste the Links table from the Nez Perce National Historic Trail page to the Glacier National Park page.

1 Select the text in the Title box on the Document toolbar, and then type `Glacier National Park` as the page title.

2 Click the Web page and then type `Glacier National Park.` Apply Heading 1 to the text and then center it on the page. Click at the end of the heading, and then press ENTER.

3 Click the Table button on the Layout tab on the Insert bar to begin inserting a new table.

4 In the Table dialog box, change the settings as follows: Rows 4, Columns 2, Table width 90 Percent, Cell padding 5, and Cell spacing 5. (Do not enter a Border thickness value.)

5 Click the Summary text box, type `Glacier National Park feature page` as the Summary text, and then click the OK button to insert the table.

6 Click the Table text box in the Property inspector, type `glacier_01` as the ID text, and then press the ENTER key to accept the new ID.

7 Click the Align button and then click Center to center the table.

8 Click the Save button on the Standard toolbar to save the table (Figure 3–55).

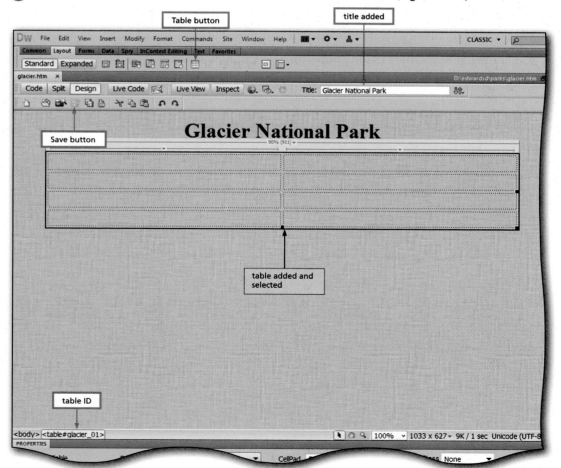

Figure 3–55

Spanning Rows and Columns

An understanding of HTML and how it relates to a table and to parts of a table provides you with the ability to use code to select a table and table components and to modify a table. Merging and varying the span of columns (as you did in the Nez Perce National Historic Trail page) and merging and varying the span of rows is helpful for grouping information, adding emphasis, creating balance, or deleting empty cells. When you merge two or more cells in a row, you are spanning a column. Continuing with the <table> example on page DW 198 and spanning the two cells in row 1, the HTML tags would be <td colspan="2">First cellSecond cell</td>. When you merge two cells in a column, you are spanning a row. The attribute rowspan would replace colspan in the above example. Understanding colspan and rowspan will help you determine when and if two columns or two rows have been merged.

To Adjust the Cell Alignment and Column Width

In the following steps, you will adjust the width for columns 1 and 2 in the Glacier National Park page, and then change the vertical alignment to Top within both columns.

1 Click in row 1, column 1, and then drag to select all the cells in the table.

2 Click the Vert button in the Property inspector, and then click Top to top-align the cells.

3 Click row 2, column 1 to adjust the width of column 1.

4 Click the W box in the Property inspector, type **60%,** and then press the ENTER key to set the width of column 1.

5 Click row 2, column 2 to adjust the width of column 2.

6 Click the W box in the Property inspector, type **40%,** and then press the ENTER key to set the width of column 2 (Figure 3–56 on the next page).

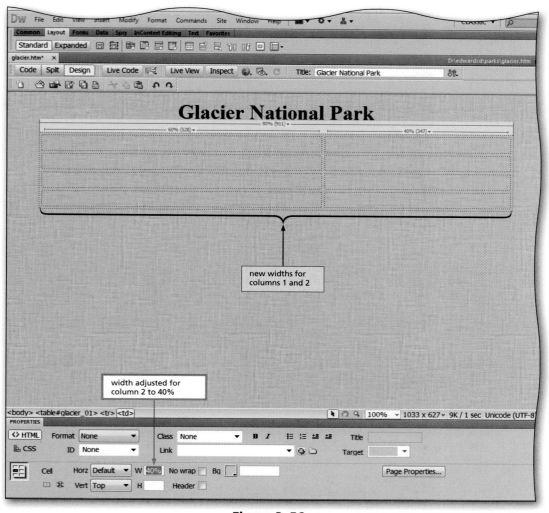

Figure 3–56

To Merge Cells in Row 1

For the Glacier National Park page, you merge columns 1 and 2 in row 1, and then merge rows 2 and 3 in column 2. The following step illustrates how to merge the cells.

- Click row 1, column 1 and then drag to select all of row 1.

- Click the 'Merges selected cells using spans' button in the Property inspector to merge the selected cells into one row.

- Click row 2, column 2 and then drag to select row 3, column 2.

- Click the 'Merges selected cells using spans' button in the Property inspector to merge the selected cells into one column (Figure 3–57).

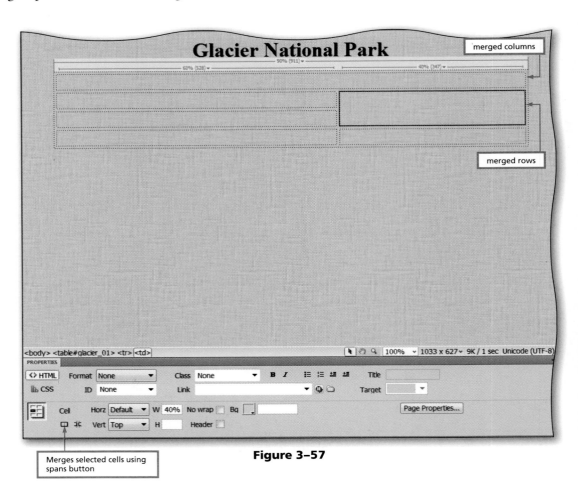

Figure 3–57

Adding Text to the Table

Now you add text to the table. Table 3–5 on the next page contains the text for the Glacier National Park Web page. You can select one of two methods to enter the text: a) copy the text from the data file and paste it into the appropriate cell in the table; or b) type the text in the appropriate cell as you did for the Nez Perce page.

To copy and paste text, open the data file in Microsoft Word or a text document. Select the text and then select Copy. Click the appropriate Dreamweaver cell and then click Paste. If the copy and paste text option is not available, use the same process you used to type the text as you did with the Nez Perce Web page.

Table 3–5 Text for the Glacier National Park Page	
Section	**Text**
Part 1	Glacier National Park is one of the largest national parks in the lower 48 states and is one of the most beautiful of America's national parks. Native Americans referred to the park as the "Shining Mountains" and the "Backbone of the World." The park is home to over seventy species of mammals including the wolverine, grizzly bear, gray wolf, and lynx. Over 260 species of birds visit or reside in the park.
Part 2	<ENTER>Many people, when they think of Glacier, think of the grizzly bear or the brown bear. Glacier contains one of the remaining grizzly bear populations in the lower 48 states. The park, however, is home to over 60 species of other animals, including elk, gray wolf, wolverine, cougar, mountain goat, and bighorn sheep, to name a few. The lynx and grizzly are threatened species, while the gray wolf is endangered.
Part 3	A park visitor also can find a number of amphibians — some quite unusual. The tailed frog, for instance, is named for the male's inside-out reproductive opening. This is the only frog in North American that fertilizes the female's eggs internally.
Part 4	Glacier Park's cold winter is not an invitation to many reptiles. However, three species of reptiles live in the park. The Western painted turtle is one of the favorite reptiles of many visitors. Their bottom shell has bright yellow and orange markings, and the skin is streaked with yellow. They can be seen basking in the sun on logs around low elevation lakes. <ENTER>
Part 5	<ENTER>The park is open 24 hours a day year round</br> Park Service Information Office:</br> Glacier National Park</br> PO Box 128</br> West Glacier, MT 59936-0128

To Add and Format Text for the Glacier National Park Web page

Now you are ready to add text to the table. The following steps illustrate how to add and format text for the Glacier National Park Web page.

1

• Click row 1, and then type the text of Part 1 as shown in Table 3–5 (Figure 3–58).

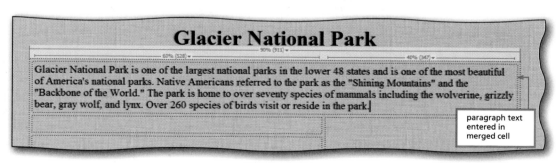

Figure 3–58

2

● Click row 2, column 1, and then type the text of Part 2 as shown in Table 3–5 on page DW 231, pressing the ENTER key as indicated (Figure 3–59).

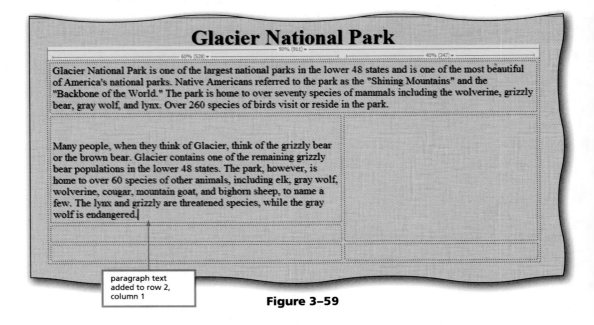

paragraph text added to row 2, column 1

Figure 3–59

3

● Click row 3, column 1, and then type the text of Part 3 as shown in Table 3–5 (Figure 3–60).

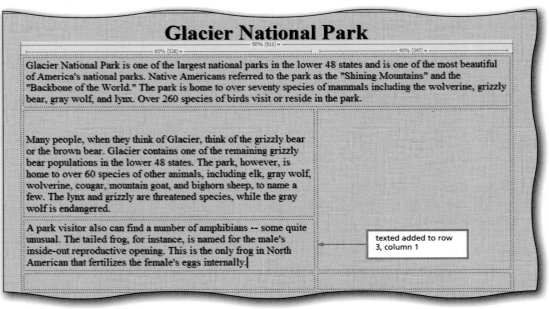

texted added to row 3, column 1

Figure 3–60

4

- Click row 4, column 1, and then type the text of Part 4 as shown in Table 3–5 on page DW 231, pressing the ENTER key as indicated (Figure 3–61).

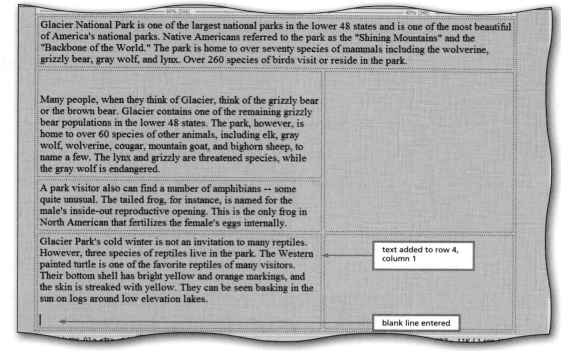

Figure 3–61

5

- Click row 4, column 2, and then type the text of Part 5 as shown in Table 3–5, pressing the ENTER key and inserting line breaks as indicated in Table 3–5.

- With the insertion point in row 4, column 2, click the <td> tag in the tag selector to select the cell.

- Click Format on the Application bar, point to Align, and then click Right to right-align the text (Figure 3–62).

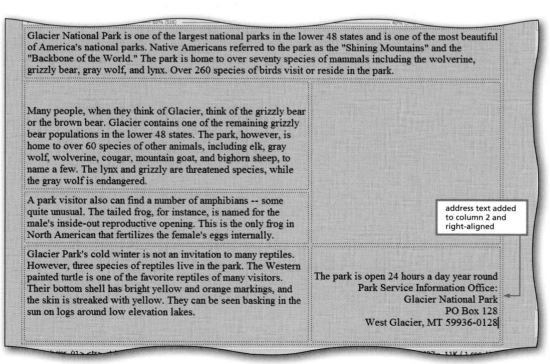

Figure 3–62

Adding Images and Image Borders

The purpose of most tables in a Web page is to provide a structure for the positioning of text and images. When a table is created within Dreamweaver, therefore, the default border is 0 (zero), or no visible border. You can add a border to a table when you create the table using the Border thickness text box in the Table dialog box. When the table is selected, the table border option also is available through the Property inspector.

Plan Ahead

Determine when to add borders.
Applying a border to a table helps to structure the table content. Adding a border to an image transforms the image into a graphical element itself. Depending on the content, a table border can become a visual cue for the reader by separating content. Experiment with border thickness to achieve the effect you want to create.

You also can add borders to images. The **Border** command specifies the width, in pixels, of the line that frames the image. The alignment options for images are listed in Table 3–6. Note that these are the same as the alignment options for table cells.

Table 3–6 Image Alignment Options

Alignment Option	Description
Default	Specifies a baseline alignment; default may vary depending on the user's browser
Baseline	Aligns the cell content at the bottom of the cell (same as Bottom)
Top	Aligns the cell content at the top of the cell
Bottom	Aligns the cell content at the bottom of the cell
TextTop	Aligns the top of the image with the top of the tallest character in the text line
Absolute Middle	Aligns the middle of the image with the middle of the text in the current line
Absolute Bottom	Aligns the bottom of the image with the bottom of the line of text
Left	Places the selected image on the left margin, wrapping text around it to the right; if left-aligned text precedes the object on the line, it generally forces left-aligned objects to wrap to a new line
Middle	Aligns the middle of the image with the baseline of the current line
Right	Places the image on the right margin, wrapping text around the object to the left; if right-aligned text precedes the object on the line, it generally forces right-aligned objects to wrap to a new line

To Add Images, Image Borders, and a Table Border

The next task is to add images to the Web page. In the following steps, you insert, resize, align, and add a border to the images, and then add a border to the table.

- Click row 2, column 1 to select the first cell in row 2, and then drag the glacier_ eagle image from the Assets panel to the insertion point.

- Click the ID text box in the Property inspector and then type `glacier_ eagle` as the image ID.

- Change the width in the W box to 335 and the height in the H box to 245 to resize the image.

- Click the H Space box and then type 50 to set the horizontal spacing.

Figure 3–63

- Click the Alt box, type `Glacier eagle,` and then press ENTER to enter the Alt text.

- Scroll to display the glacier_eagle image.

 **Experiment**

- Click the Border text box, type any value from 1 to 20, and then press ENTER.

- In the Border text box, type 2 to set the border thickness.

- Click the Align button and then click Absolute Middle to align the image in the middle of the line.

- Click Format on the Application bar, point to Align, and then click Center to center the image.

- Press the F5 key to refresh the page (Figure 3–63).

2

- If necessary, scroll down and click at the beginning of the blank line at the end of row 4, column 1 to prepare for inserting the next image.

- Drag the sunset image to the insertion point in row 4, column 1 to add the sunset image to the table.

- Click the ID text box in the Property inspector and then type **evening_ sunset** as the image ID.

- Change the width in the W box to 500 and the height in the H box to 350 to resize the image.

- Click the V Space box and then type **10** to set the vertical spacing.

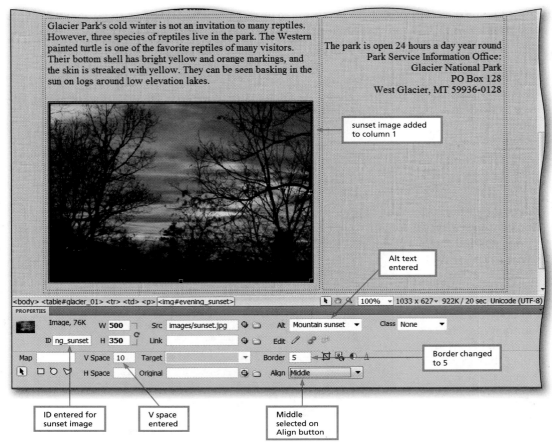

Figure 3–64

- Click the Alt box, type **Mountain sunset,** and then press ENTER to enter the Alt text.

- Click the Border text box and then type **5** to set the border thickness.

- Click the Align button and then click Middle to align the image in the middle of the line.

- Press the F5 key to refresh the page (Figure 3–64).

- Click the first line in row 2, column 2, and then drag the red_eagle_ mountain image to the insertion point to insert the image in the cell.

- Click the ID text box in the Property inspector and then type **red_eagle_ mountain** as the image ID.

- Change the width in the W box to 475 and the height in the H box to 335 to resize the image.

- Click the Alt box, type **Red Eagle Mountain** and then press ENTER to enter the Alt text for the image.

- Click the Border text box and then type 5 to set the border thickness.

- Click the Align button and then click Middle to align the image.

- Press the F5 key to refresh the page, and then scroll as necessary to display the image (Figure 3–65).

Glacier National Park

Glacier National Park is one of the largest national parks in the lower 48 states and is one of the most beautiful of America's national parks. Native Americans referred to the park as the "Shining Mountains" and the "Backbone of the World." The park is home to over seventy species of mammals including the wolverine, grizzly bear, gray wolf, and lynx. Over 260 species of birds visit or reside in the park.

Many people, when they think of Glacier, think of the grizzly bear or the brown bear. Glacier contains one of the remaining grizzly bear populations in the lower 48 states. The park, however, is home to over 60 species of other animals, including the gray wolf, wolverine, cougar, mountain goat, and bighorn sheep, to name a few. The lynx and grizzly are threatened species, while the gray wolf is endangered.

<body> <table#glacier_01> <tr> <td> <img#red_eagle_mountain>

red_eagle_mountain image added to row 2, column 2

372K / 39 sec Unicode (UTF-8

Figure 3–65

- Click the blank line at the top of row 3, column 2, and then drag the painted_ turtle image to the insertion point to insert the image in the cell.

- Click the ID box in the Property inspector, and then type **painted_turtle** as the image ID.

- Click the Alt box, type **Painted turtle** and then press ENTER to enter the Alt text.

- Click the Border box, type **5**, and then press ENTER to set the border thickness.

- Click Format on the Application bar, point to Align, and then click Center to center the image (Figure 3–66).

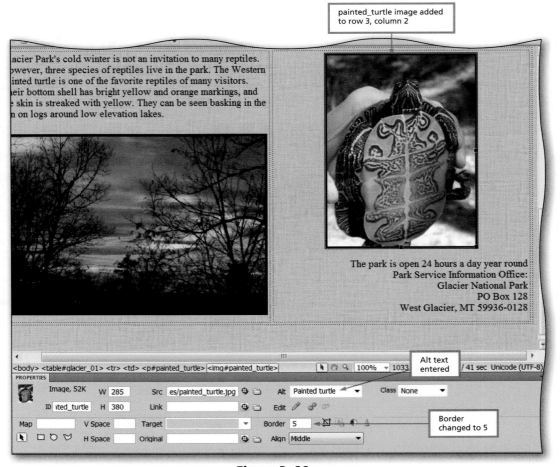

Figure 3–66

5

- Click
  <table#glacier_01>
  in the tag selector
  to select the table.

- Enter 5 in the
  Border text box,
  and then press
  ENTER to add a
  border to the table
  (Figure 3–67).

6

- Click the Save
  button to save your
  work.

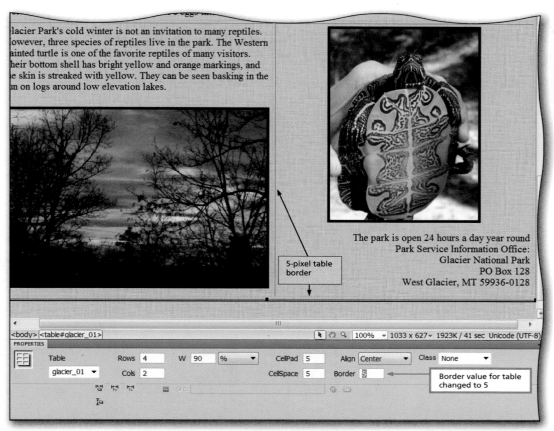

Figure 3–67

To Add Links to and Spell Check the Glacier National Park Web Page

The following steps illustrate how to add an absolute link to the Glacier National Park page, and then copy the Links table from the Nez Perce National Historic Trail page and paste it as a footer in the Glacier National Park page. You also spell check the Web page, save it, and view it in a browser.

1 If necessary, scroll down, select the text Glacier National Park in the address in row 4, column 2, type **http://www.nps.gov/glac** in the Link box, and then press ENTER to create an absolute link to the National Park Service's Web page for Glacier National Park.

2 Open the nez_perce.htm page, scroll down, and then click in the links table to set the focus on the links table.

3 Click <table#Montana_parks_links> in the tag selector to select the table, and then press CTRL+C to copy the table.

4 Click the glacier.htm document tab to return to the Glacier National Park page, click to the right of the table, press ENTER to move the insertion point to the next line, and then press CTRL+V to paste the Montana_parks_links table.

5 If necessary, select the Montana_parks_links table, click the Align button in the Property inspector, and then click Center to center the table. Click anywhere in the document to deselect the table.

6 Press the CTRL+HOME keys to move the insertion point to the beginning of the page, click Commands on the Application bar, and then click Check Spelling to begin spell checking the page. Check the spelling and make any necessary corrections.

7 Click the Save button on the Standard toolbar to save your work.

8 Press the F12 key to view the Web page in your browser (Figure 3–68).

Figure 3–68

9 Close the browser.

Head Content

HTML files consist of two main sections: the head section and the body section. The head section is one of the more important sections of a Web page. A standard HTML page contains a <head> tag and a <body> tag. Contained within the head section is site and page information. With the exception of the title, the information contained in the head is not displayed in the browser. Some of the information contained in the head is accessed by the browser, and other information is accessed by other programs such as search engines and server software. You also can display the Common category on the Insert bar and then click the Head button to display a list of commands described in the next section.

BTW

Using Meta Tags
Meta tags are information inserted into the head content area of Web pages. The meta description tag allows you to influence the description of a page in the search engines that support the tag.

Head Content Elements

Dreamweaver makes it easy to add content to the head section through the Insert menu. To access these commands, point to HTML on the Insert menu, and then point to the submenu of the command you want to select.

Meta A <meta> tag contains information about the current document. This information is used by servers, browsers, and search engines. HTML documents can have as many <meta> tags as needed. Each item uses a different set of tags.

Keywords Keywords are a list of words that someone would type into a search engine search field.

Description The description contains a sentence or two that can be used in a search engine's results page.

Refresh The <refresh> tag is processed by the browser to reload the page or load a new page after a specified amount of time has elapsed.

Base The base tag sets the base URL to provide an absolute link and/or a link target that the browser can use to resolve link conflicts.

Link The link element defines a relationship between the current document and another file. This is not the same as a link in the Document window.

Keywords, descriptions, and refresh settings are special-use cases of the meta tag.

Plan head content.

Browsers and Web search tools refer to information contained in the head section of a Web page. Although this section is not displayed in the browser window, you can set the properties of the head elements to control how your pages are identified. At a minimum, you should set properties for the following head elements:

- **Keywords:** Enter keywords you anticipate users and search engines might use to find your page. Because some search engines limit the number of keywords or characters they track, enter only a few accurate, descriptive keywords.

- **Description:** Many search engines also read the contents of the Description text. Some search engines display the Description text in the search results, so be sure to enter a meaningful description.

Plan Ahead

To Add Keywords and a Description to the Index Page

The following steps show how to add keywords and a description to the index.htm page.

1

- Open the index.htm page.

- Click Insert on the Application bar, point to HTML, point to Head Tags on the HTML submenu, and then point to Keywords on the Head Tags submenu (Figure 3–69).

Q&A

What is a keyword?

A keyword is a word or phrase that someone might type into a search engine search field.

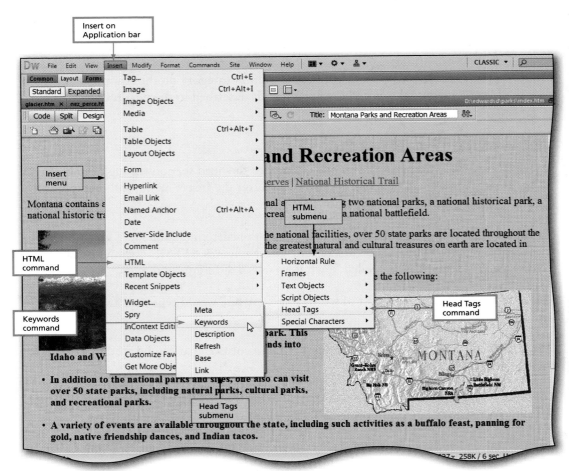

Figure 3–69

2

● Click the Keywords command to display the Keywords dialog box.

● Type **parks, Montana, national parks, national preserves** in the Keywords text box to add the keywords to the Keywords dialog box (Figure 3–70).

Q&A

What does a search engine typically do with the keywords?

When a search engine begins a search for any of the keywords, the Web site address will be displayed in the search results.

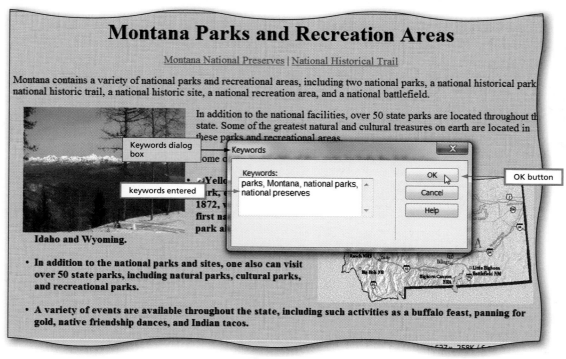

Figure 3–70

3

● Click the OK button to add the keywords to the head tag and close the Keywords dialog box.

● Click Insert on the Application bar, point to HTML, point to Head Tags on the HTML submenu, and then click Description on the Head Tags submenu to open the Description dialog box.

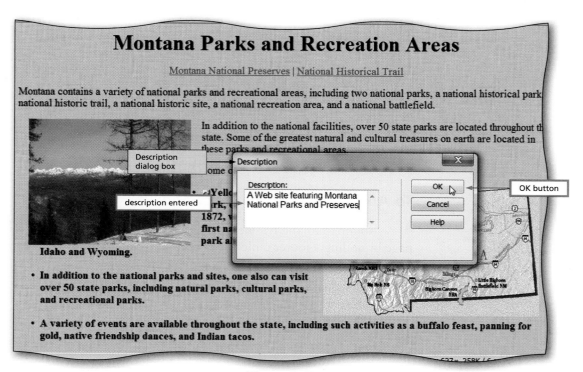

Figure 3–71

• Type **A Web site featuring Montana National Parks and Preserves** in the Description text box to describe the Web page (Figure 3–71 on the previous page).

Q&A

What is the purpose of the description?

The description contains a sentence or two that can be used in a search engine's results page.

4

• Click the OK button to close the Description dialog box.

• Click the Code button on the Document toolbar to display the page in Code view (Figure 3–72).

5

• Click the Design button on the Document toolbar to return to Design view.

• Click the Save button on the Standard toolbar to save your work.

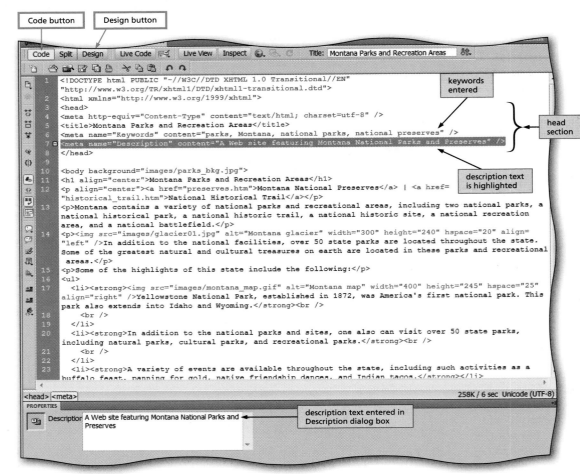

Figure 3–72

Other Ways

1. Click Code button on Document toolbar, type keywords code in code window

To Add Links to the Index Page

To integrate the two new pages in the Web site, you need to modify the index.htm page by adding a footer table at the bottom of the page. The following steps show how to delete the existing links and add a Links table.

1 Click the glacier.htm document tab to display that Web page, scroll to the bottom of the page, select the Montana_parks_links table, right-click the selection to display the context menu, and then click Copy to copy the table.

2 Click the index.htm document tab, scroll to the bottom of the page, click to the right of the last sentence (Most events are free.), and then press ENTER to move the insertion point to the next line.

3 Right-click near the insertion point to display the context menu and then click Paste to paste the Montana_parks_links table into the index page.

4 Click to the right of the Nez Perce text in the Montana_parks_links table, press the SPACEBAR, press SHIFT+| (vertical bar), press the SPACEBAR, and then type `Glacier National Park.`

5 Drag to select the space, vertical bar, and space you just entered, delete the text in the Link box in the Property inspector, click the Glacier National Park text in the Montana_parks_links table, and then change the entry in the Link box to glacier.htm (Figure 3–73).

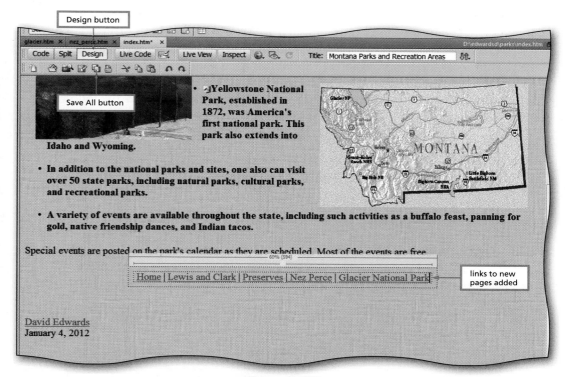

Figure 3–73

6 Scroll to the top of the index.htm page, select the two links, and then press DELETE to remove the links from the top of the page.

7 Scroll to the bottom of the page, select the space, vertical bar, space, and Glacier National Park text in the Montana_parks_links table, and then press CTRL+C to copy the linked text.

8 Click the glacier.htm document tab, click at the end of the Montana_parks_links table at the bottom of the page, and then press CTRL+V to insert the link.

9 Click the nez_perce.htm document tab, click at the end of the Montana_parks_links table at the bottom of the page, and then press CTRL+V to insert the link.

10 Click the index.htm document tab, and then click the Save All button on the Standard toolbar to save your work on the three pages.

11 Press the F12 key to preview the page in a browser, test each link to verify that it works, and then close the browser.

Publishing a Web Site

In Chapter 1 you defined a local site, and in Chapters 1, 2, and 3 you added Web pages to the local site. This local site resides on your computer's hard disk, a network drive, or possibly a USB drive. You can view the organization of all files and folders in your site through the Files panel.

To prepare a Web site and make it available for others to view requires that you publish your site by putting it on a Web server for public access. A Web server is an Internet- or intranet-connected computer that delivers, or *serves up*, Web pages. You upload files to a folder on a server and download files to a folder in the Files panel on your computer. Generally, when Web site designers publish to a folder on a Web site, they do so by using a file transfer (FTP) program such as WS_FTP, Cute FTP, or Windows Web Folders. Dreamweaver, however, includes built-in support that enables you to connect and transfer your local site to a Web server without using an additional program. To publish to a Web server requires that you have access to a Web server.

Publishing and maintaining your site using Dreamweaver involves the following steps:

1. Using the Site Setup dialog box to enter the FTP information
2. Specifying the Web server to which you want to publish your Web site
3. Connecting to the Web server and uploading the files
4. Synchronizing the local and remote sites

Your school or company may have a server that you can use to upload your Web site. Free Web hosting services such as those provided by Angelfire or Tripod are other options. These services, as well as many other hosting services, also offer low-cost Web hosting from approximately $3.95 to $9.95 a month. The FreeSite.com Web site contains a list of free and inexpensive hosting services, and FreeWebspace.net provides a PowerSearch form for free and low-cost hosting.

Table 3–7 contains a list of Web hosting services. Appendix C contains step-by-step instructions on publishing a Web site to a remote folder.

Table 3–7 Web Site Hosting Services		
Name	**Web Site**	**Cost**
Angelfire	angelfire.lycos.com	Free (ad-supported); starting at $4.95 monthly ad-free
FreeWebspace.net	freewebspace.net	A searchable guide for free Web space
The FreeSite.com	thefreesite.com/Free_Web_Space	A list of free and inexpensive hosting sites
Tripod	tripod.lycos.com	Free (ad-supported); starting at $4.95 monthly ad-free

If required by your instructor, publish the Montana Parks Web site to a remote server by following the steps in Appendix C.

Quitting Dreamweaver

After you add pages to your Web site and add the head content, Chapter 3 is complete, so you can quit Dreamweaver.

To Close the Web Site and Quit Dreamweaver

The following step illustrates how to close the Web site, quit Dreamweaver CS5, and return to Windows.

1 Click the Close button on the right corner of the Dreamweaver title bar. If prompted, click the Yes button to save any changes.

Chapter Summary

Chapter 3 introduced you to tables and to Web page design using tables. You created two Web pages. You added a border to one of the Web pages. You merged and split cells and learned how to add text and images to the tables and how to create links to other pages. Finally, you added head content to one of the Web pages. The items listed below include all the new skills you have learned in this chapter.

1. Insert a table (DW 193)
2. Select and center a table (DW 201)
3. Change vertical alignment from Middle to Top (DW 203)
4. Specify column width (DW 205)
5. Add a table ID to the Nez Perce National Historic Trail table (DW 206)
6. Add text to the Nez Perce National Historic Trail Web page (DW 208)
7. Add a second table to the Nez Perce National Historic Trail Web page (DW 210)
8. Adjust the table width, center the text, and add the table ID (DW 212)
9. Add links to the Nez Perce National Historic Trail Web page (DW 213)
10. Merge two cells in a table (DW 217)
11. Disable the Image Tag Accessibility Attributes dialog box (DW 218)
12. Add images, image borders, and a table border (DW 235)
13. Add keywords and a description to the index page (DW 242)

Learn It Online

Test your knowledge of chapter content and key terms.

Instructions: To complete the Learn It Online exercises, start your browser, click the Address bar, and then enter the Web address `scsite.com/dwcs5/learn.` When the Dreamweaver CS5 Learn It Online page is displayed, click the link for the exercise you want to complete and then read the instructions.

Chapter Reinforcement TF, MC, and SA
A series of true/false, multiple choice, and short answer questions that test your knowledge of the chapter content.

Flash Cards
An interactive learning environment where you identify chapter key terms associated with displayed definitions.

Practice Test
A series of multiple choice questions that test your knowledge of chapter content and key terms.

Who Wants to Be a Computer Genius?
An interactive game that challenges your knowledge of chapter content in the style of a television quiz show.

Wheel of Terms
An interactive game that challenges your knowledge of chapter key terms in the style of the television show *Wheel of Fortune*.

Crossword Puzzle Challenge
A crossword puzzle that challenges your knowledge of key terms presented in the chapter.

Apply Your Knowledge

Reinforce the skills and apply the concepts you learned in this chapter.

Adding a Table to a Web Page

Instructions: In this activity, you modify a Web page by adding a table and then inserting images in the table. Figure 3–74 shows the completed Web page. Make sure you have downloaded the data files for this chapter. See the inside back cover of this book for instructions for downloading the Data Files for Students, or contact your instructor for information about accessing the required files for this book.

Figure 3–74

Perform the following tasks:

1. Start Dreamweaver, and then copy the apply_ch03.htm file from the Chapter03\apply data files folder into the apply folder for your Apply Exercises local Web site. (For example, the apply folder might be stored on H:\edwardsd\apply.) Copy the three image files from the Chapter03\apply\ images folder to the apply\images folder for the Apply Exercises site. (For example, the images folder might be stored on H:\edwardsd\apply\images.)

2. Open the Apply Exercises site.

3. Open the apply_ch03.htm page. Add the apply_bkg background image to the page.

4. Click to the right of the "Plants of the Week" heading and then press ENTER.

5. Insert a one-row, three-column table with a table width of 90 percent, border thickness of 3 pixels, cell padding of 5, and cell spacing of 10.

6. Click the Summary box, type **Favorite plants**, and then click OK to insert the table.

7. Center the table and type `favorite_plants` in the Table box to enter the table ID.

8. Insert the plant01 image into row 1, column 1.

9. Use the following properties for the plant01 image:

   Image ID: sunflowers

   Width: 255 pixels

   Height: 170 pixels

   Alt text: sunflowers

10. Insert the plant02 image into row 1, column 2.

11. Use the following properties for the plant02 image:

    Image ID: purple_passion

    Width: 255 pixels

    Height: 170 pixels

    Alt text: Purple passion

12. Insert the plant03 image into row 1, column 3.

13. Use the following properties for the plant03 image:

    Image ID: roses

    Width: 255 pixels

    Height: 170 pixels

    Alt text: Roses are white

14. Center each image in its table cell.

15. Save your document and then view it in your browser. Submit the Web page in the format specified by your instructor.

Extend Your Knowledge

Extend the skills you learned in this chapter and experiment with new skills. You may need to use Help to complete the assignment.

Adding, Aligning, and Resizing an Image on a Web Page

Instructions: In this activity, you create a Web page, insert text, add a table, insert images, and then align and resize the images. Figure 3–75 shows the completed Web page. Make sure you have downloaded the data files for this chapter. See the inside back cover of this book for instructions for downloading the Data Files for Students, or contact your instructor for information about accessing the required files for this book.

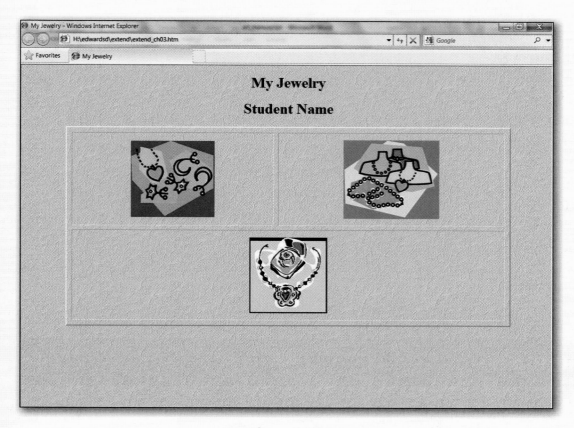

Figure 3–75

Perform the following tasks:

1. Start Dreamweaver, and then copy the three image files from the Chapter03\extend\images folder to the extend\images folder for the Extend Exercises site. (For example, the images folder might be stored on H:\edwardsd\extend\images.)

2. Open the Extend Exercises site, create a new HTML document, and then save the page as extend_ch03.htm. Apply the extend_bkg background image to the page.

3. Enter the following heading at the top of the page: My Jewelry. Press ENTER and then type your name.

4. Apply the Heading 1 format to the heading and your name, and then center both lines. Click to the right of your name and then press ENTER.

5. Insert a two-row, two-column table with a table width of 85 percent, border thickness of 3 pixels, cell padding of 15, and cell spacing of 10.

6. Use jewelry as the table ID text, and then center the table.

7. Drag the jewelry01 image to row 1, column 1. Use the following properties for the jewelry01 image:

   Image ID: purple_jewelry

   Width: 175 pixels

   Height: 165 pixels

   Alt text: purple jewelry

8. Drag the jewelry02 image to cell row 1, column 2. Use the following properties for the jewelry02 image:

   Image ID: necklaces

   Width: 200 pixels

   Height: 170 pixels

   Alt text: necklaces

9. Merge the two cells in row 2.

10. Drag the jewelry03 image to row 2. Use the following properties for the jewelry03 image:

   Image ID: jewelry_set

   Width: 163 pixels

   Height: 164 pixels

   Alt text: jewelry set

11. Align each image in the absolute middle of the cell, and then center each image.

12. Use the following text as the page title: My Jewelry.

13. Save your document and then view it in your browser. Submit the Web page in the format specified by your instructor.

Make It Right

Analyze a Web page and correct all errors and/or improve the design.

Adding an Image and E-mail Address to a Web Page

Instructions: In this activity, you modify a Web page to add a heading and a table with images. Figure 3-76 on the next page shows the completed Web page. Table 3-8 on the next page lists the properties you should use for the table and images. Make sure you have downloaded the data files for Chapter03\right. See the inside back cover of this book for instructions for downloading the Data Files for Students, or contact your instructor for information about accessing the required files for this book.

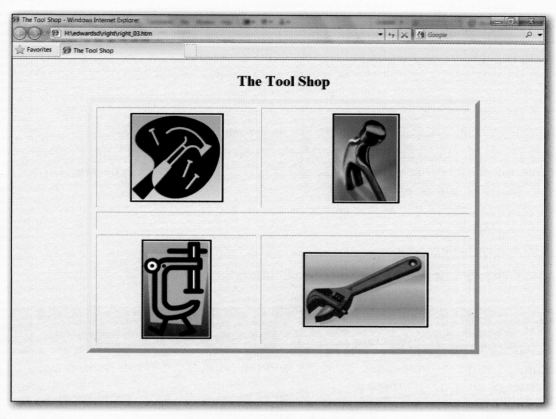

Figure 3–76

Table 3–8 Properties for Table and Images

Table Section	Image Name	Properties
Entire table	n/a	Rows: 3 Columns: 2 Width: 75 percent Border thickness: 10 Cell padding: 10 Cell spacing: 10 ID: tools Alignment: Center
Column 1, row 1	hammer01	ID: hammer_01 Alt text: regular hammer Border: 3 Alignment: Absolute Middle
Column 2, row 1	hammer02	ID: hammer_02 Alt text: special hammer Border: 3 Alignment: Absolute Middle
Column 1, row 2	blank	
Column 2, row 2	blank	
Column 1, row 3	clamp	ID: clamp Alt text: clamp Border: 3 Alignment: Middle
Column 2, row 3	wrench	ID: wrench Alt text: wrench Border: 3 Alignment: Middle

Perform the following tasks:

1. Start Dreamweaver, and then copy the right_ch03.htm file from the Chapter03\right data files folder into the right folder for your Right Exercises local Web site. Copy the four image files from the Chapter03\right\images data files folder into the right\images folder for your Right Exercises local Web site.

2. Open the Right Exercises site.

3. Open the right_ch03.htm page. Apply the right_bkg background image to the page.

4. The Web page you need to create is shown in Figure 3–76 on the previous page. Table 3–8 on the previous page lists the properties to apply to the table and the images to insert in the cells. Do not change the width or height of the images.

5. Merge the cells in row 2.

6. Center each image in its cell.

7. Save your document and then view it in your browser.

8. Submit your Web page in the format specified by your instructor.

In the Lab

Create a document using the guidelines, concepts, and skills presented in this chapter. Labs are listed in order of increasing difficulty.

Lab 1: Modifying the Computer Repair Services Web Site

Problem: Now that Bryan has a basic Web site for his Computer Repair Services business, he wants to make the site more appealing to visitors. The Web site currently contains three pages. Bryan asks you to add a fourth page with a table that includes a list of services, information about how often the services are scheduled, and the price of each service. In the table, you should merge two of the rows, add and center an image in one row, and apply a border to the entire table. You also add keywords and a description to the page. You then add a link to the home page and save the page (Figure 3–77).

Software and hardware settings determine how a Web page is displayed in a browser. Your Web page may appear different from the one shown in Figure 3–77. Appendix C contains instructions for uploading your local site to a remote site.

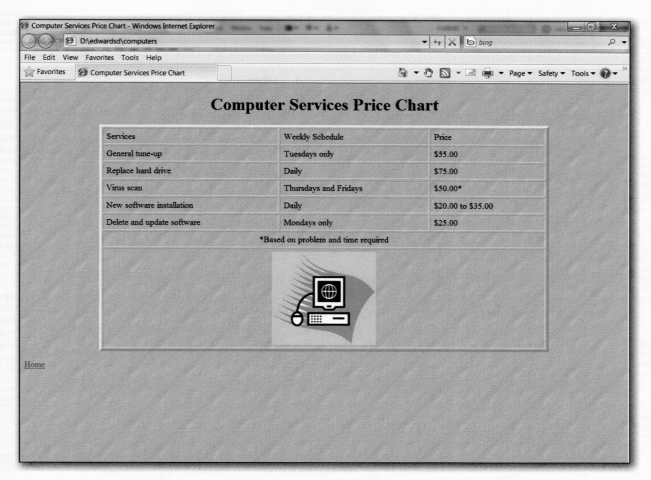

Figure 3–77

Perform the following tasks:

1. Start Dreamweaver, and then copy the price_chart data file from the Chapter03\computers data files folder into the root folder for your Computer Repair Services local Web site. (For example, the root folder might be stored on H:\edwardsd\computers.)

2. Open the Computer Repair Services site, and then open the price_chart.htm document.

3. Use the Page Properties dialog box to apply the repair_bkg background image to the page.

4. Position the insertion point after the Computer Services Price Chart heading, press the ENTER key after the heading, and then click the Layout tab on the Insert bar. Click the Table button on the Layout tab. Enter the following values in the Table dialog box and then click the OK button:

   Rows: 8

   Columns: 3

   Table width: 75%

   Border thickness: 4

   Cell padding: 5

   Cell spacing: 3

   Summary text: Pricing chart for computer services

5. In the first six rows of the table, enter the text as shown in Table 3–9. Apply the Heading 3 format to the column title cells and center-align them. Press the TAB key to move from cell to cell.

Table 3–9 Text for Table on Prices Page

Column 1	Column 2	Column 3
Services	Weekly Schedule	Price
General tune-up	Tuesdays only	$55.00
Replace hard drive	Daily	$75.00
Virus scan	Thursdays and Fridays	$50.00*
New software installation	Daily	$20.00 to $35.00
Delete and update software	Mondays only	$25.00

6. Click anywhere in row 7 and then click the <tr> tag in the tag selector to select row 7. Click the 'Merges selected cells using spans' button. Click the Horz button arrow in the Property inspector, and then select Center. Type ***Based on problem and time required** in the merged cell.

7. Click anywhere in row 8 and then click the <tr> tag in the tag selector to select row 8. Click the 'Merges selected cells using spans' button. Click the Horz button arrow in the Property inspector, and then select Center. If necessary, display the Assets panel. With the insertion point in the middle of the merged row 8, drag the computer_repair04 image to the insertion point. With the image still selected, type **computer** in the ID text box and then type **computer repair** as the Alt text.

8. Click the <table> tag in the tag selector, click the Align button, and then click Center to center the table. Click the Table text box and then type computer_services as the ID.

9. Position the insertion point outside the table by clicking to the right of the table. Press the ENTER key. Type **Home** and then create a relative link to the index.htm file.

10. Click Insert on the Application bar, point to HTML, point to Head Tags, and then click the Keywords command. When the Keywords dialog box is displayed, type the following text in the Keywords text box: **computer repair, computer service, price schedule, your name**. Click the OK button. Click Insert on the Application bar, point to HTML, point to Head Tags, and then click the Description command. When the Description dialog box is displayed, type **Bryan's Computer Repair Services price schedule** in the Description text box. Click the OK button.

11. Check the spelling of the document, and then save the price_chart.htm Web page.

12. Open the index.htm page and then scroll to the end of the page. Click at the end of the sentence that reads, "Our mission is to be a premier…" and then press the ENTER key. Type **Check our prices**. Create a link from the words Check our prices to the price_chart.htm page. Save the index.htm Web page.

13. View the pages in your browser. Verify that your links work.

14. Submit your Web pages in the format specified by your instructor.

In the Lab

Lab 2: Adding a Page with a Table to the Baskets by Carole Web Site

Problem: Publicity from the Baskets by Carole Web site has generated several requests for examples of Carole's baskets. Carole has asked you to add a page to the site that shows some of her creations and the price of each piece. The new Web page will be named specials and should include a link to the home page. The new page is shown in Figure 3–78.

Software and hardware settings determine how a Web page is displayed in a browser. Your Web page may appear different from the one shown in Figure 3–78. Appendix C contains instructions for uploading your local site to a remote site.

Figure 3–78

Perform the following tasks:

1. Start Dreamweaver, and then copy the two image data files from the Chapter03\baskets\images data files folder into the images folder for your Gift Basket Designs local Web site. (For example, the images folder might be stored on H:\edwardsd\baskets\images.)

2. Open the Gift Basket Designs site.

3. Create a new blank HTML page named specials.htm for this Web site.

4. Use the Page Properties dialog box to apply the baskets_bkg background image to the Web page. Title the page Baskets by Carole.

4. Click the upper-left corner of the page, type **Carole's Basket Specials** as the page heading, and then press the ENTER key to insert a blank line. Format the heading as Heading 1 text, and then center it.

5. Below the heading, insert a table with the following properties:

   Rows: 6

   Columns: 3

   Table width: 80 percent

   Border thickness: 3

   Cell padding: 3

   Cell spacing: 3

   Summary: Basket examples

6. Merge the three cells in row 1 into one cell. Center row 1 horizontally. Type the following heading for the table in row 1: **Baskets by Carole Specialty Pieces.** Apply Heading 2 to the table heading.

7. Center rows 2 through 6 horizontally and apply a Middle vertical alignment. Set the width of each column to 33%.

8. Using the Assets panel, drag images to row 2 as follows:

   Column 1   basket01

   Column 2   basket02

   Column 3   basket03

9. Enter the following information in row 3:

   Column 1 $18.50

   Column 2 $19.50

   Column 3 $20.00

10. Merge the three cells in row 4.

11. Add the following images in row 5:

    Column 1   basket04

    Column 2   basket05

    Column 3   basket06

12. Enter the following information in row 6:

    Column 1 $21.00

    Column 2 $28.00

    Column 3 $29.00

13. Resize each image in the table so the width and height are each 250.

14. Select the table, enter baskets as the ID, and then use the Property inspector to center-align the table.

15. Insert a blank line after the table. On the new line, type **Home** and then use this text to create a link from the specials.htm page to the index.htm page. Save the specials.htm page.

16. Open the index.htm page and click to the right of the Company History link. Press ENTER. Type **Specials** and then use this text to create a link to the specials.htm page. Save the index.htm page.

17. View the pages in your browser. Verify that your links work.

18. Submit your Web pages in the format specified by your instructor.

In the Lab

Lab 3: Adding a Page with a Table to the Credit Web Site

Problem: The Credit Protection Web site has become very popular. Jessica Minnick receives numerous e-mail messages requesting that the Web site be expanded. Several messages have included a request to provide some hints and tips about how to save money. Jessica asks you to create a new page for the Web site so she can share some of this information. Figure 3–79 shows the completed Web page.

Software and hardware settings determine how a Web page is displayed in a browser. Your Web page may appear different from the one shown in Figure 3–79. Appendix C contains instructions for uploading your local site to a remote site.

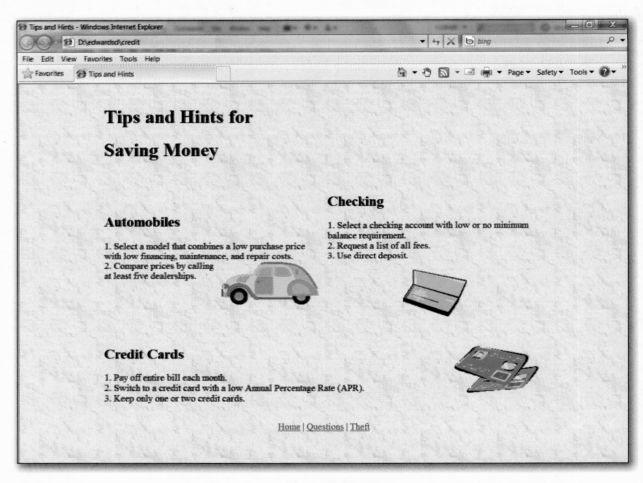

Figure 3–79

Perform the following tasks:

1. Start Dreamweaver, and then copy the three image files from the Chapter03\credit\images data files folder into the images folder for your Credit Protection local Web site.

2. Open the Credit Protection site, and then create a new blank HTML page named saving.htm for this Web site.

3. Apply the credit_bkg background image to the new page. Title the page Tips and Hints.

4. Create a table with four rows, two columns, a width of 75%, border thickness of 0, cell padding of 5, and cell spacing of 5. Add the following summary text: Tips and hints for saving money. Set the width of each column to 50%.

5. Use Figure 3–79 as a guide to add content to the table. Use the information in Table 3–10 for the specific properties and as a reference for the cell contents. Type the specified text into each cell.

Table 3–10 Credit Protection Table Guide

Cells	Merge	Cell Text	Image Name	Image Location	Image Alignment	Alt Text
Row 1, columns 1 and 2	Cells in columns 1 and 2	Tips and Hints for \<ENTER\> Saving Money	None	None	None	None
Row 2, column 1	None	Automobiles \<ENTER\> 1. Select a model that combines a low purchase price with low financing, maintenance, and repair costs.\<br /\> 2. Compare prices by calling at least five dealerships.	car.gif	End of Step 1, after "repair costs."	Right	Car
Row 2, column 2	None	Checking \<ENTER\> 1. Select a checking account with a low or no minimum balance requirement.\<br /\> 2. Request a list of all fees.\<br /\> 3. Use direct deposit. \<ENTER\>	check.gif	Below Step 3, "Use direct deposit."	Center	Checking Account
Row 3, columns 1 and 2	Cells in columns 1 and 2	Credit Cards \<ENTER\> 1. Pay off the entire bill each month. \<br /\> 2. Switch to a credit card with a low Annual Percentage Rate (APR).\<br /\> 3. Keep only one or two credit cards.	credit_card.gif	End of the "Credit Cards" heading	Right	Credit Cards
Row 4, columns 1 and 2	Cells in columns 1 and 2	Home | Questions | Theft	None	None	None	None

6. Apply Heading 1 to the text in the first cell. Apply Heading 2 to the "Automobiles," "Checking," and "Credit Cards" headings.

7. Insert the images into the cells in the locations specified in Table 3–10. Format the images as shown in Table 3–10.

8. Center the last row of the table horizontally. Add the appropriate relative links to this text, using Table 3–11 as a guide.

Table 3–11 Links for Last Row	
Text	**Link**
Home	index.htm
Questions	questions.htm
Theft	theft.htm

9. Select the table, and then center it.

10. Add the following keywords to the Head section: credit, money, tips, checking, saving, your name. Add the following description: Tips and hints on how to save money. Save the Web page.

11. Open the index.htm page and click to the right of the last bulleted item. Press the ENTER key twice. Type **Saving Tips** and create a link from this text to the saving.htm page. Save the index.htm page.

12. View the pages in your browser. Verify that your links work.

13. Submit your Web pages in the format specified by your instructor.

Cases and Places

Apply your creative thinking and problem solving skills to design and implement a solution.

● Easier ●●More Difficult

● 1: Add a Web Page to the Favorite Sports Web Site

The Favorite Sports Web site has become very popular. Several of your friends have suggested that you add a statistics page. You agree that this is a good idea. Create the new page. Using the Internet or other resources, find statistics about your selected sport. Add a background image to the page and use Standard mode to insert a table that contains your statistical information. Add an appropriate heading to the table and an appropriate title for the page. Create a link to the home page. Save the page in the sports subfolder of the Favorite Sports Web site. For a selection of images and backgrounds, visit the Dreamweaver CS5 Media Web page (scsite.com/dwcs5/media) and then click Media below Chapter 3.

● 2: Expand the Hobby Web Site

Modify your Hobby Web site. Add a new page that includes a table created in Standard mode. The table should contain a minimum of three rows and three columns, and a border. Include information in the table about your hobby. Include a minimum of two images in the table. Merge one of the rows or one of the columns and change the default border thickness. Add a background image to the page and give your page a title. Create a link to the home page. Save the page in the hobby subfolder of the Hobby Web site. For a selection of images and backgrounds, visit the Dreamweaver CS5 Media Web page (scsite.com/dwcs5/media) and then click Media below Chapter 3.

●● 3: Add a Web Page to the Politics Web Site

Your campaign for office is going well. You want to add a new page to the Politics Web site to include pictures and text listing some of your outstanding achievements. Apply a background image to the page. Insert a table with a minimum of four cells. Include your picture in one of the cells. Add an appropriate title, keywords, and a description to the page. Center the table. Save the page in the subfolder for the Politics site and then view the page in your browser. Appendix C contains instructions for uploading your local site to a remote site. For a selection of images and backgrounds, visit the Dreamweaver CS5 Media Web page (scsite.com/dwcs5/media) and then click Media below Chapter 3.

●● 4: Modify the Favorite Music Web Site

Make It Personal

Modify your Favorite Music Web site by adding a new page. The new page should contain a table with four rows and three columns. Merge one of the rows and add a background color to the row. Add at least two images to your table. Center the images in the cell. View your Web pages in your browser. Give your page a title and save the page in the folder for the Favorite Music site. Appendix C contains instructions for uploading your local site to a remote site. For a selection of images and backgrounds, visit the Dreamweaver CS5 Media Web page (scsite.com/dwcs5/media) and then click Media below Chapter 3.

• • 5: Upgrade the Student Trips Web Site

Working Together

The students at your school are requesting more information about the student trips. To accommodate the request, the members of your team decide to add another page to the Web site. Each team member is responsible for researching possible destinations and developing content for the selected destination. Add a heading to the new page and format it appropriately. Insert a table with a minimum of six cells. Each member adds at least one image and text content to a cell. One member formats the page — including the text and images. Add a title, keywords, and a description. Save the page and view it in your browser. Appendix C contains instructions for uploading your local site to a remote site. For a selection of images and backgrounds, visit the Dreamweaver CS5 Media Web page (scsite.com/dwcs5/media) and then click Media below Chapter 3.

4 Templates and Style Sheets

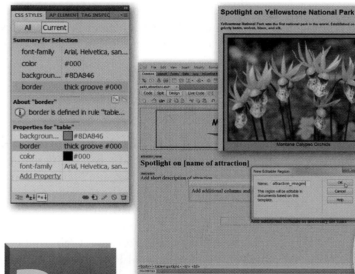

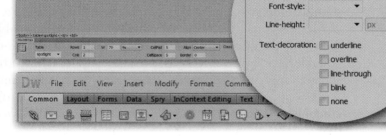

Objectives

You will have mastered the material in this chapter when you can:

- Describe a template
- Create a template
- Add a banner image to a template
- Specify editable and noneditable regions in a template
- Describe different types of style sheets
- Display the CSS Styles panel

- Create a Cascading Style Sheet
- Apply Cascading Style Sheet attributes to a template
- Use Expanded Tables mode
- Create a Web page from a template
- Specify links targets
- Describe CSS style properties

4 | Templates and Style Sheets

Introduction

Designing a Web site is a complex process that requires you to make decisions about the structure of the site and the appearance and content of each Web page within the site. As you develop a Web site, you can use a template to provide a basic framework for the structured organization of the entire Web site. For example, an educational institution could have a template for student home pages. The student supplies the content for the Web page. The template then takes care of the rest of the job and displays the page in a format that promotes consistency among student Web pages. Another example is the content within an e-commerce catalog page. Using a template, the content developer easily can add and delete new products, change prices, and make other modifications without affecting the design.

Project — Adding a Template and Applying Styles

In this chapter, you continue adding pages to the Montana Parks Web site. You learn how to create a Dreamweaver template. Using the template, you then create a Web page highlighting one of Montana's national attractions: Yellowstone National Park.

First, you create a single page that contains all the elements you want to include in your Web page, and then you save the page as a template. After creating the template, you create the style sheet and then apply the style sheet attributes to the template. Next, you use the template containing the style sheet attributes to create a Web page featuring one of Montana's natural attractions — Yellowstone National Park — shown in Figure 4–1. This Web page contains a logo and four designated regions that can be edited. The editable regions are as follows: a heading, a short description, and two tables. You use styles to apply font and color attributes to the heading and the description and to apply fonts, font color attributes, a background, and a border to the two tables. The first table contains cells for images of Yellowstone National Park. You also add a short description of each image. The second table contains cells for links. Finally, you add a relative link to your home page and an absolute link to the Yellowstone National Park Web site.

Figure 4–1

Overview

As you read this chapter, you will learn how to add to your Web site the page shown in Figure 4–1 by performing these general tasks:

- Create and save a template document.
- Add a background image and title.
- Add a logo image.
- Add editable regions.
- Add tables.
- Create editable regions.
- Add styles.
- Add images.
- Add links.

Plan
Ahead

> **General Project Guidelines**
> When adding pages to a Web site, consider the appearance and characteristics of the completed site. As you create the template page shown in Figure 4–1, you should follow these general guidelines:
>
> 1. **Plan the template and Web pages**. Determine what types of pages you will create from the template and how each will fit into the Web site.
>
> 2. **Create a template**. Determine what elements will be contained in the template.
>
> 3. **Identify editable and noneditable regions**. Consider which part of the template will be editable and which areas will be noneditable.
>
> 4. **Design the template**. Specify where images, headings, content, and footer information, if any, will appear.
>
> 5. **Create a style sheet**. In the style sheet, set the styles for all the elements that appear in the template.
>
> 6. **Set styles for links**. Determine the format you want to use for links throughout your site.

When necessary, more specific details concerning the above guidelines are presented at appropriate points in the chapter. The chapter also will identify the actions performed and decisions made regarding these guidelines during the creation of the Web page shown in Figure 4–1.

Starting Dreamweaver and Opening a Web Site

Each time you start Dreamweaver, it opens to the last site displayed when you closed the program. It therefore may be necessary for you to open the Montana Parks Web site. Clicking the Sites pop-up menu in the Files panel lists the sites you have defined. When you open the site, a list of pages and subfolders within the site is displayed.

To Start Dreamweaver and Open the Montana Parks Web Site

With a good understanding of the requirements, and an understanding of the necessary decisions and planning process, the next step is to start Dreamweaver, open the Montana Parks Web site, and create an untitled template.

1 Click the Start button on the Windows taskbar.

2 Click Adobe Dreamweaver CS5 on the Start menu or point to All Programs on the Start menu, click Adobe Design Premium, if necessary, and then click Adobe Dreamweaver CS5 on the All Programs list to start Dreamweaver.

3 If necessary, display the panel groups.

4 If the Montana Parks hierarchy is not displayed, click the Sites pop-up menu button on the Files panel, and then click Montana Parks to display the Montana Parks Web site in the Files panel (Figure 4–2).

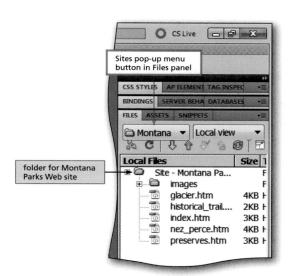

Figure 4–2

To Copy Data Files to the Parks Web Site

Before you start enhancing and adding to your Web site, you need to copy the data files into the site's folder hierarchy. In the following steps, you copy the data files for the Chapter 4 project from the Chapter04 folder on a USB drive to the parks\images folder stored in the *your name* folder. In the following steps, the data files for this chapter are stored on drive L:. The location on your computer may be different. If necessary, verify the location of the data files with your instructor.

1 Click the Sites pop-up menu button in the Files panel, and then click the name of the drive containing your data files, such as Removable Disk (L:).

2 If necessary, click the plus sign (+) next to the folder containing your data files to expand that folder, and then click the plus sign (+) next to the Chapter04 folder to expand it.

3 Expand the parks folder to display the data files.

4 Click the first file in the list to select the file.

5 Hold down the SHIFT key and then click the last file in the list to select all the data files.

6 Press CTRL+C to copy the files.

7 If necessary, click the Sites pop-up menu button, and then click the drive containing the Montana Parks Web site. Click the images folder to select it.

8 Press CTRL+V to paste the files in the images folder (Figure 4–3).

Q&A What should I do if my files are displayed in a different order?

Press the F5 key to refresh the file list.

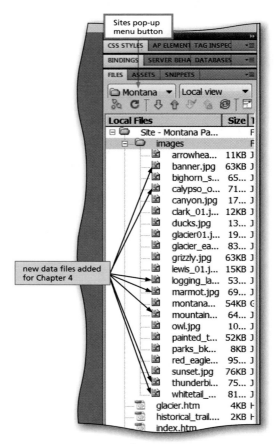

Figure 4–3

Understanding Templates

You are probably already familiar with templates. A stencil, for instance, is a type of template. Or you may have used a template in Microsoft Office or other software applications to create documents with a repeated design. In Web site development with Dreamweaver, a **template** is a predesigned Web page that defines the appearance of the page, including items such as the default font, font size, logos and images, and backgrounds. A template provides an alternative to separately creating many similar pages on your Web site. Instead, you create a basic layout and navigation system and use it as the basis for each similar page. A template page functions as a pattern for other pages. Using a template can save time and can help create a consistent and standardized design.

Planning is an important element in creating a template. Organizing the information and deciding how to structure the template will make it user-friendly and a more effective site-design tool.

<table>
<tr><td>

Plan the template and Web pages.

You use a template to create a fixed page layout. All the documents you create based on that template use the layout provided in the template, so it must be versatile and comprehensive. To make sure you consider all the types of elements you might include on your Web pages, include the following steps as you plan a template:

- Determine the look of the page, including backgrounds, fonts, and logos.
- Set the style of headings and other text, including font family, size, weight, and color.
- Set the style for various types of links, including unvisited, visited, rollover, and active links.
- Determine where you want to use tables and select design elements such as background color and border color.
- Consider where graphics and other media will be displayed

</td><td>

Plan
Ahead

</td></tr>
</table>

When the first template for a Web site is saved, Dreamweaver automatically creates a Templates folder in the Web site local root folder and then saves the template with a **.dwt extension** within that folder. Any templates added to the Web site are saved in the Templates folder automatically.

Dreamweaver provides three methods to create a template: (1) create a template from an existing file, (2) create a template from a new document Basic template page, or (3) use the File menu New command and select HTML template in the New Document dialog box.

To create a template from an existing file, you open the file, use the Save as Template command on the File menu, and then define the editable regions. In this chapter, you use the third method to create the parks_attractions template by selecting the HTML Template category in the New Document dialog box.

Using a Dreamweaver Template

A **Dreamweaver template** is a special type of HTML document. When you create a template, Dreamweaver inserts code that defines the document as a template. A **template instance**, which is a Web page based on a template, looks identical to the template. The difference, however, is that you can make changes only to designated parts of the template instance. The designated parts of the page to which you can make changes are called **editable regions**. An editable region can be any part of a page: a heading, a paragraph, a table, a table cell, and so on. You designate the editable regions when you design the template. Once the designation is complete, other parts of the page are locked so that others cannot change them.

One of the more powerful benefits that templates provide is the ability to update multiple pages at once. After a new document is created from a template, the document remains attached to the original template unless it specifically is separated. Therefore, you can modify a template and immediately update the design in all of the documents based on it.

You begin this project by creating a template for the Montana Parks Web site. Next, you add Cascading Style Sheet attributes to the template and then you use the template to create a Web page focusing on one of Montana's more popular attractions — Yellowstone National Park.

To Create and Save a Template

1

- Click File on the Application bar and then click New to display the New Document dialog box.

- If necessary, click Blank Template and then click HTML template in the Template Type column to select the document type.

- If necessary, click <none> in the Layout column to specify no particular layout (Figure 4–4).

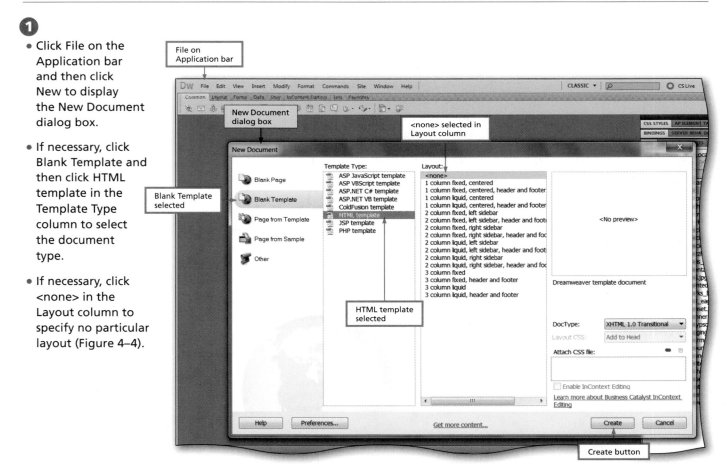

Figure 4–4

2

- Click the Create button to display a new untitled template page.

- Click File on the Application bar and then click Save as Template to display the Save As Template dialog box.

Q&A What should I do if a Dreamweaver warning box is displayed?

Click the OK button to display the Save As Template dialog box.

- Type **parks template** in the Description text box to enter a description for the template.

- Type **parks_attractions** in the Save as text box to enter a file name for the template (Figure 4–5).

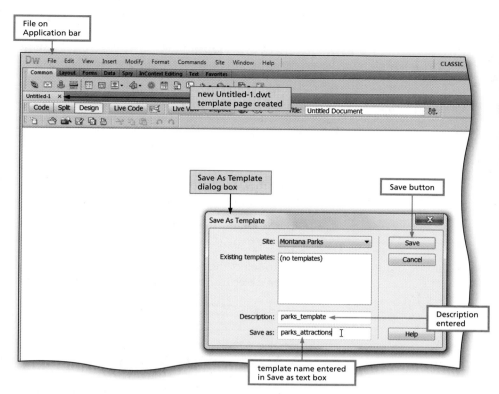

Figure 4–5

3

- Click the Save button to save the parks_attractions template in the Templates folder.

Q&A What should I do if an Update Links dialog box is displayed?

Click the Yes button to create the Templates folder in the parks local files folder.

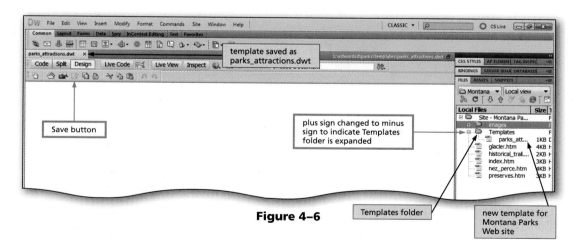

Figure 4–6

Q&A How did the Templates folder get created?

Dreamweaver created the Templates folder automatically.

- If necessary, click the minus sign to the left of the images folder to collapse the folder.

- Click the plus sign to the left of the Templates folder in the Files panel to expand the folder and display the parks_attractions.dwt template (Figure 4–6).

Q&A What does the extension .dwt indicate?

The .dwt extension indicates it is a template file.

To Add a Background Image to the Template Page

The purpose of the template created in this chapter is to use it as a foundation to spotlight a different Montana Park attraction each month. The next step shows how to begin designing the parks_attractions template page.

1 Click Modify on the Application bar and then click Page Properties to open the Page Properties dialog box.

2 Click Appearance (HTML) in the Category list, if necessary, and then click the Browse button to the right of the Background image text box to open the Select Image Source dialog box.

3 If necessary, navigate to the images folder. Click parks_bkg.jpg and then click the OK button to select the background image.

4 Click the OK button in the Page Properties dialog box to add the background image to the template page.

5 Drag to select the text in the Title text box, type `Spotlight on Montana Attractions` as the page title, and then press the ENTER key (Figure 4–7).

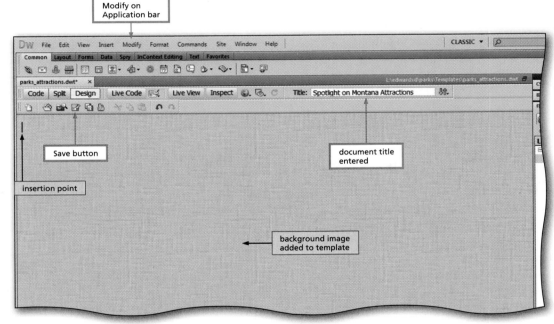

Figure 4–7

6 If necessary, click the Document window, and then click the Save button.

Q&A What should I do if a Dreamweaver warning box is displayed?

Click the OK button to continue.

To Add a Banner Image to the Template

The following steps show how to add a title image to the template. This banner image becomes part of the template and is a noneditable item. When a content developer uses this template, the banner image will remain as is and cannot be deleted or aligned to another position.

1

- If necessary, click the upper-left corner of the page to display the insertion point.

- Click the Assets tab in the panel groups to display images and other assets.

- If necessary, click the Site option button to display the assets for this site.

- Click the banner.jpg file to select it (Figure 4–8).

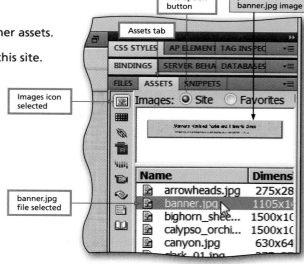

Figure 4–8

2

- Drag the banner.jpg image to the upper-left corner of the Document window.

- Collapse the panel groups to display the entire banner image in the Document window.

- If necessary, click the banner image to select it and then press CTRL+ALT+SHIFT+C to center the image.

- Click below the banner image to deselect the image (Figure 4–9).

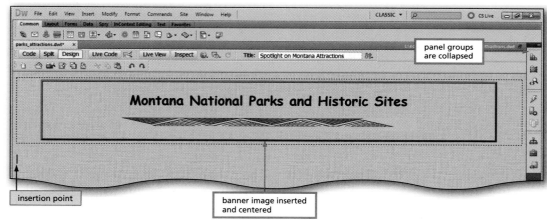

Figure 4–9

Q&A What should I do if an Image Tag Accessibility dialog box opens?

Close the dialog box without entering any information. This dialog box was disabled in Chapter 3. If necessary, repeat the steps in the "To Disable the Image Tag Accessibility Attributes Dialog Box" section to disable the dialog box again.

Q&A Why do dotted lines appear around the image?

The dotted lines indicate that this template is using a div tag to lay out the page elements. A div tag is an HTML tag that contains text, similar to a table cell in HTML layouts.

Other Ways
1. On Insert menu, click Image, select file name in Select Image Source dialog box, click OK button

Specifying Editable and Noneditable Regions

When you first create a template, Dreamweaver automatically locks most parts of the template document. The title, however, is not locked. As the template author, you define which regions of a template-based document can be edited by inserting editable regions in the template.

Plan Ahead

Identify editable and noneditable regions.
When you first create a template, most of the regions in the document are locked so that others cannot add or change text or other elements in the template or the pages created from the template. You should specify at least one editable region, however, so that other people can customize a Web page as necessary. Otherwise, all the pages created from a template will be identical.

An editable region can include a prompt, which is text that describes what content developers should enter in the region. For example, if you design part of the page to display an image of an attraction, enter a prompt such as "Insert image of attraction," so content developers know what type of content to insert.

Dreamweaver supports four different types of regions in a template: editable regions, repeating regions, optional regions, and editable tag attributes.

Editable Region   An **editable region** is the basic building block of a template and is an unlocked region. You can define any area of a template as editable. Thus, this is a section a content developer can edit; it can be a heading, a paragraph, a table, or another type of section. A template can and usually does contain multiple editable regions. For a template to be functional, it should contain at least one editable region; otherwise, pages based on the template cannot be changed.

BTW

Template Editing
To edit a template, open the Assets panel, click the template, and then click the Edit button at the bottom of the Assets panel. After you update the template, Dreamweaver asks whether you want to make the same changes to the documents that are based on the template.

Repeating Region   A **repeating region** is a section in a document that is set to repeat. You can use repeating regions to control the layout of regions that are repeated on a page. The two types of repeating template objects are tables and regions. For instance, a list of catalog products may include a name, description, price, and picture in a single row. You can repeat this table row to allow the content developer to create an expanding list, while keeping the design under your control. A repeating region is a section of a template that can be duplicated as often as desired in a template-based page. By default, the repeating region does not include an editable region, but you can insert an editable region into the repeating region. A repeating region generally is used with a table, but also can be defined for other page elements.

Optional Region An **optional region** lets the content developer show or hide content on a page-by-page basis. For example, you may want to include an optional region that would contain special promotional products.

Editable Tag Attribute An **editable tag** attribute lets the content developer unlock a tag attribute in a template and edit the tag in a template-based page. For instance, you could unlock the table border attribute, but keep locked other table attributes such as padding, spacing, and alignment.

BTW

Detaching a Page from a Template
To detach a page from a template, click Modify on the Application bar, point to Templates, and then click Detach from Template on the Templates submenu. The page becomes a regular document, and the locked regions become editable.

Designing the Template

When you are creating a template, one of the best methods is to finalize a single page that includes all the elements you want in the template. Then, save the document as a template and mark all of the editable regions.

Design the template.
Consider the following when designing your template page:

- Include as much content as possible. Structure and design will enable the content developer to produce a Web page based on the template more quickly.

- Use prompts in the editable regions to inform the content developer as to the type of content to be added to a particular region.

- Give your editable regions meaningful names.

- Use placeholders if possible, particularly for images.

Plan Ahead

To Add the Attraction Name and Attraction Description Prompts for the First Two Editable Regions

The following steps show how to add prompts for two editable regions in the template page. The prompt for the first editable region is the heading and includes instructions to add the attraction name; the prompt for the second editable region is the instruction to add a short description of the attraction.

- Press the ENTER key, and then type **Spotlight on [name of attraction]** as the heading prompt below the banner (Figure 4–10).

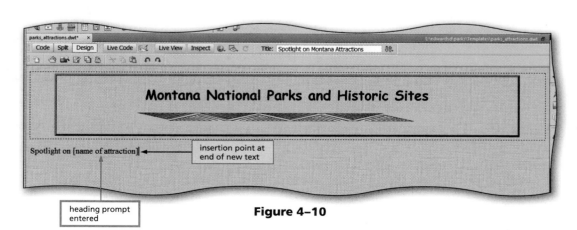

Figure 4–10

- With the insertion point at the end of the new text, click the Format button in the Property inspector, and then click Heading 2 to apply the Heading 2 format to the spotlight prompt (Figure 4–11).

Q&A

What will users do with this heading text when the page is displayed in a browser?

Users can select the [name of attraction] text and replace it with an attraction name, such as Yellowstone National Park.

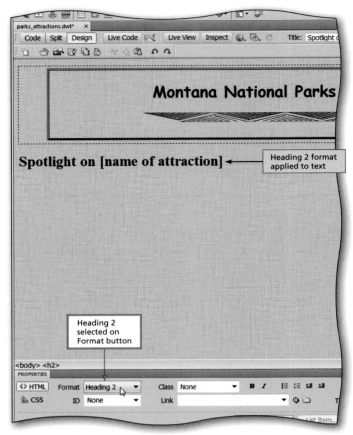

Figure 4–11

- Press the ENTER key to move the insertion point below the prompt (Figure 4–12).

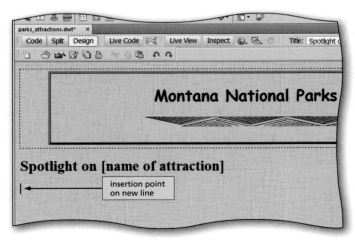

Figure 4–12

4

- Type **Add short description of attraction** as the prompt for the second editable region.

- If necessary, apply the Paragraph format to the description prompt to specify the format.

- Press the ENTER key to move the insertion point below the description prompt (Figure 4–13).

Q&A

What will users do with this paragraph text when the page is displayed in a browser?

Users can select the 'Add short description of attraction' text and replace it with text that describes the attraction, such as a fact or two about the attraction's history.

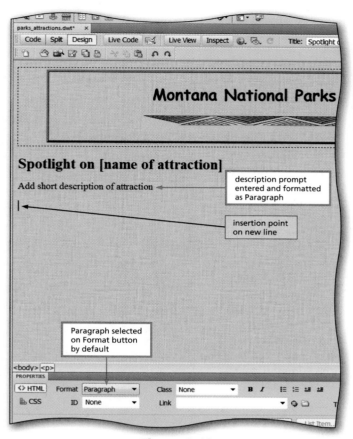

Figure 4–13

Adding Tables for Images and Links

The third editable region will consist of a one-row, two-column centered table that will contain centered images and a short description immediately below each image. The table is editable, so depending on the attraction to be spotlighted and the number of available images, the content developer can add rows and columns to the table as needed. Instructions for the table are contained in row 1, column 1, and an image placeholder is contained in row 1, column 2. A placeholder provides the Web page developer with a guide as to what is to be placed in the cell and the required placement, such as right, left, or centered.

A second table will become the fourth editable region. This one-row, two-column centered table will contain cells for a relative link to the Montana Parks and Recreation Areas index page and an absolute link to the Montana National Preserves Web page on the nps.gov Web site. This second table also is editable, which will permit the content developer to modify or add additional links as needed.

BTW

Editable Regions in Tables
You can place editable regions anywhere on a page, including an individual cell or an entire table. You cannot, however, select several nonadjacent cells and define them as one editable region.

To Add and Center a Table as the Third Editable Region

The following steps show how to add the first table as the third editable region.

1

- Click Insert on the Application bar and then click Table to display the Table dialog box.

- Enter the following data in the Table dialog box: 1 for Rows, 2 for Columns, 70 percent for Table width, 0 for Border thickness, 5 for Cell padding, and 5 for Cell spacing. Type **Spotlight on Montana national attractions** as the Summary text (Figure 4–14).

Q&A

What is the Summary text used for?

Screen readers can read the summary text, though it does not appear in the browser. The Summary text increases the accessibility of the Web page.

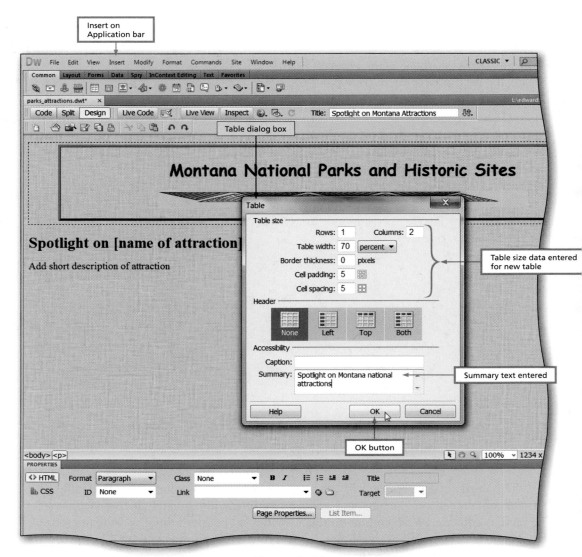

Figure 4–14

2

- Click the OK button to add the table to the template.

- Click the Align button in the Property inspector, and then click Center to center the table in the Document window (Figure 4–15).

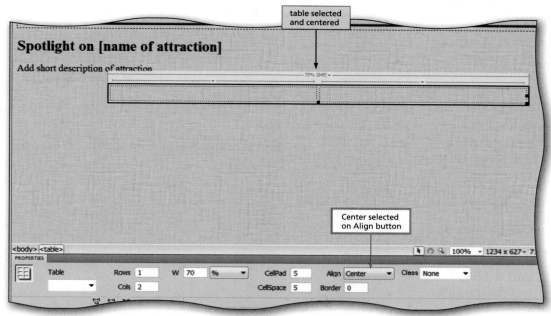

Figure 4–15

3

- Click the left cell in the table and then drag to select both cells in the table (Figure 4–16).

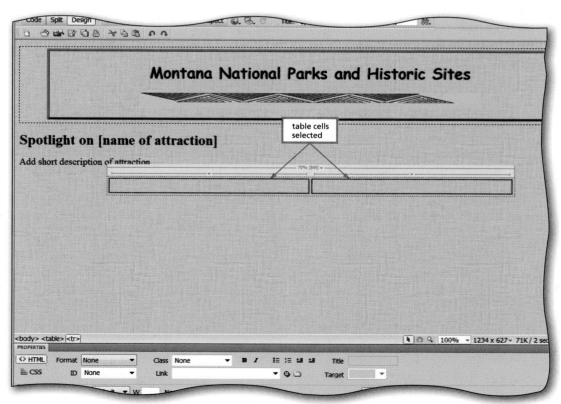

Figure 4–16

4

- Click the Horz button in the Property inspector and then click Center to center the contents of the cells horizontally.

- Click the Vert button and then click Middle to align the cell contents in the middle of the line vertically.

- Click the left cell in the table and then type **Add additional columns and rows as necessary. Add images and short descriptions of image to each cell in the table.** as the placeholder text.

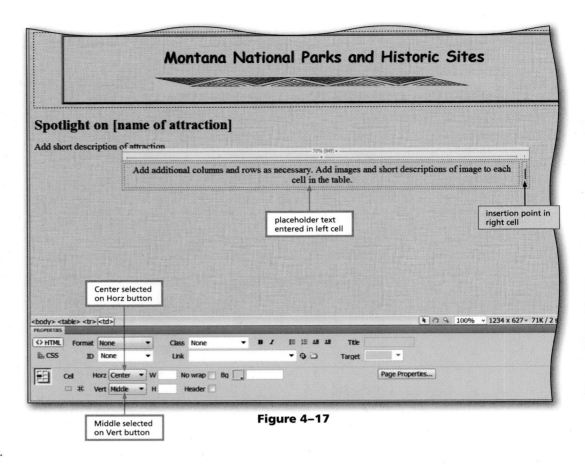

Figure 4–17

- Click the right cell to prepare for entering content in the right cell (Figure 4–17).

Q&A

Why does the left cell expand to take up most of the table?

The cell expands to accommodate the placeholder text. When you add content to the right cell, the table will adjust accordingly. By default, Dreamweaver lets the browser determine the width or height of a table cell depending on the contents of the cell. You can avoid this expansion by setting the W value for the column in the Property inspector. To do so, select the column, and then enter the width in pixels or as a percentage. When you specify a percentage, follow the value with a percent symbol (%).

5

- Click Insert on the Application bar, point to Image Objects, and then point to Image Placeholder to prepare for inserting an image placeholder (Figure 4–18).

What is an image placeholder?

An image placeholder is a generic graphic you use until you are ready to add a specific image to the page. If necessary, you can set the size and color of the placeholder and include a text label to identify it.

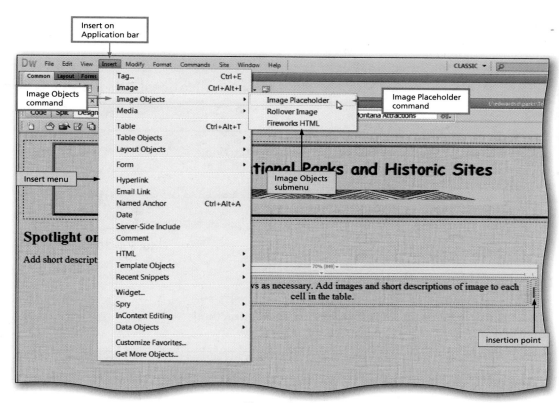

Figure 4–18

6

- Click Image Placeholder to display the Image Placeholder dialog box.

- Type **add_image** in the Name text box as the prompt.

- Press the TAB key, and then type **64** for the Width.

- Press the TAB key, and then, if necessary, type **32** for the Height (Figure 4–19).

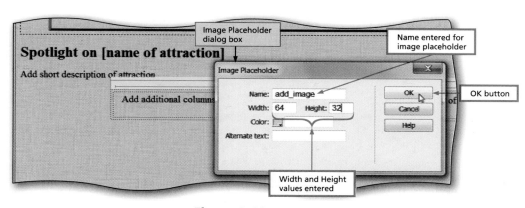

Figure 4–19

Should I always use these width and height values for an image placeholder?

No. Usually, you specify the approximate width and height of the image you plan to insert later so you can see how the image will fit into the page.

7

- Click the OK button to add the placeholder to the table (Figure 4–20).

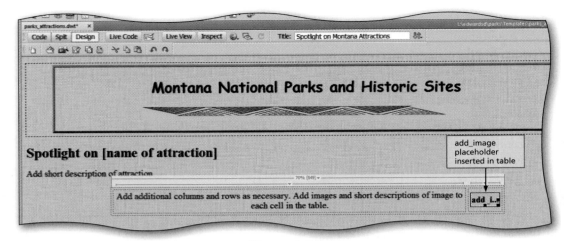

Figure 4–20

8

- Click <table> in the tag selector to select the table.

- Type **spotlight** in the Table box to name the table.

- Press the ENTER key to enter the name of the table (Figure 4–21).

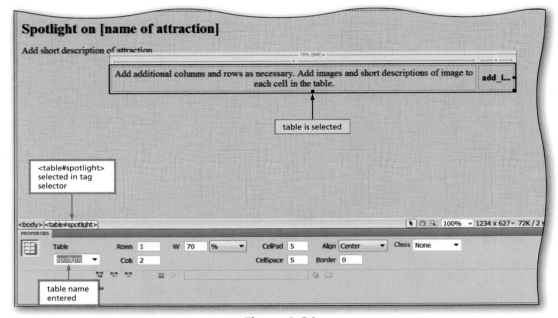

Figure 4–21

9

- Click to the right of the table and then press the ENTER key two times to insert a blank line after the table (Figure 4–22).

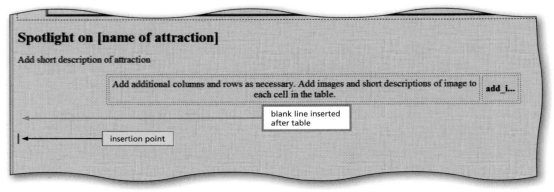

Figure 4–22

To Add and Center a Table as the Fourth Editable Region

The second table will serve as a table for links and will contain two columns. Additional columns can be added to the table as necessary. The following steps show how to add the link table as the fourth editable region.

1 Click Insert on the Application bar and then click Table to display the Table dialog box.

2 Enter the following data in the Table dialog box: 1 for Rows, 2 for Columns, 50 percent for Table width, 0 for Border thickness, 5 for Cell padding, and 0 for Cell spacing. Type `Web site links` as the Summary text. Click the OK button.

3 Click the Align button in the Property inspector, and then click Center to center the table.

4 Click the left cell and then drag to select both cells in the table.

5 Click the Horz button in the Property inspector and then click Center. Click the Vert button arrow and then click Middle.

6 Click the left cell and then type `Add additional columns as necessary for links` as the placeholder text.

7 Select the table, type `links` in the Table box, and then press the ENTER key to name the table.

8 Press CTRL+S to save the file. If a Dreamweaver warning box is displayed, click the OK button (Figure 4–23).

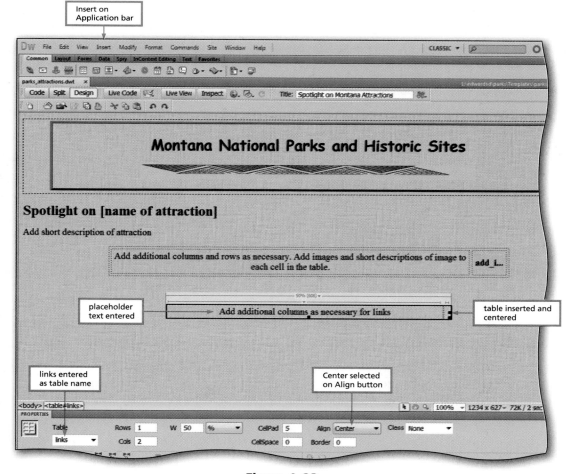

Figure 4–23

Saving an HTML File as a Template
If you have an HTML file that you want to save as a Dreamweaver template, open the document, click File on the Application bar, and then click Save As Template. You also can click the Templates button on the Common tab in the Insert panel, and then click Make Template.

Adding Editable Regions

As previously discussed on page DW 277, Dreamweaver supports four different regions in a template: editable regions, repeating regions, optional regions, and editable tag attributes. All Dreamweaver region objects, along with other template-related objects, are available through the Templates pop-up menu on the Common category tab of the Insert bar. Figure 4–24 shows the Template Objects pop-up menu.

Figure 4–24

Table 4–1 lists the commands and descriptions on the Templates pop-up menu.

Table 4–1 Commands on the Templates Pop-Up Menu	
Command Name	**Description**
Make Template	Displays the Save As Template dialog box; features in the dialog box include selecting a Web site in which to save the template, a list of existing templates, and a Save As box to name the template
Make Nested Template	Creates a template whose design and editable regions are based on another template; useful for sites in which all pages share certain elements and subsections of those pages share a subset of page elements
Editable Region	Creates an unlocked region; the basic building block of a template
Optional Region	Designates a region that can be used to show or hide content on a page-by-page basis; use an optional region to set conditions for displaying content in a document
Repeating Region	Creates a section of a template that can be duplicated as often as desired in a template-based page
Editable Optional Region	Designates a region that can be used to show or hide content on a page-by-page basis
Repeating Table	Defines a table and then defines the location of editable regions in each cell in the table

Marking Existing Content as an Editable Region

As discussed previously, an editable region is one that the content developer can change. Editable template regions control which areas of a template-based page can be edited. Each editable region must have a unique name. Dreamweaver uses the name to identify the editable region when new content is entered or the template is applied.

To Create the First Editable Region

The following steps show how to make the heading an editable region.

1

- If necessary, click the Common tab on the Insert bar to display the Common category.
- Click to the left of the heading prompt to prepare for selecting the prompt (Figure 4–25).

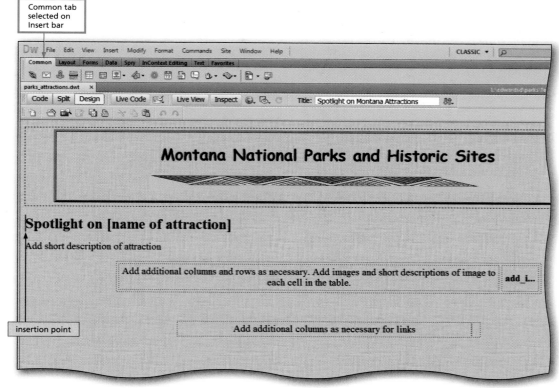

Figure 4–25

2

- Click the <h2> tag in the tag selector to select the prompt for the heading (Figure 4–26).

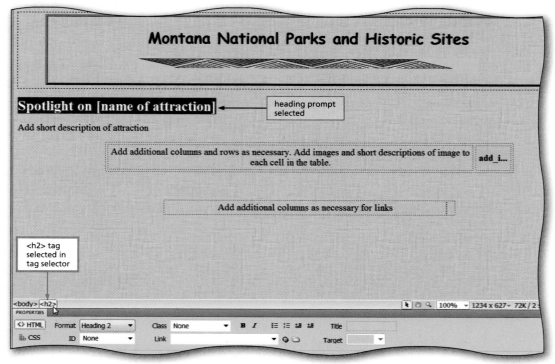

Figure 4–26

- On the Insert tab, click the Templates button arrow to display the Templates pop-up menu.
- Click Editable Region to display the New Editable Region dialog box (Figure 4–27).

Q&A

The name in my New Editable Region dialog box has a different number at the end. Why is that?

Dreamweaver numbers the name of the editable region according to how many editable regions you already have created. You rename the editable region in the next step.

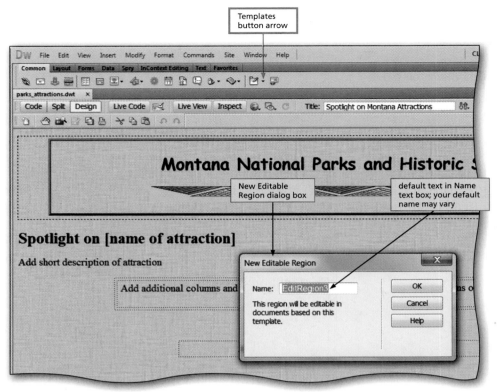

Figure 4–27

- Type **attraction_ name** in the Name text box to provide a name for the new editable region (Figure 4–28).

- Click the OK button to designate the selected text as an editable region.

Q&A

How can I tell which areas on the page are editable regions?

Editable regions appear with an outline around the text and a tab containing the region's name.

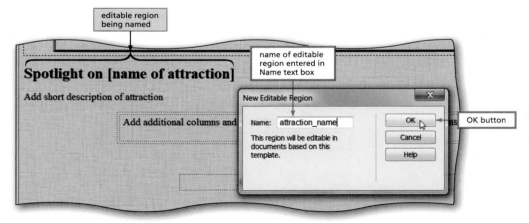

Figure 4–28

Other Ways
1. Click Insert on the Application bar, point to Template Objects, click Editable Region on Template Objects submenu   2. Right-click selected content, point to Templates, click New Editable Region on the Templates submenu

To Create the Second Editable Region

The second editable region that needs to be identified and given a name is the text area that will provide a short description of the featured attraction. The following steps illustrate how to make the attraction description section an editable region using the Insert menu instead of the Insert bar.

- Click to the left of the prompt, Add short description of attraction, in the Document window to prepare for creating a second editable region.

- Click the <p> tag in the tag selector to select the prompt (Figure 4–29).

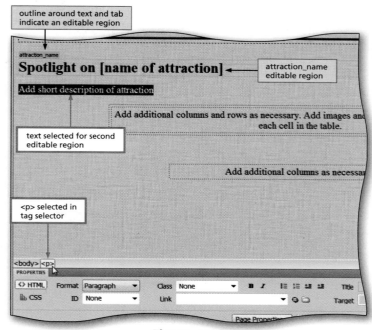

Figure 4–29

- Click Insert on the Application bar, point to Template Objects, and then point to Editable Region (Figure 4–30).

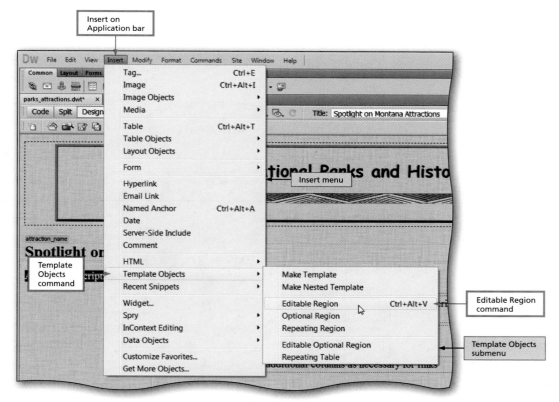

Figure 4–30

- Click Editable Region to display the New Editable Region dialog box.

- Type **description** in the Name text box to provide a name for the new editable region (Figure 4–31).

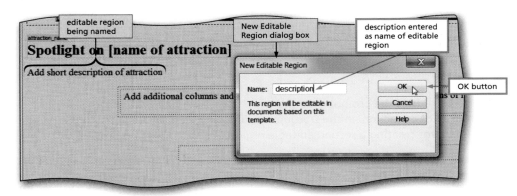

Figure 4–31

- Click the OK button to name the editable region (Figure 4–32).

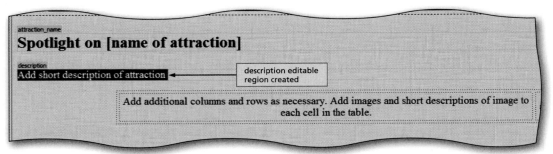

Figure 4–32

To Create the Third and Fourth Editable Regions

The third and fourth editable regions are the two tables that were added to the template. The following steps show how to name the tables and how to make both tables editable regions.

- Click a cell in the first table and then click the <table#spotlight> tag in the tag selector to select the table (Figure 4–33).

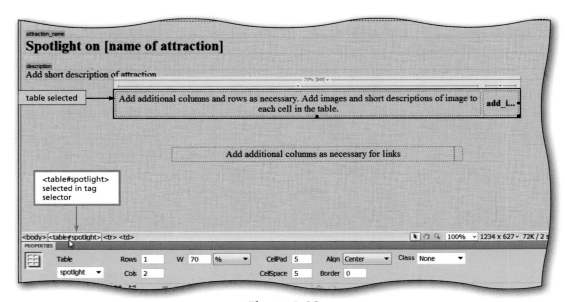

Figure 4–33

2

- Click Insert on the Application bar, point to Template Objects, and then click the Editable Region command to display the New Editable Region dialog box (Figure 4–34).

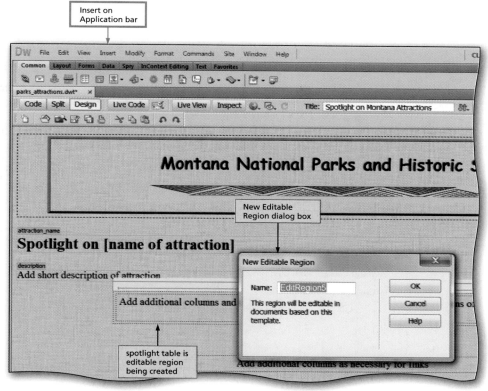

Figure 4–34

3

- Type **attraction_images** in the Name text box to name the new editable region (Figure 4–35).

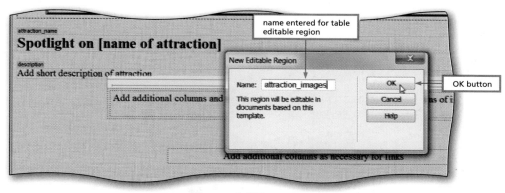

Figure 4–35

4

- Click the OK button to enter the editable region name for the selected table (Figure 4–36).

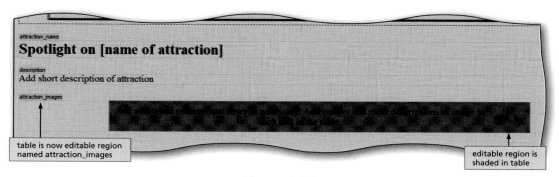

Figure 4–36

5

- Click a cell in the second table and then click the <table#links> tag in the tag selector to select the table.

- Click the Templates: Editable Region button on the Insert bar to display the New Editable Region dialog box (Figure 4–37).

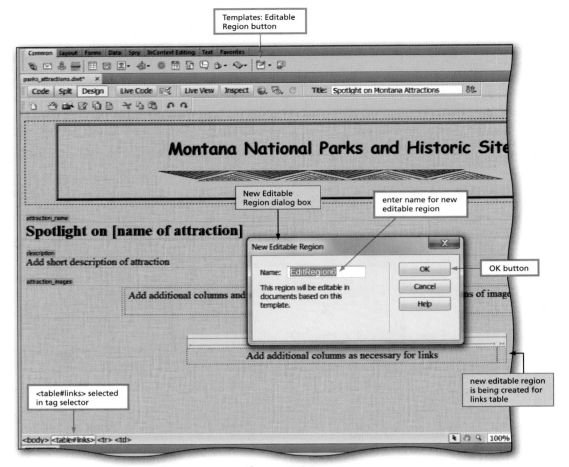

Figure 4–37

6

- Type **links** in the Name text box, click the OK button to add links as the editable region name, and then click a blank spot on the page background to deselect the links table.

- Click the Save button on the Standard toolbar to save your work (Figure 4–38).

Q&A

What should I do if a warning dialog box appears?

If a warning dialog box is displayed, indicating you have placed an editable region inside a <p> tag, click Cancel, and then repeat Steps 5 and 6.

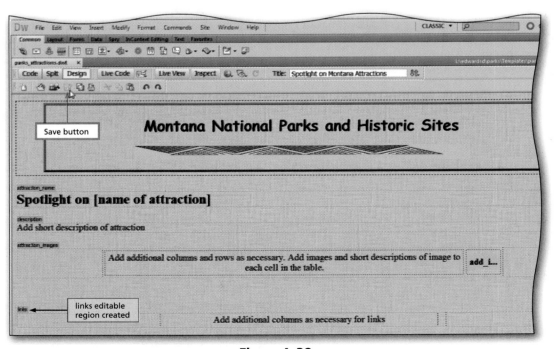

Figure 4–38

Introduction to Style Sheets

If you have used styles in a word processing program such as Microsoft Word, then the concept of styles within HTML and Dreamweaver will be familiar. A **style** is a rule describing how a specific object is formatted. A style sheet (discussed later in this section) is a file that contains a collection of these rules or styles. One style sheet, for example, can control the typography, color, and other layout elements for an entire Web site.

Dreamweaver supports two types of styles: HTML styles and Cascading Style Sheets (CSS).

Create a style sheet.

Using a style sheet that defines CSS styles separates the content of a Web page from its presentation. That means you can change text or images on a Web page, for example, without affecting the design. Before you add new Web pages to a site, consider creating a style sheet containing CSS style rules. With CSS, you can create a style rule for all the h1 (Heading 1) text, for example, and specify the font, font size, weight (such as bold or italics), text color and background color, and much more. (Tables 4–5 through 4–12 list the formatting properties you can apply to Web page content.) If you add a rule to the style sheet that formats h1 text as 28-point dark blue text, all the Web pages you create can refer to the style sheet and format the h1 text as 28-point dark blue. Also consider attaching a style sheet to a template. If you do, all the Web pages created from the template will use the styles defined in the style sheet. When you want to change the h1 text to 36-point green, you need to change only the style rule in the style sheet, not in every page in your site.

Plan Ahead

HTML Styles

Thus far, when you have formatted text, you have selected the text in the Document window and then applied font attributes using the Property inspector. You selected and then formatted each text element individually: the heading, character, word, paragraph, and so on. **HTML styles**, however, are a Dreamweaver feature that a Web page developer can use to apply formatting options quickly and easily to text in a Web page. They are similar to a template used in a word processing or spreadsheet document.

HTML styles use HTML tags such as the <h1> and <b> tags to apply the formatting. Once you have created and saved an HTML style, you can apply it to any document in the Web site. One advantage of HTML styles is that they consist only of font tags, and therefore are displayed in just about all browsers, including Internet Explorer 7.0 and earlier versions. One of the main disadvantages of HTML styles, however, is that changes made to an HTML style are not updated automatically in the document. If a style is applied and then the style is modified, the style must be reapplied to the text to update the formatting. To use HTML styles, you must deselect the Use CSS instead of HTML Tags option in the General category of the Preferences dialog box.

The HTML 4.0 specification released by the World Wide Web Consortium (W3C) discourages the use of HTML formatting tags in favor of Cascading Style Sheets (CSS). This chapter, therefore, focuses on Cascading Style Sheets.

Cascading Style Sheets

Cascading Style Sheets, also called **CSS** and **style sheets**, are a collection of formatting rules that control the appearance of content in a Web page. Cascading Style Sheets are the cornerstone of Dynamic HTML (DHTML). **DHTML** is an extension to HTML that enables a Web page to respond to user input without sending a request to the Web server. Compared with HTML styles, style sheets provide the Web site developer with more precision and control over many aspects of page design.

You can define the following types of styles in Dreamweaver:

- *Class*: Also considered a custom style, class is the most flexible way to define a style. In a **custom style**, you specify all the attributes you want the style to include. The name of a custom style always begins with a period. This type of style can be applied to any text within the document.

- *Tag*: The tag style provides the option to make global changes to existing Web pages by modifying the properties or attributes of an HTML tag. When this option is selected in the New CSS Rule dialog box, the Tag pop-up menu provides a selection of over 90 HTML tags listed in alphabetical order.

- *Advanced*: Also known as a pseudo-class, this type of style commonly is applied to hyperlinks to create a rollover effect. For example, when the mouse pointer moves over or hovers over a link, the link changes color. Dreamweaver provides the a:active, a:hover, a:link, and a:visited link options through the pop-up menu. You are not limited to these four options. You can enter one or more of any HTML tag in the Selector text box and apply a single attribute or a combination of attributes to that tag.

To define a style, you create a style rule. A CSS style rule contains two parts: the **selector**, which is the name of the style, and the **declaration**, which defines the style elements. An example of a selector is h2 (defining the HTML h2 tag) and an example of a declaration is 24 pt Courier, defining the font size and type to apply to the h2 tag.

After creating a style, you can apply it instantly to text, margins, images, and other Web page elements. Some of the advantages of style sheets include the following:

- Precise layout control
- Smaller, faster downloading pages
- Browser-friendly — browsers not supporting CSS simply ignore the code
- All attached Web pages can be updated at one time

Conflicting Styles

The term **cascading** refers to the capability of applying multiple style sheets to the same Web page. When more than one style is applied to the same Web page, an order of preference is involved. Styles are used as described and applied in the following preference order:

- An **external style sheet** is a single style sheet that is used to create uniform formatting and contains no HTML code. An external style sheet can be linked to any page within the Web site or imported into a Web site. Using the Import command creates an @import tag in the HTML code and references the URL where the published style sheet is located.

- An **internal style sheet**, or **embedded style sheet**, contains styles that apply to a specific page. The styles that apply to the page are embedded in the <head> portion of the Web page.

- A specified element within a page can have its own style.

In some instances, two styles will be applied to the same element. When this occurs, the browser displays all attributes of both styles unless an attribute conflict exists. For example, one style may specify Arial as the font and the other style may specify Times New Roman. When this happens, the browser displays the attribute of the style closest to the text within the HTML code.

The CSS Styles Panel

To develop a style sheet, you start with the **CSS Styles panel** (Figure 4–39). Styles are created and controlled through the CSS Styles panel. A **custom style** is a style you can create and name, in which you specify all the attributes you want the style to include. The name of a custom style always begins with a period.

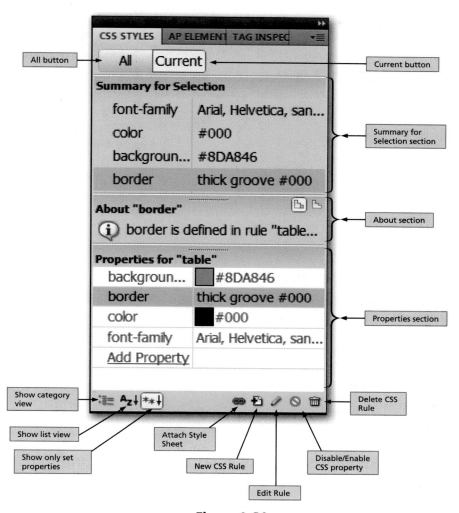

Figure 4–39

In the lower-right corner of the CSS Styles panel are five buttons. These buttons are used for the following tasks:

- The **Attach Style Sheet** button opens the Link External Style Sheet dialog box. Select an external style sheet to link to or import into your current document.

- The **New CSS Rule** button opens the New CSS Rule dialog box. Use the New CSS Rule dialog box to define a type of style.

- The **Edit Rule** button opens the CSS Style Definition dialog box. Edit any of the styles in the current document or in an external style sheet.

- The **Disable/Enable CSS property** button lets you disable or enable a property to see how it affects the design of a page.

- The **Delete CSS Rule** button removes the selected style from the CSS Styles panel, and removes the formatting from any element to which it was applied.

To Display the CSS Styles Panel

The following step shows how to display the CSS Styles panel.

1

- Click the Expand Panels button to expand the panel groups.

- Click the CSS Styles tab to display the CSS Styles panel.

- Double-click the Assets tab to minimize the other panel groups.

- If necessary, drag the Properties bar in the CSS Styles panel up to display the Properties section (Figure 4–40).

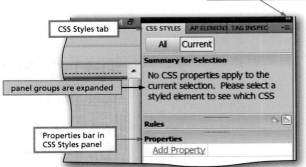

Figure 4–40

Other Ways

1. Click Window on Application bar, click CSS Styles

2. Press SHIFT+F11

Defining Style Attributes

Dreamweaver makes it easy to add style attributes to the style sheet. This is done through the CSS Rule Definition dialog box (Figure 4–41), which contains eight categories with more than 70 different CSS attributes. As you are defining a style, select a category to access the attributes for that category. Styles from more than one category can be applied to the same element. Tables 4–5 through 4–12 on pages DW 330–332 describe each attribute in each of the eight categories.

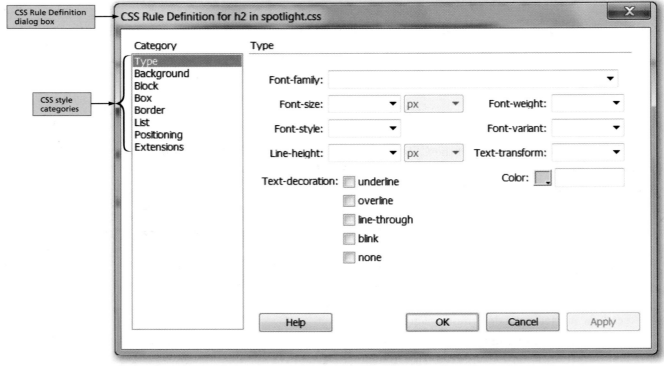

Figure 4–41

Creating a Style Sheet

Recall that styles and style sheets are applied in a variety of formats: you can link or import an external style sheet to any number of Web pages; you can work with an embedded style sheet in one Web page only; or you can apply a style to a specific element within a Web page. The spotlight style sheet you create in the following steps is an external style sheet that is linked to the spotlight template page. When you apply the first style, a Document window with a .css extension opens behind the original Document window. This window contains the code for the applied styles; it is not displayed in Design view. When you finish adding styles, you also save and close the .css window.

In this chapter, the original Document window contains a template, and you apply styles to the template. However, you also can use an external style sheet to apply styles to a basic HTML page.

To Add a Style and Save the Style Sheet

The following steps show how to create a style sheet by setting the heading style and then saving the style sheet.

1

- Click to the left of the text, Spotlight on [name of attraction], in the attraction_name editable region, and then click the <h2> tag in the tag selector to select the heading prompt.

- Click the New CSS Rule button in the CSS Styles panel to display the New CSS Rule dialog box (Figure 4–42).

Q&A

Why did I click the <h2> tag before clicking the New CSS Rule button?

You clicked the <h2> tag because you are setting the attributes for the Heading 2 style. After you complete these steps, all of the Heading 2 text in all of the documents attached to the spotlight style sheet will have these same attributes.

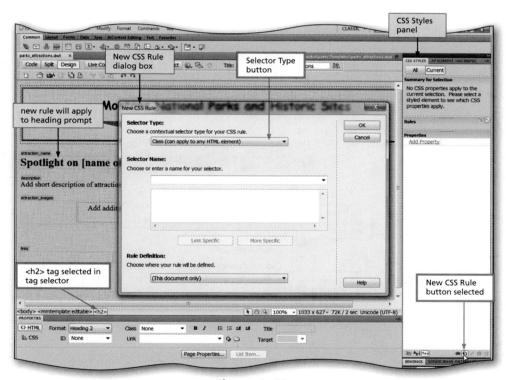

Figure 4–42

● Click the Selector Type
button and then point to Tag
(redefines an HTML element)
to prepare for selecting that
type (Figure 4–43).

Q&A

What is the effect of selecting Tag (redefines an HTML
element)?

When you select the Tag
option, you redefine the
default formatting of the
selected tag, which is <h2>
in this case.

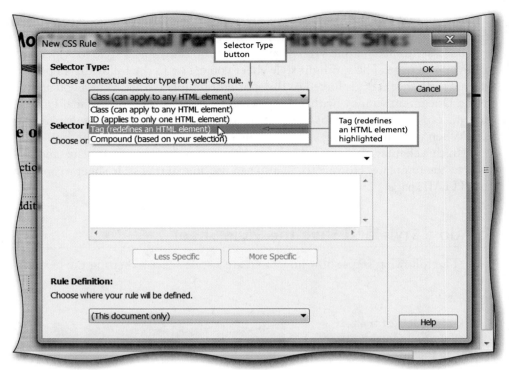

Figure 4–43

● Click Tag (redefines
an HTML element)
to select that
selector type.

● Click the
Selector Name
text box and
type **h2** as the
selector name, if
necessary.

● Click the Rule
Definition button,
and then click (New
Style Sheet File) to
specify that you
want to create an
external
style sheet
(Figure 4–44).

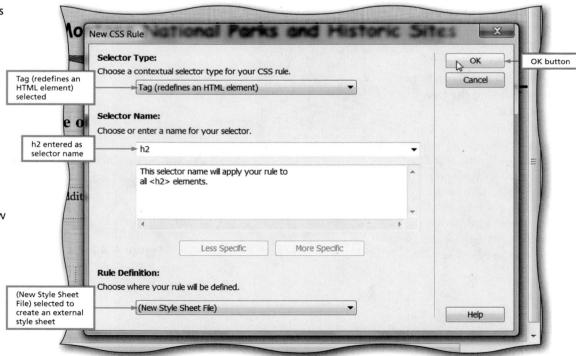

Figure 4–44

4

- Click the OK button to display the Save Style Sheet File As dialog box.

- If necessary, click the Save in box arrow and then click the parks folder to select the location for the style sheet file.

- Click the File name text box and then type **spotlight** to enter a name for the style sheet.

- Click the Save as type arrow and select Style Sheet Files (*.css), if necessary (Figure 4–45).

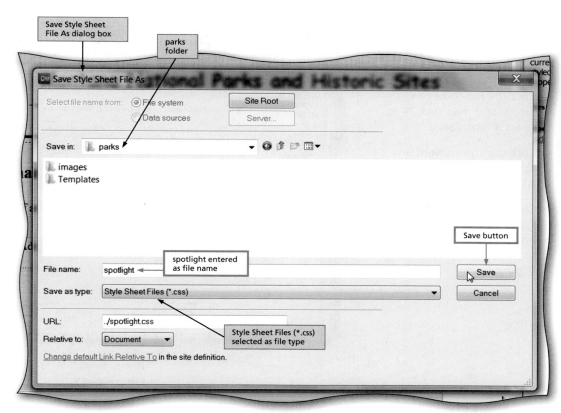

Figure 4–45

5

- Click the Save button to display the CSS Rule Definition for h2 in spotlight.css dialog box.

- If necessary, click Type in the Category list to display the properties for type (Figure 4–46).

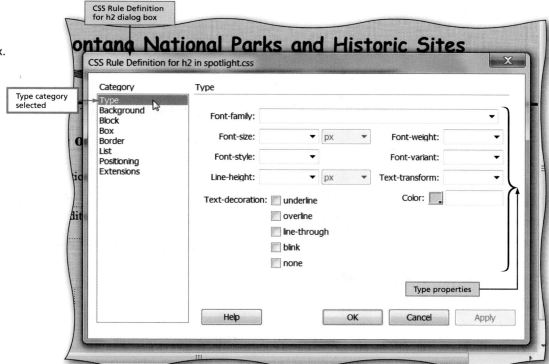

Figure 4–46

6

- Click the Font-family box arrow, and then click Arial, Helvetica, sans-serif to select a font family for h2 text.

- Click the Font-size box arrow, and then click 24 to select a font size.

- Click the Font-weight box arrow, and then click bolder to select a font weight.

- Click the Color text box, type #000 for black text, and then press the TAB key to enter the style definitions (Figure 4–47).

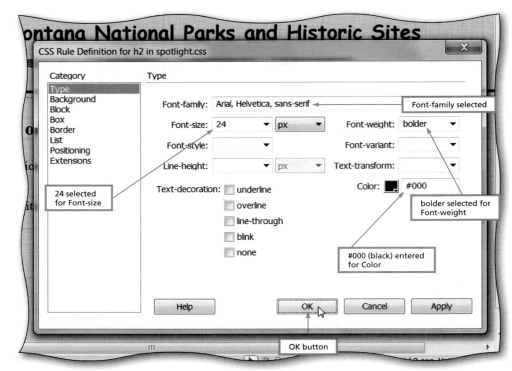

Figure 4–47

7

- Click the OK button to finish creating the new style rule.

- Click anywhere in the attraction_name editable region to deselect the heading prompt, which displays the new style (Figure 4–48).

Q&A What should I do if a Code Navigator icon appears?

Continue with the steps. The Code Navigator icon appears to help you navigate to related code sources, including CSS style rules.

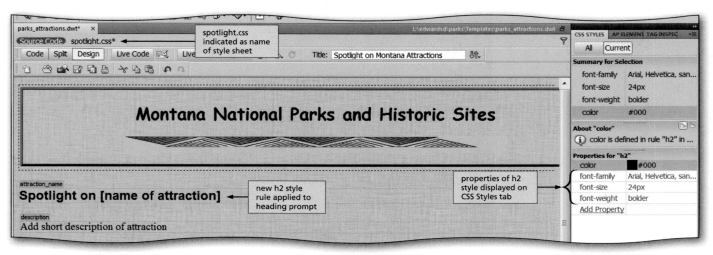

Figure 4–48

To Create a Style for the Paragraph Text

Next, you create a style for the description text. The following steps illustrate how to redefine the HTML paragraph tag for the description editable region.

1

• Click to the left of the prompt, Add short description of attraction, and then click the <p> tag in the tag selector to select the prompt (Figure 4–49).

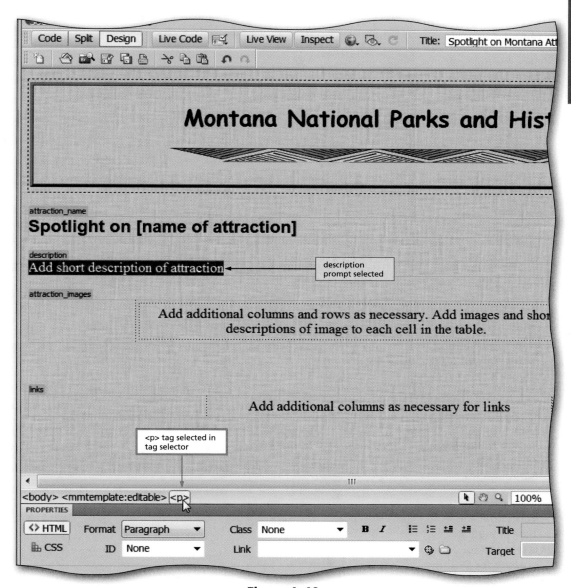

Figure 4–49

2

- Click the New CSS Rule button in the CSS Styles panel to display the New CSS Rule dialog box.

- Click the Selector Type button and then select Tag (redefines an HTML element).

- Verify that the p tag is displayed in the Selector Name text box to make sure you are creating a rule that defines paragraph text.

- Click the Rule Definition arrow, and then click (This document only) to specify where the rule will apply (Figure 4–50).

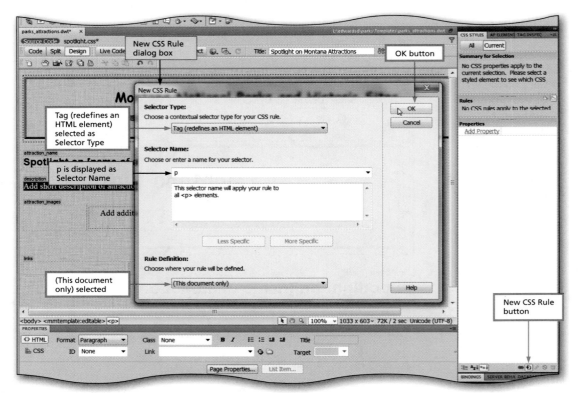

Figure 4–50

3

- Click the OK button to display the CSS Rule definition for p dialog box.

- Verify that the Type category is selected to prepare for setting Type properties (Figure 4–51).

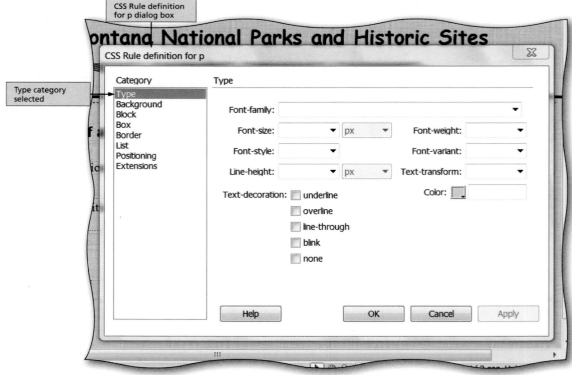

Figure 4–51

4

- Click the Font-family box arrow and then click Arial, Helvetica, sans-serif to select a font family for all <p> text in this document.

- Click the Font-size box arrow and then click 12 to select a font size.

- Click the Font-weight box arrow and then click bold to select a font weight.

- Click the Color text box, type #000 to set black as the text color, and then press the TAB key to enter the properties for <p> text (Figure 4–52).

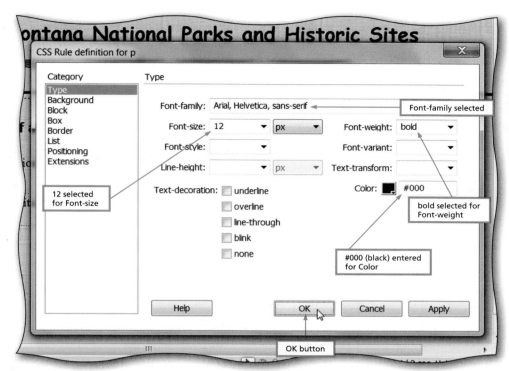

Figure 4–52

5

- Click the OK button to apply the styles to the current paragraph.

- Click to the right of the paragraph and observe the new text properties applied to the description prompt (Figure 4–53).

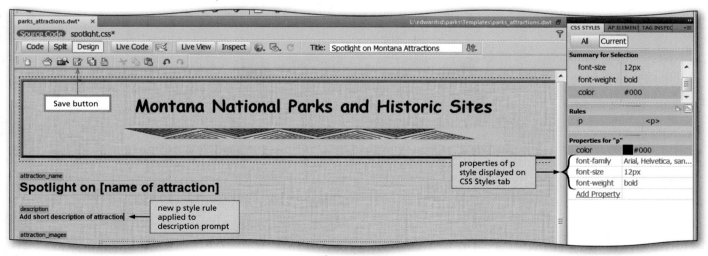

Figure 4–53

6

- Click the Save button on the Standard toolbar to save the style sheet.

BTW

Creating CSS Rules in the Property Inspector
Another way to create CSS style rules is to use the CSS Property inspector. Select text to which you want to apply a new CSS rule. Click the CSS button in the Property inspector, if necessary, to display the CSS Property inspector, and then click the Edit Rule button to open the New CSS Rule dialog box, which you use to specify the style attributes in the new rule.

To Add a Background, Border, and Text Color to a Table

Adding a background, border, and text color to the tables is your next goal. To accomplish this, you use the Type, Background, and Border categories in the New CSS Rule dialog box. The following steps show how to select a font, a background color of green, and a thick black border for each table.

• Click in the first cell of the first table.

• Click the <table#spotlight> tag in the tag selector to select the table.

• Click the New CSS Rule button in the CSS Styles panel to display the New CSS Rule dialog box.

• Click the Selector Type button and then click Tag (redefines an HTML element).

• If necessary, type **table** in the Selector Name text box (Figure 4–54).

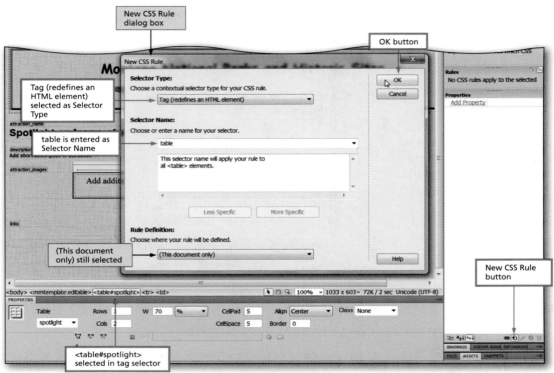

Figure 4–54

• Click the OK button to display the CSS Rule definition for table dialog box.

• Verify that the Type category is selected to prepare for setting Type properties (Figure 4–55).

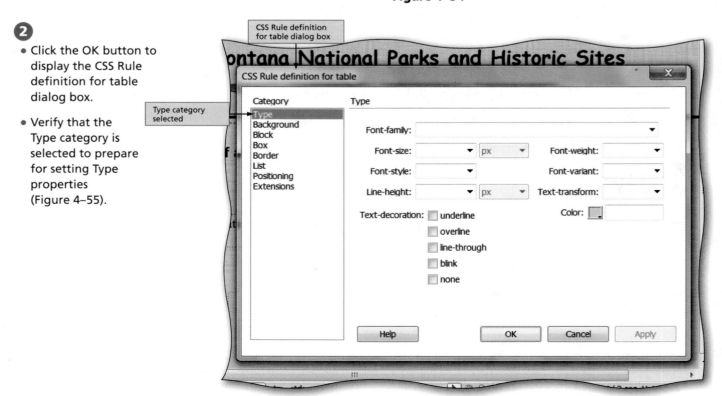

Figure 4–55

3

- Click the Font-family box arrow and then click Arial, Helvetica, sans-serif to select a font family.

- Click the Color text box, type **#000** to set black as the text color, and then press the TAB key to display the selected color (Figure 4–56).

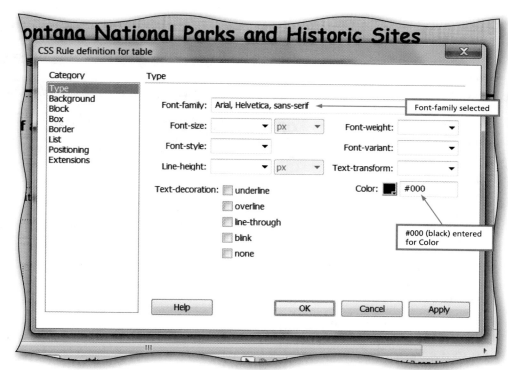

Figure 4–56

4

- Click Background in the Category list to display the Background properties.

- Click the Background-color text box, type **#8DA846** to set green as the background color, and then press the TAB key to display the background color in the Background-color box.

- Click the Apply button to apply

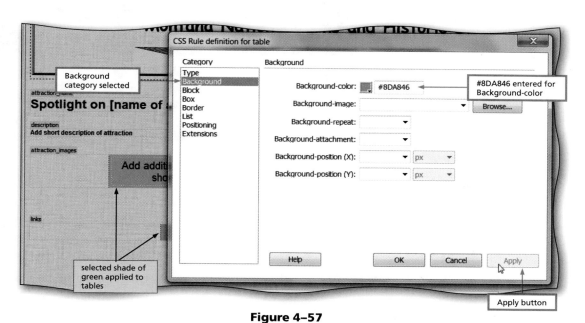

Figure 4–57

the selected shade of green to the table background (Figure 4–57).

5

- Click Border in the Category list to display the Border properties.

- Verify that the Same for all check boxes are selected for Style, Width, and Color to set the same properties to the top, right, bottom, and left borders of tables.

- Click the Top box arrow under Style and then click groove to select a groove border style.

- Click the first Width box arrow and then click thick to select a border width.

- Click the first text box in the Color column and then type #000 for the border color to set black as the border color.

- Press the TAB key to define the attributes (Figure 4–58).

Q&A

How will the CSS rule change the formatting of the current Web page?

The CSS rule being created is for the table style, so all the tables on the park_attractions page will share the same formatting: black Arial text, green background, and a grooved, thick black border.

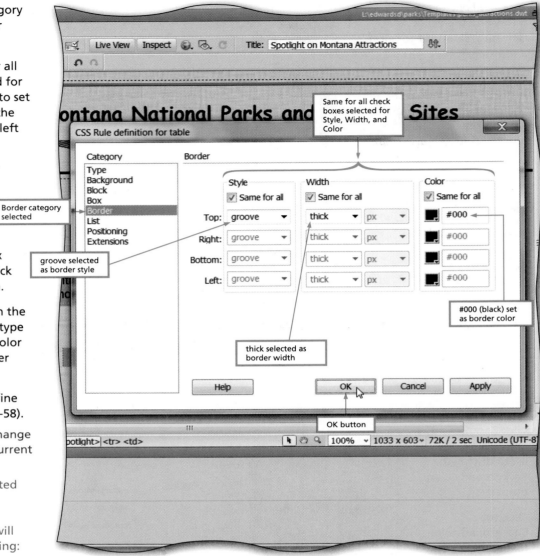

Figure 4–58

6

- Click the OK button to finish creating the CSS rule definition for the table style.

- Click anywhere in the spotlight table, and then click <table#spotlight> in the tag selector to select the table.

- If necessary, click the Current button in the CSS Styles panel to display only those styles applied to the current selection.

- In the CSS Styles panel, click the 'Show information about selected property' button to display the About section.

- In the Summary for Selection section, click the border property to select it.

- Drag the About bar and the Properties bar down to display the Summary for Selection, the About "border" section, and the Properties for "table" section (Figure 4–59).

Q&A

How do I access a full view of the attributes in the CSS Styles panel second column?

Move the pointer over the vertical bar until it turns into a two-headed arrow and then drag to the left.

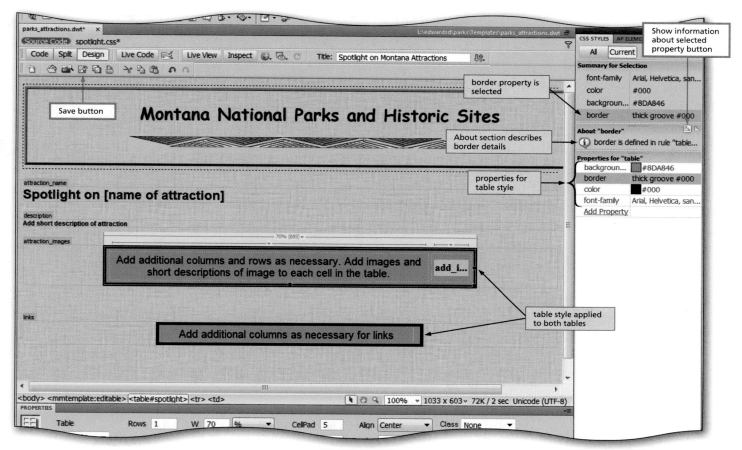

Figure 4–59

- Click a blank spot on the template page to deselect the table.

- Click the Save button on the Standard toolbar to save the page (Figure 4–60).

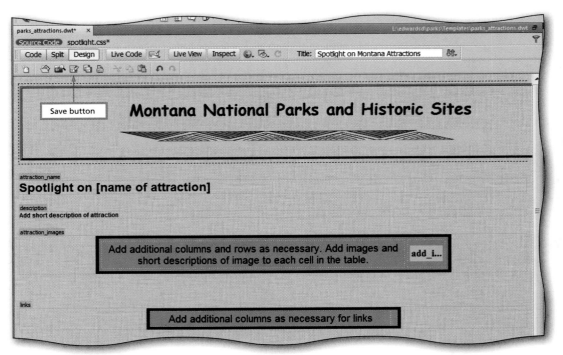

Figure 4–60

Style Sheets and Links

When you selected the <table> tag for the spotlight table and applied the attributes, you added the attributes to all tables in the template. Now you will add two links to the links table — a relative link to the index page and an absolute link to the Yellowstone National Park page.

Plan Ahead

> **Set styles for links.**
> Style sheets provide new ways to display links, which enable the content developer to match the style of the links with that of the rest of the Web page. When you are defining the style for links, you can apply the following four attributes:
>
> - **Link color** defines the style of an unvisited link.
>
> - **Visited links** defines the style of a link to a Web site that you have visited.
>
> - **Rollover links** defines the style of a link when the mouse pointer moves over the link.
>
> - **Active links** defines the style of a clicked link.

Using the Page Properties dialog box, you can specify that the links will use red for the text color and will not contain an underline when displayed in the browser. The Underline style within the Page Properties dialog box provides options to Always underline, Never underline, Show underline only on rollover, and Hide underline on rollover. The default setting for regular text is none. The default setting for links is Always underline. You also can specify that when the mouse pointer rolls over a link, the underline is displayed. This indicates to the Web page visitor that the link is available.

To Format Link Text

The following steps show how to add the attributes for formatting the links as the browser will display them.

1

- If necessary, scroll down, and then click anywhere in the links table (Figure 4–61).

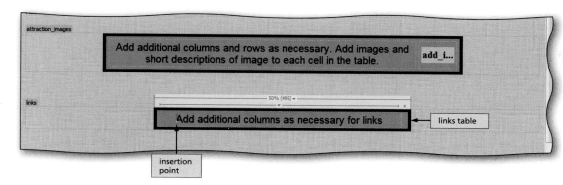

Figure 4–61

2

- Click the Page Properties button in the Property inspector to open the Page Properties dialog box.

- Click the Links (CSS) category to display the options for formatting link text (Figure 4–62).

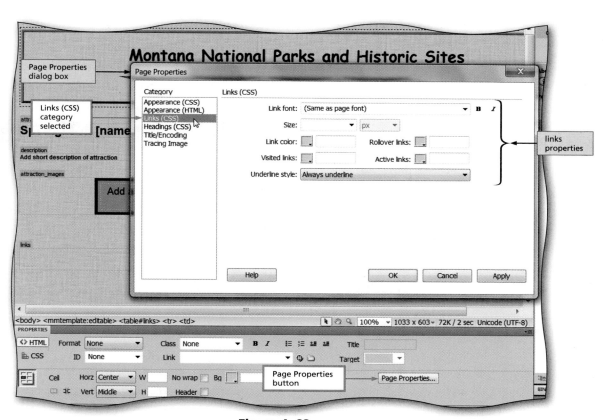

Figure 4–62

3
- Click the Link color button to display a color palette for unvisited link text (Figure 4–63).

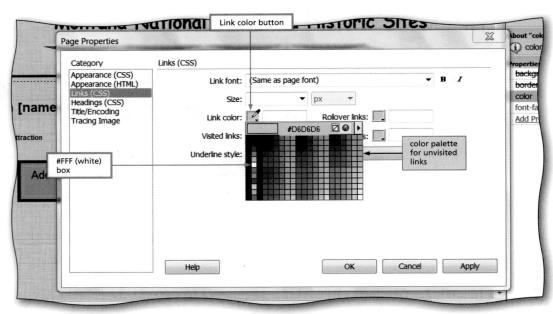

Figure 4–63

4
- In the left column of the color palette, click the white (#FFF) box, if necessary, to set white as the color for unvisited links (Figure 4–64).

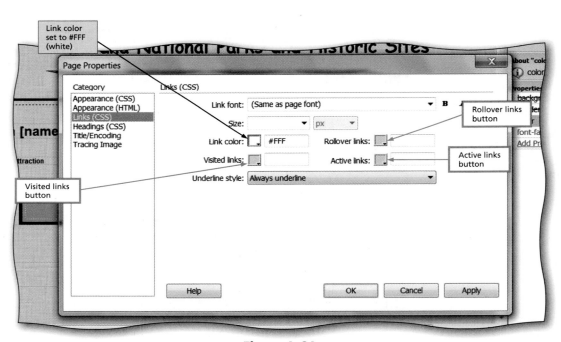

Figure 4–64

5

- Click the Rollover links color button and then click #900 (second column, seventh row) to select dark red as the Rollover links color.

- Click the Visited links color button and then click #6F9 (last column, fourth row) to select light green as the Visited links color.

- Click the Active links color button and then point to #FFF (first column, sixth row) (Figure 4–65).

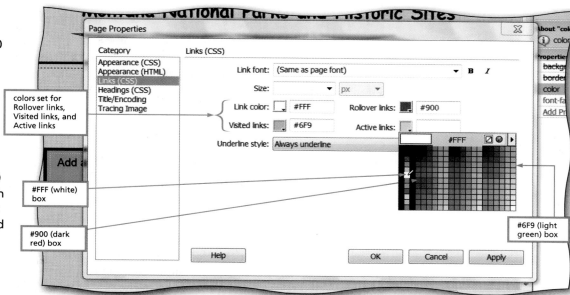

Figure 4–65

6

- Click #FFF to select white as the color for active links.

- If necessary, click the Underline style button and select Always underline to specify that link text always appears with an underline (Figure 4–66).

7

- Click the OK button to add the links attributes to the template.

- Click the Save button on the Standard toolbar to save your changes.

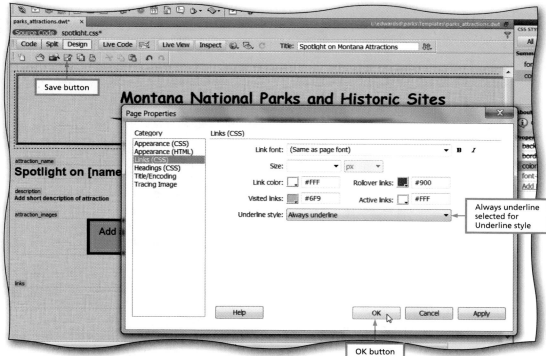

Figure 4–66

Q&A How can I remove a style?

To remove a style from an element on a Web page, select the element and then click the Delete CSS Rule button in the CSS Styles panel.

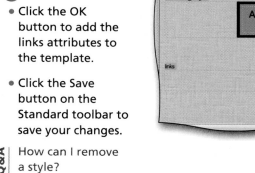

Maintaining Style Sheets

After a style is created, you can edit, delete, or duplicate it. You apply these commands using buttons at the bottom of the CSS Styles panel.

- **Current button**: When the Current button is selected, you can view the CSS rules that relate to the currently selected element.
- **All button**: When the All button is selected, the panel displays CSS rules that relate to the full document. Figure 4–67 shows an expanded view of the CSS panel with the All button selected and the properties you applied to the h2 element. Note that Current mode contains three panes — Summary for Selection, About, and Properties.

You can change any of these properties in either All view or Current view. Select the property and then click the Edit Rule button to display the CSS Rule definition dialog box. Make your changes and then click the OK button.

Below the Properties pane are three buttons that you can use to change the view in the Properties pane:

- **Show category view button**: Clicking the Show Category View button divides the CSS properties into categories. Double-clicking the property opens a box to the right of the selected text. Clicking the arrow in the box provides a list of properties that can be applied to the selected property.
- **Show list view button**: The Show List View button displays all Dreamweaver CSS properties in alphabetical order.
- **Set properties view button**: Set Properties View (default view) displays only set properties.

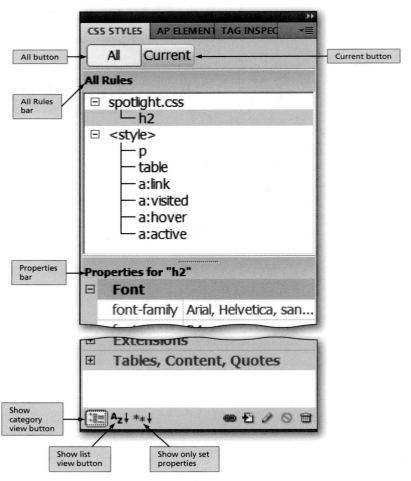

Figure 4–67

Creating a Web Page from a Template

After you create and save a template, you can use it to create a Web page. All the pages created from a template contain the same content that appears in the noneditable regions of the template. Content developers and others can change the content in the editable regions.

To Create the Yellowstone National Park Attractions Web Page

Now that you have created the template and added styles to it, you are ready to use the template to create the Yellowstone National Park Spotlight Web page.

1 If necessary, save the parks_attractions.dwt template page, and then close it.

Q&A What should I do if a Dreamweaver dialog box appears and asks whether to save changes to spotlight.css?

Click Yes to save any changes.

2 Collapse the CSS Styles panel, and then display the Files panel.

3 Click File on the Application bar and then click New.

4 Click Blank Page in the New Document dialog box, verify that HTML is selected in the Page Type column and that <none> is selected in the Layout column, and then click the Create button.

5 Click the Save button on the Standard toolbar and then save the page in the parks folder as a document named yellowstone.htm (Figure 4–68).

BTW

Updating Documents Based on Templates
When you change a template, Dreamweaver reminds you to update the documents based on that template. If you want to update documents at any other time, open the document, click Modify on the Application bar, point to Templates, and then click Update Current Page to update only the open page or click Update Pages to update all the pages based on the template.

Dreamweaver Chapter 4

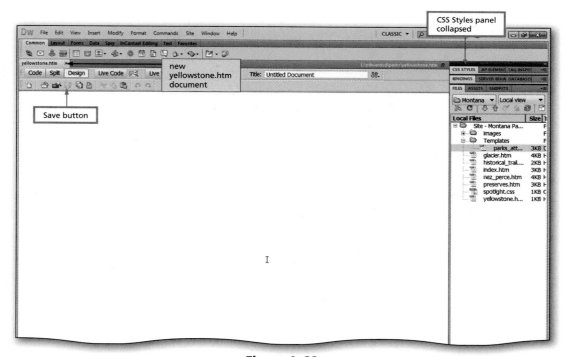

Figure 4–68

To Apply a Template to the Yellowstone National Park Web Page

To apply a template to a document, you use the Assets panel. The following steps illustrate how to display the Assets panel, apply the template to the Yellowstone National Park Web page, and add two rows to the spotlight table.

1

- Click the Assets tab in the Files group panel to display the assets for the Montana Parks Web site.

- Click the Templates icon in the Assets panel to display the templates for the site.

- Click parks_attractions to select the template (Figure 4–69).

Q&A Why does the Assets panel contain templates?

The Assets panel includes all of the assets for your site, including images, video, and other media. A template also is considered an asset.

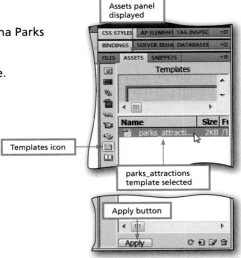

Figure 4–69

2

- Click the Apply button to apply the template.

- Collapse the panels to display the entire yellowstone.htm page (Figure 4–70).

Q&A How can I tell when a template is applied to a Dreamweaver document?

The document has a yellow border and a tab is displayed in the upper-right corner of the Document window with the name of the template.

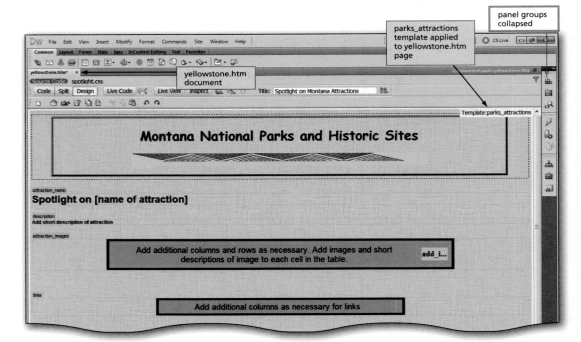

Figure 4–70

Other Ways

1. Click Document window; on Modify menu point to Templates, click Apply Template to Page on Templates submenu, select a template from list, click Select button

2. Click Document window; from Assets panel, drag template to Document window.

To Add the Name and Description of the Attraction to the Yellowstone National Park Web Page

Now you use the template to create the Yellowstone National Park Web page. You first save the page, add the name of the attraction, and then add a short description of the attraction. The following steps show how to save the page and add the attraction name and attraction description.

- If necessary, click anywhere in the document.

  Move the mouse pointer over the page and note that in the noneditable sections, such as the logo image, the pointer changes to a circle with a line through the middle.

- Select the text and brackets, [name of attraction], in the attraction_name editable region (Figure 4–71).

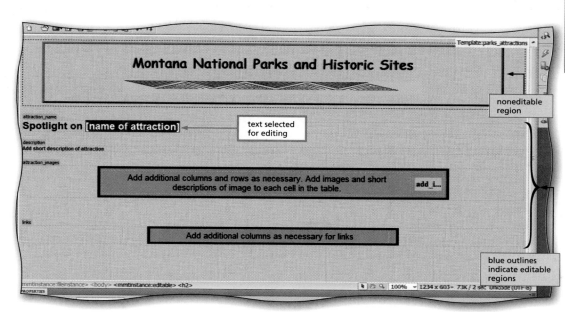

Figure 4–71

- Type **Yellowstone National Park** as the attraction name (Figure 4–72).

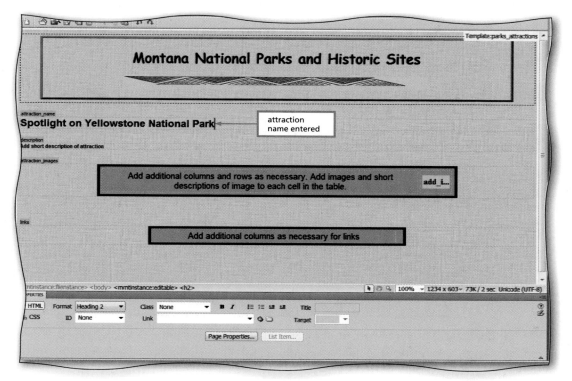

Figure 4–72

3

- Drag to select the prompt, Add short description of attraction, in the description editable region.

- Press the DELETE key to delete the prompt.

- Type the following text as the attraction description: `Yellowstone National Park was the first national park in the world. Established on March 1, 1872, the park spans an area of 3,468 square miles and is home to a large variety of wildlife, including grizzly bears, wolves, bison, and elk.` (Figure 4–73).

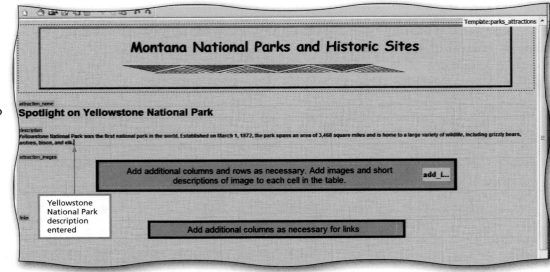

Figure 4–73

To Add Rows to the Spotlight Table

The following steps show how to add two rows to the spotlight table.

1 Click in the left cell of the spotlight table to prepare for modifying the table.

2 Click Modify on the Application bar, point to Table, and then click Insert Rows or Columns to display the Insert Rows or Columns dialog box.

3 Double-click the Number of rows text box and then type **2** for the number of rows to indicate you want to add two rows to the table.

4 Click the OK button to add the two rows to the spotlight table (Figure 4–74).

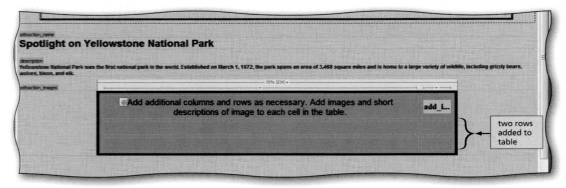

Figure 4–74

Expanded Tables Mode

Inserting an image into a table cell and then clicking to the right or left of the image is somewhat awkward in Dreamweaver. Using Expanded Tables mode will be helpful as you add images and text to the spotlight table. Expanded Tables mode provides extra cell spacing and cell padding so you can select items in tables or precisely place the insertion point. You return to Standard mode when you finish adding images and text to the table.

To Add Images to the Spotlight Table in Expanded Tables Mode

To add an image, you drag the image from the Assets panel to a table cell. You use Expanded Tables mode to assist with insertion point placement. The following steps illustrate how to add the six images and a short description of each image in Expanded Tables mode.

- Expand the panel groups to display the Assets tab and then click the Images button to display images only.

- Click to the left of the text in row 1, column 1 of the spotlight table, hold down the SHIFT key, and then press the ENTER key to insert a line break above the placeholder text.

- Press the UP ARROW key to position the insertion point in the new line.

- Click the Layout tab on the Insert bar, and then click the Expanded button to switch to Expanded Tables mode (Figure 4–75).

Q&A

What should I do if a Getting Started in Expanded Tables Mode dialog box is displayed?

Read the information and then click the OK button.

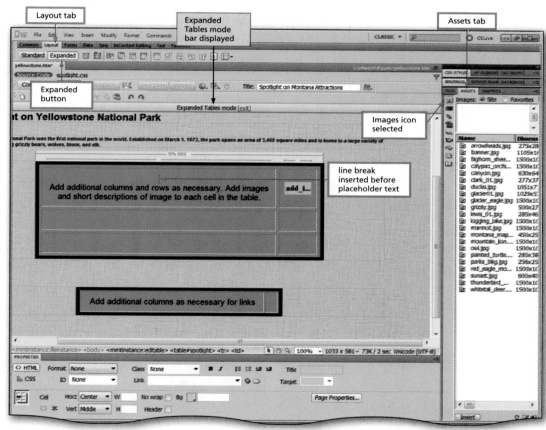

Figure 4–75

2

- Drag the calypso_ orchids.jpg file from the Assets panel to the insertion point in row 1, column 1 of the spotlight table to add the image to the table.

- Resize the image to a W of 500 and H of 350.

- Type `calypso_ orchid` in the ID text box to name the image.

- Press the F5 key to refresh the page.

- If necessary, scroll to view the complete image (Figure 4–76).

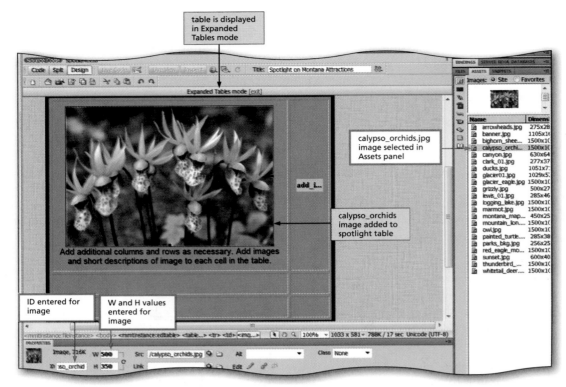

Figure 4–76

3

- Select the placeholder text below the image, and then type `Montana Calypso Orchids` as the image description (Figure 4–77).

Figure 4–77

4

- Press the TAB key to move the insertion point to row 1, column 2 to select the image placeholder (Figure 4–78).

image placeholder selected in row 1, column 2 of spotlight table

Figure 4–78

5

- Press the DELETE key to delete the image placeholder.

- Drag the logging_ lake.jpg file from the Assets panel to the insertion point in row 1, column 2 to insert the image in the table.

- Resize the image to a W of 500 and H of 350.

- In the ID text box, type **logging_lake** as the image name.

- Press the F5 key to refresh the page.

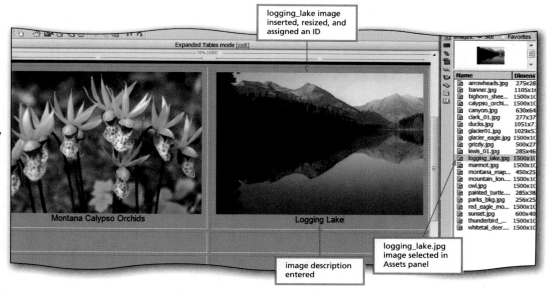

logging_lake image inserted, resized, and assigned an ID

logging_lake.jpg image selected in Assets panel

image description entered

Figure 4–79

- Click to the right of the image, hold down the SHIFT key, and then press the ENTER key to insert a line break.

Q&A Where is the insertion point?

The insertion point is below the image. You may not see the insertion point until you begin typing.

- Type **Logging Lake** as the description below the image (Figure 4–79).

6

- Add the four other images and descriptions to the spotlight table as indicated in Table 4–2 on the next page.

- Resize all of the images to a W of 500 and H of 350.

- Collapse the panel groups to display as much of the table as possible (Figure 4–80).

Q&A

How should I add the four other images and descriptions?

Scrolling as necessary, drag each image to the appropriate table cell, resize and name the image, refresh the page, click to the right of the image, insert a line break (hold down SHIFT and press the ENTER key), and then type the description. Press the TAB key to move from cell to cell.

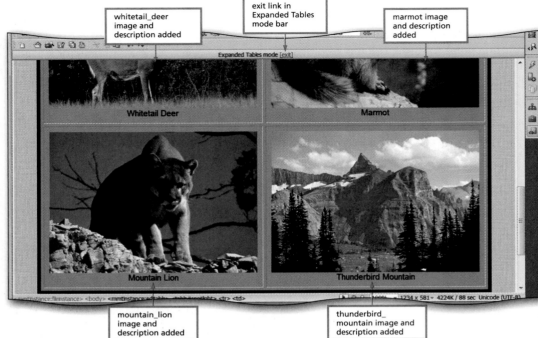

whitetail_deer image and description added

exit link in Expanded Tables mode bar

marmot image and description added

mountain_lion image and description added

thunderbird_ mountain image and description added

Figure 4–80

7

- Click each image and add the Alt text for each image as listed in Table 4–3 on the next page.

- Save the page (Figure 4–81).

Save button

Figure 4–81

Other Ways

1. Click table cell; on Insert menu click Image, select file name in Select Image Source dialog box, click OK button.

Table 4–2 Montana Parks Image File Names and Descriptions

Cell	Image	Image ID	Image Description
Row 1, Column 1	calpyso_orchids.jpg	calypso_orchids	Montana Calypso Orchids
Row 1, Column 2	logging_lake.jpg	logging_lake	Logging Lake
Row 2, Column 1	whitetail_deer.jpg	whitetail_deer	Whitetail Deer
Row 2, Column 2	marmot.jpg	marmot	Marmot
Row 3, Column 1	mountain_lion.jpg	mountain_lion	Mountain Lion
Row 3, Column 2	thunderbird_mountain.jpg	thunderbird_mountain	Thunderbird Mountain

Table 4–3 Alt Text for Yellowstone National Park Images

Image	Alt Text
calpyso_orchids.jpg	Yellowstone orchids
logging_lake.jpg	Logging Lake
whitetail_deer.jpg	Yellowstone whitetail deer
marmot.jpg	Yellowstone marmot
mountain_lion	Yellowstone mountain lion
thunderbird_mountain	Thunderbird Mountain

Specifying Link Targets

To complete the Yellowstone National Park Web page, you add two links in the links table. The first link is a relative link to the Montana Parks home page (index.htm). The second link is an absolute link to the Yellowstone National Park Web page. Thus far, when creating links, you used the default and did not specify a target. The target for your links, therefore, has been to open the linked document in the same browser window.

When you create the link to the Yellowstone National Park Web page, however, the page should open in a new browser window. Recall from Chapter 2 that the Target option in the Property inspector specifies the frame or window in which the linked page is displayed. When the _blank target is specified, the linked document opens in a new browser window. The other three choices in the Target options are _parent, _self, and _top. All the Target options are described in Table 4–4.

Table 4–4 Target Options for Links

Option	Effect
_blank	Opens the linked document in a new browser window without affecting the current window
_parent	Opens the linked document in the current window (the window containing the link text), replacing the current window
_self	Opens the linked document in the window containing the link text; has the same effect as the _parent option
_top	Opens the linked document in the full browser window, replacing the current window

To Add Targeted Links to the Links Table and Add Image Borders

The following steps show how to insert the two links to the links table and add borders to the images.

1

- If necessary, scroll down to display the links table.

- Select the text in the left cell of the links table and then press the DELETE key to delete all of the text from the cell (Figure 4–82).

Figure 4–82

2

- Type **Home** as the link text in the left cell and then select the text to prepare for linking it to a Web page.

- Click the Link text box in the Property inspector, and then type **index.htm** as the relative link.

- Press the TAB key to add the link to the Montana Parks home page and center it in the first cell of the links table.

- Click anywhere in the Home link to deselect the text (Figure 4–83).

Q&A

Why does the Home link text appear in white?

You set the link color for unvisited links to white using the Links (CSS) category in the Page Properties dialog box.

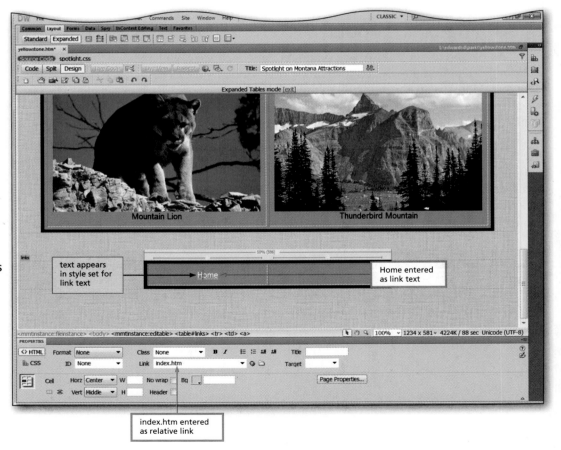

Figure 4–83

3

- Click the right cell in the links table to prepare for entering another link.

- Type **Yellowstone National Park** as the link text, and then select the text.

- Click the Link text box in the Property inspector, and then type **http://www.nps .gov/yell/index .htm** as the absolute link.

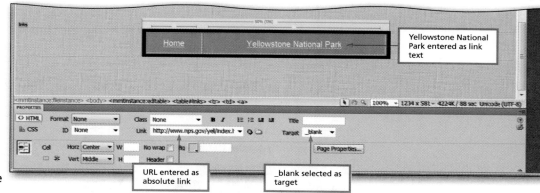

Figure 4–84

- Click the Target box arrow and select _blank.

- Press the F5 key to refresh the page.

- Click anywhere in the Yellowstone National Park link to deselect the text (Figure 4–84).

Q&A

What will happen when a user clicks the Yellowstone National Park link?

The linked page will open in a new window when the link is clicked.

4

- Click the exit link in the Expanded Tables mode bar to exit Expanded Tables mode.

- Scroll to the top of the page and select the Montana Calypso Orchids image.

- Click the Border box in the Property inspector and type 5 to add a border to the image.

- Press the TAB key to apply the border, and then click anywhere in the spotlight table to deselect the Montana Calypso Orchids image (Figure 4–85).

Figure 4–85

5

- Select each of the other images and apply a 5-pixel border.

- Click the Save button and then view the page in your browser (Figure 4–86).

6

- Close the browser window.

5-pixel border applied to each image

5-pixel border applied to each table

Figure 4–86

To Add a Link from the Index Page to the Yellowstone National Park Page

The following steps illustrate how to complete the update of the Montana Parks Web site by adding a link from the index page to the Yellowstone National Park page.

1 Expand the panel groups, click the Files tab, and then open the index.htm page.

2 Scroll down to the links table on the index.htm page, click to the right of the Glacier National Park link, press the SPACEBAR, and then insert a vertical line.

3 Select the space and line you just entered, and then delete the text in the Link box in the Property inspector.

4 Insert a space after the vertical line, and then type **Featured Attraction** as the link text.

5 Select the text and then drag yellowstone.htm from the Files panel to the Link box in the Property inspector.

6 Click the Save button on the Standard toolbar, and then press the RIGHT ARROW key to deselect the text (Figure 4–87).

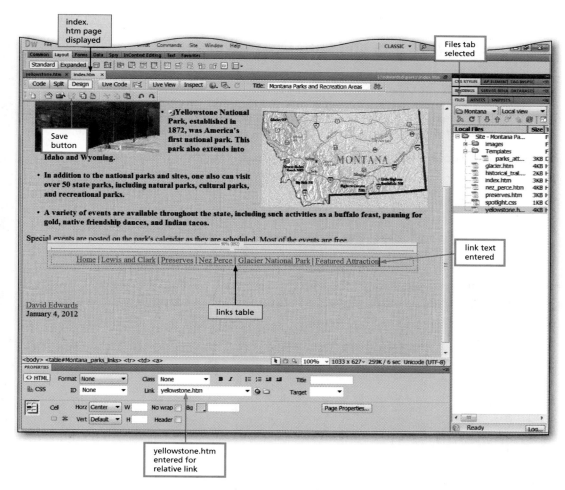

Figure 4–87

7 Press the F12 key to preview the index.htm page in your browser.

8 Scroll down and then click the Featured Attraction link to view the Yellowstone National Park Web page. Verify that the Yellowstone National Park Web page links work.

9 If instructed to do so, print a copy of the Yellowstone National Park Web page and submit it to your instructor.

10 If instructed to do so, upload your Web site to a remote server.

Q&A How do I upload the Web site to a remote server?

Appendix C contains information on uploading to a remote server. A remote folder is required before you can upload to a remote server. Generally, the remote folder is defined by the Web server administrator or your instructor.

11 Close the browser.

Quitting Dreamweaver

After you have created your Web page based on a template with applied styles, and tested and verified that the links work, Chapter 4 is complete.

To Close the Web Site and Quit Dreamweaver

The following steps show how to close the Web site, quit Dreamweaver CS5, and return control to Windows.

1 Click the Close button on the upper-right corner of the Dreamweaver title bar to close the Dreamweaver window, the Document window, and the Montana Parks Web site.

2 If you have unsaved changes, click the Yes button in response to the Dreamweaver prompt.

CSS Style Definition Category Descriptions

Tables 4–5 through 4–12 list the attributes and descriptions of the eight categories of CSS properties available through the CSS Rule Definition dialog box. Not all browsers support all properties; browser support is indicated in the Description column. The phrase "both browsers" refers to Microsoft Internet Explorer and Mozilla Firefox.

Table 4–5 CSS Style Type Properties

Attributes	Description
Font Family	Sets the font family for the style. Supported by both browsers.
Font Size	Defines the size of the text. Enter or select a number and then select a unit of measurement. Selecting pixels prevents Web site visitors from adjusting the text size in their Web browsers. Supported by both browsers.
Font Weight	Applies a specific or relative amount of boldface to the font. Normal is equivalent to 400; Bold is equivalent to 700. The weight attribute is supported by both browsers.
Font Style	Specifies Normal, Italic, or Oblique as the font style. The default setting is Normal. The style attribute is supported by both browsers.
Font Variant	Specifies small-caps or normal. Dreamweaver does not display this attribute in the Document window. Not supported by Netscape Navigator.
Line Height	Sets the height of the line on which the text is placed. This setting is traditionally called leading. Select Normal to have the line height for the font size calculated automatically, or enter an exact value and select a unit of measurement. The line height attribute is supported by both browsers.
Text Transform	Capitalizes the first letter of each word in the selection or sets the text to all up-percase or lowercase. Supported by both browsers.
Text Decoration	Adds an underline, overline, or line-through to the text, or makes the text blink. Supported by both browsers.
Color	Sets the text color. Supported by both browsers.

Table 4–6 CSS Style Background Properties

Attributes	Description
Background Color	Sets the background color for an element — a character, a word, a paragraph, or even the Web page itself. Supported by both browsers.
Background Image	Sets the background image to either a Web page or a table. Supported by both browsers.
Background Repeat	Repeats the background image. Supported by both browsers.
Background Attachment	Determines whether the background image is fixed at its original position or scrolls along with the content. Not supported by Netscape Navigator.
Background Position (X) and Background Position (Y)	Specifies a position for selected text or other Web page elements. Can be used to align a background image to the center of the page, both vertically and horizontally, or to align the element relative to the Document window.

Table 4–7 CSS Style Block Properties

Attributes	Description
Word Spacing	Sets the spacing between words; not displayed in the Document window.
Letter Spacing	Sets the spacing between letters or characters. Supported by both browsers.
Vertical Align	Specifies the vertical alignment of the element to which it is applied. Is displayed in the Document window only when applied to an image. Supported by both browsers.
Text Align	Sets the text alignment within the element. Supported by both browsers.
Text Indent	Specifies the amount of space the first line of text is indented. Supported by both browsers.
Whitespace	Determines how the browser displays extra white space. Supported by Internet Explorer 5.5 and higher.
Display	Specifies whether an element is displayed, and, if so, how it is displayed. Supported by both browsers.

Table 4–8 CSS Style Box Properties

Attributes	Description
Width and Height	Sets the width and height of an element. Supported by both browsers.
Float	Sets which side other elements, such as text, layers, and tables, will float around an element. Supported by both browsers.
Clear	Prevents an element from wrapping around an object with a right or left float. Supported by both browsers.
Padding	Specifies the amount of space between the content of an element and its border (or margin if there is no border). Supported by both browsers.
Margin	Specifies the amount of space between the border of an element (or the padding if there is no border) and another element. Supported by both browsers.
Same For All	Sets the same padding or margin attributes to the Top, Right, Bottom, and Left of the padding and element to which it is applied. Supported by both browsers.

Table 4–9 CSS Style Border Properties

Attributes	Description
Type	Sets the style appearance of the border. Appearance may be rendered differently in different browsers. Supported by both browsers.
Same For All	Applies the same style, thickness, or color to the Top, Bottom, Right, and Left of the element to which it is applied. Supported by both browsers.
Width	Sets the thickness of the element. Supported by both browsers.
Color	Sets the color of the border. Supported by both browsers.

Table 4–10 CSS Style List Properties

Attributes	Description
List style type	Sets the appearance of bullets or numbers. Supported by both browsers.
List style image	Specifies a custom image for the bullet. Supported by both browsers.
List style position	Sets whether list item text wraps and indents (outside) or whether the text wraps to the left margin (inside). Supported by both browsers.

Table 4–11 CSS Style Positioning Properties

Attributes	Description
Position	Determines how the browser should position the element (absolute, relative, fixed, or static).
Visibility	Determines the initial display condition of the content.
Z-Index	Determines the stacking order of the layer.
Height	Sets the height of the layer.
Overflow	Determines what happens if the content of a layer exceeds its size. CSS layers only.
Placement	Specifies the location and size of the layer (Left, Top, Right, or Bottom).
Clip	Defines the part of the layer that is visible (Left, Top, Right, or Bottom).

Table 4–12 CSS Style Extension Properties

Attributes	Description
Page break before	Creates a page break during printing either before or after the object controlled by the style.
Cursor	Changes the pointer image when the pointer is over the object controlled by style.
Filter	Applies special effects to the object controlled by the style.

Chapter Summary

In this chapter, you learned about templates and style sheets. You created a template document, and then defined editable and noneditable regions on the page. You designed the template by adding a logo, text, and table for images and links. You also created a style sheet and added a style to it. You created a new Web page based on the template, added images and links to the tables, and then tested the links on the new page. The items listed below include all the new skills you have learned in this chapter.

1. Create and save a template (DW 272)
2. Add a banner image to the template (DW 275)
3. Add the attraction name and attraction description prompts for the first two editable regions (DW 278)
4. Add and center a table as the third editable region (DW 280)
5. Add and center a table as the fourth editable region (DW 285)
6. Create the first editable region (DW 287)
7. Create the second editable region (DW 289)
8. Create the third and fourth editable regions (DW 290)
9. Display the CSS Styles panel (DW 296)
10. Add a style and save the style sheet (DW 298)
11. Create a style for the paragraph text (DW 302)
12. Add a background, border, and text color to a table (DW 305)
13. Format link text (DW 310)
14. Apply a template to the Yellowstone National Park Web page (DW 316)
15. Add the name and description of the attraction to the Yellowstone National Park Web page (DW 318)
16. Add images to the spotlight table in Expanded Tables mode (DW 320)
17. Add targeted links to the links table and add image borders (DW 325)

Learn It Online

Test your knowledge of chapter content and key terms.

Instructions: To complete the Learn It Online exercises, start your browser, click the Address bar, and then enter the Web address scsite.com/dwcs5/learn. When the Dreamweaver CS5 Learn It Online page is displayed, click the link for the exercise you want to complete and then read the instructions.

Chapter Reinforcement TF, MC, and SA

A series of true/false, multiple choice, and short answer questions that test your knowledge of the chapter content.

Flash Cards

An interactive learning environment where you identify chapter key terms associated with displayed definitions.

Practice Test

A series of multiple choice questions that test your knowledge of chapter content and key terms.

Who Wants To Be a Computer Genius?

An interactive game that challenges your knowledge of chapter content in the style of a television quiz show.

Wheel of Terms

An interactive game that challenges your knowledge of chapter key terms in the style of the television show *Wheel of Fortune*.

Crossword Puzzle Challenge

A crossword puzzle that challenges your knowledge of key terms presented in the chapter.

Apply Your Knowledge

Reinforce the skills and apply the concepts you learned in this chapter.

Creating a Template and Applying It to a Web Page

Instructions: In this activity, you add a background color and some text to a template and then apply the template to a Web page. Figure 4–88 shows the completed template and Web page. Make sure you have downloaded the data files for this chapter. See the inside back cover of this book for instructions for downloading the Data Files for Students, or contact your instructor for information about accessing the required files for this book.

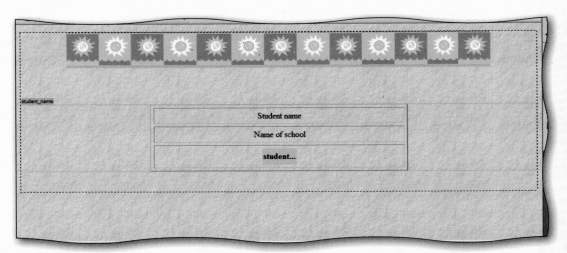

Figure 4–88a

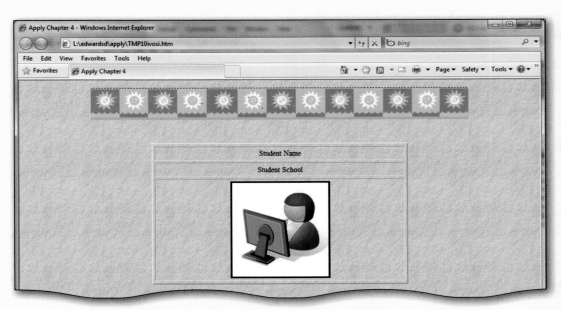

Figure 4–88b

Perform the following tasks:

1. Start Dreamweaver, and then copy the data files from the Chapter04\apply data files folder into the apply\images folder for your Apply Exercises local Web site.

2. Open the Apply Exercises site.

3. Create a blank HTML template, and then save it as a template named apply.dwt.

4. Add the apply_bkg image as the background image for the template.

5. Insert the banner.jpg image at the top of the template page and then center the banner.

6. Click to the right of the banner and then press the ENTER key two times to insert a blank line.

7. Insert a three-row, one-column table with a width of 50 percent, border thickness of 2, cell padding of 5, and cell spacing of 5. Name the table student_info.

8. Center the table on the page, if necessary. Change the Horz setting for all cells to Center.

9. Type **Student name** in the first row and **Name of school** in the second row.

10. Add an image placeholder named student to the third row. Resize the placeholder to 64 (Width) by 32 (Height) pixels.

11. Select the table, click Insert on the Application bar, point to Template Objects, and then click Editable Region.

12. Name the editable region student_name, and then click outside the editable region to deselect it.

13. Save the template (Figure 4–88a).

14. Close the apply.dwt template document. Create a new blank HTML page and save it as apply_ch04.htm. Title the page Apply Chapter 4.

15. Apply the template to the new page.

16. Enter your name in the Student name row and the name of your school in the Name of school row.

17. Insert the student_female.jpg or student_male.jpg image in the third row. Resize the image to 200 (W) by 200 (H) pixels, and add a 4-pixel border to the image.

18. Save the document, and then view it in your browser (Figure 4–88b). Submit the template and Web page in the format specified by your instructor.

Extend Your Knowledge

Extend the skills you learned in this chapter and experiment with new skills. You may need to use Help to complete the assignment.

Creating a Template

Instructions: In this activity, you create a template with a background, a table, and text, and then apply styles to a Web page. Figure 4–89 shows the completed template and Web page. Make sure you have downloaded the data files for this chapter. See the inside back cover of this book for instructions for downloading the Data Files for Students, or contact your instructor for information about accessing the required files for this book.

Figure 4–89a

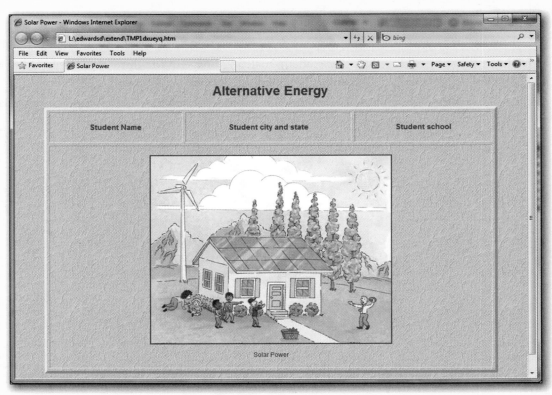

Figure 4–89b

Perform the following tasks:

1. Start Dreamweaver, and then copy the data file from the Chapter03\extend folder to the extend\images folder for the Extend Exercises site.

2. Open the Extend Exercises site.

3. Create a blank HTML template page and save it as a template named extend.dwt.

4. Add the extend_bkg image as the background image for the template.

5. Type **Alternative Energy**, format it as Heading 1, and then center the heading. Press ENTER and then insert a two-row, three-column table with a width of 90 percent, 6 for cell padding and cell spacing, and a border of 5 pixels.

6. Center the table.

7. Click row 1, column 1 and then type the following text: **Your name goes here.**

8. Click row 1, column 2, and then type the following text: **Your city and state goes here.**

9. Click row 1, column 3, and then type the following text: **Your school name goes here.**

10. Apply Heading 3 to the text in row 1.

11. Merge the cells in row 2.

12. Open the Page Properties dialog box.

13. In the Appearance (CSS) category, select Arial, Helvetica, sans-serif for the Page font and 14 for the Size. Enter #639 for the text color, and then apply the settings to the template.

14. Change the Horz setting for all cells to Center. Name the table solar_power.

15. Title the template document Solar Power.

16. Select the solar_power table and make all of the table cells editable. Name the editable region alt_energy.

17. Click outside the table, save the template (Figure 4–89a), and then close it.

18. Open a new blank HTML page and then save it as extend_ch04.

19. Apply the extend template to the new page.

20. Add your name, city and state, and the name of your school as indicated by the prompts on the template.

21. Drag the solar_power image to row 2. Resize the image to 500 (W) by 400 (H) pixels, and add a 3-pixel border to the image.

22. Below the image, type **Solar Power** as the image description.

23. Save the document, and then view it in your browser (Figure 4–89b). Submit the template and Web page in the format specified by your instructor.

Make It Right

Analyze a Web page template and correct all errors and/or improve the design.

Modifying a Template

Instructions: In this activity, you modify a template and add your name and the name of a raffle item to a Web page (Figure 4–90). Make sure you have downloaded the data files for Chapter04\right. See the inside back cover of this book for instructions for downloading the Data Files for Students, or contact your instructor for information about accessing the required files for this book.

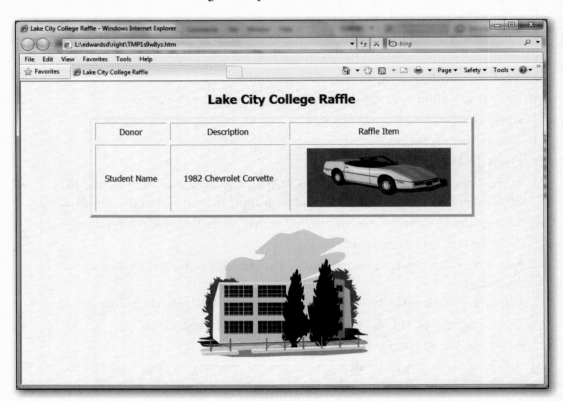

Figure 4–90

Perform the following tasks:

1. Start Dreamweaver, and then copy the right.dwt file from the Chapter04\right data files folder into a new folder named Templates for your Right Exercises local Web site. (For example, the Templates folder might be stored on L:\edwardsd\extend\Templates.) Copy the image files from the Chapter04\right\images data files folder into the right\images folder for your Right Exercises local Web site.

2. Open the Right Exercises site, and then open the right.dwt template.

3. Click at the end of the heading text, and then press the ENTER key.

4. Create a two-row, three-column table with a width of 75 percent, cell padding and cell spacing of 8, and a 5 px border. Name the table raffle_items and then center it.

5. Select the cells in row 1 and change the Horz setting to Center and the Vert setting to Middle. Select the cells in row 2 and change the Horz setting to Center and the Vert setting to Middle.

6. In row 1, column 1, type **Donor**. In row 1, column 2, type **Description**. In row 1, column 3, type **Raffle Item**.

7. In row 2, column 1, type **[Enter your first and last name]**.

8. In row 2, column 2, type **[Enter your raffle item]**.

9. In row 2, column 3, insert an image placeholder named donation. Resize the placeholder to 75 (W) by 75 (H) pixels.

10. Make the raffle_items table an editable region named donation.

11. Insert the college.jpg image from your images folder below the table. Center the image on the page, if necessary. Resize the college.jpg image to 377 (W) by 300 (H) pixels.

12. Save the template and then close it.

13. Create a new HTML page named right_ch04.htm, and then apply the template to the new page.

14. Select the placeholder text in the first column, second row in the table and then type your name.

15. Select the placeholder text in the second column, second row in the table and then type **1982 Chevrolet Corvette.**

16. Select the image placeholder in the third column and replace it with the car.jpg image. Resize the image to 300 (W) by 125 (H) pixels.

17. Title the document Lake City College Raffle. Save your document and then view it in your browser (Figure 4–90).

18. Submit the template and the Web page in the format specified by your instructor.

In the Lab

Create a document using the guidelines, concepts, and skills presented in this chapter. Labs are listed in order of increasing difficulty.

Lab 1: Creating a Template and Style Sheet for Bryan's Computer Repair Services Web Site

Problem: Bryan wants to add a page to the Computer Repair Services Web site that highlights his weekly features. He wants something that can be modified easily, so he plans to use a template to create the page. To create this template and then add styles, you copy four images from the computers folder provided with your data files to the Computer Repair Services Web site images folder. You begin the process by creating a template, and then you define styles. Next, you apply this template to a new blank page and create a page for featured computers. Finally, you add a link to and from the Bryan's Computer Repair Services home page.

The template is shown in Figure 4–91a; the Web page is shown in Figure 4–91b. Software and hardware settings determine how a Web page is displayed in a browser. Your Web page may appear different from the one shown in Figure 4–91. Appendix C contains instructions for uploading your local site to a remote site.

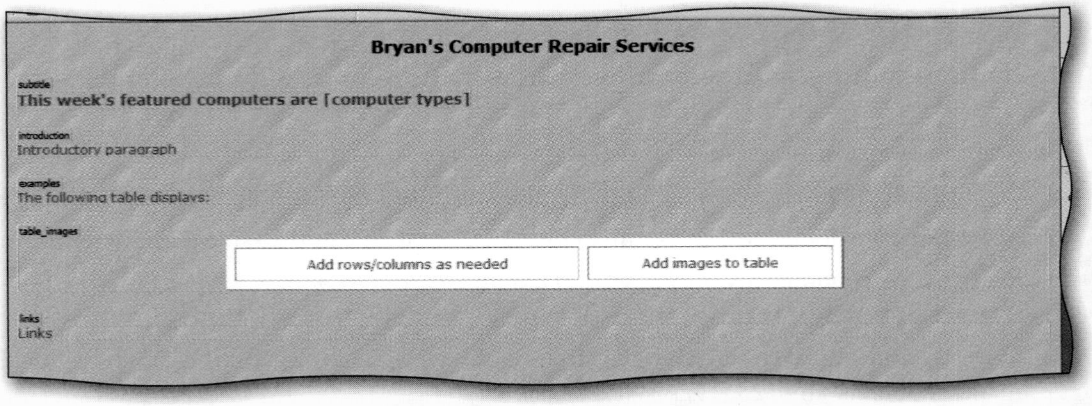

Bryan's Computer Repair Services
subtitle
This week's featured computers are [computer types]
introduction
Introductory paragraph
examples
The following table displays:
table_images
Add rows/columns as needed
Add images to table
links
Links

Figure 4–91a

Bryan's Computer Repair Services - Windows Internet Explorer
L:\edwardsd\computers\TMP9doqoe.htm
File Edit View Favorites Tools Help
Favorites
Bryan's Computer Repair Services
Page Safety Tools
Bryan's Computer Repair Services
This week's featured computers are desktop, laptop, tablet, and handheld computer.
Weekly specials include USB flash drives: once you get your hands on these high-capacity drives, you will not let go!
The following table displays this week's specials:
Desktop
Laptop
Tablet
Handheld
Home

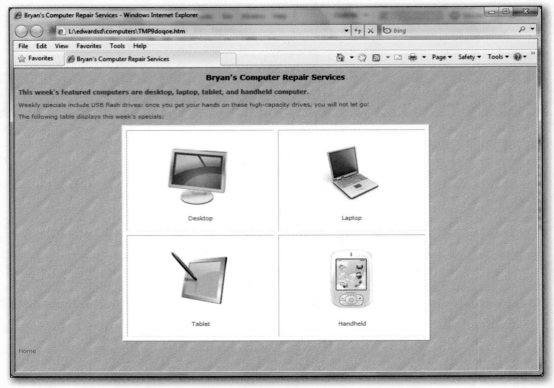

Figure 4–91b

Perform the following tasks:

1. Start Dreamweaver, and then copy the data files from the Chapter04\computers data files folder into the images folder for your Computer Repair Services local Web site.

2. Open the Computer Repair Services site.

3. Create a blank HTML template. Save it as a template named weekly_features.dwt.

4. Use the Page Properties dialog box to apply the repair_bkg background image to the page.

5. If necessary, click the upper-left corner of the Document window. Type **Bryan's Computer Repair Services** as the heading, and then press ENTER.

6. Select the heading, format it as Heading 1, and then center it.

7. Below the heading, type the following text: **This week's featured computers are [computer types]**. Apply Heading 3 and then press the ENTER key. Align the text to the left.

8. Type **Introductory paragraph** and then press the ENTER key.

9. Type **The following table displays:** and then press the ENTER key.

10. Insert a one-row, two-column table with a width of 60 percent, border of 2, cell padding of 8, and cell spacing of 8. In cell 1, type **Add rows/columns as needed** and type **Add images to table** in cell 2. Name the table computers and then center-align it. Change the Horz setting for all cells to Center.

11. Click to the right of the table, press the ENTER key, and then type **Links**.

12. Using the Editable Region command on the Templates pop-up menu, create the five editable regions indicated in Table 4–13.

13. Click the CSS button in the Property inspector, if necessary, to display the CSS properties. Double-click the CSS Styles tab in the panel group, if necessary, to display the CSS Styles panel.

14. Click anywhere in the heading, Bryan's Computer Repair Services, and then click the <h1> tag in the tag selector. Click the New CSS Rule button in the CSS Styles panel. In the New CSS Rule dialog box, select Tag (redefines an HTML element), h1, and (This document only) as necessary, and then click the OK button. In the CSS Rule definition for h1 dialog box, set the following values in the Type category: Verdana, Geneva, sans-serif for the Font-family; 16 pixels for the Font-size; and bold for the Font-weight. Click the OK button.

15. Click anywhere in the subtitle prompt, This week's featured computers are [computer types], and then click the <h3> tag in the tag selector. Click the New CSS Rule button in the CSS Styles panel. In the New CSS Rule dialog box, select Tag (redefines an HTML element), h3, and (This document only) as necessary, and then click the OK button. Set the following values in the Type category: Verdana, Geneva, sans-serif for the Font-family; 14 pixels for the Font-size; 600 for the Font-weight; and #336633 for the Color. Click the OK button.

16. Click anywhere in the Introductory paragraph prompt, and then click the <p> tag in the tag selector. Click the New CSS Rule button in the CSS Styles panel. In the New CSS Rule dialog box, select Tag (redefines an HTML element), p, and (This document only) as necessary, and then click the OK button. Set the following values in the Type category: Verdana, Geneva, sans-serif for the Font-family; 12 pixels for the Font-size; and #336633 for the Color. Click the OK button. Verify that the style is applied to the examples text, table_images, and the links text.

17. Click in the computers table and then click the <table#computers> tag in the tag selector. Click the New CSS Rule button in the CSS Styles panel. In the New CSS Rule dialog box, select ID (applies to only one HTML element), #computers, and (This document only), and then click the OK button. Select the Background category, and then choose white (#FFF) as the background color. Click the OK button.

18. Select the text, Links, and then click the Page Properties button in the Property inspector. In the Category list, click Links (CSS). Enter #336633 as the Link color. Click the Rollover links text box and type #0F0 for the color, #F00 for Visited links, and #336633 for Active links. Click the Underline style arrow and then select Show underline only on rollover. Click the Apply button and then click the OK button.

19. Title the template Bryan's Computer Repair Services, and then save it. (Click OK if any Dreamweaver dialog boxes appear.) Close the template.

20 Open a new blank HTML page, and save it as computer_types.htm in the computers folder.

21. Collapse the CSS Styles panel, click the Assets tab in the Files panel group, and then click the Templates icon. Click the Apply button to apply the weekly_features template to the computer_types.htm page.

22. Use Table 4–14 as a guide to add content to each of the editable regions. Change the dimensions of each image to 150 (W) by 150 (H) pixels.

23. Select the Home text and link it to the index.htm page.

24. Save the document. Open the index.htm file. Scroll to the bottom of the page and then click to the right of the current date. Insert a line break, and then type **Weekly Specials** as the link text. Add a link to the computer_types.htm page. Save the index.htm page.

25. Press the F12 key to view the page in your browser. Click the Weekly Specials link, and then click the Home link to verify they work. Submit your assignment in the format specified by your instructor.

Table 4–13 Bryan's Computer Repair Services Editable Regions

Region Text	Region Name
This week's featured computers are [computer types]	subtitle
Introductory paragraph	introduction
The following table displays:	examples
computers table	table_images
Home	links

Table 4–14 Bryan's Computer Repair Services Page Content

Region Text	Region Name
This week's featured computers are desktop, laptop, tablet, and handheld computers.	subtitle
Weekly specials include USB flash drives; once you get your hands on these high-capacity drives, you will not let go!	introduction
The following table displays this week's specials:	examples
(Note: Press Tab to move from cell to cell): Row 1, column 1 Row 1, column 2 Row 2, column 1 Row 2, column 2	table_images image: desktop.jpg; description: Desktop image: laptop.jpg; description: Laptop image: tablet.jpg; description: Tablet image: handheld.jpg; description: Handheld
Home	links

In the Lab

Lab 2: Creating a Template for the Baskets by Carole Web Site

Problem: The Baskets by Carole Web site is receiving a large number of hits every day, and Carole is receiving increasingly more orders each day. She foresees a time when she will need to expand the Web site and is considering a standard design for her pages. Carole is not sure exactly how a template works within a Web site and has requested that you put together an example. You know that she has been considering a promotional page for her business, so you decide to create a template and Web page using this topic. The template is shown in Figure 4–92a and the Web page is shown in Figure 4–92b. The template contains five tables — one noneditable table and four editable tables.

Software and hardware settings determine how a Web page is displayed in a browser. Your template and Web page may appear different from the ones shown in Figure 4–92. Appendix C contains instructions for uploading your local site to a remote site.

Figure 4–92a

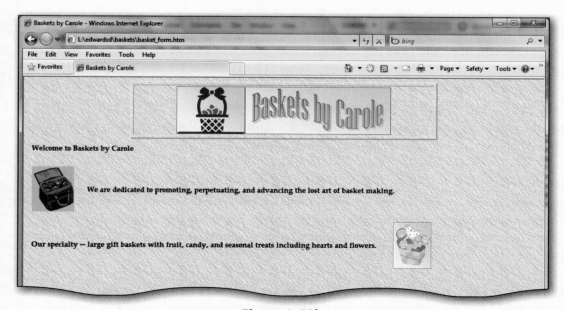

Figure 4–92b

Perform the following tasks:

1. Start Dreamweaver, and then copy the image data files from the Chapter04\baskets data files folder into the images folder for your Gift Basket Designs local Web site.

2. Open the Gift Basket Designs site.

3. Create a blank HTML template and then save it as a template named basket_form.dwt.

4. Use the Page Properties button in the Property inspector to add the baskets_bkg.jpg background image to the page.

5. Create a one-row, one-column table with a table width of 60 percent, border of 2, cell padding of 3, and cell spacing of 5. Type **Baskets by Carole logo table** as the Summary text. Center the table on the page. Select the table cell and set Horz to Center and the Vert to Middle. Name the table logos.

6. Drag the logo01.jpg image to the table cell and then enter Logo Image 1 as the Alt text. Resize logo01 to 143 (W) by 100 (H) pixels. Drag the logo02.jpg image to the right of logo01 and then enter Logo Image 2 as the Alt text. Resize logo02 to 305 (W) by 100 (H) pixels.

7. Click to the right of the logos table and then press the ENTER key. Add a one-row, one-column table with a width of 90 percent, border of 0, cell padding of 5, and cell spacing of 5. Name the table promo_heading. Left-align the table on the page. Click in the table and type **Heading goes here** as the prompt. Make the table an editable region named heading.

8. Select the "Heading goes here" text and then click the New CSS Rule button in the CSS Styles panel. In the New CSS Rule dialog box, select Tag (redefines an HTML element), td, and (This document only) as necessary, and then click the OK button. Select the Palatino Linotype, Book Antiqua, Palatino, serif Font-family, 16-point Font-size, and bold Font-weight for the "Heading goes here" text.

9. Click to the right of the promo_heading table and then press the ENTER key two times. Add a third table to the template with one row and two columns, width of 80 percent, border thickness of 0, cell padding of 5, and cell spacing of 5. Name the table promos. Type **Image or text goes here** in the first cell and **Add as many columns/rows as necessary** in the second cell. Make the table an editable region named image01.

10. Click below the image01 table and then insert a fourth table — a one-row, two-column table with a width of 80 percent, border thickness of 0, cell padding of 5, and cell spacing of 5. Name the table descriptions. Left-align the table on the page. Type **Add as many columns/rows as necessary** in the first table cell and **Basket descriptions or images go here** in the second table cell. Make the table an editable region named image02.

11. Enter Baskets by Carole as the title of the template, and then save and close the template document.

12. Open a new blank HTML page and save it as basket_form.htm. Click the Assets tab in the Files panel group. Apply the template to the basket_form document.

13. Select the Heading goes here text and then type **Welcome to Baskets by Carole** in the heading editable region.

14. Delete the text in the left column of the image01 editable region and then insert the basket_promo01 image. Resize the image to 88 (W) by 97 (H) pixels. Select the text in the right column, and then type **We are dedicated to promoting, perpetuating, and advancing the lost art of basket making.**

15. Select the text in the first cell of the second table and then type **Our speciality — large gift baskets with fruit, candy, and seasonal treats including hearts and flowers.** Delete the text in the second cell of the image02 editable region and then insert the basket_promo02 image. Resize the image to 80 (W) by 100 (H) pixels.

16. Save the basket_form.htm page and then open the index.htm page. Scroll to the bottom of the page, click to the right of the Specials link, and then press the END key. Insert a line break and then type **Featured Baskets** as the link text. Create a link to the baskets_form.htm page. Save the index page.

17. Press the F12 key to view the page in your browser. Click the Featured Baskets link to verify that it works. Submit your assignment in the format specified by your instructor.

In the Lab

Lab 3: Creating a Template and Applying a Style Sheet for the Credit Protection Web Site

Problem: Jessica Minnick has decided to add Web pages to the Credit Protection Web site emphasizing the ABCs of Credit. She would like to have a uniform format for these pages and has asked you to create a template. She has provided you with content for the first page. The template is shown in Figure 4–93a and the Web page is shown in Figure 4–93b. Appendix C contains instructions for uploading your local site to a remote server.

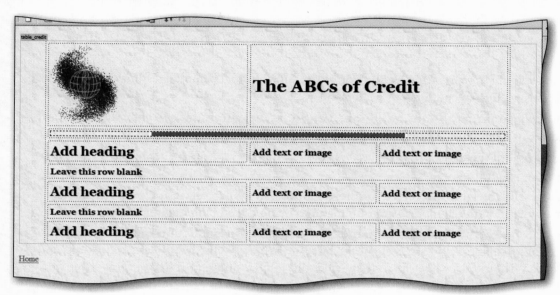

Figure 4–93a

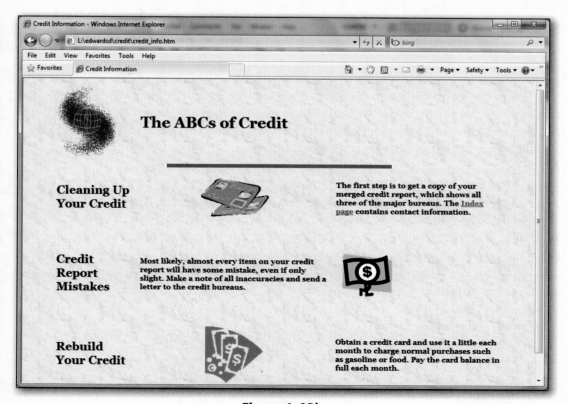

Figure 4–93b

Perform the following tasks:

1. Start Dreamweaver, and then copy the image data files from the Chapter04\credit data files folder into the images folder for your Credit Protection local Web site.

2. Open the Credit Protection site, and then create a blank HTML template named credit.dwt. Apply the credit_bkg.jpg background image to the page.

3. Insert a seven-row, three-column table with a width of 90 percent, border thickness of 0, cell padding of 5, cell spacing of 5, and Summary text of ABCs of Credit. Center the table. Drag the logo.gif image to the first cell in the first row. Merge the last two cells in row 1. Type **The ABCs of Credit** in the merged cells and apply the Heading 1 format.

4. Merge all three cells in row 2. Drag the line.gif image to the merged row, and then center the line in the cell.

5. Merge all three cells in row 4 and then type **Leave this row blank** in the cell. Repeat this step for row 6.

6. Click row 3, column 1, type **Add heading** as the entry, and then apply Heading 2 to this text. Repeat this instruction in column 1 of rows 5 and 7.

7. Click row 3, column 2; type **Add text or image** as the entry; and then copy this text. Paste the text into row 3, column 3; row 5, columns 2 and 3; and row 7, columns 2 and 3.

8. Click to the right of the table, press the ENTER key, and then type **Home**. Create a link from this text to the index.htm page.

9. Click anywhere in the table and then click the <table> tag in the tag selector. Use the Editable Region menu item on the Templates pop-up menu to name the editable region table_credit.

10. Open the CSS Styles panel and then click the New CSS Rule button. In the New CSS Rule dialog box, select Tag (redefines an HTML element), table, and (New Style Sheet File) as necessary, and then click the OK button. Name the style sheet credit_info.css and save it in your credit folder. Apply the following attributes in the Type category: Georgia, Times New Roman, Times, serif for the Font-family; 16 for the Font-size; and bold for the Font-weight. Click the OK button and close the template. Save and close the credit_info.css style sheet and the credit.dwt template.

11. Open a new blank HTML page and save it as credit_info.htm. Click the Assets panel tab and apply the credit template to the page. Delete the text, Leave this row blank, from all cells.

12. Select the "Add heading" text in row 3, column 1; type **Cleaning Up Your Credit** as the entry; and then select the text in row 3, column 3. Type **The first step is to get a copy of your merged credit report, which shows all three of the major bureaus. The Index page contains contact information.** Select the text "Index page" and add a link to the index.htm page. Delete the text in row 3, column 2, and drag the credit_card.gif image to the cell, and then center the image.

13. Select the "Add heading" text in row 5, column 1, type **Credit Report Mistakes** as the entry, and then select the text in row 5, column 2. Type **Most likely, almost every item on your credit report will have some mistake, even if only slight. Make a note of all inaccuracies and send a letter to the credit bureaus.** Delete the text in row 5, column 3 and then drag the money2.gif image to the cell.

14. Select the text in row 7, column 1; type **Rebuild Your Credit** as the entry; and then select the text in row 7, column 3. Type **Obtain a credit card and use it a little each month to charge normal purchases such as gasoline or food. Pay the card balance in full each month.** Delete the text in row 7, column 2, drag the rebuild. gif image to the cell, and then center the image.

15. Title the page Credit Information, and then save the credit_info.htm document.

16. Open the index.htm file. Scroll to the bottom of the page, click to the right of the current date, and then press the ENTER key. Type **Credit Information** as the link text. Create a link to the credit_info.htm page. Save the page.

17. Press the F12 key to view the page in your browser. Click the Credit Information link. Submit your assignment in the format specified by your instructor.

Cases and Places

Apply your creative thinking and problem solving skills to design and implement a solution.

• EASIER   ••MORE DIFFICULT

• 1: Create a Template for the Favorite Sports Web Site

Your sports Web site has become very popular. You have received many e-mails asking for statistics and other information. You decide to add a Web page that will contain statistics and will be updated on a weekly basis. Add a background image to the page and add a title to the page. Create a template using tables. Add descriptive prompts and then create editable regions. Add styles to the headings and text. Then create a page, apply the template, and save the page in your sports Web site. Create links to and from the home page.

• 2: Create a Template and New Web Page for the Hobby Web Site

You have decided to add a do-it-yourself section to your hobby Web site and want to use a consistent format and look for the page. You decide to use a template to create this new section. Create the template using a logo, tables, and links. Add descriptive prompts to the editable regions and apply styles to enhance the text and text size. Create the first do-it-yourself Web page and apply the template. Create links to and from the home page. Upload the pages to a remote server, if instructed to do so.

•• 3: Create a Template and Style Sheet for the Politics Web Site

Your campaign for political office is progressing well, and you are one of the top two candidates. You have decided to add a new section to your Web site featuring your campaign supporters. To provide consistency and control, you use a template for this site. After completing the template, attach styles. Next, create two new pages for the site and then apply the template. Create links to and from the home page. Upload the new pages to a remote server, if instructed to do so.

•• 4: Create a Template for the Favorite Music Web Site

Make It Personal
Create a template for your music hobby Web site and then add a background to the page. Insert logos, tables, and other appropriate elements. Add a background image to a table. Apply a border to the table. Use the CSS Styles panel and apply styles to the elements on the page. Create a new Web page featuring a new topic for your Web site and apply the template. Create links to and from the home page. Upload the page to a remote server, if instructed to do so.

•• 5: Create a Template and New Web Page for the Student Trips Web Site

Working Together
Each member of the group decides to create a template for the three vacation sites previously selected. Include on the templates headings, tables, links, and graphics. Present the three templates to the group and determine which one best meets the needs of the Web site. Next, add appropriate styles, including styles from the Type, Background, and Border categories. Include at least two images and a logo on the template. Create the three vacation site Web pages and apply the template. Then create links to and from the home page. Upload the new pages to a remote server, if instructed to do so.

5 Absolute Positioning, Image Maps, the History Panel, and Date Objects

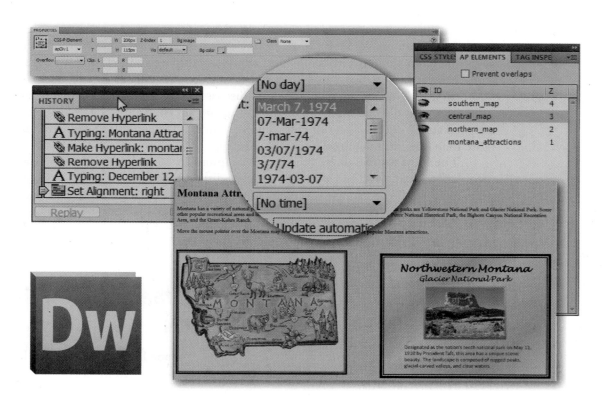

Objectives

You will have mastered the material in this chapter when you can:

- Explain the concept of AP elements
- Insert, select, resize, and move an AP element
- Display the AP Elements panel
- Name an AP element
- Align AP elements
- Add an image to an AP element

- Create and select stacked AP elements
- Describe an image map
- Create an image map
- Add and edit behaviors
- Use the History panel
- Insert a Date object

5 | Absolute Positioning, Image Maps, the History Panel, and Date Objects

Introduction

Chapter 5 introduces four unique Dreamweaver features: absolute positioning (AP elements), image maps, the History panel, and the Date object. Web developers have long dreamed of being able to position graphics, text, and other HTML objects at specific pixel coordinates. Tables provide some placement control, but not absolute precision. Dreamweaver's AP elements, however, can be positioned anywhere on the page. They remain in the same position relative to the top and left margins of the window regardless of how a user resizes the browser window.

An image map is the second feature discussed in this chapter. An image map is a picture that is divided into regions, called hotspots. When a user clicks a hotspot, an assigned action occurs. You can create multiple hotspots in an image, and you can have more than one image map on a single Web page.

The third feature introduced in this chapter is the History panel. This panel records formatting and editing tasks and then displays them in the order in which they were completed. You can use this panel to undo steps you want to reverse or redo steps that you perform repetitively.

With the fourth feature, you delete the static date at the bottom of the index page and replace it with the Date object, which is updated automatically.

Project — Using AP Elements, Image Maps, the History Panel, and Date Objects

In this chapter, you continue adding pages to the Montana Parks Web site. You learn how to use and apply four Dreamweaver tools as you develop the Montana Parks Web site. You begin the chapter by adding a new page to the Web site that contains an image map and AP elements, also previously known as layers (Figure 5–1a). You add four separate elements to the page, and then embed images in each element. One element contains a Montana map, which serves as the image map. Within the image map, moving the mouse pointer over different spots will display a list of the parks and other attractions in northern, central, and southern Montana. Next, you learn how to use the History panel to streamline your work and Date objects to provide the current date on Web pages.

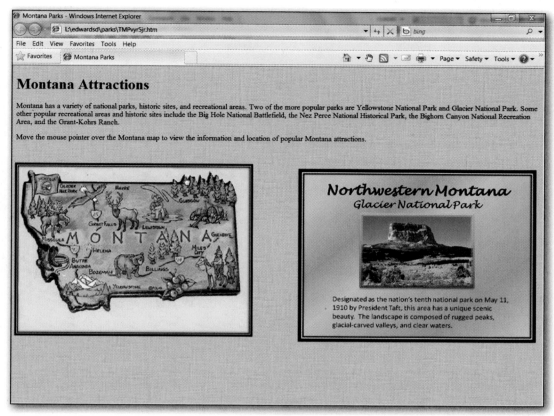

Figure 5–1a

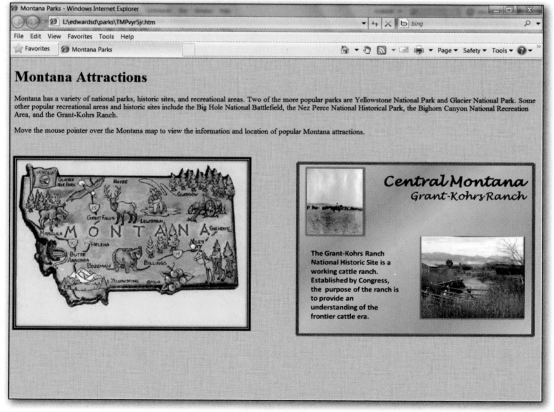

Figure 5–1b

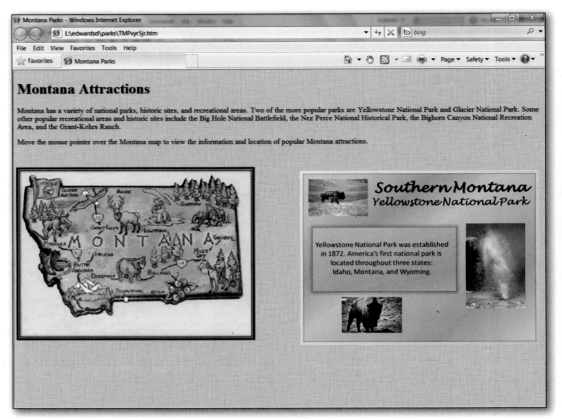

Figure 5–1c

Overview

As you read this chapter, you will learn how to add to your Web site the pages shown in Figure 5–1 by performing these general tasks:

- Insert, select, resize, and align an AP element.
- Create and save an image map.
- Add and edit behaviors.
- Use the History panel.
- Insert a Date object.

Plan
Ahead

General Project Guidelines

When adding pages to a Web site, consider the appearance and characteristics of the completed site. As you create the Web pages shown in Figure 5–1, you should follow these general guidelines:

1. **Determine whether to use AP elements to lay out a page.** An AP element is absolutely positioned on a Web page and does not change when the browser window changes. If you want a section such as a menu or banner always to appear in the same spot, using AP elements is an effective technique.

2. **Decide where AP elements should appear on a page.** Because AP elements hold content such as text, images, media, or other objects, you can determine where and how to use AP elements by deciding where you want to place content such as images that are not moved or resized when users resize the browser window or its text.

3. **Consider using an image map.** If you want to create links for parts of an image, but do not want to divide the image into separate files, create an image map. Consider where the image map will be displayed on the page and how the sections will be divided.

4. **Plan behaviors for AP elements.** You can assign behaviors to AP elements to make your Web pages engaging and interactive. For example, when a user points to part of an image, appropriate information or objects will appear on the page.

5. **Decide where to use the Date object.** Insert a Date object that automatically is updated when a page is opened and saved.

When necessary, more specific details concerning the above guidelines are presented at appropriate points in the chapter. The chapter also will identify the actions performed and decisions made regarding these guidelines during the creation of the Web pages shown in Figure 5–1.

Starting Dreamweaver and Opening a Web Site

Each time you start Dreamweaver, it opens to the last site displayed when you closed the program. It therefore may be necessary for you to open the Montana Parks Web site. Clicking the Sites pop-up menu in the Files panel lists the sites you have defined. When you open the site, a list of pages and subfolders within the site is displayed.

To Start Dreamweaver and Open the Montana Parks Web Site

With a good understanding of the requirements, and an understanding of the necessary decisions and planning process, the first step is to start Dreamweaver and open the Montana Parks Web site.

1 Click the Start button on the Windows taskbar.

2 Click Adobe Dreamweaver CS5 on the Start menu or point to All Programs on the Start menu, click Adobe Design Premium, if necessary, and then click Adobe Dreamweaver CS5 on the All Programs list to start Dreamweaver.

3 If necessary, display the panel groups.

4 If the Montana Parks hierarchy is not displayed, click the Sites pop-up menu button on the Files panel, and then click Montana Parks to display the Montana Parks Web site in the Files panel.

To Copy Data Files to the Parks Web Site

Before you start enhancing and adding to your Web site, you need to copy the data files into the site's folder hierarchy. In the following steps, you copy the data files for the Chapter 5 project from the Chapter05 folder on a USB drive to the parks and the parks\images folders stored in the *your name* folder on the same USB drive. In the following steps, the data files for this chapter are stored on drive L:. The location on your computer may be different. If necessary, verify the location of the data files with your instructor.

1 Click the Sites pop-up menu button in the Files panel, and then click the name of the drive containing your data files, such as Removable Disk (L:).

2 If necessary, click the plus sign (**+**) next to the folder containing your data files to expand that folder, and then click the plus sign (**+**) next to the Chapter05 folder to expand it.

3 Expand the parks folder to display the data files.

4 Click the montana_attractions document to select it and then copy and paste it to the parks folder.

5 Double-click the images folder. Click the first file in the list, hold down the SHIFT key, and then click the last file in the list to select the four image files.

6 Copy the files and then paste them in the parks\images folder (Figure 5–2).

Q&A How can I alphabetize the files in the Local Files list?

Click the Refresh button in the Files panel to refresh the list.

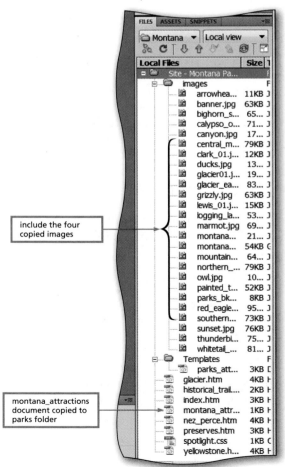

include the four copied images

montana_attractions document copied to parks folder

Figure 5–2

Understanding AP Elements

An **AP element** is similar to a table — it is a container that holds other types of content, such as images, text, and even other AP elements (nested elements). Anything you can put in an HTML document, you also can put into an AP element. The AP elements can be stacked on top of one another, placed side by side, or overlapped. They easily can be moved, dragged, or resized. Web site developers use AP elements for page layout much as they use tables. An AP element, however, provides more flexibility than a table because it can be placed in an exact spot anywhere on the page with pixel-perfect precision. It remains in this position (relative to the top and left margins of the page) regardless of how the Web page visitor resizes the browser window or views the text size. This is called **absolute positioning** (AP) and is possible because AP elements are positioned using a standard x-, y-, and z-coordinate system, similar to what you would use to create a graph on graph paper. Instead of having the point of origin in the lower-left corner, however, the x- and y-coordinates correspond to the AP element's top and left positions within the page. The z-coordinate, also called the **z-index**, determines an AP element's stacking order when more than one element is added to a page.

AP Divs and DHTML

Absolute positioning is a component of dynamic HTML (DHTML) — an extension of HTML that allows Web page developers to precisely position objects on the Web page. DHTML combines AP Divs, Cascading Style Sheets (CSS), and JavaScript coding, enabling the creation of dynamic page elements. Additionally, because an AP Div uses both DHTML and CSS, it offers a wide range of flexibility and control. Some possible effects you can accomplish using DHTML are as follows:

- Add images that are hidden from view initially and then display when a user clicks a button or hotspot.
- Create pop-up menus.
- Position objects side by side.
- Drag and drop objects.
- Create animations.
- Provide feedback to right and wrong answers.

A disadvantage of using AP elements is that older browsers do not support them. Internet Explorer 4.0 and Netscape Navigator 4.0 (and later) support AP Divs under the original W3C Cascading Style Sheets-Positioning (CSS-P) specifications. Navigator 4.0 in particular has a difficult time with AP elements and often displays them incorrectly. Browsers older than version 4.0, however, ignore the AP Div code and display the content in the normal flow of the page (no absolute positioning).

Determine whether to use AP elements on a Web page.
Because an AP element does not move from its specified position, you can use it to create certain effects. For example, use an AP element to fix the position of menus or navigation bars. You can also overlap AP elements, such as overlapping an image with text. Another effective use of AP elements is to turn on visibility so certain content appears when the user performs an action (such as clicking a button), and then turn off visibility when the user performs a different action.

Plan Ahead

Dreamweaver provides two options for creating AP elements: the Draw AP Div button located on the Layout tab on the Insert bar, and the Layout Objects submenu available through the Insert menu. In this chapter, you use the Draw AP Div button on the Layout tab on the Insert bar, modify attributes through the CSS-P Elements Property inspector, and control visibility through the AP Elements panel. Displaying Dreamweaver's layout tools, such as the rulers or the grid, helps with precise positioning. In this chapter, you use the rulers.

You copied the files necessary to begin creating your new Web page to the Montana Parks local root folder in the Files panel. You begin the chapter by adding a new page to the Web site, containing an image map and AP elements, also previously known as layers. You add four separate elements to the page, and then embed images in each element. One element contains a Montana map, which serves as the image map. With the image map, moving the mouse pointer over different spots will display a list of the parks and other attractions in northern, central, and southern Montana. Each image also has alternate text to address accessibility issues.

To Open the Montana Attractions Page and Display the Rulers

The following steps show how to open the montana_attractions.htm page and to display the rulers.

1

- If necessary, collapse the images folder in the Files panel to reduce the number of files displayed.

- Double-click the montana_attractions.htm file to open the file and display the insertion point at the top of the window (Figure 5–3).

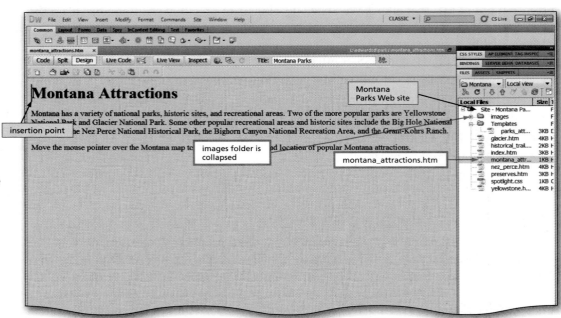

Figure 5–3

2

- Click View on the Application bar, point to Rulers, and then point to Show to highlight the Show command on the Rulers submenu (Figure 5–4).

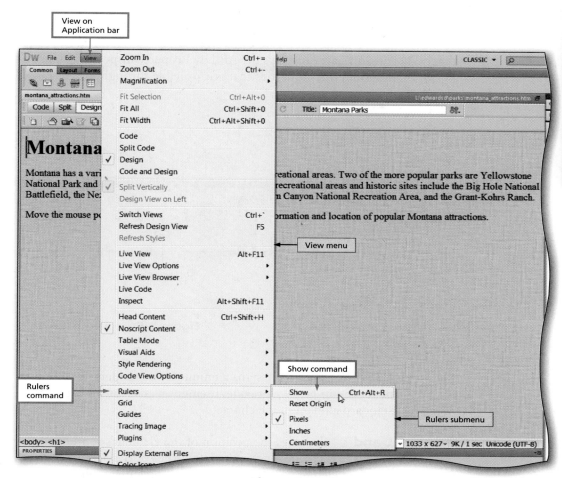

Figure 5–4

3

- Click Show to display the rulers in the Document window and to display the ruler-origin icon in the upper-left corner (Figure 5–5).

Q&A

What should I do if my ruler shows inches?

Right-click the ruler and then click Pixels.

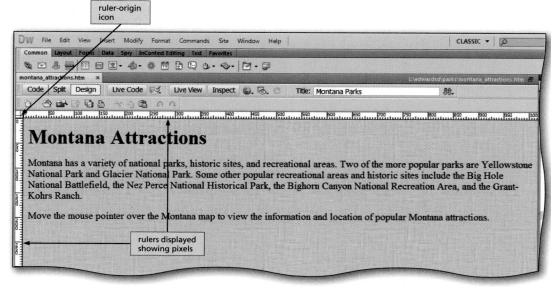

Figure 5–5

AP Div Property Inspector

When you insert an AP element into a Web page and the element is selected, Dreamweaver displays the AP Div Property inspector (Figure 5–6). The following section describes the properties that are available through the AP Div Property inspector.

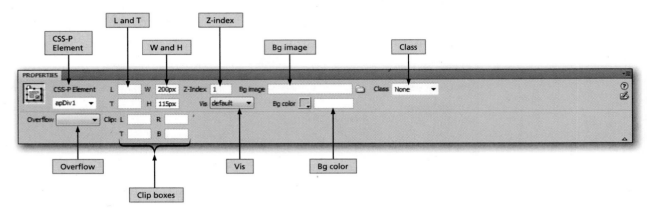

Figure 5–6

CSS-P Element   Assigns a unique name to identify the element in the AP Elements panel and in JavaScript code. Element names must start with a letter and can contain only standard alphanumeric characters.

L and T   Specifies the position of the element's top-left corner relative to the top-left corner of the page, or the top-left corner of the parent element if the element is nested. A nested element, or child element, is an element whose code is contained in another element. Nesting often is used to group elements together. A nested element moves with its parent element and can be set to inherit visibility from its parent. Parent and child elements are discussed in more detail in the section on nesting, overlapping, and stacking elements, later in this chapter.

W and H   Specifies the width and height of the element in Design view. In Design view, if the content of the element exceeds the specified size, the bottom edge of the element stretches to accommodate the content. When the element appears in a browser, however, the bottom edge does not stretch unless the Overflow property is set to visible. The default unit for position and size is pixels (px). Other units include pc (picas), pt (points), in (inches), mm (millimeters), cm (centimeters), and % (percentage of the parent element's corresponding value). The abbreviations must follow the value without a space: for example, 3mm indicates 3 millimeters.

Z-Index   Determines the stacking order of the element. In a browser, higher-numbered elements appear in front of lower-numbered ones. The z-index values can be positive or negative. The stacking order can be changed through the AP Elements panel.

Vis   Specifies whether the element is visible initially or not. The following options are available:

- **default** does not specify a visibility property. When no visibility is specified, most browsers default to inherit.

- **inherit** uses the visibility property of the element's parent.

- **visible** displays the element contents, regardless of the parent's value.

- **hidden** hides the element contents, regardless of the parent's value. Note that hidden elements created with ilayer (a tag unique to Netscape Navigator) still take up the same space as if they were visible.

Bg Image   Specifies a background image for the element.

Bg Color   Specifies a background color for the element. Leave this option blank to specify a transparent background.

Class   Lets you apply CSS rules to the selected object.

Overflow   Works only with the <div> and <span> tags and controls how elements appear in a browser when the content exceeds the element's specified size. The following options are available:

- **visible** indicates that the extra content appears in the element.

- **hidden** specifies that the extra content is not displayed in the browser.

- **scroll** specifies that the browser should add scroll bars to the element whether or not they are needed.

- **auto** causes the browser to display scroll bars for the element only when the element's contents exceed its boundaries.

Clip   Defines the visible area of an element. Specify left, top, right, and bottom coordinates to define a rectangle in the coordinate space of the element (counting from the top-left corner of the element). The element is clipped so that only the specified rectangle is visible.

BTW

<div> versus <span> Tags
The difference between the <div> and <span> tags is that browsers that do not support AP elements place extra line breaks before and after the <div> tag. In most cases, it is better for AP element content to appear in a paragraph of its own in browsers that do not support elements. Therefore, in most cases, it is better to use <div> tags than <span> tags.

Using the Rulers as a Visual Guide

You use the rulers as a visual guide to create an AP element that will be a container for the Montana map image. When you draw the AP element in the Document window, a rectangular image appears, representing the element. (If the AP element borders are not displayed in the Document window, they can be turned on by selecting AP Element outlines through the Visual Aids submenu accessed through the View menu.) This rectangular box, however, is not displayed when the page is viewed in a browser. Instead, only the content of what is displayed within the AP element is displayed in the browser.

The default rulers appear on the left and top borders of the Document window, marked in pixels. The **ruler origin** is the 0 point, or the location on the page where the horizontal and vertical lines meet and read 0. The 0 point is represented by the **ruler-origin icon**, which is located in the Document window when the page is displayed in Design view and the rulers are displayed (see Figure 5–6 on the previous page). Generally, this location is the upper-left corner of the Document window.

BTW

Rulers
You can change the ruler unit of measurement from the default pixels to inches or centimeters by right-clicking anywhere on the rulers and then selecting a different unit of measurement on the context menu.

Using the rulers as a drawing guideline can be somewhat difficult to manage if done from the default 0 point. To make measuring easier, however, you can move the 0 point anywhere within the Document window. To move the 0 point, move the mouse pointer to the upper-left corner where the vertical and horizontal lines meet, and then click and drag the crosshairs to the desired location. When you move the 0 point, the crosshairs are displayed in the Document window and follow the mouse pointer. The mouse pointer position is indicated with a dotted line on both the vertical and horizontal ruler lines.

Relocating the 0 point does not affect the page content. You can relocate the 0 point as many times as necessary. You also can reset the ruler origin by right-clicking anywhere on the rulers and then selecting Reset Origin on the context menu.

The AP Element Marker

When you insert an AP element, a **code marker** appears in the Document window. This small yellow icon indicates that an AP element is on the page. To show the code marker, the Anchor points for AP elements check box must be selected through the Invisible Elements category in the Preferences dialog box. When the Invisible Elements option is turned on, the markers may cause the elements on the page in the Document window to appear to shift position. These markers, however, are not displayed in the browser. When you view the page in your browser, the AP elements and other objects are displayed in the correct positions.

The code marker is similar in appearance to the invisible element marker that displayed when you inserted images into a Web page in Chapter 2. In Chapter 2, dragging the image marker to another position in the Document window also moved the image to another position. Normally, the position of HTML objects in the Document window and in the browser is determined by their order in the HTML source code. They are displayed in a top-to-bottom sequence that mirrors their order in the source code.

Dragging or moving the AP element marker, however, generally does not reposition the element and has no effect on the way a Web page displays the AP element in a browser. When you move an AP element marker, you are not moving the element; instead, you are repositioning the element's code in the HTML of the page. Moving an element marker, therefore, can affect how the code is interpreted and the order in which the element content is loaded. It is possible to have an element's content displayed at the top of the Web page while the source code is at the end of the page.

If your Web page contains tables, do not drag the element marker into a table cell. This can cause display problems in some browsers. You can drag an AP element, however, to overlap a table or make a label appear to be inside the table cell, as long as the code marker itself is not in the table cell. When you use the AP Div button to create the AP element, Dreamweaver will not let you insert the code into a table cell.

To Create and Select an AP Element for the montana_attractions Image

The following steps illustrate how to create and select an AP element.

1

- If necessary, display the Insert bar and then select the Layout tab to display the buttons for working with AP elements.

- Click at the end of the last line of text in the Document window, and then press ENTER to move the insertion point to a new line.

- Click the ruler-origin icon and drag it to the insertion point to position the ruler 0 point where you will begin to draw the AP element (Figure 5–7).

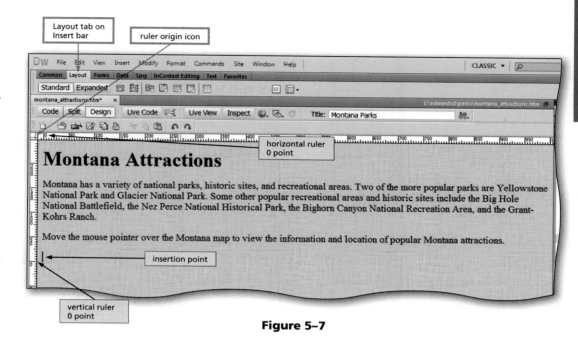

Figure 5–7

Q&A

How do I know that the insertion point and ruler 0 point are in the right positions?

The insertion point should be blinking below the last line of text in the Document window and the vertical ruler 0 point should be to the left of the insertion point.

2

- Click the Draw AP Div button on the Layout tab to prepare for drawing an AP element.

- Move the pointer to the insertion point so that the AP element pointer is at the 0, 0 point on the rulers (Figure 5–8).

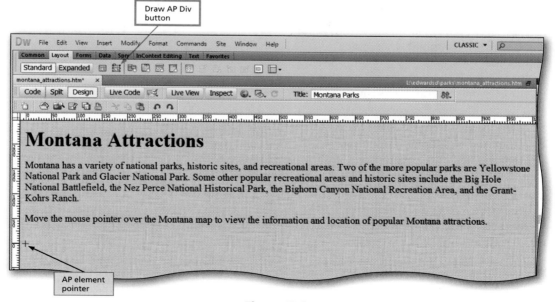

Figure 5–8

● Using the rulers as a guide, draw an AP element approximately 470 pixels wide and 375 pixels high.

● Click the AP element to select it.

● If necessary, make the following changes in the CSS-P Element Property inspector to set the properties for the AP element: L – 5px, T – 210px, W – 470px, and H – 375px.

● Right-click anywhere on the rulers and click Reset Origin on the context menu to reset the origin to the upper-left corner of the Document window (Figure 5–9).

Q&A What should I do if the element outline does not appear in the Document window?

If the element outline does not appear in the Document window, click View on the Application bar, point to Visual Aids, and then click AP Element Outlines on the Visual Aids submenu.

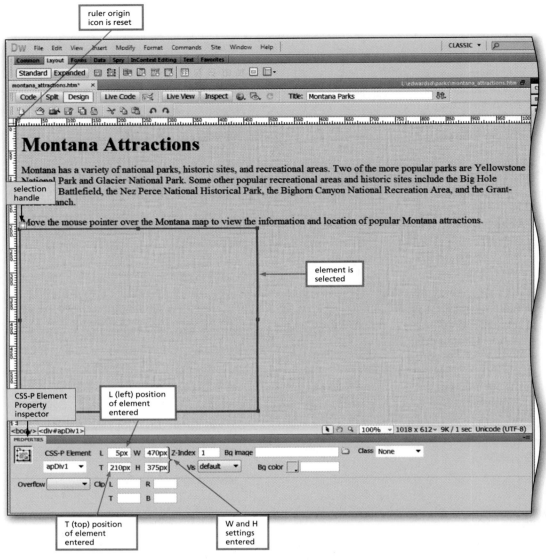

Figure 5–9

Q&A What should I do if the element marker is not displayed?

If the element marker is not displayed, click Edit on the Application bar, select Preferences, and then click the Invisible Elements tab. Click the Anchor points for AP elements check box and then click the OK button.

Q&A What should I do if the element marker overlaps some text?

The AP element overlaps text in some cases depending on the location of the element starting point and on your computer settings. If this occurs, it will be corrected later in this chapter when the element's coordinates are added.

Other Ways
1. On Insert menu, click Layout Objects, click AP Div

The AP Elements Panel

The **AP Elements panel**, part of the CSS panel group, is helpful in managing the elements in your document. Use the AP Elements panel to prevent overlaps, to change the visibility of elements, to nest or stack elements, and to select one or more elements. All of the AP elements on a Web page are listed in the panel. The AP Elements panel contains three columns: Visibility, Name, and Z-Index. The Visibility column uses eye icons. A **closed-eye icon** indicates that an element is hidden; an **open-eye icon** indicates that the element is visible. The absence of an eye icon indicates that the element is in its default state — that it is showing, but not defined as showing in the HTML code. The middle column displays the names of the elements. Clicking an element name in the AP Elements panel is another way to select an element. In the Z-Index column, elements are displayed in order of their z-index values. The first element created appears at the bottom of the list, and the most recently created element at the top of the list. Nested elements are displayed as indented names connected to parent elements (as discussed later in this chapter). The Prevent overlaps check box, when clicked, prevents elements from overlapping. When the Prevent overlaps option is on, an element cannot be created in front of, moved or resized over, or nested within an existing element.

To Display the AP Elements Panel

The following step illustrates how to display the AP Elements panel.

1

- Click Window on the Application bar and then click AP Elements to display the AP Elements panel.

- If necessary to view the complete AP Elements panel, move the mouse pointer over the bottom of the AP Elements panel until the pointer changes to a two-headed arrow.

- If necessary, drag the border of the AP Elements panel up or down so that it is displayed fully (Figure 5–10).

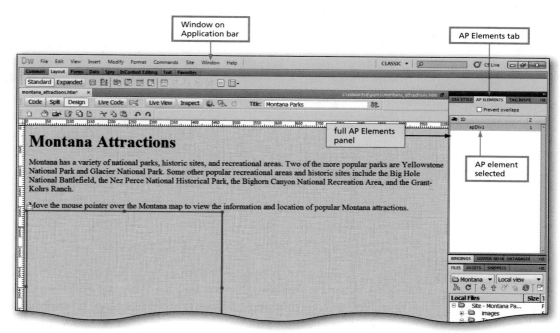

Figure 5–10

Other Ways
1. Press the F2 key

To Name the AP Element

The default name for AP elements is apDiv1, apDiv2, and so on. The next step is to use the Property inspector to rename the element and to adjust the element width and height properties.

1

- Click the CSS-P Element text box in the Property inspector.

- Type **montana_ attractions** as the element name.

- Press the ENTER key to make the change in the Property inspector (Figure 5–11).

Q&A

I noticed that the L and T values changed and that Vis was changed to visible in the Property inspector. What should I do?

Leave those settings as they are for now. You will change them later.

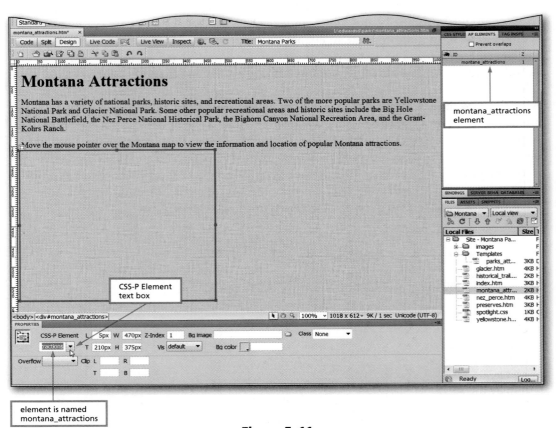

Figure 5–11

Other Ways

1. Double-click element name in AP Elements panel

Adding Objects to AP Elements

As indicated previously, an AP element is a container that can hold objects. The objects can be anything that can be added to an HTML page and include such items as images, text, form objects, and even other elements (nested elements). Objects, including images, can be inserted onto elements through the Insert menu. Images also can be dragged from the Files or Assets panels onto the element.

To Add an Image to the montana_attractions AP Element

The following steps show how to add the montana_attractions image to the AP element.

1

- In the Files panel, click the plus sign next to the images folder to expand the folder.

- Scroll to locate and click the montana_attractions.jpg image.

- Drag the montana_attractions.jpg image onto the AP element (Figure 5–12).

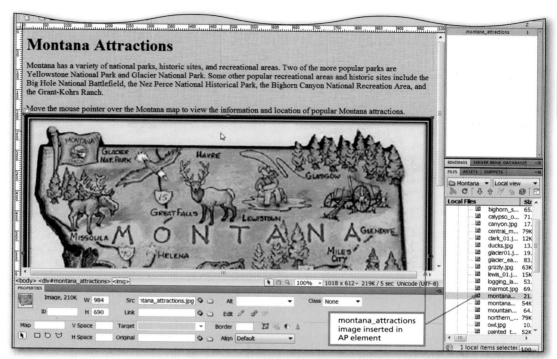

Figure 5–12

2

- Change the W to 500 and the H to 375 to resize the map image (Figure 5–13).

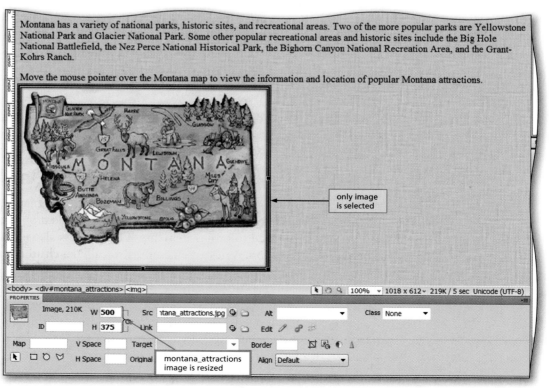

Figure 5–13

- Click the image ID box in the Property inspector and type **montana_map** to name the image.

- Click the Alt text box and type **Montana Attractions** to provide Alt text for the image.

- Click the Save button on the Standard toolbar to save your work (Figure 5–14).

- Press F12 and view the Web page in your browser.

- Close the browser.

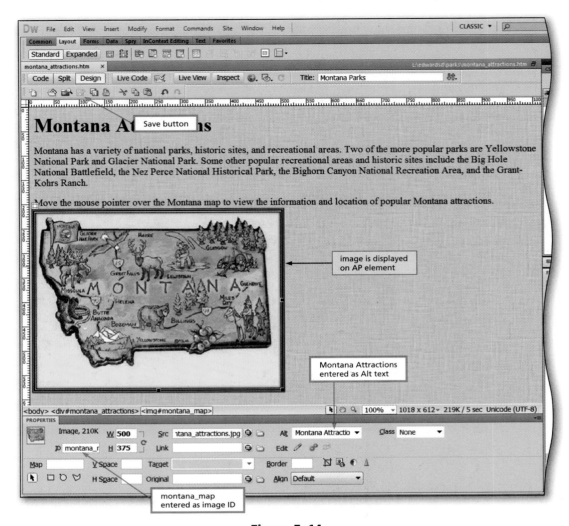

Figure 5–14

Other Ways

1. On Insert menu, click Image, select file name in the Select Image Source dialog box, click OK

Nesting, Overlapping, and Stacking Elements

Several methods are available to manage and manipulate elements. As noted previously, elements can be nested, overlapped, or stacked one on top of another.

Nesting is used to group elements. This process also is referred to as creating a parent-child relation. A nested element, also called a **child element**, is similar in concept to a nested table or a nested frame. Having a nested element, however, does not necessarily mean that one element resides within another element. Rather, it means that the HTML code for one element is written inside the code for another element. The nested element can be displayed anywhere on the page. It does not even have to touch the **parent element**, which is the element containing the code for the other elements. The primary advantage of nested elements is that the parent element controls the behavior of its child elements. If the parent element is moved on the screen, the nested elements move with it. Additionally, if you hide the parent element, you also hide any nested elements. In the AP Elements panel, nested elements are indented below the parent element.

To create a nested element, draw the element inside an existing element while holding down the CTRL key. To unnest a nested element, drag the element marker to a different location in the Document window, or, in the AP Elements panel, drag the nested element to an empty spot.

Elements also can overlap or be stacked one on top of another. Elements that float on top of each other have a **stacking order**. In the HTML source code, the stacking order, or z-index, of the elements is determined by the order in which they are created. The first element you draw is 1, the second is 2, and so on. The element with the highest number appears on top or in front of elements with lower numbers. Stacking elements provides opportunities for techniques such as hiding and displaying elements or parts of elements, creating draggable elements, and creating animation.

Two different methods are available through the AP Elements panel to change the z-index for an element and set which element appears in front of or behind another element. First, you can click the element name and then drag it up or down in the list. A line appears, indicating where the element will be placed. The second method is to click the number of the element you want to change in the Z column, and then type a higher number to move the element up or a lower number to move the element down in the stacking order. After you change the z-index, Dreamweaver automatically rearranges the elements from highest to lowest, with the highest number on top. You also can turn off the overlapping feature in the AP Elements panel. When the Prevent overlaps check box is selected, elements cannot be overlapped or stacked.

To Create Stacked Elements

The following steps illustrate how to draw three stacked elements, one on top of the other. The placement of the elements in Figures 5–15 through 5–18 on pages DW 365–DW 368 is approximate. Later in this chapter, you align and position the elements.

1

- Collapse the panel groups to provide more room for working with AP elements.

- Click the ruler-origin icon and drag it about 75 pixels to the right of and to top-align with the montana_attractions element to prepare for adding the stacked elements.

- Click the Draw AP Div button on the Layout tab.

- Move the AP element pointer to the 0, 0 position on the page.

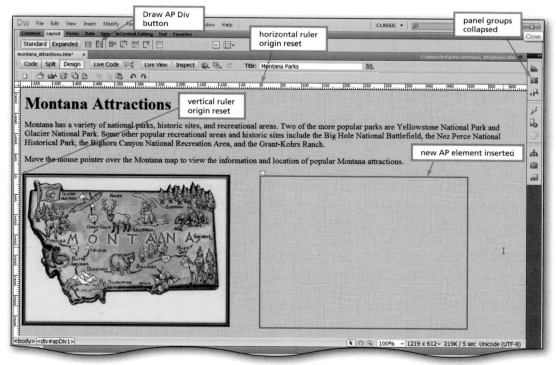

Figure 5–15

- Use the rulers as a visual guide to draw an AP element measuring approximately 500px in width and 375px in height to the right of the montana_attractions element (Figure 5–15).

2

- Click the border of the AP element to select the element.

- Click the CSS-P Element text box and then type **northern_map** as the name of the new AP element.

- Enter the following properties for the northern_map element: W – 500px, H – 375px, and Vis – hidden.

Q&A Why is the Vis property set to Hidden?

The contents of the AP element should not appear in the browser by default. Later, you will modify the page so that the contents appear in certain conditions.

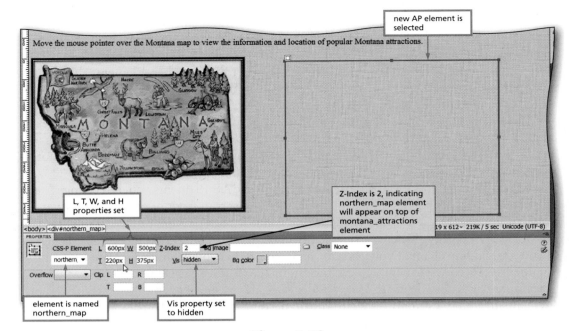

Figure 5–16

- If necessary, change L to 600px and T to 210px (Figure 5–16).

Q&A What should I do to prevent problems when drawing overlapping AP elements?

Make sure the Prevent Overlaps option is not selected in the AP Elements panel. To do so, open the AP Elements panel by clicking Window on the Application bar and then clicking AP Elements. If the Prevent Overlaps check box is selected, click the check box to deselect the option.

Q&A What should I do if the border of the AP element does not appear in the Document window?

Change the Visual Aids setting to show not hide the AP element border. To do so, click View on the Application bar, and then point to Visual Aids. If AP Div Outlines or CSS Layout Outlines is not selected, click the option to select it. Note that Dreamweaver displays borders for AP elements by default.

Q&A How do you add content to an AP element?

Click in the AP element to place the insertion point within the border. You can then enter text and other content such as images in the AP element.

3

- Right-click anywhere on the rulers and then click Reset Origin on the context menu.

- Scroll as necessary to display the entire northern_map element.

- Click the Draw AP Div button on the Layout tab.

- Draw a second AP element directly on top of the northern_map element.

- Select the new AP element.

- Add and modify the following properties in the Property inspector: CSS-P Element – central_ map, W – 500px, H – 375px, and Vis – hidden.

- If necessary, change L to 600px and T to 210px (Figure 5–17).

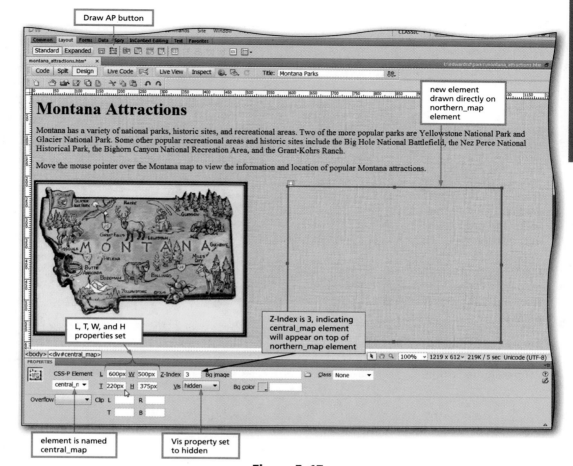

Figure 5–17

Q&A

I drew the second AP element inside of the first AP element. Is that a problem?

When you draw an AP element inside of another AP element, you are creating nested elements. Nesting elements is one way to group AP Divs together. However, in these steps, you are creating overlapping AP elements, not nested elements. Click the Undo button on the Document toolbar as many times as necessary to remove the second AP element, and then repeat Step 3.

4

- With the central_ map AP element still selected, click the Draw AP Div button on the Layout tab and then draw a third element on top of the central_map element.

- Select the new AP element.

- Add and modify the following properties in the Property inspector: CSS-P Element – southern_ map, W – 500px, H – 375px, and Vis – hidden.

- If necessary, change L to 600px and T to 210px (Figure 5–18).

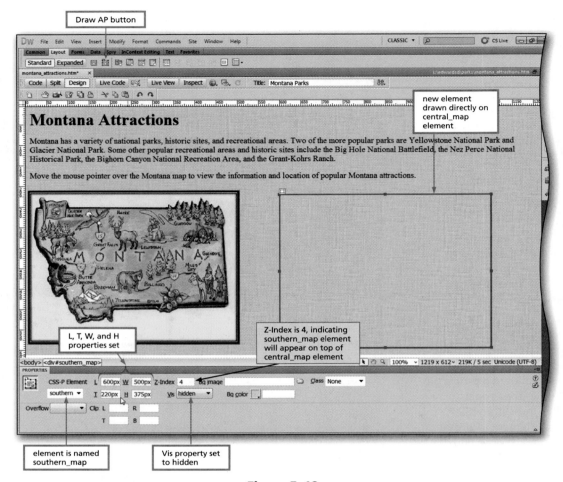

Figure 5–18

Selecting Stacked AP Elements

The next step is to add images to each of the AP elements, but before you add the images, you first must select the correct element. Dreamweaver provides the following options for selecting AP elements:

- Click the name of the desired element in the AP Elements panel.
- Click an element's selection handle. If the selection handle is not visible, click anywhere inside the element to make the handle visible.
- Click an element's border.
- Press and hold CTRL+SHIFT and then click. If multiple elements are selected, this deselects all other elements and selects only the one that you clicked.
- Click the AP element marker (in Design view) that represents the element's location in the HTML code.

To Select AP Elements and Add Images

When elements are stacked, the easiest way to select an element is to click the name in the AP Elements panel. The following steps illustrate how to select AP elements and to add the images to each element.

1

• Expand the panel groups and then display the AP Elements panel, if necessary.

• In the AP Elements panel, click the eye icon next to the southern_map element to display an open-eye icon.

• Click the eye icon next to the central_map element one or more times to display a closed-eye icon.

• Click the eye icon next to the northern_map element one or more times to display a closed-eye icon.

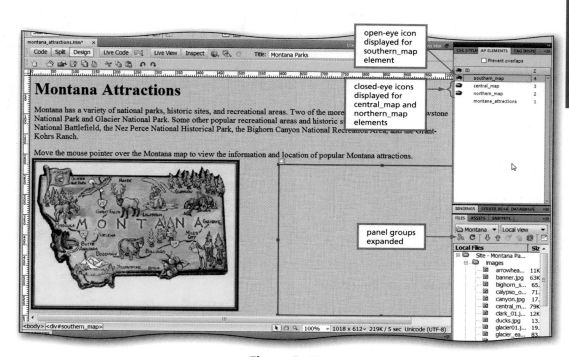

Figure 5–19

What is the effect of the changes made in this step?

Because the southern_map element is displayed with an open-eye icon and the central_map and northern_map elements are displayed with closed-eye icons, when the image in the southern_map element is displayed, the images in the northern_map and central_map elements will be hidden.

• Click the southern_map element name to select the element (Figure 5–19).

What does the order of the AP elements mean in the AP Elements panel?

In the AP Elements panel, AP elements are listed by name in order of their z-index. By default, the first AP element you created appears at the bottom of the list and has a z-index of 1. This means the AP element appears at the bottom of the stacking order. The most recently created AP element appears at the top of the list. This means the AP element appears at the top of the stacking order. To change the stacking order, you change the z-index value in the AP Elements panel. You also can change the z-index value in the Property inspector.

What does it mean if no eye icon appears next to an AP element in the AP Elements panel?

No eye icon means that the AP element inherits visibility from its parent. If the parent element is visible, so is the element without an eye icon. If the AP element is not nested, it inherits visibility from the document body, which is always visible.

2

- If necessary, scroll to the right in the Document window so that the entire AP element is displayed.

- Drag the southern_ map.jpg image from the Files panel onto the southern_map AP element.

- Click the image ID box and type **southern_ montana** as the image ID.

- Click the Alt text box and type **Southern Montana Features** as the Alt text.

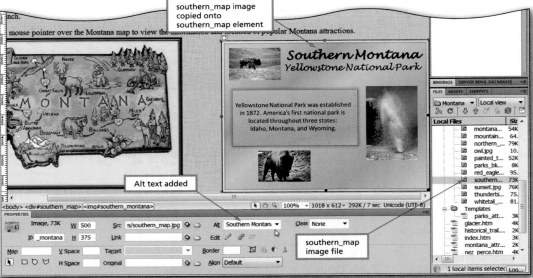

Figure 5–20

- If necessary, press the TAB key so that the southern_map.jpg image is displayed in the southern_map element (Figure 5–20).

3

- In the AP Elements panel, click the eye icon next to the southern_map element one or more times to display a closed-eye icon.

- Click the eye icon next to the central_ map element to display an open eye.

- Click the central_ map element name to select the element.

- Drag the central_ map.jpg image from the Files panel onto the central_map AP element.

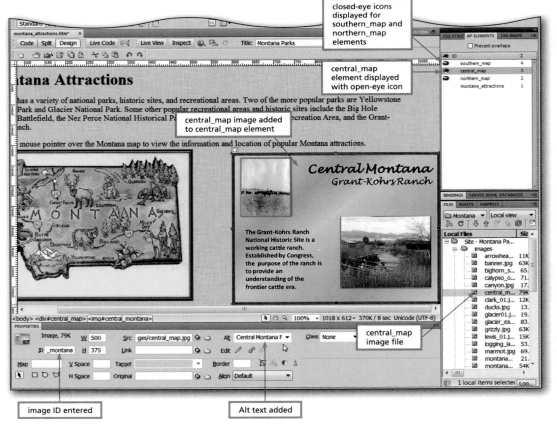

Figure 5–21

What is the effect of the changes made in this step?

Because the central_map element is displayed with an open-eye icon and the southern_map and northern_map elements are displayed with closed-eye icons, when the image in the central_map element is displayed, the images in the northern_map and southern_map elements will be hidden.

- Click the image ID box and type **central_montana** as the image ID.

- Click the Alt text box and type **Central Montana Features** as the Alt text.

- Press the TAB key to have Dreamweaver accept the entry (Figure 5–21).

4

- In the AP Elements panel, click the eye icon next to the central_map one or more times to display a closed-eye icon.

- Click the eye icon next to the northern_map element to display an open eye.

- Click the northern_map element name to select the element.

- Drag the northern_map image from the Files panel onto the northern_map AP element.

- Click the image ID box and type **northern_montana** as the image ID.

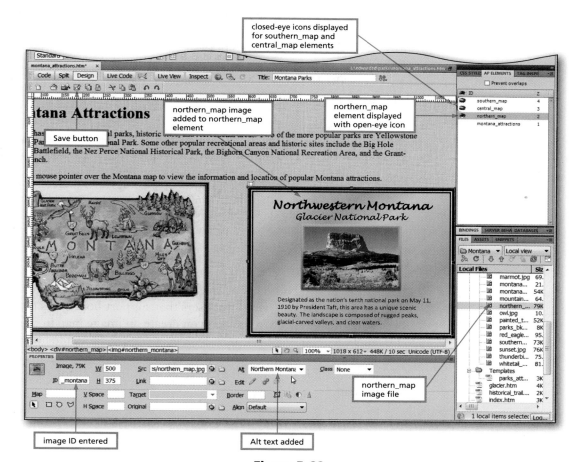

Figure 5–22

- Click the Alt text box and type **Northern Montana Features** as the Alt text.

- Press the TAB key to have Dreamweaver accept the entry (Figure 5–22).

What should I do if the AP elements change position?

After adding the images to the AP elements, select each element in the AP Elements panel, and then verify that L is set to 600px, T to 200px, W is set to 500px, and H is set to 375px, except for the montana_attractions element. For montana_attractions, verify that L is set to 5px and T to 210px.

5

- Save the montana_attractions page.

Image Maps

Image maps are an exciting and interesting way to liven up your Web site. An **image map** is an image that has one or more hotspots placed on top of it. A **hotspot** is a designated area on an image map that the user clicks to cause an action to occur. You can create a hotspot on an image map to link to different parts of the same Web page, to link to other Web pages within the Web site or outside the Web site, or to display content within a hidden AP element.

Two types of image maps exist: server-side and client-side. The way in which **map data** is stored and interpreted depends on the type of map. Map data is the description in the HTML code of the mapped regions or hotspots within the image. A Web server interprets the code or map data for **server-side maps**. When a visitor to a Web page clicks a hotspot in a server-side image map, the browser transfers data to a program running on a Web server for processing. The code for **client-side maps** is stored as part of the Web page HTML code. The Web browser, therefore, interprets the code for client-side maps. When a visitor to a Web page clicks a hotspot in a client-side image map, the browser processes the HTML code without interacting with the Web server. The code for client-side maps is processed faster because it does not have to be sent to a server.

Plan Ahead

> **Consider using an image map.**
> An image map is basically a picture on a Web page that users point to or click. Depending on where users point or click, the image map provides links to other Web pages or to specified content. If you want to condense information an image provides, an image map is an excellent way to do so. For example, if you have an image of a map of the world, you can create an image map so that when users click each country, information about the country appears on the Web page.

You can add both client-side image maps and server-side image maps to the same document in Dreamweaver. Browsers that support both types of image maps give priority to client-side image maps. When you create an image map in the Document window, Dreamweaver automatically creates the code for client-side image maps. To include a server-side image map in a document, you must write the appropriate HTML code in Code view and be connected to a Web server. In this chapter, you create a client-side image map.

Creating a Client-Side Image Map

The first step in creating the image map is to place the image on the Web page. In this chapter, the image is a Montana map. Earlier in this chapter, you placed the image on the montana_attractions element. It is not necessary to place an image on an element to create an image map. You can insert the image anywhere on the page, just as you previously have inserted images in earlier chapters. Placing the image on an element, however, provides absolute positioning. Using this method, you can be assured that the image map will be displayed properly in all browsers supporting CSS-P.

When you create an image map and add a hotspot, you are creating an area that is clickable on the image. To define a hotspot, use one of three shapes: a rectangle, a circle (or oval), or a polygon. Select the tool you want to use and then drag the pointer over the image to create the hotspot. Use the **Rectangular Hotspot Tool** to create a rectangular-shaped hotspot. Use the **Circle Hotspot Tool** to define an oval or circular hotspot area. Use the **Polygon Hotspot Tool** to define an irregularly shaped hotspot. Click the **Pointer Hotspot Tool** (arrow) to close the polygon shape.

When an image is selected, the Property inspector for images is displayed. The Map name text box and hotspot tools are available in the lower portion of the Property inspector (Figure 5–23a).

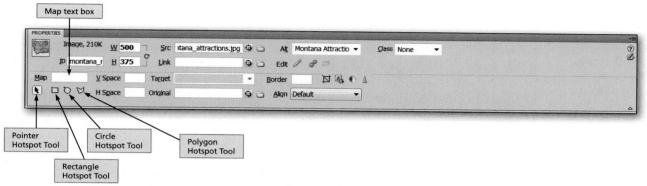

Figure 5–23a

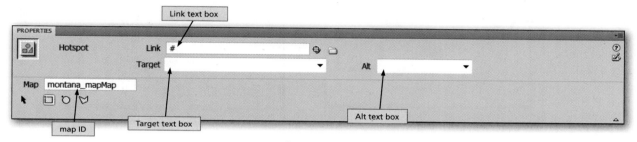

Figure 5–23b

The **Map name** and the **hotspot tools** allow you to label and create a client-side image map. The other properties in the Image Property inspector are described in Chapter 2 on pages DW 126–DW 127.

After you create a hotspot, Dreamweaver displays the Property inspector for a hotspot (Figure 5–23b). If you are linking to other locations within the same Web page or to Web pages outside of your existing Web site, the link or URL is inserted into the Link text box. On the Target pop-up menu, choose the window in which the file should open in the Target field. You also can select from the reserved target names: _blank, _parent, _self, and _top. The target option is not available unless the selected hotspot contains a link.

In this image map, you will not link to another Web site or Web page. Instead, you add behaviors to the hotspots to link to and to display hidden AP elements. Behaviors are discussed later in this chapter. Clicking the top third of the Montana map displays an image listing some of the more popular features in northern Montana. Clicking the middle portion of the map displays an image listing some of the more popular features in central Montana. Clicking the lower third of the map displays an image listing some of the more popular features in southern Montana.

If Windows 7, Windows Vista, or Windows XP SP2 is installed on your computer, the Internet Explorer security settings can prevent the display of active content such as the AP elements associated with the hotspots. To display the content, right-click the information bar at the top of the Internet Explorer window, and choose to allow blocked content.

Earlier in this chapter, you used the View menu to select Visual Aids, and then verified that AP Element Outlines was selected. This same menu also contains an Image Maps command. To see a visual of the hotspot on the image, the Image Maps command must be active.

To Create Hotspots on the montana_attractions Image

The following steps illustrate how to verify that the Image Maps command is selected and how to create three rectangular hotspots on the montana_attractions image.

● Collapse the panel groups to provide more room in the Document window.

● If necessary, scroll to display the upper-left corner of the montana_attractions AP element.

● Click the montana_attractions map image in the montana_attractions element to select the image (Figure 5–24).

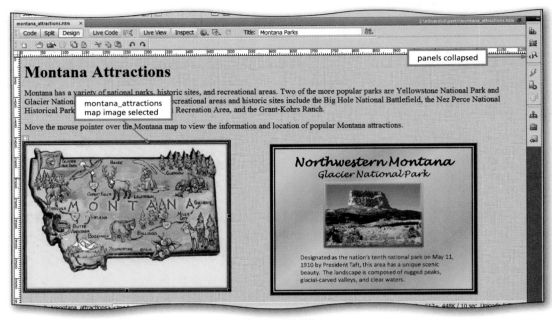

Figure 5–24

● Click the Rectangle Hotspot Tool in the Property inspector to change the pointer to a crosshair pointer for drawing a hotspot.

● Move the crosshair pointer to the upper-left corner of the montana_attractions image (Figure 5–25).

Q&A

How large should I draw the hotspot on the image?

When drawing more than one hotspot on a single image, take care to draw the hotspots as precisely as possible so they do not overlap. When drawing only one hotspot on an image, it is a good idea to draw the hotspot slightly larger than the image. In both cases, consider where and how users will click the hotspot on the Web page as you draw.

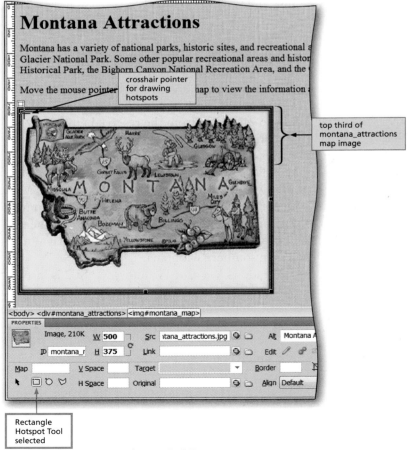

Figure 5–25

3

- Drag to draw a rectangle encompassing approximately the top third of the montana_attractions image (Figure 5–26).

What should I do if the rectangular hotspot does not appear?

If the rectangular hotspot does not appear, click View on the Application bar, point to Visual Aids, and then click Image Maps on the Visual Aids submenu to display the rectangular hotspot.

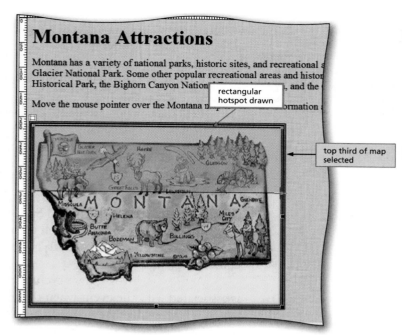

Figure 5–26

4

- Draw a second hotspot on the montana_attractions image by dragging the crosshair pointer over the middle third of the image.

- Draw a third hotspot on the montana_attractions image by dragging the crosshair pointer over the lower third of the image.

- Click anywhere in the window to cancel the crosshair pointer.

- If necessary, scroll down to display the entire montana_attractions image (Figure 5–27).

Can I set properties for hotspots?

Yes. You can use the hotspot Property inspector to set properties for hotspots as you do for other elements. For example, in the Link box, you can enter a link to a document that opens when users click a hotspot.

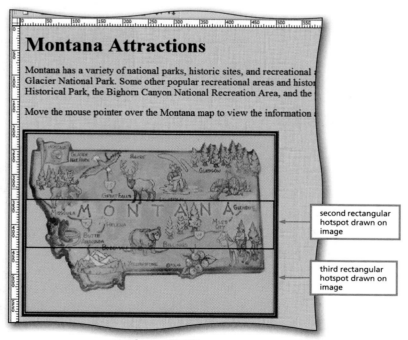

Figure 5–27

Behaviors

A **behavior** is a combination of an event and an action. Behaviors are attached to a specific element on the Web page. The element can be a table, an image, a link, or even a hotspot on an image map. Some of the actions you can attach to hotspots (or other elements) include Show Pop-Up Menu, Play Sound, Drag AP Element, Swap Image, and Show-Hide AP Elements.

When a behavior is initiated, Dreamweaver uses JavaScript to write the code. JavaScript is a scripting language written as a text file. After a behavior is attached to a page element, and when the event specified occurs for that element, the browser calls the action (the JavaScript code) that is associated with that event. A scripting language, such as JavaScript, provides flexibility, interaction, and power to any Web site.

Dreamweaver contains two standard events designed expressly for working with AP Elements: Drag AP Element and Show-Hide Elements. **Drag AP Element** is used to set up an interactive process in which the user can drag or rearrange elements of the design. **Show-Hide Elements** is used to make visible or to hide an element and the element's content.

Actions to invoke these events are **onMouseOut**, which initiates whatever action is associated with the event when the mouse is moved out of an object; **onMouseOver**, which initiates whatever action is associated with the event when the mouse is moved over the object; **onClick**, which initiates whatever action is associated with the event when the object is clicked; and **onDblClick**, which initiates whatever action is associated with the event when the object is double-clicked. These actions are selected through the Tag Inspector panel with the Behaviors button selected, also called the Behaviors panel. The default is onMouseOver. To change the action for an event, click the existing event in the Behaviors panel. An arrow then is displayed to the right of the event, listing the four actions. Click the arrow to display a pop-up menu and to select another action: onClick, onDblClick, onMouseOut, or onMouseOver. Note that the arrow for the pop-up menu is not displayed until the existing event is clicked.

Plan Ahead

> **Plan behaviors for AP elements.**
> Determine whether you want to set up an interaction where the user can drag or rearrange elements of the design. If so, use the Drag AP Element event. If you want to show and hide image, text, or other objects, use the Show-Hide Elements event. Also consider how you want users to initiate these events: when they move the mouse pointer away from an object or to an object or when they click or double-click an object.

Adding Behaviors

Selecting a hotspot and then clicking the Add behavior (+) pop-up menu in the Behaviors panel displays a menu of actions that can be attached to the hotspot. When you choose an action on this menu, Dreamweaver displays a dialog box in which you can specify the parameters for the action. In this chapter, you use the Show-Hide Elements action.

To Add the Show-Hide Elements Action to the Image Map Hotspots

The following steps show how to attach the Show-Hide Elements action to each of the three image map hotspots.

1

- Display the panel groups to prepare for displaying the Behaviors panel.

- Collapse the Property inspector to provide more room to work (Figure 5–28).

Q&A

What other behaviors can I add in Dreamweaver?

Another built-in behavior is Swap Image, which swaps one image for another, such as to create a button rollover effect. Use the Open Browser Window behavior to open a page in a new browser window. This behavior is often used with thumbnail images. When users click a thumbnail image, an appropriate page opens in a new browser window.

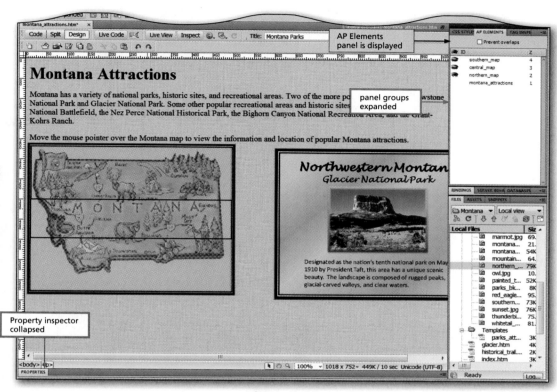

Figure 5–28

- Click the top hotspot on the montana_ attractions image to select the hotspot (Figure 5–29).

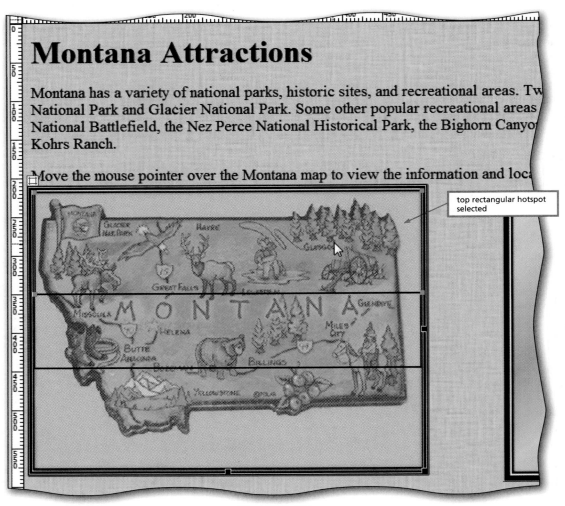

Figure 5–29

- Click Window on the Application bar, and then click Behaviors to display the Behaviors panel.

- Click the Add behavior button to display the Actions pop-up menu in the Behaviors panel.

- Point to Show-Hide Elements (Figure 5–30).

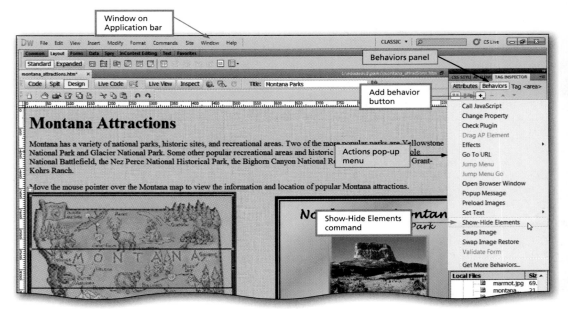

Figure 5–30

4

- Click Show-Hide Elements to open the Show-Hide Elements dialog box.

- If necessary, click div "montana_ attractions" in the Elements list to select it (Figure 5–31).

Q&A

The order of the elements is different in my dialog box. Is that a problem?

No. The order of the elements in your dialog box may differ.

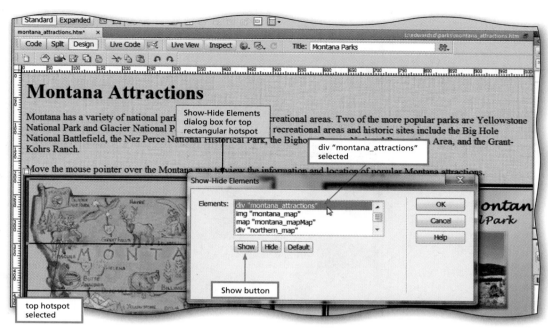

Figure 5–31

5

- Click the Show button to set the montana_attractions element to appear when the pointer is over the top hotspot.

- Click div "northern_ map" and then click the Show button to display this element when the pointer is over the top hotspot (Figure 5–32).

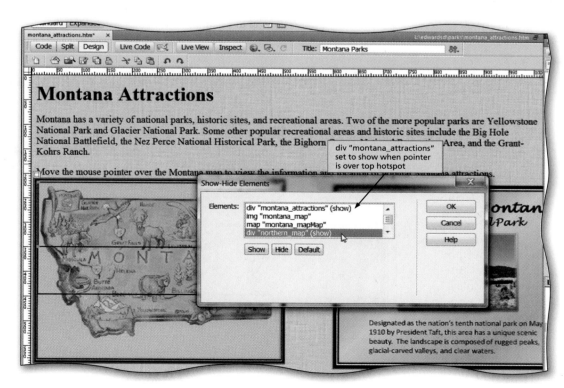

Figure 5–32

6

- Click div "central_map" and then click the Hide button to hide the element when the pointer is over the top hotspot.

- Click div "southern_map" and then click the Hide button to hide the element when the pointer is over the top hotspot (Figure 5–33).

Q&A What is the effect of the selections in this step?

First, you set the montana_attractions element and the map image it contains to appear when the pointer is over the hotspot. The map image will appear on the left side of the browser window. Next, you set the northern_map element and its image to appear when the pointer is over the hotspot. The northern_map image will appear to the right of the montana_attractions image. You also set the central_map and southern_map elements to be hidden when the pointer is over the top hotspot. The complete effect is that when the pointer is over the top hotspot, the montana_attractions image will appear on the left and only the northern_map image will appear on the right.

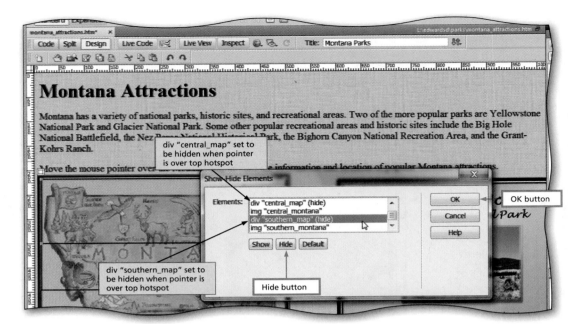

Figure 5–33

7

- Click the OK button to accept the settings for the top hotspot.

- Click the middle hotspot on the montana_attractions image to select the middle hotspot.

- Click the Add behavior button in the Behaviors panel to display the Actions pop-up menu.

- Click Show-Hide Elements on the Actions pop-up menu to display the Show-Hide Elements dialog box.

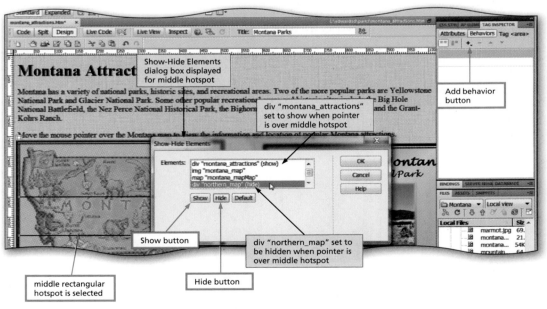

Figure 5–34

- If necessary, click div "montana_attractions" in the Elements list to select it.

- Click the Show button to display the montana_attractions element when the pointer is over the middle hotspot.

- Click div "northern_map" and then click the Hide button to hide the element when the pointer is over the middle hotspot (Figure 5–34).

8

- Click div "central_map" and then click the Show button to show the element when the pointer is over the middle hotspot.

- Click div "southern_map" and then click the Hide button to hide the element when the pointer is over the middle hotspot (Figure 5–35).

What is the effect of the selections in this step?

The complete effect is that when the pointer is over the middle hotspot, the montana_attractions image will appear on the left and only the central_map image will appear on the right.

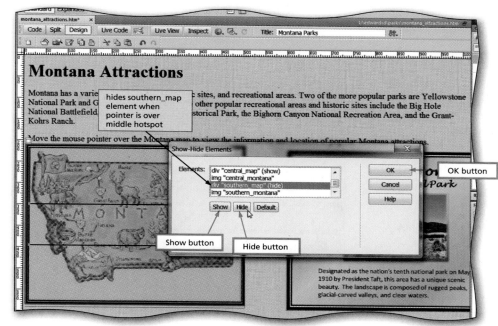

Figure 5–35

9

- Click the OK button to accept the settings for the middle hotspot.

- Click the bottom hotspot on the montana_attractions image.

- Click the Add behavior button in the Behaviors panel to display the Actions pop-up menu.

- Click Show-Hide Elements on the Actions pop-up menu to display the Show-Hide Elements dialog box

- With div "montana_attractions" selected in the Elements list, click the Show button to show the element when the pointer is over the bottom hotspot.

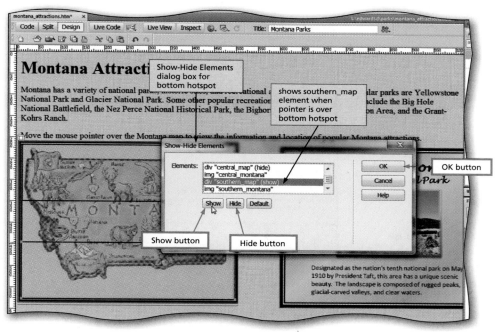

Figure 5–36

- Click div "northern_map" and then click the Hide button to hide the element when the pointer is over the bottom hotspot.

- Click div "central_map" and then click the Hide button to hide the element when the pointer is over the bottom hotspot.

- Click div "southern_map" and then click the Show button to show the element when the pointer is over the bottom hotspot (Figure 5–36).

Q&A What is the effect of the selections in this step?

The complete effect is that when the pointer is over the bottom hotspot, the montana_attractions image will appear on the left and only the southern_map image will appear on the right.

10

- Click the OK button to accept the settings for the bottom hotspot.

- Click the Save button on the Standard toolbar to save your work.

- Press the F12 key to display the Web page in your browser.

- If necessary, maximize the browser window.

Q&A What should I do if a message appears about allowing blocked content?

Click the message, click Allow Blocked Content, and then click the Yes button to confirm. When you are testing the Web pages created in this chapter, you can allow blocked content because you created the content yourself.

- Move the mouse pointer over the hotspots on the montana_attractions image to display each of the hidden elements (Figure 5–37, Figure 5–38, and Figure 5–39).

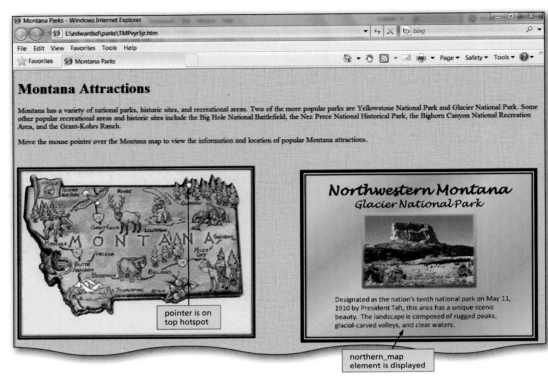

Figure 5–37

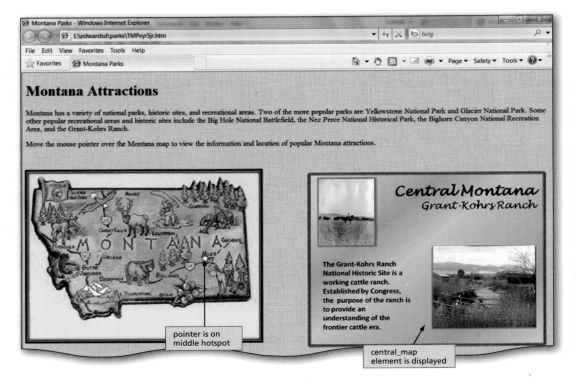

Figure 5–38

11
- Close the browser window and return to Dreamweaver.

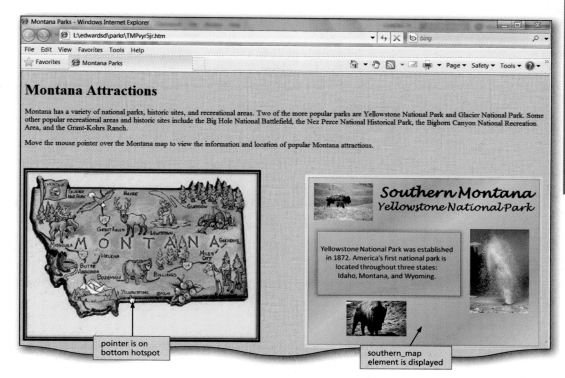

Figure 5–39

Positioning AP Elements

When you displayed the montana_attractions image and the images in the browser, you might have noticed that the spacing between the images and the text was not quite right. One advantage of using AP elements is that they can be positioned on the page. In some instances, to eliminate extra space, it is necessary to drag the image over existing text. Even though the text is covered in the Document window, it is displayed correctly in the browser.

Positioning AP elements sometimes can be a trial-and-error process. You can select and drag the element by the selection handle or you can move the element pixel by pixel by selecting the image, holding down the SHIFT key, and then pressing one of the arrow keys.

If you are having trouble positioning AP elements, you can use the Dreamweaver layout grid. The grid appears in the Document window to help you place objects precisely. AP elements will snap to the grid as you move them, which is especially useful when placing elements in relation to other objects on the page. To display the grid, click View on the Application bar, point to Grid, and then click Show Grid. To have AP elements snap to the grid, click View on the Application bar, point to Grid, and then click Grid Settings. In the Grid Settings dialog box, select the Snap to Grid option.

To Adjust AP Element Placement

In some instances, the map and the AP element may overlap the text. If this happens, the following steps show how to adjust the position of the montana_attractions element. If the elements do not overlap, you do not need to complete these steps.

1 Display the Property inspector and the AP Elements panel.

2 Click montana_attractions in the AP Elements panel.

3 If necessary, double-click the T text box in the Property inspector and type **210px** as the T value.

4 Press the TAB key and then click anywhere in the Document window.

Q&A What should I do if some of the text overlaps?

Leave it as is. The overlapped text will not be displayed as overlapped when viewed in the browser.

5 Click the Save button on the Standard toolbar to save any changes.

Selecting, Aligning, and Resizing Multiple AP Elements

Dreamweaver contains yet another command that you can use to lay out your Web page: the **Arrange command.** This command, which is accessed through the Modify menu, lets you align elements to their left, right, top, or bottom edges. The Arrange command also provides an option to make the width or height of selected elements the same. When you are using the Arrange command, the element you select last controls the alignment selection. For instance, if you first select northern_map, then central_map, and finally southern_map, the alignment placement is determined by southern_map. Likewise, if you select the option to make the width or height of selected elements the same, the last element selected is the one whose values are used as the values for the other elements.

To align two or more elements, you first must select the elements. To select multiple elements in the AP Elements panel, you select one element, hold down the SHIFT key, and then click the other elements you want to align. A second method for selecting multiple elements is to click the border of one element, hold down the SHIFT key, and then click the border of any other elements. When multiple elements are selected, the handles of the last selected element are highlighted in black. The resize handles of the other elements are highlighted in white.

AP elements do not have to be stacked or overlapped to be aligned. The three elements you need to align, however, are stacked one on top of the other. Thus, the best method for selecting the three elements is through the AP Elements panel.

To Select and Align Multiple AP Elements

The final steps for this Web page are to use the Align command to align the tops of the three hidden elements with the montana_attractions element, make the three hidden elements the same height and width if necessary, and then align the three elements to the left. Finally, you add a link from the index.htm Web page to this new montana_attractions.htm page.

The following steps illustrate how to complete the alignment options and add the link.

1

- Click the southern_map element in the AP Elements panel to select the first element to align.

- Hold down the SHIFT key and then click the central_map, northern_map, and montana_attractions elements to select all four elements (Figure 5–40).

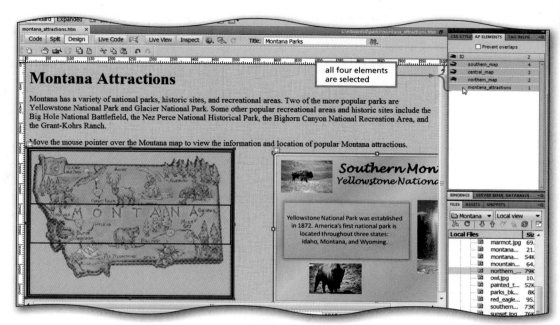

Figure 5–40

2

- Click Modify on the Application bar, point to Arrange, and then point to Align Top on the Arrange submenu to highlight the command (Figure 5–41).

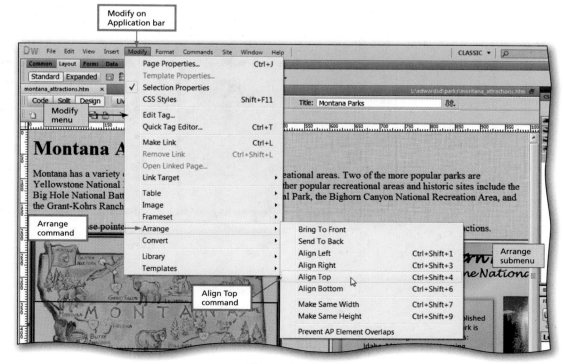

Figure 5–41

3

- Click Align Top to align all four elements along their tops (Figure 5–42).

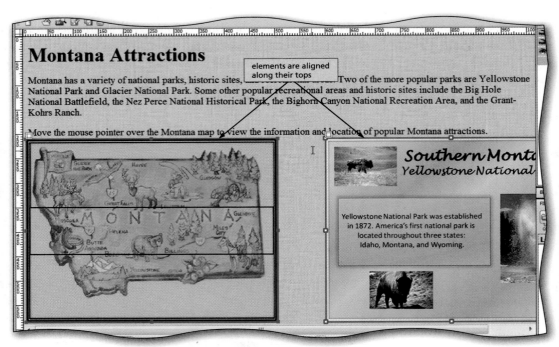

Figure 5–42

4

- Hold down the CTRL key and then click montana_attractions in the AP Elements panel to deselect it (Figure 5–43).

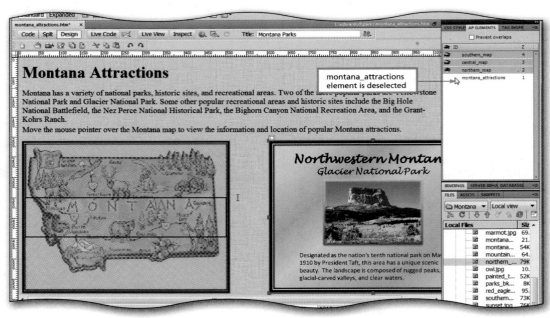

Figure 5–43

- Click Modify on the Application bar, point to Arrange, and then click Align Left on the Arrange submenu to align all elements to the left.

- Click Modify on the Application bar, point to Arrange, and then click Make Same Width on the Arrange submenu to make all elements the same width.

- Click Modify on the Application bar, point to Arrange, and then click Make Same Height on the Arrange submenu to make all elements the same height.

Figure 5–44

- Click View on the Application bar, point to Rulers, and then click Show on the Rulers submenu to hide the rulers (Figure 5–44).

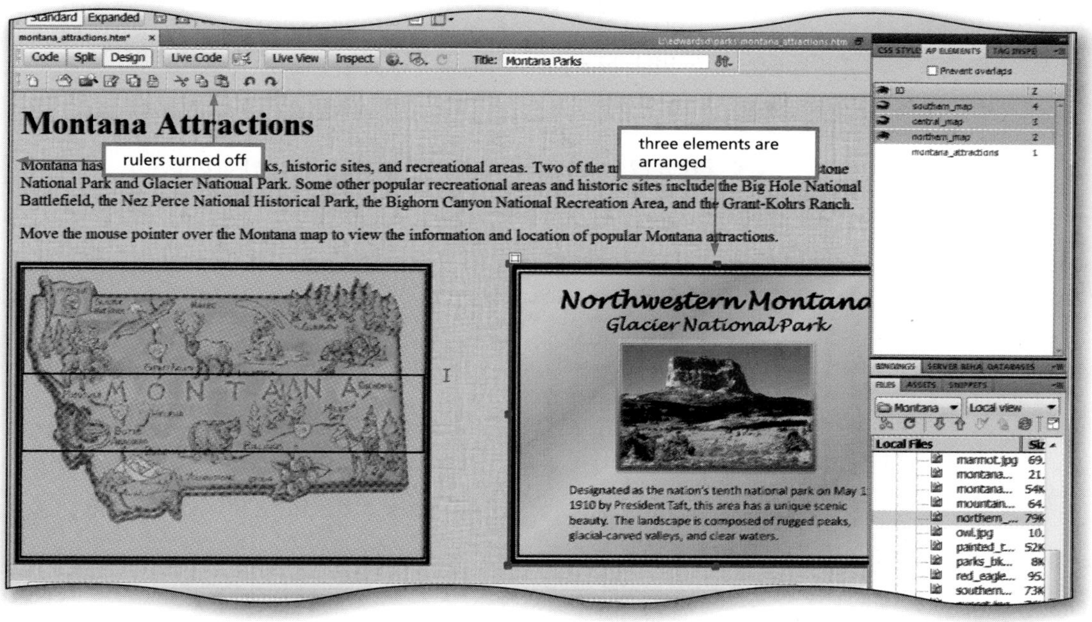

6

- Click the Save button on the Standard toolbar to save your work.

- Press the F12 key to view the Web page in your browser.

Q&A What should I do if I receive a browser message about whether to allow blocked content?

Because you are creating and testing the content, you can allow blocked content to display the Web page.

- Move the mouse pointer over the Montana map to verify that the images are displayed and that they are aligned properly.

- Close the browser and return to Dreamweaver.

Create a Link to the Montana Attractions Page

The following steps add a link to the index page that opens the Montana Attractions page, which contains the map of Montana attractions.

1 Close the montana_attractions.htm document.

2 Press F2 to collapse the AP Elements panel group.

3 In the Files panel, open the index.htm document and scroll to the bottom of the page.

4 Click to the right of the Featured Attraction link in the links table, press the SPACEBAR, and then insert a vertical line.

5 Select the space and line you just entered, and then delete the text in the Links text box to make sure the previous link does not continue to the new one.

6 Insert a space after the vertical line, and then type **Montana Attractions Map** as the link text.

7 Create a link to the montana_attractions.htm page, and then save the index.htm file (Figure 5–45).

8 Press F12 to view the Web page and test the link. Close the browser to return to Dreamweaver.

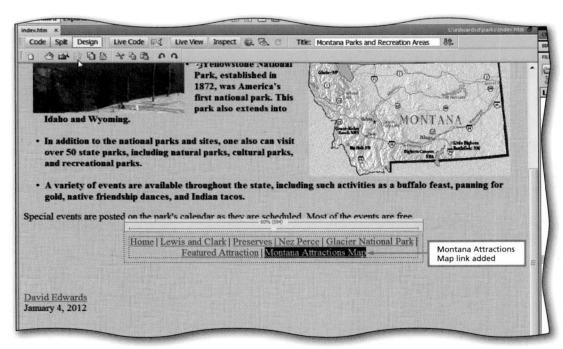

Figure 5–45

The History Panel

If you find yourself repeating or needing to undo or redo a step or steps, you can use Dreamweaver's History panel to undo one step or multiple steps at one time. The History panel includes a slider that can be dragged up and down to redo or undo code. The default number of steps is 50, but that number can be increased in the Preferences dialog box. You also can click the bar to the left of a step to undo all steps below the selected step.

To Use the History Panel

The following steps provide practice for using the History panel.

- If necessary, display the index.htm page.

- Click the link for your name at the end of the page and then remove the text from Link text box in the Property inspector.

- Select the date displayed at the bottom of the page and then replace it with December 12, 2012.

- Select the links table and then align it to the right (Figure 5–46).

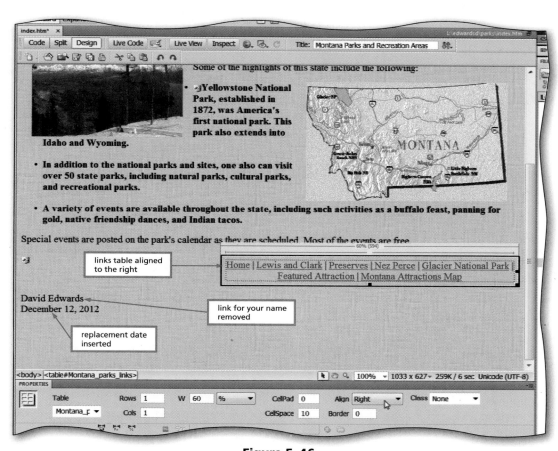

Figure 5–46

2

- Click Window on the Application bar and then click History to display the History panel.

- Drag the title bar of the History panel to move the panel to the middle of the Document window (Figure 5–47).

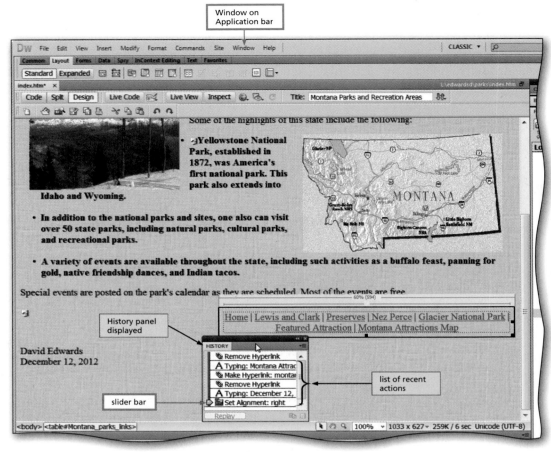

Figure 5–47

3

- Drag the slider bar up one notch to undo the Set Alignment: right command (Figure 5–48).

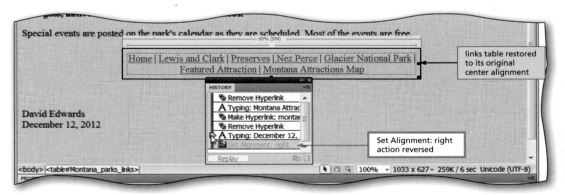

Figure 5–48

4

- Drag the slider bar to the top to undo two more commands (Figure 5–49).

- Type and format text and then use the History panel to redo and undo the actions. Before performing the next step, make sure the History panel looks like the one in Figure 5–49.

5

- Click the Close button on the History panel title bar to close the History panel.

Can the History panel display any action you can perform in the Dreamweaver window?

No. The History panel cannot record some mouse movements, such as clicking to select an object in the Document window. To select an object and record that action in the History panel, use the arrow keys instead of the mouse. Other actions such as dragging an element from one location to another are not recorded in the History panel. These actions appear as an icon with a red x or as a black line in the History panel.

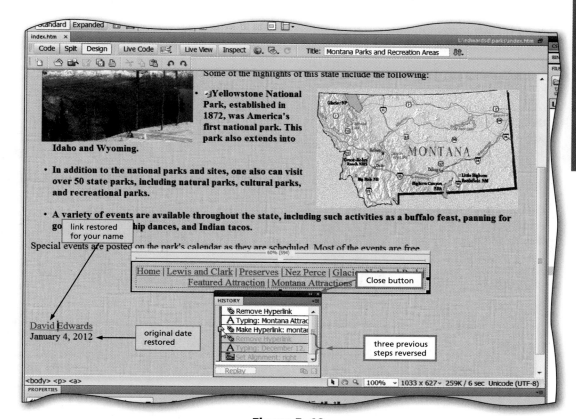

Figure 5–49

Adding the Date Object

Another feature that Dreamweaver provides is the **Date object,** which inserts the current date in a format of your preference and provides the option of updating the date (with or without the time) whenever you save the file.

To Insert the Date Object

The first step in modifying the index page is to remove the static date placed at the bottom of the page. The second step is to replace it with the current date and then format it using the Dreamweaver Date object. The following steps show how to insert the Date object.

- At the bottom of the index.htm page, select the date and then press the DELETE key to delete the date.

- Click Insert on the Application bar to display the Insert menu and then point to Date (Figure 5–50).

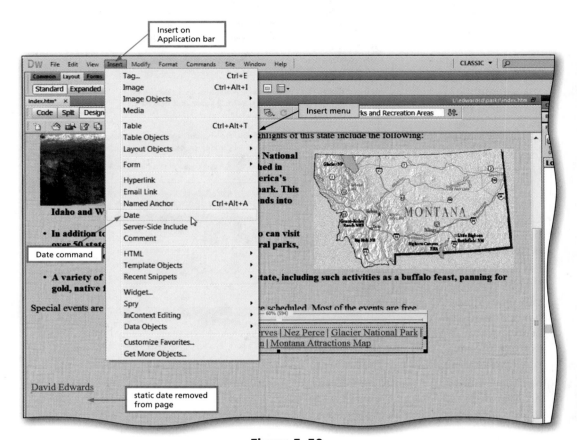

Figure 5–50

- Click Date to display the Insert Date dialog box, which includes a list of date formats.

- Click the Update automatically on save check box to have Dreamweaver display the current date when the page is saved (Figure 5–51).

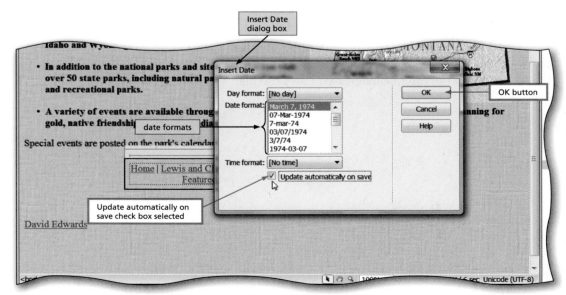

Figure 5–51

- Click the OK button to display the current date in the default format on the index page.

How can I change the date format after inserting a Date object?

Click the Date object on the page and then click the Edit date format button in the Property inspector.

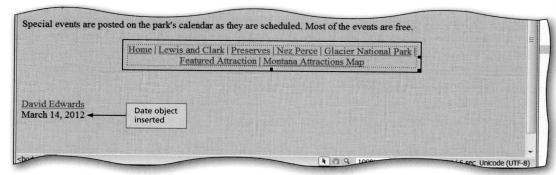

Figure 5–52

- Click anywhere on the page to deselect the date.

- Click the Save button on the Standard toolbar to save your work (Figure 5–52).

Other Ways

1. Click Common tab on Insert bar, click Date button on Common tab, select Date format in Insert Date dialog box, click OK

To Close the Web Site and Quit Dreamweaver

After you have created your Web page based on a template with applied styles, and tested and verified that the links work, Chapter 5 is complete. The following step closes the Web site and quits Dreamweaver.

1 Click the Close button in the upper-right corner of the Dreamweaver title bar to close the Dreamweaver window, the Document window, and the Montana Parks Web site.

Chapter Summary

Chapter 5 introduced you to AP elements, image maps, the History panel, and the Date object. You added single AP elements and stacked elements. You selected and aligned several elements. Next, you created an image map and then added hotspots that displayed hidden AP elements. Then, you modified the existing index page by deleting links and replacing those links with a navigation bar. You also inserted a Date object on the index page. The items listed below include all the new skills you have learned in this chapter.

1. Open the Montana Attractions page and display the rulers (DW 354)
2. Create and select an AP element for the Montana map image (DW 359)
3. Display the AP Elements panel (DW 361)
4. Name the AP element (DW 362)
5. Add an image to the montana_attractions AP element (DW 363)
6. Create stacked elements (DW 365)
7. Select AP elements and add images (DW 369)
8. Create hotspots on the montana_attractions image (DW 374)
9. Add the Show-Hide Elements action to the image map hotspots (DW 377)
10. Adjust AP element placement (DW 384)
11. Select and align multiple AP elements (DW 385)
12. Use the History panel (DW 389)
13. Insert the Date object (DW 392)

Learn It Online

Test your knowledge of chapter content and key terms.

Instructions: To complete the Learn It Online exercises, start your browser, click the Address bar, and then enter the Web address scsite.com/dwcs5/learn. When the Dreamweaver CS5 Learn It Online page is displayed, click the link for the exercise you want to complete and then read the instructions.

Chapter Reinforcement TF, MC, and SA

A series of true/false, multiple choice, and short answer questions that test your knowledge of the chapter content.

Flash Cards

An interactive learning environment where you identify chapter key terms associated with displayed definitions.

Practice Test

A series of multiple choice questions that test your knowledge of chapter content and key terms.

Who Wants To Be a Computer Genius?

An interactive game that challenges your knowledge of chapter content in the style of a television quiz show.

Wheel of Terms

An interactive game that challenges your knowledge of chapter key terms in the style of the television show *Wheel of Fortune*.

Crossword Puzzle Challenge

A crossword puzzle that challenges your knowledge of key terms presented in the chapter.

Apply Your Knowledge

Reinforce the skills and apply the concepts you learned in this chapter.

Inserting a Date Object

Instructions: In this activity, you insert a Date object on a Web page (Figure 5–53). Data files are not required for this exercise.

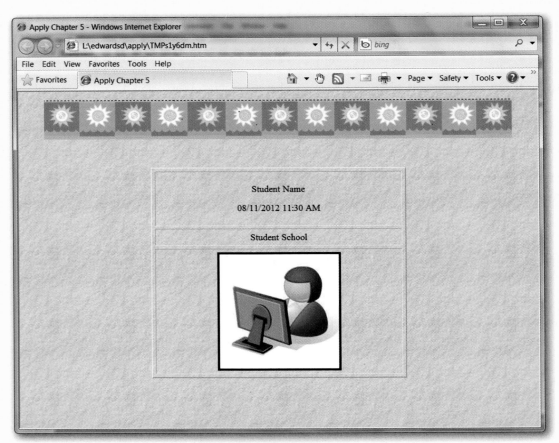

Figure 5–53

Perform the following tasks:

1. Start Dreamweaver, and then open the Apply Exercises site.
2. Open the apply_ch04 document, which you created in Chapter 4.
3. Save the document as apply_ch05, and then change the title to Apply Chapter 5.
4. Click to the right of your name and then press the ENTER key.
5. Click Insert on the Application bar and then click Date.
6. In the Insert Date dialog box, select a date format that you prefer.
7. Click the Time format button and select a time format that you prefer.
8. Click the Update automatically on save check box, and then click the OK button to insert the date and time.
9. Save the document, display it in a browser, and then submit it to your instructor as requested.

Extend Your Knowledge

Extend the skills you learned in this chapter and experiment with new skills. You may need to use Help to complete the assignment.

Using the History Panel

Instructions: In this activity, you increase your knowledge of using the History panel. Data files are not required for this exercise.

Perform the following tasks:

1. If necessary, start Dreamweaver and then open the Extend Exercises Web site.
2. Open the extend_ch04 page, which you created in Chapter 4, and then save the document as extend_ch05.
3. Display the History panel.
4. Delete your name and then type **Mary Smith**.
5. Delete your school's name and then type **WCCC**.
6. Click the solar power image and then align it to the right.
7. Below the table, insert the current date and time in the formats of your choice (Figure 5–54).

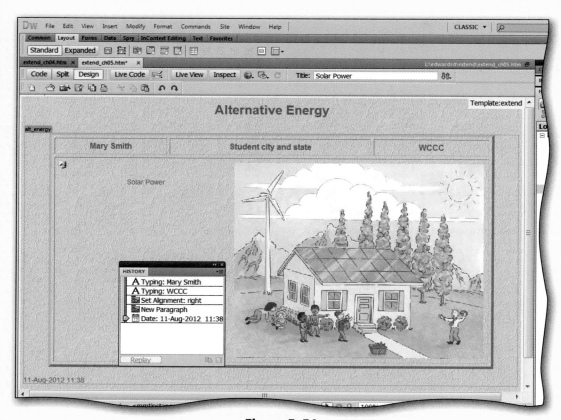

Figure 5–54

8. Undo all changes, and then insert the date and time again.
9. Save the document, display it in a browser, and then submit it to your instructor as requested.

Make It Right

Analyze a Web page template and correct all errors or improve the design.

Adding Hotspots and Behaviors

Instructions: In this activity, you modify a Web page so it correctly displays images when the mouse pointer is over a hotspot (Figure 5–55). Make sure you have downloaded the data files for this chapter. See the inside back cover of this book for instructions for downloading the Data Files for Students, or contact your instructor for information about accessing the required files for this book.

Perform the following tasks:

1. Start Dreamweaver, and then copy the data file from the Chapter05\right data files folder into the right folder for your Right Exercises local Web site. Copy the image files from the Chapter05\right\images data files folder into the right\images folder for your Right Exercises local Web site.

2. Open the Right Exercises Web site, and then open the right_ch05 document.

3. Draw three hotspots on the map image on the left. The top hotspot should include the picture of France, the middle hotspot should include the picture of Germany, and the bottom hotspot should include the picture of the Netherlands.

4. Use the Show-Hide Elements dialog box for each hotspot to show and hide AP elements as specified in Table 5–1.

Table 5–1 Show-Hide Settings

Hotspot	Elements to Show	Elements to Hide
top	div "france_sights"	div "germany_sights" div "netherlands_sights"
middle	div "germany_sights"	div "france_sights" div "netherlands_sights"
bottom	div "netherlands_sights"	div "france_sights" div "germany_sights"

5. Save the document and display it in a browser. Move the mouse pointer over the maps on the left to display the corresponding images on the right (Figure 5–55).

6. Submit the document to your instructor as requested.

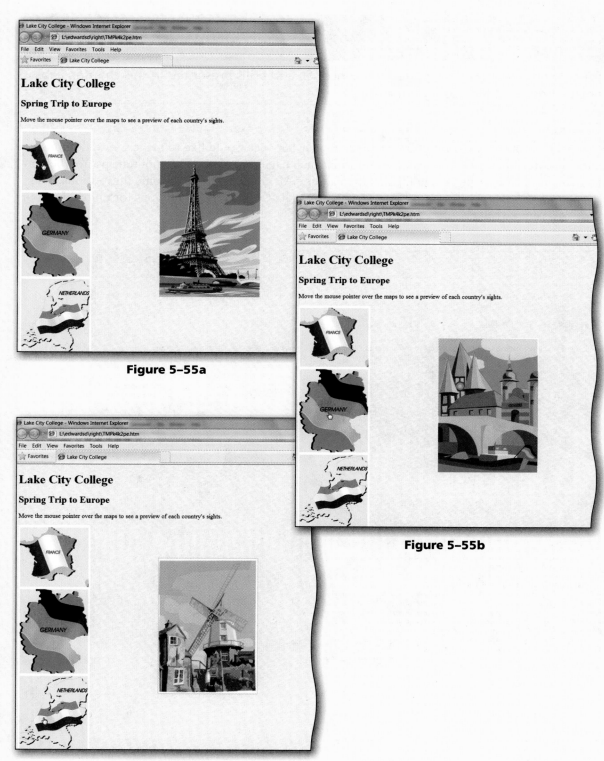

Figure 5–55a

Figure 5–55b

Figure 5–55c

In the Lab

Create a document using the guidelines, concepts, and skills presented in this chapter. Labs are listed in order of increasing difficulty.

Lab 1: Adding AP Elements to the Bryan's Computer Repair Services Web Site

Problem: The proprietors of Bryan's Computer Repair Services would like to make some additions to their Web site. They want to include an informational page that provides computer tips. You begin creating the page by opening a data file and then adding AP elements to show some illustrations. The new computer_tips page is shown in Figure 5–56. Appendix C contains instructions for uploading your local site to a remote server.

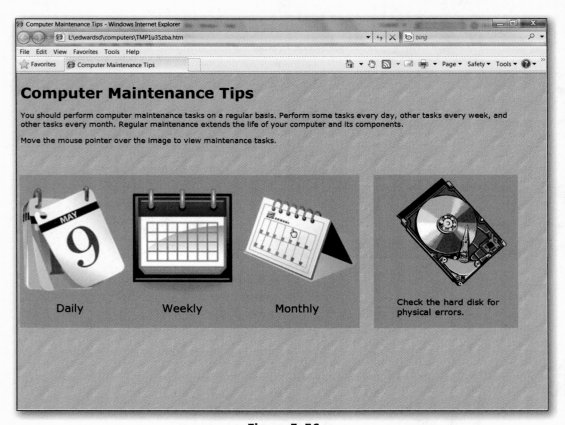

Figure 5–56

Perform the following tasks:

1. Start Dreamweaver, and then copy the data file from the Chapter05\computers data files folder into the computers folder for your Computer Repair Services local Web site. Copy the data files from the Chapter05\computers\images data files folder into the images folder for your Computer Repair Services local Web site.

2. Open the Computer Repair Services site, and then open the computer_tips page.

3. Display the rulers. Click the ruler-origin icon and drag it to about the 5-pixel mark on the horizontal ruler and the 220-pixel mark on the vertical ruler.

4. Click the Draw AP Div button on the Layout tab, and then draw an AP element about 715 by 335 pixels in size.

5. Select the AP element, and then type **map** in the CSS-P Element ID text box. Enter 5px in the L box and 220px in the T box. Specify 715px as the width and 335px as the height.

6. Drag the calendars image from the Files panel to the map element.

7. Click the ruler-origin icon and drag it to about the 750-pixel mark on the horizontal ruler and the 220-pixel mark on the vertical ruler.

8. Click the Draw AP Div button on the Layout tab, and then use the rulers as a guide to draw an AP element about 303 by 335 pixels in size.

9. Select the AP element, type **day_tip** in the CSS-P Element ID text box, and then specify 303px as the width and 335px as the height of the element. Enter 750px in the L text box and 220px in the T text box. Set the Vis property to hidden.

10. Drag the shutdown image onto the day_tip AP element. Enter shutdown as the image ID and Daily Tip as the Alt text.

11. Add two more AP elements on top of the day_tip element. Use the rulers to approximate the L and T positions on the page, as indicated in Table 5–2. Name the elements and drag the corresponding images onto each element, using the data indicated in the table. Before you drag an image to the element, make sure an insertion point appears in the element. Make any other necessary adjustments in the Property inspector.

Table 5–2 AP Element Properties

AP Element ID	L and T	W and H	Vis	Image Name	Image ID	Alt Text
week_tip	750px, 220px	303px, 335px	hidden	backup	backup	Weekly Tip
month_tip	750px, 220px	303px, 335px	hidden	checkdisk	checkdisk	Monthly Tip

12. Add three hotspots to the calendars image. Each hotspot should cover about one-third of the image. The first hotspot should cover the Daily calendar, the second hotspot should cover the Weekly calendar, and the third hotspot should cover the Monthly calendar.

13. Display the Behaviors panel. Select the first hotspot, click the Add behavior button in the Behaviors panel, and then click Show-Hide Elements on the Add behavior pop-up menu. In the Show-Hide Elements dialog box, show div "day_tip" and div "map". Hide div "week_tip" and div "month_tip". Click the OK button.

14. Click the second hotspot, click the Add behavior button in the Behaviors panel, and then click Show-Hide Elements on the Add behavior pop-up menu. Show div "week_tip" and div "map". Hide div "day_tip" and div "month_tip". Click the OK button to close the Show-Hide Elements dialog box.

15. Click the third hotspot, click the Add behavior button in the Behaviors panel, and then click Show-Hide Elements on the Add behavior pop-up menu. Show div "month_tip" and div "map". Hide div "day_tip" and div "week_tip". Click the OK button to close the Show-Hide Elements dialog box.

16. Hide the rulers and display the AP Elements panel. Select the four elements and top-align them.

17. Click the Save button and then press the F12 key to view the Web page in your browser. Allow blocked content, if necessary. Test all the hotspots and links.

18. Submit your files in the format provided by your instructor.

In the Lab

Lab 2: Baskets by Carole Web Site

Problem: The Baskets by Carole Web site has become very popular. Carole would like to redesign the index page to make it more interactive and keep it up to date. She has requested that you help her with this project rearranging some of the text by using AP elements, adding an automatic Date object so the current date is displayed on the page, and aligning existing AP elements. You agree to help her. The revised Web page is shown in Figure 5–57. Appendix C contains instructions for uploading your local site to a remote server.

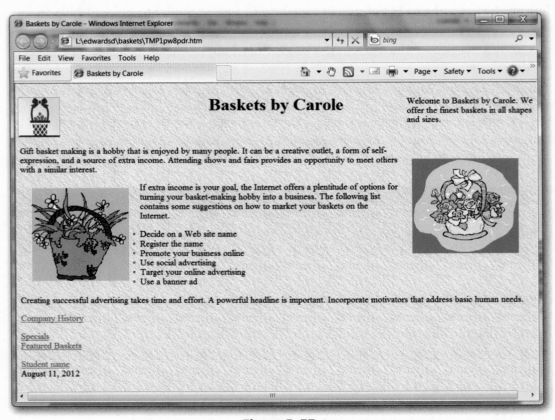

Figure 5–57

Perform the following tasks:

1. Start Dreamweaver, open the Gift Basket Designs site, and then open the index page.

2. Click after the heading text, and then press the ENTER key twice to insert a blank line and to move the element marker to a new line. Center the Baskets by Carole heading. Display the rulers, if necessary.

3. The next task is to add an AP element for the logo. Click the Draw AP Div button on the Layout tab and then draw an element in the upper-left corner of the page with an approximate width of 75px and height of 75px. Name the element logo. Change the L to 5px and the T to 25px. If necessary, change the W to 75px and the H to 75px. Change the Vis setting to visible. Drag the logo01 image onto the AP element. Resize the logo01 image to 75 (W) by 75 (H) pixels.

4. Next, you add an AP element to the right of the Baskets by Carole heading. Draw an AP element about 100 pixels to the right of the heading. Set the following properties for the element: ID – heading, L – 700px, T – 25px, W – 250px, H – 65px, Vis – hidden.

5. Click in the heading AP element to move the insertion point to the element. Type the following text:

   Welcome to Baskets by Carole. We offer the finest baskets in all shapes and sizes.

6. Draw a hotspot on the complete basket01 image on the right side of the page.

7. Select the hotspot, open the Behaviors panel, click the Add behavior button, and then click Show-Hide Elements on the pop-up menu. Show the logo and the heading elements when the pointer is over the hotspot.

8. Display the AP Elements panel. Select the two elements and then top-align them.

9. Delete the date at the end of the page, and then insert a date that is automatically updated on save. Select the format that matches March 7, 1974.

10. Save your work, and then press the F12 key to view the page in your browser. Allow blocked content, if necessary. Point to the basket image to display the logo and text. Submit your files in the format provided by your instructor.

In the Lab

Lab 3: Modifying the Questions Web Page for the Credit Protection Web Site

Problem: Jessica would like to add more interaction to the Credit Protection Web site and has asked you for ideas. You suggest that the questions page could be revised so that when a user points to a question, the answer is displayed. Jessica likes your suggestion, and you agree to revise the page. The revised page is shown in Figure 5–58; it displays the answer to a question when the pointer is over the question. Appendix C contains instructions for uploading your local site to a remote server.

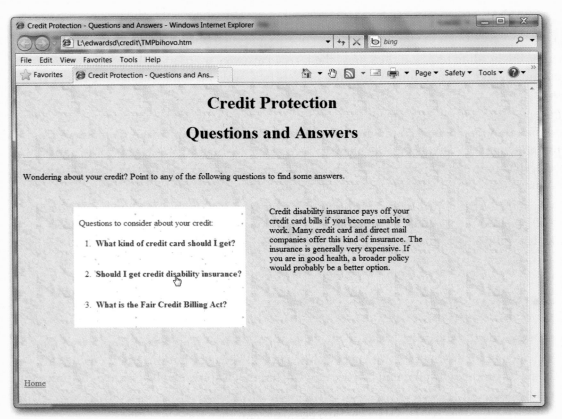

Figure 5–58

Perform the following tasks:

1. In Dreamweaver, open the Credit Protection Web site, and then copy the credit data files to the credit folder and the images folder for your Credit Protection Web site. The data files contain a questions.htm file, which will replace the existing questions.htm file. If necessary, click the Copy and Replace button in response to the Copy File dialog box.

2. If necessary, display the panel groups and the Layout tab.

3. Open the questions document. Display the rulers. Position the insertion point below the horizontal line and type `Wondering about your credit? Point to any of the following questions to find some answers.` Press the ENTER key two times.

4. Click the Draw AP Div button on the Layout tab and use the rulers as a guide to draw an AP element with the following properties: CSS-P Element ID – questions, L – 100px, T – 225px, W – 305px, H – 220px, Vis – visible. Drag the questions image from the Files panel onto the questions element.

5. Draw three more AP elements to the right of the questions element. Use the rulers as a guide to draw the elements. Use Table 5–3 to enter the properties for each element. After you create each element, type the text as listed in the Text column.

Table 5–3 AP Element Properties

AP Element ID	L and T (px)	W and H (px)	Vis	Text
quest01	450/225	280/205	hidden	Consider how you will use the card. Do you pay the entire balance at the end of every month? Or, do you make minimum payments? For those individuals who pay the entire balance each month, interest rate is not a priority. Most likely, you will not have to pay finance charges. Instead, look for a company that does not charge an annual fee. If you tend to carry an outstanding balance, search for a card issuer that charges very low interest rates.
quest02	450/225	275/145	hidden	Credit disability insurance pays off your credit card bills if you become unable to work. Many credit card and direct mail companies offer this type of insurance. The insurance is generally very expensive. If you are in good health, a broader policy would probably be a better option.
quest03	450/225	285/160	hidden	The Fair Credit Billing Act is a federal law that determines how billing errors and disputes involving credit and charge cards are handled. If you check the back of your monthly statement, generally you will find information about this process. If the company violates any provision of the law, you can sue to recover any damages.

6. Select the questions element and then draw a hotspot over the first question. With the hotspot selected, click the Add behavior button in the Behaviors panel and then click Show-Hide Elements on the Add behavior pop-up menu. Show the questions and quest01 elements. Hide the quest02 and quest03 elements.

7. Draw a second hotspot over the second question. With the hotspot selected, click the Add behavior button in the Behaviors panel and then click Show-Hide Elements on the Add behavior pop-up menu. Show the questions and quest02 elements. Hide the quest01 and quest03 elements.

8. Draw a third hotspot over the third question. With the hotspot selected, click the Add behavior button in the Behaviors panel and then click Show-Hide Elements on the Add behavior pop-up menu. Show the questions and quest03 elements. Hide the quest01 and quest02 elements.

9. Press CTRL+S to save the questions Web page.

10. Press the F12 key to view the page in your browser. Allow blocked content, if necessary. Roll over each of the hotspots to verify that they work correctly. Submit your files in the format provided by your instructor.

Cases and Places

Apply your creative thinking and problem solving skills to design and implement a solution.

● Easier ●●More Difficult

● 1: Add a Date and a New Image for the Favorite Sports Web Site

You would like to add an additional image to your sports Web site. You decide to modify the index page and add a Date object so the date will be updated automatically when you save the page. Insert the Date object at the end of the page. Insert the new image at the top-right side of the page.

● 2: Add an Image Map and Links to Other Online Hobby Web Sites

Your hobby Web page has become very popular and you want to give it a more professional look. Use AP elements to create a new layout for one of your pages. Determine which page in your Web site you will revise and then add at least four AP elements to the page. Name each element and place it appropriately on the page. Add images or text to the elements. Upload the page to a remote site if instructed to do so.

●● 3: Add an Image Map to the Politics Web Site

You are receiving a lot of e-mail about what a great Web site you have for your political office campaign. You decide to make the site more interactive by adding an AP element with an image map, and then adding two other AP elements. Create the three elements — the first one with the image map and the other two displaying images related to your politics site. Add hotspots to your image map to show and hide the two images. Upload the revised pages to a remote site.

●● 4: Add an Image Map and the Date Object to the Favorite Music Web Site

Make It Personal

You are receiving a lot of e-mail about what a great Web site you have to showcase your music interest. You decide to make the site more interactive by adding an AP element with an image map, and then adding two other AP elements. Create the three elements — the first one with the image map and the other two displaying images related to your music site. Add hotspots to your image map to show and hide the two images. Include a Date object showing the date and time in the formats of your choice. Upload the revised pages to a remote site.

●● 5: Add an Image Map to the Student Trips Web Site

Working Together

The student trips Web site still is receiving numerous hits, and the debate about which location to pick for the trip is continuing. Add a new page to the Web site. Add an image map with at least four AP elements to the Web site. The first element should contain a map of the United States. The other three elements should contain pictures of possible trip locations. Add hotspots to the image map on the individual states and then set the AP elements to appear as appropriate. Upload the new pages to a remote server.

6 | Forms

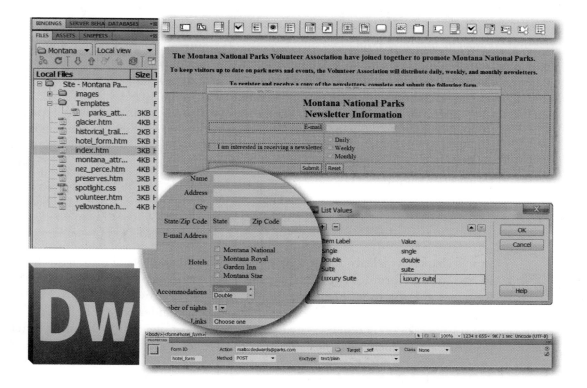

Objectives

You will have mastered the material in this chapter when you can:

- Discuss form processing

- Describe the difference between client-side and server-side form processing

- Add a horizontal rule to a Web page

- Create a form

- Insert a table into a form

- Describe form objects

- Describe and add text fields and text areas to a form

- Describe and add check boxes and radio buttons to a form

- Describe and add lists and menus to a form

- Describe and add form buttons to a form

- Describe form accessibility options

- Apply behaviors to a form

- View and test a form

6 | Forms

Introduction

As you learned in Chapter 3, Dreamweaver's table feature is an effective tool for designing a Web page. A table allows you to add vertical and horizontal structure to a Web page. Using a table, you can put just about anything on your page and have it be displayed in a specific location. Using Dreamweaver's table features, you can create columns of text or navigation bars and lay out tabular data. You can delete, split, and merge rows and columns; modify table, row, or cell properties to add color and adjust alignment; and copy, paste, and delete cells in the table structure.

Tables also enable the Web site designer to use this format to lay out and create forms. Forms enable the Web page designer to provide visitors with dynamic information and to obtain and process information and feedback from the people viewing the Web page. Web forms are highly versatile tools that can be used for surveys, guest books, order forms, tests, automated responses, user questions, and reservations.

Project — Adding Forms to a Web Site

BTW

Form Design
When designing a form, keep the form simple and to the point. Before you create the form, sketch it on paper. The layout should be clear and uncomplicated.

In this chapter, you learn to use tables to create forms and to add form fields to the forms. You add forms to two Web pages — a general information page and a Hotel Reservation Form page. The Hotel Reservation Form, shown in Figure 6–1a, also contains a relative link to the Montana National Parks index page. The Hotel Reservation Form page contains a request for a hotel reservation at one of four Montana hotels and provides a jump menu with absolute links to pages on the National Park Service Web site. The general information page, sponsored by the Montana National Parks Volunteer Association, is shown in Figure 6–1b. This Web page contains a small form that allows the viewer to subscribe to a free newsletter. This page also contains a link to the Montana National Parks index page. Both forms contain the same background used for the previous pages in the Montana Parks Web site and each contains a horizontal rule separating the heading and the form.

As you complete the activities in this chapter, you will find that forms are one of the more important sources of interactivity on the Web and are one of the standard tools for the Web page designer.

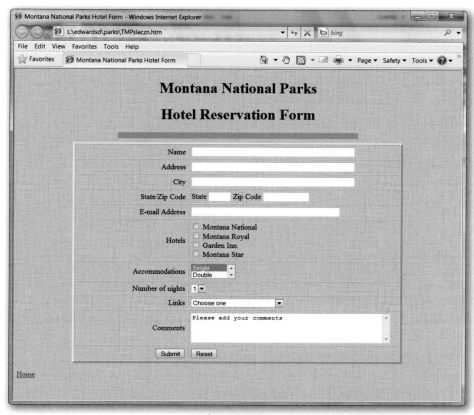

Figure 6–1a

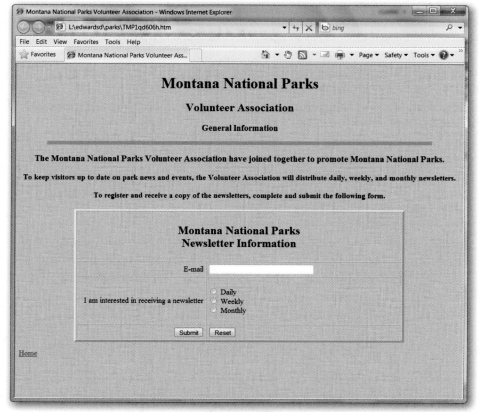

Figure 6–1b

Overview

As you read this chapter, you will learn how to add to your Web site the pages shown in Figure 6–1a and Figure 6–1b by performing these general tasks:

- Insert and center a heading.
- Insert a table into a Dreamweaver Web page.
- Insert a form and set the form properties.
- Specify column width and merge cells.
- Add form objects.
- Add accessibility attributes.
- Add text to the table.
- Add links.

Plan Ahead

General Project Guidelines

When adding pages to a Web site, you must consider the appearance and characteristics of the completed page. As you create and add the two Web pages to the Montana Parks Web site shown in Figure 6–1a and Figure 6–1b, you should follow these general guidelines.

1. **Plan the format of the form pages.** Determine the purpose of the form. Consider how the form pages will best fit into the Web site. Where will the data be stored?

2. **Organize your content.** Create and organize the content for the two new pages.

3. **Consider the data you will collect.** Use the data to determine rows and columns that will be included as part of the form. Decide if column headings will be named and, if so, what names will be given to the columns. Consider the audience that will use the form and what is the best way to collect the data.

4. **Images.** Decide if you will add images to your form and, if so, where you will place them. Consider the vertical and horizontal space that will need to be designated to place the image better. Determine if the image will need to be resized, and if so, how much resizing will need to be done.

5. **Determine the types of controls you will add to the form.** The controls you add will determine and affect the type of data you can collect.

6. **Consider Web content accessibility factors.** When an object is inserted into an HTML form, you can make the form object accessible.

7. **Link the new content.** Consider the content of each new page and how it will link to and from the other pages in the Web site.

8. **Create, test, and validate the form.** After creating the form, it should be tested to verify that all controls work as intended, including the Submit and Reset buttons. The Validate Form behavior checks the contents of specified text fields to ensure that the user has entered the correct type of data.

When necessary, more specific details concerning the above guidelines are presented at appropriate points in the chapter. The chapter also will identify the actions performed and decisions made regarding these guidelines during the creation of the Web pages shown in Figures 6–1a and 6–1b.

Starting Dreamweaver and Opening a Web Site

Each time you start Dreamweaver, it opens to the last site displayed when you closed the program. It therefore may be necessary for you to open the Montana Parks Web site. Clicking the Sites pop-up menu in the Files panel lists the sites you have defined. When you open the site, a list of pages and subfolders within the site is displayed.

To Start Dreamweaver and Open the Montana Parks Web Site

With a good understanding of the requirements, and an understanding of the necessary decisions and planning process, the first step is to start Dreamweaver and open the Montana Parks Web site.

1 Click the Start button on the Windows taskbar.

2 Click Adobe Dreamweaver CS5 on the Start menu or point to All Programs on the Start menu, click Adobe Design Premium, if necessary, and then click Adobe Dreamweaver CS5 on the All Programs list to start Dreamweaver.

3 If necessary, display the panel groups.

4 If the Montana Parks hierarchy is not displayed, click the Sites pop-up menu button on the Files panel, and then click Montana Parks to display the Montana Parks Web site in the Files panel.

To Copy Data Files to the Parks Web Site

Before you start enhancing and adding to your Web site, you need to copy the data files into the site's folder hierarchy. In the following steps, you copy the data files for the Chapter 6 project from the Chapter06 folder on a USB drive to the parks folder stored in the *your name* folder on the same USB drive. In the following steps, the data files for this chapter are stored on drive L:. The location on your computer may be different. If necessary, verify the location of the data files with your instructor.

1 Click the Sites pop-up menu button in the Files panel, and then click the name of the drive containing your data files, such as Removable Disk (L:).

2 If necessary, click the plus sign (+) next to the folder containing your data files to expand that folder, and then click the plus sign (+) next to the Chapter06 folder to expand it.

3 Expand the parks folder to display the data files.

4 Click the volunteer document to select it and then copy and paste it in the parks folder (Figure 6–2).

Q&A

Is there another method for copying a data file into the Web site folder?

Yes, you can copy the file using the Windows Computer tool.

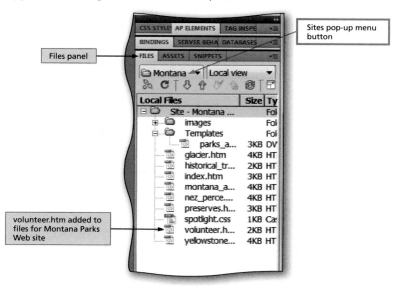

Figure 6–2

Creating the Hotel Reservation Form Web Page

You start by creating the Hotel Reservation Form page and then applying a background image. This is the same background image you used for the Montana Parks Web site pages in previous chapters.

Plan Ahead

> **Plan the format of the form pages.**
> To integrate a form page into your Web site, format it the same way you format other pages on the site. Use the same background image, for example, and the same font and styles for the text. To minimize the amount of scrolling users must do to complete the form, sketch a form and plan where to insert the controls such as text boxes and labels. If you are converting a paper-based form into a Web form, identify how you can condense the form to fit the screen and what types of electronic controls you will use where users enter information on the printed form.

To Create a New Document

The following steps illustrate how to create a new document and save the page as hotel_form.htm.

1 Click File on the Application bar and then click New to open the New Document dialog box. If necessary, click Blank Page, click HTML in the Page Type list, click <none> in the Layout list, and then click the Create button to create a Web page.

2 Click the Save button on the Standard toolbar to display the Save As dialog box.

3 Type **hotel_form** as the file name. If necessary, select the parks folder, and then click the Save button to save the hotel_form.htm page in the Montana Parks local folder (Figure 6–3).

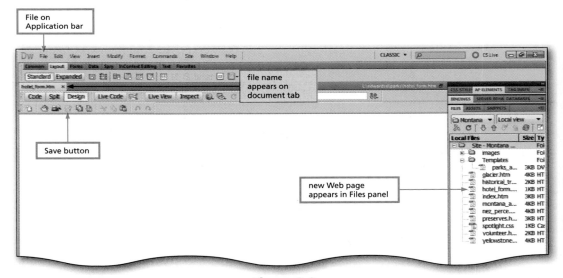

Figure 6–3

To Add a Background Image to the hotel_form Page

To provide additional space in the Document window and to create a better overview of the layout, you start by collapsing the panel groups. Then you apply the background image to the hotel_form page.

1 If necessary, click the panel groups Collapse to Icons button to collapse the panel groups, and click the Property inspector expander arrow to display both the upper and lower sections.

2 Click the Page Properties button in the Property inspector to display the Page Properties dialog box.

3 Click Appearance (HTML) in the Category column to display the HTML options.

4 Click the Browse button to the right of the Background image box to open the Select Image Source dialog box.

5 If necessary, navigate to the parks\images folder. Click parks_bkg and then click the OK button in the Select Image Source dialog box to select the image.

6 Click the OK button in the Page Properties dialog box to apply the background image to the page. If necessary, click the Document window to display the hotel_form Web page with the background applied and the insertion point aligned at the left (Figure 6–4).

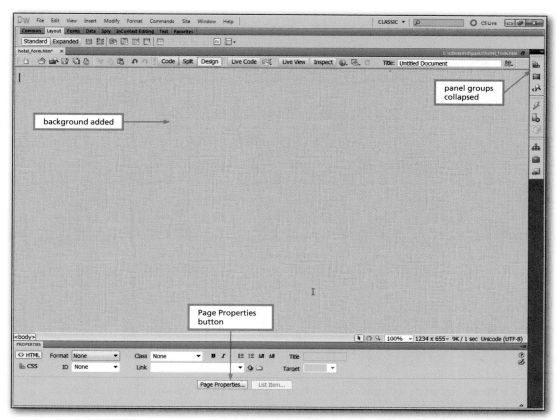

Figure 6–4

To Insert and Format the Page Headings

Next, you insert and format the page headings. You apply the same heading format you applied to the heading in the index page. The following steps show how to add the headings and apply the Heading 1 format.

1 In the Title text box, type **Montana National Parks Hotel Form** as the page title, and then press the ENTER key.

2 Click the Document window to display the insertion point, and then type **Montana National Parks** as the heading.

3 Press the ENTER key and then type **Hotel Reservation Form** as the second heading.

4 Select both headings, click Format on the Application bar, point to Align, and then click Center to center the headings.

5 Apply Heading 1 to both lines to format the headings, and then press the ENTER key to move the insertion point below the second heading.

6 Click the Save button on the Standard toolbar to save the page with the centered and formatted headings (Figure 6–5).

Figure 6–5

Understanding How Forms Work

Forms are interactive elements that provide a way for the Web site visitor to interact with the site. A form provides a method for a user to give feedback, submit an order for merchandise or services, request information, and so on. Forms are created using HTML tags. Each form must have a beginning <form> tag and an ending </form> tag. You cannot nest forms. Each HTML document, however, may contain multiple forms.

Form Processing

A form provides a popular way to collect data from a Web site visitor. Forms, however, do not process data. Forms require a script to process the form input data. Such a script generally is a text file that is executed within an application and usually is written in Perl, VBScript, JavaScript, Java, or C++. These scripts reside on a server. Therefore, they are called **server-side scripts**. Other server-side technologies include Adobe ColdFusion, ASP, ASP.NET, PHP, and JavaServer Pages (JSP). Some type of database application typically supports these technologies.

A common way to process form data is through a **Common Gateway Interface (CGI)** script. When a browser collects data, the data is sent to a Hypertext Transfer Protocol (HTTP) server (a gateway) specified in the HTML form. The server then starts a program (which also is specified in the HTML form) that can process the collected data. The gateway can process the input however you choose. It may return customized HTML based on the user's input, log the input to a file, or e-mail the input to someone.

The **<form> tag** includes parameters that allow you to specify a path to the server-side script or application that processes the form data and indicate which HTTP method to use when transmitting data from the browser to the server. The two HTTP methods are GET and POST, and both of these methods are attributes of the <form> tag. The **GET method** sends the data with a URL. This method is not widely used because it places a limitation on the amount and format of the data that is transmitted to the application. Another limitation of the GET method is that the information being sent is visible in the browser's Address bar. The **POST method** is more efficient because it sends the data to the application as standard input with no limits. The POST method can send much more information than the typical GET method. With POST, the information is not sent with the URL, so the data is invisible to the site visitor.

As an example of form data processing, when a user enters information into a form and clicks the Submit button, the information is sent to the server, where the server-side script or application processes it. The server then responds by sending the requested information back to the user, or performing some other action based on the content of the form.

The specifics of setting up scripts and database applications are beyond the scope of this book. Another option for form data processing exists, however, in which a form can be set up to send data to an e-mail address. The e-mail action is not 100 percent reliable and may not work if your Internet connection has extensive security parameters. In some instances, submitting a mailto form results in a blank mail message being displayed. Nothing is harmed when this happens, but no data is attached to and sent with the message. Additionally, some browsers display a warning message whenever a form button using mailto is processed. This book uses the e-mail action, however, because this is the action more widely available for most students and users. On the other hand, your instructor may have server-side scripting available. Verify with your instructor the action you are to use.

Between the <form> and </form> tags are the tags that create the body of the form and collect the data. These tags are <input>, <select>, and <textarea>. The most widely used is the **<input> tag**, which collects data from check boxes, option buttons (called radio buttons in Dreamweaver), single-line text fields, form/image buttons, and passwords. The **<select> tag** is used with list and pop-up menu boxes. The **<textarea> tag** collects the data from multiline text fields.

BTW

Form Processing
Forms can contain form objects that enable user interaction and allow the Web page designer to interact with or gather information from visitors to a Web site. After the data is collected from a user, it is submitted to a server for processing or e-mailed to a designated e-mail address.

If you are using Internet Explorer with Windows 7, Windows Vista, or Windows XP Service Pack 2 (SP2), in many instances, Internet Explorer automatically blocks content such as form elements. Thus, for all instances in this chapter where pages containing forms are displayed in Internet Explorer, you may have to choose to "allow blocked content" by right-clicking the Information Bar and selecting the Allow Blocked Content command from the context menu, or modify the Internet Explorer security settings to display form elements.

Using Horizontal Rules

A horizontal rule (or line) is useful for organizing information and visually separating text and objects. You can specify the width and height of the rule in pixels or as a percentage of the page size. The rule can be aligned to the left, center, or right, and you can add shading or draw the line in a solid color. These attributes are available through the Property inspector. The HTML tag for a horizontal rule is <hr>.

To Insert and Format a Horizontal Rule

In the following steps, you insert a horizontal rule below the document headings on the Hotel Reservation Form Web page. You also change the width and the height of the rule, and select no shading.

1
- Click Insert on the Application bar, point to HTML, and then point to Horizontal Rule to highlight the Horizontal Rule command (Figure 6–6).

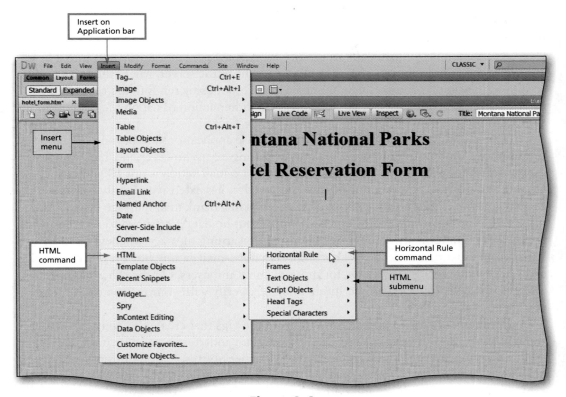

Figure 6–6

2

- Click Horizontal Rule to insert the horizontal rule below the heading and to display the Horizontal rule Property inspector (Figure 6–7).

When should horizontal rules be used on a Web page?

Horizontal rules are useful for separating sections of content on a Web page, such as a form from headings or other text.

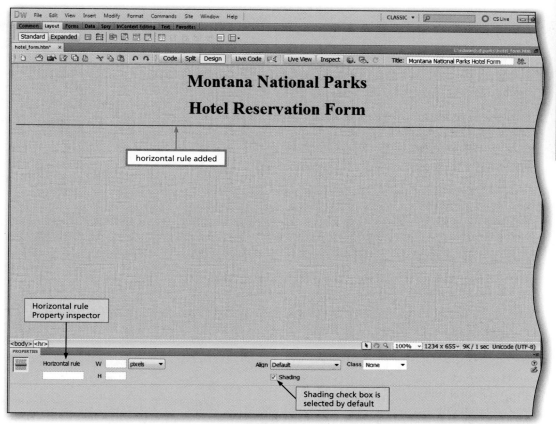

horizontal rule added

Horizontal rule Property inspector

Shading check box is selected by default

Figure 6–7

3

- Click the Horizontal rule text box in the Property inspector and type **horz_rule** as the ID for the horizontal rule.

- Click the W (Width) text box and type **500** to decrease the line width.

- Press the TAB key two times to move the insertion point to the H box.

- Type **12** in the H (Height) text box to increase the line height.

- Click the Shading check box to remove the check mark and to format the horizontal rule with no shading (Figure 6–8).

4

- Click below the horizontal rule, and then click the Save button to save the Hotel Reservation Form page.

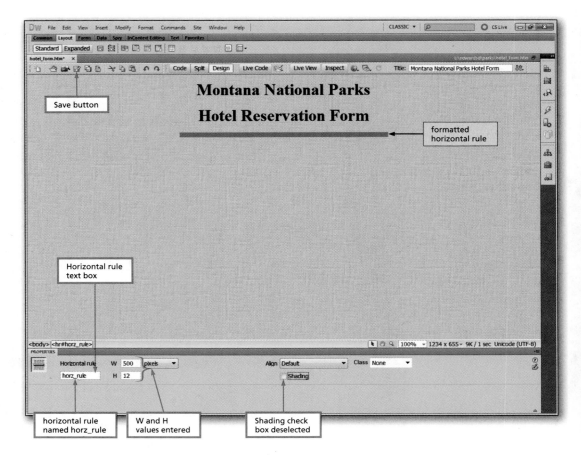

Figure 6–8

Forms and Web Pages

Web page designers create forms consisting of a collection of input fields so users can obtain useful information and enter data. When a user clicks the form's Send or Submit button, the data is processed with a server-side script or is sent to a specified e-mail address. A typical form, such as the one created in this chapter, is composed of form objects. A **form object** can be a text box, check box, radio button, list, menu, or other button. Form objects are discussed in more detail later in this chapter.

**Plan
Ahead**

Consider the data you will collect.
List the data you want to collect and consider how the server will process it. If the server will store the data in a database, for example, you might need to request the first and last names of the user in separate input fields, which is how databases often store names. If the server will use the data to send order verifications to users, you should be sure to include an input field for an e-mail address. When identifying fields on a form, place the label for an input field close to the form object. Use familiar labels that clearly describe the data users should enter. For example, "Phone" is an appropriate label for a phone number field, though "Home Phone (including area code)" is more specific and descriptive. If necessary, include simple, clear instructions about what information users should provide. Indicate which data users are required to provide. Finally, organize the input fields so the order is logical and predictable to users.

Inserting a Form

You insert a form in the same manner as you would a table or any other object in Dreamweaver. Position the insertion point where you want the form to start and then click the Form button on the Forms tab on the Insert bar. Dreamweaver inserts the <form> and </form> tags into the source code and then displays a dotted red outline to represent the form in Design view. You cannot resize a form by dragging the borders. Rather, the form expands as you insert objects into the form. When viewed in a browser, the form outline is not displayed; therefore, no visible border exists to turn on or off.

BTW

Dreamweaver and Forms
Dreamweaver makes it easy to add forms to your Web pages. The Forms tab on the Insert bar contains all of the traditional form objects. When the object is entered into the form, Dreamweaver creates the JavaScript necessary for processing the form.

To Insert a Form on a Web Page

The following steps illustrate how to insert a form into the hotel_form page.

1
- Click the Forms tab on the Insert bar to display the Form buttons (Figure 6–9).

Figure 6–9

2

- Click View on the Application bar, and then point to Visual Aids to verify that Invisible Elements is selected (Figure 6–10).

Q&A Should I have the same items checked on the Visual Aids submenu as in Figure 6–10?

The checked items on your Visual Aids submenu might be different. To make sure your screens match the figures in this chapter, your checked items should match those in Figure 6–10.

Q&A Why should I check to make sure invisible elements are displayed?

In Design view, form outlines are displayed as a dotted red outline. This outline is an invisible element because it does not appear in the browser. To see this outline as you are creating a form, you must display invisible elements in the Document window.

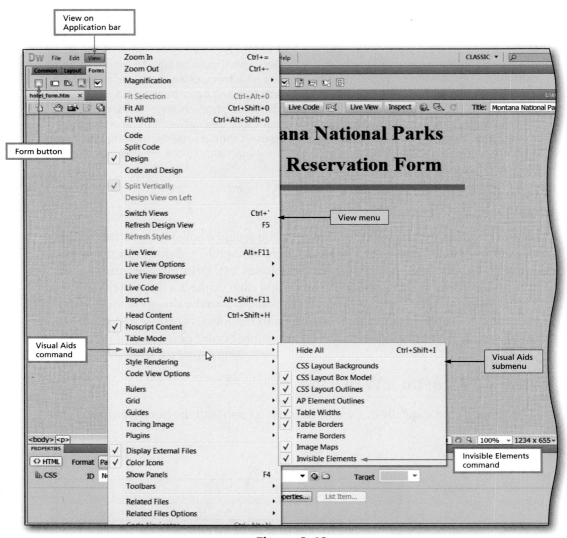

Figure 6–10

3

- If necessary, click Invisible Elements on the Visual Aids submenu to select it.

- Click the Form button on the Forms tab to insert a form into the Document window and to display the Form Property inspector (Figure 6–11).

Figure 6–11

Other Ways
1. On Insert menu, point to Form, click Form

Form Property Inspector

As you have seen, the Property inspector options change depending on the selected object. The following section describes the form-related features of the Property inspector shown in Figure 6–12.

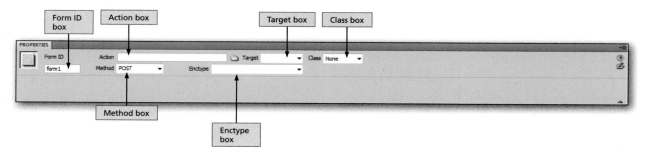

Figure 6–12

Form ID Naming a form makes it possible to reference or control the form with a scripting language, such as JavaScript or VBScript.

Action Contains the mailto address or specifies the URL to the dynamic page or script that will process the form.

Target Specifies the window or frame in which to display the data after processing if a script specifies that a new page should be displayed. The four targets are _blank, _parent, _self, and _top. The _blank target opens the referenced link (or processed data) in a new browser window, leaving the current window untouched. The **_blank** target is the one most often used with a jump menu, which is discussed later in this chapter. The **_self** target opens the destination document in the same window as the one in which the form was submitted. The two other targets mostly are used with frames.

Method Indicates the method by which the form data is transferred to the server. The three options are POST, which embeds the form data in the HTTP request; GET, which appends the form data to the URL requesting the page; and **Default**, which uses the browser's default setting to send the form data to the server. Generally, the default is the POST method. The POST and GET methods were discussed earlier in this chapter.

Enctype Specifies a **MIME (Multipurpose Internet Mail Extensions)** type for the data being submitted to the server so the server software will know how to interpret the data. The default is application/x-www-form-urlencoded and typically is used with the POST method. This default automatically encodes the form response with non-alphanumeric characters in hexadecimal format. The multipart/form-data MIME type is used with a form object that enables the user to upload a file. You can select one of these two values from the Enctype list box or manually enter a value in the Enctype list box. The text/plain value is useful for e-mail replies, but is not an option in the Enctype list box and must be entered manually. This value enables the data to be transmitted in a readable format instead of as one long string of data.

Class Sets style sheet attributes and/or attaches a style sheet to the current document.

Setting Form Properties

When naming the form and the form elements (discussed later in this chapter), use names that identify the form or form element. Be consistent with your naming conventions and do not use spaces or other special characters, except the underscore. This chapter uses lowercase letters to name the form and form elements. If you are using server-side scripting, be aware of and avoid reserved words in the scripting language.

BTW

Naming Forms
A form does not need a name to work, but a name is helpful if you use Dreamweaver behavior or JavaScript to interact with the form.

To Set the Form Properties

The following steps illustrate how to name the form and to set the other form properties, including using the mailto action. Verify with your instructor that this is the correct action and that the form data is not to be processed with a server-side script.

- Double-click the Form ID text box in the Property inspector to select the default form name.

- Type **hotel_ form** and then press the TAB key to name the form (Figure 6–13).

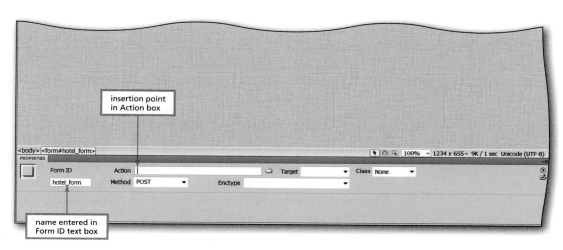

Figure 6–13

- Type your e-mail address in the Action text box in the format mailto:dedwards@ parks.com (Figure 6–14).

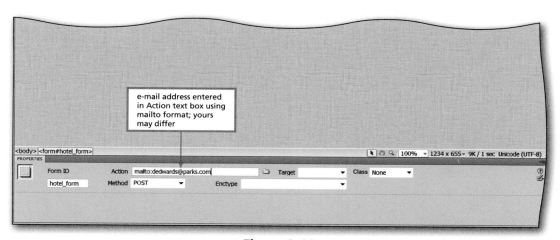

Figure 6–14

- Click the Target box arrow, select _self to display the data in the same window as the one displaying the form, and then press the TAB key to move the insertion point to the Enctype box.

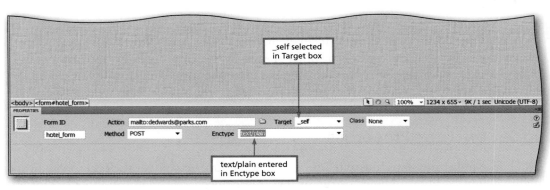

Figure 6–15

- Type **text/ plain** in the Enctype box, and then press the ENTER key to specify you want to receive the e-mail response from the server as plain text (Figure 6–15).

Inserting a Table into a Form

Adding and aligning labels within a form sometimes can be a problem. The text field width for labels is measured in **monospace**, meaning that each character has the same width. Most regular fonts, however, are not monospaced; they are proportional. To align labels properly using preformatted text requires the insertion of extra spaces. Two options to solve this problem are preformatted text and tables. Using tables and text alignment, therefore, is a faster and easier method to use when creating a form.

To Insert a Table into a Form

The following steps show how to add an 11-row, 2-column table to the form.

- If necessary, click inside the form (the dotted red outline) to display the insertion point in the form.

- Click Insert on the Application bar to display the Insert menu, and then point to Table (Figure 6–16).

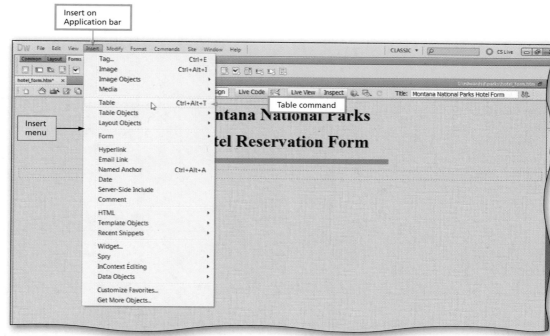

Figure 6–16

- Click Table to display the Table dialog box.

- Type the following values in the Table dialog box:

  Rows: **11**

  Columns: **2**

  Table width: **7 5** percent

  Border thickness: **4**

  Cell padding: **5**

  Cell spacing: **0**

- Summary text: **Hotel reservation form for Montana National Parks** (Figure 6–17).

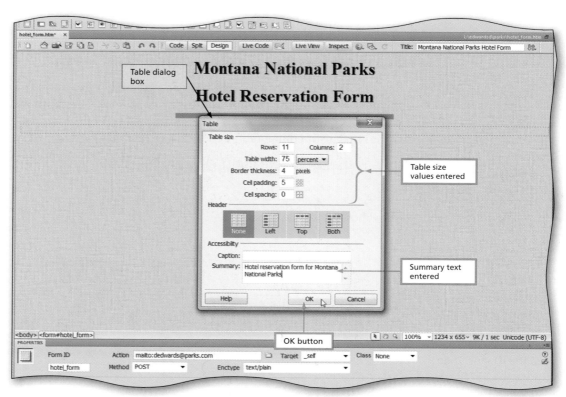

Figure 6–17

3

- Click the OK button to insert the table into the form.

- With the table selected, click the Align button in the Property inspector, and then select Center to center the table in the form outline and to display the table properties in the Property inspector (Figure 6–18).

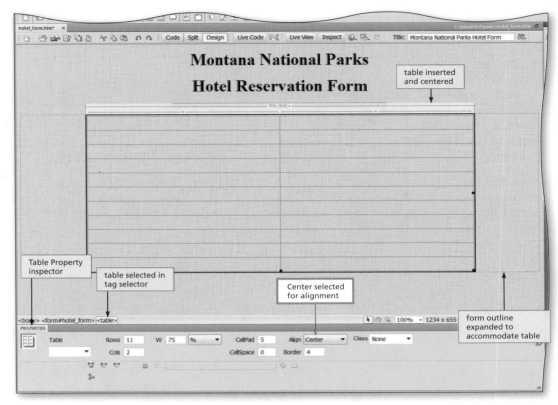

Figure 6–18

Formatting the Table within the Form

Formatting a form creates a more attractive page. In this instance, formatting includes changing the column widths in the table and aligning the text for the labels in column 1 to the right. Based on the settings within Dreamweaver, when alignment is set to right or justified in a table cell, a dotted line may be displayed within the cell.

To Format the Form

The following steps show how to format the form.

1

- If necessary, select the table.

- In the Property inspector, click the Table box, type **reservations** as the ID, and then press the ENTER key to name the table (Figure 6–19).

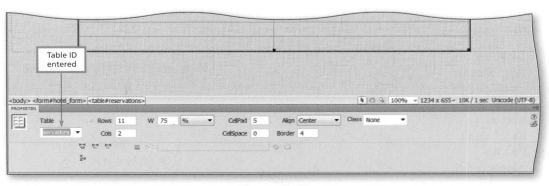

Figure 6–19

2

- Click row 1, column 1, and then drag to select all of column 1.

- Click the W text box, type 35%, and then press the ENTER key to set the column width to 35 percent (Figure 6–20).

Q&A

Why should I use a percentage as the width (W) value?

Using a percentage for the width of column 1 creates a more flexible layout. If users resize the browser window, column 1 adjusts to be 35 percent of the total table width.

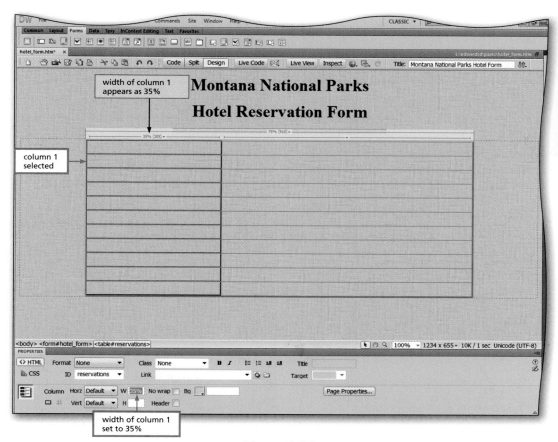

Figure 6–20

3

- With column 1 still selected, click Format on the Application bar, point to Align, and then click Right to right-align the text entered into column 1.

- Click the Save button on the Standard toolbar to save the table (Figure 6–21).

Q&A

Why doesn't the appearance of column 1 change after right-aligning it?

The right-alignment applies to the text the column will contain. When you enter text in column 1, it will be right-aligned.

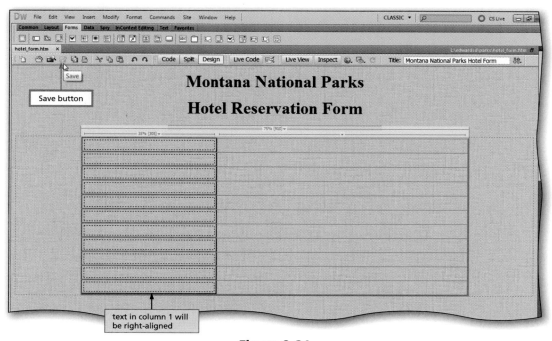

Figure 6–21

Form Objects

In Dreamweaver, data is entered through form input types called form objects. After you add a form to your Web page, you begin creating the form by adding form objects such as text fields, check boxes, and radio buttons. Each form object should have a unique name — except radio buttons within the same group, which should share the same name. To insert a form field in a Web page, (1) add the form field and any descriptive labels, and (2) modify the properties of the form object. All Dreamweaver form objects are available on the Forms tab on the Insert bar (Figure 6–22). Table 6–1 lists the button names and descriptions.

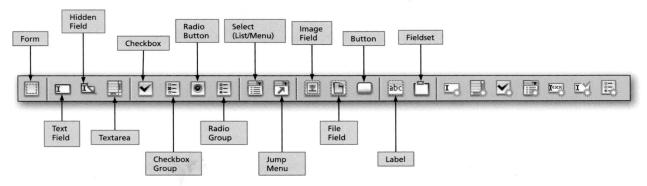

Figure 6–22

Table 6–1 Buttons on the Insert Bar Forms Tab	
Button Name	**Description**
Form	Inserts a form into the Document window
Text Field	Accepts any type of alphanumeric text entry
Hidden Field	Stores information entered by a user and then uses that data within the site database
Textarea	Provides a multiline text entry field
Checkbox	Represents a selection
Checkbox Group	Allows multiple responses in a single group of options, letting the user select as many options as apply
Radio Button	Represents an exclusive choice; only one item in a group of buttons can be selected
Radio Group	Represents a group of radio buttons
Select (List/Menu)	List displays option values within a scrolling list that allows users to select multiple options; Menu displays the option values in a pop-up menu that allows users to select only a single item
Jump Menu	Special form of a pop-up menu that lets the viewer link to another document or file
Image Field	Creates a custom, graphical button
File Field	Allows users to browse to a file on their computers and upload the file as form data
Button	Performs actions when clicked; Submit and Reset buttons send data to the server and clear the form fields
Label	Provides a way to associate the text label for a field with the field structurally
Fieldset	Inserts a container tag for a logical group of form elements

**Plan
Ahead**

> **Determine the types of controls you will add to the form.**
> After creating a form and inserting a table to align the form contents, you add objects to the form that users select to enter information into the form. Select objects depending on the type of information you want to collect: Text Fields and Textareas for text entries such as addresses, Checkboxes, RadioButtons, and List/Menus for options users select, and Buttons for submitting and resetting the form.

Text Fields

A **text field** is a form object in which users enter a response. Forms support three types of text fields: single-line, multiple-line, and password. Input into a text field can consist of alphanumeric and punctuation characters. When you insert a text field into a form, the TextField Property inspector is displayed (Figure 6–23).

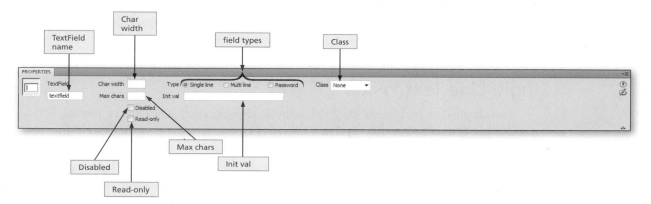

Figure 6–23

The following section describes the text field attributes for a single-line and password form. The multiple-line attributes are described later in this chapter.

TextField   Assigns a unique name to the form object.

Char width   Specifies the width of the field in characters.

Max chars   Specifies the maximum number of characters that can be entered into the field.

Type   Designates the field as a single-line, multiple-line, or password field.

Init val   Assigns the value that is displayed in the field when the form first loads.

Class   Establishes an attribute used with Cascading Style Sheets.

Disabled   Disables the text area.

Read-only Makes the text area a read-only text area.

Typically, a **single-line text field** allows a single word or short phrase response. A **password text field** is a single-line text box that contains special characters. When a user types in a password field, asterisks or bullets replace the text as a security precaution. Note, however, that passwords sent to a server using a password field are not encrypted and can be intercepted and read as alphanumeric text. For this reason, you always should provide encryption for data you want to keep secure. A **multiple-line text field** provides a larger text area in which to enter a response.

Inserting Text in a Form

You will notice as you insert form objects in a Web page that typically they contain no text label. **Labels** identify the type of data to be entered into the TextField form object. Adding a descriptive label to the form that indicates the type of information requested provides a visual cue to the Web site visitors about the type of data they should type into the text box. Inserting text in a form is as simple as positioning the insertion point and then typing.

Single-Line Text Fields

Use single-line text fields for short, concise answers such as a word or phrase. Set the following properties in the TextField Property inspector after entering single-line text fields:

- *TextField*: Enter a unique name for each text field in the form. Server-side scripts use this name to process the data. If you use the mailto option, the name is contained within the data in the e-mail that is sent to your e-mail address. Form object names are case sensitive and cannot contain spaces or special characters other than underscores.

- *Char width*: The default setting is 20 characters. You can change the default, however, by entering another number. If the Char width is left as the 20-character default and a user enters 50 characters, the text scrolls to the right and only the last 20 of those characters are displayed in the text field. Even though the extra characters are not displayed, they all are recognized by the form field object and will be sent to the server for processing or contained within the data if mailto is used.

- *Max chars*: Entering a value into the Max chars field defines the size limit of the text field and is used to validate the form. If a user tries to exceed the limit, an alert is sounded. If the Max chars field is left blank, users can enter any amount of text.

- *Init val*: To display a default text value in a field, type the default text in the Init val text box. When the form is displayed in the browser, this text is displayed.

To Add Descriptive Labels and Single-Line Text Fields to the Hotel Reservation Form

The following steps show how to add name, address, and e-mail single-line text boxes to the Hotel Reservation Form.

1

- Click row 1, column 1 to place the insertion point in the cell (Figure 6–24).

Q&A

Why does the insertion point appear on the right side of the cell?

In the previous set of steps, you right-aligned column 1 so that any text entered in column 1 will be right-aligned.

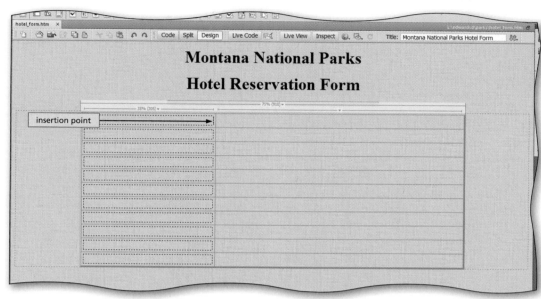

Figure 6–24

2

- Type **Name** as the descriptive label, and then press the TAB key to place the insertion point in row 1, column 2 (Figure 6–25).

Figure 6–25

3

- Click the Text Field button on the Forms tab to insert a TextField form object for Name (Figure 6–26).

Q&A

The Input Tag Accessibility Attributes dialog box is displayed after I add the TextField form object. What should I do?

If the Input Tag Accessibility Attributes dialog box is displayed, click the Cancel button.

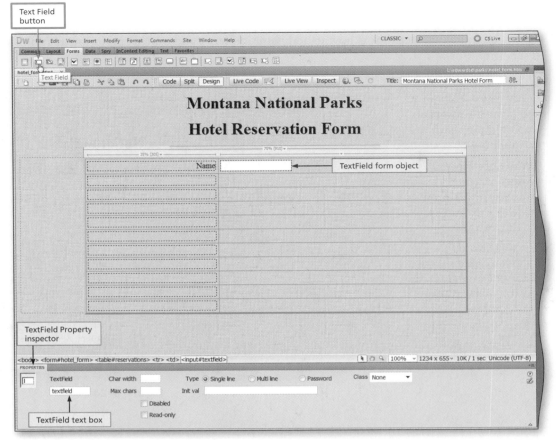

Figure 6–26

4

- Double-click the TextField text box in the Property inspector to select the default name, type **name** to rename the TextField object, and then press the TAB key to move the insertion point to the Char width text box.

- Type **50** in the Char width text box and then press the TAB key to increase the width of the Name text field to 50 characters.

- If necessary, click the Single line option button in the Type area to select the text field type (Figure 6–27).

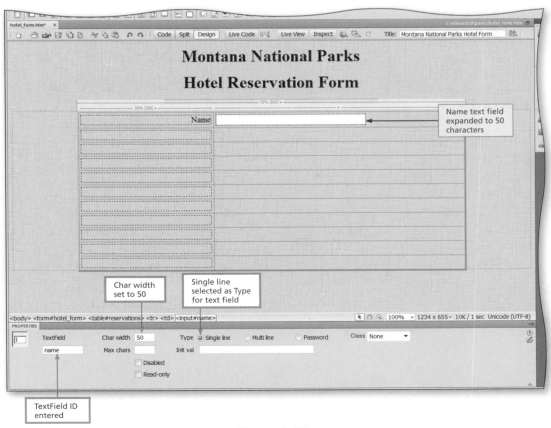

Figure 6–27

5

- Click row 2, column 1, type **Address** as the descriptive label, and then press the TAB key to move the insertion point to column 2.

- Click the Text Field button on the Forms tab to insert a TextField form object for Address (Figure 6–28).

Q&A

Why is the new TextField form object narrower than the first TextField form object?

The width of all TextField form objects is determined by the Char width property. By default, TextField form objects are 20 characters wide when they are inserted.

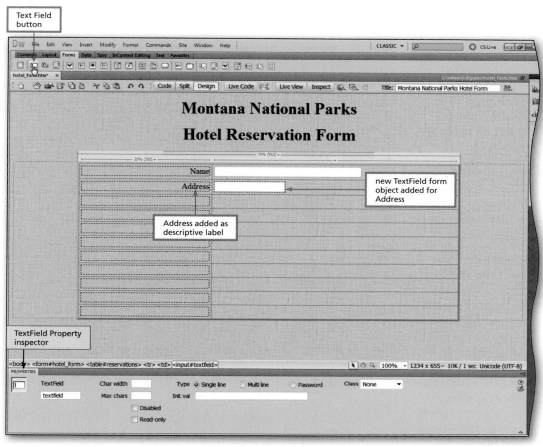

Figure 6–28

6

- Double-click the TextField text box in the Property inspector to select the default name, type **address** to rename the TextField object, and then press the TAB key to move the insertion point to the Char width text box.

- Type **50** in the Char width text box and then press the TAB key to increase the width of the Address text field to 50 characters.

- If necessary, click the Single line option button in the Type area to select the text field type (Figure 6–29).

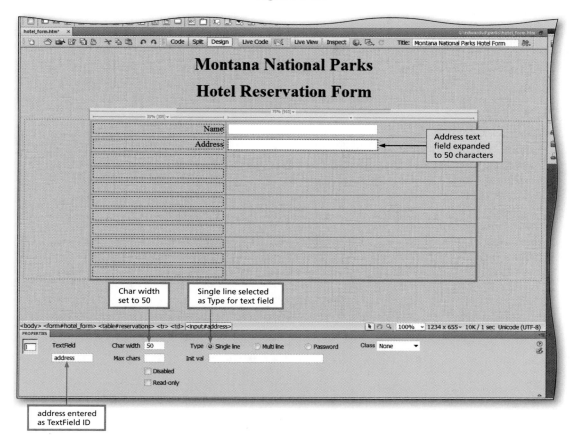

Figure 6–29

7

- Click row 3, column 1, type **City** as the descriptive label, and then press the TAB key to move the insertion point to column 2.

- Click the Text Field button on the Forms tab to insert a TextField form object for City.

- Double-click the TextField text box in the Property inspector to select the default name, type **city** to rename the TextField object, and then press the TAB key to move the insertion point to the Char width text box.

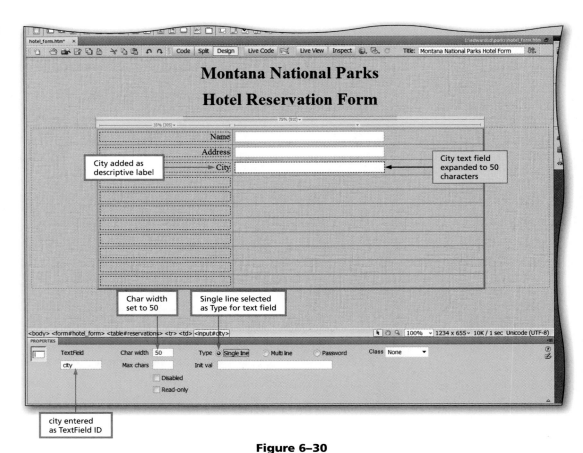

Figure 6–30

- Type **50** in the Char width text box and then press the TAB key to increase the width of the City text field to 50 characters.

- If necessary, click the Single line option button in the Type area to select the text field type (Figure 6–30).

8

- Click row 4, column 1, type **State/ Zip Code** as the descriptive label, and then press the TAB key to move the insertion point to column 2 (Figure 6–31).

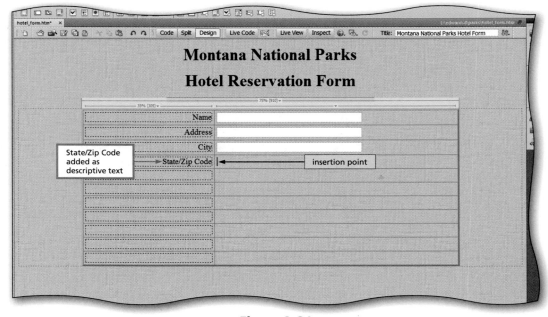

Figure 6–31

9

- Type **State** and then press the SPACEBAR to add the State descriptive label in column 2 (Figure 6–32).

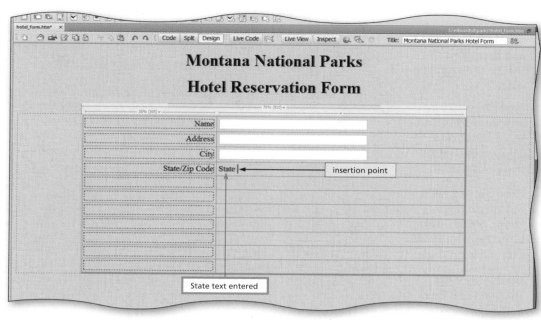

Figure 6–32

10

- Click the Text Field button on the Forms tab to insert a TextField form object for State.

- Double-click the TextField text box in the Property inspector to select the default name, type **state** to rename the TextField object, and then press the TAB key to move the insertion point to the Char width text box.

- Type **2** in the Char width text box and then press the TAB key to decrease the width of the text field to two characters.

- Type **2** in the Max chars text box

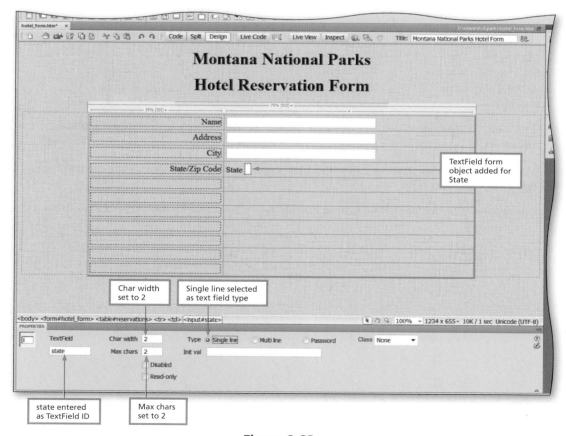

Figure 6–33

to specify the maximum number of characters allowed in the State text field, and then press the TAB key to resize the text field.

- If necessary, click the Single line option button in the Type area to select the text field type (Figure 6–33).

11

- Click to the right of the State text field and then press the SPACEBAR to insert a space.

- Type **Zip Code** and then press the SPACEBAR to add Zip Code as the descriptive label.

- Click the Text Field button on the Forms tab to insert a TextField form object for Zip Code.

- Double-click the TextField text box in the Property inspector to select the default name, type **zip** to rename the TextField object, and then press the TAB key to move the insertion point to the Char width text box.

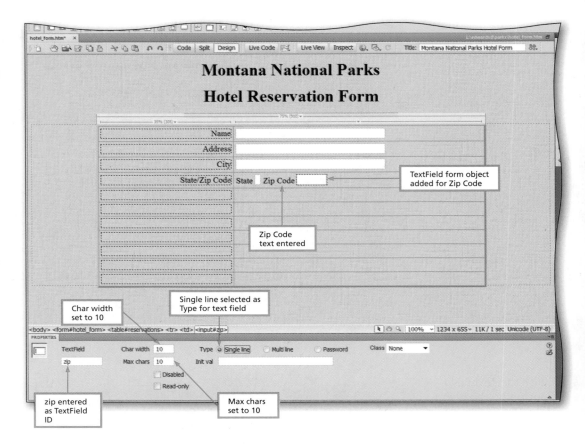

Figure 6–34

- Type **10** in the Char width text box and then press the TAB key to decrease the width of the Zip Code text field to 10 characters.

- Type **10** in the Max chars text box and then press the TAB key to specify the maximum number of characters allowed in the Zip Code text field.

- If necessary, click the Single line option button in the Type area to select the text field type (Figure 6–34).

- If necessary, scroll down, click row 5, column 1, and then type **E-mail Address** as the descriptive label.

- Press the TAB key and then click the Text Field button to insert a text field for E-mail Address (Figure 6–35).

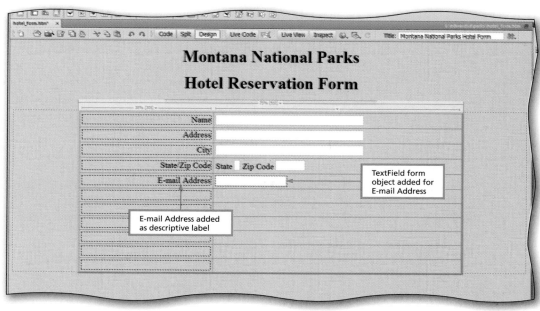

Figure 6–35

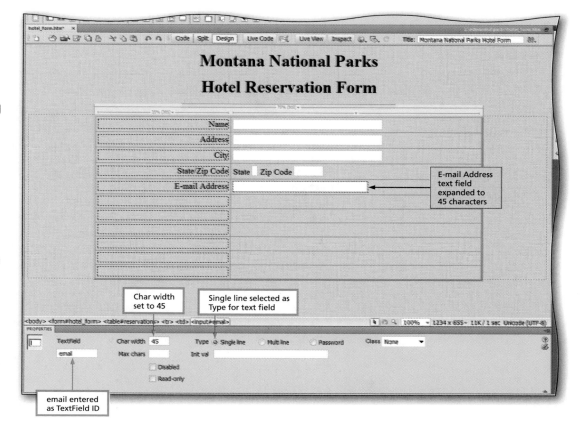

- Double-click the TextField text box in the Property inspector to select the default name, type **email** to rename the TextField object, and then press the TAB key to move the insertion point to the Char width text box.

- Type **45** in the Char width text box and then press the TAB key to adjust the width of the E-mail Address text field to 45 characters.

- If necessary, click the Single line option button in the Type area to select the text field type (Figure 6–36).

Figure 6–36

- Press CTRL+S to save the page.

Other Ways

1. On Insert menu, point to Form, click Text Field

Check Boxes

Check boxes allow the Web visitor to click a box to toggle a value to either yes or no. Check boxes frequently are used to enable the visitor to select as many of the listed options as desired. Figure 6–37 displays the Property inspector for a check box. Just like a text field, each check box should have a unique name. The Checked value text box contains the information you want to send to the script or include in the mailto information to identify the data. For the Initial state, the default is Unchecked. Click Checked if you want an option to appear selected when the form first loads in the browser.

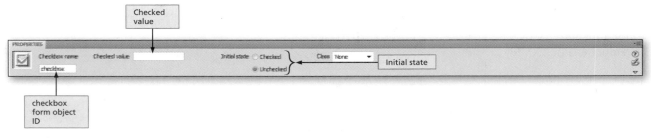

Figure 6–37

To Add Check Boxes

The following steps illustrate how to add four check boxes to the Hotel Reservation Form.

1

- Click row 6, column 1, type **Hotels** as the descriptive label, and then press the TAB key to move the insertion point to column 2.

- Click the Checkbox button on the Forms tab to add the check box to the form (Figure 6–38).

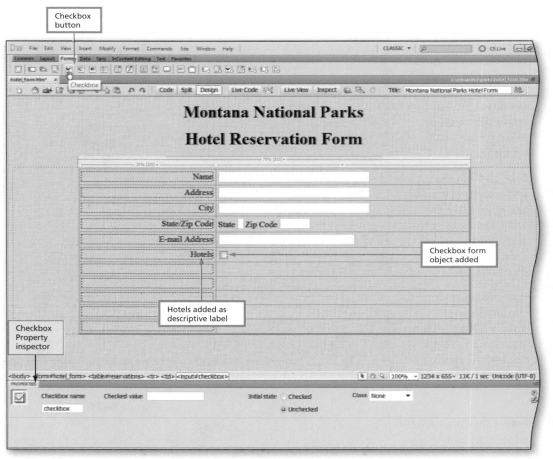

Figure 6–38

2

- Double-click the text in the Checkbox name text box, and then type **hotel01** as the Checkbox name.

- Press the TAB key and then type **montana_ national** in the Checked value text box.

- Press the TAB key to add the first check box to the form (Figure 6–39).

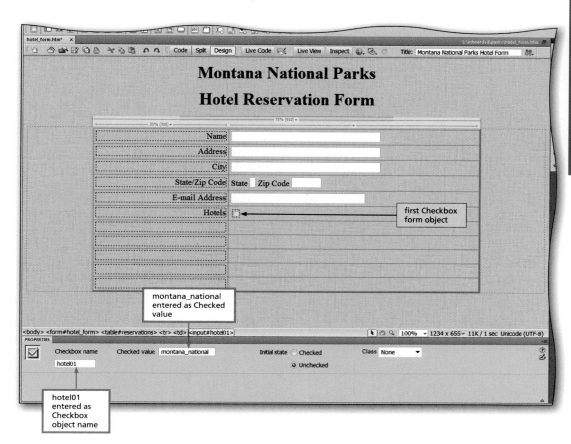

Figure 6–39

3

- Click to the right of the Checkbox form object and then press the SHIFT+ENTER keys to add a line break and to position the insertion point below the first check box (Figure 6–40).

Q&A

My insertion point is very small. Is that correct?

Yes. The insertion point is always small after a line break.

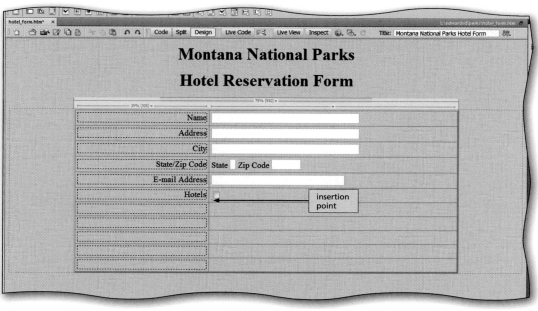

Figure 6–40

4

- Click the Checkbox button on the Forms tab to insert a second check box.

- Double-click the text in the Checkbox name text box, and then type `hotel02` as the Checkbox name.

- Press the TAB key and then type `montana_royal` in the Checked value text box.

- Press the TAB key to add the second check box to the form (Figure 6–41).

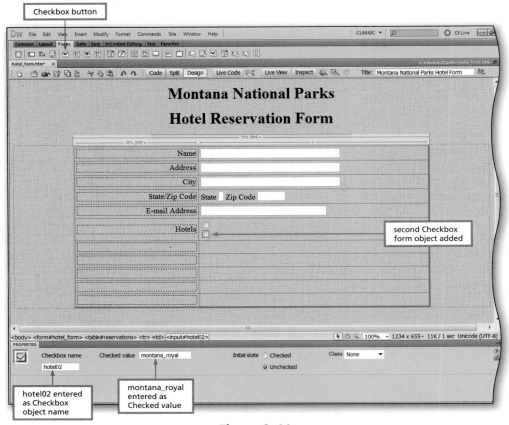

Figure 6–41

5

- Click to the right of the second check box, press the SHIFT+ENTER keys to add a line break, and then click the Checkbox button on the Forms tab to insert a third check box.

- Double-click the text in the Checkbox name text box, and then type `hotel03` as the Checkbox name.

- Press the TAB key and then type `garden_inn` in the Checked value text box.

- Press the TAB key to add the third check box to the form (Figure 6–42).

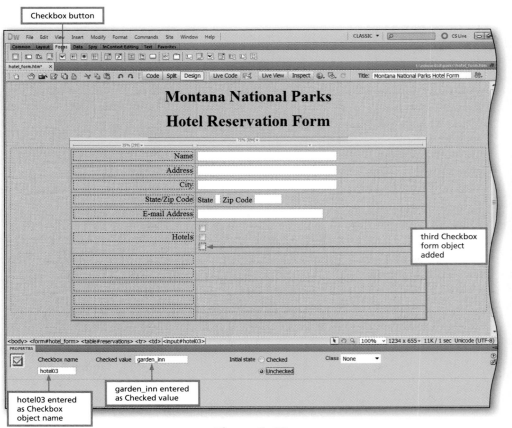

Figure 6–42

6

- Click to the right of the third check box, press the SHIFT+ENTER keys to add a line break, and then click the Checkbox button on the Forms tab to insert a fourth check box.

- Double-click the text in the Checkbox name text box, and then type **hotel04** as the Checkbox name.

- Press the TAB key and then type **montana_star** in the Checked value text box.

- Press the TAB key to add the fourth check box to the form (Figure 6–43).

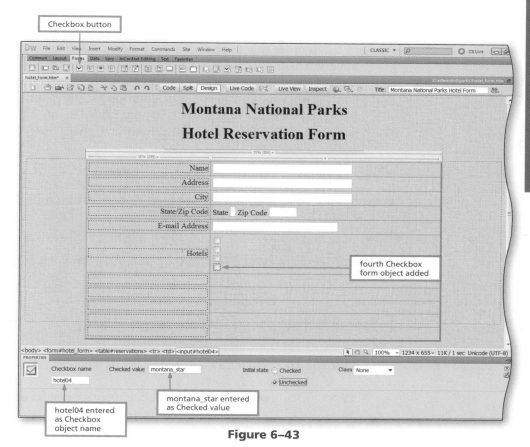

Figure 6–43

7

- Click to the right of the first check box, type **Montana National** as the descriptive label for the first check box, and then press the DOWN ARROW key.

- Type **Montana Royal** as the descriptive label for the second check box, and then press the DOWN ARROW key.

- Type **Garden Inn** as the descriptive label for the third check box, and then press the DOWN ARROW key.

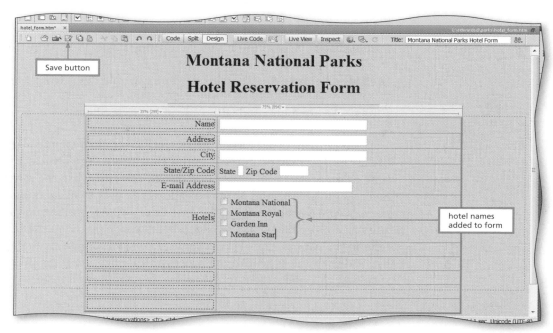

Figure 6–44

- Type **Montana Star** as the descriptive label for the fourth check box to add the descriptive labels for all four check boxes (Figure 6–44).

8

- Click the Save button on the Standard toolbar to save your work.

Select (List/Menu)

Another way to provide form field options for your Web site visitor is with lists and menus. These objects let users select one or more options from many choices within a limited space. A **list** provides a scroll bar with up and down arrows that lets a user scroll the list, whereas a menu contains a pop-up list. Multiple selections can be made from a list, while users can select only one item from a menu. The menu option is discussed later in this chapter. Figure 6–45 illustrates the Property inspector for a list.

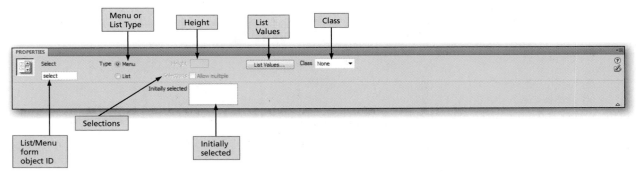

Figure 6–45

List/Menu Assigns a name to the list or menu.

Type Designates if the form object is a pop-up menu or a scrolling list.

Height Specifies the number of lines that are displayed in the form; the default is 1.

Selections Designates if the user can select more than one option; not available with the menu option.

List Values Opens the List Values dialog box.

Initially selected Contains a list of available items from which the user can select.

Class An attribute used with Cascading Style Sheets.

As with all other form objects, the list should be named. You control the height of the list by specifying a number in the Height box. You can elect to show one item at a time or show the entire list. If you display the entire list, the scroll bar is not displayed. Selecting the Selections check box allows the user to make multiple selections. Clicking the List Values button opens the List Values dialog box so you can add or remove items on a list or pop-up menu. These added items are displayed in the Initially selected box. Each item in the list has a label and a value. The label represents the text that appears in the list, and the value is sent to the processing application if the item is selected. If no value is specified, the label is sent to the processing application instead.

To Create a Scrolling List

The following steps show how to add a scrolling list to the Hotel Reservation Form.

1

- Click row 7, column 1, type **Accommodations** to add a descriptive label, and then press the TAB key to move the insertion point to column 2.

- Click the Select (List/Menu) button on the Forms tab to add a scrolling list to the form (Figure 6–46).

Q&A

Why is the Select (List/Menu) object inserted as a menu with an arrow button?

The default type for the Select (List/Menu) object is Menu. You will change the type to List in the next step.

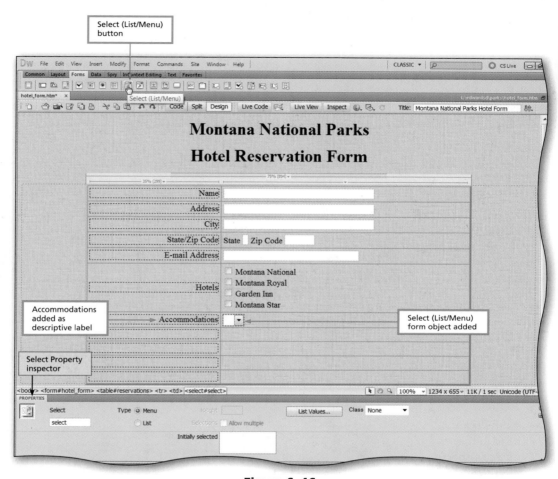

Figure 6–46

2

- Double-click the text in the Select text box, and then type **accommodations** to name the Select (List/Menu) object.

- Click the List option button in the Type area to select the list type of form object.

- Select the value in the Height box, and then type **2** to set the height of the List object to 2 lines.

- Click the Selections check box to allow multiple selections (Figure 6–47).

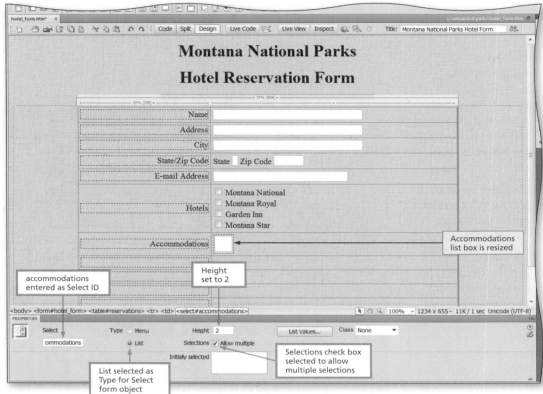

Figure 6–47

3

- Click the List Values button in the Property inspector to display the List Values dialog box (Figure 6–48).

Q&A

What do I enter in the List Values dialog box?

You enter the Item Label, which is the text that appears in the list box. For the Hotel Reservation Form, the Item Labels are the types of hotel rooms users can reserve. You also enter the Value, which is the data sent to the server when the form is processed.

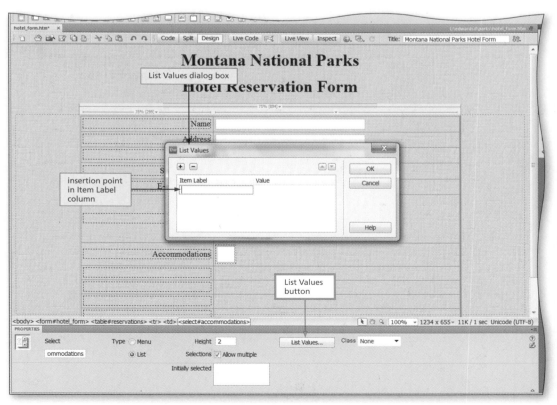

Figure 6–48

4

- Type **Single** as the first Item Label, and then press the TAB key to move the insertion point to the Value column.

- Type **single** as the Value and then press the TAB key to add the first item to the Item Label list (Figure 6–49).

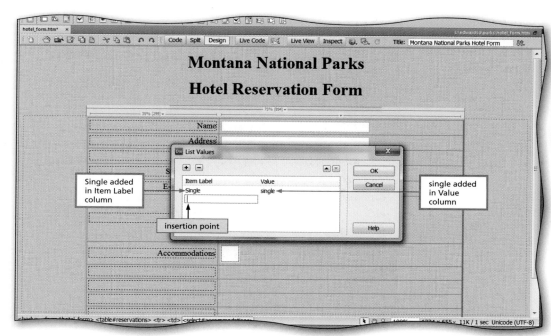

Figure 6–49

5

- Type **Double** as the second Item Label, and then press the TAB key.

- Type **double** as the Value, and then press the TAB key.

- Type **Suite** as the third Item Label, and then press the TAB key.

- Type **suite** as the Value, and then press the TAB key.

- Type **Luxury Suite** as the fourth Item Label, and then press the TAB key.

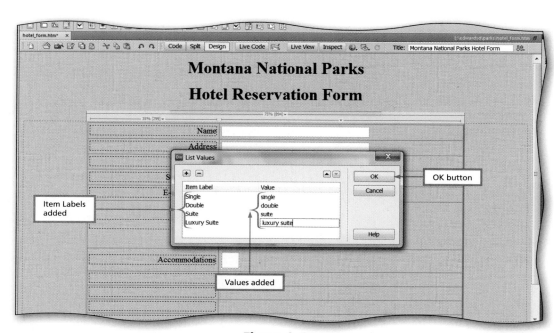

Figure 6–50

- Type **luxury_suite** as the Value to complete the items list (Figure 6–50).

6

- Click the OK button to display the item labels in the list box (Figure 6–51).

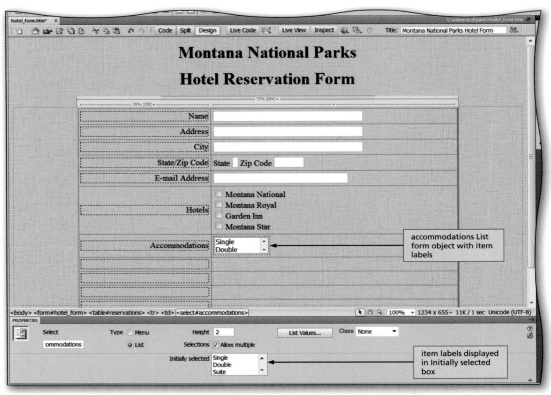

Figure 6–51

7

- Click Single in the Initially selected box in the Property inspector to designate it as the default item in the list (Figure 6–52).

8

- Click the Save button on the Standard toolbar to save your work.

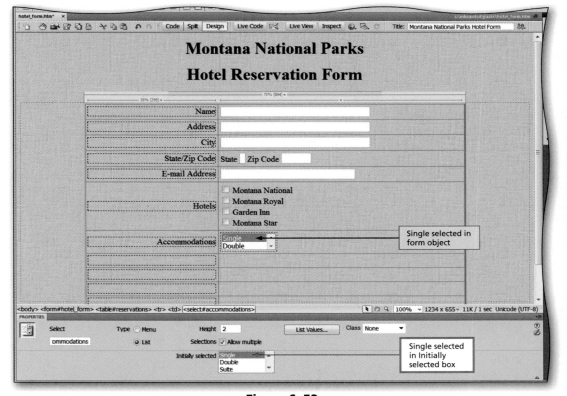

Figure 6–52

Other Ways

1. On Insert menu, point to Form, click Select (List/Menu)

Pop-Up Menus

You can offer your Web site visitors a range of choices by using a pop-up menu. This type of menu (also called a drop-down menu) lets a user select a single item from a list of many options. A **pop-up menu** is useful when you have a limited amount of space because it occupies only a single line of vertical space in the form. Only one option is visible when the menu form object is displayed in the browser. Clicking an arrow button displays the entire list. The user then clicks one of the menu items to make a selection.

To Create a Pop-Up Menu

The following steps illustrate how to create a pop-up menu.

1

- If necessary, scroll down and then click row 8, column 1.

- Type **Number of nights** as the descriptive label, and then press the TAB key to move the insertion point to column 2.

- Click the Select (List/ Menu) button on the Forms tab to insert a Select (List/Menu) form object (Figure 6–53).

Q&A

Why am I inserting this form object as a pop-up menu?

Pop-up menus display only one option on the form. Users must click the arrow button to display the other options. Users also can select only one option from a pop-up menu. Users can select more than one option from a list.

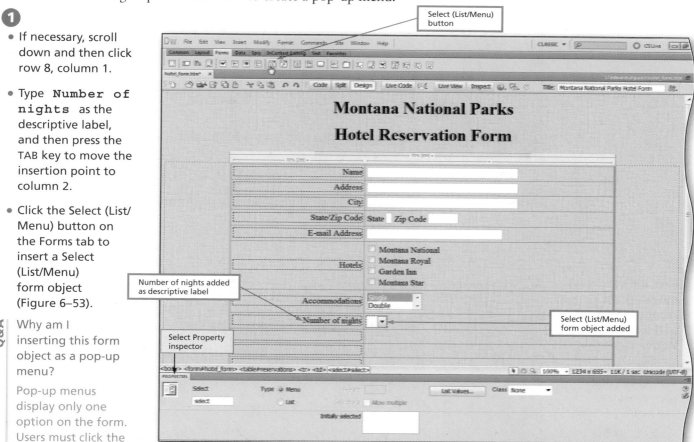

Figure 6–53

2

- Double-click the text in the Select text box, and then type **nights** to name the form object.

- If necessary, click the Menu option button in the Type area to select the menu type of form object (Figure 6–54).

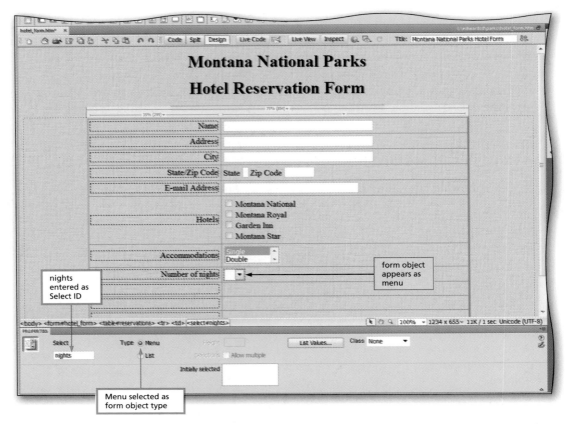

Figure 6–54

3

- Click the List Values button in the Property inspector to display the List Values dialog box.

- Type **1** as the Item Label, and then press the TAB key.

- Type **1** as the Value, and then press the TAB key (Figure 6–55).

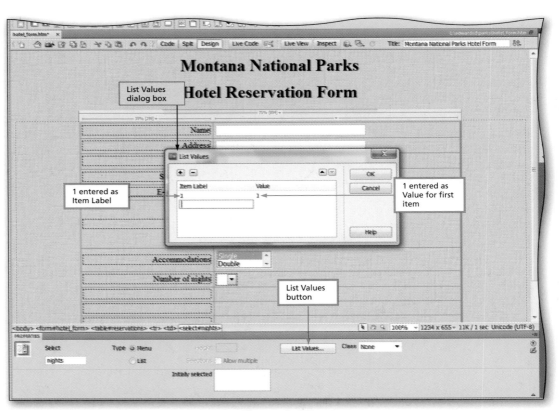

Figure 6–55

4

- Repeat Step 3, incrementing the number each time by 1 in the Item Label and Value fields, until the number 7 is added to the Item Label field and the Value field (Figure 6–56).

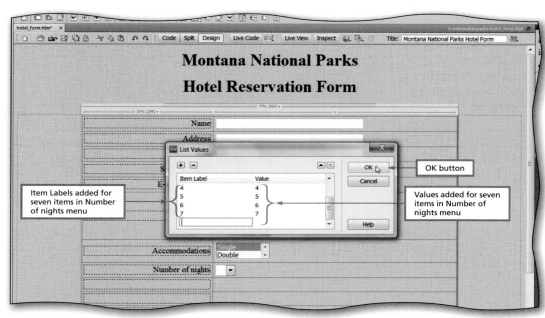

Figure 6–56

5

- Click the OK button to include the item labels in the Number of nights pop-up menu and the Initially selected box (Figure 6–57).

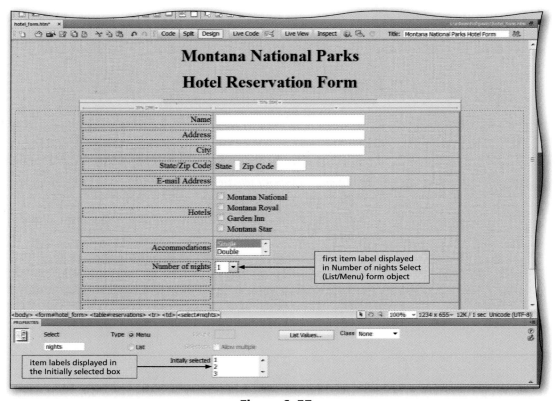

Figure 6–57

● Click the number 1 in the Initially selected box in the Property inspector to create the default value (Figure 6–58).

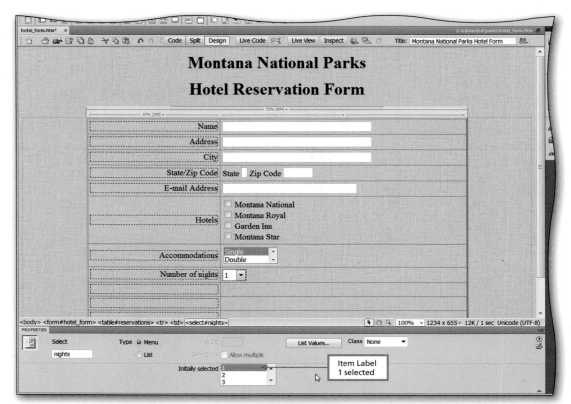

Figure 6–58

Jump Menus

A **jump menu** is a special type of pop-up menu that provides options that link to documents or files. You can create links to documents on your Web site, links to documents on other Web sites, e-mail links, links to graphics, or links to any other file type that can be opened in a browser. A jump menu can contain three basic components:

- *An optional menu selection prompt*: This could be a category description for the menu items or instructions, such as Choose one.
- *A required list of linked menu items*: When the user chooses an option, a linked document or file is opened.
- *An optional Go button*: With a Go button, the user makes a selection from the menu, and the new page loads when the Go button is clicked. Without a Go button, the new page loads as soon as the user makes a selection from the menu.

To Insert a Jump Menu

The following steps illustrate how to add a jump menu with a link to the Web sites for four national parks in Montana. The menu will contain a "Choose one" selection prompt, and the linked Web pages will open in the main window.

- Click row 9, column 1, type **Links**, and then press the TAB key to move the insertion point to column 2 (Figure 6–59).

Figure 6–59

2

- Click the Jump Menu button on the Forms tab to display the Insert Jump Menu dialog box.

- If necessary, double-click the Text text box to select its text, and then type **Choose one** as the menu selection prompt.

- Click the plus (+) button to add "Choose one" as a menu item (Figure 6–60).

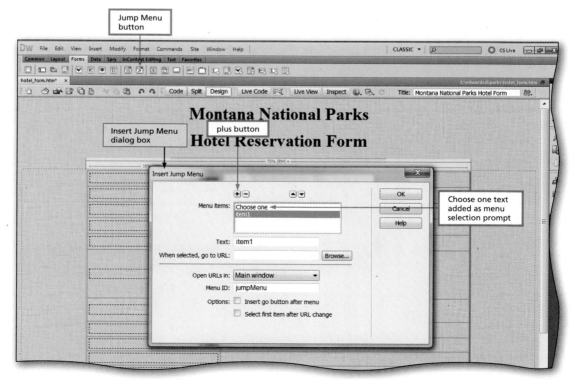

Figure 6–60

3

● Double-click the Text text box to select its text, and then type **Glacier National Park** as the text for the second menu item (Figure 6–61).

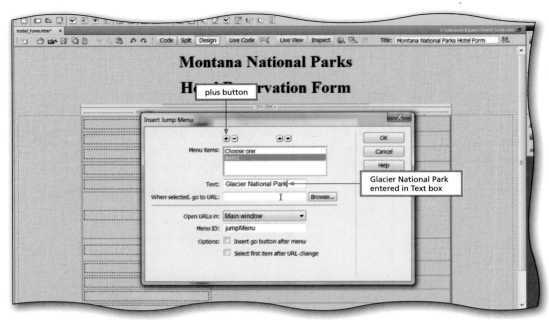

Figure 6–61

4

● Press the TAB key to move the insertion point to the When selected, go to URL text box.

● Type **http:// www.nps.gov/ glac/index.htm** as the URL for the Glacier National Park menu item (Figure 6–62).

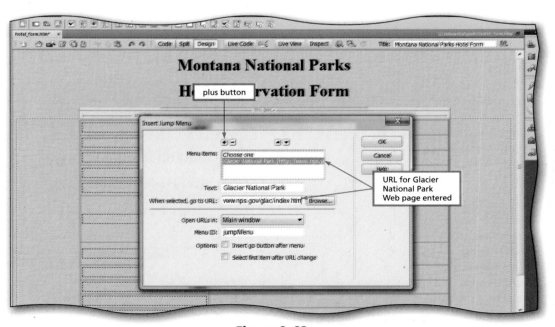

Figure 6–62

5

- Click the plus (+) button to add Glacier National Park and the URL as the second menu item.

- Double-click the Text text box to select its text, and then type **Badlands National Park** as the text for the third menu item.

- Press the TAB key to move to the When selected, go to URL text box.

- Type **http:// www.nps.gov/ badl/index.htm** as the URL for the Badlands National Park menu item (Figure 6–63).

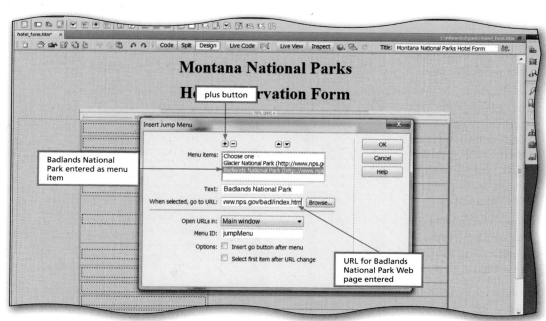

Figure 6–63

6

- Click the plus (+) button to add Badlands National Park and the URL as the third menu item.

- Double-click the Text text box to select its text, and then type **Grand Teton National Park** as the text for the fourth menu item.

- Press the TAB key to move to the When selected, go to URL text box.

- Type **http:// www.nps.gov/ grte/index.htm** as the URL for the Grand Teton National Park menu item (Figure 6–64).

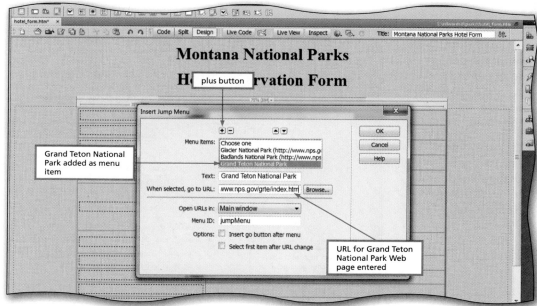

Figure 6–64

7

- Click the plus (+) button to add Grand Teton National Park as the fourth menu item.

- Double-click the Text text box to select its text, and then type **Mammoth Cave National Park** as the text for the fifth menu item.

- Press the TAB key to move to the When selected, go to URL text box.

- Type **http:// www.nps.gov/ maca/index.htm** as the URL for the

Mammoth Cave National Park menu item (Figure 6–65).

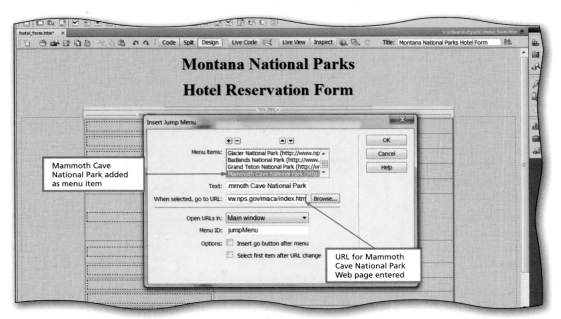

Figure 6–65

8

- Double-click in the Menu ID text box to select the default text, and then type **park_web_ sites** to name the menu.

- Click the 'Select first item after URL change' check box to select the option (Figure 6–66).

Figure 6–66

9

- Click the OK button to add the jump menu to the form.

- Click Choose one in the Initially selected box in the Property inspector.

- Click the Save button on the Standard toolbar to save the form (Figure 6–67).

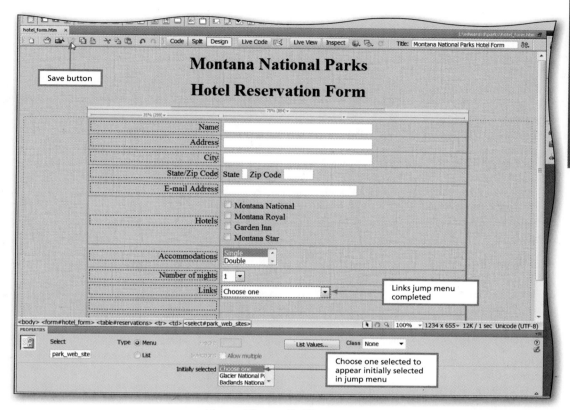

Figure 6–67

Other Ways

1. On Insert menu, point to Form, click Jump Menu

Textarea Text Fields

Earlier in this chapter, you added several single-line TextField form objects to the Hotel Reservation Form. A second type of text field is the Textarea form object, which supports multiline objects. The Property inspector settings for the Textarea form object are similar to those for single-line text fields, except you can specify the maximum number of lines the user can enter. The Property inspector for a Textarea text field is shown in Figure 6–68.

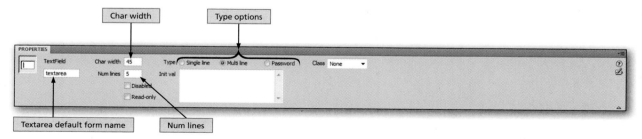

Figure 6–68

An initial value can be added to the Init val box. When the user clicks the Textarea text field, this initial value is highlighted and then deleted when the user begins to enter text.

To Add a Textarea Text Field

The following steps illustrate how to add a multiline text field to create a comments text area in your Hotel Reservation Form.

- If necessary, scroll down to row 10, and then click row 10, column 1.

- Type **Comments** as the descriptive label, and then press the TAB key to move the insertion point to column 2.

- Click the Textarea button on the Forms tab to add the Textarea form object to the form (Figure 6–69).

Q&A

How is a Textarea form object different from a TextField form object?

A Textarea form object allows users to enter more than one line of text. A TextField form object allows users to enter only a single line of text.

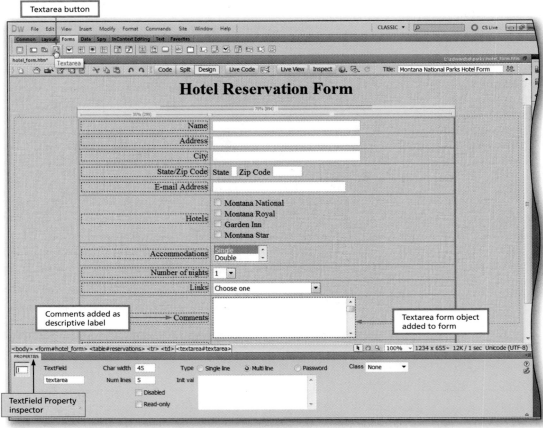

Figure 6–69

2

- Double-click the TextField box in the Property inspector to select the default name, and then type **comments** as the name of the Textarea form object.

- Press the TAB key and type **50** for the Char width value.

- Press the TAB key and type **4** for the Num lines value.

- Click the Init val box, and then type **Please add your comments** as the entry.

- Verify that the Multi line option button is selected in the Type area.

- Click the Textarea object in the form to display the initial value.

- Click the Save button on the Standard toolbar to save the form (Figure 6–70).

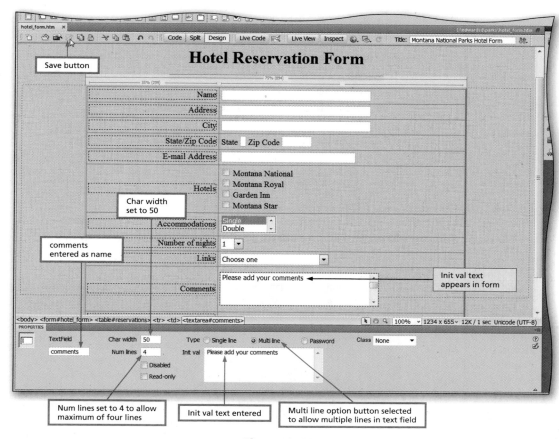

Figure 6–70

Form Buttons

Form buttons control form operations. HTML provides three basic types of form buttons: Submit, Reset, and Command. Submit and Reset buttons are standard features of almost every form. When the user clicks the Submit button, the data entered into a form is sent to a server for processing or forwarded to an e-mail address. In some instances, the data is edited by JavaScript or other code prior to processing. The Reset button clears all the fields in the form. You also can assign to a Command button other processing tasks that you have defined in a script. For example, a Command button might calculate the total cost of a hotel room for a week. Command buttons require that additional code be added using Code view. The Button name Property inspector is displayed in Figure 6–71.

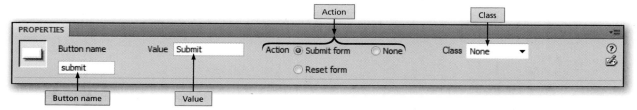

Figure 6–71

Button name Assigns a name to the button. Submit and Reset are reserved names.

Value Determines the text that appears on the button.

Action Determines what happens when the button is clicked and how the data is to be processed. Form processing was discussed earlier in this chapter. The three processing options are to submit the contents of the form (Submit form), to clear the contents of the form (Reset form), or to do nothing (None).

Class An attribute used with Cascading Style Sheets.

To Add the Submit and Reset Buttons

The following steps illustrate how to add the Submit and Reset buttons to the Hotel Reservation Form.

1

• If necessary, scroll down and then click row 11, column 1 (Figure 6–72).

Q&A

Should every form include a Submit button and a Reset button?

Yes. A form needs a Submit button so that users can submit the form data for processing. A form also needs a Reset button so users can clear the form data.

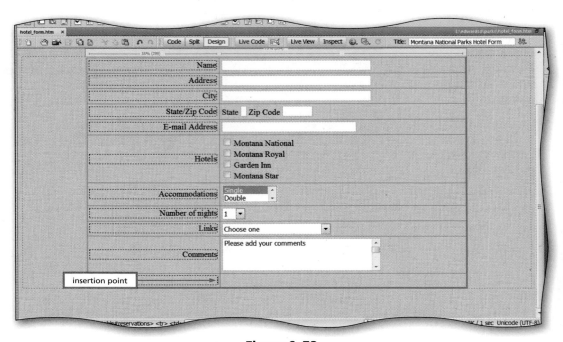

Figure 6–72

2

- Click the Button button on the Forms tab to add a Submit button to the form.

Q&A

The Input Tag Accessibility Attributes dialog box is displayed after I add the Submit button. What should I do?

If the Input Tag Accessibility Attributes dialog box is displayed, click the Cancel button.

- Double-click the Button name text box, type **submit** to name the button, and then press the TAB key to select the text in the Value text box.

- If necessary, type **Submit** in the Value text box.

- If necessary, click the Submit form option button in the Action area to select Submit form as the action (Figure 6–73).

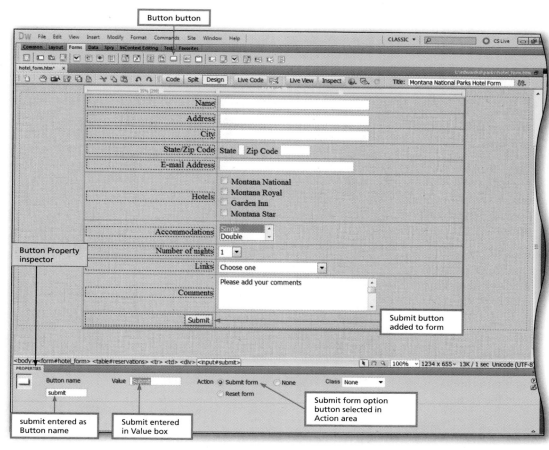

Figure 6–73

3

- Click row 11, column 2, and then click the Button button on the Forms tab to add the Submit button form object to the form (Figure 6–74).

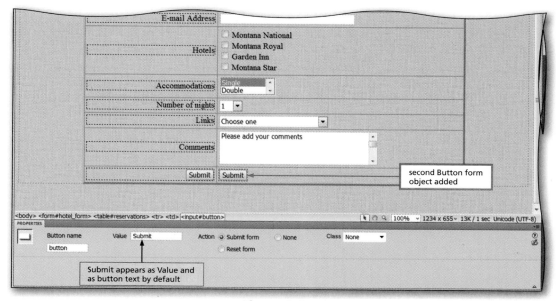

Figure 6–74

4

- Double-click the Button name text box, type **Reset** to name the button, and then press the TAB key to select the text in the Value text box.

- Type **Reset** in the Value text box so that Reset appears on the new button.

- Click the Reset form option button in the Action area (Figure 6–75).

5

- Click the Save button on the Standard toolbar to save the form.

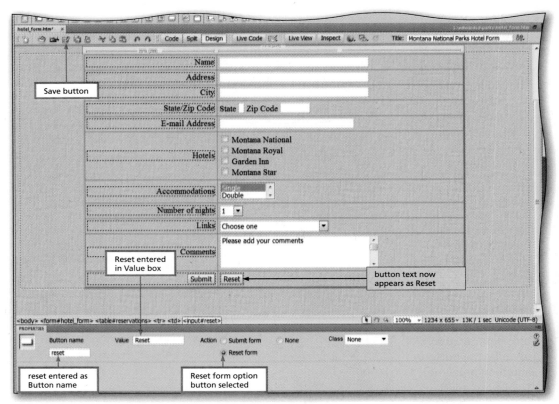

Figure 6–75

Other Ways

1. On Insert menu, point to Form, click Button

Radio Buttons and Radio Button Groups

Radio buttons provide a set of options from which the user can select only one button. Clicking a second button automatically deselects the first choice. Each button in a form consists of a radio button and a corresponding descriptive label. In Dreamweaver, you can insert radio buttons one at a time or insert a radio button group. When you insert an individual radio button, the Property inspector shown in Figure 6–76 is displayed. In the Property inspector's Radio Button text box, type a descriptive name. If you are inserting individual radio buttons to create a group, you must label each button. In the Checked value text box, enter the value you want to send to the server-side script or application when a user selects this radio button. For the Initial state, click Checked if you want an option to appear selected when the form first loads in the browser.

Figure 6–76

A radio button group is a commonly used option. If you are adding multiple radio buttons to a form, each set of radio buttons must have a unique name. When you click the Radio Group button on the Forms tab, the Radio Group dialog box is displayed. Radio button groups are discussed later in this chapter.

Form Objects, the Label Button, and Accessibility

So far, when you added a form object to a page, you also added a descriptive label to identify the object. Traditionally, this is the way most Web page authors label form objects. The current HTML specifications, however, provide the <label> tag. This tag adds functionality to the form object by associating the descriptive label for the form object directly with that object. This is particularly helpful for the users of speech-based browsers.

BTW

Customizing Forms
Some organizations develop a template form for use throughout their Web sites. The Web site developer then uses this template to design a custom form for a particular need.

Plan Ahead

Consider Web content accessibility factors.
Web forms are a popular way for Web site visitors to select and purchase merchandise, complete surveys and questionnaires, and perform many other online tasks. Web forms should be useful to their audience, even those who use screen readers. Start making your Web form accessible by organizing the information logically and designing the content with all of your users in mind. As you create a form, provide names and labels for each form object so that screen readers can read them. Group form controls logically. For example, request personal information such as name and address in one area, and let users select products or services in another area.

The Insert bar Forms tab contains a Label button. To add a label, select the specific form object to which you want to associate the label, and then click the Label button. When you click a radio button, for instance, and then click the Label button, Code view is displayed. You then manually type the descriptive text between the <label> and </label> tags. Similarly, Dreamweaver does not provide a Property inspector for labels, so any editing of labels is done in Code view.

Manual editing of the <label> tag can be time-consuming and error-prone, but Dreamweaver provides an alternative with the Accessibility options for form objects. When the Accessibility options for form objects are enabled, Dreamweaver displays the Input Tag Accessibility Attributes dialog box (Figure 6–77). Table 6–2 contains a description of the options in this dialog box. Recall that Accessibility options are turned on by clicking Edit on the menu bar and then selecting Preferences. In the Preferences dialog box, click the Accessibility category and then click the check box for Form objects. Appendix B contains an expanded discussion of accessibility options.

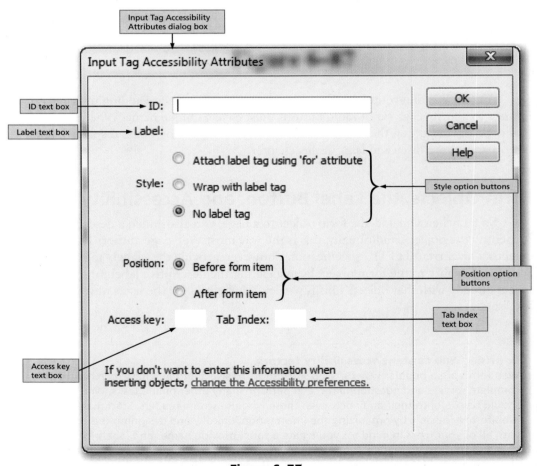

Figure 6–77

Table 6–2 Input Tag Accessibility Attributes

Attribute Name	Description
ID	Assigns an ID value that can be used to refer to a field from JavaScript and also used as an attribute value.
Label	The descriptive text that identifies the form object.
Style	Provides three options for the <label> tag: *Attach label tag using 'for' attribute* allows the user to associate a label with a form element, even if the two are in different table cells. *Wrap with label tag* wraps a label tag around the form item. *No label tag* turns off the Accessibility option.
Position	Determines the placement of the label text in relation to the form object — before or after the form object.
Access key	Selects the form object in the browser using a keyboard shortcut (one letter). This key is used in combination with the CTRL key (Windows) to access the object.
Tab Index	Specifies the order in which the form objects are selected when pressing the TAB key. The tab order goes from the lowest to highest number.

To Add a Form to the Volunteer Web Page

The next step is to add a form to the volunteer Web page.

1 Click the Expand Panels button to display the panel groups.

2 Double-click volunteer.htm in the Files panel to open the document.

3 Click the Collapse to Icons button to collapse the panel groups and provide more room to work (Figure 6–78).

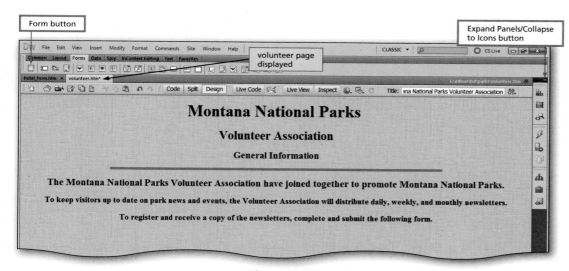

Figure 6–78

4 Click below the last line of text to position the insertion point, and then click the Form button on the Forms tab to insert a form.

5 In the Property inspector, type **newsletter** as the Form ID.

6 Use the mailto: format and type your e-mail address in the Action text box.

7 Click the Target arrow button and then click _self to display the data in the same window as the one displaying the form.

8 Type **text/plain** in the Enctype box, and then press the ENTER key to set the properties for the newsletter form (Figure 6–79).

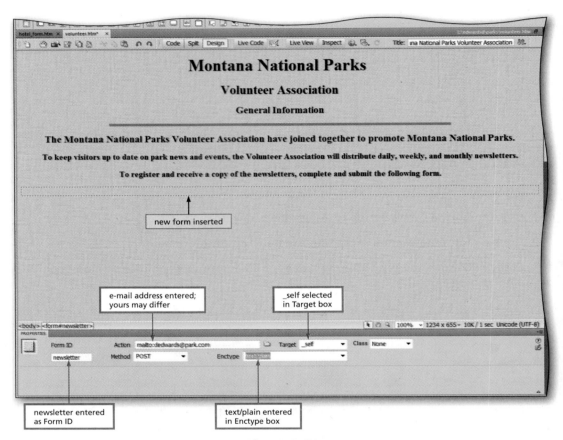

Figure 6–79

To Add a Table to the Volunteer Web Page

The following steps show how to add a table to the volunteer Web page and then format it.

1 If necessary, click in the form in the Document window to place the insertion point in the form.

2 Click Insert on the Application bar and then click Table to display the Table dialog box.

3 Create a four-row, two-column table, with a width of 75%, border thickness of 4, cell padding of 5, and cell spacing of 0. Type **Montana National Parks newsletter** in the Summary text box (Figure 6–80).

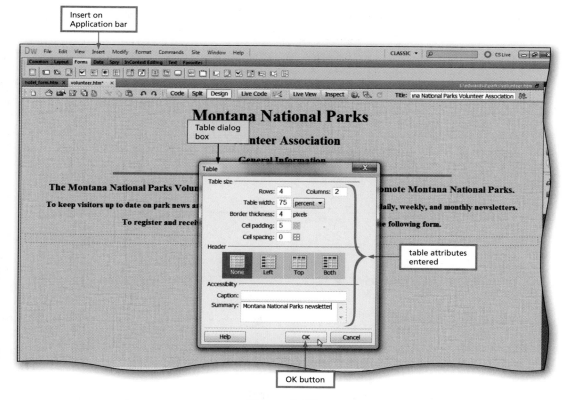

Figure 6–80

4 Click the OK button to insert the table in the form.

5 With the table selected, click Format on the Application bar, point to Align, and then click Center to center the table.

6 Click the Table text box in the Property inspector and then type **newsletter_form** as the ID.

7 Select row 1, columns 1 and 2, and then merge the cells.

8 Click in row 1, type **Montana National Parks** as the entry, and then press SHIFT+ENTER to insert a line break.

Q&A My insertion point is not visible. What should I do?

The insertion point is very small, but should be located on the line below the first entry.

9 Type **Newsletter Information**, select the two lines of text, apply Heading 2, and then center the headings (Figure 6–81).

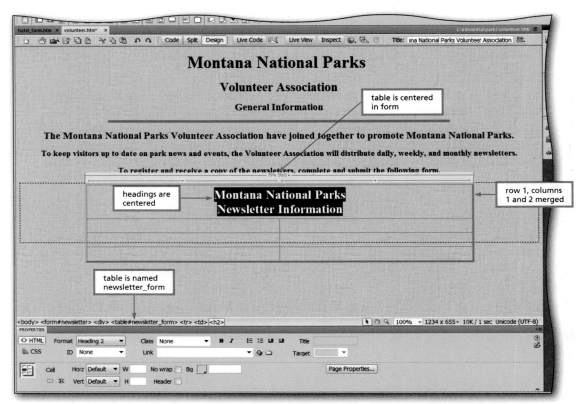

Figure 6–81

10 Select rows 2 through 4 in column 1, click Format on the Application bar, point to Align, and then click Right to right-align the text.

11 Select rows 2 through 4 in column 2, click the Horz button in the Property inspector, and then click Left to left-align the cells.

12 Click the last row in column 2 to deselect the cells. Click the Save button on the Standard toolbar to add the table (Figure 6–82).

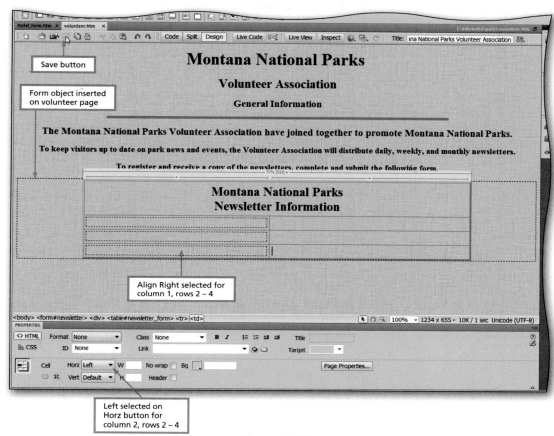

Figure 6–82

To Add an E-mail Address Field to a Form

Next, you adjust the column width and add descriptive text for the e-mail address and a single-line text field for user input to row 2. The following steps illustrate how to adjust the column width and how to add the e-mail address and a single-line text form object.

1 Select rows 2 through 4, column 1, and then set the column width to 40%.

2 Click row 2, column 1, type **E-mail** as the descriptive label, and then press the TAB key.

3 Click the Text Field button on the Forms tab to insert a text field.

4 Double-click the TextField text box in the Property inspector, type **email** as the ID, and then press the TAB key.

5 Type **3 0** as the Char width and then press the TAB key to set the properties for the e-mail text form object (Figure 6–83).

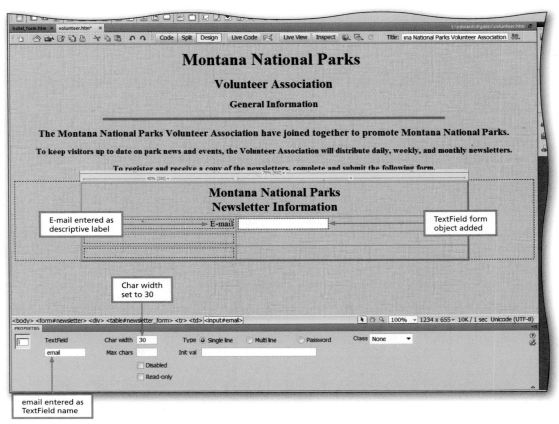

Figure 6–83

Radio Groups

When you are adding multiple radio buttons to a form, the **Radio Group** form object is the fastest and easiest method to use. At times, the table may extend outside the form boundaries. If this happens, ignore it.

To Add a Radio Group

The following steps show how to add descriptive text and a radio group to the Newsletter Information form.

1

• Click row 3, column 1, type **I am interested in receiving a newsletter** as the descriptive text, and then press the TAB key to move the insertion point to column 2 (Figure 6–84).

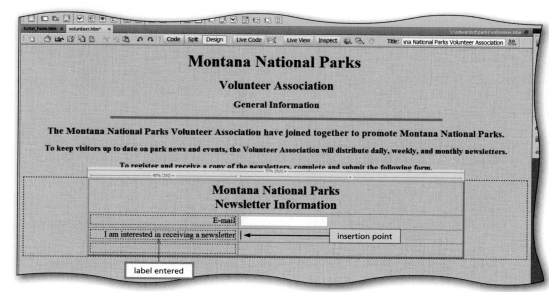

Figure 6–84

2

• Click the Radio Group button on the Forms tab to display the Radio Group dialog box (Figure 6–85).

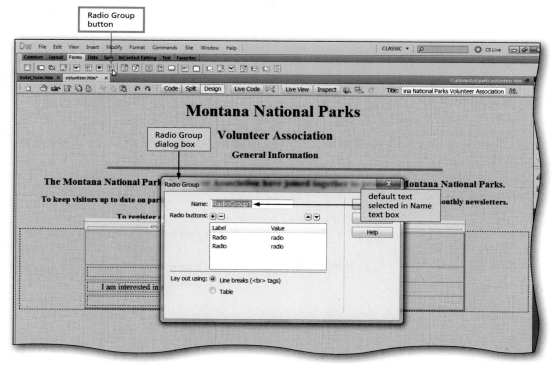

Figure 6–85

3

- Type **newsletter** in the Name text box to provide a name for the radio group.

- Click the first instance of Radio in the Label column to select it (Figure 6–86).

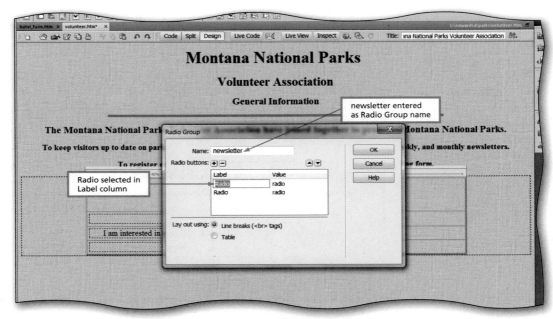

Figure 6–86

4

- Type **Daily** in the Label column, and then press the TAB key to enter the label for the first radio button.

- Type **daily** in the Value column and then press the TAB key to enter the value for the first radio button (Figure 6–87).

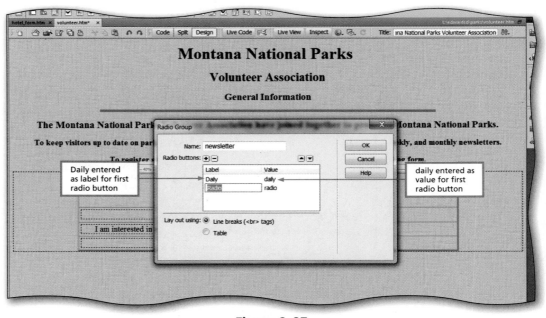

Figure 6–87

5

- Type **Weekly** in the Label column, and then press the TAB key to enter the label for the second radio button.

- Type **weekly** in the Value column and then press the TAB key to enter the value for the second radio button.

- Click the plus (+) button to insert another pair of values in the Radio buttons area.

- Click Radio in the Label column, type **Monthly**, and then press the TAB key to enter the label for the third radio button.

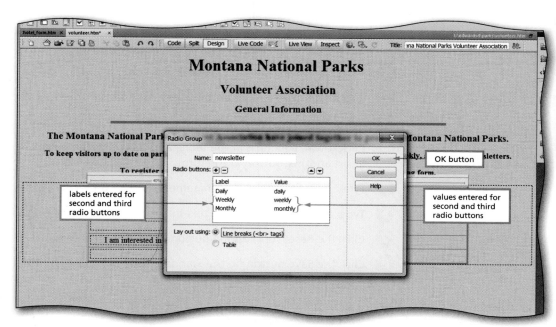

labels entered for second and third radio buttons

values entered for second and third radio buttons

OK button

Figure 6–88

- Type **monthly** in the Value column and then press the TAB key to enter the value for the third radio button (Figure 6–88).

6

- Click the OK button to insert the radio group and labels in the form (Figure 6–89).

Q&A What should I do if a dialog box appears asking if I want to add a form tab?

Click the Yes button to continue.

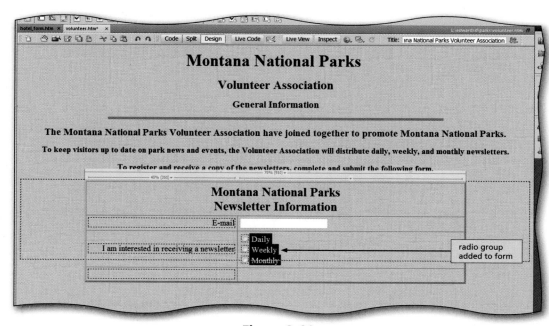

radio group added to form

Figure 6–89

To Add the Submit and Reset Buttons to the Volunteer Form

The final step is to add the Submit and Reset buttons to the volunteer form. The following steps show how to add these two buttons.

1 If necessary, scroll down to click row 4, column 1.

2 Click the Button button on the Forms tab to insert the Submit button.

3 In the Property inspector, type **submit** as the Button name.

4 Click row 4, column 2 in the table, and then click the Button button on the Forms tab to insert another button in the form.

5 Type **reset** as the Button name, and then press the TAB key to name the Reset button.

6 Type **Reset** in the Value text box to specify the label that should appear on the button.

7 Click the Reset form option button in the Action area.

8 Click the Save button on the Standard toolbar to save the form with the new buttons (Figure 6–90).

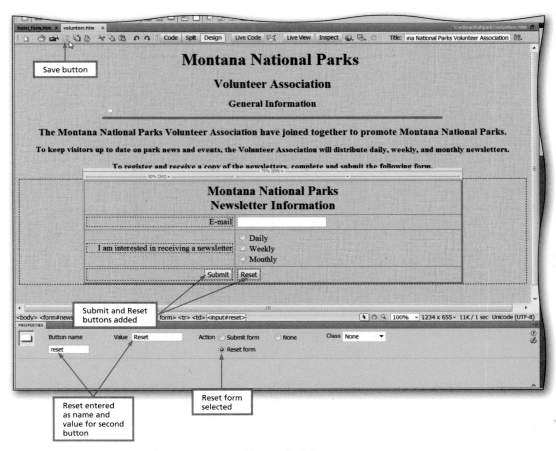

Figure 6–90

Other Ways

1. On Insert menu, point to Form, click Radio Group

To Add Links to and from the volunteer, hotel_form, and index Web Pages

Chapter 2 discussed the different types of links, including relative links, absolute links, named anchors, and e-mail links. The following steps illustrate how to add links to the volunteer and hotel_form Web pages, and how to add links from the index Web page to the volunteer and hotel_form Web pages.

1 Display the panel groups, open the index.htm Web page, scroll to the end of the page, and then add a line break after your name.

2 Type **Montana National Parks Volunteer Association** as the first link text, add a line break, and then type **Montana National Parks Hotel Reservations** as the second link text.

3 Select the text Montana National Parks Volunteer Association and create a link to the volunteer.htm Web page.

4 Select the text Montana National Parks Hotel Reservations and create a link to the hotel_form.htm Web page.

5 Save the index.htm Web page, press the F12 key to display the page in your browser, verify that the links work, and then close the browser and the index.htm Web page.

6 If necessary, click the volunteer.htm tab and then scroll to the bottom of the page. Click below the table, type **Home**, and then left-align the text.

7 Select the Home text and then create a link to the index.htm Web page.

8 Save the volunteer.htm Web page, and then press the F12 key to display the Web page in your browser (Figure 6–91).

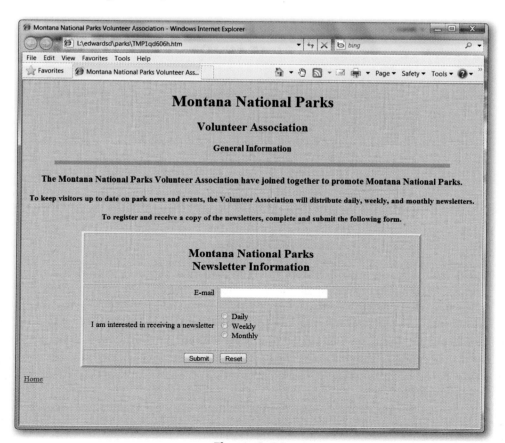

Figure 6–91

9 Verify that the link works, and then close the browser.

10 Click the hotel_form.htm tab to display the page, click below the table, type **Home**, and then left-align the text.

11 Select the Home text and then create a link to the index.htm Web page.

12 Save the hotel_form.htm Web page, and then press the F12 key to display the Web page in your browser. Allow blocked content, if necessary (Figure 6–92).

13 Close the browser.

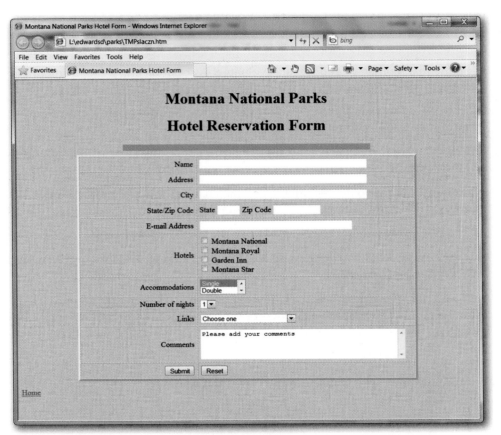

Figure 6–92

Using Behaviors with Forms

As you learned in Chapter 5, a **behavior** is a combination of an event and an action. Behaviors are attached to a specific element on the Web page. The element can be a table, an image, a link, a form, a form object, and so on. When a behavior is initiated, Dreamweaver uses JavaScript to write the code. **JavaScript** is a scripting language written as a text file. After a behavior is attached to a page element, and when the event specified occurs for that element, the browser calls the action (the JavaScript code) that is associated with that event. A scripting language, such as JavaScript, provides flexibility, interaction, and power to any Web site.

To create this type of user interaction with almost any other software program requires that you write the JavaScript. When you attach a behavior in Dreamweaver, however, the JavaScript is produced and inserted into the code for you.

Create, test, and validate the form.

Dreamweaver provides two form-related behaviors: Validate Form and Set Text of Text Field. These behaviors are available only if a text field has been inserted into the form:

- **Validate Form**: This behavior verifies that the user has entered data into each designated field. The form is checked when the user clicks the Submit button. If omissions or other errors occur, a Microsoft Internet Explorer (or other browser) dialog box is displayed. The errors then must be corrected before the form can be submitted successfully.

- **Set Text of Text Field**: This action replaces the content of a form's text field with the content you specify when creating the behavior. For example, you could use this behavior to insert the current date.

    The Behaviors panel is displayed in Figure 6–93.

Plan Ahead

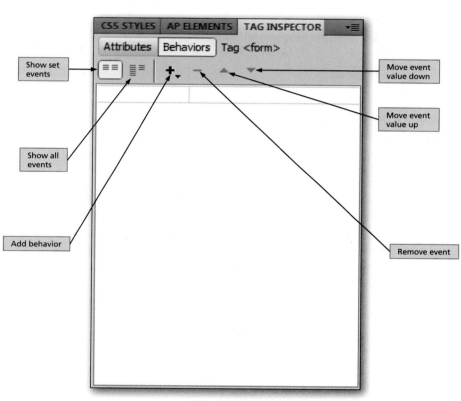

Show set events

Show all events

Add behavior

Move event value down

Move event value up

Remove event

Figure 6–93

To Add the Validate Form Behavior

The following steps show how to add the Validate Form behavior to the Hotel Reservation Form.

- Collapse the Property inspector to provide additional room for working with forms.

- If necessary, click the hotel_form.htm tab to display the page in the Document window.

- Click Window on the Application bar to display the Window menu and then point to Behaviors to highlight the command (Figure 6–94).

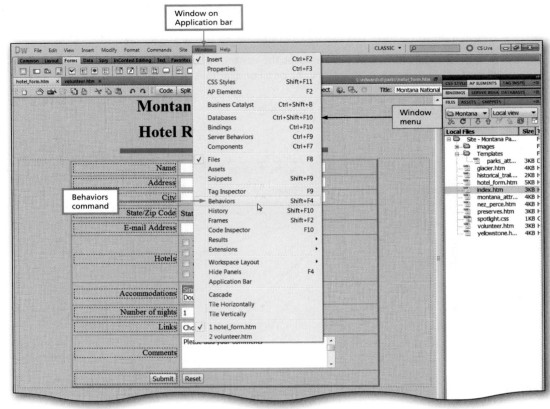

Figure 6–94

②
- Click Behaviors to display the Behaviors panel (Figure 6–95).

Figure 6–95

3

- If necessary, click anywhere inside the form to move the insertion point to the form.

- Click <form#hotel_form> in the tag selector to select the form.

- Click the Add behavior button in the Behaviors panel and then point to Validate Form on the pop-up menu to highlight the command (Figure 6–96).

Q&A

What should I do if form#hotel_form is not displayed in the tag selector?

Verify that the insertion point is in the form.

Figure 6–96

4

- Click Validate Form to display the Validate Form dialog box (Figure 6–97).

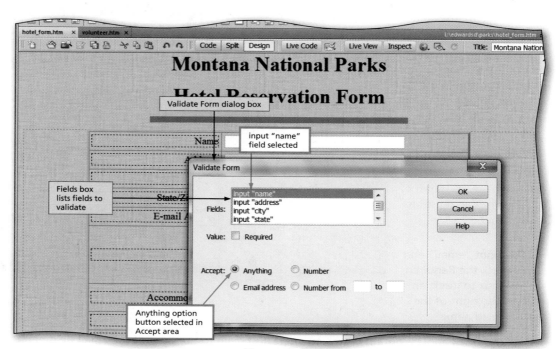

Figure 6–97

5

- Click the Value Required check box to insert an (R) to the right of the name field name.

- Click input "address" and then click the Required check box to insert an (R) to the right of the address field name.

- Click input "city" and then click the Required check box to insert an (R) to the right of the city field name.

- Click input "state" and then click the Required check box to insert an (R) to the right of the state field name.

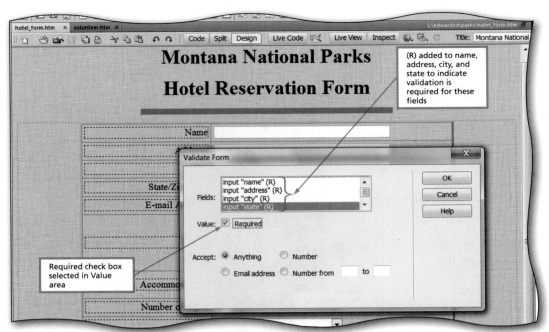

Figure 6–98

- Scroll up to verify that the first four entries include an (R) for required (Figure 6–98).

6

- Scroll down to click input "zip" and then click the Required check box to insert an (R) to the right of the zip field name.

- Click the Number option button in the Accept section to insert (RisNum) to the right of the zip field name.

Q&A What does RisNum mean?

RisNum means that the value entered must be a number.

- Click input "email" and then click the Required check box to insert an (R) to the right of the email field name.

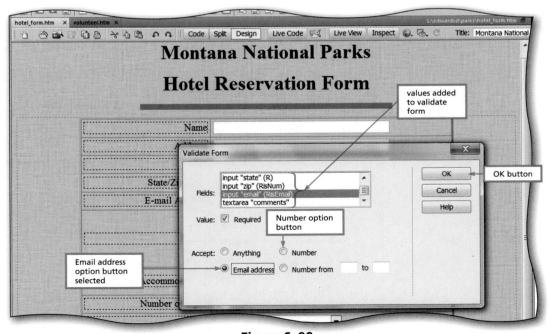

Figure 6–99

- Click the Email address option button to insert (RisEmail) to the right of the email field name (Figure 6–99).

Q&A What does RisEmail mean?

RisEmail means that the value entered must be an e-mail address.

7

• Click the OK button to accept the entries in the Validate Form dialog box.

• Click in the form outside the table to deselect the form and display the OnSubmit event and the Validate Form action in the Behaviors panel.

Q&A When you are using form validation, what is the difference between the onBlur event and the onSubmit event?

Use the onBlur event to validate the fields as the user is filling out the form, and use the onSubmit event to validate several text fields at once when the user clicks the Submit button.

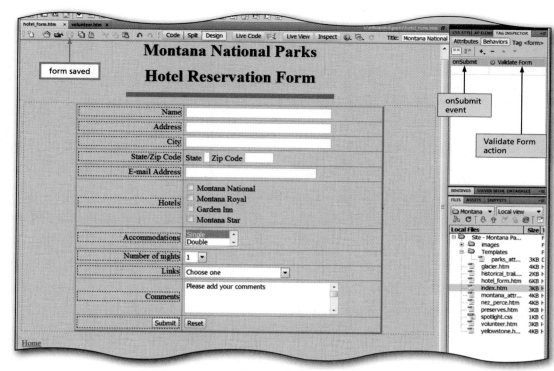

Figure 6–100

• Click the Save button on the Standard toolbar to save the form (Figure 6–100).

Q&A I clicked Save, but nothing happened. Is that correct?

Yes. At this point, no visible changes are evident in the Document window.

To View and Test the Hotel Reservation Form

The following steps illustrate how to view and test the Hotel Reservation Form.

1

- Press the F12 key to display the hotel_ form page in the browser.

An information bar appears in the browser window. What should I do?

Click the bar to allow the content, and then click the Yes button in the Security Warning dialog box.

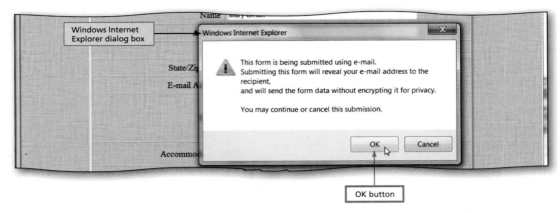

Figure 6–101

- Complete the form, typing data in each field, but skipping the Links jump menu.
- Click the Submit button to display a Windows Internet Explorer dialog box (Figure 6–101).

2

- Read the information in the dialog box, and then click the OK button to process the form and to have the data automatically e-mailed to you.
- Check your e-mail to verify that the data is e-mailed to you.

Q&A What should I do if the e-mail message does not include the form data?

In some instances, your e-mail message may not include the form data. This is determined by the e-mail program server and the security set up on your computer.

- Close the browser and return to Dreamweaver.

Q&A What should I do if I receive an error message when I try to process the form?

Most likely, you need to publish the Web site before you can process the form.

To Add Behaviors, View, and Test the Volunteer Form

Next, you add behaviors to validate the form on the volunteer Web page, and then you view and test the form.

1 Click the volunteer.htm tab to display the page in the Document window, click inside the form, and then click <form#newsletter> in the tag selector to select the form.

2 Click the Add behavior button on the Behaviors panel and then click Validate Form on the pop-up menu to display the Validate Form dialog box.

3 Click the Required check box and the Email address option button to specify that the e-mail address is required for processing the form (Figure 6–102).

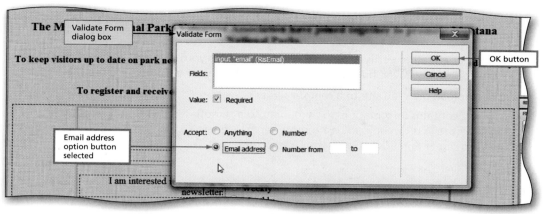

Figure 6–102

4 Click the OK button to accept the entries in the Validate Form dialog box.

5 Save the document, press the F12 key to display the form in your browser, and allow blocked content, if necessary.

6 Click the E-mail text box, type your e-mail address, and then click the Weekly radio button to specify that you want to receive a newsletter each week (Figure 6–103).

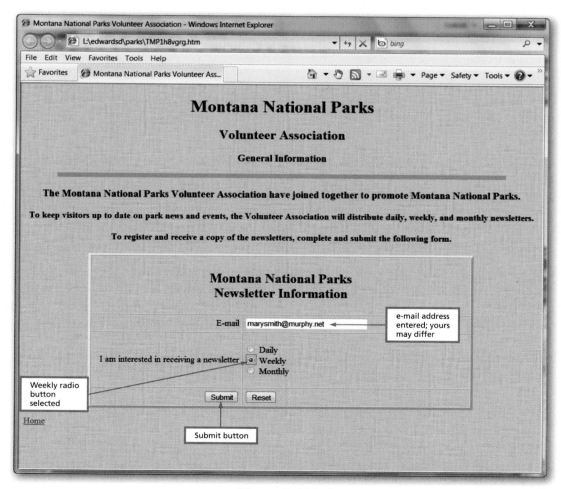

Figure 6–103

7 Click the Submit button to submit the form, and then click the OK button in the Windows Internet Explorer dialog box to e-mail the data.

8 Check your e-mail to verify that the data is e-mailed to you, close the browser, and then return to Dreamweaver. If instructed to do so, upload your Web site to a remote server.

Q&A How do I upload my Web site to a remote server?

Appendix C contains information on uploading to a remote server. A remote folder is required before you can upload to a remote server. Generally, the remote folder is defined by the Web server administrator or your instructor.

Quitting Dreamweaver

After you have created your forms, tested and verified that the forms work, and uploaded the Web site to a remote server, Chapter 6 is complete.

To Close the Web Site and Quit Dreamweaver

The following steps show how to close the Web site, quit Dreamweaver CS5, and return control to Windows.

1 Click the Close button on the upper-right corner of the Dreamweaver title bar to close the Dreamweaver window, the Document windows, and the parks Web site.

2 If you have unsaved changes, click the Yes button in the Dreamweaver dialog box to save the page.

Chapter Summary

In this chapter, you have learned how to create forms on Web pages. You created two forms and added a table to each of the forms to format them. In the Hotel Reservation Form, you added the following form objects: text fields, check boxes, a list and pop-up menu, a jump menu, a text area, and Submit and Reset buttons. You added a text field, radio group buttons, and Submit and Reset buttons to the Newsletter Information form. You then used the Behaviors panel to attach the Validate Form behavior to both forms. Finally, you viewed and tested the forms in your browser. The items listed below include all the new skills you have learned in this chapter.

1. Insert a horizontal rule (DW 416)
2. Insert a form (DW 419)
3. Set the form properties (DW 423)
4. Insert a table into a form (DW 425)
5. Format the form (DW 426)
6. Add descriptive labels and single-line text fields to the Hotel Reservation Form (DW 431)
7. Add check boxes (DW 438)
8. Create a scrolling list (DW 443)
9. Create a pop-up menu (DW 447)
10. Insert a jump menu (DW 451)
11. Add a Textarea text field (DW 456)
12. Add the Submit and Reset buttons (DW 458)
13. Add an e-mail address (DW 468)
14. Add a radio group (DW 469)
15. Add the validate form behavior (DW 476)
16. Add behaviors, view, and test the volunteer form (DW 481)

Learn It Online

Test your knowledge of chapter content and key terms.

Instructions: To complete the Learn It Online exercises, start your browser, click the Address bar, and then enter the Web address scsite.com/dwcs5/learn. When the Dreamweaver CS5 Learn It Online page is displayed, click the link for the exercise you want to complete and then read the instructions.

Chapter Reinforcement TF, MC, and SA

A series of true/false, multiple choice, and short answer questions that test your knowledge of the chapter content.

Flash Cards

An interactive learning environment where you identify chapter key terms associated with displayed definitions.

Practice Test

A series of multiple choice questions that test your knowledge of chapter content and key terms.

Who Wants To Be a Computer Genius?

An interactive game that challenges your knowledge of chapter content in the style of a television quiz show.

Wheel of Terms

An interactive game that challenges your knowledge of chapter key terms in the style of the television show *Wheel of Fortune*.

Crossword Puzzle Challenge

A crossword puzzle that challenges your knowledge of key terms presented in the chapter.

Apply Your Knowledge

Reinforce the skills and apply the concepts you learned in this chapter.

Adding a Form to a Web Page

Instructions: In this activity, you create a new Web page, add a background, and then add a general information form to the page (Figure 6–104). Data files are not required for this exercise.

Figure 6–104

Perform the following tasks:

1. Start Dreamweaver and then open the Apply Exercises site.
2. Create a blank HTML document and save it as apply_ch06 in the apply folder.
3. Add the apply_bkg image to the background of the page.
4. Type **Input Data** as the heading, apply Heading 1, and then center the title.
5. Click to the right of the heading and then press ENTER two times.
6. Click the Form button to insert a form.
7. In the new form, insert a three-row, two-column table with a table width of 90 percent, border of 7 pixels, and cell padding and cell spacing of 4 pixels each.
8. Click the Form ID box and then type **Data Input**.
9. Center the table in the form, and then right-align the contents of column 1.
10. Select column 2, click the Horz button in the Property inspector, and then select Left.
11. With column 2 still selected, click the Vert button and select Middle.
12. Click column 1, row 1 and type **Name**.
13. Click column 1, row 2 and type **Address**.
14. Click column 1, row 3 and type **City and State**.
15. Click column 2, row 1.
16. Insert a text field and name the text field username.
17. Set the Char width and Max chars to 35. Verify that Single line is selected.
18. Click column 2, row 2.

19. Insert a text field and name it address.

20. Set the Char width and Max chars to 45. Verify that Single line is selected.

21. Click column 2, row 3.

22. Insert a text field and name it city.

23. Set the Char width and Max chars to 25. Verify that Single line is selected.

24. Click to the right of the city text field, press the SPACEBAR, and insert another text field. Name the new text field state.

25. Set the Char width and Max chars to 2 and verify that Single line is selected.

26. Title your page Data Input Form and then save the apply_ch06.htm Web page.

27. View the form in your browser. Verify that you can input data in the form.

28. Submit the form in the format specified by your instructor.

Extend Your Knowledge

Extend the skills you learned in this chapter and experiment with new skills. You may need to use Help to complete the assignment.

Adding a Form to a Web Page

Instructions: In this activity, you create a Web page by adding a form and then adding a table with images and form objects to the form (Figure 6–105). You use data files provided for previous chapters.

Figure 6–105

Perform the following tasks:

1. Start Dreamweaver and then open the Extend Exercises Web site.

2. Create a blank HTML document, save it as extend_ch06 in the extend folder, and then apply the extend_bkg image to the background of the page.

3. Add and then center your name at the top of the page.

4. Apply Heading 1 to your name and then press the ENTER key.

5. Insert a horizontal rule and name it rule. Set the Width to 650 and the Height to 6. Shading should be selected.

6. Click at the end of the horizontal rule line and press the ENTER key.

7. Insert a form below the horizontal rule and name the form images.

8. If necessary, click inside the form and insert a two-row, three-column table with a table width of 70 percent, a Border thickness of 4 pixels, and cell padding and cell spacing of 6 pixels. Center the table and name the table jewelry.

9. In row 1, column 1 of the table, insert the jewelry01 image. In row 1, column 2, insert the jewelry02 image. In row 1, column 3, insert the jewelry03 image. Resize all images to a width of 200 and a height of 200.

10. In row 2, column 1, type **Earrings**. In row 2, column 2, type **Necklaces**. In row 2, column 3, type **Ring**.

11. Using Table 6–3 as a guide, insert a check box in row 2 to the left of the text you just entered. Enter the name, checked value, and initial state as specified in Table 6–3.

12. Click to the right of the table, and then press ENTER to insert a blank line at the bottom of the form. Add Submit and Reset buttons centered at the bottom of the form. Name the Submit button submit, and the Reset button reset. Set the value of the Reset button to Reset. Assign appropriate actions to the buttons.

13. Enter Jewelry in the Title text box to title the page.

14. Save your document and then view it in your browser. Submit it in the format specified by your instructor.

Table 6–3 Properties for the Checkboxes			
Property	**Checkbox 1**	**Checkbox 2**	**Checkbox 3**
Location	Row 2, column 1	Row 2, column 2	Row 2, column 3
Check box name	jewelry01	jewelry02	jewelry03
Checked value	Earrings	Necklace	Ring
Initial state	unchecked	unchecked	unchecked

Make It Right

Analyze a Web page with a form and correct all errors and/or improve the design.

Modifying a Web Page Form

Instructions: In this activity, you modify an existing Web page by correcting errors within a form (Figure 6–106). Make sure you have downloaded the data files for this chapter. See the inside back cover of this book for instructions for downloading the Data Files for Students, or contact your instructor for information about accessing the required files for this book.

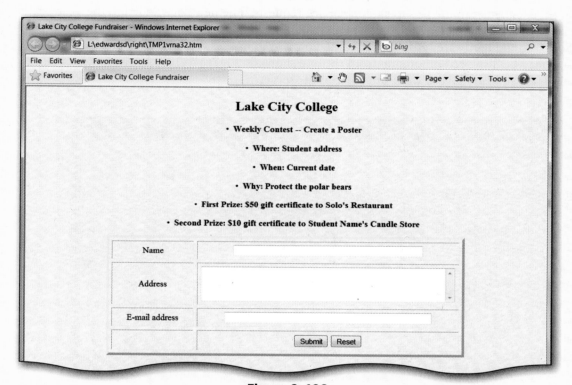

Figure 6–106

Perform the following tasks:

1. Start Dreamweaver, and then copy the data file from the Chapter06\right data files folder into the right folder for your Right Exercises local Web site.

2. Make changes as necessary so that the page looks similar to Figure 6–106. The table width is 70 percent, with a border of 4 pixels, cell spacing of 6 pixels, and cell padding of 6 pixels. Specify a width of 30% for column 1. Use a character width of 50 for the Name text box, 55 characters and four lines for the Address Textarea object, and 55 characters for the e-mail address text box. Provide an appropriate name for each form object and the form itself.

3. Add the Submit and Reset buttons with appropriate names and actions.

4. Save your document and then view it in your browser.

5. Submit your Web page in the format specified by your instructor.

In the Lab

Create a document using the guidelines, concepts, and skills presented in this chapter. Labs are listed in order of increasing difficulty.

Lab 1: Creating a Web Form for the Bryan's Computer Repair Services Web Site

Problem: Bryan's Computer Repair Services is growing, and he needs a way for clients to request services on his Web site. The Web site currently contains five pages. You will add a sixth page with a form containing a table. You add to this page a heading and a form with single-line text fields and Textarea fields, a list, Submit and Reset buttons, and links to and from the Bryan's Computer Repair Services page. Clients can use this to submit service requests. The new page added to the Web site is shown in Figure 6–107.

Software and hardware settings determine how a Web page is displayed in a browser. Your Web page may be displayed differently from the one shown in Figure 6–107. Appendix C contains instructions for uploading your local site to a remote server.

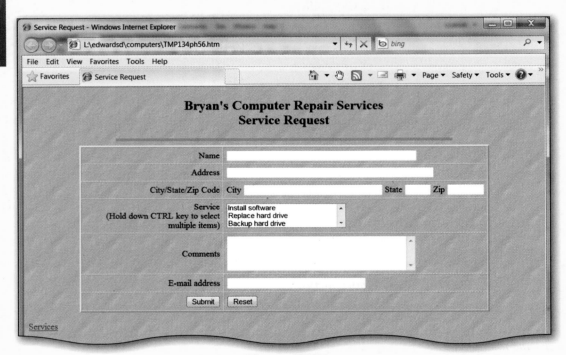

Figure 6–107

Perform the following tasks:

1. Start Dreamweaver, open the Computer Repair Services site, and then open a new HTML document. Save the page as services_form.htm.

2. Apply the repair_bkg background image, which can be found in the images folder.

3. If necessary, display the Insert bar and then click the Forms tab.

4. In the upper-left corner of the Document window, type **Bryan's Computer Repair Services** and then press the SHIFT+ENTER keys. Type **Service Request** and then press the ENTER key.

5. Select both lines. Apply Heading 2 and then center the two lines of text.

6. Click below the headings. Click Insert on the menu bar, point to HTML, and then click Horizontal Rule. Specify a width of 600 pixels, a height of 4, center alignment, and no shading.

7. Click below the horizontal rule. Click the Form button on the Forms tab. Double-click the Form ID text box in the Property inspector and then type **services** as the form name. Click the Action text box and then type **mailto:bryan@hometown.com** (substitute your name and e-mail address). Click the Target box arrow and then select _self. Click the Enctype box and then type **text/plain** as the entry.

8. Click inside the form. Click Insert on the menu bar and then click Table. Insert a seven-row, two-column table with a width of 80%, a border thickness of 3, a cell padding of 5, and a cell spacing of 0.

9. If necessary, select the table. Click the Align button arrow in the Property inspector and then click Center. Name the table service_request.

10. Select column 1, click the Horz button, and then click Right. Set the column W (width) to 35%. Select column 2, click the Horz button, and then click Left.

11. Click row 1, column 1; type **Name** as the entry; and then press the tab key.

12. Click the Text Field button on the Forms tab. In the Property inspector, type **name** as the form object name. Press the TAB key, type **50** as the Char width, and then press ENTER.

13. Click row 2, column 1; type **Address** as the entry; and then press the tab key. Insert a TextField form object, type **address** as the form object name, and then specify a Char width of 55.

14. Click row 3, column 1; type **City/State/Zip Code** as the entry; and then press the TAB key.

15. Type **City** and then press the SPACEBAR. Insert a TextField form object named city with a Char width of 35. Click to the right of the text field and then insert a space.

16. Type **State** and then press the SPACEBAR. Insert a TextField form object named state with a Char width of 2. Click to the right of the text field and then insert a space.

17. Type **Zip** and then press the SPACEBAR. Insert a TextField form object named zip with a Char width of 5.

18. Click row 4, column 1; type **Service** as the entry; and then press SHIFT+ENTER. Type the following text as the entry, including the parentheses: **(Hold down CTRL key to select multiple items).**

19. Click row 4, column 2, and then click the Select (List/Menu) button on the Forms tab. Type **services** as the List/Menu form object name, click the List option button in the Property inspector Type area, specify a height of 3, click the Allow multiple check box in the Selections area, and then click the List Values button. Type each Item Label and Value as shown in Table 6–4. Press the TAB key to move from field to field.

Table 6–4 Computer Services List Values	
Item Label	**Value**
Install software	$50 – $75
Replace hard drive	$150
Back up hard drive	$100
Update drivers	$75
Remove conflicts	$75
Optimize speed and performance	$100

20. Click the OK button; click row 5, column 1; type **Comments** as the entry; and then press the TAB key. Insert a Textarea form object named comments with a Char width of 40. Type **4** for the Num lines value.

21. Click row 6, column 1; type **E-mail address** as the entry; and then press the TAB key. Insert a TextField form object named email with a Char width of 35.

22. Click row 7, column 1, and then insert a Submit button named submit. Click row 7, column 2, and then insert another Button object named reset. Type **Reset** in the Value text box, and then click the Reset form option button in the Action area.

23. If necessary, display the Behaviors panel. Click form#services in the tag selector and then click the Add behavior button in the Behaviors panel. Click Validate Form on the Add behavior menu.

24. In the Validate Form dialog box, click the Required check box for all fields except the Comments text area. In the Accept area, make sure the Anything option button is selected for all fields except the email field. For the email field, click Email address. Click the OK button in the Validate Form dialog box.

25. Click below the form. Type **Services**, select the text, and then create a link to the services.htm Web page. Title the page Service Request, and then click the Save button on the Standard toolbar.

26. Open the services.htm Web page and then scroll down to the bottom of the page. Insert a line break after the Home link. Type **Service Request Form** and then create a link to the services_form.htm Web page. Save the Web page.

27. Press F12 to display the services.htm Web page in your browser. Click the Service Request Form link to display the services_form.htm Web page. Allow blocked content, if necessary. Input data into the form and then click the Submit button to test the form. Test the link to the services.htm Web page. Close the browser.

28. Submit your assignment in the format specified by your instructor. Close Dreamweaver.

In the Lab

Lab 2: Creating a Web Form for the Baskets by Carole Web Site

Problem: Carole has decided she would like to conduct a survey to determine which baskets her Web site visitors like best. She wants to include a comments section and to provide a copy of the results to those visitors who are interested. To create the survey, she has requested that you add a form to the Baskets by Carole site. The completed form is shown in Figure 6–108. Appendix C contains instructions for uploading your local site to a remote server.

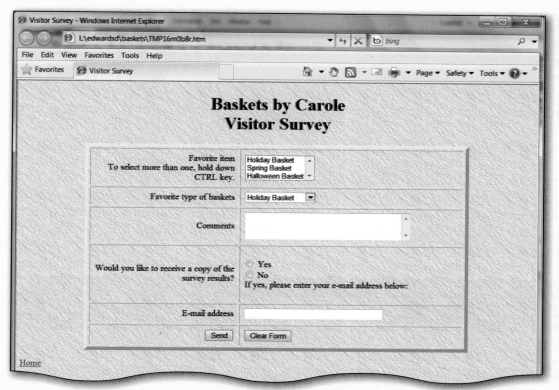

Figure 6–108

Perform the following tasks:

1. Start Dreamweaver, open the Baskets by Carole Web site, and then open a new HTML document. Save the page as survey_form.htm.

2. Apply the baskets_bkg background image to the page, which can be found in the images folder.

3. Use Visitor Survey as the title for the Web page.

4. In the upper-left corner of the Document window, add and center the two-line heading, Baskets by Carole Visitor Survey, as shown in Figure 6–108. Apply Heading 1 to both lines.

5. Press the ENTER key after the second heading. If necessary, click the Forms tab on the Insert bar and then click the Form button. Type **survey_form** as the Form ID. Type **mailto:carole@hometown.com** (substitute your e-mail address) as the action. Select _self in the Target box. Click the Enctype box and then type **text/plain** as the entry.

6. Click inside the form and then insert a table with the following attributes: 6 rows, 2 columns, width of 75%, border thickness of 6, cell padding of 7, and cell spacing of 3. Center the table in the form and then specify a width of 40%, right-alignment for column 1, and left-alignment for column 2.

7. Click row 1, column 1; type **Favorite item** as the entry; and then insert a line break. Type the following text (including the period): **To select more than one, hold down CTRL key.** Press the TAB key.

8. Click the Select (List/Menu) button on the Forms tab. Type **favorites** as the object name, click List in the Type area, type **3** in the Height box, and then click the Allow multiple check box.

9. Click the List Values button. Type each Item Label and Value as shown in Table 6–5. Press the TAB key to move from field to field. Click the OK button when you are finished entering the list values.

Table 6–5 Favorite Item List Values	
Item Label	**Value**
Holiday Basket	$75
Spring Basket	$75
Halloween Basket	$30
Food Basket	$30 to $75 based on type of food
Birthday Basket	$25 to $100 based on accessories

10. Click row 2, column 1. Type **Favorite type of baskets** and then press the TAB key. Click the Select (List/Menu) button on the Forms tab. Type **favorite_baskets** as the object name. If necessary, click Menu in the Type area, and then click the List Values button. Type each Item Label and Value as shown in Table 6–6. Press the TAB key to move from field to field. Select Holiday Basket in the Initially selected list box.

Table 6-6 Favorite Type of Baskets Values	
Item Label	**Value**
Holiday Basket	holiday
Spring Basket	spring
Halloween Basket	halloween
Food Basket	food
Birthday Basket	birthday

11. Click row 3, column 1; type **Comments** as the entry; and then press the TAB key. Insert a Textarea form object named comments with a Char width of 35 and Num lines of 3.

12. Click row 4, column 1. Type the following text and then press the TAB key: **Would you like to receive a copy of the survey results?**.

13. Insert a Radio Group form object named group_results. Click the first instance of Radio below Label, type **Yes** as the Label, and then press the TAB key. Type **yes** for the Value and then press the TAB key. Type **No** for the second Label field, press the TAB key, and then type **no** for the second Value. Click the OK button.

14. Position the insertion point to the right of No and then insert a line break. Type the following text and then press the TAB key: **If yes, please enter your e-mail address below:**.

15. If necessary, click in row 5, column 1. Type the following text and then press the tab key: **E-mail address**. Insert a TextField form object named email and then set a Char width of 35.

16. Click row 6, column 1, and then insert a Button form object named send. Type **Send** in the Value text box.

17. Click row 6, column 2, and then insert a Button form object named clear. Type **Clear Form** in the Value text box, and then click Reset form in the Action area.

18. Below the form, type **Home**, insert a line break, left-align the text, and then add a link to the index. htm Web page. Save the document. Press the F12 key to view the Web page in your browser. Input data into the form and then click the Send button to test the form.

19. Open the index.htm Web page and then scroll down to the bottom of the page. Click at the end of the Featured Baskets link and insert a line break. Type **Survey** and create a link to the survey_form.htm Web page.

20. Save the Web page and then test the link in your browser. Submit your assignment in the format specified by your instructor.

In the Lab

Lab 3: Creating a Form Web Page for the Credit Protection Web Site

Problem: Jessica Minnick recently received several e-mails asking for suggestions on how to spend money wisely. She has created three informational articles and would like to provide these articles to her Web site visitors. Jessica asks you to create a form so she can provide this information. The form is shown in Figure 6–109. Appendix C contains instructions for uploading your local site to a remote server.

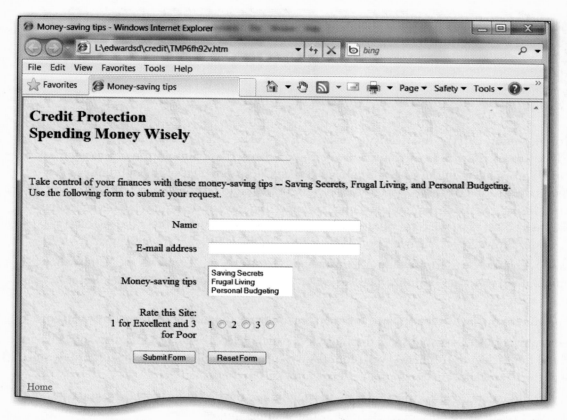

Figure 6–109

1. Using Dreamweaver or Windows Explorer, copy the tips_form.htm file from the Chapter06\credit folder provided with your data files to your credit folder.

2. Start Dreamweaver, if necessary, and then open the Credit Protection Web site.

3. Open the tips_form Web page.

4. Click to the right of the last sentence and then press the ENTER key. If necessary, click the Forms tab on the Insert bar and then click the Form button. Name the form guest_comments. Type `mailto:jessica@credit.com` (substitute your e-mail address) as the action. Select _self in the Target box. Click the Enctype box and then type `text/plain` as the entry.

5. Click inside the form and then insert a table with the following attributes: 5 rows, 2 columns, width of 75%, border thickness of 0, cell padding of 7, and a cell spacing of 3. Center the table in the form and specify a width of 30% for column 1.

6. Right-align the text in column 1.

7. Click row 1, column 1; type **Name** as the entry; and then press the TAB key. Add a single-line text field named name with a Char width of 40.

8. Click row 2, column 1; type **E-mail address** as the entry; and then press the TAB key. Add a single-line text field named email with a Char width of 40.

9. Click row 3, column 1; type the following text and then press the TAB key: **Money-saving tips**. Insert a Select (List/Menu) form object named saving, with a Type of List and a Height of 3. Allow multiple lines in the form object.

10. In the List Values dialog box, type each Item Label and Value as shown in Table 6–7.

Table 6–7 Credit Protection List Values	
Item Label	**Value**
Saving Secrets	saving
Frugal Living	frugal
Personal Budgeting	budget

11. Click row 4, column 1. Type the following text: **Rate this Site:** and then insert a line break. Type **1 for Excellent and 3 for Poor**. Insert a Radio Button object named excellent. Type excellent in the Checked value text box. Click to the left of the radio button, type **1** and press the SPACEBAR. Insert a space to the right of the radio button, type **2** and press the SPACEBAR. Insert a Radio Button object named average. Type **average** in the Checked value text box. Insert a space to the right of the radio button, type **3** and then press the SPACEBAR. Insert a Radio Button object named poor. Type **poor** in the Checked value text box.

12. Click row 5, column 1. Insert the Submit button and type **Submit Form** as the Value. Click row 5, column 2. Insert another button, type **Reset Form** as the Value, and then click Reset form in the Action area.

13. At the bottom of the page, type **Home**, and then make the text a link to the index.htm Web page.

14. If necessary, press SHIFT+F4 to display the Behaviors panel. Select the form. Click the Add behavior button and then select the Validate Form command to open the Validate Form dialog box. Require a value in the name field, and accept only e-mail addresses in the e-mail field.

15. Insert a left-aligned horizontal rule under the second line in the heading. The horizontal rule should have a width of 400 pixels, a height of 3, and shading applied.

16. Save the form.

17. Open the index.htm Web page, scroll down to the bottom of the page, click to the right of Credit Information, and then add a line break. Type **Information Request** as the entry, select the text, and then create a link to the tips_form.htm Web page.

18. View the Web pages in your browser. Input data into the form and then click the Submit Form button to test the form. Close the browser. Submit your assignment in the format specified by your instructor.

Cases and Places

Apply your creative thinking and problem solving skills to design and implement a solution.

● EASIER ●● MORE DIFFICULT

● 1: Add a Form to the Favorite Sports Web Site

Your sports Web site is receiving more hits each day. You have received many e-mails asking for statistics and other information. You decide to start a weekly newsletter and want to add a form so your visitors can subscribe to the newsletter. Add a background image to the page and add a title to the page. Insert a form and name the form appropriately. Add a horizontal rule below the heading on your page. Next, add a table to your form. Include text fields for name and e-mail address and a text area for comments. Add descriptive text asking if the visitor would like to subscribe to the newsletter and then include a radio group with Yes and No options. Add Submit and Reset buttons. Create links to and from the home page. Save the page in your sports Web site. Open the pages in your browser and then check your links and forms.

● 2: Add a Survey to the Hobby Web Site

You would like to add some interactivity to your hobby Web site. You decide to do this by adding a survey. First, add a background image to the page and then add an appropriate title. Add a horizontal rule below the heading on your page. Insert a form and then add a table to your form. Add a four-pixel border to the form. Add a list form object that contains a list of hobbies. Ask your viewers to select their favorite hobbies. Create an e-mail text field for those visitors who would like a copy of your survey results. Add Submit and Reset buttons. Create links to and from the home page. Save your Web pages, open the pages in your browser, and then check your links and forms. Upload the page to a remote site, if instructed to do so.

●● 3: Create a Companion Web Site for the Politics Web Site

Your campaign for political office is progressing well. Create a new Web site and name it office_form. Add two pages with forms to the new site. The first page should contain a form asking for opinions and comments about your political views. The second form should contain form objects requesting donations and campaign volunteers. Add a horizontal rule below the headings on each of your two pages. Create links to and from the home page. Save your pages, open your pages in your browser, and then check your links and forms. Upload the office_form Web site to a remote server.

●● 4: Add a Form to the Favorite Music Web Site

Make It Personal

Add an informational form to your music hobby Web site and then add a background to the page. Add a horizontal rule below the heading on your page. Insert a form and a table. Include form objects for name, address, telephone number, and e-mail address. Include a menu with at least five choices and then add the Submit and Reset buttons. Rename the buttons. Fill in all relevant attributes in the Property inspector for each object. Create links to and from the home page. Save your Web pages, open the pages in your browser, and then check your links and forms. Upload the page to a remote site.

STUDENT ASSIGNMENTS

•• 5: Add a Form to the Student Trips Web Site

Working Together

Last week, the student government officers selected three possible vacation sites to visit. Now they would like to have a form page for students to provide feedback about each of the three sites. Each student in your group creates a page with introductory text and a form listing each of the three student trip locations. Provide form objects so the Web site visitors can vote on which trip they would like to take and offer feedback regarding the number of days, minimum and maximum costs, and other related information. Integrate the three pages into one. Add a horizontal rule below the heading on your page. Create links to and from the home page. Save your Web pages, open the pages in your browser, and then check your links and forms.

7 Using Spry to Create Interactive Web Pages

Objectives

You will have mastered the material in this chapter when you can:

- Describe the Spry framework
- Describe Spry widgets
- Add the Spry Collapsible Panel widget to a Web page
- Add headings to a Collapsible Panel widget
- Copy and paste text to a Collapsible Panel widget
- Add and customize a Spry Menu Bar widget on a Web page
- Format a Spry widget
- Describe Spry effects

7 | Using Spry to Create Interactive Web Pages

Introduction

Chapter 7 introduces the **Spry framework for AJAX** and explains how to use and apply reusable Spry widgets. **AJAX (Asynchronous JavaScript and XML)** is a collection of Web technologies that communicate with a server in the background. AJAX is not a new programming language, but it is a new way to use the following existing standards: JavaScript, XML, HTML, and CSS. A **Spry widget** is an element you insert on a Web page so that users can interact with it. For example, they can use widgets to show or hide content on the page, change the background color of the page, or select menu options.

One of the more well-known applications that uses AJAX is Google Maps. In Google Maps, you can change views and manipulate the map in real time. Applications developed using AJAX generally are referred to as Rich Internet Applications (RIA). AJAX applications do not require you to install a plug-in such as those used with programs such as QuickTime, Photoshop, Flash, and others. Instead, they use a technique that enables a JavaScript file to communicate and exchange data directly with the server. This technique does not require the browser to reload an entire page. Instead, it allows the Web page to request small bits of information, which enhances download speed.

Project — Interactive Web Pages

In this chapter, you continue creating the Montana Parks Web site. You learn about Spry and how to apply this technology by creating and adding two new Web pages to the Montana Parks Web site.

You begin the chapter by creating a page that contains a Spry Collapsible Panel widget. The page focuses on the different types of animals (bears, moose, and mountain lions) found in Montana, so you add three separate panels — one panel for each animal. The panels can be closed to show only the panel names (Figure 7–1a) or opened to display detailed content (Figure 7–1b).

The second new page contains a horizontal Spry Menu Bar widget, which enables you to incorporate numerous links into a compact space (Figure 7–1c on page DW 500). The Spry Menu Bar widget supports two levels of pop-up submenus. Each menu button can include a pop-up menu, and each pop-up menu can have yet another pop-up menu.

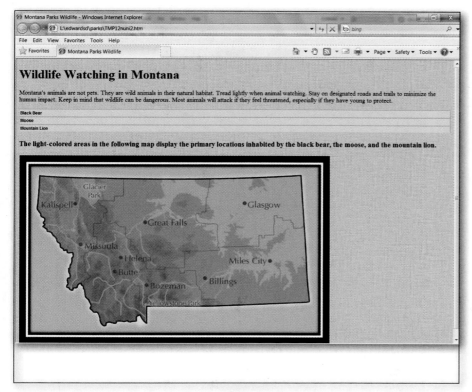

Figure 7–1a

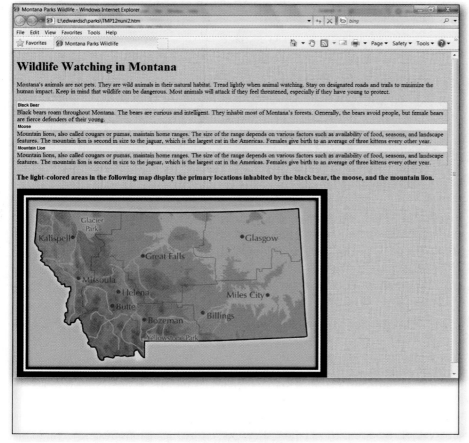

Figure 7–1b

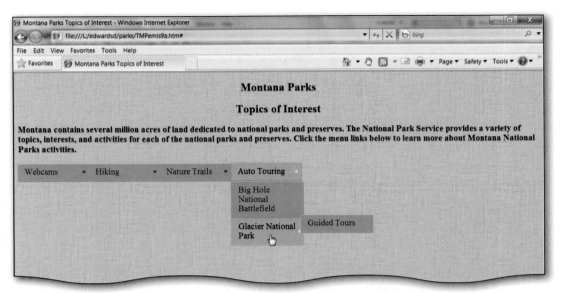

Figure 7–1c

Overview

As you read this chapter, you will learn how to add to your Web site the pages shown in Figure 7–1 by performing these general tasks:

- Add two new pages to the Montana Parks Web site.
- Explore Spry options and how they work.
- Add the Spry Collapsible Panel widget to a Web page.
- Add headings to a Collapsible Panel widget.
- Copy and paste text from a data file to a Web page.
- Add the Spry Menu Bar widget to a Web page.
- Add text and links to the Menu Bar widget.
- Format the Menu Bar widget.

Plan Ahead

General Project Guidelines

When adding pages to a Web site, consider the appearance and characteristics of the completed site. As you create the Web pages shown in Figure 7–1, you should follow these general guidelines:

1. **Review what you need to publish a Web site that uses Spry widgets.** A Web page containing a Spry widget needs support files that specify its formatting and behavior. Dreamweaver creates these files for you automatically. You need to upload these files to the server when you publish the site.

2. **Select Spry widgets.** Determine which Spry widgets you will use and how you will place them on the page.

3. **Edit and format Spry widgets.** Change the content and format of the widgets to match the design of your Web site.

4. **Add text to a Web page from another source.** To use text from another Dreamweaver document or from other sources, such as a basic text file, you can copy or move the text. If you want to use text from a file created in a program such as Microsoft Word or Microsoft Excel, you need to import the text.

When necessary, more specific details concerning the above guidelines are presented at appropriate points in the chapter. The chapter also will identify the actions performed and decisions made regarding these guidelines during the creation of the Web pages shown in Figure 7–1.

Starting Dreamweaver and Opening a Web Site

Each time you start Dreamweaver, it opens to the last site displayed when you closed the program. It therefore may be necessary for you to open the parks Web site. Clicking the Files pop-up menu in the Files panel lists the sites you have defined. When you open the site, a list of pages and subfolders within the site is displayed.

To Start Dreamweaver and Open the Montana Parks Web Site

With a good understanding of the requirements, and an understanding of the necessary decisions and planning process, the next step is to start Dreamweaver and open the Montana Parks Web site.

1 Click the Start button on the Windows taskbar.

2 Click Adobe Dreamweaver CS5 on the Start menu or point to All Programs on the Start menu, click Adobe Design Premium, if necessary, and then click Adobe Dreamweaver CS5 on the All Programs list to start Dreamweaver.

3 If necessary, display the panel groups.

4 If the Montana Parks hierarchy is not displayed, click the Sites pop-up menu button on the Files panel, and then click Montana Parks to display the Montana Parks Web site in the Files panel.

To Copy Data Files to the Montana Parks Web Site

Before you start enhancing your Web site, you need to copy the data files into the site's folder hierarchy. In the following steps, you copy the data files for the Chapter 7 project from the Chapter07 folder on a USB drive to the parks and the parks\images folders stored in the *your name* folder on the same USB drive. In the following steps, the data files for this chapter are stored on drive L:. The location on your computer may be different. If necessary, verify the location of the data files with your instructor.

1 Click the Sites pop-up menu button in the Files panel, and then click the name of the drive containing your data files, such as Removable Disk (L:).

2 If necessary, click the plus sign (+) next to the folder containing your data files to expand that folder, expand the Chapter07 folder, and then expand the parks folder.

3 Copy the wildlife_watching file from the data files, click the Sites pop-up menu button in the Files panel, click Montana Parks, and then paste the wildlife_watching file in the parks folder for the Montana Parks site.

4 Navigate again to the Chapter07 folder containing your data files. If necessary, expand the parks folder.

5 Copy the montana_map03 image file from the data files, click the Sites pop-up menu button in the Files panel, click Montana Parks, click the images folder, and then paste the montana_map03 file in the images folder for the Montana Parks site (Figure 7–2).

Q&A What should I do with the other six files in the Chapter07\parks folder?

You do not need to copy the other six files. Keep the drive containing your data files handy, however, because you will open the files later.

Q&A How can I display the files in the Files panel in alphabetic order?

Click the Refresh button on the Files panel toolbar to display the files in alphabetic order.

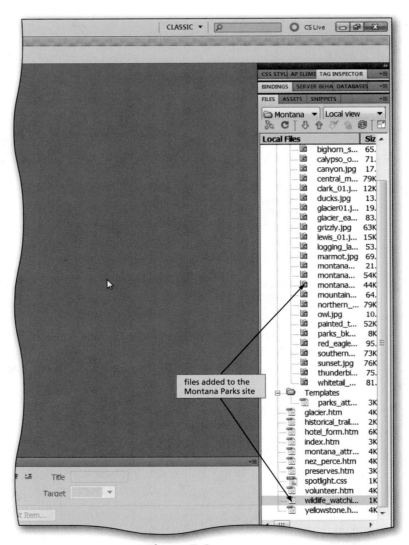

Figure 7–2

Understanding the Spry Framework

The Adobe Spry framework for AJAX was introduced in Dreamweaver CS3. The Spry framework consists of a library of JavaScript components and behaviors that you can use to add interactive functionality to a Web site. The Spry category on the Insert bar contains three groups of Spry widgets. The first group controls data and describes how to display it with widgets. The second group focuses on form elements, and the third group provides dynamic elements such as menu bars, tabbed panels, accordion bars, and collapsible panels.

Plan Ahead

Select Spry widgets.

Spry widgets are page elements that let you interact with a Web page to make selections, navigate the site, link to related files, and perform other tasks you typically perform on a Web page, such as entering a password. The Spry Collapsible Panel and the Spry Menu Bar are two popular widgets covered in this chapter. Choose to use them on a Web site in the following circumstances:

- **Spry Collapsible Panel widget:** Select this type of Spry widget when you want to provide detailed descriptions or supplemental content but do not want to take up a lot of screen space. Users can click the tab in a Collapsible Panel widget to show or hide related details.

- **Spry Menu Bar widget:** Select this type of Spry widget when you want to include a lot of navigational information in a compact space. Users point to menu items to display options, which they can click to link to other Web pages.

Table 7–1 describes the tools in the Spry category on the Insert bar shown in Figure 7–3.

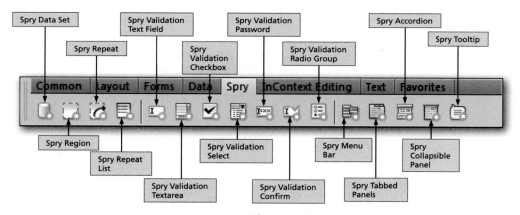

Figure 7–3

Table 7–1 Spry Tools on the Insert Bar	
Command	**Description**
Spry Data Set	JavaScript object containing pointers to XML data sources
Spry Region	JavaScript object used to enclose data objects, which includes two types of regions — the Spry Region wraps around data objects such as tables and the Spry Detail Region works with a master table object to allow dynamic updating of data
Spry Repeat	Data structure that can be formatted to present data as needed
Spry Repeat List	Data structure that displays data as an ordered list, an unordered or bulleted list, a definition list, or a drop-down list
Spry Validation Text Field	Text field that displays valid or invalid data when a site visitor enters text
Spry Validation Textarea	Widget that validates the text entered into a Textarea field
Spry Validation Checkbox	Widget that displays valid or invalid states when the user selects or fails to select a checkbox
Spry Validation Select	Drop-down menu that displays valid or invalid states when the user makes a selection
Spry Validation Password	Widget that validates password input
Spry Validation Confirm	Widget that confirms valid data was entered
Spry Validation Radio Group	Widget that validates an option is selected within the radio group
Spry Menu Bar	Widget that displays a set of navigational menu items that display submenus or links when a site visitor points to the item
Spry Tabbed Panels	Widget used to organize content into panels; users can access panels by clicking a tab at the top of the panel
Spry Accordion	Widget that resembles a standard vertical menu bar; the panels collapse and expand to display or hide content panels
Spry Collapsible Panel	Widget that stores content in a compact space; users can hide or reveal the content by clicking a tab
Spry Tooltip	Widget that displays an on-screen tip when users point to forms and other data

BTW

Finding Other Widgets
The Adobe Exchange provides other widgets you can use on a Web page besides those that are provided with Dreamweaver. Click the Extend Dreamweaver button on the Application bar, and then click Browse for Web Widgets to find additional widgets.

Using Spry Widgets in Dreamweaver

Dreamweaver supports a number of widgets as described in Table 7–1. You can change the appearance of most of the widgets by editing the widget's CSS code. Editing the code is beyond the scope of this book. You also can use HTML and CSS properties to format widgets, such as by changing their font type and size, the same way you format other objects in Dreamweaver. Some of the more popular widgets are described in Table 7–2.

Table 7–2 Spry Widgets

Widget	Name	Description
	Spry Collapsible Panel	This widget stores content in a compact space. Clicking a panel tab expands or collapses the content stored in the widget. You can open one or all of the panels at the same time.
	Spry Accordion	Similar to the Collapsible Panel widget, this widget can store a large amount of content in a compact space. Unlike the Collapsible Panel widget, you can open only one content panel at a time.
	Spry Menu Bar	You can use the Spry Menu Bar widget to create menus with items and submenus. You can select a horizontal or vertical layout and then use the Menu Bar Property inspector to format the widget. Using the Menu Bar plus and minus symbol buttons, you can add and remove items from a menu. The arrow symbols let you move items up or down the sort order.
	Spry Tabbed Panels	The Tabbed Panels widget contains a set of panels that can store content in a small space. You click the panel tab to view or hide the content. You can open only one content panel at a time.
	Spry Tooltip	When you point to a particular element on a Web page, the Tooltip widget displays additional information. The content disappears when you move the mouse pointer.

These widgets have attached behaviors that you can access and modify through the Behaviors panel. When you do so, you are adding Spry effects to the widgets or other object.

Plan Ahead

Review what you need to publish a Web site that uses Spry widgets.
When you insert a Spry widget into your Web page, Dreamweaver automatically creates a folder named SpryAssets and adds it to the root level of your Web site. Each time you insert a Spry widget into a Web page, Dreamweaver adds a corresponding CSS file and a JavaScript file to the SpryAssets folder. The CSS file contains all the style specifications for the widget, and the JavaScript file contains code that determines the widget's behavior. The CSS and JavaScript file names contain the name of the widget with which they are associated. For example, the files associated with the Collapsible Panel widget are named SpryCollapsiblePanel.css and SpryCollapsiblePanel.js.

If you are uploading your page to a file server, you also must upload the SpryAssets folder and its contents for the widget to properly function.

You insert all of the widgets described in Table 7-2 into a Web page the same way as you insert the Spry Collapsible Panel widget in the following steps. Once you insert them, you can customize the widgets and modify their styles through the CSS Styles panel.

You copied the files necessary to begin creating an interactive Web page for the Montana Parks Web site. You start the chapter by opening the wildlife_watching file. You then add three Spry collapsible panels to the page. The first panel will contain information about Montana's black bears, the second panel about Montana's moose, and the third panel about Montana's mountain lions.

Later, you add another new page that incorporates a multitiered horizontal menu. This page, named montana_topics.htm, provides menu options for topics of interest for several of Montana's national parks.

Spry Collapsible Panels

As indicated previously, the Collapsible Panel widget is one of the more popular Spry widgets in Dreamweaver. Use this widget to store content in a compact space. The user then can hide or reveal the content by clicking a widget tab.

To Add the Spry Collapsible Panel Widget

The following steps illustrate how to add the Spry Collapsible Panel widget to the wildlife_watching page. The widget will contain three panels describing three types of wildlife found in Montana.

- Open the wildlife_watching file.

- Apply the parks_bkg image to the background of the page.

- If necessary, click at the end of the last sentence and then press the ENTER key to prepare for adding a Spry Collapsible Panel widget (Figure 7–4).

Figure 7–4

- Collapse the panel groups to create more room to work.

- Click the Spry tab on the Insert bar to display the Spry widgets (Figure 7–5).

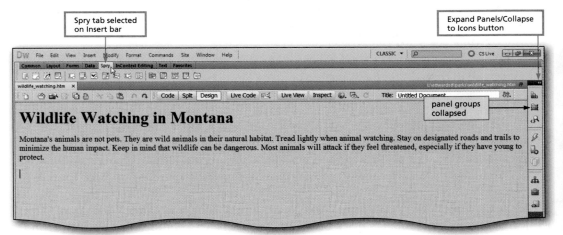

Figure 7–5

3

• Point to the Spry Collapsible Panel button to identify it (Figure 7–6).

Figure 7–6

4

• Click the Spry Collapsible Panel button to insert the first Collapsible Panel widget (Figure 7–7).

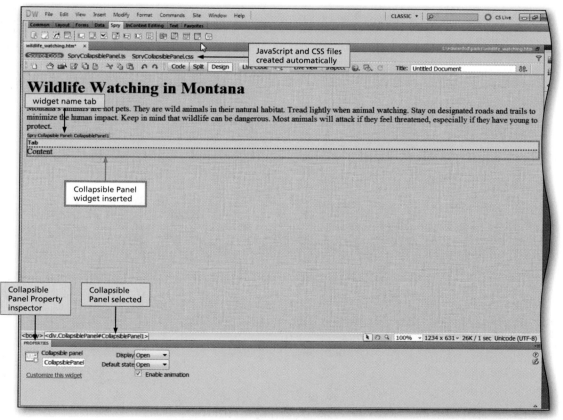

Figure 7–7

- If necessary, click the widget name tab to select the Collapsible Panel widget.

- Double-click the Collapsible panel text box in the Property inspector to select the default name, and then type **black_bear** to name the widget.

- Press the TAB key to accept the new name (Figure 7–8).

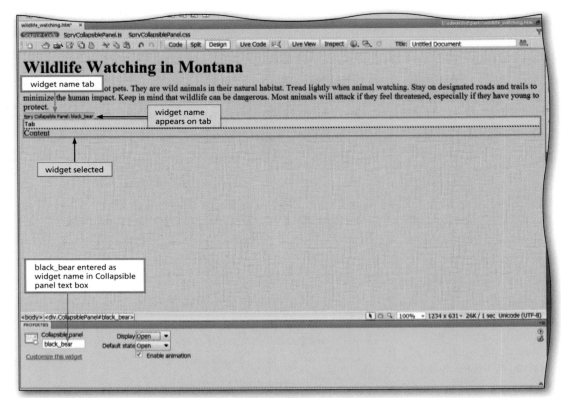

Figure 7–8

- In the Collapsible Panel widget, move the mouse pointer to the end of the Tab box to display the closed-eye icon (Figure 7–9).

Q&A What does the eye icon indicate?

An open-eye icon indicates that the Content box in the collapsible panel is open on the Web

Figure 7–9

page as you are developing it. A closed-eye icon indicates that the Content box is closed on the Web page, which hides the content as you are developing the Web page.

7

- If necessary, click the eye icon to close the panel so you can focus on changing the properties of the tab, not the contents of the panel.

- Double-click the word Tab in the Collapsible Panel widget.

- In the tag inspector, click <div. CollapsiblePanelTab> to select the tab only and to display the Div ID Property inspector.

- Type **black_ bear_tab** in the Div ID box to name the tab, and then press the TAB key to name the panel tab (Figure 7–10).

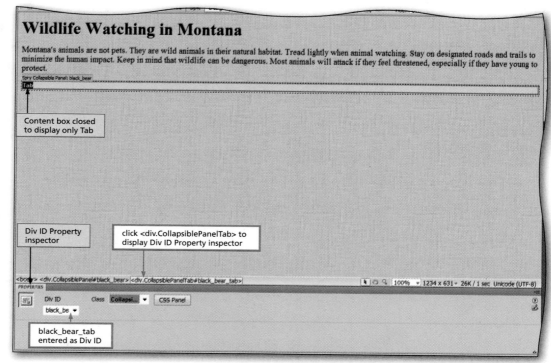

Figure 7–10

8

- Move the mouse pointer to the end of the Tab box to display the eye icon.

- Click the eye icon to display the Content box.

- Click the widget name tab to select the entire black_ bear collapsible panel (Figure 7–11).

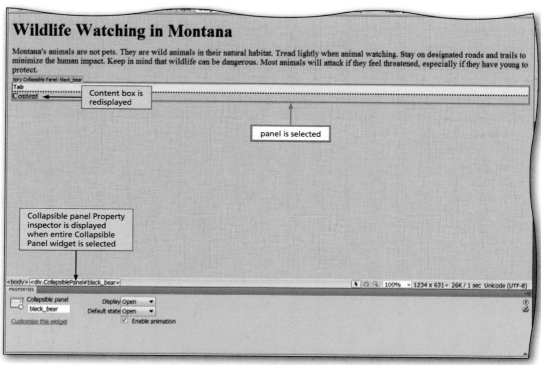

Figure 7–11

9

- Click the Spry Collapsible Panel button on the Spry toolbar to add a second panel directly below the first panel (Figure 7–12).

Q&A

Why does the second panel overlap the first panel?

Only the name tab of the second panel overlaps the first panel. The name tab does not appear in the browser window, so the tab will appear properly placed when the Web page is displayed.

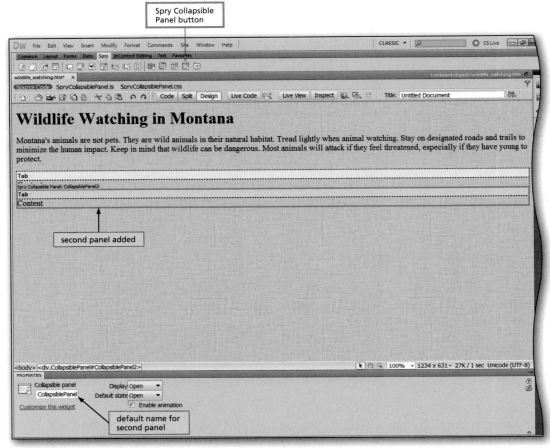

Figure 7–12

10

- Verify that the second collapsible panel is selected.

- Select the default name in the Collapsible panel text box in the Property inspector, type **moose**, and then press the TAB key to name the second panel (Figure 7–13).

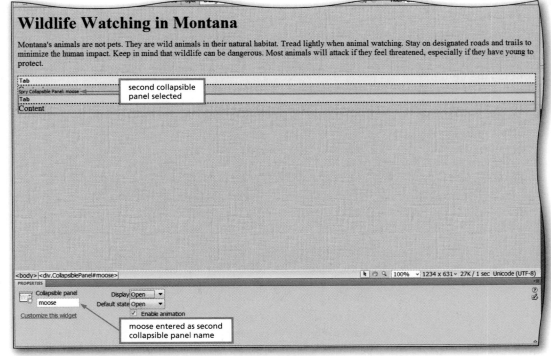

Figure 7–13

- Verify that the second collapsible panel still is selected.

- Click the Spry Collapsible Panel button on the Spry toolbar to add a third panel directly below the second panel.

- Select the default name in the Collapsible panel text box in the Property inspector, type **mountain_lion**, and then press the TAB key to name the third panel (Figure 7–14).

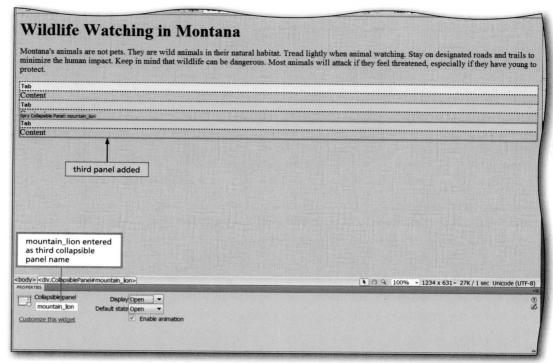

Figure 7–14

Other Ways
1. On Insert menu, point to Spry, click Spry Collapsible Panel

Panel Headings

Each panel contains a heading with "Tab" as the default text. To identify the content of each panel, you need to change "Tab" to a more descriptive name.

To Add the Panel Headings

The following steps change the Tab text to text that identifies the panel content.

- Double-click the text, Tab, in the first panel to select the text (Figure 7–15).

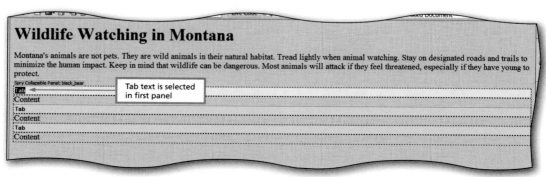

Figure 7–15

2

- Type **Black Bear** to provide a descriptive heading for the first panel.

- Double-click the Tab text in the second panel and then type **Moose** to add the second panel heading.

- Double-click the Tab text in the third panel and then type **Mountain Lion** to add the third panel heading.

Figure 7–16

Q&A What is the effect of entering the panel heading text?

This text appears on the Web page whether the panel is open or closed.

- Click the Save button on the Standard toolbar to save your work and display the Copy Dependent Files dialog box.

Q&A Why is the Copy Dependent Files dialog box displayed?

Dreamweaver displays this dialog box to remind you about the files you need to upload to the server when you publish the page.

- Click the OK button to copy the files (Figure 7–16).

Q&A What are the dependent files that Dreamweaver copies?

The file with a CSS filename extension is the CSS file that specifies the appearance of the widget. The file with a JS filename extension is the JavaScript file that controls how the widget responds to user actions. When you insert a widget, Dreamweaver links these files to the page so that the widget works correctly and is styled to suit the page.

Using the Paste Special Command

To save time and ensure accuracy, you can add text to a Web page from a source such as another Dreamweaver file, a basic text file, or a document created in a program such as Microsoft Word or Microsoft Excel.

Plan
Ahead

Add text to a Web page from another source.
In this chapter and in previous chapters, you have typed text directly into the document. Dreamweaver, however, also provides other options, including the following techniques, for adding text to a Dreamweaver document:

- **Copy or move text from another Dreamweaver document:** You can copy or cut text from one Dreamweaver document and paste the text into another Dreamweaver document.

- **Copy or move text from another type of text document:** You can copy or cut text from a text-editing program such as TextEdit, WordPad, Notepad, or even your e-mail program and then paste it into a Dreamweaver document.

- **Import text:** You can import tabular data or complete text files from other programs such as Microsoft Office Word or Microsoft Office Excel. If the text is updated frequently, consider creating a link to the document instead of importing or copying and pasting the text.

To control the format of text that you paste into a Dreamweaver document, you can use the Paste Special command on the Edit menu. This command lets you specify the format of the pasted text using the following four options:

- **Text only** This option pastes text without any formatting, and is the most basic of the four options. Line breaks and paragraphs are ignored and the text is pasted as plain text in one long sentence. Choose this option when you want to use formatted text from another document, but want to apply styles to it in Dreamweaver.

- **Text with structure** This format can retain structural text elements such as paragraphs, bulleted text, heaters/footers, lists, and tables. Formatting such as bold and italics is not preserved.

- **Text with structure plus basic formatting** This format includes the same elements as Text with structure, but also includes additional formatting options such as bold, italics, and underlining. Choose this option to paste Microsoft Word or Excel data with basic formatting.

- **Text with structure plus full formatting** This format includes the basic formatting options plus styles. In some instances, CSS information such as margins, font size, and font color are retained. Full formatting is available only when copying and pasting from a Word or Excel document.

To Copy and Paste Formatted Text with Paste Special

Next, you copy and paste text from a data file to a Dreamweaver page. The data file is available in three formats. Based on the programs available on your computer, you can select Microsoft Word 2010 (.docx and the same as Microsoft Word 2007), Microsoft Word 2003 (.doc), or a text file (.rtf). The Word 2010 file format is used in the following figures. The following steps show how to copy text from the data file and paste it into your Dreamweaver document.

- Use your word processing program or text-editing program to open one of the following three documents in the Chapter07\parks folder provided with your data files: wildlife_Office2010, wildlife_Office2003, or wildlife_text.

- Select the paragraph describing black bears in the data file.

- Press the CTRL+C keys to copy the selected paragraph (Figure 7–17).

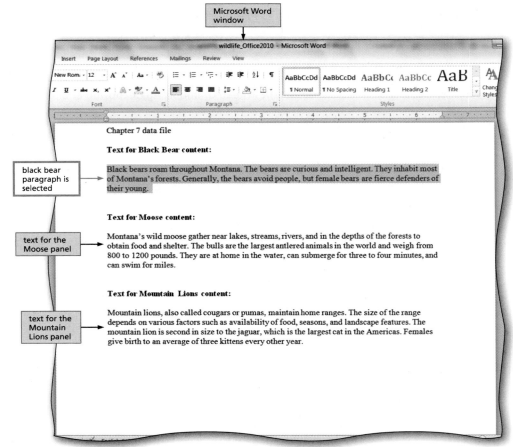

Figure 7–17

- Click the Adobe Dreamweaver CS5 program button on the taskbar to return to the wildlife_ watching page in Dreamweaver.

- In the black_bear Collapsible Panel widget, select the text, Content, below the Black Bear heading (Figure 7–18).

Figure 7–18

Q&A

The name tab from the second collapsible panel covers the Content text. How can I select it?

Click in the first collapsible panel, and then use the arrow keys to move to the Content box. Press and hold the SHIFT key while pressing an arrow key to select the text.

3

- Click Edit on the Application bar and then point to Paste Special to highlight the command (Figure 7–19).

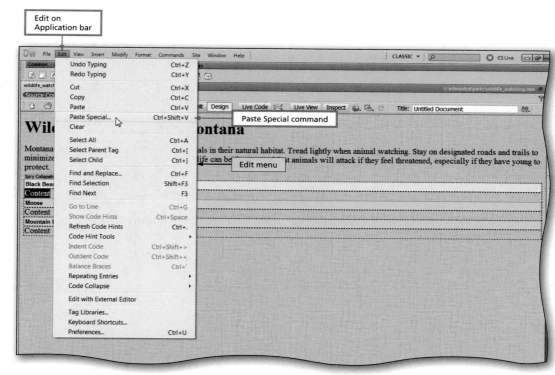

Figure 7–19

4

- Click Paste Special to display the Paste Special dialog box.

- Click the Text with structure plus full formatting (bold, italic, styles) option button (Figure 7–20).

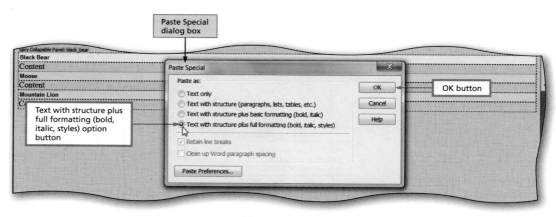

Figure 7–20

5

● Click the OK button to paste the text (Figure 7–21).

Q&A

Can I enter text by typing instead of copying and pasting it?

Yes, you can enter text directly by clicking in the panel, typing the text, and then formatting it using Dreamweaver's text formatting tools.

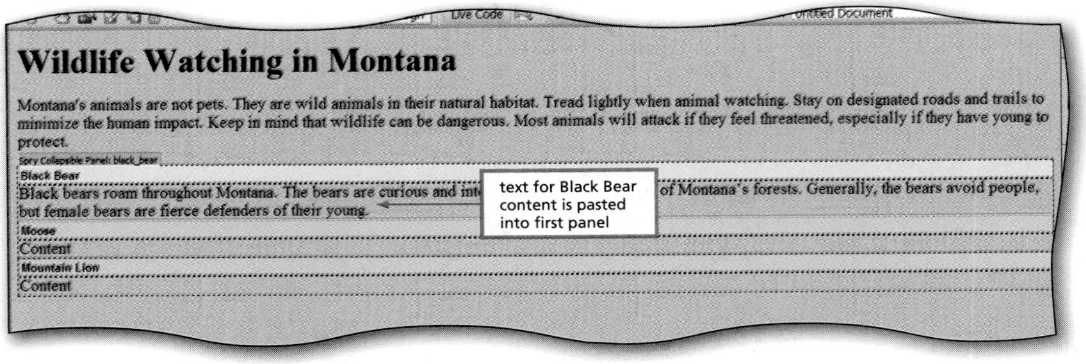

Wildlife Watching in Montana

Montana's animals are not pets. They are wild animals in their natural habitat. Tread lightly when animal watching. Stay on designated roads and trails to minimize the human impact. Keep in mind that wildlife can be dangerous. Most animals will attack if they feel threatened, especially if they have young to protect.

Spry Collapsible Panel: black_bear

Black Bear
Black bears roam throughout Montana. The bears are curious and int... [text for Black Bear content is pasted into first panel] ...of Montana's forests. Generally, the bears avoid people, but female bears are fierce defenders of their young.

Moose
Content

Mountain Lion
Content

Figure 7–21

6

● Repeat Steps 1–5 to copy the Moose and Mountain Lion text to the appropriate Content boxes (Figure 7–22).

Q&A

The Collapsible Panel widget seems similar to the Accordion widget. How are they different?

The Collapsible Panel widget can display more than one tab open at once, whereas the Accordion widget can display only one tab open at a time. Also, the Collapsible Panel widget can display tabs horizontally across the Web page instead of vertically. The Accordion widget can display tabs only vertically.

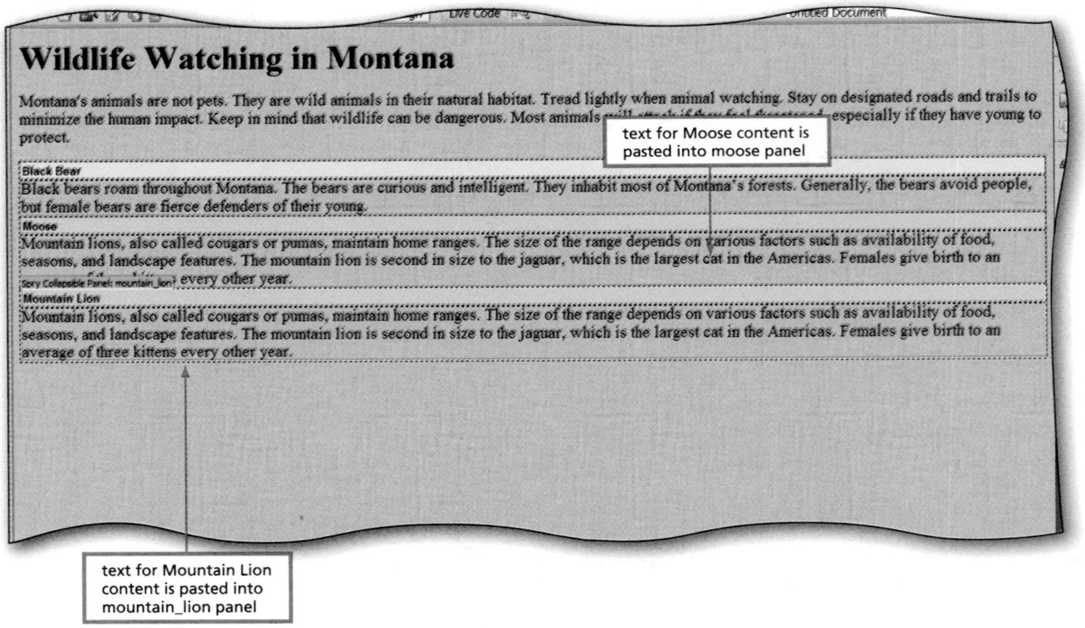

Wildlife Watching in Montana

Montana's animals are not pets. They are wild animals in their natural habitat. Tread lightly when animal watching. Stay on designated roads and trails to minimize the human impact. Keep in mind that wildlife can be dangerous. Most animals will attack if they feel threatened, especially if they have young to protect.

Black Bear
Black bears roam throughout Montana. The bears are curious and intelligent. They inhabit most of Montana's forests. Generally, the bears avoid people, but female bears are fierce defenders of their young.

Moose
Mountain lions, also called cougars or pumas, maintain home ranges. The size of the range depends on various factors such as availability of food, seasons, and landscape features. The mountain lion is second in size to the jaguar, which is the largest cat in the Americas. Females give birth to an [text for Moose content is pasted into moose panel]

Spry Collapsible Panel: mountain_lion ... every other year.

Mountain Lion
Mountain lions, also called cougars or pumas, maintain home ranges. The size of the range depends on various factors such as availability of food, seasons, and landscape features. The mountain lion is second in size to the jaguar, which is the largest cat in the Americas. Females give birth to an average of three kittens every other year. [text for Mountain Lion content is pasted into mountain_lion panel]

Figure 7–22

Other Ways

1. Press CTRL+SHIFT+V to select Paste Special options

To Add an Image and Descriptive Text to the Web Page

You want to provide an overview of where someone could see wildlife when visiting Montana. In the following steps, you add a map image, a sentence describing the image, and the Web page title.

1 Click below the third collapsible panel to place the insertion point. Type the following text: **The light-colored areas in the following map display the primary locations inhabited by the black bear, the moose, and the mountain lion.**

2 Apply Heading 3 to the text to format it.

3 Display the panel groups and then open the images folder in the Files panel, if necessary. Drag the montana_map03 file to the insertion point. Type **Montana map** for the Alt text in the Property inspector.

4 In the Title text box, enter **Montana Parks Wildlife** as the title of the Web page.

5 Collapse the panel groups and the Property inspector to provide room to work (Figure 7–23).

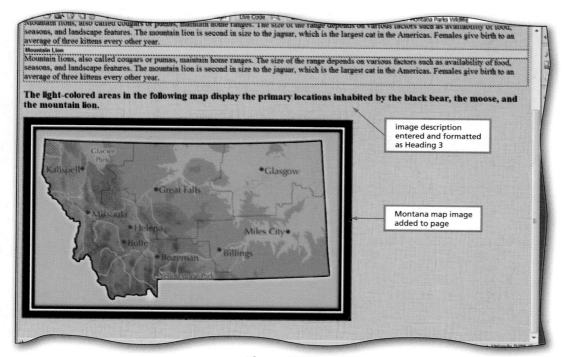

Figure 7–23

6 Click the Save button on the Standard toolbar to save the document.

7 Quit Word.

To View the Web Page in Your Browser

As you create your Web page, it always is a good idea to preview the content. This helps you to determine if the spacing is correct. In the following steps, you view the Web page in your browser and then expand and collapse the panels.

1

- Press the F12 key to view the Web page with expanded panels in your browser (Figure 7–24).

Q&A

What should I do if a message appears about allowing blocked content?

Click the message, click Allow Blocked Content, and then click the Yes button to confirm. When you are testing the Web pages created in this chapter, you can allow blocked content because you created the content yourself.

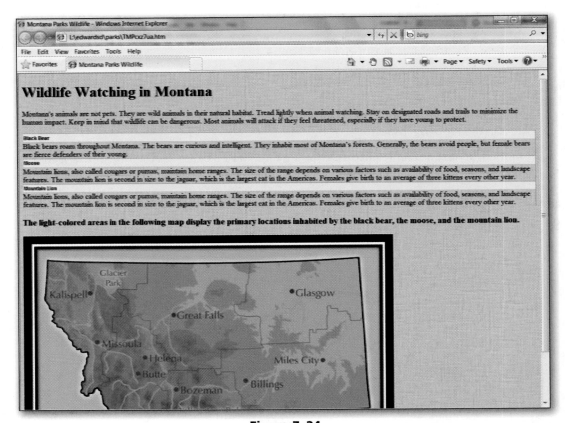

Figure 7–24

2

- Click the Black Bear tab to collapse the first panel (Figure 7–25).

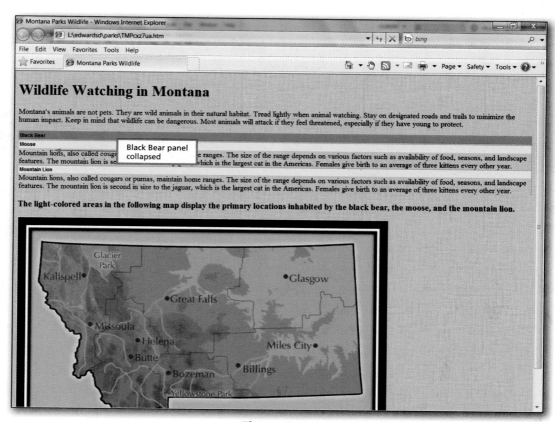

Figure 7–25

3

- Click the Moose tab to collapse the second panel.

- Click the Mountain Lion tab to collapse the third panel (Figure 7–26).

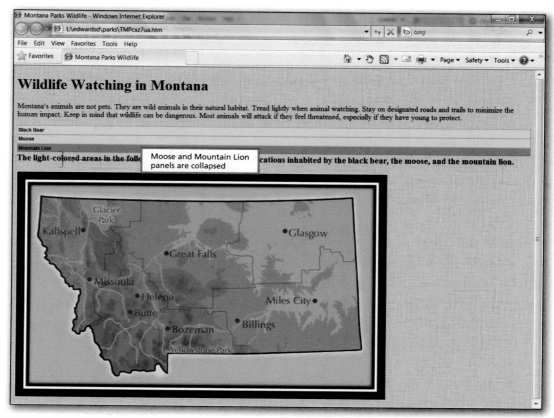

Figure 7–26

- Click the Black Bear tab again to expand the first panel (Figure 7–27).

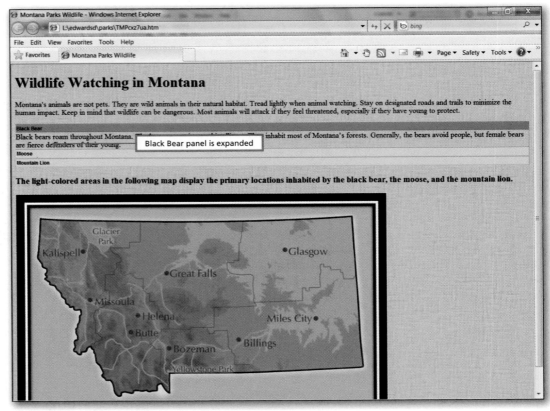

Figure 7–27

- Click the Moose and Mountain Lion tabs to expand the panels (Figure 7–28).

- Collapse all three panels and then close the browser.

- Close the wildlife_ watching document.

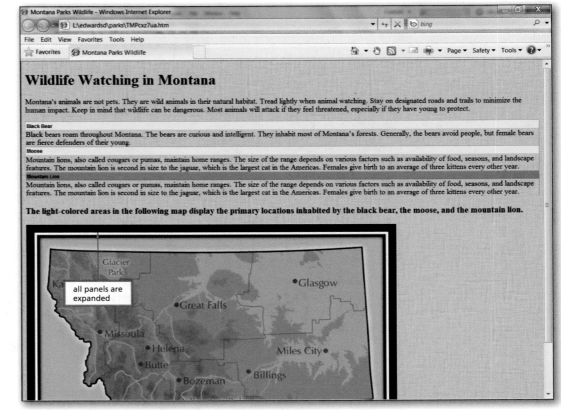

Figure 7–28

Using the Menu Bar Widget

As described previously, Dreamweaver also contains a Spry Menu Bar widget. You use this widget to create a fly-out menu, which is a menu that lists buttons horizontally or vertically along the menu bar. You point to a menu button to display a list of menu items. Each menu item can contain a submenu listing menu items. You use this type of menu to include a number of links within a small area of the screen, and to allow the Web site visitor to navigate quickly throughout the site's structure.

To Create the Montana Topics Page

The second new page that you add to your Web site will contain a horizontal navigational menu that provides links to a number of topics that visitors might find interesting. In the following instructions, you add a new page to the Montana Parks Web site and then add a background and text to the page.

1 Create a blank HTML page in the Montana Parks Web site. Save the page as montana_topics and enter **Montana Parks Topics of Interest** in the Title text box to provide the Web page title.

2 Display the Property inspector, and then apply the parks_bkg image to the background of the new page.

3 Type **Montana Parks** at the top of the page and then press ENTER to insert the first heading on the page.

4 Type **Topics of Interest** and then press ENTER to insert the second heading on the page.

5 Center and apply Heading 2 to both lines (Figure 7–29).

Figure 7–29

6 Open the topics_Office2010, topics_Office2003, or topics_text document provided with your data files, depending on what word processing program you have installed on your computer.

7 Select and copy the text, and then quit Word.

8 In the montana_topics page, click under the Topics of Interest heading to set the insertion point. Make sure the new line is left-aligned.

9 Click Edit on the Application bar, click Paste Special, and then select the Text with Structure plus full formatting (bold, italic, styles) option button. Click OK to paste the text.

10 Apply Heading 3 to the text you pasted, click at the end of the new text, and then press ENTER to start a new line.

11 Save the page (Figure 7–30).

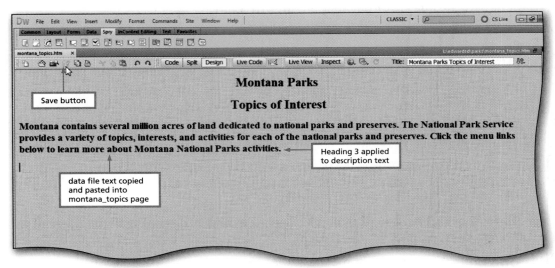

Figure 7–30

Designing Menu Bars

The Spry Menu Bar widget consists of a set of four main menu items, with each item a link for navigating the Web page. Each menu item can support two levels of menu options. To display menu options, the Web site visitor points to a menu item. To display a submenu, the Web site visitor points to a menu option. This enables the Web site visitor to quickly move from page to page and to pages located deep within the site's structure.

Adobe recommends that you include links only to the main pages of your Web site in the top level of the Menu Bar widget. Many people turn off JavaScript in their browsers, which means that only the top level of the menu bar appears on the page.

To Insert the Spry Menu Bar

The following steps illustrate how to add a horizontal Spry Menu Bar widget to the new montana_topics Web page.

1

- If necessary, click the Spry tab on the Insert bar to display the Spry toolbar.

- Click the Spry Menu Bar button to display the Spry Menu Bar dialog box (Figure 7–31).

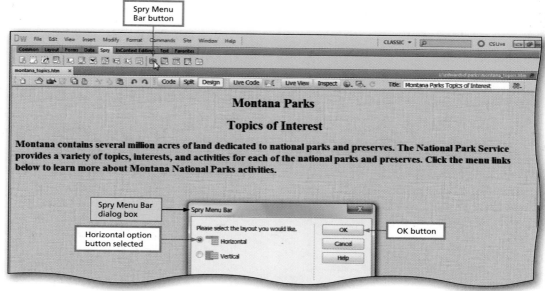

Figure 7–31

2

- If necessary, select the Horizontal option button to specify a horizontal layout.

- Click the OK button to insert a horizontal menu bar (Figure 7–32).

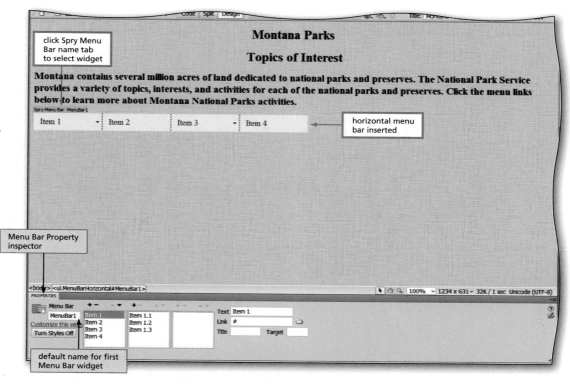

Figure 7–32

Other Ways

1. On Insert menu, point to Spry, click Spry Menu Bar

To Add Text and Links to the Menu Bar

Now that you have inserted the menu bar into your Web page, you can add text and links for the menu items. These links, when clicked, will be listed as options below each menu item. The first menu item will link to Webcams in Montana's national parks. To add text and links, you use the Menu Bar Property inspector.

- If necessary, select the Menu Bar widget by clicking the Spry Menu Bar tab above Item 1.

- Select the Menu Bar default name (such as MenuBar1) in the Property inspector, type **montana_ nav**, and then press the TAB key to name the Menu Bar widget (Figure 7–33).

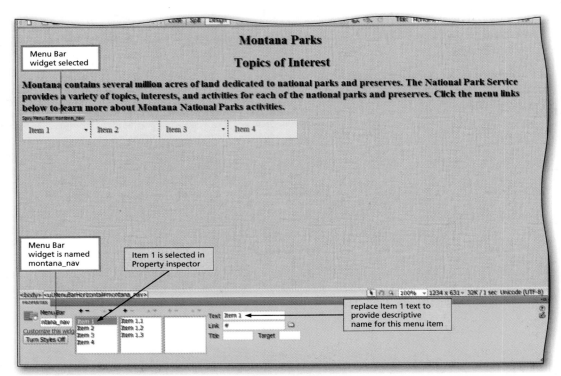

Figure 7–33

- Verify that Item 1 in the first list box is selected in the Property inspector.

- In the Text text box, select the Item 1 text, type **Webcams**, and then press the ENTER key to provide a name for the first menu item (Figure 7–34).

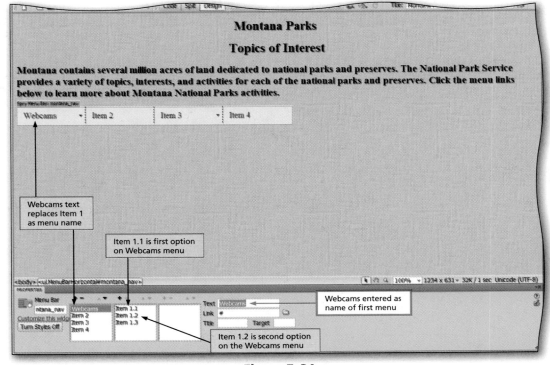

Figure 7–34

3

- In the Property inspector, click Item 1.1 to select it in the second list box.

- In the Text text box, select the Item 1.1 text and then type `Webcam01` to name the first option on the Webcams menu.

- Select the entry in the Link box, and then type `http:// www.nps.gov/glac/ photosmultimedia/ webcams.htm` to specify the link for the first menu option on the Webcams menu.

- Click the Target text box, type `Blank` to specify that the linked page opens in a new browser window, and then press the ENTER key (Figure 7–35).

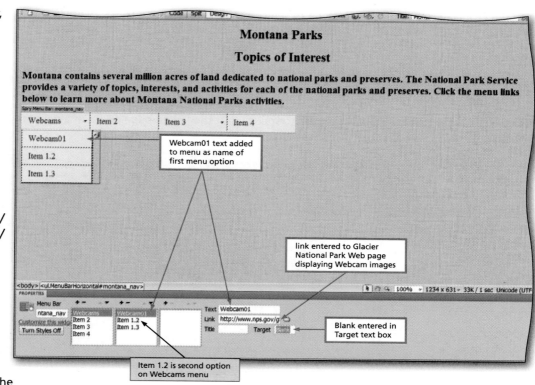

Figure 7–35

4

- In the Property inspector, click Item 1.2 to select it in the second list box.

- In the Text text box, select the Item 1.2 text, and then type `Webcam02` as the name of the second option on the Webcams menu.

- Select the entry in the Link text box, and then type `http:// www.tetoncam. com` to specify the link for the second menu option on the Webcams menu.

- Click the Target text box, type `Blank` to specify that the linked page opens in a new browser window, and then press the ENTER key (Figure 7–36).

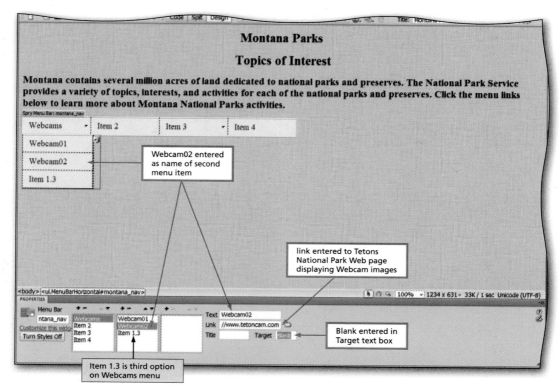

Figure 7–36

- In the Property inspector, click Item 1.3 to select it in the second list box.

- In the Text text box, select the Item 1.3 text, and then type `Webcam03` as the name of the third option on the Webcams menu.

- Select the entry in the Link text box, and then type `http://www.nationalparkreservations.com/info/glacier/index.php` to specify the link for the third menu option on the Webcams menu.

- Click the Target text box, type `Blank` to specify that the linked page opens in a new browser window, and then press the ENTER key.

- Click the Save button on the Standard toolbar to save your work and display the Copy Dependent Files dialog box.

- Click the OK button to copy the files (Figure 7–37).

Q&A

Why is the Copy Dependent Files dialog box displayed again?

Each time you insert a Spry widget on a Web page, Dreamweaver creates dependent files that you need to display the widget correctly. Be sure to copy the files by clicking the OK button in the Copy Dependent Files dialog box.

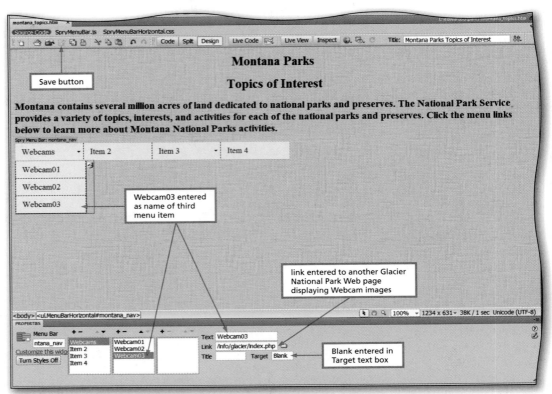

Figure 7–37

To Add Text and Links to Items 2 through 4

The following steps illustrate how to continue to build the menu by adding data for the remaining menu items.

1

- If necessary, select the Spry Menu Bar widget by clicking its name tab.

- Click Item 2 in the first list box in the Property inspector.

- In the Text text box, select the Item 2 text, type **Hiking** as the name of the second menu in the Menu Bar widget, and then press the TAB key to enter the name of the second menu.

- Point to the plus sign (the Add menu item button) above the second box to prepare for adding menu options to the Hiking menu (Figure 7–38).

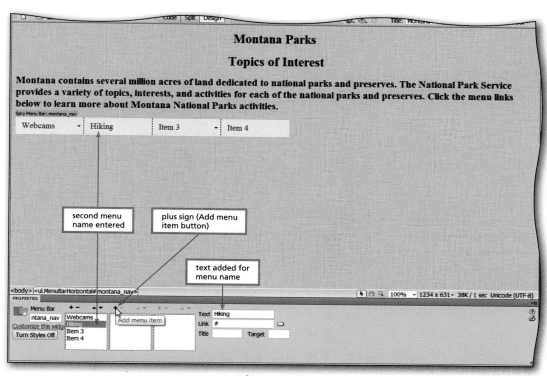

Figure 7–38

2

- In the Property inspector, click the plus sign (the Add menu item button) above the second list box to display Untitled Item, which is the placeholder text for the first option on the Hiking menu (Figure 7–39).

 Why doesn't the second menu item include options named Item 2.1, Item 2.2, and so on, as the first menu item did?

This design is determined by the default behavior and style provided by the Spry framework.

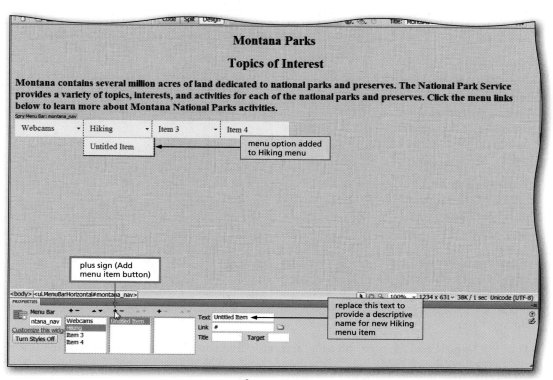

Figure 7–39

- In the Text text box, select the Untitled Item text, and then type **Bighorn Canyon** as the name of the first option on the Hiking menu.

- Select the entry in the Link text box, and then type **http:// www.nps.gov/ bica/** to specify the link for the first menu option on the Hiking menu.

- Click the Target text box, type **Blank** to specify that the linked page opens in a new browser window, and then press the ENTER key (Figure 7–40).

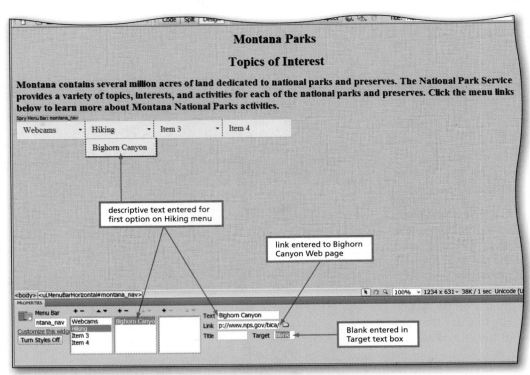

Figure 7–40

④

- In the Property inspector, click the plus sign above the second list box to add a second option to the Hiking menu.

- In the Text text box, select the Untitled Item text, and then type **Lake McDonald** as the name of the second option on the Hiking menu.

- Select the entry in the Link text box, and then type **http:// enjoyyourparks. com/ glaciermcdonald. html** to specify the link for the second menu option on the Hiking menu.

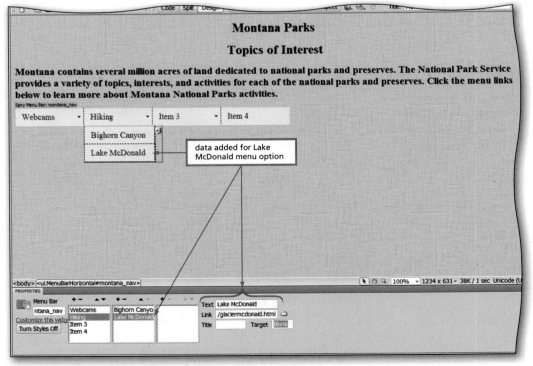

Figure 7–41

- Click the Target text box, type **Blank** to specify that the linked page opens in a new browser window, and then press the ENTER key (Figure 7–41).

Q&A If I enter text in the Title text box, where does it appear on the Web page?

When you enter text in the Title text box for a menu item, that text appears in a ToolTip when users point to the menu option on the Web page.

5

- In the Property inspector, click Item 3 in the first list box to prepare for adding a third menu item.

- In the Text text box, select the Item 3 text, and then type **Nature Trails** as the name of the third menu item.

- Click Item 3.1 in the second list box to select it.

- In the Text text box, select the Item 3.1 text, and then type **Cracker Lake** to name the first option on the Nature Trails menu.

- Select the entry in the Link text box, and then type **http://www.nps.gov/archive/glac/maps/crackerl.htm** to specify the link for the first menu on the Nature Trails menu.

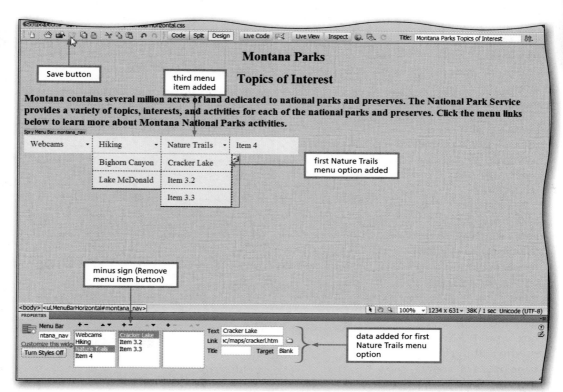

Figure 7–42

Q&A Should I enter the number 1 or the letter l at the end of the URL?

Be sure to enter the letter l in the crackerl.htm part of the URL.

- Click the Target text box, type **Blank** to specify that the linked page opens in a new browser window, and then press the ENTER key.

Q&A Why does the Cracker Lake menu option include a submenu?

By default, the first option on the third menu item includes a submenu.

- In the third list box, click Item 3.1.1 to select it, and then click the minus sign (Remove menu item button) to delete the first submenu option.

- With Item 3.1.2 selected, click the minus sign to delete the second submenu option.

- Click the Save button on the Standard toolbar to save the file (Figure 7–42).

6

• In the Property inspector, click Item 3.2 in the second list box to select it.

• In the Text text box, select the Item 3.2 text, and then type **Trail of the Cedars** to name the second option on the Nature Trails menu.

• Select the entry in the Link text box, and then type **http:// www.nps.gov/ archive/ glac/eHikes/ avalanche/ avalanche2.htm** to specify the link for the second option on the Nature Trails menu.

• Click the Target text box, type **Blank** to specify that the linked page opens in a new browser window, and then press the ENTER key (Figure 7–43).

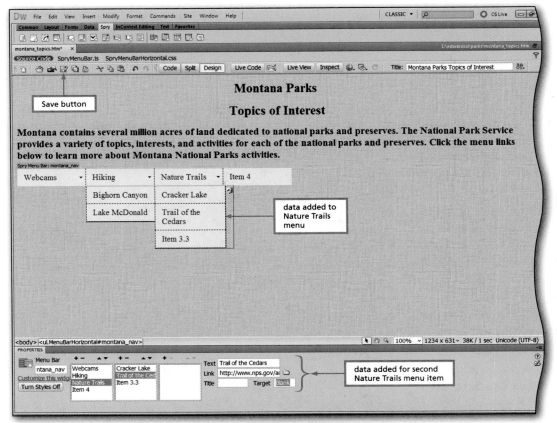

Figure 7–43

Q&A

Can I create a Menu Bar widget that lists the menu options vertically from top to bottom on a Web page instead of horizontally from left to right?

Yes, you can create a vertical Menu Bar widget as well as a horizontal Menu Bar widget. Recall that after you clicked the Spry Menu Bar button on the Insert tab, the Spry Menu Bar dialog box was displayed. Click the Vertical option button to insert a vertical Menu Bar widget.

7

- In the second list box in the Property inspector, click Item 3.3 to select it.

- In the Text text box, select the Item 3.3 text, type **Rainbow Falls** to name the third option on the Nature Trails menu, and then press the ENTER key to select Rainbow Falls and to prepare for adding submenu options to the Rainbow Falls option.

- Click the plus sign above the third list box to add Untitled Item to the list of submenu options.

- Select Untitled Item in the Text text box, and then type **Goat Haunt Montana** to name the first option on the Rainbow Falls submenu.

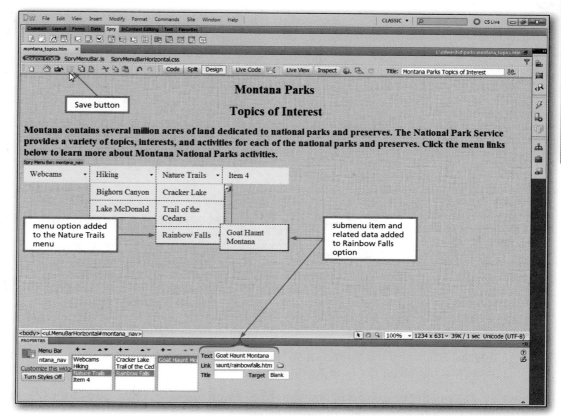

Figure 7–44

- Select the entry in the Link text box, and then type **http://www.glacierparkinformation.com/goat_haunt/rainbowfalls.htm** to specify the link for the option on the Rainbow Falls submenu.

- Click the Target text box, type **Blank** to specify that the linked page opens in a new browser window, and then press the ENTER key.

- Click the Save button on the Standard toolbar to save the file (Figure 7–44).

Q&A

What would happen if I did not enter Blank in the Target text box?

Dreamweaver would apply the default Target setting, which is Self. When you click a menu option, such as Goat Haunt Montana, the Goat Haunt Montana Web page would open in the same browser window as the current page, the Montana Parks Topics of Interest page in this case.

- If necessary, select the Spry Menu Bar widget and then click Item 4 in the Property inspector to prepare for adding a fourth menu on the menu bar.

- In the Text text box, select the Item 4 text, type **Auto Touring** as the name of the fourth menu in the Menu Bar widget, and then press the TAB key.

Figure 7–45

- In the Property inspector, click the plus sign above the second list box to add the first option to the Auto Touring menu.

- In the Text text box, select the Untitled Item text, and then type **Big Hole National Battlefield** as the name of the first option on the Auto Touring menu.

- Select the entry in the Link text box, and then type **http://www.nps.gov/biho/index.htm** to specify the link for the first option on the Auto Touring menu.

- Click the Target text box, type **Blank** to specify that the linked page opens in a new browser window, and then press the ENTER key.

- Click the plus sign above the second list box to add the second option to the Auto Touring menu.

- In the Text text box, select the Untitled Item text, and then type **Glacier National Park** as the name of the second option on the Auto Touring menu.

- Select the entry in the Link text box, and then type **http://www.nps.gov/glac/index.htm** to specify the link for the second option on the Auto Touring menu.

- Click the Target text box, type **Blank** to specify that the linked page opens in a new browser window, and then press the ENTER key (Figure 7–45).

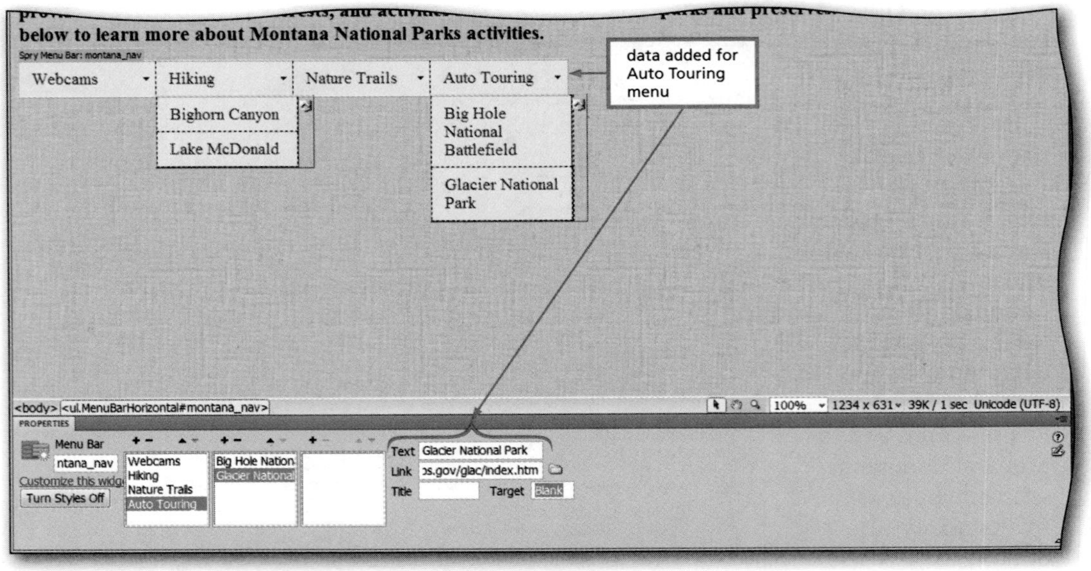

9

- Click the plus sign above the third box in the Property inspector to display Untitled Item as the submenu option for the Glacier National Park menu option (Figure 7–46).

Q&A

Can I change the order of the menu and submenu options?

Yes. Click a menu option to select it, and then click the Move item up or Move item down button in the Property inspector to change the order.

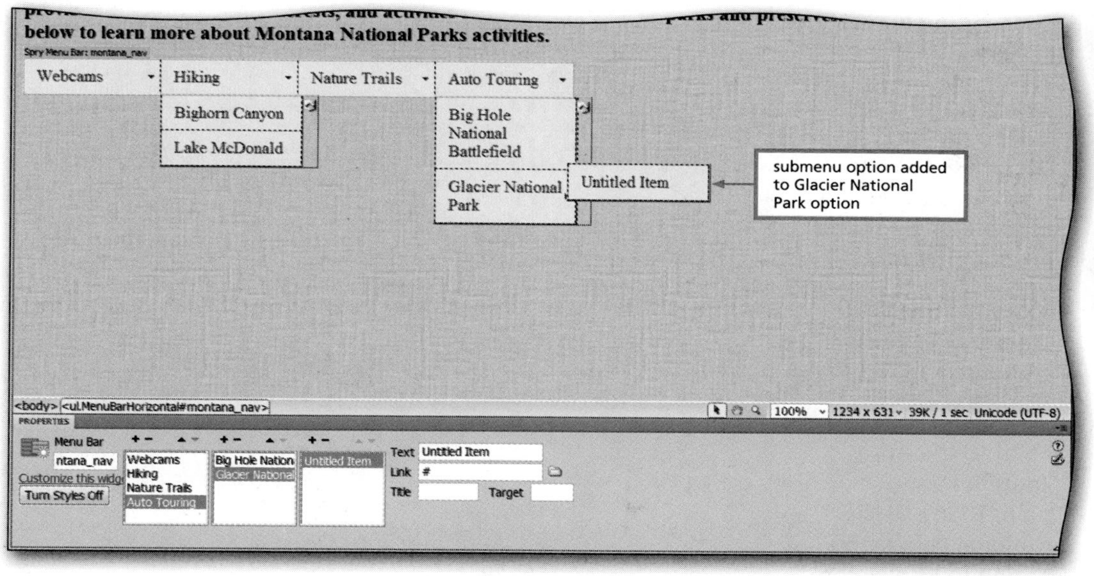

Figure 7–46

10

- In the Text text box, select the Untitled Item text, and then type **Guided Tours** as the name of the submenu option.

- Select the entry in the Link text box, and then type **http://www. nps.gov/wrst/ planyourvisit/ guidedtours. htm** to specify the link for the submenu option.

- Click the Target text box, type **Blank** to specify that the linked page opens in a new browser window, and then press the ENTER key.

- Click the Save button on the Standard toolbar to save the file (Figure 7–47).

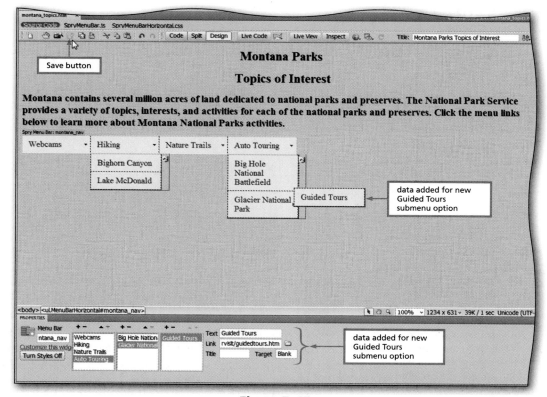

Figure 7–47

11

- Collapse the Property inspector.

- Click the Live View button on the Document toolbar to view the document as it would be displayed in your browser.

- Move the mouse pointer over each menu item in the Menu Bar widget.

- Point to the Auto Touring menu, point to the Glacier National Park menu option to display the submenu, and then point to the Guided Tours link (Figure 7–48).

12

- Press the F12 key to view the page in a browser, and then allow blocked content, if necessary.

- Check each of the links to verify that they work, and then close the browser.

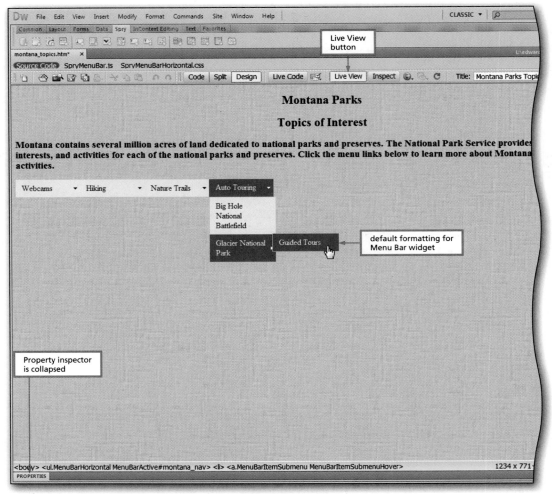

Figure 7–48

Customizing the Menu Bar Widget

You can customize the Menu Bar widget and many other widgets. You can set properties for the entire Menu Bar widget or for individual components only. If you are familiar with JavaScript and CSS, you can modify the text within the appropriate JavaScript or CSS file located in the SpryAssets folder. A simpler way to customize the widget is to use the CSS Styles panel. This requires some detective work, however, to determine which CSS rules apply to what element. For example, the ul.MenuBarHorizontal rule specifies the properties for the outermost container of the menu bar. The ul.MenuBarHorizontal li rule specifies the properties for the top-level menu items. The ul.MenuBarHorizontal ul rule specifies the properties for the menu options.

Plan Ahead

Edit and format Spry widgets.
After inserting a Spry widget on a Web page, you can use the Property inspector and the CSS Styles panel to edit and format the widget. For example, you can make the following changes to a Menu Bar widget:

- **Add or delete menu options and submenu options:** Use the same techniques you used to enter the initial menu option information — select a menu item or option name, and then use the plus or minus buttons to add or remove options.

- **Change the order of the menu options:** Select a menu item or option name, and then use the Move item up and Move item down buttons to change the order of the menu options.

- **Format the text:** You format menu text by using the CSS Styles panel to change the default CSS style properties. You can change the font, font size, and text color for example.

- **Format the menu bar:** You can also use the CSS Styles panel to change the background color of menu items when they are inactive, when the user points to an item, and when the user clicks an item.

To Customize the Font Style and Size of the Menu Bar Widget

The following steps illustrate how to modify the menu bar's font style and size.

1

- Click the Live View button to turn off Live View.

- Expand the panel groups so you can access the CSS Styles tab.

- Double-click the Files tab in the panel groups to collapse the Files panel.

- Double-click the CSS Styles tab and then click the All button, if necessary, to display all the CSS style rules on the page.

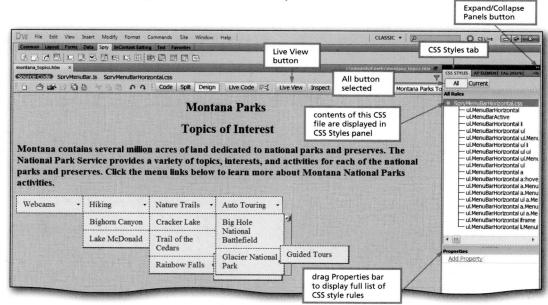

Figure 7–49

- Click the plus sign next to SpryMenuBarHorizontal.css to expand the styles for the Menu Bar widget.

- If necessary, drag the Properties bar down to display the complete list of CSS style rules (Figure 7–49).

Q&A

How can I learn which CSS rule to select to customize a particular part of the Menu Bar widget?

Dreamweaver Help provides detailed information about the CSS rules used in the Spry widgets. Press the F1 key to open Dreamweaver Help, and then search for the widget item you want to change. To learn about the text styles for menu items, for example, search for *change text styling of a menu item*.

• In the CSS Styles panel, locate and then click the ul.MenuBarHorizontal li rule to display the properties for the top-level menu bar items (Figure 7–50).

Q&A

Some of the submenus are not displayed as they are in Figure 7–50. Is that a problem?

No. If you deselect the Menu Bar widget, and then reselect it, Dreamweaver does not display the submenus.

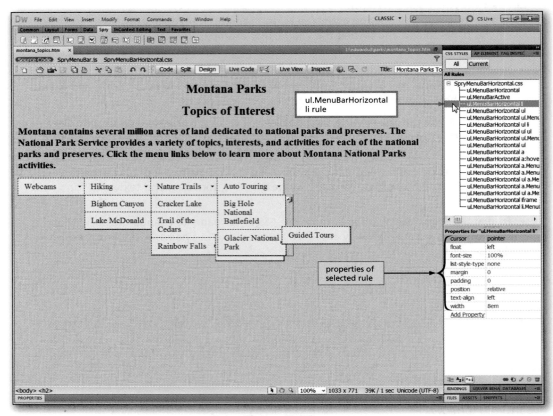

Figure 7–50

• Click to the right of the font-size property to display two list boxes (Figure 7–51).

Q&A

What am I changing when I select the ul.MenuBarHorizontal li rule and then change its properties?

The ul.MenuBarHorizontal li rule specifies settings for all menu items in a horizontal menu bar. (You would use the ul.MenuBarVertical li rule for a vertical menu bar.) In this case, you are changing the size of the text for all menu items.

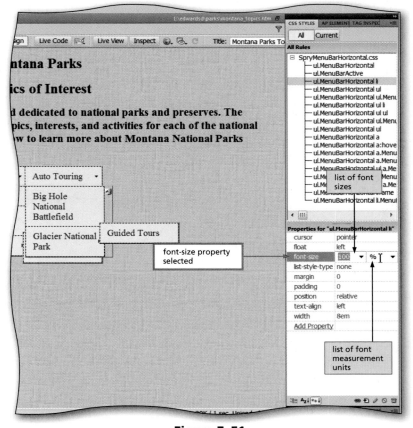

Figure 7–51

4

- Click the arrow on the right and then point to pt (Figure 7–52).

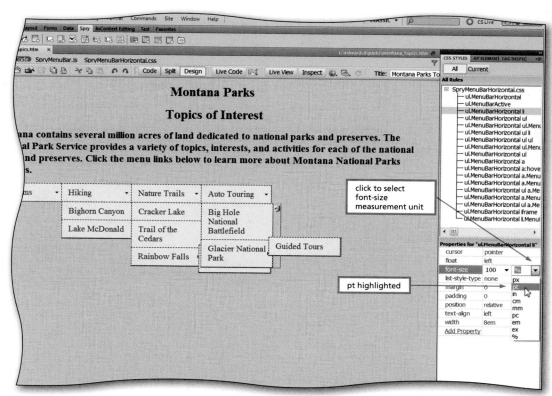

Figure 7–52

5

- Click pt to select pt as the font-size measurement unit.

- Click the arrow on the left to display the font size, and then click 14 to change the font size of the top-level menu items (Figure 7–53).

Q&A

Why do the menu and submenu options also appear in 14-point text?

They display the same size as the menu items by default. However, it is good practice to specifically set a size for the menu and submenu options.

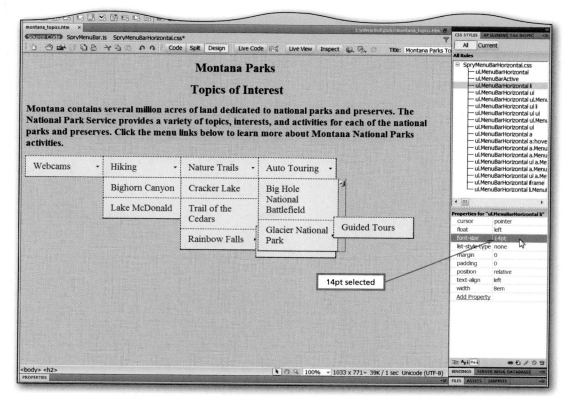

Figure 7–53

6

- In the CSS Styles panel, click the ul.MenuBarHorizontal ul rule to display the properties for the menu options.

- Repeat Steps 3–5 to change the font size of the menu options to 14pt.

- Click the Save All button on the Standard toolbar to save the CSS file (Figure 7–54).

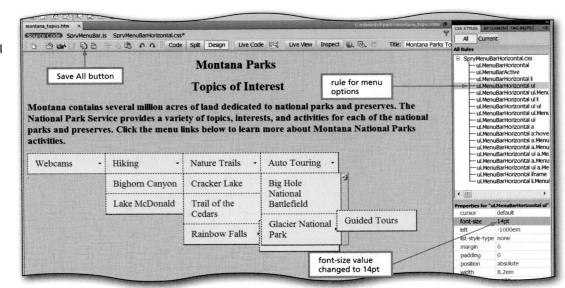

Figure 7–54

To Change the Menu Background Color

The ul.MenuBarHorizontal a rule specifies the color scheme (including background color), border, and fonts for menu items. The three-part rule called ul.MenuBarHorizontal a.MenuBarItemHover, ul.MenuBarHorizontal a.MenuBarItemSubmenuHover, ul.MenuBarHorizontal a.MenuBarSubmenuVisible specifies the same properties for selected menu items. Complete the following steps to change the background color of the menu.

1

- If necessary, select the menu bar on the Montana Parks page.

- Click the ul.MenuBarHorizontal a rule to display its properties (Figure 7–55).

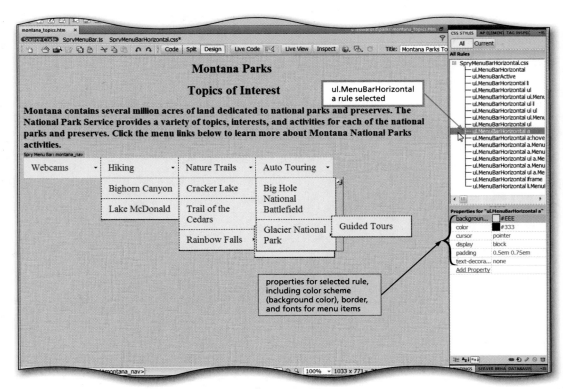

Figure 7–55

2

- Click the background-color box to display the color palette.

- Move the pointer to #3C6 (column 11, row 3 in the main palette), a shade of green (Figure 7–56).

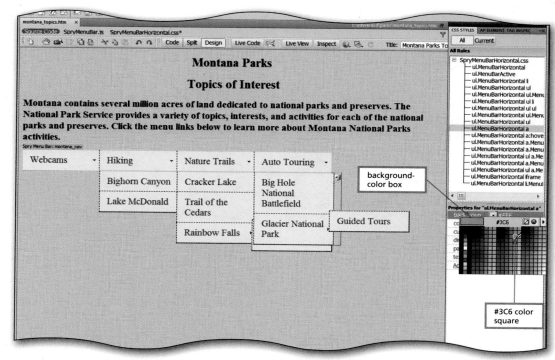

Figure 7–56

3

- Click the #3C6 color square to apply the background color to the menu items and options (Figure 7–57).

Can I add properties to the Properties list on the CSS Styles panel?

Yes. Click the Add Property link in the Properties list, and then click the arrow button to select a property from the list or enter the name of the property. You can also select or enter the property attribute. For example, you can add the font-weight property to the Properties list, and then select the bolder attribute.

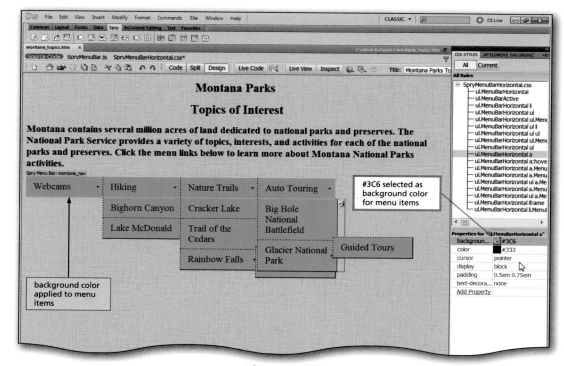

Figure 7–57

4

- Click the Live View button on the Document toolbar to display the page in Live View.

- Move the mouse pointer over the menu and note that the background color is blue when each menu item is selected, which is the default background color (Figure 7–58).

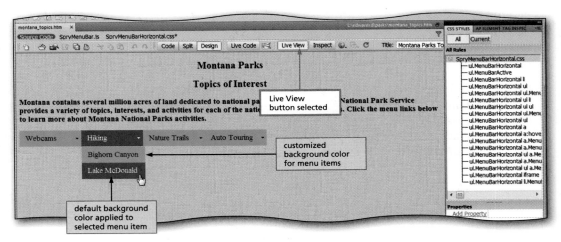

Figure 7–58

5

- In the CSS Styles panel, click the ul.MenuBarHorizontal a.MenuBarItemHover, ul.MenuBarHorizontal a.MenuBarItemSubmenuHover, ul.MenuBarHorizontal a.MenuBarSubmenuVisible rule (rule 12 from the top) to select it.

- Click the background-color box and then point to #9C0 (column 5, row 7 in the main part of the palette), a lighter shade of green (Figure 7–59).

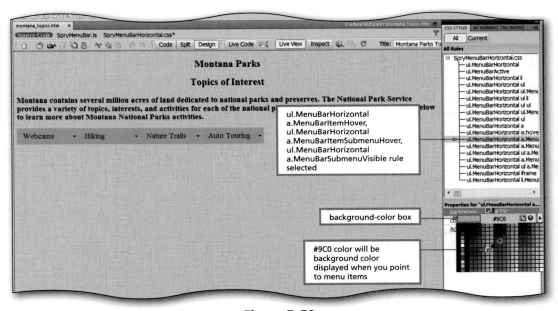

Figure 7–59

6

- Click the #9C0 color square to select that color as the background color to display when you point to a menu item.

- Click the color property in the Properties list to set the text color displayed when you point to a menu item.

- Select the entry to the right of the color box, type #000 and then press the ENTER key to specify black as the text color.

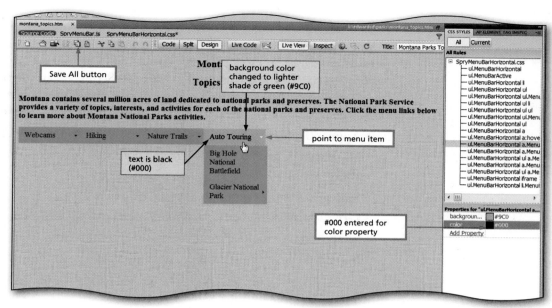

Figure 7–60

- In the Document window, click the menu to activate it, and then point to the Auto Touring menu item to verify that the background color is light green and the text is black when you point to a menu option (Figure 7–60).

7

- Click the Save All button on the Standard toolbar to save all your changes.

- Press the F12 key to view the Web page in your browser.

- Allow blocked content, if necessary, and then point to each menu item (Figure 7–61).

8

- Close the browser.

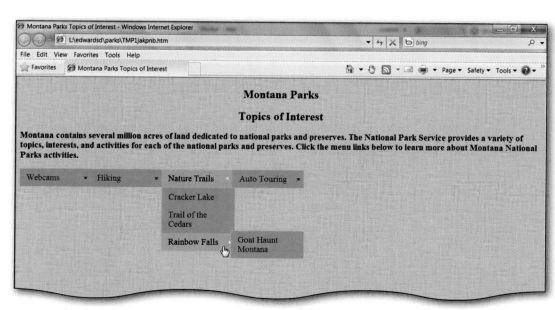

Figure 7–61

Spry Effects

Besides adding Spry widgets to Web pages, you can add **Spry effects**, which are visual enhancements and animations you can apply to text and other elements on a Web page. Dreamweaver uses JavaScript to apply effects to HTML elements without needing additional custom tags so that you do not need to learn JavaScript. When you perform an action, such as clickingtext, the browser only needs to update the text or other element that includes an effect, not the entire Web page. Dreamweaver includes the following Spry effects:

- **Appear/Fade** Gradually displays or fades the text or other element
- **Highlight** Changes the background color of the text or element
- **Blind** Hides or reveals text or another element
- **Slide** Moves the text or element up or down
- **Grow/Shrink** Increases or reduces the size of the text or element
- **Shake** Shakes the text or element from left to right
- **Squish** Fades the text or element into the upper-left corner of the page

You practice applying specific Spry effects in Chapter 8. To apply a Spry effect, you would perform the following general steps:

1. Select the content, such as text, or a layout element, such as a list.
2. Open the Behaviors panel, if necessary, by clicking Window on the Application bar, and then clicking Behaviors. In the Behaviors panel, click the Plus button, point to Effects, and then select a Spry effect.
3. To apply the effect to the selected element, make sure <Current Selection> appears as the target. Otherwise, click the target button and then select the ID of the element to which you want to apply the Spry effect. A dialog box is displayed where you can select settings appropriate for the effect.
4. Select settings to create the effect you want, and then click OK.

Note that some of these effects can be applied only to certain elements. Search for *Spry effects* in the Dreamweaver Help to find detailed information about each Spry effect.

To Close the Web Site and Quit Dreamweaver

After you create your interactive Web pages using Spry widgets, and test and verify that the widgets work, Chapter 7 is complete. The following step closes the Web site and quits Dreamweaver.

1 Click the Close button in the upper-right corner of the Dreamweaver title bar to close the Dreamweaver window, the document window, and the Montana Parks Web site.

Chapter Summary

In this chapter, you learned about the Spry widgets available in Dreamweaver. You added a Collapsible Panel widget to a Web page, and then inserted meaningful labels on the panel's tabs. You also inserted text on the page by copying and pasting it from a Microsoft Word document. Next, you added a Menu Bar widget to a new Web page, and then customized and formatted the widget. The items listed below include all the new skills you have learned in this chapter.

1. Add the Spry Collapsible Panel widget (DW 506)
2. Add the panel headings (DW 511)
3. Copy and paste formatted text with Paste Special (DW 514)
4. Insert the Spry Menu Bar (DW 523)
5. Add text and links to the menu bar (DW 524)
6. Customize the font style and size of the Menu Bar widget (DW 535)
7. Change the menu background color (DW 538)

Learn It Online

Test your knowledge of chapter content and key terms.

Instructions: To complete the Learn It Online exercises, start your browser, click the Address bar, and then enter the Web address scsite.com/dwCS5/learn. When the Dreamweaver CS5 Learn It Online page is displayed, click the link for the exercise you want to complete and then read the instructions.

Chapter Reinforcement TF, MC, and SA

A series of true/false, multiple choice, and short answer questions that test your knowledge of the chapter content.

Flash Cards

An interactive learning environment where you identify chapter key terms associated with displayed definitions.

Practice Test

A series of multiple choice questions that test your knowledge of chapter content and key terms.

Who Wants To Be a Computer Genius?

An interactive game that challenges your knowledge of chapter content in the style of a television quiz show.

Wheel of Terms

An interactive game that challenges your knowledge of chapter key terms in the style of the television show *Wheel of Fortune*.

Crossword Puzzle Challenge

A crossword puzzle that challenges your knowledge of key terms presented in the chapter.

Apply Your Knowledge

Reinforce the skills and apply the concepts you learned in this chapter.

Adding Content to a Spry Collapsible Panel

Instructions: In this activity you create a new Web page, and add a background, two collapsible panels, and data. Figure 7–62a shows the panel expanded and Figure 7–62b shows the panel collapsed.

Figure 7–62a

Figure 7–62b

Perform the following tasks:

1. If necessary, start Dreamweaver and then open the Apply Exercises Web site. Create a new, blank HTML page and then save it as apply_ch07.htm.

2. Apply the apply_bkg image to the background of the Web page.

3. Type `Green Cleaning Tips` at the top of the page and then press the ENTER key. Apply the Heading 1 style to the heading text you just entered, and then center the heading.

4. Click below the heading, and then click the Spry Collapsible Panel button on the Spry toolbar to insert a Spry Collapsible Panel widget.

5. Enter `green_tips` as the name of the Collapsible Panel widget.

6. Select the text, Tab, in the panel and then type `Use Household Ingredients` as the panel heading.

7. Select the text, Content, in the panel and then type the following text: `Vinegar, lemon juice, baking soda, Borax, Castille soap, olive oil and many things you have in your pantry can all be used to create non-toxic cleaning solutions inexpensively.`

8. Insert a second collapsible panel below the first one. Enter `recipes` as the name of the Collapsible Panel widget.

9. Select the text, Tab, in the second panel and then type `Featured Recipe` as the panel heading.

10. Select the text, Content, in the second panel and then type the following text: `Furniture Polish: in a new, clean spray bottle, mix 1 cup olive oil and 1/2 cup lemon juice. Shake well before each use. Apply mixture to the cleaning cloth.`

11. Title the Web page `Green Cleaning Tips`.

12. Bold the two content sentences.

13. Save the document, copy dependent files if necessary, and then view the page in your browser. Allow blocked content, if necessary. Click each tab to collapse the panels.

14. Submit the document in the format specified by your instructor.

Extend Your Knowledge

Extend the skills you learned in this chapter and experiment with new skills. You may need to use Help to complete the assignment.

Adding a Spry Menu Bar to a New Web Page

Instructions: In this activity, create a Web page and then add a Spry Menu Bar. You will customize the menu bar by deleting items, reordering items, adding a link to a local page, and changing the font family (Figure 7–63).

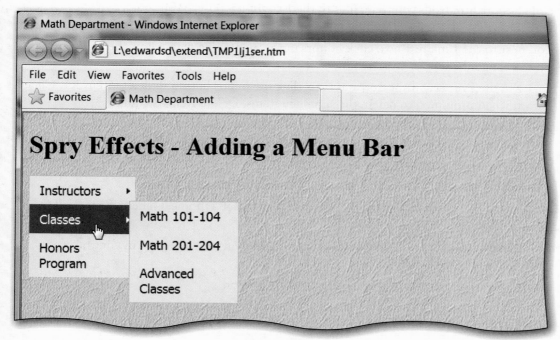

Figure 7–63

Perform the following tasks:

1. If necessary, start Dreamweaver and then open the Extend Exercises Web site.

2. Create a new, blank HTML page, and then save it as extend_ch07.htm. Title the Web page **Math Department**.

3. Apply the extend_bkg image as the background for the page.

4. Type the following heading at the top of the page: **Spry Effects - Adding a Menu Bar**. Apply Heading 1 to this text.

5. Press ENTER at the end of the heading to insert a new line.

6. Click the Spry Menu Bar button on the Spry toolbar, click the Vertical option button in the Spry Menu Bar dialog box, and then click OK.

7. Click Item 1 in the first list box in the Property inspector, select the text, Item 1, in the Text text box, and then enter **Classes**. Replace Item 2 with **Instructors** and replace Item 3 with **Honors Program**.

8. Select Item 4 in the first list box, and then click the minus button to remove it.

9. Click Instructors in the first list box to select Instructors, and then click the Move item up button to change the order of the menu items.

10. In the second list box, click the plus button to insert a new, untitled menu option on the Instructors menu. Click the plus button three more times to insert four menu options for Instructors.

11. Select the first Untitled Item text, and then enter **Dr. Barron** in the Text text box. Replace the Untitled Item text for the remaining three menu options with the names of the following three instructors, in order: **Ms. Ortiz**, **Dr. Weinstein**, and **Mr. Shah**.

12. Select Classes in the first list box, and then replace the Item 1.1 text with **Math 101-104**, the Item 1.2 text with **Math 201-204**, and the Item1.3 text with **Advanced Classes**.

13. Copy the file honors.htm from your data files to the Extend Exercises Web site.

14. Select the Menu Bar widget, and then click Honors Program in the Property inspector. Click the Browse icon next to the Link text box, click honors in the Select File dialog box, then click the OK button to change the link to honors.htm.

15. Click Item 3.1 in the Property inspector, and then click the minus button to delete Item 3.1. Click the OK button when prompted to delete the submenu items. Delete Items 3.2 and 3.3.

16. Enter **math_dept** as the name of the Menu Bar widget.

17. Display the CSS Styles panel, if necessary. Select the widget, and then click the SpryMenuBarVertical.css expand button to expand the list.

18. Click ul.MenuBarVertical li to select it, and then click the Add Property link.

19. Type **font-family** in the new property box, and then select Tahoma, Geneva, Sans Serif from the menu in the right text box.

20. Save your document, copy dependent files if necessary, and then view the page in your browser. Allow blocked content, if necessary.

21. Submit the document in the format specified by your instructor.

Make It Right

Reinforce the skills and apply the concepts you learned in this chapter.

Modifying a Menu Bar

Instructions: In this activity, you modify an existing Web page with a Spry Menu Bar widget by adding and deleting items on the Spry Menu Bar (Figure 7–64).

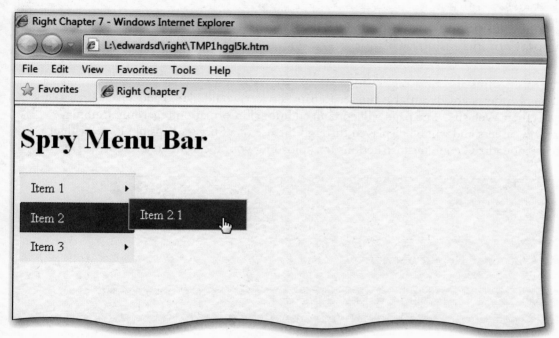

Figure 7–64

Perform the following tasks:

1. If necessary, start Dreamweaver and then copy the right_ch07.htm document and the SpryAssets folder from the Chapter07\right folder provided with your data files to the Right Exercises Web site. (*Hint:* To see the Spry Assets folder, you may need to change your Windows settings. Search for "display hidden files and folders" in the Windows Control Panel to do so.)

2. Open the Right Exercises Web site, and then open the right_ch07.htm file. Apply the right_bkg image to the background of the page. The menu bar on this page contains five items — you need to delete three of the items from the menu bar (two menu items and one submenu item) and add one new item.

3. If necessary, select the blue widget name tab at the top of the Menu Bar widget to display the Menu Bar Property inspector. Type `right_menubar` as the name of the Menu Bar widget.

4. If necessary, click Item 1 in the Property inspector.

5. In the second list box, click Item 1.3 and then click the minus button to delete this menu item.

6. Click Item 4 and then click the minus button to delete this menu item.

7. Click Item 5 and then click the minus button to delete this menu item.

8. Click Item 2.

9. Click the plus button above the second list box to add a new Untitled Item.

10. Select Untitled Item in the Text text box and then type `Item 2.1`. Link the menu item to http://www.cengage.com.

11. Title your Web page **Right Chapter 7**.

12. Save your document, copy dependent files, if necessary, and then view the page in your browser. Allow blocked content, if necessary. Test each item in the menu bar.

13. Submit the document in the format specified by your instructor.

In the Lab

Create Web pages using the guidelines, concepts, and skills presented in this chapter. Labs are listed in order of increasing difficulty.

Lab 1: Adding a Collapsible Panel Widget to a Web Page

Problem: The proprietors of Bryan's Computer Repair Services would like to add a page on careers and training to their Web site. The page will contain additional information regarding training, certification, and careers and will be displayed through the use of a Spry Collapsible Panel widget (Figure 7–65). Appendix C contains instructions for uploading your local site to a remote server.

Figure 7–65

Perform the following tasks:

1. If necessary, start Dreamweaver, and then open the Computer Repair Services Web site.

2. Create a new page, save it as careers.htm, and apply the repair_bkg background image. Title the page **Careers**. If necessary, display the Property inspector, the Spry category on the Insert bar, and panel groups.

3. Type **Careers in Computer Repair Services** at the top of the page, and then apply Heading 1 to the text. Press ENTER at the end of the heading to insert a new line.

4. Click the Spry Collapsible Panel button on the Spry toolbar to insert a new collapsible panel and display the Collapsible panel Property inspector. Enter **training** as the name of the Collapsible Panel widget.

5. Select the text, Tab, in the widget and then type **Training**.

6. Use the word processing program installed on your computer to open the careers_Office2010, careers_Office2003, or careers_text file. Copy the Training content text from that document.

7. Select the text, Content, in the widget and then use the Paste Special command to paste the text into the panel widget.

8. Insert a new Collapsible Panel widget below the first one. Enter `certification` as the name of the Collapsible Panel widget. Replace the text, Tab, by typing `Certification`.

9. Copy the Certification text from the careers_Office2010, careers_Office2003, or careers_text file. Use the Paste Special command to paste the text into the second panel widget.

10. Insert a third Collapsible Panel widget below the second one. Enter `careers` as the name of the Collapsible Panel widget. Replace the text, Tab, by typing `Careers`.

11. Copy the Careers text from the careers_Office2010, careers_Office2003, or careers_text file. Use the Paste Special command to paste the text into the third panel widget.

12. Save your document and copy dependent files, if necessary. View the page in your browser. Allow blocked content, if necessary. Click each tab to verify that it works.

13. Submit the document in the format specified by your instructor

In the Lab

Lab 2: Creating a Menu Bar for the Baskets by Carole Web Site

Problem: Carole would like to add a menu bar to all pages on her site. You agree to help her and suggest that the Spry Menu Bar widget is an appropriate object for what she has in mind. You want to create and format a horizontal menu bar as a prototype (Figure 7–66). If she likes it, she will add it to all of the pages on her site. Appendix C contains instructions for uploading your local site to a remote server.

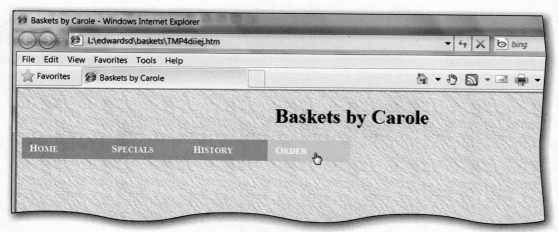

Figure 7–66

Perform the following tasks:

1. If necessary, start Dreamweaver and then open the Gift Basket Designs Web site.

2. Create a blank HTML page, and save the page as menu_bar.htm. Enter `Baskets by Carole` as the Web page title. Apply the baskets_bkg image to the background.

3. At the top of the page, type `Baskets by Carole` and press ENTER. Apply Heading 1 to the text and center it.

4. Click below the heading, and then click the Spry Menu Bar button on the Spry toolbar to display the Spry Menu Bar dialog box.

5. Click the Horizontal option button if necessary, and then click the OK button.

6. Enter `basket_menu` as the name of the Menu Bar widget.

7. Select Item 1 in the widget, and then type **Home** in the Text text box to replace the default text. Replace Items 2–4 with: Specials, History, and Order.

8. Click the Spry Menu Bar name tab to select the widget. Delete all levels of subitems under Home and History.

9. Expand the panel groups, if necessary. Double-click the CSS Styles tab in the panel groups and then click the All button, if necessary. Expand the styles for the SpryMenuBarHorizontal.css widget.

10. Click the property that starts with ul.MenuBarHorizontal a.MenuBarItemHover, ul.MenuBarHorizontal a.MenuBarSubmenuHover to display its properties. Next to background-color, click the Color box, and then click #CF9 (column 12, row 13).

11. Click the ul.MenuBarHorizontal a property. Change the background-color to #F69. Click the black color box next to color, and then click #FFF to change the text color to white. Use the Add Property link to add two new properties: font-weight, bolder and font-variant, small-caps.

12. Save your document. If a Copy Dependent Files dialog box is displayed, click OK and then view the page in your browser. Allow blocked content, if necessary. Click each menu option to verify that it works as designed.

13. Submit the document in the format specified by your instructor.

In the Lab

Lab 3: Modifying the Questions Web Page for the Credit Protection Web Site

Problem: Jessica would like to update and modify the Credit Protection Web site by adding a navigation menu. She is considering a vertical menu format instead of a horizontal format. She also would like to add some additional information to the Questions and Credit Information links. This will require additional links from those two pages. Jessica asks you to prepare a sample showing how the vertical menu would display with the additions. The revised page is shown in Figure 7–67.

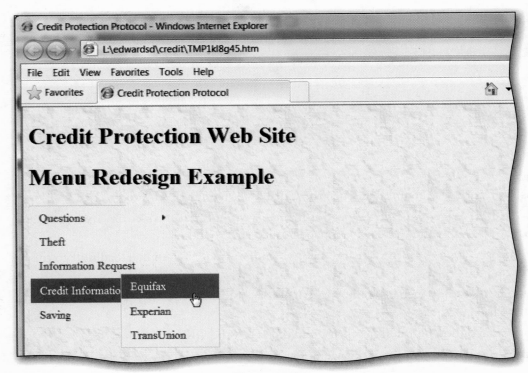

Figure 7–67

Perform the following tasks:

1. If necessary, start Dreamweaver and then open the Credit Protection Web site. Create a blank HTML page and save it as testing_effects.htm. Apply the credit_bkg background image to the Web page. Title the Web page `Credit Protection Protocol`.

2. At the top of the page, type the following two lines and then apply Heading 1 to both lines:

   `Credit Protection Web Site`

   `Menu Redesign Example`

3. Press ENTER after the second heading, click the Spry Menu Bar button on the Spry toolbar, and then select the Vertical layout.

4. Click the OK button to insert the menu. The menu will contain links to the following five pages on the Credit Protection Web site: Questions, Theft, Information Request, Credit Information, and Saving.

5. Click the Spry Menu Bar name tab, and then enter `example_01` as the name of the Menu Bar widget.

6. Click Item 1 in the Property inspector and change the text to `Questions`. Link to questions.htm and then type `Blank` in the Target text box.

7. Create the other four menu items with links as shown in Table 7–3. (*Hint:* Click the Credit Information item, then click the plus button to add a fifth menu item after Credit Information).

Table 7–3 Links for the Menu Bar Widget

Default Name	Customized Name	Link	Target
Item 2	Theft	theft.htm	Blank
Item 3	Information Request	tips_form.htm	Blank
Item 4	Credit Information	credit_info.htm	Blank
Item 5	Saving	saving.htm	Blank

8. Select Questions in the first list box in the Property inspector and then click Item 1.1 in the second list box. Enter `Credit Card Questions` in the Text text box and the following link in the Link text box: `http://wiki.answers.com/Q/FAQ/1785`. Type `Blank` in the Target text box.

9. Click Item 1.2 in the second list box. Enter `Closing Credit Card` in the Text text box. Add the following link to the Link box: `http://www.sunvirtual.com`. Type `Blank` in the Target text box. Delete the Questions Item 1.3.

10. Click Information Request in the first list box, and then delete Items 3.1 through 3.3. (*Hint:* Item 3.1 contains submenu items. Click Yes in the dialog box to delete them.)

11. Click Credit Information and then add three items to the second list box with the following titles: `Equifax, Experian`, and `TransUnion`.

12. Add the following links for each of the Credit Information links, using Blank as the Target property:

    Equifax: http://www.equifax.com/home

    Experian: http://www.experian.com

    TransUnion: http://www.transunion.com

13. Change the ul.MenuBarVertical li width style to 12em.

14. Save your document. If a Copy Dependent Files dialog box is displayed, click OK and then view the page in your browser. Allow blocked content, if necessary. Click each of the menu items to verify that they work.

15. Submit the document in the format specified by your instructor.

Cases and Places

Apply your creative thinking and problem solving skills to design and implement a solution.

● Easier ●● More Difficult

● 1: Create a Menu Bar for the Favorite Sports Web Site

You would like to add some navigation to your sports Web site. You decide to create a page with a horizontal menu bar that contains links to all of the other pages in the Web site as well as to two external pages. Add your background image and a title to the page. Create the horizontal menu linking to all of the site pages. Then create a new menu item that has at least two external links. Give the menu item an appropriate name. Save the page in your sports Web site. For a selection of images and backgrounds, visit the Dreamweaver CS5 Media Web page (scsite.com/dwcs5/media) and then click Media below Chapter 7.

● 2: Create Collapsible Panels for the Hobby Web Site

You would like to add some interactivity to your hobby Web site. You decide to do this by adding four Spry Collapsible Panel widgets. First, create a new page, add a background image, and then add an appropriate title. Next, insert four collapsible panels. Provide appropriate names for the panels and then add content to each panel. Create a link to your home page from this new page. Upload the new page to a remote site, if instructed to do so. For a selection of images and backgrounds, visit the Dreamweaver CS5 Media Web page (scsite.com/dwcs5/media) and then click Media below Chapter 7.

●● 3: Add a Menu Bar to the Politics Web Site

Your campaign for political office is going well, and you want to enhance your campaign Web site by adding pages that link to issues that are important to you. You want to create a Spry Menu Bar to help users navigate to the new content. Create a new Web page, and then add an appropriate background image and title. Add a menu bar with at least four menu items and two submenu items and then link them to pages with content about important campaign issues. Upload the revised Web site to a remote server. For a selection of images and backgrounds, visit the Dreamweaver CS5 Media Web page (scsite.com/dwcs5/media) and then click Media below Chapter 7.

●● 4: Add Collapsible Panels to the Favorite Music Web Site

Make It Personal

Add a page to your music Web site, and then add an appropriate background image and title. Decide what kind of content you want to include in one or more panels: album covers, links to venues you like to visit, or something of your choosing. Upload the page to a remote site. For a selection of images and backgrounds, visit the Dreamweaver CS5 Media Web page (scsite.com/dwcs5/media) and then click Media below Chapter 7.

●● 5: Add Widgets to the Student Trips Web Site

Working Together

You and your team would like to add a more attractive index page to the student trips Web site that will catch the attention of more students. You decide to add a vertical menu bar and Spry Collapsible Panels. Individual team members are each responsible for creating one of the items. Upload the new pages to a remote server. For a selection of images and backgrounds, visit the Dreamweaver CS5 Media Web page (scsite.com/dwcs5/media) and then click Media below Chapter 7.

8 | Advanced Spry Activities

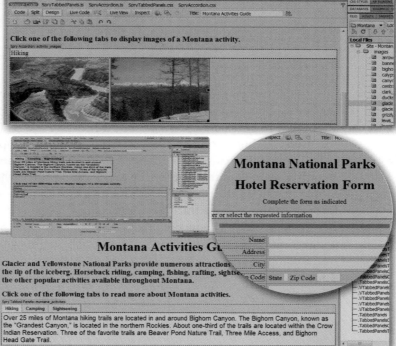

Objectives

You will have mastered the material in this chapter when you can:

- Insert a tooltip
- Create a Spry Tabbed Panels widget
- Add content to the Spry Tabbed Panels widget
- Format a Spry Tabbed Panels widget
- Add a Spry Accordion widget to a Web page
- Format a Spry Accordion widget
- Apply a Spry effect

8 | Advanced Spry Activities

Introduction

Chapter 7 introduced the Spry framework for AJAX and described how to use and apply reusable Spry widgets. The Spry framework, developed by Adobe Systems, is an open-source code that can be used to add and incorporate dynamic content to a Web page. In Chapter 7, you learned how to create and customize a Spry Collapsible Panel widget and a Spry Menu Bar widget. Chapter 8 continues with describing and illustrating how to use three other Spry widgets and apply Spry effects.

Project — Advanced Spry Activities

BTW

Finding Other Widgets
The Adobe Exchange provides other widgets you can use on a Web page besides those that are provided with Dreamweaver. Click the Extend Dreamweaver button on the Application bar, and then click Browse for Web Widgets to find additional widgets.

In this chapter, you continue to develop the Montana Parks Web site by adding interactive activities. You begin the chapter by inserting a Tooltip widget in the Hotel Reservations Form that you created in Chapter 6. The Tooltip widget (Figure 8–1a) will remind Web site users making a hotel reservation that they must complete all the fields in the form.

Next, you create a Spry Tabbed Panels widget. The Tabbed Panels widget provides information to Montana visitors by highlighting three types of popular activities: hiking, camping, and sightseeing. You add three separate panels — one panel for hiking, a second one for camping, and a third for sightseeing. The panels can be opened to display detailed content or closed to show only the panel names (Figure 8–1b). The third type of Spry widget you add is an Accordion widget, which enables you to incorporate numerous links into a compact space (Figure 8–1b). Finally, you apply Spry effects such as Shake and Squish to created animated effects on the pages in the Montana Parks Web site (Figure 8–1c).

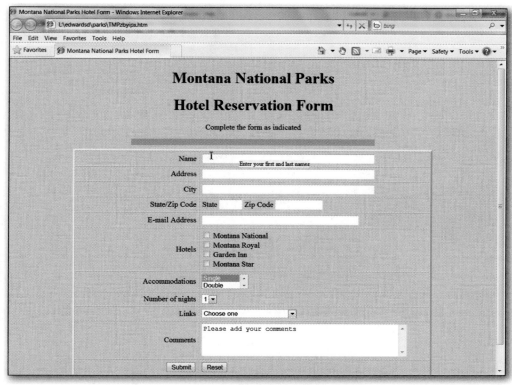

Figure 8–1a

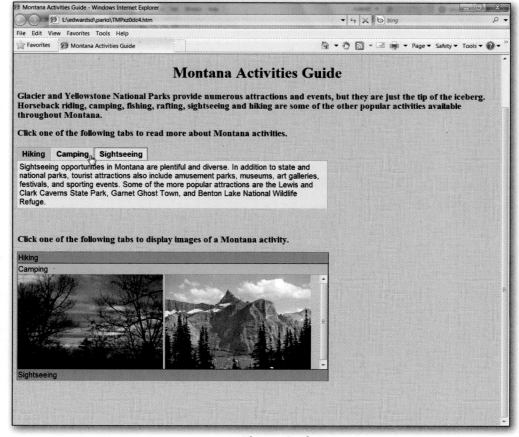

Figure 8–1b

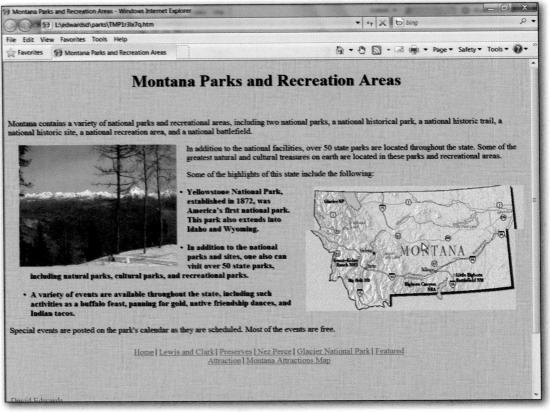

Figure 8–1c

Overview

As you read this chapter, you will learn how to add to your Web site the pages shown in Figure 8–1 by performing these general tasks:

- Enhance the Hotel Reservation Form page by adding a Tooltip widget.
- Add the Spry Tabbed Panels widget to a new Web page.
- Add headings and content to the Spry Tabbed Panels widget.
- Format the headings in the Spry Tabbed Panels widget.
- Add a Spry Accordion widget to a Web page.
- Add labels and text to the Spry Accordion widget.
- Apply Spry effects to Web pages.

Plan
Ahead

General Project Guidelines

When adding Spry widgets to a Web page, consider the appearance and characteristics of the completed page. As you create the Web pages shown in Figure 8–1, you should follow these general guidelines:

1. **Select the appropriate Spry widget.** Determine which Spry widget will best enhance the Web page.

2. **Determine how to customize the Spry widget.** Customize the Spry widget so that it is easy for Web site visitors to use and invites interaction.

3. **Format the Spry widget.** Work with CSS styles to change the format of elements such as text and background colors.

4. **Consider applying Spry effects to objects on the Web page.** To attract the attention of Web site visitors, you can apply Spry effects to objects such as images and text.

When necessary, more specific details concerning the above guidelines are presented at appropriate points in the chapter. The chapter also will identify the actions performed and decisions made regarding these guidelines during the creation of the Web pages shown in Figure 8–1.

Starting Dreamweaver and Opening a Web Site

Each time you start Dreamweaver, it opens to the last site displayed when you closed the program. It therefore may be necessary for you to open the parks Web site. Clicking the Files pop-up menu in the Files panel lists the sites you have defined. When you open the site, a list of pages and subfolders within the site is displayed.

To Start Dreamweaver and Open the Montana Parks Web Site

With a good understanding of the requirements, and an understanding of the necessary decisions and planning process, the next step is to start Dreamweaver and open the Montana Parks Web site.

1 Click the Start button on the Windows taskbar.

2 Click Adobe Dreamweaver CS5 on the Start menu or point to All Programs on the Start menu, click Adobe Design Premium, if necessary, and then click Adobe Dreamweaver CS5 on the All Programs list to start Dreamweaver.

3 If necessary, display the panel groups.

4 If the Montana Parks hierarchy is not displayed, click the Sites pop-up menu button on the Files panel, and then click Montana Parks to display the Montana Parks Web site in the Files panel.

To Copy Data Files to the Montana Parks Web Site

Before you start enhancing and adding to your Web site, you need to copy the data files into the site's folder hierarchy. In the following steps, you copy the data files for the Chapter 8 project from the Chapter08 folder on a USB drive to the parks folder stored in the *your name* folder on the same USB drive. In the following steps, the data files for this chapter are stored on drive L:. The location on your computer may be different. If necessary, verify the location of the data files with your instructor.

1 Click the Sites pop-up menu button in the Files panel, and then click the name of the drive containing your data files, such as Removable Disk (L:).

2 If necessary, click the plus sign (+) next to the folder containing your data files to expand that folder, expand the Chapter08 folder, and then expand the parks folder.

3 Copy the montana_guide file from the data files, click the Sites pop-up menu button in the Files panel, click Montana Parks, and then paste the montana_guide file in the parks folder for the Montana Parks site.

Q&A What should I do with the other three files in the Chapter08\parks folder?

You do not need to copy the other three files. Keep the drive containing your data files handy, however, because you will open the files later.

BTW

Using Copyrighted Material
When you add images and text to widgets or any other elements on a Web page, be aware of copyright issues. Copyright protects content creators against unauthorized use of their work. If you improperly use copyrighted material, you could be violating the copyright law and be legally liable for damages to the content creator. To protect yourself, find and use materials that fall under public domain, which means that it is not protected by copyright. The U.S. government, for example, releases images, videos, and other material to the public domain. If you are quoting an author's material or citing other works, you may be able to incorporate the material under fair use, which typically allows educational use. Otherwise, seek permission from the content creator to use their material.

Adding Advanced Spry Widgets to Web Pages

As you learned in Chapter 7, the Spry framework consists of a library of JavaScript components and behaviors that you can use to add interactivity to a Web site. The Spry category on the Insert bar contains three groups of Spry widgets. The first group controls data and describes how to display it with widgets. The second group focuses on form elements, and the third group provides dynamic elements such as menu bars, tabbed panels, accordion bars, and collapsible panels. Refer to Table 7-1 in Chapter 7 for a description of the tools in the Spry category on the Insert bar.

Recall that Dreamweaver supports a number of widgets, including the Collapsible Panel widget and the Menu Bar widget. You also can use HTML and CSS properties to format widgets, such as by changing their font type and size, the same way you format other objects in Dreamweaver. This chapter explores three other widgets: the Accordion, Tabbed Panel, and Tooltip widgets. Table 8-1 provides a visual overview of all five of these widgets.

Table 8–1 Selected Spry Widgets

Name	Widget	Description
Accordion		Similar to the Collapsible Panel widget, this widget can store a large amount of content in a compact space. Unlike the Collapsible Panel widget, you can open only one content panel at a time.
Collapsible Panel	Expanded Collapsed	This widget stores content in a compact space. Clicking a panel tab expands or collapses the content stored in the widget. You can open one or all of the panels at the same time.
Menu Bar		You can use the Spry Menu Bar widget to create menus with items and submenus. You can select a horizontal or vertical layout and then use the Menu Bar Property inspector to format the widget. Using the Menu Bar plus and minus symbol buttons, you can add and remove items from a menu. The arrow symbols let you move items up or down the sort order.
Tabbed Panels		The Tabbed Panels widget contains a set of panels that can store content in a small space. You click the panel tab to view or hide the content. You can open only one content panel at a time.
Tooltip		When you point to a particular element on a Web page, the Tooltip widget displays additional information. The content disappears when you move the mouse pointer.

The widgets described in Table 8-1 have attached behaviors that you can access and modify through the Behaviors panel. When you do so, you are adding Spry effects to the widgets or other objects.

As you learned in Chapter 7, when you insert a Spry widget into your Web page, a folder named SpryAssets is created automatically and added to the root level of your Web site. Each time you insert a Spry widget into a Web page, Dreamweaver adds a corresponding CSS file and a JavaScript file to the SpryAssets folder. If you are uploading your page to a file server, remember that you must upload this folder and its contents for the widget to properly function.

You insert all of the widgets in the preceding list into a Web page the same way that you inserted the Spry Collapsible Panel and the Spry Menu Bar widgets in Chapter 7. After you insert the widgets, you can customize them and modify their styles using the Property inspector and the CSS Styles panel.

Select the appropriate Spry widget.
As you are planning a Web page, consider whether a Spry widget will enhance the page and make it easier for Web site visitors to interact with the content. Most Spry widgets condense a large amount of content into a small space. Appropriate Spry widgets for this purpose are the Tabbed Panels, Accordion, and Collapsible Panel widgets. If your Web page contains a form, a Spry Tooltip or Validation widget is more appropriate because they provide feedback to users completing a form.

Plan Ahead

You start the chapter by adding Spry Tooltip widgets to the Hotel Reservation Form you created in Chapter 6.

Using Tooltips

The Spry Tooltip widget allows users to move the mouse over page elements to expose additional information in a small pop-up window. When the mouse is moved away, the additional content is no longer displayed. A Tooltip widget can be used to display text and pictures, provide a definition, or point to another Web link that contains additional information. In this chapter, you create two Tooltip widgets — one that appears when users point to text on the Web page and another that appears when users point to a text box in the form.

To Insert a Spry Tooltip Widget for a Web Page

The following steps illustrate adding a Spry Tooltip widget to the Hotel Reservation Form Web page to provide general instructions for completing the form.

- Open the hotel_form document that you created in Chapter 6 to prepare for adding a Tooltip widget.

- Click to the right of the Hotel Reservation Form heading to position the insertion point.

- Press the ENTER key to insert a new blank line.

- If necessary, center the new line on the page.

- If necessary, click the Spry tab on the Insert bar to display the Spry category.

- Point to the Spry Tooltip button to display its ScreenTip and identify the button (Figure 8-2).

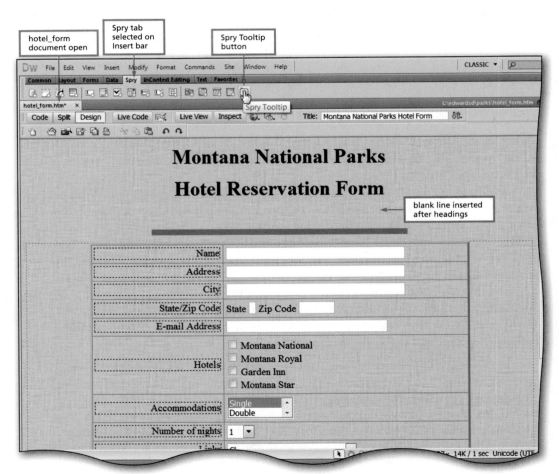

Figure 8–2

2

- Click the Spry Tooltip button to insert the Spry Tooltip widget and the tooltip trigger text (Figure 8-3).

What is the tooltip trigger text?

The tooltip must be attached to an element on the page. If you insert a Tooltip widget without selecting an element on the page first, Dreamweaver inserts the placeholder trigger text, which you can change as necessary. When users point to the trigger text, the tooltip content appears.

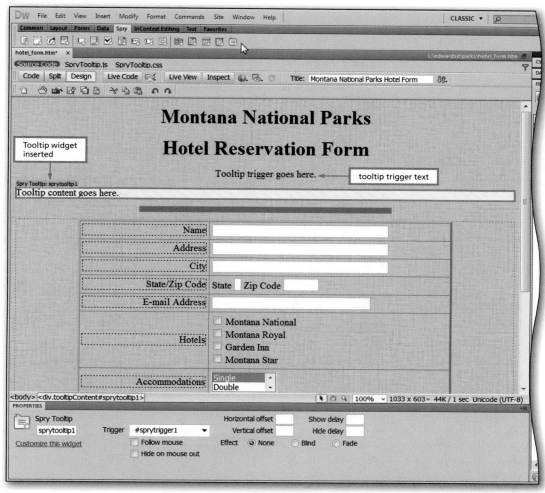

Figure 8–3

3

- Select the 'Tooltip trigger goes here.' text to prepare for changing it.

- Type **Complete the form as indicated** to enter the tooltip trigger text below the page titles (Figure 8-4).

Figure 8–4

4

- Select the 'Tooltip content goes here.' text in the Tooltip widget to prepare for entering customized text.

- Type `Click each field and then enter or select the requested information` to enter the tooltip text (Figure 8–5).

Q&A

What do users see when they open the page?

When users open the page, they see the tooltip trigger text, which is "Complete the form as indicated" in this case.

When does the tooltip text appear on the page?

Figure 8–5

When users point to the tooltip trigger text (Complete the form as indicated), the tooltip text appears, which is "Click each field and then enter or select the requested information" in this case.

5

- Click the div tag in the tag selector to display the Tooltip widget properties in the Property inspector.

- Double-click the text in the Spry Tooltip text box to select it.

- Type **form_ instructions** and then press the ENTER key to provide a name for the Tooltip widget.

- Click the Follow mouse check box so that the tooltip follows the mouse pointer if the pointer moves when it is over the trigger text.

- Click the 'Hide on mouse out' check box so that the tooltip is displayed as long as the mouse pointer is over the tooltip text (Figure 8–6).

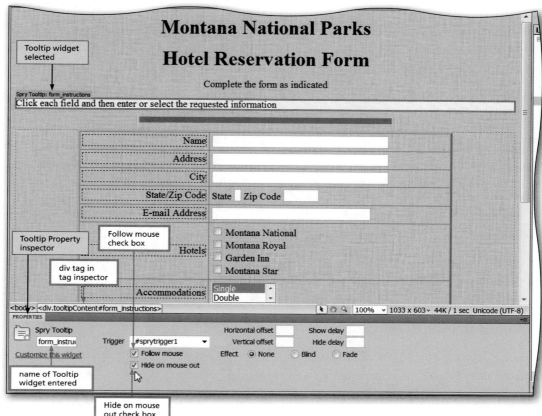

Figure 8–6

Q&A

When should I use the 'Hide on mouse out' check box?

Select this option when you want to display the tooltip text even if the mouse is moved from the trigger text. This gives users plenty of time to read the tooltip. It also is useful if the tooltip includes links, buttons, or other interactive elements.

6

- Click the Fade option button in the Property inspector to indicate that the tooltip should fade in when it is displayed and fade out when it is removed from the page.

- Click the Hide delay text box, type 8000, and then press the ENTER key to delay the fading of the tooltip to 8,000 milliseconds (Figure 8–7).

Q&A

What are the purposes of the other option buttons in the Effect area?

Select the Blind option button to reveal the tooltip from bottom to top and then hide the tooltip from top to bottom, similar to a window blind. Select the None option button to display the tooltip without any effect.

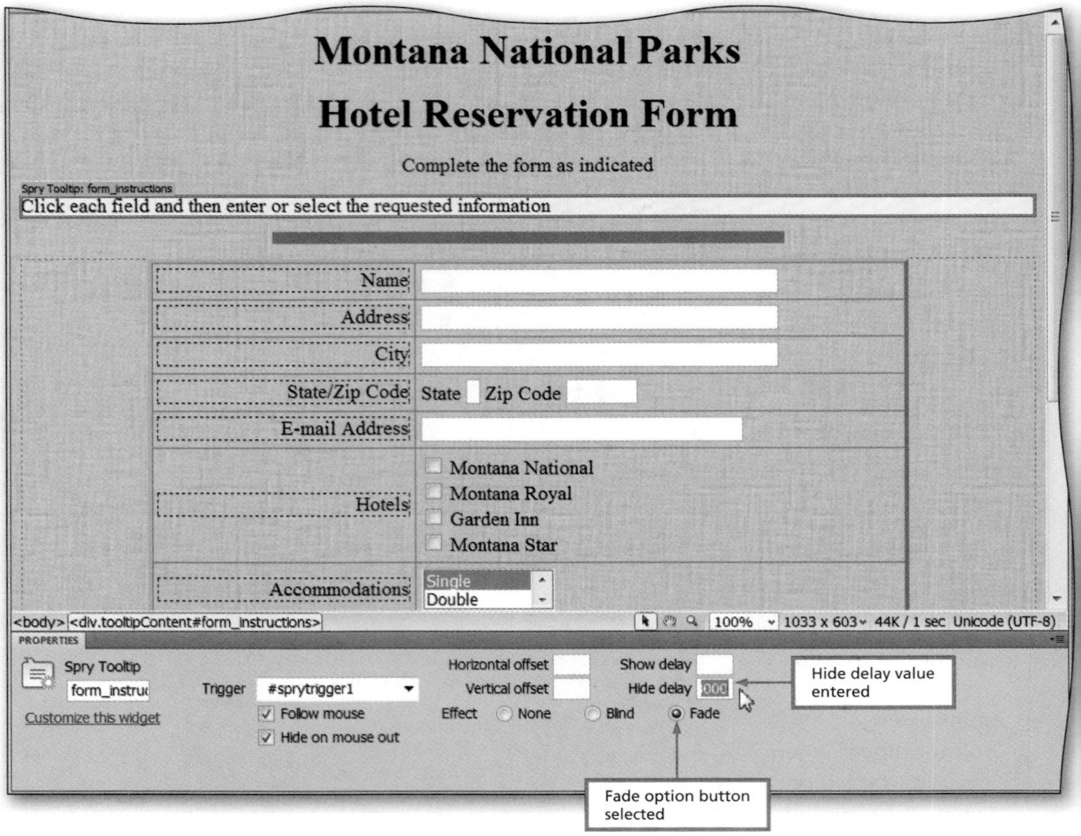

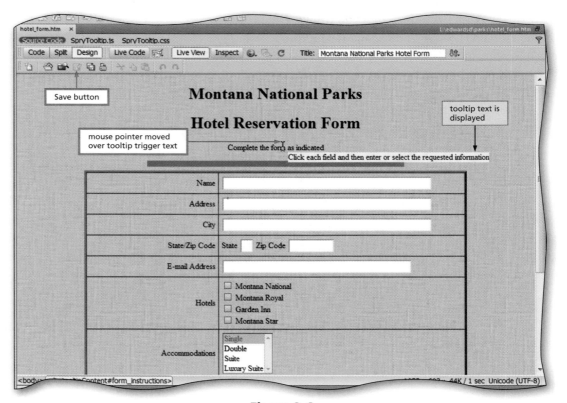

Figure 8–7

7

- Click the Save button on the Standard toolbar to save the document.

- Click the OK button in the Copy Dependent Files dialog box to copy the files.

- Click the Live View button on the Document toolbar to test the Tooltip widget.

- Move the mouse pointer over the tooltip trigger text to display the tooltip (Figure 8–8).

Figure 8–8

- Move the mouse pointer to make sure the tooltip follows the pointer.

- Point to part of the tooltip that does not appear on the trigger text to make sure the tooltip stays open.

8

- Click the Live View button on the Document toolbar to return to Design view.

To Insert a Spry Tooltip Widget for a Form Element

The following steps illustrate adding a Spry Tooltip widget to the Name text box on the Hotel Reservation Form Web page to provide instructions for entering information in the text box.

1

- Click the Name Textfield object to select it.

- Click the Spry Tooltip button on the Insert bar to insert the Spry Tooltip widget for the Name text box.

- If necessary, scroll the page to display the Tooltip widget (Figure 8–9).

Q&A

Why does no tooltip trigger text appear for the Name Textfield object?

When you click an element in the document, and then click the Spry Tooltip button, the Tooltip widget is attached to the element, so the tooltip trigger text is unnecessary.

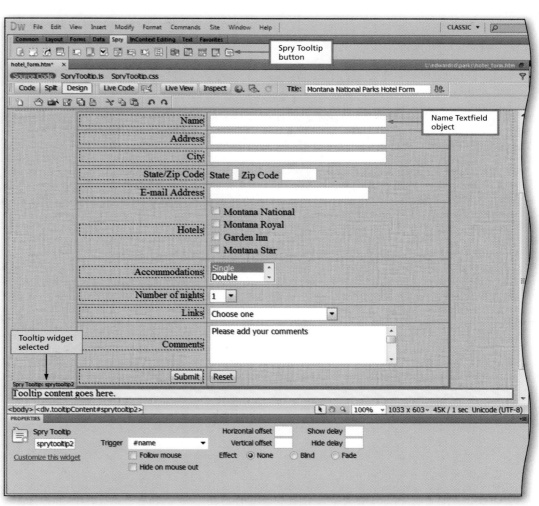

Figure 8–9

2

- Select the 'Tooltip content goes here.' text in the Tooltip widget to prepare for entering customized text.

- Type **Enter your first and last names** to enter the tooltip text (Figure 8–10).

Q&A

When does this tooltip text appear on the page?

When users point to the Name text box, the tooltip text appears to provide instructions for entering information in the text box. In other words, the Name text box is the trigger for the tooltip text.

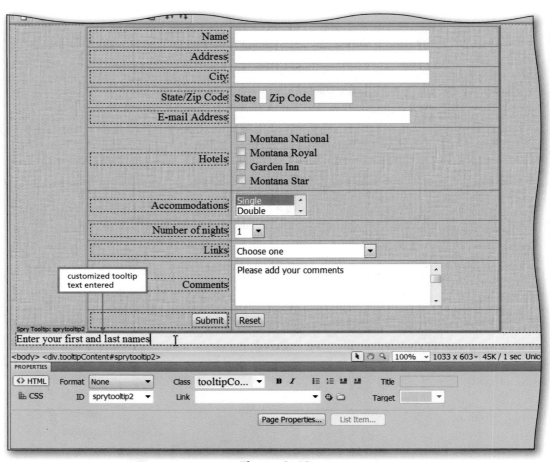

Figure 8–10

3

- Click the div tag in the tag selector to display the Tooltip widget properties in the Property inspector.

- Double-click the text in the Spry Tooltip text box to select it.

- Type **name_tip** and then press the ENTER key to provide a name for the Tooltip widget.

- Click the Follow mouse check box so that the tooltip follows the mouse pointer if the pointer moves when it is over the Name text box.

- Click the 'Hide on mouse out' check box so that the tooltip is displayed as long as the mouse pointer is over the tooltip text.

- Click the Fade option button in the Property inspector to indicate that the tooltip should fade in when it is displayed and fade out when it is removed from the page.

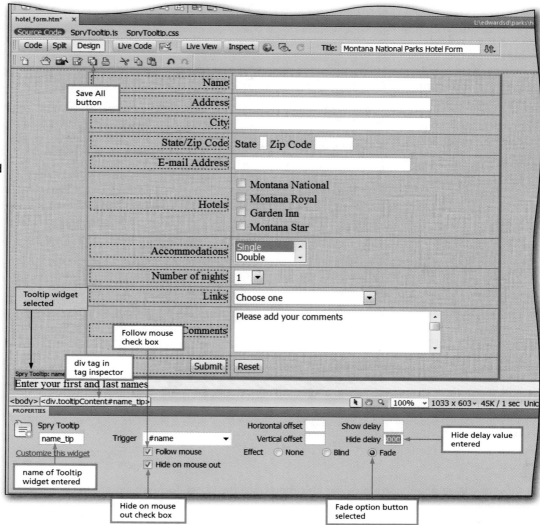

Figure 8–11

- Click the Hide delay text box, type **8000** and then press the ENTER key to delay the fading of the tooltip to 8,000 milliseconds (Figure 8–11).

4

- Click the Save All button on the Standard toolbar to save the document and related files.

- Press the F12 key to view the page in your browser.

- If necessary, allow blocked content.

- Move the mouse pointer over the Name text box to display the tooltip (Figure 8–12).

Q&A

Can I format the tooltip text?

Yes, you can format the tooltip text using the same tools you use to format any other text. For example, if the tooltip text provides cautionary information, you could format it in a red font color.

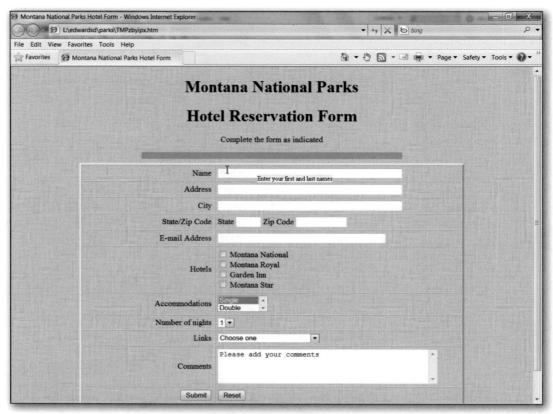

Figure 8–12

5

- Close the Web page in the browser and then close the hotel_form document in Dreamweaver.

Spry Tabbed Panels Widget

Your next activity is to add a Tabbed Panels widget to the montana_guide page to provide information about Montana activities such as sightseeing, hiking, and camping. The first tabbed panel will contain information about Montana's popular sightseeing opportunities, the second tabbed panel about Montana's hiking trails, and the third tabbed panel about Montana's camping sites.

Determine how to customize the Spry widget.
You can customize most Spry widgets to change the order of the contents or set their size or position on the Web page. For example, you can change the order of the panels in a Tabbed Panels widget and change the width of an Accordion widget. Examine the options in the Property inspector for a widget to learn which properties you can customize.

Plan Ahead

As indicated previously, the Spry Tabbed Panels widget is one of the more popular Spry widgets in Dreamweaver. Use this widget to store content in a compact space. The user then can hide or reveal the content by clicking a tab on the widget. In a Tabbed Panels widget, only one content panel is open at a time.

To Add the Spry Tabbed Panels Widget to a Web page

The following steps illustrate how to open the new Montana Activities Guide page, apply a background image, and then add the Spry Tabbed Panels widget to the page. The widget will contain three panels describing Montana activities.

- Open the montana_ guide document to prepare for enhancing it for the Montana Parks site.

- Apply the parks_ bkg image to the background of the page so it uses the same background as the other pages on the site.

- Enter **Montana Activities Guide** in the Title text box to provide a document title (Figure 8–13).

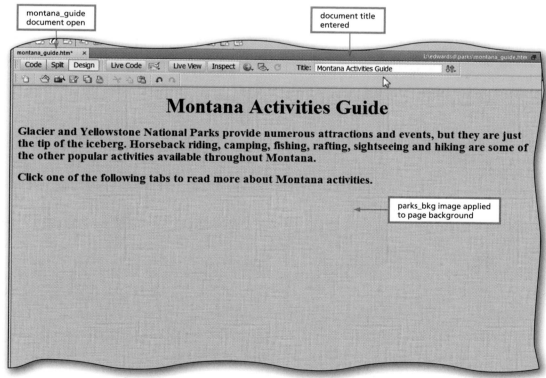

Figure 8–13

- Click below the last line on the page.
- Point to the Spry Tabbed Panels button on the Insert bar to identify the button (Figure 8–14).

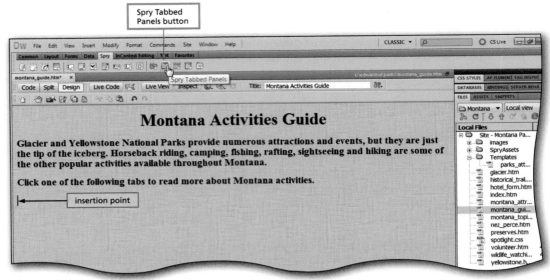

Figure 8–14

- Click the Spry Tabbed Panels button to insert a Tabbed Panels widget on the page (Figure 8–15).

Q&A

Only two tabs are displayed in the Tabbed Panels widget. Can I add other tabbed panels to the widget?

Yes, you can add panels to the widget as necessary. You will see how to do so shortly.

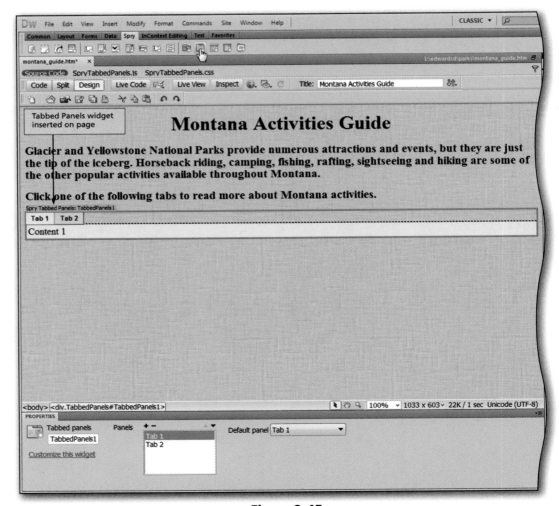

Figure 8–15

4

- If necessary, click the widget name tab to select the Tabbed Panels widget.

- Double-click the text in the Tabbed panels text box in the Property inspector to select the default name.

- Type **montana_ activities** and then press the ENTER key to name the widget (Figure 8–16).

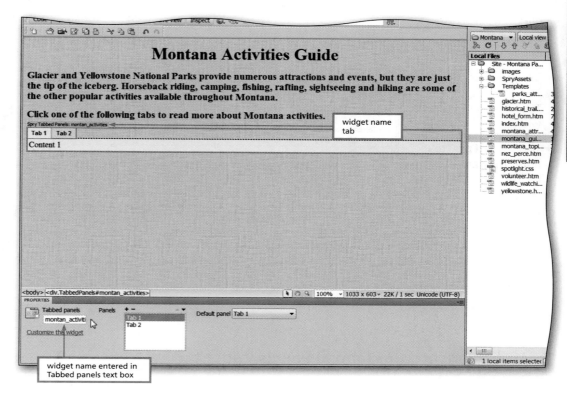

Figure 8–16

5

- In the Tabbed Panels widget, drag to select the Tab 1 text to prepare for customizing it.

- Type **Sightseeing** to enter the name of the first tab.

- Move the mouse pointer over Tab 2 to display the open eye icon (Figure 8–17).

 What does the eye icon indicate?

An open eye icon indicates that the Content panel in the tabbed panel is closed on the Web page; click the open eye icon to open the panel.

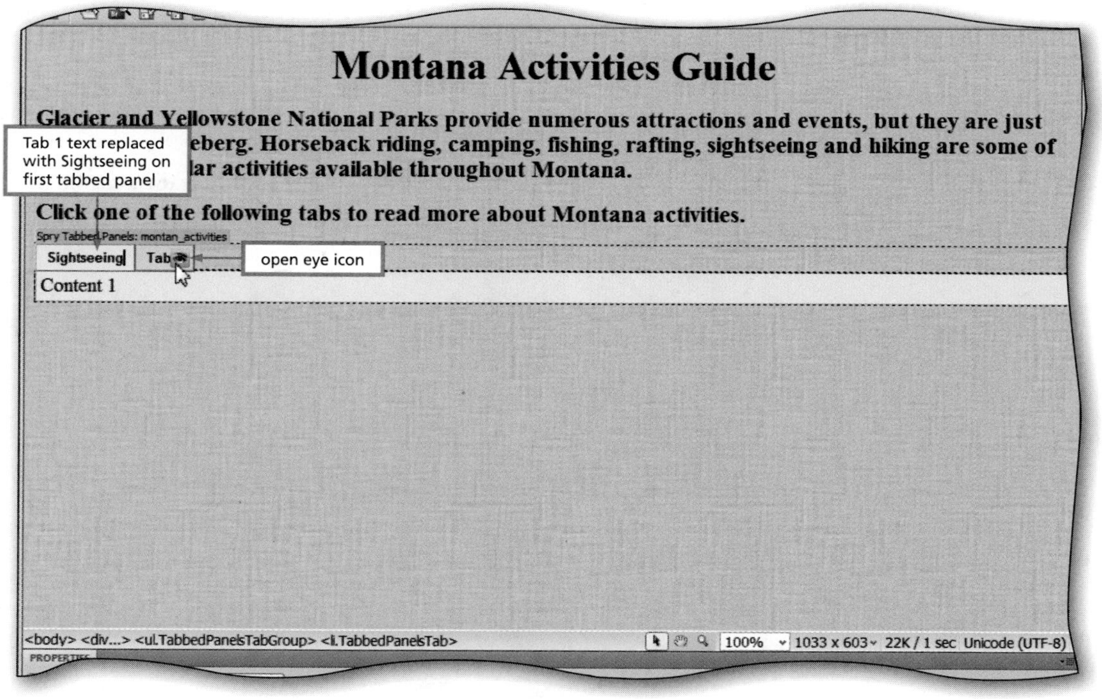

Figure 8–17

6

- Click the eye icon to open the second panel for editing.

- Drag to select the Tab 2 text in the Tabbed Panels widget.

- Type **Hiking** to enter the name of the second tab (Figure 8–18).

Q&A When should I enter text in the Content box for each tab?

You enter the text for the Content boxes later in the chapter.

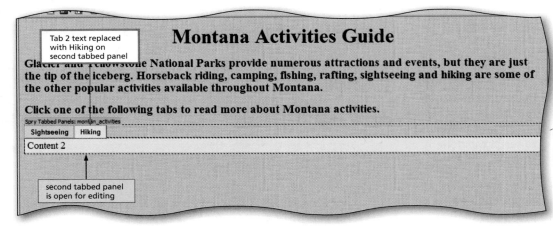

Figure 8–18

Other Ways
1. On Insert menu, point to Spry, click Spry Tabbed Panels

To Add a Panel to the Tabbed Panels Widget

The montana_activities Tabbed Panels widget includes two tabs — one for Sightseeing information and the other for Hiking information. The widget also should include a third tab for Camping information. The following steps illustrate how to add a third tabbed panel to the Tabbed Panels widget.

1

- Click div.TabbedPanels #montana_activities in the tag inspector to select the entire widget (Figure 8–19).

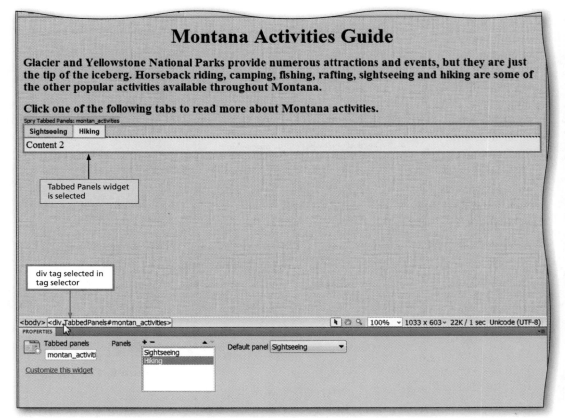

Figure 8–19

2

- Click the plus sign (Add panel button) in the Property inspector to add a third panel to the Tabbed Panels widget with the default name Tab 3 (Figure 8–20).

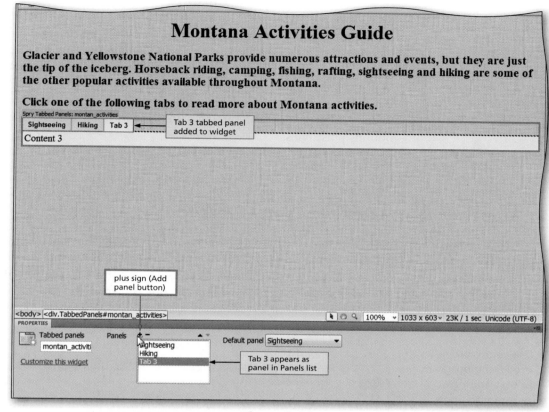

Figure 8–20

3

- Drag to select the Tab 3 text in the widget.

- Type **Camping** as the name of the third tab (Figure 8–21).

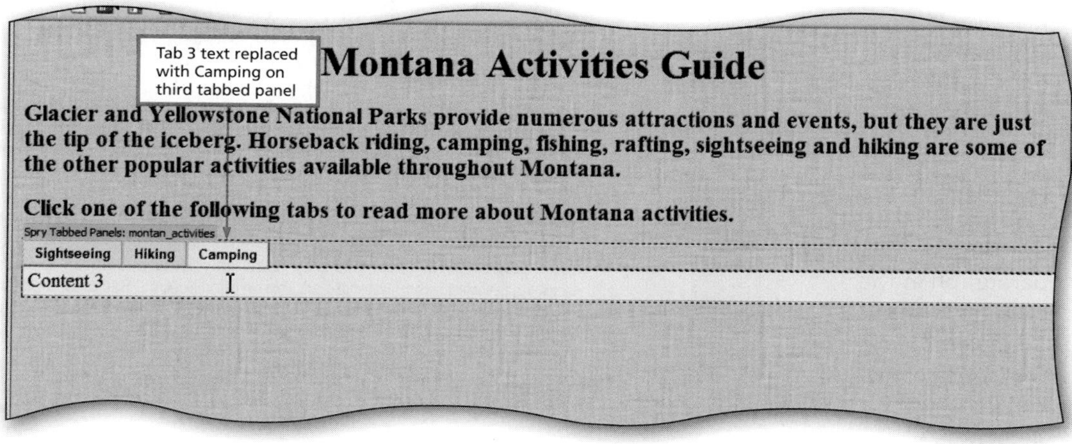

Figure 8–21

Inserting Text with the Paste Special Command

To control the format of text that you paste into a Dreamweaver document, you can use the Paste Special command on the Edit menu. Recall that this command lets you specify the format of the pasted text using the following four options: Text only, which pasts text without any formatting; Text with structure, which retains structural text elements such as paragraphs and tables, but not formatting such as bold and italics; Text with structure plus basic formatting, which preserves structure along with formatting such as bold and italics; and Text with structure plus full formatting, which includes all the basic formatting options plus styles.

To Copy and Paste Formatted Content Text

Next, you copy and paste text from a data file to a Dreamweaver page. The data file is available in three formats. Based on the programs available on your computer, you can select Microsoft Word 2010 (which is the same as Microsoft Office Word 2007), Microsoft Office Word 2003, or a text file. The Word 2010 file format is used in the following figures. The following steps show how to copy text from the data file and paste it into your Dreamweaver document.

1

- Use your word processing program or text-editing program to open one of the following three documents in the Chapter08\parks folder provided with your data files: activities_Office2010.docx, activities_Office2003.doc, or activities_text.rtf.

- Select the Sightseeing description paragraph in the data file, which is labeled "Text for Sightseeing content."

- Press the CTRL+C keys to copy the selected paragraph (Figure 8–22).

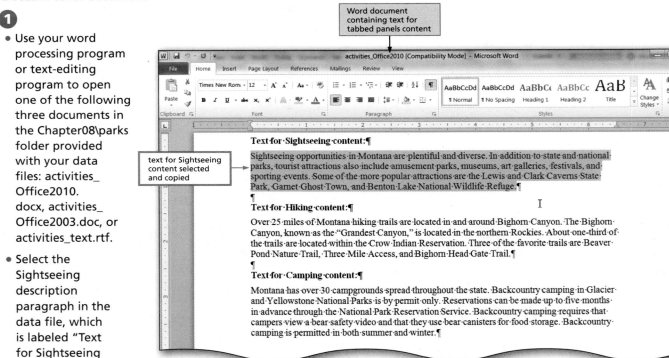

Figure 8–22

- Click the Adobe
Dreamweaver
program button
to return to the
Montana Activities
Guide page in
Dreamweaver.

- Point to the
Sightseeing tab in
the Tabbed Panels
widget, and then, if
necessary, click the
eye icon to open the
Sightseeing tabbed
panel.

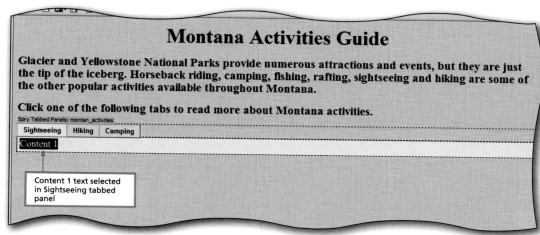

Content 1 text selected
in Sightseeing tabbed
panel

Figure 8–23

- Select the Content 1
text in the Sightseeing tabbed panel to prepare for replacing it (Figure 8–23).

---

❸

- Click Edit on the
Application bar
and then click Paste
Special to display the
Paste Special dialog
box.

- If necessary, click the
Text with structure
plus full formatting
(bold, italic, styles)
option button
(Figure 8–24).

Edit on
Application bar

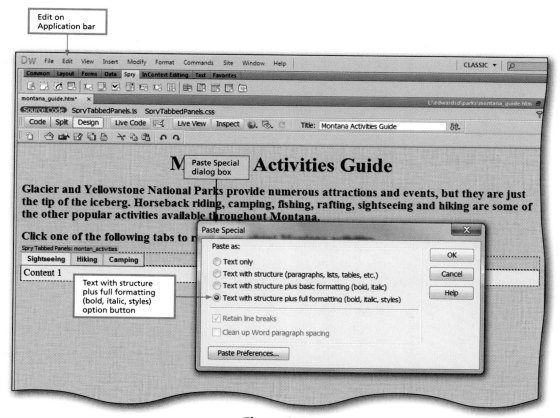

Paste Special
dialog box

Text with structure
plus full formatting
(bold, italic, styles)
option button

Figure 8–24

- Click the OK button to paste the text (Figure 8–25).

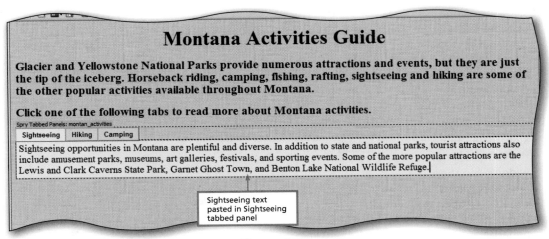

Figure 8–25

- Display the activities document you used in Step 1 to prepare for copying and pasting the text for the Hiking tabbed panel.

- Select the Hiking description paragraph in the data file, which is labeled "Text for Hiking content."

- Press the CTRL+C keys to copy the selected paragraph.

Figure 8–26

- Repeat Steps 2–4 to paste the Hiking text in the Hiking tabbed panel (Figure 8–26).

6

- Display the activities document you used in Step 1 to prepare for copying and pasting the text for the Camping tabbed panel.

- Select the Camping description paragraph in the data file, which is labeled "Text for Camping content."

- Press the CTRL+C keys to copy the selected paragraph.

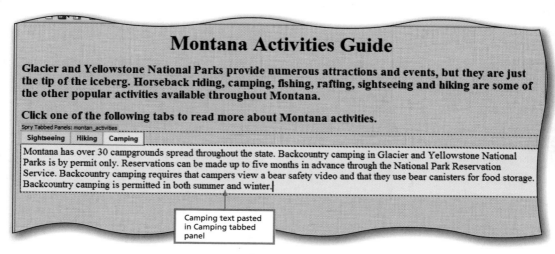

Figure 8–27

- Repeat Steps 2–4 to paste the Camping text in the Camping tabbed panel (Figure 8–27).

Other Ways
1. Press CTRL+SHIFT+V to select Paste Special options

To Change the Order of the Panels

Hiking and camping might be more popular activities for Montana visitors than sightseeing. You can change the order of the panels so that the Hiking panel is first, Camping is second, and Sightseeing is third. The following steps show how to change the order of the panels in the Tabbed Panels widget.

1

- Click the widget name tab to select the montana_ activities Tabbed Panels widget.

- Click Sightseeing in the Panels list box to select it (Figure 8–28).

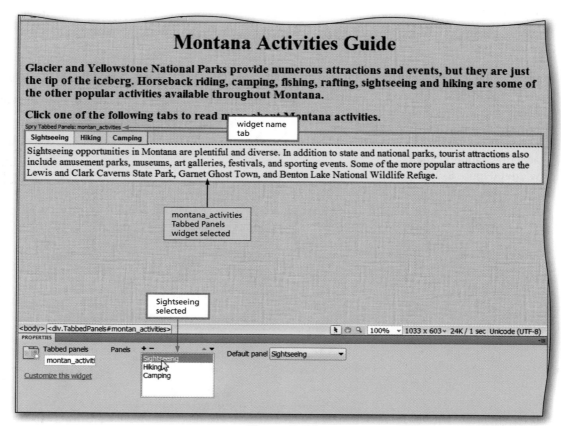

Figure 8–28

● Click the 'Move panel down in list' button twice to move Sightseeing to the bottom of the list (Figure 8–29).

Q&A

How do I move a tabbed panel up in the Panels list box?

Click the 'Move panel up in list' button.

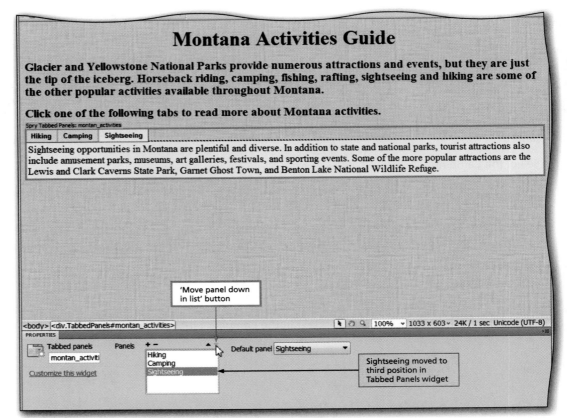

Figure 8–29

Set the Default Panel

The default panel is the one that opens when the Web page is displayed in the browser. The following steps illustrate setting the Hiking panel as the default panel in the montana_activities Tabbed Panels widget.

● Click Hiking in the Panels list box to select it.

● Click the Default panel button to display the panels in the montana_activities Tabbed Panels widget (Figure 8–30).

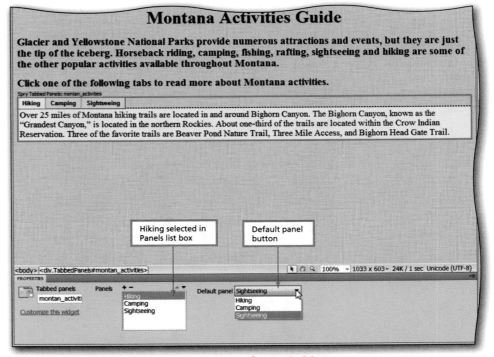

Figure 8–30

2
- Click Hiking to set that panel as the one to open by default when the Montana Activities Guide page is displayed in the browser (Figure 8–31).

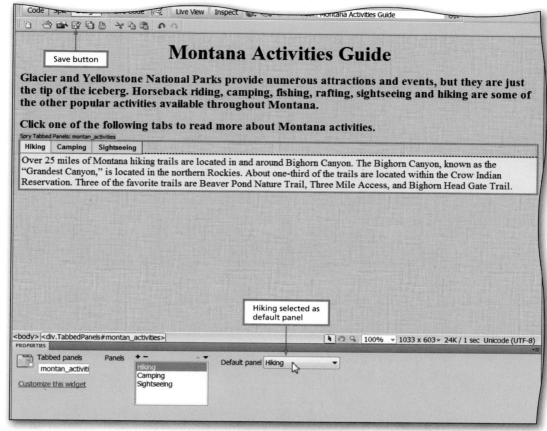

Figure 8–31

To View the Web Page in Your Browser

As you create your Web page, it always is a good idea to preview the content. This helps you determine if the spacing is correct. In the following steps, you view the Web page in your browser and then display the tabbed panels.

1
- Click the Save button on the Standard toolbar to save the document.
- Click the OK button in the Copy Dependent Files dialog box to copy the files.
- Press the F12 key to view the Web page in your browser, and allow blocked content, if necessary (Figure 8–32).

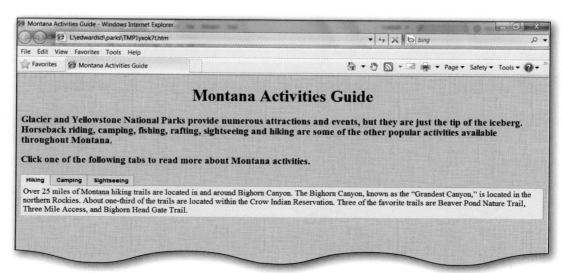

Figure 8–32

● Click the Camping tab to display the Camping tabbed panel (Figure 8–33).

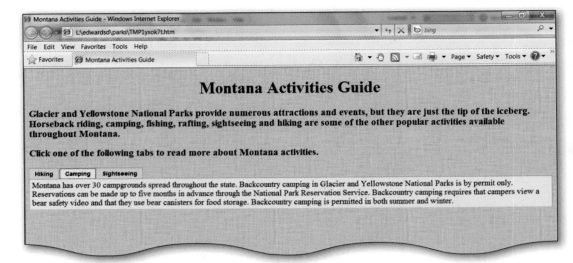

Figure 8–33

● Click the Sightseeing tab to display the Sightseeing tabbed panel (Figure 8–34).

● Close the browser.

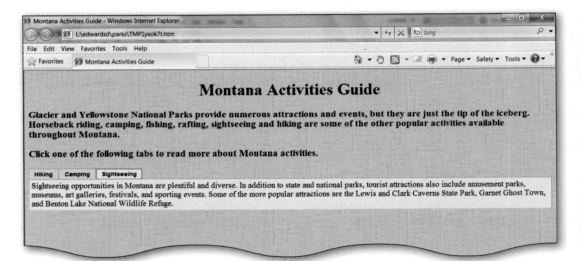

Figure 8–34

Customizing the Tabbed Panels Widget

You can customize the Tabbed Panels widget and many other widgets. You can set properties for the entire Tabbed Panels widget or for individual components only. If you are familiar with JavaScript and CSS, you can modify the text within the appropriate JavaScript or CSS file located in the SpryAssets folder. A simpler way to customize the widget is to use the CSS Styles panel. The Dreamweaver Help system provides details about the CSS rules to use to customize the Tabbed Panels widgets and other Spry widgets.

Format the Spry widget.
Although you can use the Property inspector to make some types of changes to a Spry widget, such as the number and name of the panels in a Tabbed Panels widget, you need to use the CSS Styles panel to customize the style and format of the widget. Examine the style rules in the CSS Styles panel for a widget to learn which attributes you can customize.

Plan Ahead

Table 8-2 shows information Dreamweaver Help provides for selecting the appropriate CSS rule to format text in a Tabbed Panels widget.

Table 8-2 CSS Rules for Tabbed Panels Widget Text	
Tabbed Panels widget text	**CSS rule**
Text in the entire widget	.TabbedPanels
Text in panel tabs only	.TabbedPanelsTabGroup or .TabbedPanelsTab
Text in content panels only	.TabbedPanelsContentGroup or .TabbedPanelsContent

As with Menu Bar widgets, you can change the background color of various parts of a Tabbed Panels widget. Table 8-3 shows information Dreamweaver Help provides for selecting the appropriate CSS rule to change the background color of the parts of a Tabbed Panels widget.

Table 8-3 CSS Rules for Tabbed Panels Widget Background Color	
Tabbed Panels widget part	**CSS rule**
Panel tabs	.Tabbed PanelsTabGroup or .TabbedPanelsTab
Content panels	.TabbedPanelsContentGroup or .TabbedPanelsContent
Selected tab	.TabbedPanelsTabSelected
Panel tab in focus (mouse pointer is pointing to the tab)	.TabbedPanelsTabHover

Besides changing the style of the text and background colors in a Tabbed Panels widget, you can specify the width of the entire widget. By default, the Tabbed Panels widget expands to fill the browser window. You can make sure the widget only takes up a certain amount of space across the page by setting the width property for the widget.

To Change the Font Style and Size of the Tabbed Panels Widget Text

The content text in the montana_activities Tabbed Panels widget appears in 12-point Times Roman, which are the font and font size of the text copied from the Word document. You can change the font to Arial to match the default font used on the tabs. The tab text is 9-point bold Arial by default. You can specify 12 points as the font size for all the text in the widget, and continue to bold the text displayed on the tabs. The following steps illustrate how to modify the font and font size in the Tabbed Panels widget.

- If necessary, expand the panel groups.

- Double-click the CSS Styles tab in the panel groups to display the CSS Styles tab.

- If necessary, click the All button to display all the CSS style rules on the page.

- Click the plus sign next to SpryTabbedPanels.css to expand the style rules for the Tabbed Panels widget.

- Double-click the Files tab to collapse its panel group.

- If necessary, drag the Properties bar down to display the complete list of CSS style rules (Figure 8–35).

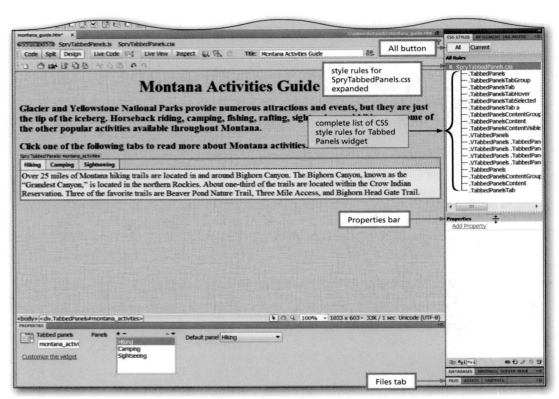

Figure 8–35

2

- In the CSS Styles panel, locate and then click the .TabbedPanelsContent rule in the All Rules area to display the properties for content text in the Tabbed Panels widget (Figure 8–36).

Q&A

What styles does the .TabbedPanelsContent rule set?

The .TabbedPanelsContent rule sets the styles for the content panels in the widget, including the text that appears in the tabbed panels.

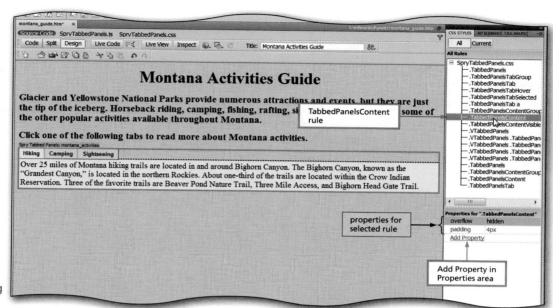

Figure 8–36

3

- Click Add Property in the Properties area of the CSS Styles panel to display a list box with an arrow button.

- Click the arrow button to display a list of properties (Figure 8–37).

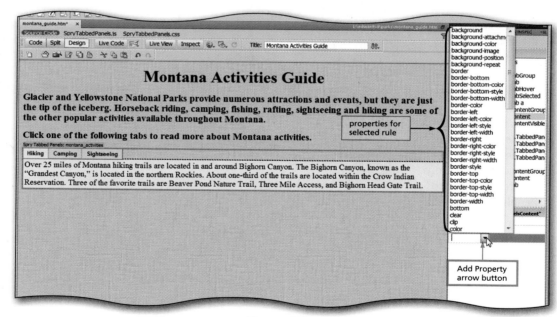

Figure 8–37

4

- Scroll in the list, and then click font to select it as the property to add to the .TabbedPanelsContent rule (Figure 8–38).

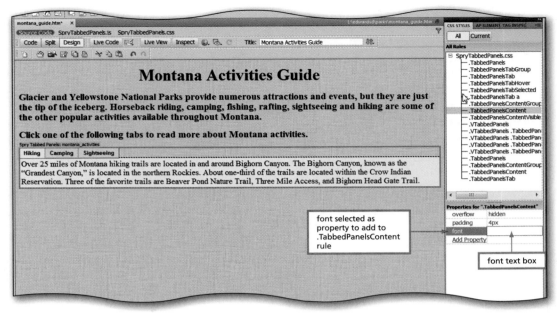

Figure 8–38

5

- Type `12pt arial; sans-serif` in the text box to the right of the font property to specify a 12-point Arial or sans-serif font.

- Press the ENTER key to specify Arial as the font and 12 points as the font size for the Tabbed Panels widget text (Figure 8–39).

Q&A

Why did I add sans-serif to the style rule?

In case a user does not have the Arial font installed on their computer, you specify sans-serif so that the browser can use a similar font that the user does have installed. Dreamweaver does not display "sans-serif" in the CSS Styles panel, though it does use it if necessary.

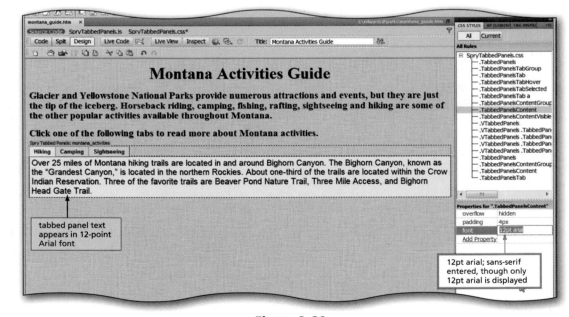

Figure 8–39

6

- Locate and then click the .TabbedPanelsTab rule in the All Rules area to display the properties for tab text in the Tabbed Panels widget (Figure 8–40).

Q&A

What styles does the .TabbedPanelsTab rule set?

The .TabbedPanelsTab rule sets the styles for the tab in the widget, including the text that appears on the tabs in the Tabbed Panels widget.

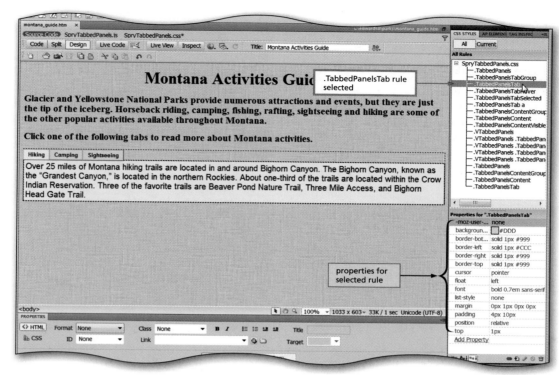

Figure 8–40

7

- Click to the right of the font property in the Properties area.

- Type **bold 12pt arial; sans-serif** and then press the ENTER key to specify a bold 12-point Arial or sans-serif font for the tab text (Figure 8–41).

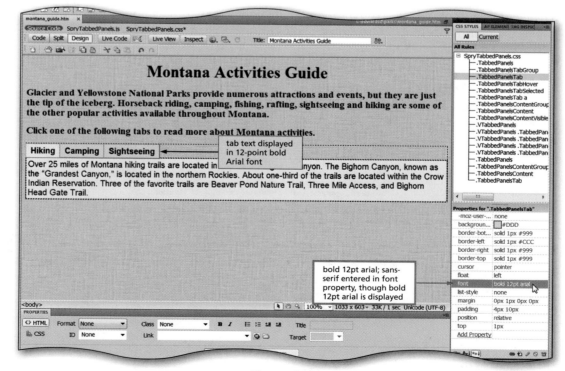

Figure 8–41

8
- Click the Save All button on the Standard toolbar to save your work.
- Click the Live View button on the Document toolbar to test the changes on the page.
- Click each tab in the Tabbed Panels widget to display the new formatting (Figure 8–42).

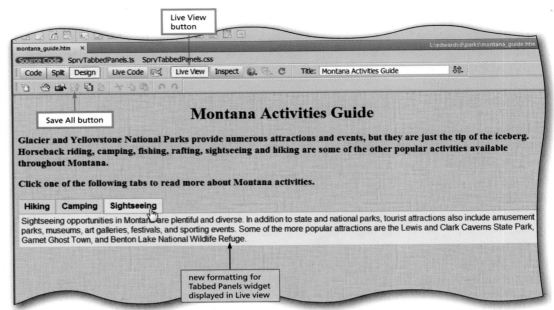

Figure 8–42

To Change the Background Color of the Panels

The default background color of unselected tabs is light gray (#DDD), while the default background color of selected tabs is white (#FFF). You can change the color of unselected tabs to a different, more eye-catching color by changing the background-color property of the .TabbedPanelsTab rule in the CSS Styles panel. You can also change the color of the selected tab, and provide interactivity by changing the color of an unselected tab when the mouse pointer points to it. The following steps illustrate changing the background color of the tabs in the montana_activities Tabbed Panels widget.

1
- Click the Live View button on the Document toolbar to return to Design view.
- If necessary, locate and then click the .TabbedPanelsTab rule in the All Rules area to display the properties for tabs in the Tabbed Panels widget.
- Click the color picker icon in the background-color text box to display a color palette (Figure 8–43).

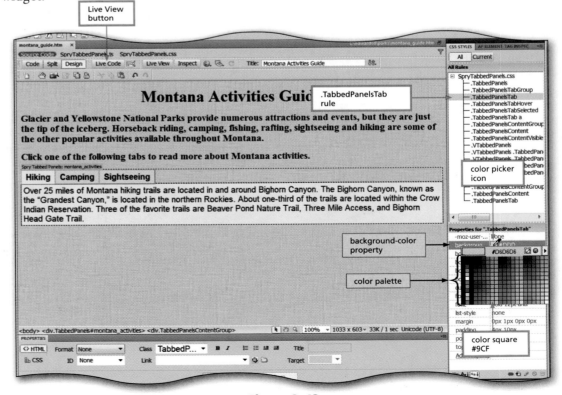

Figure 8–43

2

- Click color square #9CF (column 5, bottom row) to apply the color to the tabs (Figure 8–44).

Q&A

Can I type the hexadecimal value for the color instead of selecting it from the color palette?

Yes, you can enter the hexadecimal value by typing the value in the background-color text box.

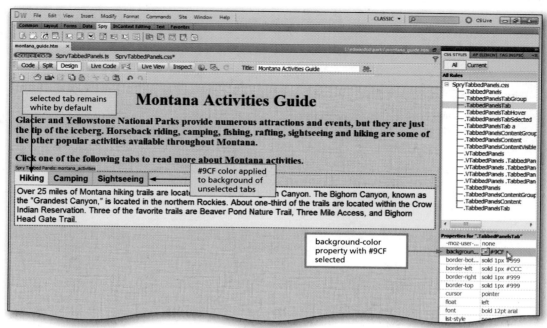

Figure 8–44

3

- Click the .TabbedPanels TabSelected rule in the All Rules area to display the properties for the selected tab in the Tabbed Panels widget.

- Click the color picker icon in the background-color text box to display a color palette (Figure 8–45).

Q&A

What styles does the .TabbedPanels TabSelected rule set?

The .TabbedPanels TabSelected rule sets the styles for the selected tab in the widget, including the background color.

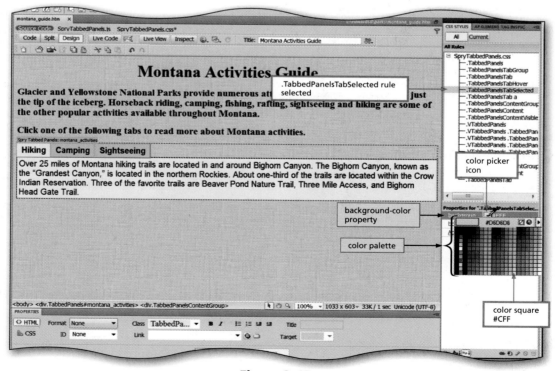

Figure 8–45

- Click color square #CFF (column 12, bottom row) to apply the color to the selected tab (Figure 8–46).

Figure 8–46

- Click the .TabbedPanelsTabHover rule in the All Rules area to display the properties applied to an unselected tab when the mouse pointer points to it.

- Click the color picker icon in the background-color text box to display a color palette (Figure 8–47).

Q&A

What styles does the .TabbedPanelsTabHover rule set?

The .TabbedPanelsTabHover rule sets the styles for an unselected tab when the mouse pointer is pointing to the tab, including the background color.

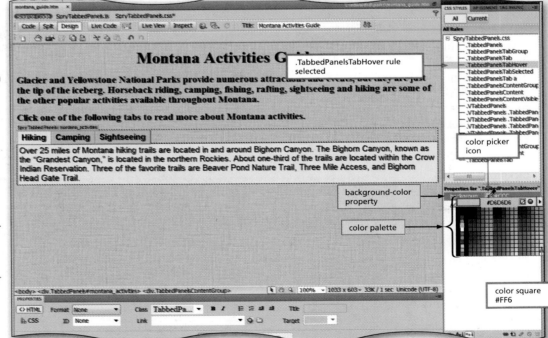

Figure 8–47

6

- Click color square #FF6 (last column, row 9) to apply the color that appears on an unselected tab when the mouse pointer points to it (Figure 8–48).

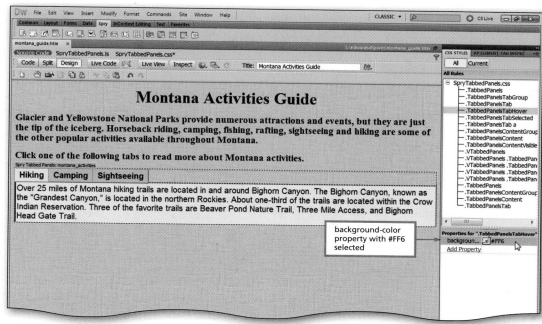

Figure 8–48

7

- Click the Save All button on the Standard toolbar to save your work.

- Click the Live View button on the Document toolbar to test the changes on the page.

- Point to and then click each tab in the Tabbed Panels widget to display the new formatting (Figure 8–49).

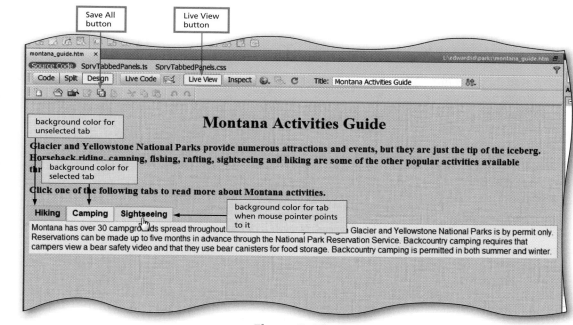

Figure 8–49

To Change the Background Color of the Tabs

The default background color of the tabbed content panels is very light gray (#EEE). You can change this to a color that coordinates with the tab colors by changing the background-color property of the .TabbedPanelsContent rule in the CSS Styles panel. The following steps illustrate changing the background color of the content panels in the montana_activities Tabbed Panels widget.

1
- Click the Live View button on the Document toolbar to return to Design view.

- Locate and then click the .TabbedPanelsContent rule in the All Rules area to display the properties for content panels in the Tabbed Panels widget (Figure 8–50).

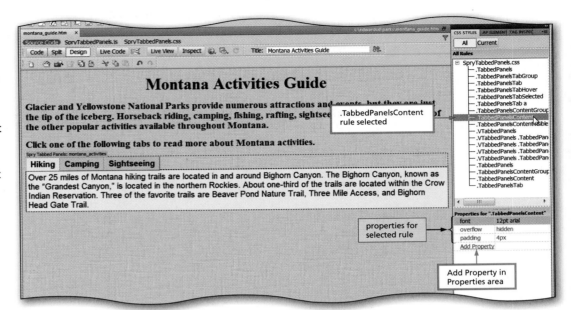

Figure 8–50

2
- Click Add Property in the Properties area of the CSS Styles panel to display a list box with an arrow button.

- Click the arrow button to display a list of properties.

- Click background-color to select it as the property to add to the .TabbedPanelsContent rule (Figure 8–51).

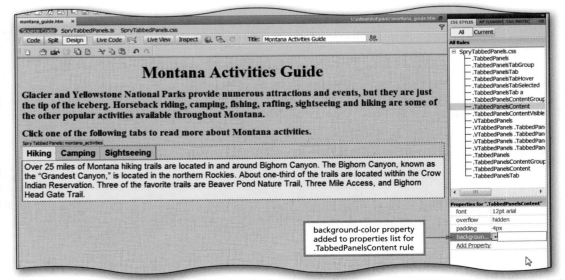

Figure 8–51

3

- Click the color picker icon in the background-color text box to display a color palette.

- Click color square #CFF (column 12, bottom row) to apply the color to the content panels (Figure 8–52).

Can I apply a different color to the selected panel?

No, you can change only the color of all the content panels.

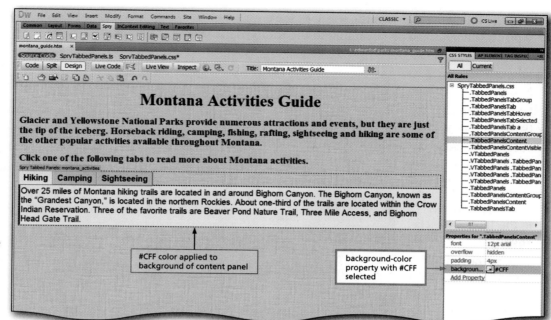

Figure 8–52

4

- Click the Save All button on the Standard toolbar to save your work.

- Click the Live View button on the Document toolbar to test the changes on the page.

- Click each tab in the Tabbed Panels widget to display the new formatting (Figure 8–53).

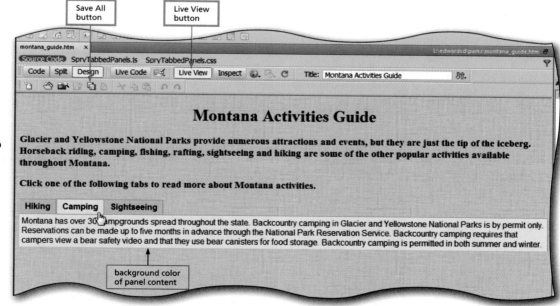

Figure 8–53

To Set the Width of the Tabbed Panels Widget

The following steps set the width of the entire montana_activities Tabbed Panels widget so it is always 640 pixels wide, instead of expanding to the width of the browser window.

- Click the Live View button on the Document toolbar to return to Design view.

- Locate and then click the .TabbedPanels rule in the All Rules area to display the properties for content panels in the Tabbed Panels widget.

- Click to the right of the width property to display two text boxes (Figure 8–54).

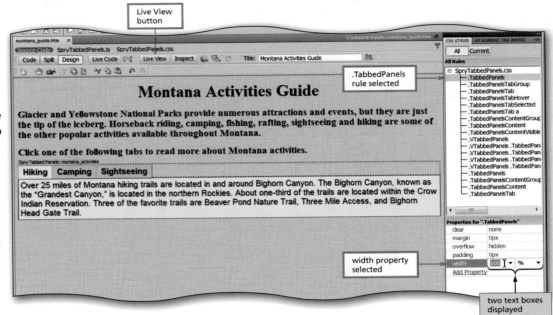

Figure 8–54

❷

- Enter 640 as the value in the first text box.

- Click the arrow button in the second text box, and then click px to set the measurement value to pixels.

- Click outside of the text box to deselect the width value (Figure 8–55).

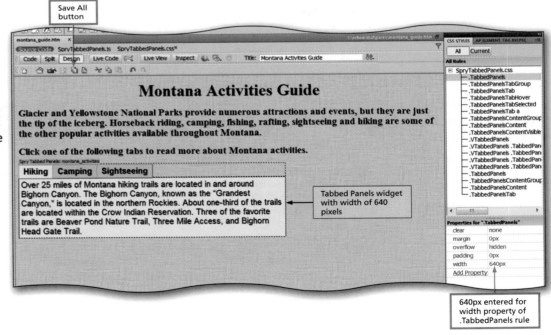

Figure 8–55

- Click the Save All button on the Standard toolbar to save your work.

- Press the F12 key to view the Web page in your browser, and allow blocked content, if necessary.

- Point to and then click each tab in the Tabbed Panels widget (Figure 8–56).

- Close the browser.

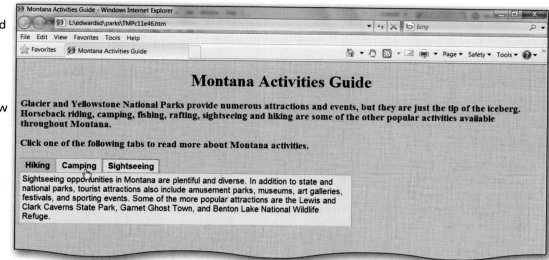

Figure 8–56

Spry Accordion Widgets

Your next activity is to add an Accordion widget to the montana_guide page to display images of hiking, camping, and sightseeing in Montana.

Similar to a Collapsible Panel widget, an Accordion widget is a set of collapsible panels that can store a large amount of content in a compact space. You display or hide the content by clicking a tab on the Accordion widget. While a Collapsible Panel widget can display the content of more than one tab at a time, the Accordion widget displays only one tab at a time.

To Add the Spry Accordion Widget to a Web Page

The following steps illustrate how to add the Spry Accordion widget to the montana_guide page. The widget will contain three panels displaying images of Montana activities.

- If necessary, open the montana_guide document to prepare for adding an Accordion widget.

  Click to the right of the Tabbed Panels widget, and then press the ENTER key twice to insert a blank line below the widget.

- Type **Click one of the following tabs to display images of a Montana activity.** to introduce the new widget.

- Apply Heading 3 to the new text.

- Click at the end of the new text, and then press the ENTER key to start a new line (Figure 8-57).

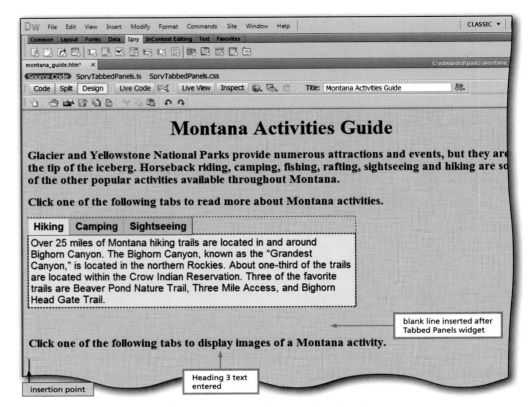

Figure 8–57

- Point to the Spry Accordion button on the Insert bar to identify the button (Figure 8–58).

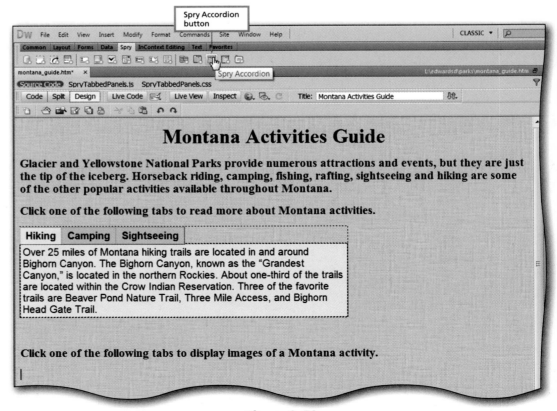

Figure 8–58

3

- Click the Spry Accordion button to insert an Accordion widget on the page.

- If necessary, scroll down to display the entire widget (Figure 8-59).

Only two tabs are displayed in the Accordion widget. Can I add other tabs to the widget?

Yes, you can add tabs to the widget as necessary. You will see how to do so shortly.

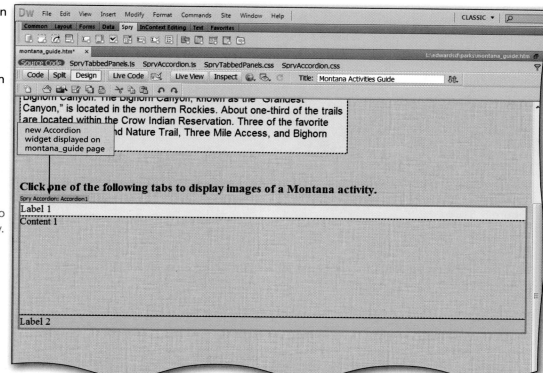

Figure 8–59

4

- If necessary, click the widget name tab to select the Accordion widget.

- Double-click the text in the Accordion text box in the Property inspector to select the default name.

- Type **activity_ images** and then press the ENTER key to name the widget (Figure 8-60).

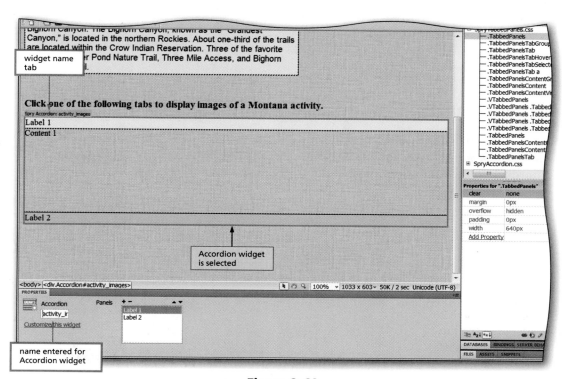

Figure 8–60

- In the Accordion widget, drag to select the Label 1 text to prepare for customizing it.
- Type **Hiking** to enter the name of the first tab.
- Move the mouse pointer over the Label 2 text to display the eye icon on the second tab (Figure 8–61).

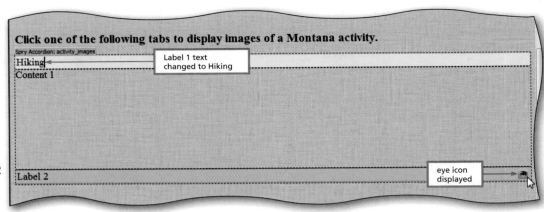

Figure 8–61

Q&A What does the eye icon indicate?

An open eye icon indicates that the Content panel in the Accordion widget is closed on the Web page; click the open eye icon to open the panel.

- Click the eye icon to open the second panel for editing.
- Drag to select the Label 2 text in the Accordion widget.
- Type **Camping** to enter the name of the second tab (Figure 8–62).

Figure 8–62

Other Ways

1. On Insert menu, point to Spry, click Spry Accordion

To Add a Panel to the Accordion Widget

The activity_images Accordion widget includes two tabs — one for hiking images and the other for camping images. The widget also should include a third tab for sightseeing images. The following steps illustrate how to add a third tab to the Accordion widget.

- If necessary, click in the activity_images Accordion widget to position the insertion point in the widget.
- Click div. Accordion#activity_ images in the tag inspector to select the entire widget (Figure 8–63).

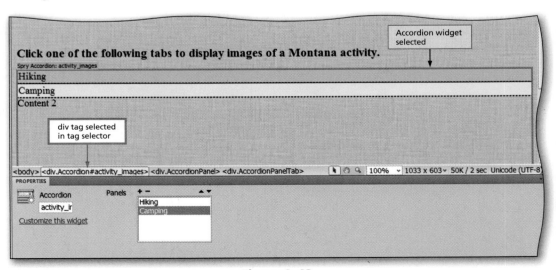

Figure 8–63

2
- Click the plus sign (Add panel button) in the Property inspector to add a third panel to the Accordion widget with the default name Label 3 (Figure 8–64).

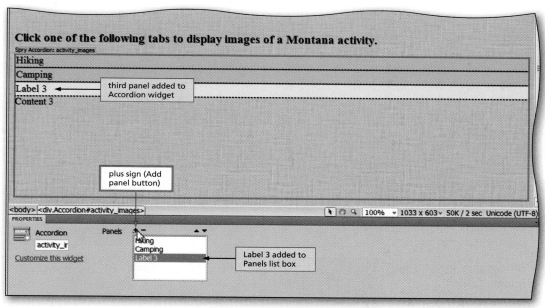

Figure 8–64

3
- Drag to select the Label 3 text in the widget.
- Type **Sightseeing** as the name of the third tab (Figure 8–65).

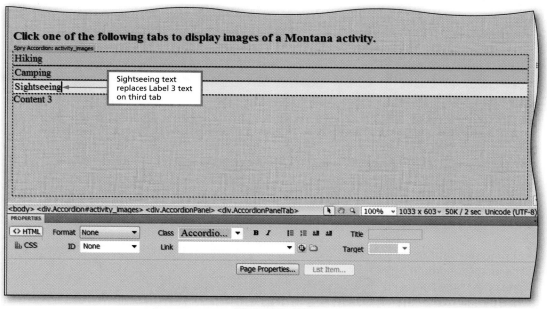

Figure 8–65

To Add Images to the Accordion Widget

Now that the activity_images Accordion widget has three tabs, you can add images to each panel that illustrate a Montana activity. The following steps show how to add images to the content panels in the Accordion widget.

1

- Drag to select the Content 3 text in the Sightseeing panel, and then press the DELETE key to delete the text.

- Double-click the CSS Panels tab to collapse the panel group.

- Click the Files tab to display the Files panel.

- If necessary, expand the images folder.

- Drag the whitetail_deer image to the Sightseeing content panel.

Q&A

What should I do if the Image Tag Accessibility Attributes dialog box is displayed?

Enter the alternate text (in this case, Whitetail deer) as the Alternate text, and then click the OK button. Do the same for the other images added to the Accordion widget.

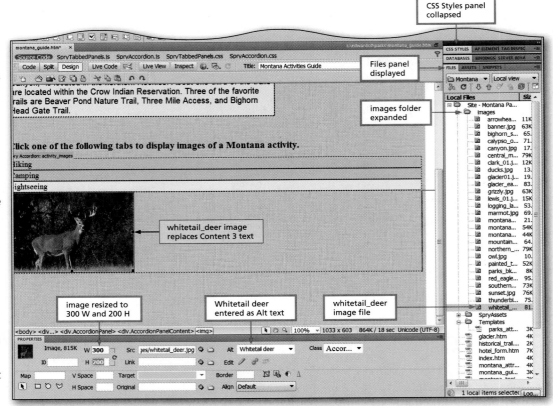

Figure 8–66

- Enter **Whitetail deer** as the Alt text for the image.

- Resize the image to 300 W and 200 H (Figure 8–66).

2

- Click to the right of the image, and then press the SPACEBAR to insert a space after the whitetail_deer image.

- Drag the red_eagle_ mountain image to the insertion point.

- Enter **Red Eagle Mountain** as the Alt text for the image.

- Resize the image to 300 W and 200 H (Figure 8–67).

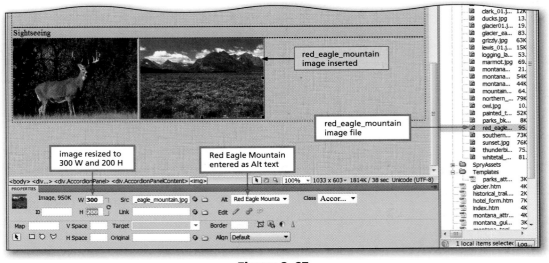

Figure 8–67

3

- Click the eye icon in the Camping tab to select the Camping panel.

- Drag to select the Content 2 text in the Camping panel, and then press the DELETE key to delete the text.

- Drag the sunset image to the Camping content panel.

- Enter **Montana sunset** as the Alt text for the image.

- Resize the image to 300 W and 200 H.

- Click to the right of the image, and then press the SPACEBAR to insert a space after the sunset image.

- Drag the thunderbird_ mountain image to the insertion point.

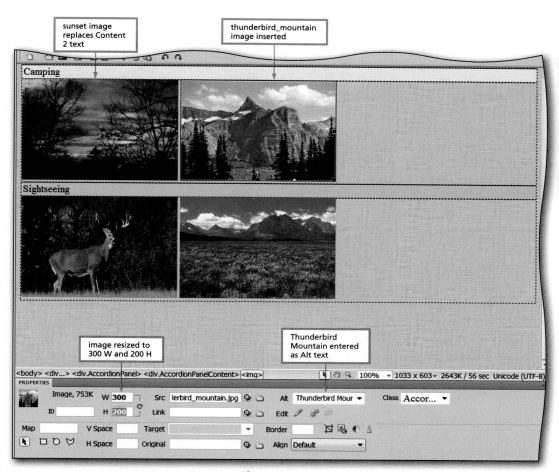

Figure 8–68

- Enter **Thunderbird Mountain** as the Alt text for the image.

- Resize the image to 300 W and 200 H (Figure 8–68).

4

- If necessary, scroll up and then click the eye icon in the Hiking tab to select the Hiking panel.
- Drag to select the Content 1 text in the Hiking panel, and then press the DELETE key to delete the text.
- Drag the canyon image to the Hiking content panel.
- Enter **Canyon** as the Alt text for the image.
- Resize the image to 300 W and 200 H.
- Click to the right of the image, and then press the SPACEBAR to insert a space after the canyon image.
- Drag the glacier01 image to the insertion point.
- Enter **Glacier** as the Alt text for the image.
- Resize the image to 300 W and 200 H (Figure 8-69).

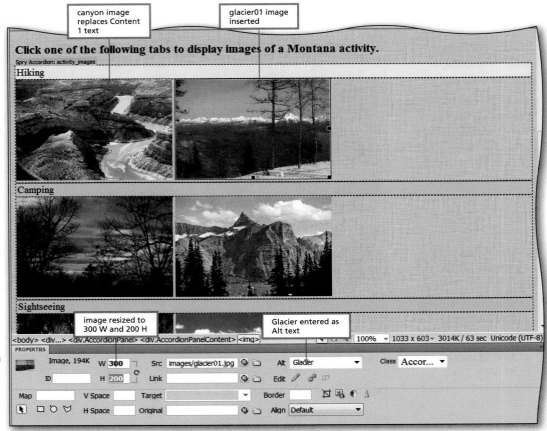

Figure 8–69

5

- Click the Save All button on the Standard toolbar to save your work.
- Click the OK button in the Copy Dependent Files dialog box to copy the files.
- Click the Live View button on the Document toolbar to test the changes on the page.
- Click each tab in the Accordion widget to display the images (Figure 8–70).

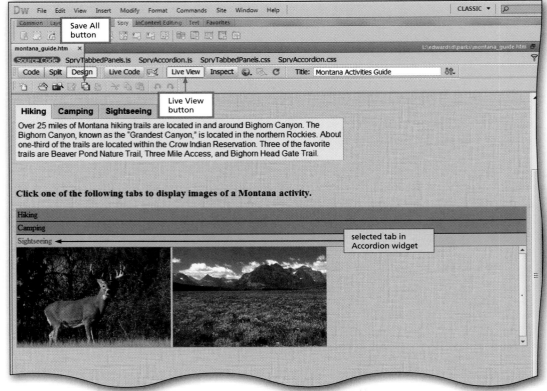

Figure 8–70

To Set the Width of the Accordion Widget

The following steps set the width of the entire activity_images widget so it is always 640 pixels wide, instead of expanding to the width of the browser window.

1

- Click the Live View button on the Document toolbar to return to Design view.

- Click the widget name tab to select the entire Accordion widget.

- Click the CSS Styles tab in the panel groups to display the CSS Styles panel.

- If necessary, click the Current button to display the CSS style rules for the current object, in this case, the activity_images Accordion widget (Figure 8–71).

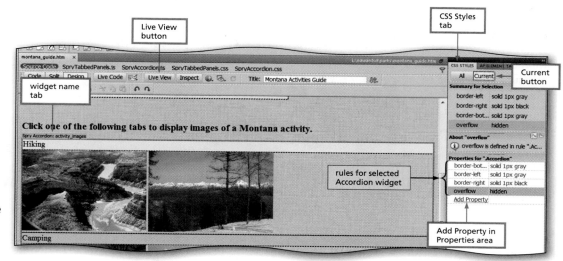

Figure 8–71

2

- Click Add Property in the Properties area of the CSS Styles panel to display a list box with an arrow button.

- Click the arrow button to display a list of properties.

- Scroll down and then click width to select it as the property to add to the .Accordion rule and display two text boxes for setting the width (Figure 8–72).

Figure 8–72

Q&A | What does the .Accordion rule cover?

The .Accordion rule covers styles for the entire Accordion widget.

3

- Enter 640 as the value in the first text box.

- If necessary, click the arrow button in the second text box, and then click px to set the measurement value to pixels.

- Click outside of the text box to deselect the width value (Figure 8–73).

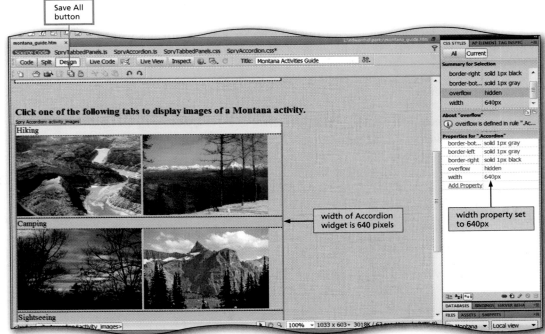

Figure 8–73

4

- Click the Save All button on the Standard toolbar to save your work.

- Press the F12 key to view the Web page in your browser, and allow blocked content, if necessary.

- Click each tab in the Accordion widget (Figure 8–74).

5

- Close the browser.

- Close the montana_ guide document.

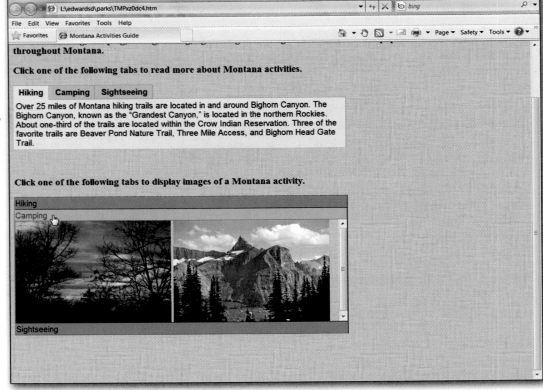

Figure 8–74

Spry Validation and Data Set Widgets

When you request information from Web site visitors, such as when you provide a form on a Web page, you can use Spry Validation widgets to test form content before the form is submitted to the server. The Validation widgets make sure certain rules are met to prevent problems processing the form. For example, if a form contains an E-mail Address field, you can attach a Spry Validation Text Field widget to the E-mail Address text field that checks to be sure users enter the @ symbol in the e-mail address.

All Spry Validation widgets generate JavaScript that allows a form field to test the field entry before processing the form. As with other widgets, the Spry Validation widgets generate CSS files that contain style rules for formatting the widget.

A Spry Data Set is a JavaScript object that contains a collection of data from a data source (such as an XML file or HTML file). When displayed in the browser, the data set appears as a standard table containing rows and columns. You select the layout for the table as you create the Data Set widget.

Spry Data Set widgets include all of the data from the selected data source by default. You can refine this selection by using CSS data selectors to include only some of the data from the data source.

Table 7-1 describes the Spry Validation and Spry Data Set widgets. You insert both types of widgets using the same techniques you use to insert and modify other types of Spry widgets. You also can practice using a Spry Validation widget and a Spry Data Set widget in the exercises at the end of the chapter.

Adding Spry Effects to Web Pages

Recall from Chapter 7 that you can apply Spry effects to Web pages to add visual enhancements and animations to text and other elements on a Web page. Dreamweaver uses JavaScript to apply effects to HTML elements without needing additional custom tags so that you do not need to learn JavaScript. Dreamweaver uses Spry to apply these effects because when you click an item or perform another action, such as pointing to text or double-clicking it, the browser only needs to update the text or other element that includes an effect, not the entire Web page.

Consider applying Spry effects to objects on the Web page.
Spry effects can change a Web page element's opacity, scale, position, and styling properties such as background color. You can apply one or more Spry effects to create the enhancement you want. Spry effects should attract rather than distract your Web site visitors, so apply Spry effects sparingly and only as appropriate to the content.

Plan Ahead

In this chapter, you complete the Montana Parks project by applying the Shake effect to the Montana map image located in the index.htm page and the Shrink effect to the glacier image.

To Apply the Spry Shake Effect

The following steps show how to apply the Spry Shake effect to the montana_map image on the index page.

1

- Open the index.htm document.

- Click the montana_map image on the page to select it.

- Click the Tag Inspector tab in the panels group to display the Behaviors panel.

- If necessary, click the Behaviors button to prepare for selecting a behavior for the montana_map image.

- Point to the Add behavior button to identify the button (Figure 8-75).

The Tag Inspector tab does not appear in the panels group. How do I open it?

Click Window on the Application bar, and then click Behaviors.

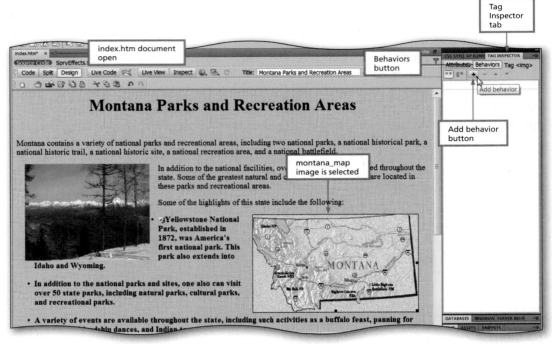

Figure 8–75

2

- Click the Add behavior button to display a list of behaviors to add to the image.

- Point to Effects to display the submenu and then point to Shake (Figure 8-76).

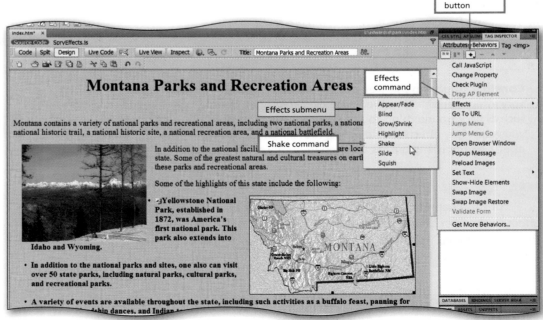

Figure 8–76

3

- Click Shake to display the Shake dialog box (Figure 8-77).

Figure 8–77

4

- Click the OK button to apply the Shake effect to the selected image.

The montana_map image did not change after I applied the Shake effect. Did I do something wrong?

No. The Shake effect does not appear until you display the Web page in a browser or in Live view.

- Click the Save button on the Standard toolbar to save the document.

- Click the OK button in the Copy Dependent Files dialog box to copy the files.

- Press the F12 key to view the Web page in your browser, and allow blocked content, if necessary.

- Click the map to create the Shake effect (Figure 8-78).

Figure 8–78

5

- Close the browser.

To Apply the Spry Squish Effect

The following steps show how to apply the Spry Squish effect to the glacier01 image on the index page.

- Click the glacier01 image on the index page to select it.
- Click the Add behavior button in the Behaviors panel.
- Point to Effects to display the submenu and then point to Squish (Figure 8–79).

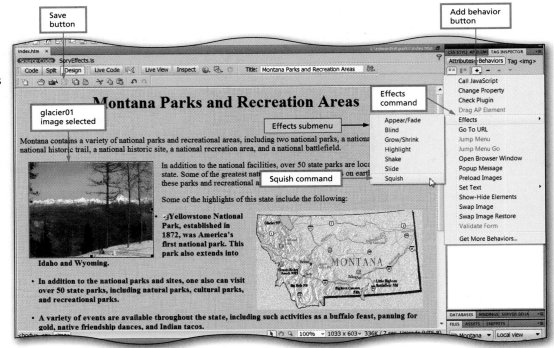

Figure 8–79

- Click Squish to display the Squish dialog box.
- Click the OK button to apply the Squish effect to the selected image.
- Click the Save button on the Standard toolbar to save the document.
- Press the F12 key to view the Web page in your browser, and allow blocked content, if necessary.
- Click the glacier image to create the Squish effect (Figure 8–80).

- Close the browser.

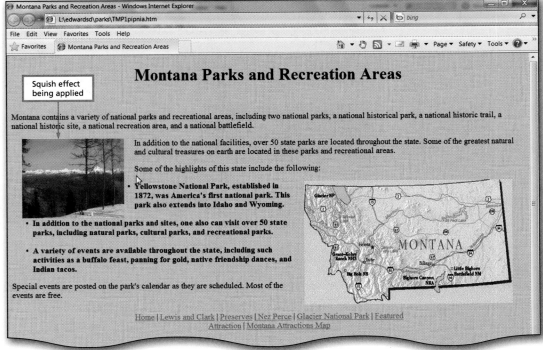

Figure 8–80

To Close the Web Site and Quit Dreamweaver

After you create your interactive Web pages using Spry widgets and effects, and test and verify that the widgets and effects work, Chapter 8 is complete. The following step closes the Web site and quits Dreamweaver.

1 Click the Close button in the upper-right corner of the Dreamweaver title bar to close the Dreamweaver window, the Document window, and the Montana Parks Web site.

Chapter Summary

In this chapter, you learned about the Spry widgets available in Dreamweaver. You added Tooltip widgets to a Web page, and then opened a new page for the Montana Parks Web site. You added a Tabbed Panels widget to the new page, included descriptive text on the panel's tabs, and then inserted text on the page by copying and pasting it from a Microsoft Word document. You also customized and formatted the Tabbed Panels widget. Next, you added an Accordion widget to the page, and then customized the widget. Finally, you applied two Spry effects to images on the index page. The items listed below include all the new skills you have learned in this chapter.

1. Insert a Spry Tooltip widget for a Web page (DW 560)
2. Insert a Spry Tooltip widget for a form element (DW 565)
3. Add the Spry Tabbed Panels widget to a Web page (DW 569)
4. Add a panel to the Tabbed Panels widget (DW 572)
5. Change the order of the panels (DW 576)
6. Set the default panel (DW 578)
7. Change the font style and size of the Tabbed Panels widget text (DW 577)
8. Change the background color of the tabs (DW 586)
9. Change the background color of the panels (DW 590)
10. Set the width of the Tabbed Panels widget (DW 592)
11. Add the Spry Accordion widget to a Web page (DW 594)
12. Add a panel to the Accordion widget (DW 596)
13. Add images to an Accordion widget (DW 598)
14. Apply the Spry Shake effect (DW 604)
15. Apply the Spry Squish effect (DW 606)

Learn It Online

Test your knowledge of chapter content and key terms.

Instructions: To complete the Learn It Online exercises, start your browser, click the Address bar, and then enter the Web address scsite.com/dwCS5/learn. When the Dreamweaver CS5 Learn It Online page is displayed, click the link for the exercise you want to complete and then read the instructions.

Chapter Reinforcement TF, MC, and SA
A series of true/false, multiple choice, and short answer questions that test your knowledge of the chapter content.

Flash Cards
An interactive learning environment where you identify chapter key terms associated with displayed definitions.

Practice Test
A series of multiple choice questions that test your knowledge of chapter content and key terms.

Who Wants To Be a Computer Genius?
An interactive game that challenges your knowledge of chapter content in the style of a television quiz show.

Wheel of Terms
An interactive game that challenges your knowledge of chapter key terms in the style of the television show *Wheel of Fortune*.

Crossword Puzzle Challenge
A crossword puzzle that challenges your knowledge of key terms presented in the chapter.

Apply Your Knowledge

Reinforce the skills and apply the concepts you learned in this chapter.

Using a Squish Effect

Instructions: In this activity you create a new Web page, add a background, text, and images, and then apply a Squish effect. Figure 8-81a shows the page as it appears when opened. Figure 8-81b shows the page during the effect.

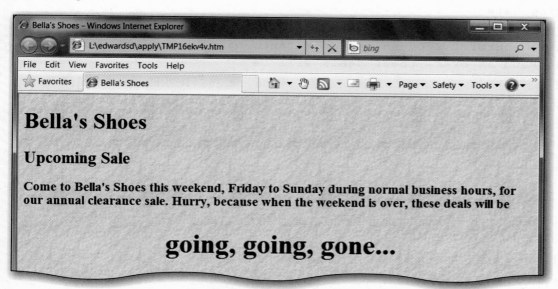

Figure 8–81a

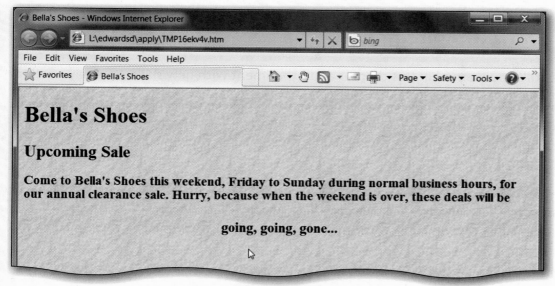

Figure 8–81b

Perform the following tasks:

1. If necessary, start Dreamweaver and then open the Apply Exercises Web site. Copy the going image file provided with your data files to the images folder for the Apply Exercises Web site. Create a new, blank HTML page and then save it as apply_ch08.htm.

2. Apply the apply_bkg image to the background of the Web page.

3. Title the Web page **Bella's Shoes**.

4. Insert the following lines of text:

   Bella's Shoes

   Upcoming Sale

   Come to Bella's Shoes this weekend, Friday to Sunday during normal business hours, for our annual clearance sale. Hurry, because when the weekend is over, these deals will be

5. Apply Heading 1 to the first line, Heading 2 to the second line, and Heading 3 to the text "Come to Bella's... will be". Press the ENTER key to insert a new line, and then center the new line.

6. Drag the going image to the insertion point.

7. Open the Behaviors panel, if necessary, by clicking Window on the Application bar and then clicking Behaviors.

8. In the Behaviors panel, click the Add behavior button, point to Effects, and then click Squish. Click OK in the Squish dialog box.

9. Save the document, copy dependent files if necessary, and then view the page in your browser. Allow blocked content, if necessary.

10. Click the going, going, gone image to test the Squish effect.

11. Submit your document in the format specified by your instructor.

Extend Your Knowledge

Extend the skills you learned in this chapter and experiment with new skills. You may need to use Help to complete the assignment.

Adding and Modifying Spry Effects

Instructions: In this activity, you create a new Web page, add text, and then add and modify several Spry effects (Figure 8-82).

Perform the following tasks:

1. If necessary, start Dreamweaver and then open the Extend Exercises Web site.

2. Create a new, blank HTML page, and then save it as extend_ch08.htm. Title the Web page **Spry Effects**.

3. Apply the extend_bkg image as the background for the page.

4. Type the following heading at the top of the page: **Adding and Modifying Spry Effects**. Apply Heading 1 to this text.

5. Press ENTER at the end of the heading to insert a new line.

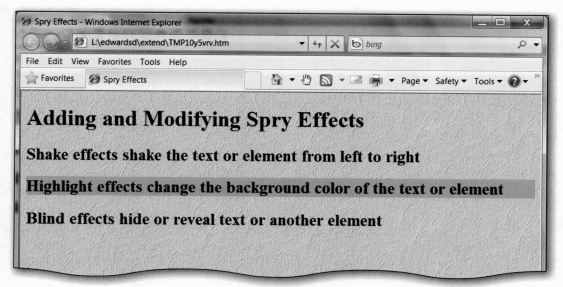

Figure 8–82

6. Type the following lines of text, pressing ENTER after each, and then apply Heading 2 to each line:

   `Shake effects shake the text or element from left to right`

   `Highlight effects change the background color of the text or element`

   `Blind effects hide or reveal text or another element`

7. Open the Behaviors panel, if necessary, by clicking Window on the Application bar, and then clicking Behaviors.

8. Select the line of text that begins with "Shake effects."

9. In the Behaviors panel, click the Add behavior button, point to Effects, and then click Shake. Click OK in the Shake dialog box.

10. Select the line of text that begins with "Highlight effects." In the Behaviors panel, click the Add behavior button, point to Effects, and then click Highlight. Click OK in the Highlight dialog box.

11. Select the line of text that begins with "Blind effects." In the Behaviors panel, click the Add behavior button, point to Effects, and then click Blind. Click OK in the Blind dialog box.

12. Save your document, copy dependent files if necessary, and then view the page in your browser. Allow blocked content, if necessary.

13. Click each of the lines of text to view the effect, and then close the browser.

14. Return to Dreamweaver.

15. Click the Highlight line. In the Behaviors panel, right-click Highlight, and then click Edit Behavior.

16. In the Highlight dialog box, click the End Color text box, type **#3399FF,** and then click OK.

17. Click the Blind line. In the Behaviors panel, right-click Blind, and then click Edit Behavior.

18. In the Blind dialog box, click the Effect duration text box, type **20000,** and then click OK.

19. Save your document, and then refresh the browser window. Click each of the lines of text to view the changes, and then close your browser window.

20. Submit your document in the format specified by your instructor.

STUDENT ASSIGNMENTS

Make It Right

Reinforce the skills and apply the concepts you learned in this chapter.

Modifying a Spry Effect

Instructions: In this activity, you modify an existing Web page with a Spry effect by modiyfing the effect (Figure 8-83).

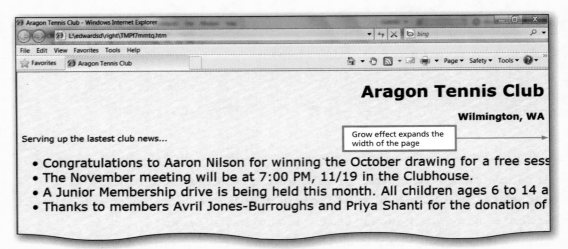

Figure 8–83

Perform the following tasks:

1. If necessary, start Dreamweaver and then copy the right_ch08.htm document provided with your data files to the Right Exercises Web site. Copy the SpryEffects.js file into the SpryAssets folder in Right Exercises Web site. (*Hint:* To see the SpryAssets folder, you may need to change your Windows settings. Search for "display hidden files and folders" in the Windows Control Panel).

2. Open the Right Exercises Web site, and then open the right_ch08.htm file.

3. View the page in your browser. Allow blocked content, if necessary.

4. Click the bulleted list to make it shrink. Click the area where the list was again to confirm that the list does not reappear.

5. Close your browser window.

6. In Dreamweaver, select the bulleted list.

7. Open the Behaviors panel, if necessary, by clicking Window on the Application bar, and then clicking Behaviors.

8. In the Behaviors panel, right-click the Grow/Shrink effect, and then click Edit Behavior.

9. In the Grow/Shrink dialog box, select Grow in the Effect list, and then enter **50** as the Grow from value and enter **150** as the Grow to value. Click the Grow from button and then click Top Left Corner. Click OK.

10. Title your Web page **Aragon Tennis Club.**

11. Save your document and then view the page in your browser. Allow blocked content, if necessary.

12. Click the bulleted list to make it shrink and then grow.

13. Submit your Web page in the format specified by your instructor.

In the Lab

Create Web pages using the guidelines, concepts, and skills presented in this chapter. Labs are listed in order of increasing difficulty.

Lab 1: Adding a Tabbed Panels Widget to the computer_tips Web Page

Problem: The proprietors of Bryan's Computer Repair Services would like to add a list of the management team to their Web site. The page will contain additional information regarding computer repair services and will be displayed through the use of the Spry Tabbed Panels widget (Figure 8-84).

Figure 8–84

Perform the following tasks:

1. If necessary, start Dreamweaver, and then open the Computer Services Repair Web site. Create a new, blank HTML page and then save it as management.htm.

2. Apply the repair_bkg image to the background of the Web page. Title the page `Management`.

3. Type `Bryan's Computer Repair Services`, and then apply Heading 1. Press ENTER. Type `Management Team`, and then apply Heading 2. Press ENTER.

4. Click the Spry Tabbed Panels button on the Insert bar.

5. Name the Tabbed Panels widget `mgmt_team`.

6. Select Tab 1 in the first panel and then type `Bryan Caruso, President`.

7. Select Content 1 in the first panel and then type the following text: `Bryan is the president and founder. He has a degree in computer science from Estes Community College, and numerous networking, security, and computer repair certifications, including A+, MCP, CCNA and Network+.`

8. Display the second panel in the widget.

9. Select Tab 2 in the second panel and then type `Aliya Bartini, Vice President`.

10. Select Content 2 in the second panel and then type the following text: `Aliya was Bryan's first staff member. Previously, she worked as a freelance quality assurance tester for several software and networking companies. She graduated with honors from the University of New Hampshire with a degree in government. She holds certifications in many networking, security, and computer repair areas, including A+ and Server+. She teaches A+ certification at Estes Community College.`

11. Add a third tabbed panel to the widget by selecting the widget and then clicking the plus sign (Add panel button) in the Property inspector.

12. Select Tab 3 in the third panel and then type `Mike Ping, Senior Technician.`

13. Select Content 3 in the third panel and then type the following text: `Mike oversees the scheduling and hiring of the technicians. He has a degree in computer science from Estes Community College, where he worked in the technical services department for four years. Included in his many computer repair, networking, and security certifications are A+, Server+, and CCSP.`

14. Save the document, copy dependent files if necessary, and then view the page in your browser. Allow blocked content, if necessary. Click each tab to test the panels.

15. Submit your document in the format specified by your instructor.

In the Lab

Lab 2: Creating a Data Set for the Baskets by Carole Web Site

Problem: Carole would like to add a page that lists some common flowers and their meanings. She asks you to help her with this project by adding a Spry Data Set. The completed Web page is shown in Figure 8-85.

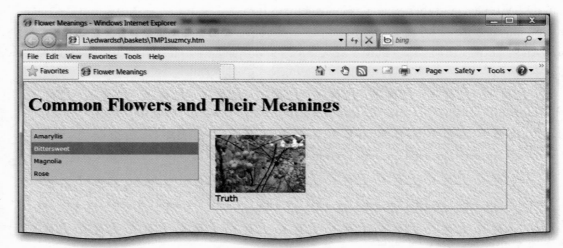

Figure 8–85

Perform the following tasks:

1. If necessary, start Dreamweaver and then open the Gift Basket Designs Web site. Copy the flower_ data document and the four floral image files provided with your data files to the Gift Basket Designs Web site (magnolia, red_rose, amaryllis, and bittersweet).

2. Create a blank HTML page, and save the page as flower_meanings. Title the Web page **Flower Meanings**. Apply the baskets_bkg image to the background.

3. At the top of the page, type **Common Flowers and Their Meanings** and then apply Heading 1 to the text.

4. Press ENTER at the end of the heading, and then save the document.

5. Click the Spry Data Set button on the Insert bar to open the Spry Data Set dialog box.

6. Select the text in the Data Set Name text box, and then type **Meanings**.

7. Click the Browse button. In the Select file source dialog box, navigate to the baskets folder if necessary, click flower_data, and then click OK.

8. Click the yellow arrow next to the table to select it, and then click the Next button. Click the Next button again.

9. In the next window, click the Insert master/detail layout option button, and then click the Done button.

10. Save your document. If a Copy Dependent Files dialog box is displayed, click OK. Start your browser (do not preview the image), and then open the flower_meanings file. Allow blocked content, if necessary. Click the flower names in the left column to view the change in the right column.

11. Submit the document in the format specified by your instructor.

In the Lab

Lab 3: Adding Spry Validation Groups to the Credit Protection Web Site

Problem: Jessica would like to create a form for setting up an account and use the Spry Validation Text Field widgets to make sure customers enter the correct information. The completed form is shown in Figure 8-86.

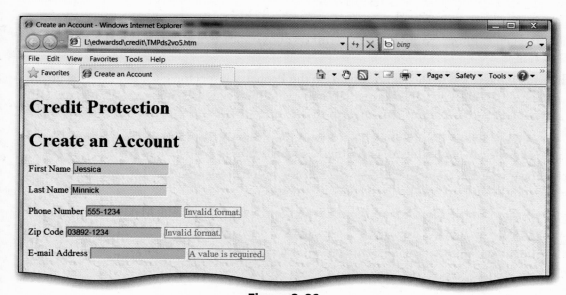

Figure 8–86

Perform the following tasks:

1. If necessary, start Dreamweaver and then open the Credit Protection Web site. Create a blank HTML page and save it as validation_form. Apply the credit_bkg background image to the Web page. Title the Web page `Create an Account`.

2. At the top of the page, type the following two lines and then apply Heading 1 to both lines:

    `Credit Protection`

    `Create an Account`

3. Press ENTER after the second heading, click the Insert on the Application bar, point to Form, and then click Form.

4. In the Property inspector, change the Form ID to `Account`.

5. In the new form, type `First Name` as the label, and then press the SPACEBAR.

6. On the Insert bar, click the Spry Validation Text Field button. Enter `First_Name` as the Spry TextField ID.

7. Click after the text field, press ENTER, type `Last Name` as the label, press the SPACEBAR, and then create a new text field with the ID `Last_Name`. Click after the text field and press ENTER.

8. Type `Phone Number` as the label, press the SPACEBAR, and then create a new text field with the ID `Phone`. Click after the text field and press ENTER.

9. Type `Zip Code` as the label, press the SPACEBAR, and then create a new text field with the ID `Zip`. Click after the text field and press ENTER.

10. Type `E-mail Address` as the label, press the SPACEBAR, and then create a new text field with the ID `Email`.

11. Click the widget name tab of the First Name text field. In the Property inspector, click the Blur check box. Type `1` in the Min chars text box.

12. Click the widget name tab of the Last Name text field. In the Property inspector, click the Blur check box. Type `1` in the Min chars text box.

13. Click the widget name tab of the Phone text field. In the Property inspector, click the Type list arrow, and then click Phone Number. In the Hint text box, type `(xxx) xxx-xxxx`. Click the Blur check box.

14. Click the widget name tab of the Zip text field. In the Property inspector, click the Type list arrow, and then click Zip Code. Click the Format list arrow, and then click US-5, if necessary. In the Hint text box, type `01234`. Click the Blur check box.

15. Click the widget name tab of the Email text field. In the Property inspector, click the Type list arrow, and then click E-mail Address. Click the Blur check box.

16. Save your document. If a Copy Dependent Files dialog box is displayed, click OK and then view the page in your browser. Allow blocked content, if necessary.

17. Enter values, both valid and invalid, in the text fields. Try to skip a text field. Make sure the form works as intended.

18. Submit the document in the format specified by your instructor.

Cases and Places

Apply your creative thinking and problem solving skills to design and implement a solution.

• Easier ••More Difficult

• 1: Create a Tabbed Panels Widget for the Favorite Sports Web Site

You decide to create a page with a tabbed panel to your Sports Web site so that you can add information about multiple topics in a compact space. Add your background image and a title to the page. Save the page in your sports Web site. Insert the Tabbed Panels widget. Include at least three tabs. Name the tabs, and add content to all of them. For a selection of images and backgrounds, visit the Dreamweaver CS5 Media Web page (scsite.com/dwcs5/media) and then click Media below Chapter 8.

• 2: Create Accordion Panels for the Hobby Web Site

You would like to add some interactivity to your Hobby Web site. You decide to do this by adding a Spry Accordion widget. First, create a new page, add a background image, and then add an appropriate title. Next, insert the Accordion widget and then add a panel so the widget has three panels. Provide appropriate names for the panels and then add content to each panel. Create a link to your home page from this new page. Upload the new page to a remote site, if instructed to do so. For a selection of images and backgrounds, visit the Dreamweaver CS5 Media Web page (scsite.com/dwcs5/media) and then click Media below Chapter 8.

•• 3: Add Tabbed Panels to the Politics Web Site

Your campaign for political office is going well, and you want to enhance your campaign Web site by adding additional pages. However, you do not want to have a lot of confusing text on one page. Therefore, you decide to add a Tabbed Panels widget with three tabs instead of three new pages. Create the new Web page and then add an appropriate background image and title. Add the widget and appropriate title and text for each of the tabs and panels. Upload the revised Web site to a remote server. For a selection of images and backgrounds, visit the Dreamweaver CS5 Media Web page (scsite.com/dwcs5/media) and then click Media below Chapter 8.

•• 4: Add Spry Validation Groups to the Favorite Music Web Site

Make It Personal

Add a new page to your Music Web site. Add Spry Validation elements, such as Text Fields and Radio Buttons, to make a form for users of your site to create an account. Add validation rules for the text fields to verify the correct format. For a selection of images and backgrounds, visit the Dreamweaver CS5 Media Web page (scsite.com/dwcs5/media) and then click Media below Chapter 8.

•• 5: Add Spry Effects to the Student Trips Web Site

Working Together

The Student Trips Web site has become even more popular. You and your team would like to add a more attractive index page that will catch the attention of more students. You decide to add Spry effects to each page. Individual team members are each responsible for creating one of the effects. Decide as a group who is doing which effect so that you use a variety of effects. Modify the effects as necessary to achieve the desired results. Upload the new pages to a remote server. For a selection of images and backgrounds, visit the Dreamweaver CS5 Media Web page (scsite.com/dwcs5/media) and then click Media below Chapter 8.

9 | Media Objects

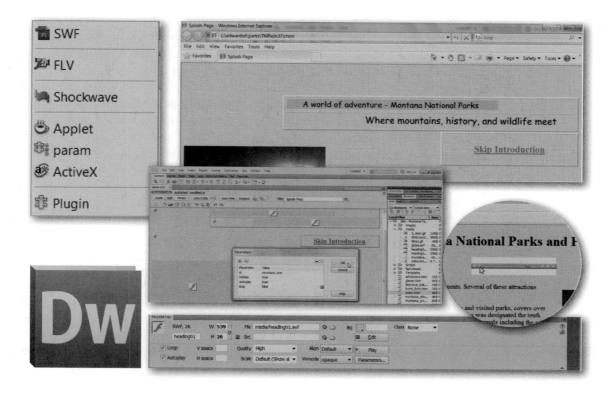

Objectives

You will have mastered the material in this chapter when you can:

- Describe media objects
- Insert Flash text into a Web page
- Insert a Flash movie into a Web page
- Add a background sound to a Web page
- Embed a sound file in a Web page
- Insert a video into a Web page
- Insert an animated GIF file into a Web page

- Use the Results panel group to validate a Web page and check links
- Check for plug-ins
- Describe Shockwave and how to insert a Shockwave movie into a Web page
- Describe a Java applet and how to insert an applet into a Web page
- Describe the ActiveX control and how it differs from plug-ins

9 | Media Objects

Introduction

Media objects, also called multimedia, are files that can be displayed or executed within HTML documents or in a stand-alone fashion. Examples include graphics such as GIFs and JPEGs, video, audio, Flash objects (SWF), Shockwave objects (DIR or DCR), PDFs (Adobe's Portable Document Format), Java applets, and other objects that can be viewed through a browser using a helper application or using a plug-in. A **helper application** is a program such as the Flash player or Shockwave viewer. These two examples are Adobe programs and are handled easily through Dreamweaver. A **plug-in** is a program application that is installed on your computer and used to view plug-in programs through the Web browser. Once a plug-in is installed, its functionality is integrated into the HTML file, and the Web browser generally recognizes the plug-in application. In this chapter, you learn how to add interactive media to a Web page. Interactive media, or multimedia, is not suitable for all Web sites. You most likely have visited Web sites that contained so many bits and pieces of multimedia that, instead of being a constructive part of the site, the multimedia elements were detrimental to the Web experience. Therefore, when adding this type of element to your Web page, you need to consider the value of each element and how it will enhance or detract from your site.

Project — Designing with Interactive Media

As you read this chapter, you will learn how to add to your Web site the page shown in Figure 9–1a and how to add an embedded sound and a video to the preserves page shown in Figure 9–1b. You add a **splash page** that will contain Flash text, a Flash movie, and a background sound. A splash page generally consists of a default home page that displays the Web site logo or some other Web site promotion. Many splash pages use various types of interactive media — from Flash movies to animated graphics — and are good mood setters. After one or two visits to the splash page, however, the frequent Web site visitor most likely would prefer to skip the page and move on to the main Web site. Therefore, a link is added to the splash page that, when clicked, will take the visitor directly to the Web site's index page. The splash page with the link is shown in Figure 9–1a. These two elements use the Windows Media Player as the helper application to display the media within the browser window. Finally, you learn how to use the Link Checker to test links on your Web site.

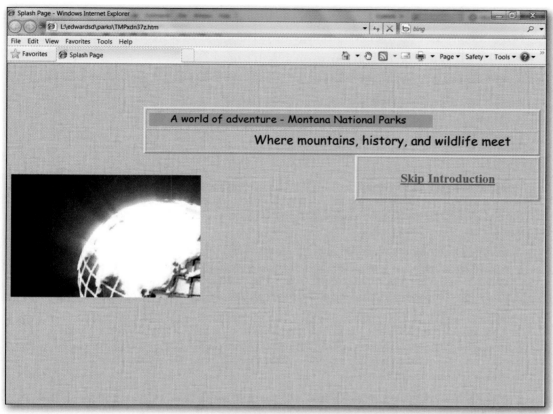

Figure 9–1a

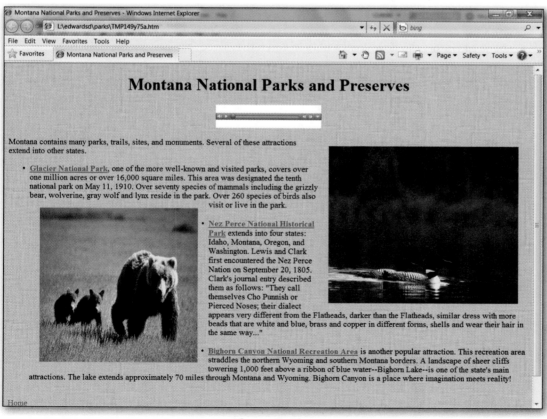

Figure 9–1b

Overview

As you read this chapter, you will learn how to add media objects to the Web pages shown in Figure 9–1 on the previous page by performing these general tasks:

- Insert Flash text or a Flash movie on a Web page.
- Add sounds to a Web page.
- Include video on a Web page.
- Work with plug-ins.
- Validate a Web page.

Plan Ahead

General Project Guidelines

When adding interactive multimedia to a Web site, consider the purpose and audience of the site. As you create the Web pages shown in Figure 9–1, you should follow these general guidelines:

1. **Insert a Flash object to provide entertainment and direct attention to certain elements.** Animated images and text, video, and sound can make your Web site more entertaining and appealing. By placing elements such as Flash text on a Web page, you can direct attention to headings, links, and changing features. Select the right type of Flash object to create the effect you want.

2. **Add sound to a Web page.** If spoken language or music will add an entertainment or instructional value, consider adding sound to a Web page, such as the splash page. You can use sound elements to guide visitors through your site, especially if you use interactive media controls.

3. **Play video on the Web page**. Video is especially effective for training visitors or displaying demonstrations.

4. **Prepare a Web site for publication.** Before you publish a Web site that uses multimedia files, test the site to make sure it works as designed.

5. **Add the Check Plugin behavior.** As a courtesy to Web site visitors, add a link to a Web page so visitors can download a plug-in when they need it to play media objects.

When necessary, more specific details concerning the above guidelines are presented at appropriate points in the chapter. The chapter also will identify the actions performed and decisions made regarding these guidelines during the creation of the Web pages shown in Figure 9–1.

Starting Dreamweaver and Opening a Web Site

Each time you start Dreamweaver, it opens to the last site displayed when you closed the program. It therefore may be necessary for you to open the parks Web site. Clicking the Files pop-up menu in the Files panel lists the sites you have defined. When you open the site, a list of pages and subfolders within the site is displayed.

To Start Dreamweaver and Open the Montana Parks Web Site

With a good understanding of the requirements, and an understanding of the necessary decisions and planning process, the next step is to start Dreamweaver and open the Montana Parks Web site.

1 Click the Start button on the Windows taskbar.

2 Click Adobe Dreamweaver CS5 on the Start menu or point to All Programs on the Start menu, click Adobe Design Premium, if necessary, and then click Adobe Dreamweaver CS5 on the All Programs list to start Dreamweaver.

3 If necessary, display the panel groups.

4 If the Montana Parks hierarchy is not displayed, click the Sites pop-up menu button on the Files panel, and then click Montana Parks to display the Montana Parks Web site in the Files panel.

To Copy Data Files to the Montana Parks Web Site

Before you start enhancing and adding to your Web site, you need to copy the data files into the site's folder hierarchy. In the following steps, you copy the data files for the Chapter 9 project from the Chapter09 folder on a USB drive to the parks folder stored in the *your name* folder on the same USB drive. In the following steps, the data files for this chapter are stored on drive L:. The location on your computer may be different. If necessary, verify the location of the data files with your instructor.

1 Click the Sites pop-up menu button in the Files panel, and then click the name of the drive containing your data files, such as Removable Disk (L:).

2 If necessary, click the plus sign (+) next to the folder containing your data files to expand that folder, expand the Chapter09 folder, and then expand the parks folder.

3 Copy the adventure file and the media folder in the data files, click the Sites pop-up menu button in the Files panel, click Montana Parks, and then paste the adventure file and media folder in the parks folder for the Montana Parks site (Figure 9–2).

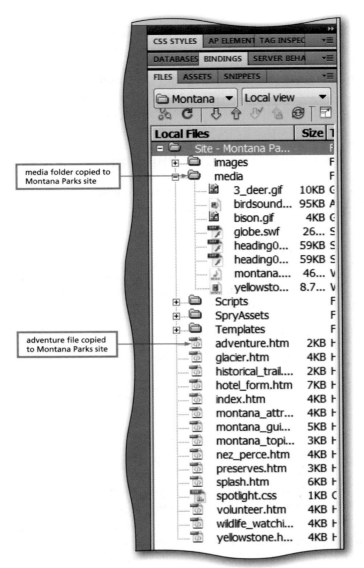

media folder copied to Montana Parks site

adventure file copied to Montana Parks site

Figure 9–2

You copied the folder and file necessary to begin creating your new Web page. You begin the project by adding a new page to the Web site. This new page will contain a Flash movie and a table containing Flash text.

Media Objects

Dreamweaver provides two methods to insert media objects: the Media pop-up menu on the Insert bar and the Insert menu located on the Application bar. When you click the Media button arrow in the Common category on the Insert bar, the Media pop-up menu lists options for inserting these special configurable objects (Figure 9–3). You use the Media pop-up menu to complete the steps in this chapter. Table 9–1 describes the options on the Media pop-up menu. Recall from Chapter 1 that when you select an option from a pop-up menu in some categories, that option becomes the default action for the button. If you select another option from this pop-up menu, the Media pop-up icon changes to that of the option you selected.

Figure 9–3

Table 9–1 Options on the Media Pop-Up Menu	
Command	**Description**
SWF	Places a Flash movie at the insertion point, using the <object> tag
	When you insert an SWF file, a dialog box is displayed in which you can browse to an SWF file. An SWF file is a compressed version of a Flash (.fla) file, and is optimized for viewing on the Web.
FLV (Flash Video)	Inserts Flash video into a Web page
Shockwave	Places an Adobe Shockwave movie at the insertion point, using the <object> and <embed> tags
Applet	Places a Java applet at the insertion point
	When you insert a Java applet, a dialog box is displayed in which you can specify the file that contains the applet's code, or click Cancel to leave the source unspecified. The Java applet is displayed only when the document is viewed in a browser.
ActiveX	Places an ActiveX control at the insertion point; use the Property inspector to specify a source file and other properties for the ActiveX control
Plugin	Used if the object you want to insert is not a Shockwave, Applet, or ActiveX object; displays a dialog box in which you can specify the source file and specify parameters for the media object

Adobe Flash

The **Adobe Flash program** is an excellent way to create and add animation and interactivity to a Web page. It is a collection of tools for animating and drawing graphics, adding sound, creating interactive elements, and playing movies. It is a standard for Web animation. Objects within Flash are created using vector graphics. Recall from Chapter 2 that mathematical formulas are used to describe vector images and produce relatively small file sizes. By contrast, GIF and JPEG graphics use **bitmap technology**, which includes data for every pixel within an object. Bitmap technology therefore produces large file sizes. Thus, vector images are a more efficient method of delivering graphics over the Internet because they are displayed faster on a downloading Web page.

    Creating **Flash files** (also called Flash movies) requires that you use the Flash program. Learning to use this program and developing Flash movies can be time-consuming. A search of the Internet, however, produces many Web sites with free or nominally priced Flash animations that can be downloaded and added to your Dreamweaver Web page.

BTW

Indicating Copyright
If you use Flash movies or other content on your Web site that is copyrighted by someone else, make sure you have permission to use the content. Indicate that the material is copyrighted by including the word "copyright," displaying the © copyright symbol, or referencing the date of publication and the name of the creator.

Most media objects require a helper program or plug-in before they can be displayed in the browser. For instance, the **Flash player** is required to view Flash files. Plug-ins are discussed in more detail later in this chapter. The Flash player is available as an add-on for Firefox and an ActiveX control for Microsoft Internet Explorer. It also is incorporated into the latest versions of Microsoft Internet Explorer, and Firefox. Adobe also provides this player as a free download at the Adobe Web site. You will learn more about plug-ins and ActiveX controls later in this chapter.

Note that although Netscape stopped being developed as a browser in March 2008, some people still use it to view Web pages. If you want to provide multimedia content for these users, or if you use the Netscape browser yourself, your Web page must include the appropriate HTML tags to embed and play multimedia files such as Flash movies in Netscape. Dreamweaver provides a Plugin tool to automate the steps of including media objects for Netscape users.

Flash Objects

The splash page for the Montana Parks Web site contains three Flash objects. The main heading (heading01) is an animated text object saved as a Flash movie file. The subheading (heading02) is a static Flash text object. The animated graphic (globe) also is a Flash movie file. When you add a static Flash text object to a Web page, the Dreamweaver Document window displays the text on the page as it would any other text. When you add an animated text object to a Web page, however, the Dreamweaver Document window displays an SWF file placeholder, which is a gray rectangle with the Flash logo and a tabbed blue outline. The tab indicates the type of object, such as an SWF file, and the object name.

Plan Ahead

Insert a Flash object to provide entertainment and direct attention to certain elements.

You add animated media objects to a Web page to make the page more appealing or to provide instructions. You also can use multimedia elements to guide visitors through your site, especially if you use interactive media controls. You can use three types of Flash objects:

- **Flash file (.fla)** This is the source file for any Flash movie and is created in the Flash program. Opening an .fla file requires the Flash program. Using Flash, you then can export the .fla file as an .swf or .swt file that can be viewed in a browser.

- **Flash movie file (.swf)** This is a compiled version of the Flash (.fla) file, and is optimized for viewing on the Web. This file can be played back in browsers and previewed in Dreamweaver, but cannot be edited in Flash.

- **Flash video file (.flv)** This file type is used to deliver encoded audio and video over the Internet using Adobe Flash Player. To view FLV files, users must have Flash Player 9 or later installed on their computers. If they do not, a dialog box appears that lets users install the latest version of Flash Player.

Adding a Table and Flash Text Objects

To begin creating your splash page, you create a one-column, two-row table and then add Flash text objects to the table.

To Add a Table and Flash Text

The splash page includes a table to help you lay out the page and to add borders to the Flash text objects. The table is named table01 and contains two rows. You first insert the Flash text objects into the table cells of table01. The following steps show how to add a table and then add Flash text to the table.

1

- Create a blank HTML page for the Montana Parks Web site. Save the page as **splash.htm**.

- Apply the parks_bkg background image to the page to add a page background.

- Type **Splash Page** as the document title.

- Click the page and then press the ENTER key two times to prepare for inserting a table on the page.

- Add a table with two rows, one column, a width of 75 percent, Border thickness of 3 pixels, and Cell padding of 5. Leave the Cell spacing text box blank.

- Type **table01** as the table name.

- If necessary, click the Common tab on the Insert bar to prepare for inserting a media object (Figure 9–4).

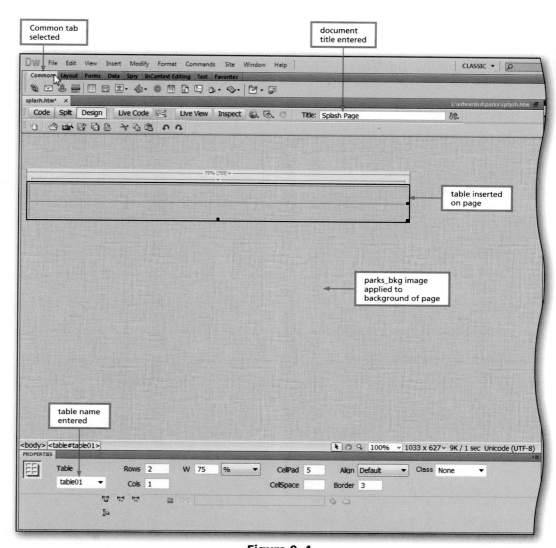

Figure 9–4

- Click the first cell in table01 to move the insertion point to this cell.

- If necessary, double-click the media folder in the Files panel to open the media folder.

- Drag the heading01 Flash file to the first cell in the table.

- Enter **heading01** in the SWF text box in the Property inspector and then press the TAB key to name the media object (Figure 9–5).

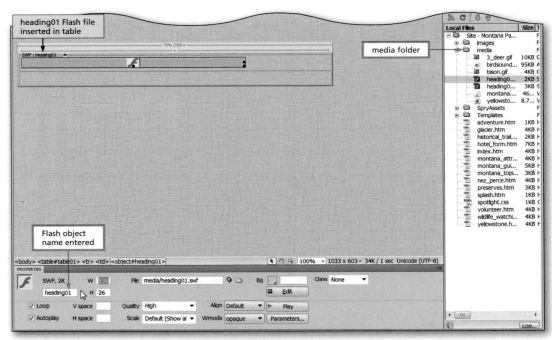

Figure 9–5

- Drag the heading02 Flash file to the second cell in the table.

- Enter **heading02** in the SWF text box in the Property inspector and then press the TAB key to name the second media object (Figure 9–6).

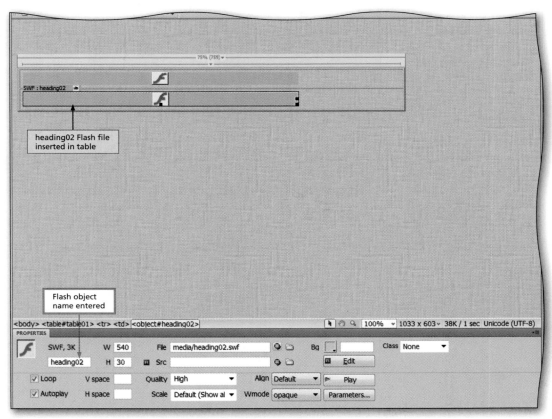

Figure 9–6

4

- Press the CTRL+S keys to save the Web page.

- Collapse the panel groups to provide more room for working in the Document window.

- Select the table, click the Align button in the Property inspector, and then click Right to align the table to the right (Figure 9–7).

Q&A

What should I do if a Copy Dependent Files dialog box is displayed?

If a Copy Dependent Files dialog box is displayed, read the information and then click the OK button.

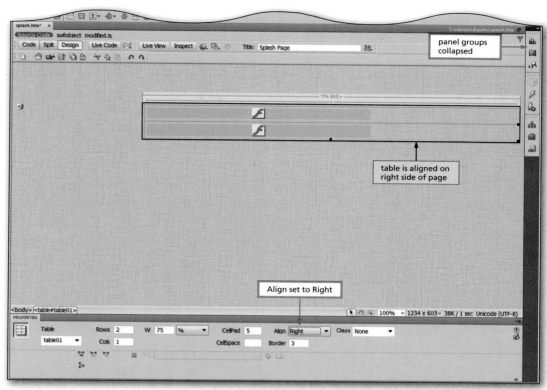

Figure 9–7

5

- Click the heading02 object in row 2 to select the heading.

- Click the Align button in the Property inspector and then click Right to align the heading to the right.

- Click anywhere on the page to deselect the heading (Figure 9–8).

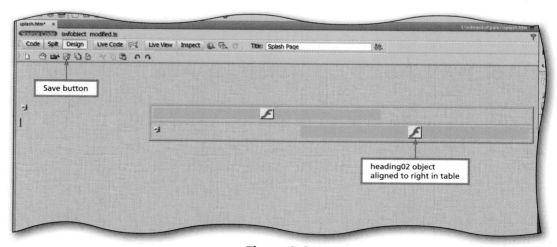

Figure 9–8

6

• Click the Save button on the Standard toolbar to save the page.

• Press F12 to view the page in the browser.

• If necessary, allow blocked content (Figure 9–9).

7

• Close the browser.

Figure 9–9

Flash Property Inspector

You can edit some elements of a Flash file through the Property inspector. For example, you can set the Loop property so the heading01 Flash object plays only once. If you select the Flash file, the Property inspector displays attributes that can be modified (Figure 9–10).

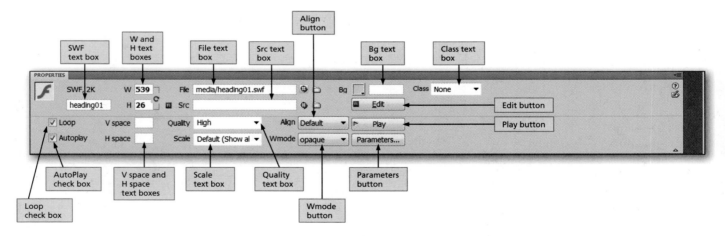

Figure 9–10

The following section describes the Flash Text Property inspector.

SWF The **SWF** text box displays the name of the Flash object.

W and H The **W** and **H** boxes indicate the width and height of the object in pixels.

File The **File** text box allows you to include a file name that specifies the path to the Flash object file. Click the Browse for File icon to browse to a file, or type a path name in the File text box.

Src This setting indicates the path to the source file when Dreamweaver and Flash are both installed on your computer.

Bg **Bg** specifies a background color for a text object; this might not be displayed until the page is viewed in a browser.

Class Select a CSS class to apply to the Flash object.

Loop Checking the **Loop** box sets the file to replay continuously; uncheck the box to play the file only once.

Autoplay Checking the **Autoplay** box causes the file to begin to play as soon as the page is loaded into the browser.

V Space and H Space The **V space** and **H space** values add space, in pixels, along the sides of the object. V space adds space along the top and bottom of an object. H space adds space along the left and right of an object.

Quality The **Quality** setting determines the quality of the media object during playback.

Scale The **Scale** setting determines how the media fits into the dimensions specified in the W and H text boxes. The Default setting displays the entire media.

Align **Align** sets the alignment of the object in relation to other elements on the page.

Wmode This button provides options to change the background of a Flash movie to transparent, opaque, or window. The default value is **opaque**, which allows DHTML elements to appear on top of SWF files in a browser. **Transparent** allows an image or background to show through; the **window** option removes the Wmode parameter from the code and allows the SWF file to appear on top of other DHTML elements.

Edit The **Edit** button opens the file in Adobe Flash if Flash is installed on your computer.

Play/Stop The **Play** button plays the object in the Document window. Click the **Stop** button to stop the object from playing. This toggle button is used primarily for Flash or Shockwave movies.

Parameters The **Parameters** button opens a dialog box for entering additional parameters to pass to the object. The object must be designed to receive these additional parameters.

To Turn Off Looping

To play the heading01 Flash object only once, you can turn off looping for that object.

- Click the heading01 media object in the Document window to select the animated text object.

- Click the Loop check box in the Property inspector to remove the check mark (Figure 9–11).

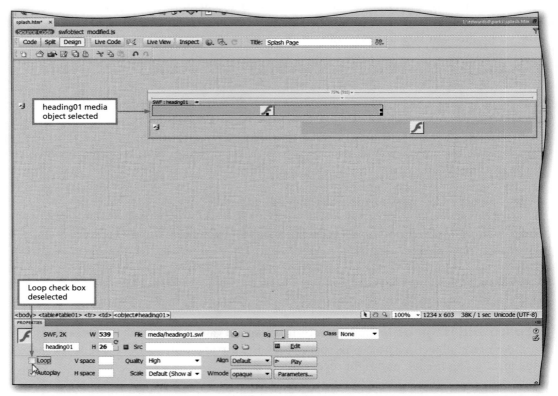

Figure 9–11

To Change Background Colors with the Wmode Element

Next, you use the Wmode element to change the background color of the Flash text objects. You display heading01 with a blue background and heading02 with a transparent background. Before you can change the background color for heading01, you need to change the Wmode setting to window.

- If necessary, click the heading01 media object in the Document window to select the animated text object.

- In the Property inspector, click the Wmode button and then click window so you can specify a background color for the object (Figure 9–12).

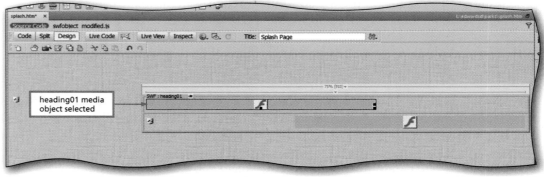

Figure 9–12

2

• Type #00CCCC in the Bg text box and then press TAB to display a light blue background color for the heading01 Flash text object (Figure 9–13).

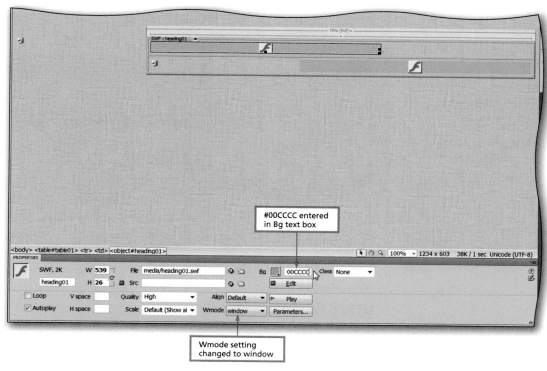

Figure 9–13

3

• Click the heading02 media object in the Document window to select the object.

• Click the Wmode button and then select transparent to display the text with a transparent background when the page is displayed in the browser (Figure 9–14).

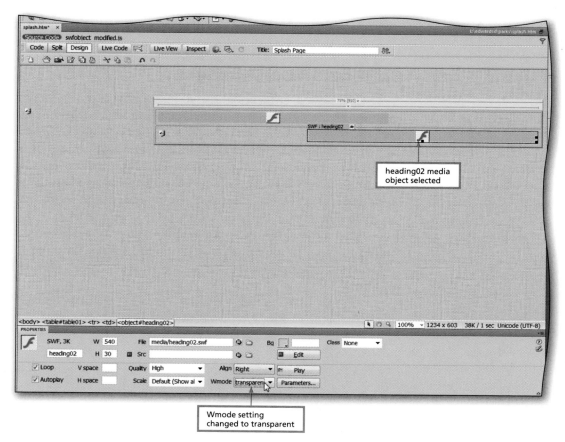

Figure 9–14

4
- Click the Save button on the Standard toolbar to save the splash page.

- Press the F12 key to view the page in your browser.

- If necessary, allow blocked content (Figure 9–15).

5
- Close the browser.

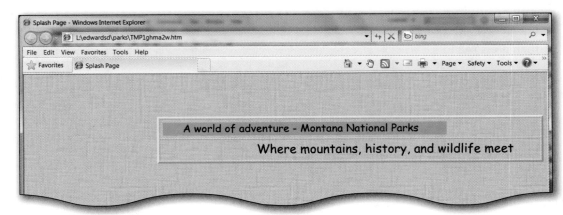

A world of adventure - Montana National Parks

Where mountains, history, and wildlife meet

Figure 9–15

Flash Movies

The earliest Web pages were plain, consisting mostly of text with links on a gray or white background. Eventually, typefaces changed, and colors and static images were added. In 1997, Macromedia purchased a software program known as FutureSplash and changed the name to Flash. Macromedia later was sold to Adobe. Flash is a multimedia program developed especially for the Internet and the World Wide Web, and it has changed the look of and added interactivity to Web pages. Today, it is a popular program for creating movies, Web graphics, and other multimedia elements.

Adding a Flash Movie

Dreamweaver makes it easy to insert a Flash movie into a Web page. Simply position the insertion point in the Document window at the location where you would like the movie to play. Then click the SWF option on the Media pop-up menu and select the file name. Flash movie files end with .swf extensions. When you insert a movie, Dreamweaver adds the code for the movie. After the movie is inserted into the Document window, a gray SWF placeholder rectangle is displayed on the page as it is for the heading01 Flash object. This rectangle represents the width and height of the movie. The width and height are determined when the developer creates the movie. When a Flash file is inserted into a Dreamweaver document, Dreamweaver automatically creates a Scripts folder and a script file, which is stored in the Scripts folder for the Web site. The Scripts folder should be uploaded to the server when the Web page containing the Flash file is published.

Similar to Flash text, when a Flash movie is inserted and selected, Dreamweaver displays the Flash Property inspector.

To Add a Flash Movie

The following steps show how to add a Flash movie to the splash page.

1
- Click to the right of table01 and then press ENTER four times to insert three blank lines on the page (Figure 9–16).

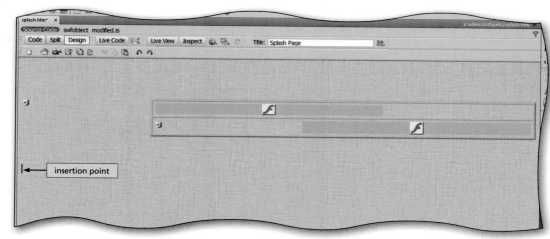

Figure 9–16

2
- Expand the panel groups and then click the Assets tab to display the Assets panel.

- Click the SWF icon in the Assets toolbar to display SWF files.

- Click the globe file in the Assets panel to select the file.

- Drag the globe file to the insertion point to add it to the splash page.

- Scroll as necessary to display the entire SWF placeholder (Figure 9–17).

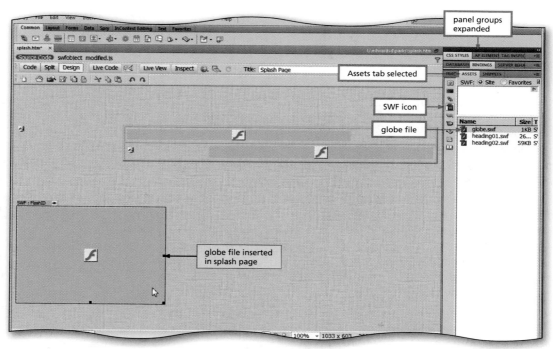

Figure 9–17

3
- Collapse the panel groups to provide more room to work in the Document window.
- Double-click the Flash ID text box in the Property inspector, type **globe** as the object name, and then press the TAB key to name the object (Figure 9–18).

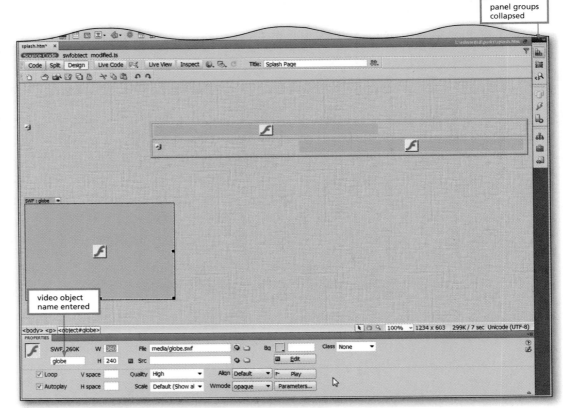

Figure 9–18

4
- Click the Play button in the Property inspector to play the movie in the Document window (Figure 9–19).

5
- Click the Stop button in the Property inspector to stop the movie and change the button back to Play.

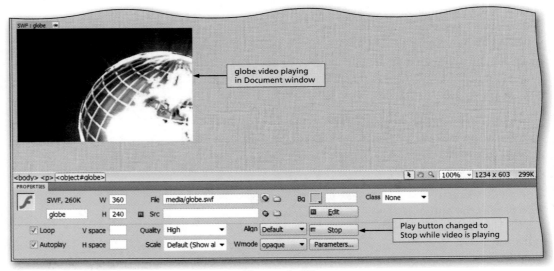

Figure 9–19

Adding a Link to Go to the Index Page

A splash page adds interest to a Web site, but may annoy frequent visitors. It is always best, therefore, to provide a link for the visitor to go directly to the index or home page.

To Add a Link to Go to the Index Page

The following steps add a link in a new table named table02. Clicking the link takes visitors directly to the index page.

1 In the Document window, click below table01 and above the Flash movie to prepare for adding a table to the page (Figure 9–20).

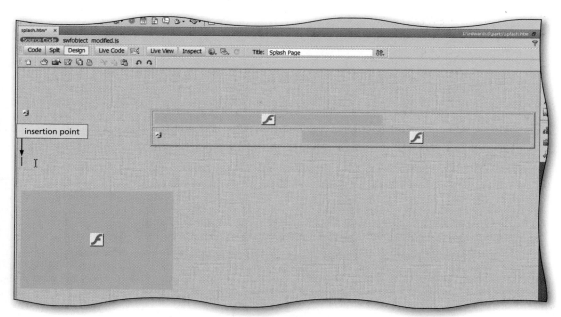

Figure 9–20

2 Insert a one-row, one-column table with a width of 35 percent, a Border thickness of 3, and Cell padding of 5. Align the table to the right, and name the table **table02**.

3 Type **Skip Introduction** in the table, select the text, and then apply Heading 2 and center the text (Figure 9–21).

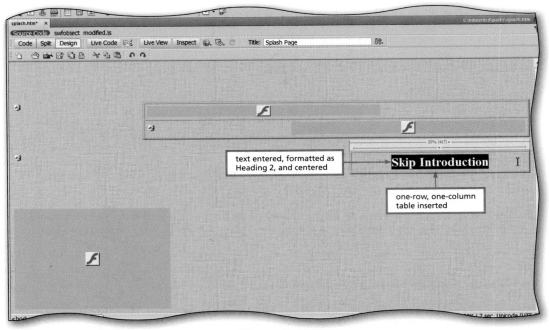

Figure 9–21

4 With the text still selected, display the panel groups and then click the Files tab. If necessary, scroll down in the Files panel and then drag index to the Link box in the Property inspector (Figure 9–22).

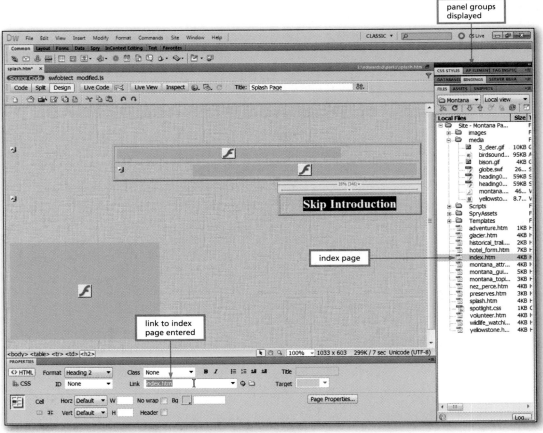

Figure 9–22

5 Press the ENTER key to accept the link to the index.htm page, and then click anywhere in the Document window.

6 Click the Save button on the Standard toolbar and then press the F12 key to view the page in your browser, allowing blocked content if necessary (Figure 9–23).

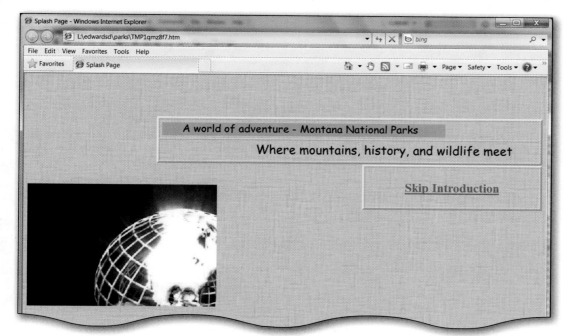

Figure 9–23

7 Click the Skip Introduction link to verify that it works, and then close the browser and return to Dreamweaver.

Audio on the Web Page

Adding sound to your Web page can add interest and set a mood. Background music can enhance your theme. Attaching sounds to objects, such as the sound of clicking buttons, can provide valuable feedback to the Web site visitor. Sound, however, can be expensive in terms of the Web site size and download time, particularly for those visitors with baseband access. Another consideration is that adding sound to a Web page can be a challenging and confusing task. Most computers today have some type of sound card and some type of sound-capable plug-in that works with the browser. The difficult part, though, is generating the desirable sounds. As you work with sound, you will discover that the Web supports several popular sound file formats, along with their supporting plug-ins; a standard format does not exist. The trick is to find the one most widely used that most browsers handle the same way. Table 9–2 contains a list and description of the commonly used sound file formats. Some factors to consider before deciding on a format and method for adding sound are the sound's purpose, your audience, the file size, the sound quality you want, and the differences between browsers.

Table 9–2 Sound File Formats

File Name Extension	Description
.aif (Audio Interchange File Format, or AIFF)	The AIFF format can be played by most browsers and does not require a plug-in; you also can record AIFF files from a CD, tape, microphone, and so on. The large file size, however, limits the length of sound clips that you can use on your Web pages.
.midi or .mid (Musical Instrument Digital Interface, or MIDI)	The MIDI format is for instrumental music. MIDI files are supported by many browsers and do not require a plug-in. The sound quality is good, but it can vary depending on a visitor's sound card. A small MIDI file can provide a long sound clip. MIDI files cannot be recorded and must be synthesized on a computer with special hardware and software.
.mp3 (Motion Picture Experts Group Audio, or MPEG-Audio Layer-3, or MP3)	The MP3 format is a compressed format that allows for substantially smaller sound files, yet the sound quality is very good. You can stream the file so that a visitor does not have to wait for the entire file to download before hearing it. To play MP3 files, visitors must download and install a helper application or plug-in such as QuickTime, Windows Media Player, or RealPlayer.
.qt, .qtm, .mov (QuickTime)	These formats are designed for audio and video files by Apple Computer. QuickTime is included with the Macintosh operating system, and most Macintosh applications can use it. PCs also can play media in the QuickTime format, though they need a QuickTime driver to do so.
.ra, .ram, .rpm (RealAudio)	The RealAudio format has a very high degree of compression, with smaller file sizes than the MP3 format. Whole song files can be downloaded in a reasonable amount of time. The files also can be streamed, so visitors can begin listening to the sound before the file has been downloaded completely. The sound quality is poorer than that of MP3 files. Visitors must download and install the RealPlayer helper application or plug-in to play these files.
.wav (Waveform Extension, or WAV)	WAV-formatted files have good sound quality, are supported by many browsers, and do not require a plug-in. The large file size, however, severely limits the length of sound clips that you can use on your Web pages.

ActiveX and Plug-ins

In addition to Flash files, you can insert other media objects, though you need special technology to do so. A Web browser basically is an HTML/scripting decoder. Recall that a plug-in is a program that is used to view plug-in applications through the Web browser. A plug-in adds functionality to the browser — it is not a stand-alone program and cannot start and run on its own. To work correctly, plug-in programs must be present in the browser's Plugins folder. Internet Explorer, Firefox, and Netscape include Plugins folders within their own application folders. When the browser encounters a file with an extension of .swf, for example, it looks for and attempts to start the Flash player plug-in.

Several years ago, Netscape developed the capability of incorporating plug-ins within the browser by creating the nonstandard HTML tag, <embed>. This tag never was made part of the W3C's official HTML specifications, but it became widely used.

Some of the more popular plug-ins are Adobe Acrobat Reader, Flash, and Shockwave, RealAudio and RealVideo, Apple QuickTime, and VRML (Virtual Reality Modeling Language). Using these plug-ins, Web site visitors can use their browsers to view specialized content, such as animation, virtual reality, streaming audio and video, and formatted content. These plug-in programs and information are available for download at their related Web sites.

In contrast, **ActiveX** is a set of technologies developed by Microsoft and is an outgrowth of OLE (object linking and embedding). An **ActiveX control** uses ActiveX technologies and currently is limited to Windows environments. ActiveX objects use the <object> tag instead of the <embed> tag. When ActiveX is inserted, a ClassID or ActiveX control is specified; in many instances, parameters also are added. Parameters are discussed in more detail later in this chapter.

As a result, you have two ways to insert media content into browsers: as plug-ins using the <embed> tag and as ActiveX objects using the <object> tag. Until recently, both Internet Explorer and Netscape supported Netscape-style plug-ins, but newer versions of Internet Explorer support only ActiveX controls, although Internet Explorer still supports the <embed> tag for ActiveX content.

When adding media to a Web page, you should try to predict how Web site visitors have their browsers configured. One of the more common problems is that a particular plug-in may not be available on a visitor's computer. Fortunately, Dreamweaver helps by offering support for both plug-ins and ActiveX controls.

Windows Media Player is one of the more popular platforms for playing audio and video. This player is Internet Explorer's default multimedia player. It plays the standard audio formats, including AIFF, AU, MIDI, WAV, and MP3. The WAV format (.wav), for example, is one of the more popular sound formats on the Internet. A compatibility issue exists, however, with the default Netscape installation and the .wav format. If you are using Netscape to view pages that contain the .wav format, most likely you will need to download a compatible plug-in.

Add sound to a Web page.

As with any other technology, you first determine what you want to accomplish by adding a sound. Your sound should serve a clear and useful purpose or have an entertaining or instructional value. Web site developers primarily use one of three methods to add sound to a Web page:

- **Link to an audio file:** This is the simplest and easiest way to add sound to a Web page. The link can be any object, such as text, an image, or a table. The object is selected and then a link to a sound file is created. Clicking the link opens the user's designated player, such as Windows Media Player, in a separate window. You might consider using the linking method, for example, to provide instructional enhancement.

- **Add a background sound:** If you want to appeal to novelty, a background sound can serve this purpose. A background sound starts to play as soon as the Web page opens in the browser. In most instances, when you add a background sound, keep the sound short, do not loop the sound, and do provide your visitor with an option to stop the sound.

- **Embed an audio file:** Embedding a sound file integrates the audio into the Web page. The sound player, along with controls, is inserted directly into the Web page. This process lets Web site visitors choose whether they want to listen to the audio and how many times they want to hear it.

Plan Ahead

To Add a Background Sound and Set Parameters

In the next steps, you add the Montana background sound file to the splash page. When the Web site visitor opens the page, the Montana sound file plays in the background, and the visitor has no control over the sound.

1

- If necessary, display the Files panel.
- Collapse the Property inspector to provide room to work in the Document window.
- Scroll down to the bottom of the page to prepare for inserting a sound file.
- Click to the right of the Flash movie and then press the ENTER key so that the insertion point is blinking at the left margin below the movie object (Figure 9–24).

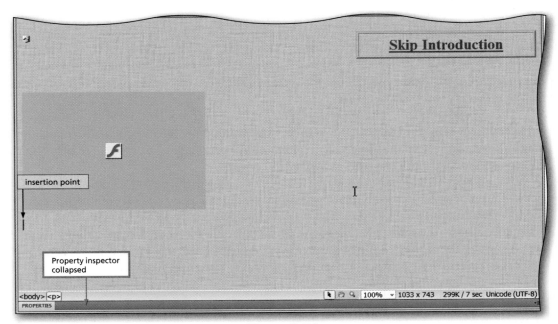

Figure 9–24

2

- Click the Media button arrow in the Common category on the Insert bar to display the Media pop-up menu, and then point to Plugin to prepare for inserting the background sound file (Figure 9–25).

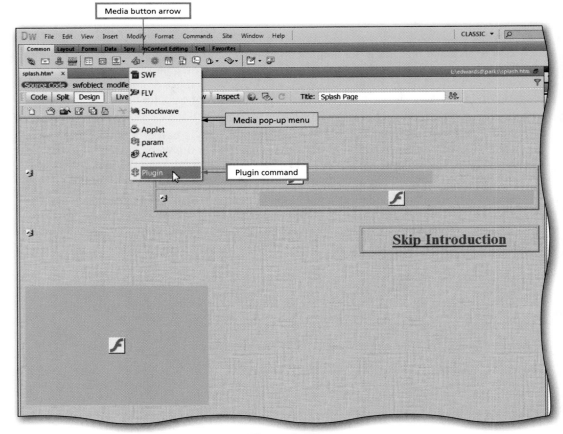

Figure 9–25

3

- Click Plugin to display the Select File dialog box (Figure 9–26).

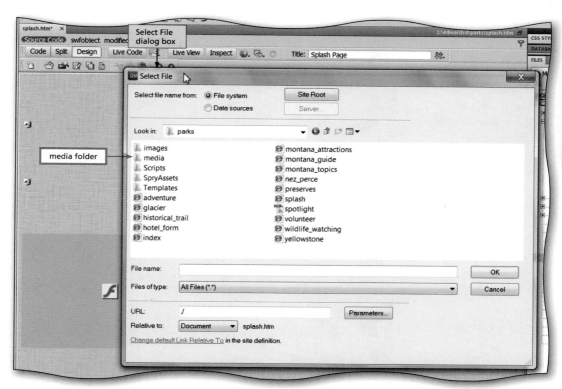

Figure 9–26

4

- Navigate to and open the media folder, and then click montana in the list of files to select the sound file for the splash page (Figure 9–27).

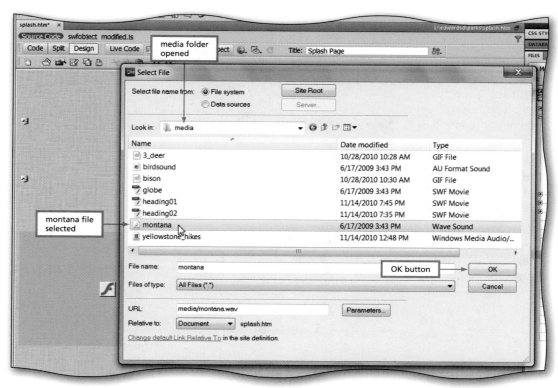

Figure 9–27

5

- Click the OK button to insert a 32 x 32 pixel placeholder for the background sound (Figure 9–28).

Why does Dreamweaver insert a placeholder for the sound file?

When you add a background sound to a page, Dreamweaver inserts a placeholder as a cue that the page includes a media object.

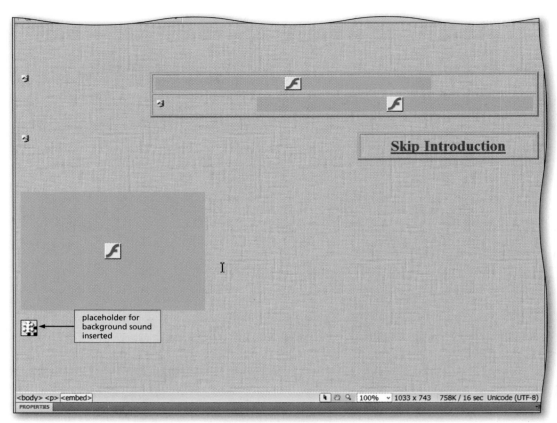

Figure 9–28

6

- With the placeholder still selected, expand the Property inspector to prepare for naming the sound object.

- Scroll as necessary to display the placeholder in the Document window.

- Type **montana_ wav** in the Plugin text box and then press the TAB key to name the sound object (Figure 9–29).

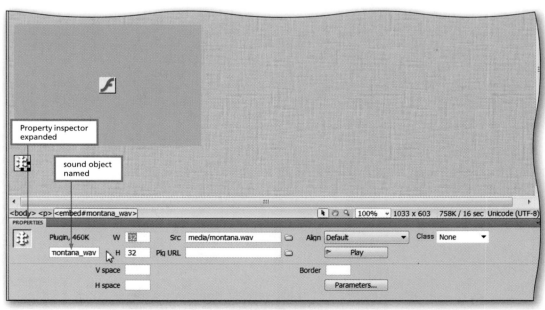

Figure 9–29

7

- Click the Parameters button to display the Parameters dialog box (Figure 9–30).

Q&A

What should I do if the Parameters dialog box already contains a parameter for the montana_wav id?

Click the plus (+) button to prepare for entering a new parameter.

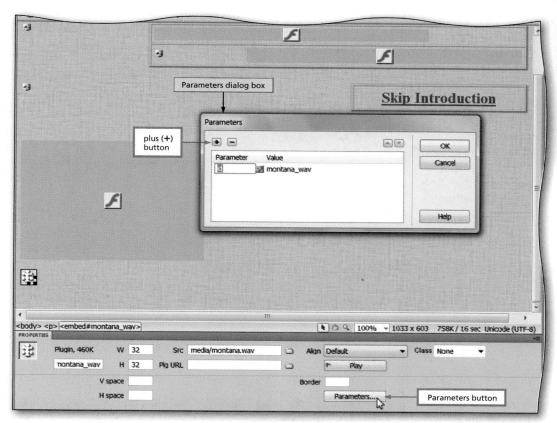

Figure 9–30

8

- Click the plus (+) button in the Parameter dialog box to display a text box for entering a parameter.

- Type **hidden** in the text box to enter the parameter.

- Press the TAB key twice to move the insertion point to a text box in the Value column (Figure 9–31).

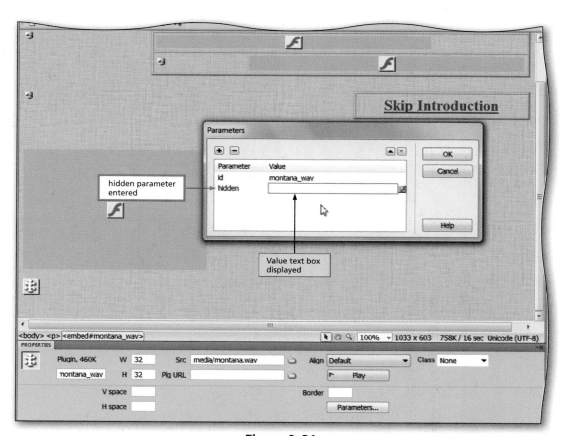

Figure 9–31

9

- Type **true** in the Value column text box to enter the parameter value for hiding the plug-in controls.

- Press the TAB key two times to move the insertion point to a blank text box in the Parameter column (Figure 9–32).

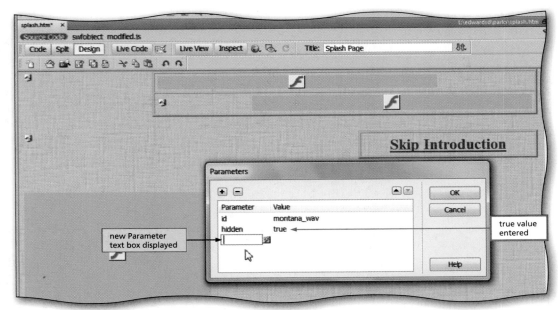

Figure 9–32

10

- Type **autoplay** to enter the new parameter.

- Press the TAB key two times to move the insertion point to a blank text box in the Value column.

- Type **true** in the Value column to enter the parameter value to have the sound start playing automatically (Figure 9–33).

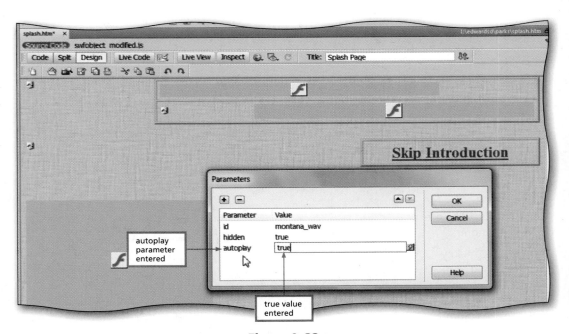

Figure 9–33

- Press the TAB key two times, and then type `loop` in the Parameter column to enter the third new parameter.

- Press the TAB key two times, and then type `false` in the Value column to enter the parameter value that specifies the media does not loop (or start playing again when it reaches the end of the file).

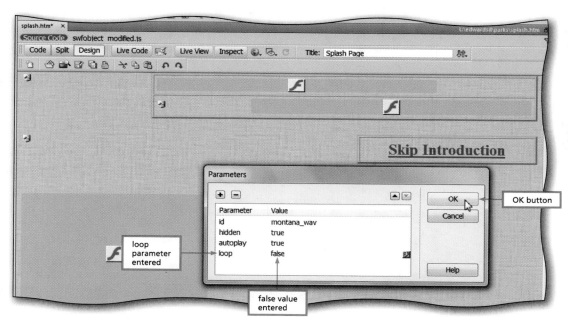

Figure 9–34

- Press the TAB key to finish adding the values (Figure 9–34).

⑫

- Click the OK button to apply the parameters you set to the background sound file.

- Click the Save button on the Standard toolbar to save the splash page.

- Press the F12 key to open the browser, allow blocked content, and verify that the audio works.

Q&A The audio file seems to play, but I don't hear any sound. What is the problem?

A speaker or headphones must be attached to the computer for you to hear the audio.

- Close the browser and then close the splash page.

Embedding an Audio File

Embedding a sound in a Web page provides the Web site visitor with control over the audio player. The content developer determines the amount of control through parameters. Next, you embed an audio player into the preserves.htm page. When the user clicks a control, a bird sound is heard through the Windows Media Player. An ActiveX control is used, thereby requiring specific parameters. A parameter defines the characteristics of something. For example, AutoRewind, AutoStart, and font specifications are parameters.

Table 9–3 contains a list of frequently used parameters. This list is an example only; several other parameters also are available.

Table 9–3 ActiveX Parameters		
Parameter	**Default**	**Description**
AutoStart	True	Defines whether the player should start automatically
AnimationAtStart	True	Defines whether an animation should show while the file loads
AutoRewind	False	Defines whether the player should rewind automatically
ClickToPlay	True	Defines whether the player should start when the user clicks the play area
DisplayBackColor	False	Shows a background color
EnablePositionControls	True	Provides the user with position controls
EnableFullScreenControls	False	Provides the user with screen controls
Filename	N/A	Indicates the URL of the file to play
InvokeURLs	True	Links to a URL
ShowControls	True False	Defines whether the player controls should show 'Mutes the sound'
ShowAudioControls	True	Defines whether the audio controls should show
ShowDisplay	False	Defines whether the display should show
Volume	–200	Specifies the volume

ActiveX controls also require a ClassID. Dreamweaver uses the ClassID to define the object when generating the code for the ActiveX control. You add this hexadecimal ID using the ActiveX Property inspector. Once added, it will become an option within the ClassID pop-up menu. The following section describes the ActiveX Property inspector (Figure 9–35).

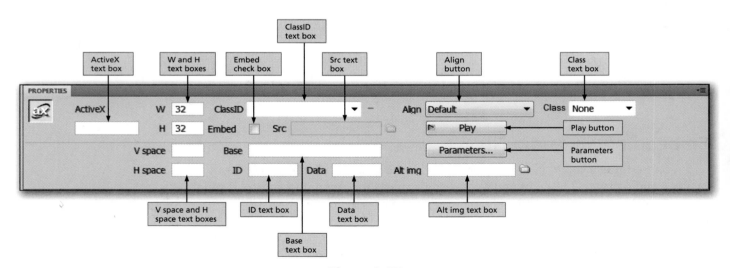

Figure 9–35

ActiveX   The name in the ActiveX text box identifies the ActiveX object for scripting purposes.

W and H   W and H are the width and height, respectively, of the object, in pixels. When embedding a sound file, these values determine the size at which the audio controls are displayed in the browser.

ClassID   The **ClassID value** identifies the ActiveX control to the browser. Enter a value or choose one on the pop-up menu. When the page is loaded, the browser uses the ClassID to locate the ActiveX control required for the ActiveX object associated with the page. For all versions of Windows Media Player from version 7 on, use the following ClassID: CLSID:22d6f312-b0f6-11d0-94ab-0080c74c7e95. You assign this number in the ActiveX Property inspector.

Embed   Checking the **Embed** check box adds an <embed> tag within the <object> tag for the ActiveX control. If the ActiveX control has a Netscape Navigator plug-in equivalent, the <embed> tag activates the plug-in. Dreamweaver assigns the values you enter as ActiveX properties to their Netscape Navigator plug-in equivalents.

Align   **Align** sets the alignment of an ActiveX object on the page. Ten different alignments are available, including the Default.

Parameters   The **Parameters** button opens a dialog box for entering additional parameters to pass to the ActiveX object.

Src   The **Src** value defines the data file to be used for a Netscape Navigator plug-in if the Embed check box is selected. If a value is not entered, Dreamweaver attempts to determine the value from the ActiveX properties already entered.

V space and H space   The **V space** and **H space** values add space, in pixels, along the sides of the object. V space adds space along the top and bottom of an object. H space adds space along the left and right of an object.

Base   The **Base value** specifies the URL containing the ActiveX control. Internet Explorer downloads the ActiveX control from this location if the control has not been installed already in the visitor's system. If the Base parameter is not specified and if the Web site visitor does not have the relevant ActiveX control installed, the browser cannot display the ActiveX object.

Alt Img   The **Alt img** parameter indicates an image to be displayed if the browser does not support the <object> tag. This option is available only when the Embed check box is not selected.

Data   The **Data** parameter specifies a data file for the ActiveX control to load. Many ActiveX controls, such as Shockwave and RealPlayer, do not use this parameter.

ID   This option specifies the data file ID.

Play/Stop   The Play/Stop button plays and stops the movie, sound, or other selected media in the Document window.

Class   Used for scripting with Cascading Style Sheets.

To Embed an Audio File

The following steps illustrate how to embed an audio file in the preserves Web page. A speaker or headphones are required to hear the sound.

- Open the preserves page to display it in the Document window.

- Collapse the panel groups to provide more room to work in the Document window.

- Click to the right of the heading text, Montana National Parks and Preserves, and then press the ENTER key to insert a new line.

- If necessary, center the insertion point to prepare for inserting a media object.

- Click the Media button arrow and then point to ActiveX on the pop-up menu (Figure 9–36).

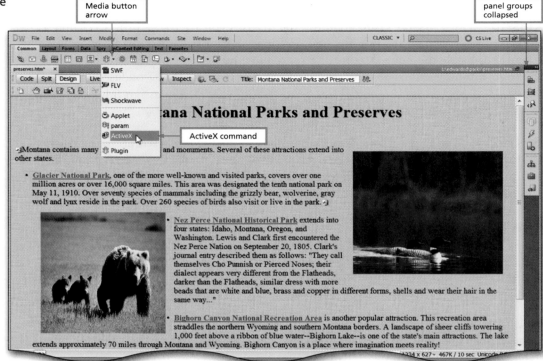

Figure 9–36

- Click ActiveX to insert an ActiveX placeholder on the page (Figure 9–37).

Figure 9–37

3

- Click the ActiveX name box in the Property inspector, type `birdsound`, and then press the TAB key to enter a name for the ActiveX control.

- Change the W value to `200` and the H value to `45` to increase the size of the control.

- Type `CLSID: 22d6f312-b0f6-11d0-94ab-0080c74c7e95` in the ClassID text box to enter the required Class ID for the ActiveX control.

- Press the ENTER key to add the ClassID number.

- Check the number to verify that it is correct and that alphabetic letters are lowercase (Figure 9–38).

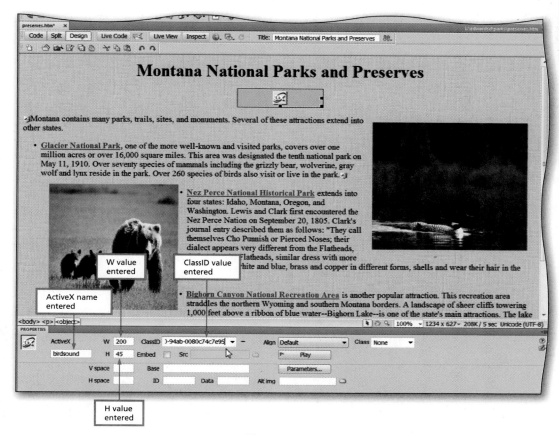

Figure 9–38

Q&A

Do I have to type the ClassID value if I need it again?

No. Once you type in the ClassID number, it becomes part of the pop-up menu. It will not be necessary to add the number again.

4

- Click the Embed check box to specify that you want to embed the ActiveX sound file.

- Click the Browse for File icon to the right of the Src text box to display the Select Netscape Plug-In File dialog box.

Q&A
Why should I link to a sound file instead of embedding it on a Web page?

Linking to sound files lets visitors choose to listen to the file and makes the file available to the widest audience.

- If necessary, navigate to the media folder to open the folder containing the ActiveX sound file (Figure 9–39).

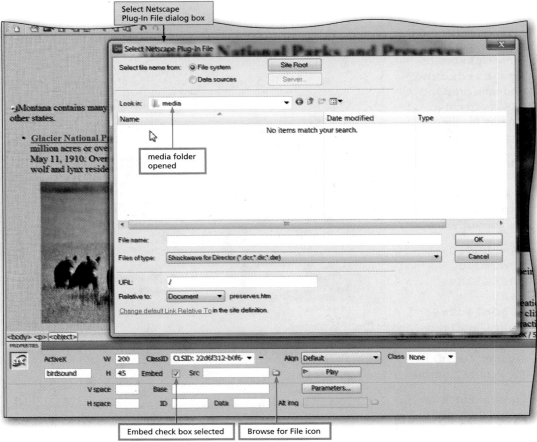

Figure 9–39

5

- Click the Files of type button and then click All Files to display all the files in the media folder.

- Click the birdsound file to select it.

- Verify that Document is selected in the Relative to button to use a relative path to the file (Figure 9–40).

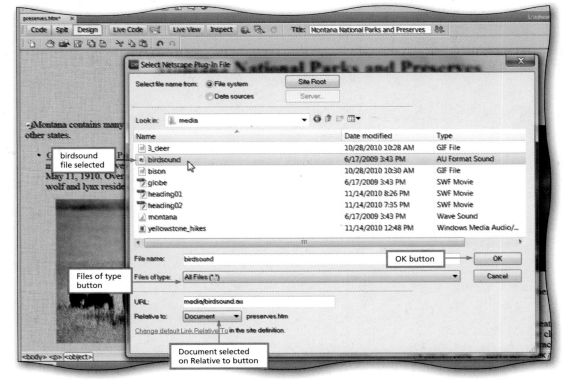

Figure 9–40

6

- Click the OK button to embed the birdsound file on the preserves page (Figure 9–41).

Q&A What will happen to the placeholder when the page is viewed in a browser?

When viewed in a browser, this placeholder will contain the audio controls.

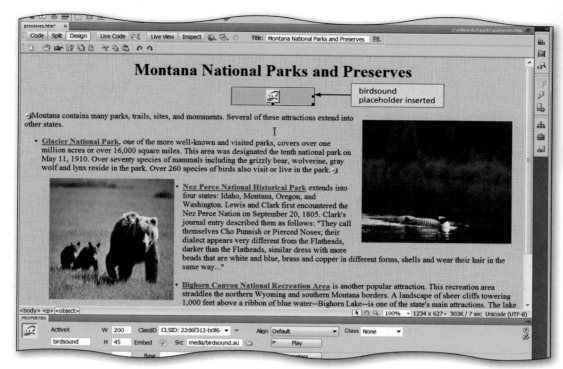

Figure 9–41

7

- Click the Parameters button in the Property inspector to set parameters for the ActiveX control you just inserted (Figure 9–42).

Figure 9–42

8

- Type **FileName** as the first parameter.

- Press the TAB key two times to move the insertion point to the Value column.

- Type **media/ birdsound.au** in the Value column to specify the path and file name of the embedded sound object (Figure 9–43).

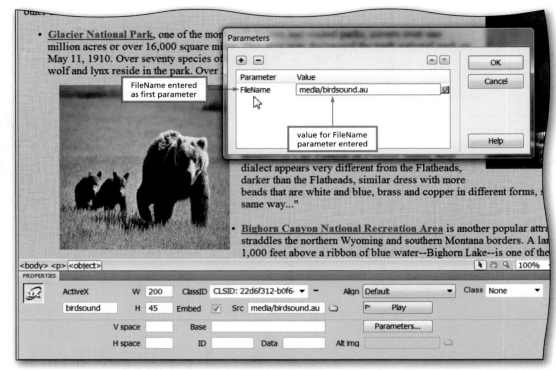

Figure 9–43

9

- Press the TAB key two times to move the insertion point to the Parameter column and prepare for adding the second parameter.

- Use Table 9–4 on page DW 656 to add the other parameters and values to the Parameters dialog box.

- Press the TAB key after the last entry to finish entering parameters (Figure 9–44).

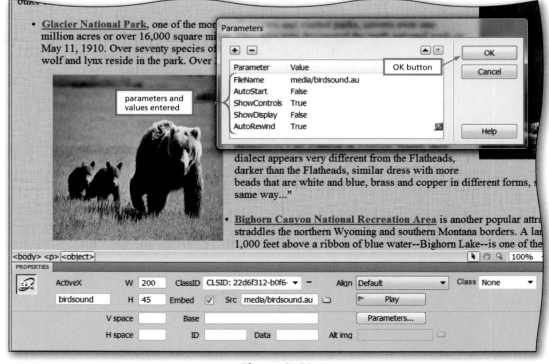

Figure 9–44

10

- Click the OK button to accept the parameters for the birdsound file.

- Click the Save button on the Standard toolbar to save the Web page.

Q&A What should I do if a Copy Dependent Files dialog box is displayed?

If a Copy Dependent Files dialog box is displayed, click the OK button.

- Expand the panel groups to display the Files panel again.

- If necessary, expand the Scripts folder to view the files stored in this folder (Figure 9–45).

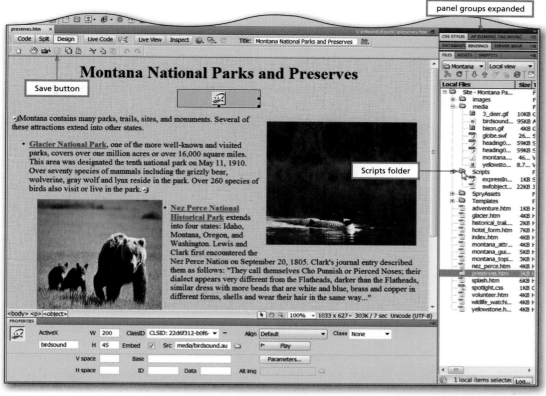

Figure 9–45

11

- Press the F12 key to view the Windows Media Player audio control in the Web page in your browser.

- Allow blocked content, if necessary.

- Click the Play button to listen to the audio file (Figure 9–46).

Q&A What do I need to hear the sound?

You need a speaker or headphones to hear the sound.

Q&A What should I do if a Dreamweaver dialog box is displayed?

If a Dreamweaver dialog box is displayed, read the information and then click the OK button.

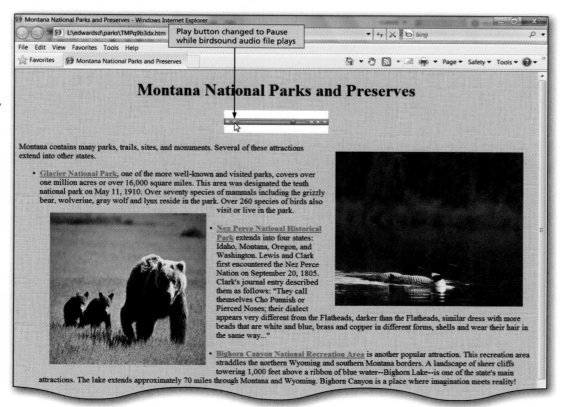

Figure 9–46

12

• Close the browser and then close the preserves page.

Other Ways

1. On Insert menu, point to Media, click ActiveX

Table 9–4 Parameters and Values

Parameter	Value
AutoStart	False
ShowControls	True
ShowDisplay	False
AutoRewind	True

Adding Other Types of Video

Earlier in this chapter, you inserted a Flash movie into the splash page. Inserting the Flash movie was a fairly simple process because Flash also is an Adobe product, and Dreamweaver comes with built-in controls to display a Flash movie. Movies, however, come in several other formats, and most likely occasions will arise when you will want to insert a movie in another format. Table 9–5 contains a description of video file formats that are used on the Internet. Most browsers can display all of these formats.

Table 9–5 Video File Formats

File Name Extension	Description
.avi (Audio Video Interleave, or AVI)	The AVI format is supported by all computers running Windows.
.mov (QuickTime, developed by Apple)	QuickTime is a common format on the Internet for both Windows and Macintosh computers. Playing QuickTime movies on a Windows computer requires the QuickTime Player.
.mpg or .mpeg (Moving Pictures Expert Group, or MPEG)	The MPEG format is one of the more popular formats on the Internet. It is cross-platform, running on Windows and Macintosh computers.
.rm or .ram (RealVideo, developed by RealMedia)	The RealVideo format allows the streaming of video, which reduces downloading time.
.swf (Flash SWF)	The SWF format requires the Adobe Flash Player.
.wmv, .wvx (Windows Media Format, or WMF)	The WMF format allows the streaming of video, uses the Windows Media Player, and plays on both Windows and Macintosh computers.

Plan Ahead

Play video on the Web page.
You can add video to your Web page by downloading to the user or by streaming it so that it plays while it is downloading. As with other non-Flash media objects, Web site visitors need to use a plug-in to view common streaming formats such as Windows Media, Real Media, and QuickTime. You then can use parameters to control the video object and how it is played on the Web page.

To Add Video to a Web Page

The following steps show how to add a Windows Media Player video file to the index Web page.

1

- Open the index page to display it in the Document window.

- Collapse the panel groups to provide more room to work.

- Scroll to the bottom of the page and then click to the right of the date, which is where the Windows Media Player video file will be added.

- Press the ENTER key to insert a new blank line.

- Click Format on the Application bar, point to Align, and then click Right to

right-align the paragraph and move the insertion point to the right of the page (Figure 9–47).

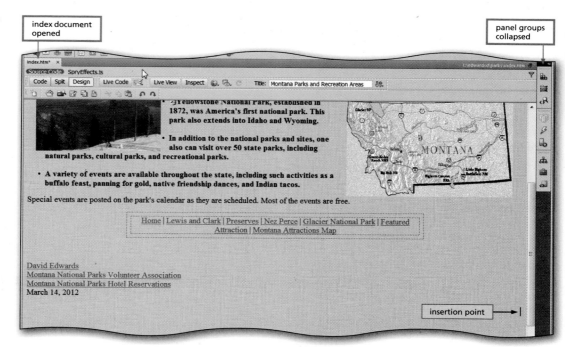

Figure 9–47

2

- Click the Media button arrow, and then point to ActiveX on the pop-up menu (Figure 9–48).

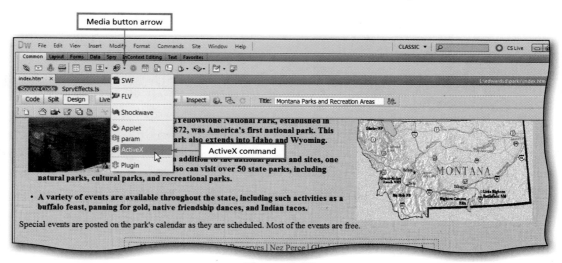

Figure 9–48

3

- Click ActiveX to insert an ActiveX control on the page.

- Click the ActiveX text box in the Property inspector to prepare for entering a name for the ActiveX control.

- Type **yellowstone_ video** as the name for the ActiveX object and then press the TAB key to enter the name.

- Change the W value to **320** and then press the TAB key to enter the width of the ActiveX control.

- Change the H value to **240** and then press the TAB key to enter the height of the ActiveX control.

- Click the ClassID box arrow and then click the ClassID value you entered earlier in this chapter.

- Click the Align button and then click Right to right-align the control.

- Scroll down to view the right-aligned ActiveX control, if necessary (Figure 9–49).

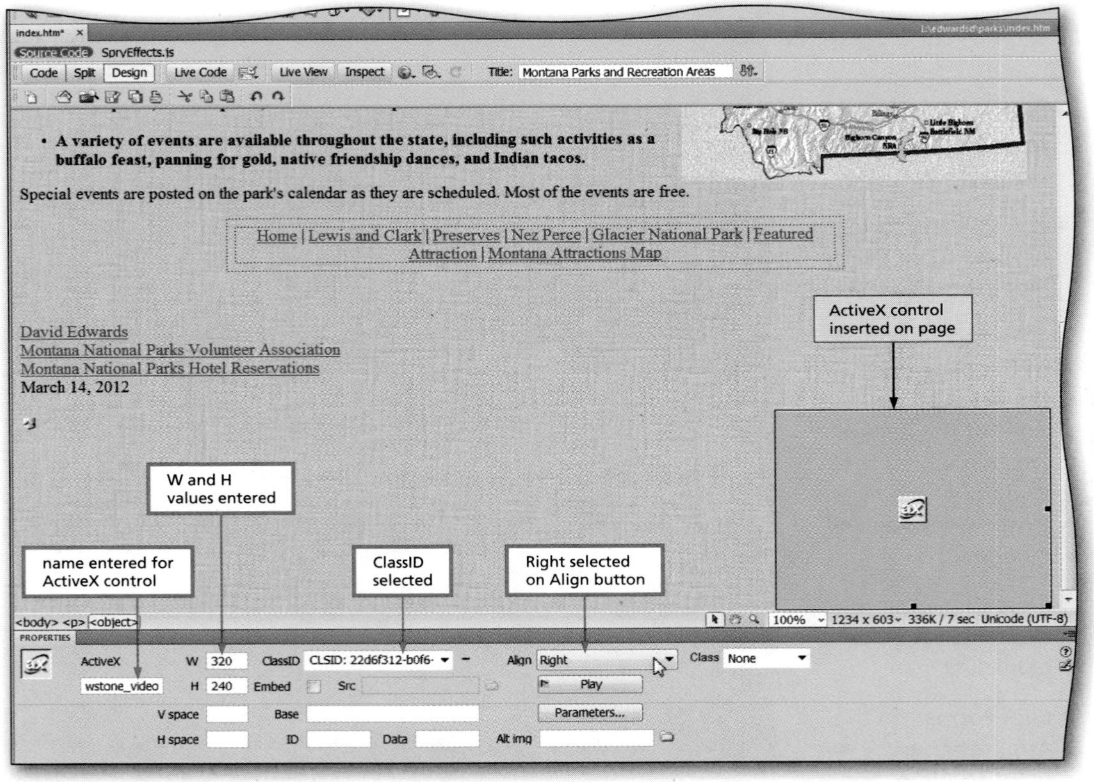

Figure 9–49

4

- Click the Embed check box in the Property inspector to embed the control on the page.

- Click the Browse for File icon to the right of the Src text box to browse for the Windows Media Player video file.

- If necessary, open the media folder, click the Files of type button, and then select All Files to display all the files in the media folder.

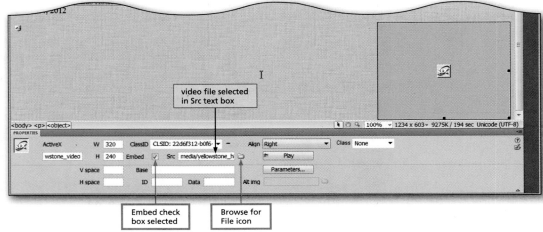

Figure 9–50

- Double-click the yellowstone_hikes file to insert it on the index page (Figure 9–50).

5

- Verify that the ActiveX placeholder is selected so you can specify parameters for the object.

- Click the Parameters button in the Property inspector to display the Parameters dialog box.

- If necessary, click the plus (+) button in the Parameters dialog box to prepare for adding a parameter (Figure 9–51).

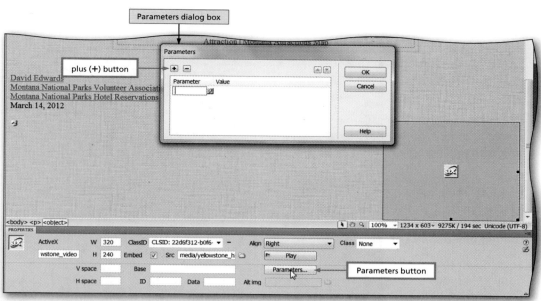

Figure 9–51

6

- Apply the steps you used on pages DW 653-654 to add the parameters and values shown in Table 9–6 (on the next page) to the Parameters dialog box (Figure 9–52).

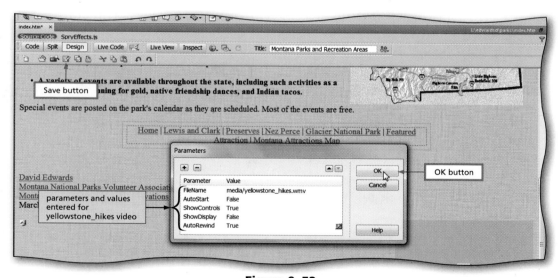

Figure 9–52

- Click the OK button to accept the parameters and values for the ActiveX video file.

- Click the Save button on the Standard toolbar to save the page.

- Press the F12 key to display the page in your browser, and allow blocked content if necessary.

- Scroll down to display the video file, and then click the Play button to play the video (Figure 9–53).

8

- Close the browser to return to Dreamweaver.

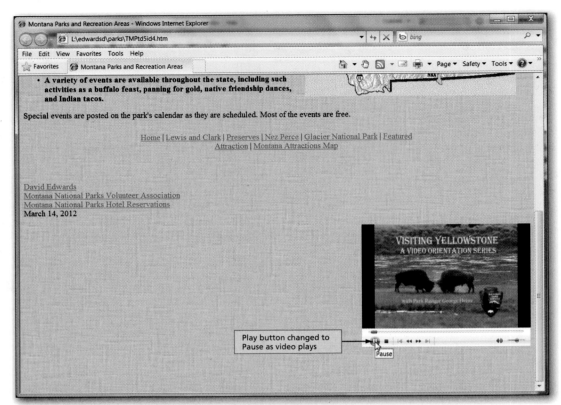

Figure 9–53

Table 9–6 Parameters and Values	
Parameter	**Value**
FileName	media/yellowstone_hikes.wmv
AutoStart	False
ShowControls	True
ShowDisplay	False
AutoRewind	True

Using the Results Panel Group

Dreamweaver's Results panel group (Figure 9–54) provides several options to help maintain your site.

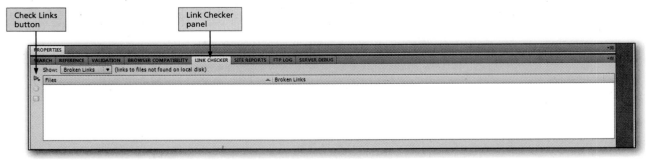

Figure 9–54

**Plan
Ahead**

Prepare a Web site for publication.
Before publishing a Web site, use the Dreamweaver Results panel group to make sure your Web pages are professional and complete. Use the following features to check your Web site before producing it for a wider audience:

- **Search** Use this option to search for and replace text, source code, and specific tags for the current document, open documents, selected files in a site, or the entire current local site.

- **Validation** Use this option to locate tag or syntax errors. You can validate the current document or a selected tag.

- **Browser Compatibility** This feature checks the code in your documents to see if any of the tags, attributes, CSS properties, or CSS values are unsupported by your target browser.

- **Link Checker** This searches for broken links and unreferenced files in a portion of a local site or throughout an entire local site. External links are not checked.

- **FTP Log** This option keeps track of all FTP activity. If an error occurs when you are transferring a file using FTP, the site FTP log can help you determine the problem.

- **Server Debug** This option is a tool to assist with server problems, and is used primarily with dynamic data.

Using the Link Checker

Be sure to check and verify that the links work on your Web page. Links are not active within Dreamweaver; that is, you cannot open a linked document by clicking the link in the Document window. You can check any type of link by displaying the page in a browser. Using a browser is the only available validation option for absolute or external links and e-mail links. For relative or internal links, Dreamweaver provides the Link Checker feature. Use the Link Checker to check internal links in a document, a folder, or an entire site.

A large Web site can contain hundreds of links that can change over time. Dreamweaver's **Link Checker** searches for broken links and unreferenced files in a portion of a local site or throughout an entire local site. This feature is limited, however, because it verifies internal links only. A list of external links is compiled, but not verified. As discussed previously, external links must be checked through a browser.

The Link Checker does have advantages, however. When you use this feature, the Link Checker displays a statistical report that includes information about broken links, orphaned files, and external links. An **orphaned file** is a file that is not connected to any page within the Web site. The orphaned file option is for informational purposes only. The orphaned file report, however, is particularly valuable for a large site, because it displays a list of all files that are not part of the Web site. Deleting unused files from a Web site increases disk space and streamlines your site. You can use the Link Checker to check links throughout your entire site from any Web page within the site. After you run the Link Checker, you can fix broken links in the Property inspector or directly in the Link Checker panel. In this exercise, you fix a broken link in the Property inspector.

To Verify Internal Links with the Link Checker

The following steps show how to use the Link Checker to verify the internal links for the index.htm page. You change the link to the Montana National Historical Sites on the index page from historical_trail to historicaltrail intentionally to illustrate how the Link Checker works and how to make corrections. Your results may be different from the ones shown.

- Make sure the index page is open in Dreamweaver to prepare for adding links to it.

- Scroll to the top of the page, display the panel groups, and then collapse the Property inspector to provide room to work.

- Click historical_trail in the Files list to select the file and then press the F2 key to select the file name.

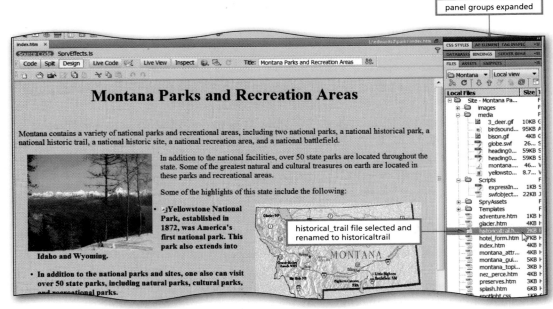

Figure 9–55

- Type **historicaltrail** and then press the ENTER key to rename the file (Figure 9–55).

Q&A The Update Files dialog box is displayed after I press ENTER. What should I do?

If the Update Files dialog box is displayed, click the Don't Update button.

- Press the F5 key to refresh the panel groups.

- Collapse the panel groups to provide more room to work.

- Click Window on the Application bar, point to Results, and then point to Link Checker to highlight the command (Figure 9–56).

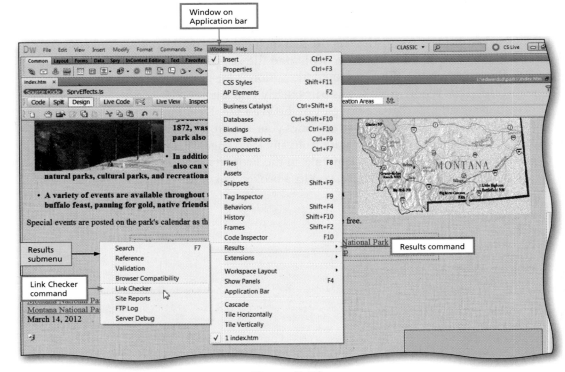

Figure 9–56

3

- Click Link Checker to display the Link Checker panel in the panel group (Figure 9–57).

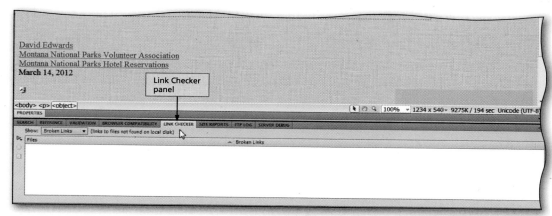

Figure 9–57

4

- Click the Check Links button (the green arrow) to the left of the Files heading to display Link Checker options (Figure 9–58).

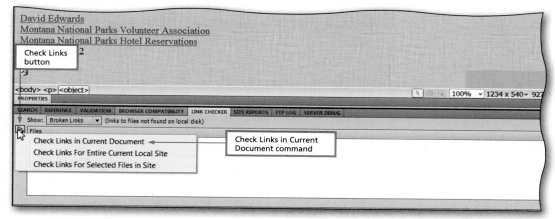

Figure 9–58

5

- Click Check Links in Current Document to check the links (Figure 9–59).

Q&A

How should I interpret the results?

The statistical report in Figure 9–59 shows information about the links in the site, including 1 Total, 1 HTML, 38 All links, 34 OK, 1 Broken, and 3 External. External links are not verified. Your report may include different results.

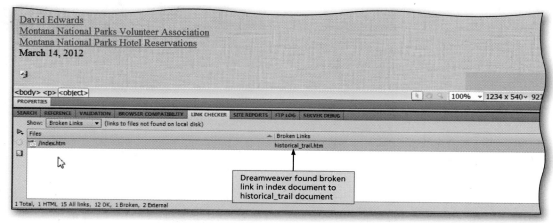

Figure 9–59

6

- Display the Files panel and rename the historicaltrail.htm file to the original file name — historical_trail.htm.

- Close the Results panel group.

Q&A What do the other commands in the Link Checker panel mean?

Use Check Links For Entire Current Local Site and Check Links For Selected Files in Site to check links sitewide or to change a link sitewide.

Adding Animated GIFs to a Web Page

An animated GIF (Graphics Interchange Format) is another alternative that provides an option to add animation to a Web page. An animated GIF can loop continuously or it can present one or a few sequences and then stop the animation.

To Add Animated GIFs to a Web Page

In the following steps, you open a new Web page and then add two animated GIFs to it.

1

- Open the adventure Web page to display it in the Document window (Figure 9–60).

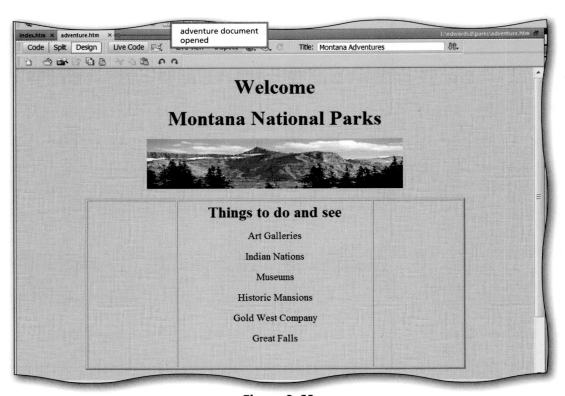

Figure 9–60

- Click the first cell in the table to move the insertion point to the cell.

- If necessary, expand the media folder to display its contents.

- Drag the bison image file to the insertion point.

- Click the third cell in the table to move the insertion point to the cell.

- Drag the 3_deer image to the insertion point (Figure 9–61).

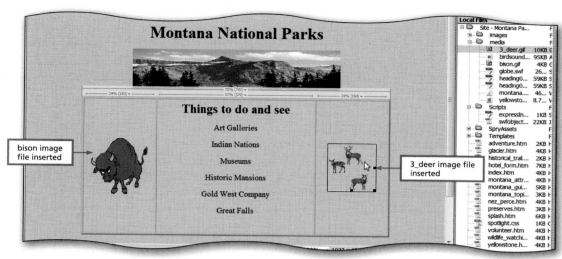

Figure 9–61

- Click the Save button on the Standard toolbar to save the page.

- Press the F12 key to view the page in your browser (Figure 9–62).

❹

- Close the browser and the adventure and index documents.

Figure 9–62

Checking for Plug-Ins

If a visitor accesses a Web page and does not have the appropriate plug-in, it is helpful to provide a link where the visitor can download the plug-in. This is done through the Check Plugin behavior. This is particularly helpful for RealMedia, RealAudio, and other media applications that are not part of a standard Windows installation (such as Windows Media Player).

Plan Ahead

> **Add the Check Plugin behavior.**
> Be sure to include a link on the appropriate Web page so visitors can download a plug-in when necessary. Adding the Check Plugin behavior to an object guides visitors to download and install a plug-in.

You add the Check Plugin behavior as follows:

1. Select an object in the Document window and then open the Behaviors panel.
2. Click the Action (+) button in the Behaviors panel and then click Check Plugin on the Actions pop-up menu.
3. Select a plug-in in the Plugin list in the Check Plugin dialog box, or click the Enter option button and then type the exact name of the plug-in in the adjacent text box.
4. In the 'If found, go to URL' text box, specify a URL for visitors who have the plug-in.
5. In the 'Otherwise, go to URL' text box, specify an alternative URL for visitors who do not have the plug-in.
6. Click the 'Always go to first URL if detection is not possible' check box to select it. Click the OK button.

Shockwave

Another popular media type is **Shockwave**. Adobe's Director program is used to create Shockwave files. Director often is referred to as an authoring tool or development platform. A developer can use a combination of graphics, video, sound, text, animation, and other elements to create interactive multimedia. After the developer creates the multimedia, it can be compressed into a Shockwave file and then added to a Web page. To play Shockwave content within your browser, the Shockwave player must be installed on your computer. You can download the latest version of the player from the Adobe Web site. Information on Adobe's Web site indicates that more than 280 million users have the Shockwave player installed.

Several file formats associated with Director and Shockwave are described below.

- **.dcr** The .dcr file is a compressed Shockwave file that can be previewed in Dreamweaver and viewed in your browser.
- **.dir** The .dir file is the source file created by Director. These files usually are exported through Director as .dcr files.
- **.dxr** The .dxr file is a locked Director file.
- **.cst** The .cst file contains additional information that is used in a .dxr or .dir file.
- **.cxt** The .cxt file is a file locked for distribution purposes.

The software that plays Shockwave movies is available both as a Netscape Navigator and Firefox plug-in and as an ActiveX control. When you insert a Shockwave movie into a Web page, Dreamweaver uses both the <object> tag (for the ActiveX control) and the <embed> tag (for the plug-in) to get the best results in all browsers. When you make changes in the Property inspector for the movie, Dreamweaver maps your entries to the appropriate parameters for both the <object> and <embed> tags.

Inserting a Shockwave file is similar to inserting a Flash movie. The following steps explain how to insert a Shockwave file into the Dreamweaver Document window.

1. Click the Document window where you want to insert the movie.
2. Click the Shockwave command on the Media pop-up menu in the Common category on the Insert bar.
3. Select a movie file in the Select File dialog box.
4. Enter the W and H values of the movie in the W and H text boxes in the Property inspector.
5. Add any necessary parameters.

Java Applets

An **applet** is a small program written in **Java**, which is a programming language for the Web. The applet can be downloaded by any computer. The applet also runs in HTML and usually is embedded in an HTML page on a Web site. Thus, it can be executed from within a browser. Hundreds, or even thousands, of applets are available on the Internet — many of them for free. Some general categories of applets include text effects, audio effects, visual effects, navigation, games, and utilities. Inserting a Java applet is similar to inserting a Flash or Shockwave movie. The following steps explain how to insert a Java applet into the Dreamweaver Document window.

1. Click the Document window where you want to insert the applet.
2. Click the Applet command on the Media pop-up menu in the Common category on the Insert bar.
3. Select an applet file in the Select File dialog box.
4. Set all necessary properties in the Property inspector.
5. Add any necessary parameters.

Adobe Smart Objects

Another type of media object you can insert on a Web page is a Photoshop image file. Photoshop files have a PSD file name extension. When you insert them in a Web page, Dreamweaver optimizes them as Web-ready images in a GIF, JPEG, or PNG format. To do so, Dreamweaver inserts the Photoshop image as a Smart Object, which maintains a connection to the original Photoshop (PSD) file. That means that if the original Photoshop file is modified, the Smart Object in Dreamweaver is also modified. If the Smart Object in Dreamweaver is not in sync with the original Photoshop file, Dreamweaver displays an icon so you can update the image without accessing Photoshop or the original file. The following steps explain how to insert a Smart Object into the Dreamweaver Document window.

1. Click the Document window where you want to insert the Smart Object.
2. Drag the Photoshop file from the Files panel to the insertion point.

3. In the Image Preview dialog box, set optimization settings as necessary and then click OK.

4. To update a Smart Object, select the Smart Object and then click the Update from Original button in the Property inspector.

BTW

Using Fireworks to Insert Navigation Bars, Rollover Images, and Buttons

If you use Fireworks as your primary image editor, you can create images in Fireworks and then use them as interactive content such as navigation bars, rollover images, and buttons in Dreamweaver. To insert a rollover image, for example, click Insert on the Application bar, point to Image Objects, click Rollover Image, and then select the Fireworks images you want to use.

Adobe Fireworks

Adobe Fireworks allows you to create static images (usually as GIF or JPEG files), animated GIFs, large images that have been divided, or sliced, into smaller components, rollover buttons, navigation bars, and partial Web pages. If you use Fireworks, you can create and optimize these objects in Fireworks, and then export them into a Dreamweaver site. To do so, you should set Fireworks as the primary external image editor. The following steps explain how to set Fireworks as the primary image editor in Dreamweaver.

1. In Dreamweaver, click Edit on the Application bar and then click Preferences.

2. Select File Types/Editors.

3. In the Extensions list, select a file extension (.gif, .jpg, or .png).

4. In the Editors list, select Fireworks, and then click Make Primary.

Web Site Project Management

Including media objects on a Web page introduces more complications than adding images or text. Typically, Web developers work in teams to complete a Web project. The project team works together to develop a project plan, which usually outlines the tasks and responsibilities of each team member. Roles include project manager, Web page engineer (who might use Dreamweaver to develop the site), designers for Web graphics and interactive media objects, and a site editor. The project manager is primarily responsible for defining the project scope, assigning tasks to team members, setting and tracking due dates, and allocating resources such as computer equipment, software, and people. The site editor ensures editorial quality, but also must make sure that the material on the site does not violate copyright laws. The site editor verifies that rights are secured for protected material, that material is original, or is free of copyright.

The project plan is organized by phase. Most Web site projects progress through the following phases from initial proposal of the Web site to completion:

- **Site definition and planning** During this phase, the Web site project team defines objectives for the Web site and begins to collect and analyze the information it needs. When the site involves media objects, part of the planning includes identifying the technologies the site will use, such as Flash or Java, and plug-ins visitors will need. Identifying the purpose and audience of the Web site and communicating with project stakeholders and users at this phase helps to avoid **scope creep**, the gradual process of adding unplanned content or features to respond to people involved with the Web site, resulting in a bloated Web site with poor focus.

- **Information design** After planning the Web site, the project team identifies the content and proposes an organization for the Web site. Recall from the Introduction chapter that a Web site can be organized in many ways depending on its content. During this phase, the team builds prototype pages to test the design and navigation of the site.

The goal of this phase is to create a site map, flowchart, or storyboard for the team. A **flowchart** is a diagram representing how Web site users can navigate the site. The flowchart uses shapes such as rectangles to represent Web pages and connects the shapes with arrows or lines to show how they are related. A **storyboard** is another graphic organizer that includes a series of screen shots or sketches that represent Web pages. These graphics are organized in sequence to visualize a Web site and test interactivity. A detailed storyboard includes filenames, Web page titles and images, and brief content descriptions, and shows how pages are linked. For a large Web site, the team might create **wireframes**, which are visual guides to a Web site that shows the relationship among Web pages.

- **Site design** The project begins to take shape during this phase. The team creates a page grid and defines the overall design of Web pages and the entire site. Members begin to gather the graphics and media for the site. Writers and editors begin to organize the text content. The goal is to produce the basic content so the Web pages can be created. Deliverables include completed text files, graphics for navigation and page backgrounds, and completed templates and style sheets.

- **Site construction** Now the Web site can be built according to the design and using the content developed in previous phases. Deliverables during this phase include finished HTML files for all Web pages, images such as graphics and photos saved in appropriate folders, and other components such as scripts and style sheets saved in an appropriate folder structure. When all the pages are completed and linked, the site is ready for user testing. Users should be people outside of the project team who record errors and report on the experience of using the site. After collecting the results of user testing, the team might need to return to the site design phase or begin the site construction phase again to correct errors.

- **Site launch** The Web site files are published to a Web server (see Appendix C) and the URL for the site is publicized.

Quitting Dreamweaver

After you have added the Flash text, Flash movie, audio, and video, and verified that the media objects work, Chapter 9 is complete.

To Close the Web Site and Quit Dreamweaver

To close the Web site, quit Dreamweaver CS5, and return control to Windows, complete the following step.

1

- Click the Close button on the upper-right corner of the Dreamweaver title bar.

BTW

After developing each version of a Web site, compare it to your storyboard to make sure you can navigate to all the pages as identified in your design. Test the site navigation from your users' perspective to determine if you need additional links or elements that identify pages.

BTW

Linking to Microsoft Word and Excel Documents
In Dreamweaver, you can insert a link to a Microsoft Word or Excel document in an existing page. To do so, open the page where you want to include the link. Drag the Word or Excel file to the Dreamweaver page. On the context menu, click Create A Link, and then click OK. When you upload the page to a Web server, be sure to upload the Word or Excel file with the other documents.

Chapter Summary

In this chapter, you learned about Dreamweaver's media objects. You added a splash page with Flash text, a Flash movie, and a link to an audio file. Then you added a link to the index page from the splash page. Next, you opened the preserves.htm page and embedded an audio file with controls. Then you added a video to the index.htm page. You also learned about the Results panel group and how to use the Link Checker. Finally, you learned the general procedure for adding Shockwave movies and Java applets to Web pages. The items listed below include all the new skills you have learned in this chapter.

1. Add a table and Flash text (DW 627)
2. Add a Flash movie (DW 635)
3. Add a background sound and set parameters (DW 642)
4. Embed an audio file (DW 650)
5. Add video to a Web page (DW 657)
6. Verify internal links with the Link Checker (DW 662)
7. Add animated GIFs to a Web page (DW 664)

Learn It Online

Test your knowledge of chapter content and key terms.

Instructions: To complete the Learn It Online exercises, start your browser, click the Address bar, and then enter the Web address scsite.com/dwCS5/learn. When the Dreamweaver CS5 Learn It Online page is displayed, click the link for the exercise you want to complete and then read the instructions.

Chapter Reinforcement TF, MC, and SA
A series of true/false, multiple choice, and short answer questions that test your knowledge of the chapter content.

Flash Cards
An interactive learning environment where you identify chapter key terms associated with displayed definitions.

Practice Test
A series of multiple choice questions that test your knowledge of chapter content and key terms.

Who Wants To Be a Computer Genius?
An interactive game that challenges your knowledge of chapter content in the style of a television quiz show.

Wheel of Terms
An interactive game that challenges your knowledge of chapter key terms in the style of the television show *Wheel of Fortune*.

Crossword Puzzle Challenge
A crossword puzzle that challenges your knowledge of key terms presented in the chapter.

Apply Your Knowledge

Reinforce the skills and apply the concepts you learned in this chapter.

Adding Flash Files to a New Web Page

Instructions: In this activity, you add two Flash files — one aligns to the left and one aligns to the right (Figure 9–63). Be sure you have the data files for Chapter 9 before starting this activity.

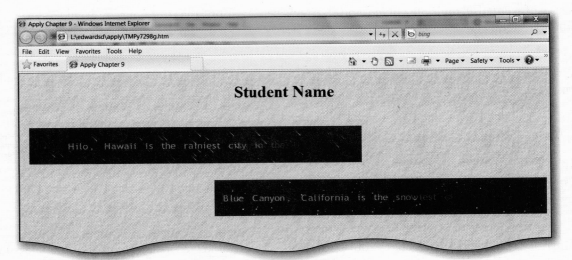

Figure 9–63

Perform the following tasks:

1. If necessary, start Dreamweaver and then copy the apply/media folder from your data files to the Apply Exercises Web site.
2. Open the Apply Exercises Web site. Create a new blank HTML page, and then save it as **apply_ch09.htm**. Title the document **Apply Chapter 9**.
3. Add the apply_bkg.jpg image to the background of the Web page.
4. Enter your name at the top of the page, format it as Heading 1, and then center the text. Press ENTER at the end of the line.
5. Click the rain_fact file located in the media folder and then drag it onto the page below the heading.
6. Name the object **rain**, and then align it to the left, if necessary.
7. Click at the end of the rain Flash object and then press ENTER four times.
8. Drag the snow_fact file onto the page at the insertion point.
9. Name the object **snow**, and then align it to the right.
10. Save the document, copy dependent files if necessary, and then view the page in your browser.
11. Submit your document in the format specified by your instructor.

Extend Your Knowledge

Extend the skills you learned in this chapter and experiment with new skills. You may need to use Help to complete the assignment.

Adding Media Objects to a New Web Page

Instructions: In this activity, you insert a table and then add a Flash file movie and Flash text to the table. You also add a plug-in to play a sound file in the page (Figure 9–64).

Figure 9–64

Perform the following tasks:

1. If necessary, start Dreamweaver and then copy the extend\media folder from your data files to the Extend Exercises Web site. Copy the ocean file from your data files to the images folder in the Extend Exercises Web site.

2. Open the Extend Exercises Web site. Create a new blank HTML page, and then save it as `extend_ch09.htm`. Title the document `Extend Chapter 9`.

3. Apply the extend_bkg image as the background for the page.

4. Insert a table with two rows, one column, a width of 50 percent, border of 5 pixels, and 5 pixels for cell padding and cell spacing.

5. Center the table.

6. Drag the sunset file in the media folder to row 1, and center the object. Name the object `Ocean Sunset`.

7. Drag the ocean file in the images folder to row 2, and center the image.

8. Select the Flash file and change the W to 420 and the H to 75.

9. On a blank line after the table, click the Media button arrow, and then click Plugin.

10. Select the ocean_waves file in the media folder as the media object.

11. Enter `ocean_waves` in the Plugin text box to name the media object.

12. Enter the following parameters and values for the media object:

hidden	false
loop	true
autoplay	true

13. Resize the media object to 200 W and 25 H.

14. Save your document, copy dependent files if necessary, and then view the page in your browser. A speaker or headphones are required to hear the audio.

15. Submit your document in the format specified by your instructor.

Make It Right

Analyze a Web page and correct all errors and/or improve the design.

Adding a Flash File to a Web Page

Instructions: In this activity, you modify an existing Web page by adding a Flash text file (Figure 9–65). Make sure you have downloaded the data files provided for this exercise.

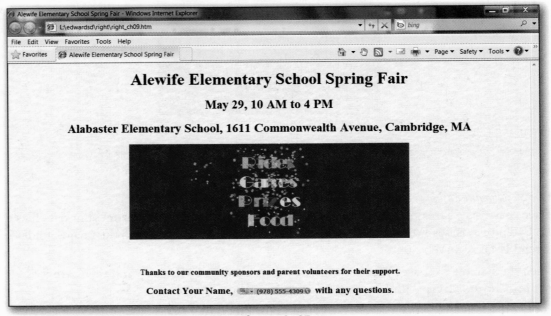

Figure 9–65

Perform the following tasks:

1. If necessary, start Dreamweaver and then copy the right_ch09 file and the media folder to the Right Exercises Web site.

2. Open the Right Exercises Web site, and then open the right_ch09 file. Apply the right_bkg image to the page background. Replace the words, Your Name, with your name.

3. Click to the right of the line ending with "Cambridge, MA".

4. Press ENTER three times, and then press the UP ARROW key once. The insertion point should be centered.

5. Open the media folder and then drag the right_09 file to the insertion point. Name the object **Rides, Games, Prizes, Food**.

6. Save your document, copy dependent files if necessary, and then view the page in your browser.

7. Submit your Web page in the format specified by your instructor.

In the Lab

Create Web pages using the guidelines, concepts, and skills presented in this chapter. Labs are listed in order of increasing difficulty.

Lab 1: Creating a Splash Page for Bryan's Computer Repair Services Web Site

Problem: Bryan's Computer Repair Services would like to add a splash page to its Web site. The management prefers something interesting and eye-catching. You decide to create a splash page with Flash text, a Flash movie, and a link to the index page. The splash page is shown in Figure 9–66. Appendix C contains instructions for uploading your local site to a remote server.

Figure 9–66

Perform the following tasks:

1. If necessary, start Dreamweaver and then copy the media folder from the computers data files to the Computer Repair Services Web site.

2. Open the Computer Repair Services Web site, create a new blank HTML page, and then save it as `computer_splash`.

3. Apply the repair_bkg image to the background. Title the page `Bryan's Computer Repair Services`.

4. Insert a one-cell table with a width of 500 pixels, cell padding of 5, and border of 10. Leave the other properties blank. Align the table to the left.

5. Click the heading01 file in the media folder and then drag the file into the table. Name the Flash object `heading`, and resize the width to 500 pixels.

6. Click to the right of the table and then press the ENTER key four times.

7. Insert a second one-cell table with a width of 350 pixels, a border of 10, and cell padding of 5. Align the table to the right, and leave the other properties blank.

8. Click the computers file in the media folder and then drag the file into the table. Name the Flash object `computers`. Change the width to 322 pixels and the height to 215 pixels.

9. Press ENTER seven times after the second table. Type the following text: `Click here to access` and then press ENTER two times. Type `Bryan's Computer Repair Services Web site` on the blank line.

10. Format both lines as Heading 2 and center-align them.

11. Link both lines to the index page for the current Web site.

12. Save the page and copy dependent files, if necessary.

13. Press the F12 key to view the page in your browser. Allow blocked content. If a Security Warning dialog box is displayed, click the Yes button. Click the index link and then click the browser Back button.

14. Submit the document in the format specified by your instructor.

In the Lab

Lab 2: Creating a Splash Page for the Baskets by Carole Web Site

Problem: Carole would like a splash page for the Baskets by Carole Web site. Carole decides to use the same background, but wants a two-row table containing Flash text at the top of the page. She has found an animated GIF that she would like to add to the splash page. She also wants to add a link to the index page. The splash page is shown in Figure 9–67. Appendix C contains instructions for uploading your local site to a remote server.

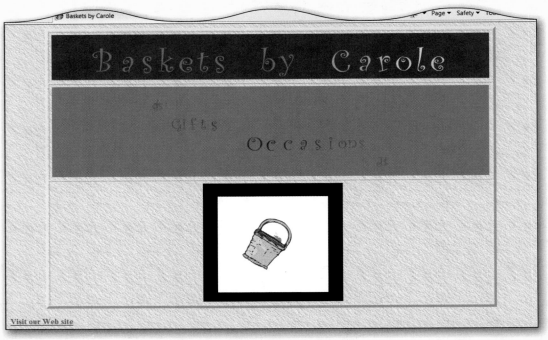

Figure 9–67

Perform the following tasks:

1. If necessary, start Dreamweaver and then copy the media folder from the baskets folder provided with your data files to the Gift Basket Designs Web site.

2. Open the Gift Baskets Web site. Create a new blank HTML page, and save the page as **basket_ splash**. Title the page **Baskets by Carole**. Apply the baskets_bkg image to the background of the page.

3. If necessary, click the top of the page and then insert a three-row, one-column table with a width of 800 pixels, a border of 5, and cell padding of 5. Leave the other properties blank. Center the table.

4. Click in the table and then drag the heading01 file in the media folder to the first row. Name the object **heading**. Click the Align button and select Absolute Middle.

5. Drag the center file in the media folder to the second row. Name the object **types**. Click the Align button and select Absolute Middle.

6. Click in the table and then drag the basket file in the media folder to the third row.

7. Enter **Falling flower basket** as the alternate text, then center the image.

8. Click to the right of the table and then press the ENTER key.

9. Type **Visit our Web site** and then select the text.

10. Bold the text and then create a link to the index page.

11. Save the basket_splash page, copy dependent files if necessary, and then press the F12 key to view the page in your browser. Allow blocked content. If a Security Warning dialog box is displayed, click the Yes button. Check your link to verify that it works, and then close the browser.

12. Submit the document in the format specified by your instructor.

In the Lab

Lab 3: Adding Video and Sound to the Credit Web Site

Problem: Jessica is interested in identity theft and identity security. She recently read about a proposal requiring that a person's driver's license become part of a national database. She has mixed feelings about this suggestion and has located a video file detailing this proposal. She would like to create a dramatic splash page for her Web site and add this movie to the site. The splash page would contain a title, the movie, and a link to the credit index.htm page. The splash page is shown in Figure 9–68. Appendix C contains instructions for uploading your local site to a remote server.

Figure 9–68

Perform the following tasks:

1. If necessary, start Dreamweaver and then copy the media folder provided with your data files to your credit folder.

2. Open the Credit Protection Web site, and then create a blank HTML page. Save the new page as **credit_splash** in the Credit Protection Web site and then title the page **Identity Security**. Apply the credit_bkg image to the background of the page.

3. At the top of the page, insert and center a one-row, one-column table with a width of 60 percent and cell padding of 10. Leave the other table properties blank. Center the table.

4. Drag the heading1 file in the media folder to the table. Name the Flash object **heading**. Change the Wmode of the Flash object to window with a background color of #000000 (black).

5. Click to the right of the table (outside the table) and then press the ENTER key twice.

6. Insert an ActiveX media element. Add the following properties in the ActiveX Property inspector — ActiveX name: identity; W: 320; and H: 320. Click the ClassID box arrow and then click the CLSID number you entered earlier in this chapter. Center the object.

7. Click the Embed check box and then click the Browse for File icon located to the right of the Src text box. Navigate to the credit media folder. Click the Files of type arrow and then click All Files. Select the ID security.wmv file in the media folder and then click the OK button.

8. Click the Parameters button and then add the parameters listed in Table 9–7.

9. Click outside the ActiveX control. Press the ENTER key several times or scroll down to move to the end of the document. Type **Home Page** and then bold the text. Select the text and then create a link to the index page for the current site.

10. Save the document. Copy dependent files, if necessary. Press the F12 key to view the page in your browser. Allow blocked content. If a Security Warning dialog box is displayed, click the Yes button. Note that settings on some computers may display the movie in a different location from that shown in Figure 9–68 on the previous page.

11. Click the Play button to view the movie, and then close the browser.

12. Submit the document in the format specified by your instructor.

Table 9–7 Parameters for Credit Web Site	
Parameter	**Value**
FileName	security.wmv
AutoStart	True
ShowControls	True
ShowDisplay	False
AutoRewind	True

Cases and Places

Apply your creative thinking and problem solving skills to design and implement a solution.

• Easier •• More Difficult

• 1: Create a Splash Page for the Favorite Sports Web Site

You would like to add a splash page to your sports Web site. Add a background image and a title to the page. Add some Flash text and then create a link to an audio file. Create a link to the home page. Save the page in your sports Web site. For a selection of images and backgrounds, visit the Dreamweaver CS5 Media Web page (scsite.com/dwCS5/media) and then click Media below Chapter 9.

• 2: Create a Splash Page with a Flash Movie for the Hobby Web Site

Your hobby Web site is receiving more and more hits each day. You would like to add some interactivity to your site. You decide to do this by adding a splash page. First, add a background image to the page and then add an appropriate title. Next, insert Flash text and Flash buttons. Then insert a Flash movie. Create a link to your home page. Upload the new page to a remote site, if instructed to do so. For a selection of images and backgrounds, visit the Dreamweaver CS5 Media Web page (scsite.com/dwcs5/media) and then click Media below Chapter 9.

•• 3: Add a Splash Page with Audio and Video to the Politics Web Site

Your campaign for political office is going well, and you want to enhance your campaign Web site by adding a splash page. Create a new Web page and then add an appropriate background image and title. Add Flash text and Flash buttons. Embed an audio file and then add a video file. Create a link to your index page. Upload the revised Web site to a remote server. For a selection of images and backgrounds, visit the Dreamweaver CS5 Media Web page (scsite.com/dwcs5/media) and then click Media below Chapter 9.

•• 4: Add a Splash Page with Audio and Video to the Favorite Music Web Site

Make It Personal

Add a new page to your music hobby Web site and then add a background image to the page. Add relevant content and then add Flash text. Add a Flash movie and then embed an audio file. Create links to and from your home page. Upload the page to a remote site. For a selection of images and backgrounds, visit the Dreamweaver CS5 Media Web page (scsite.com/dwcs5/media) and then click Media below Chapter 9.

•• 5: Add a Splash Page with Video to the Student Trips Web Site

Working Together

You and your team would like to add a splash page to the student trips Web site. You also would like to add videos to the page that describe various locations available for the student trips. Each team member is responsible for locating an appropriate Flash movie. On the splash page, add one of the Flash movies, Flash text, and a link to an audio file. On the page that includes trip locations, add two or three Flash movies illustrating some of the activities available at the different sites. Create a link to the index page. Upload the new pages to a remote server. For a selection of images and backgrounds, visit the Dreamweaver CS5 Media Web page (scsite.com/dwcs5/media) and then click Media below Chapter 9.

Special Feature
New and Updated Features in Dreamweaver CS5

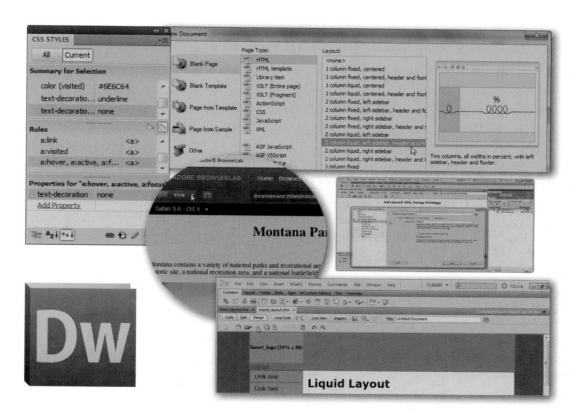

Objectives

You will have mastered the material in this chapter when you can:

- Describe the site setup process in Dreamweaver

- Describe Dreamweaver's advanced settings for site setup

- Access the Adobe BrowserLab and review key features

- Use Adobe BrowserLab to display a Web page in different browsers

- Describe and use the CSS starter layouts

- List the steps required to create a CSS page

- Inspect a Web page with CSS Inspect

- Describe Live View navigation

- Describe a software widget

Special Feature
New and Updated Features in Dreamweaver CS5

Introduction

A number of new features were added to Dreamweaver CS5 and several older features were updated. The more popular of these new and updated features are described in this Special Feature chapter.

Setting Up Sites

BTW

Page Design Considerations
As you develop Web sites and pages, keep design concepts and principles in mind. Balance your pages using symmetrical layouts (such as those that evenly distribute the page elements horizontally, vertically, diagonally, or radially--around a central point on the page). Or use an asymmetrical layout, which does not evenly distribute page elements, similar to the layout shown in Figure 14. Avoid design elements that merely decorate, such as too much color or extraneous graphics.

In CS5 and earlier versions of Dreamweaver, using Site Definition to create a local site was a fairly lengthy process that required about 10 to 11 steps. The new CS5 setup process has been streamlined and requires only three steps. Using the Site Setup dialog box, you can specify four categories of settings, although only the first category is required:

- **Site** Provide a name for the site and select a local folder on your computer where you will store the files and subfolders for the site. You can begin working on a site after completing these two settings.

- **Servers** Specify the servers you will use; most of the details are provided by your ISP. You can use more than one server, such as a testing server and a live server, for the same site.

- **Version Control** If you are connecting to a server that uses Subversion (SVN), set up the connection using this category of the Site Setup dialog box.

- **Advanced Settings** You can specify the following advanced settings in the Site Setup dialog box: Local Info, Cloaking, Design Notes, File View Columns, Contribute, Template, and Spry.

To Set Up a Practice Web Site

The following steps show how to set up a practice Web site.

- Create a folder on a USB or the computer's hard drive, and then name the folder **practice.**

- If necessary, start Dreamweaver.

- Click Site on the Application bar and then click New Site on the Site menu to display the Site Setup dialog box (Figure 1).

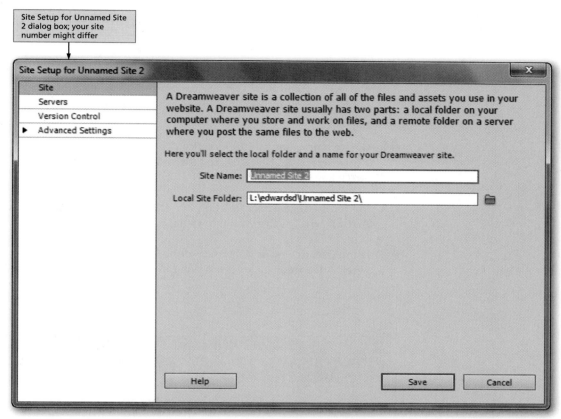

Site Setup for Unnamed Site 2 dialog box; your site number might differ

Figure 1

- If necessary, select the text in the Site Name text box and then type **practice** as the name of the site (Figure 2).

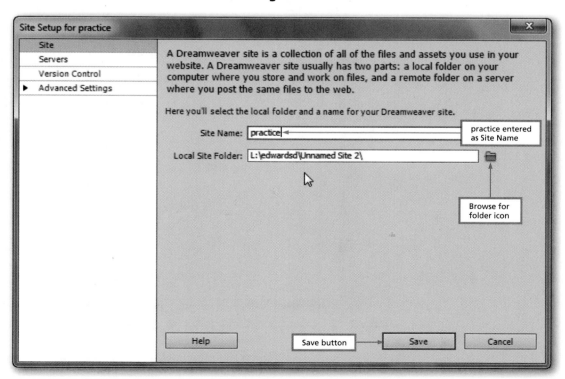

practice entered as Site Name

Browse for folder icon

Save button

Figure 2

3

- Click the Browse for folder icon and then select the location where you want to store the site, in this case, in the practice folder.

- Click the Save button to create the new Web site.

To Research Advanced Settings

The following steps show how to research the advanced settings of the Site Setup dialog box.

1 Create a new page in the practice site named `advanced_settings,` type `Advanced Site Setup Settings` at the top of the page, and then press the ENTER key to insert a new line.

2 Center the text, apply Heading 2 to the text, and then type `Advanced Site Setup Settings` as the Web page title.

3 Using Dreamweaver Help and Adobe Web sites, research the definition for each of the seven Advanced Settings contained in the Site Setup dialog box (Figure 3).

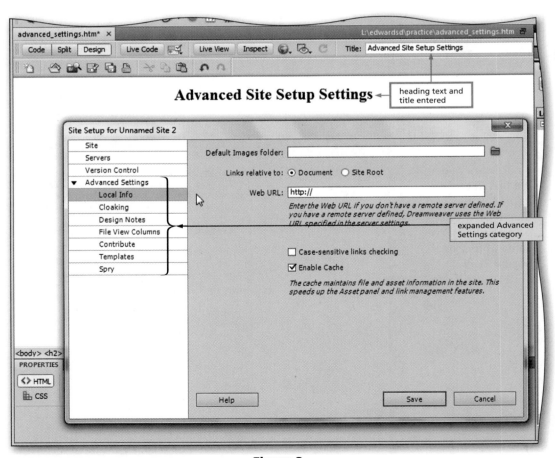

Figure 3

4 Type and bold the first term: `Local Info.`

5 Type two hyphens (--) and then type a definition or description of the term.

6 Complete Steps 3–5 to define and describe the remaining six terms.

7 Save and close the advanced_settings document.

BrowserLab Integration

The Adobe BrowserLab feature lets you preview local Web content from within your local Dreamweaver site or from a remote or testing server. This new CS Live online service lets you test Web content quickly and accurately across various Web browsers and operating systems.

BrowserLab previews your Web pages so you can see how they will be displayed in various Web browsers, even if all the browsers are not installed on your computer. Dreamweaver also includes an Adobe BrowserLab panel you can use to preview any open page in your local site.

To Preview a Web Page Using BrowserLab

The following steps show how to open the Adobe BrowserLab panel and then preview a Web page in the Montana Parks Web site. You must be connected to the Internet to use this feature.

1

- In Dreamweaver, open the Montana Parks Web site.

- Open the index page.

- Click Window on the Application bar, point to Extensions, and then click Adobe BrowserLab to open the Adobe BrowserLab panel (Figure 4).

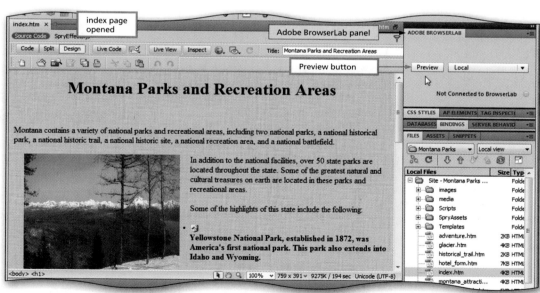

Figure 4

2

- Click the Preview button in the Adobe BrowserLab panel to connect to the Adobe BrowserLab Web page and preview the index page in the default browser (Figure 5).

What should I do if I need to sign in first?

Enter your Adobe ID (usually your e-mail address) and password, and then click the Sign In button. Click the check box indicating you read the agreement, and then click the Accept button. If you do not have an Adobe ID, create one first.

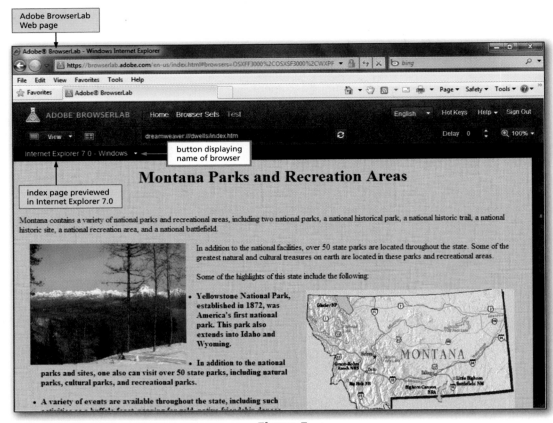

Figure 5

3

- Click the button displaying the browser name on the Adobe BrowserLab Web page to display a list of browsers selected for previewing Web pages (Figure 6).

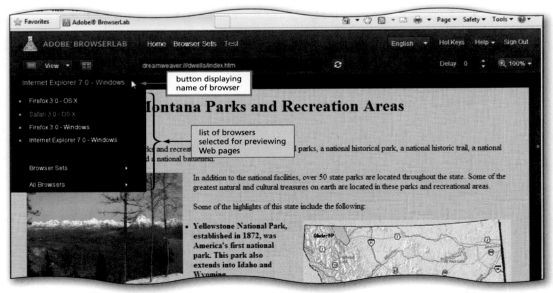

Figure 6

4

- Point to All Browsers to display a list of browsers you can use to preview Web pages in Adobe BrowserLab (Figure 7).

Q&A

How does Adobe BrowserLab preview the Web page?

When you click the Preview button in the Adobe BrowserLab panel, Dreamweaver connects you to the Adobe BrowserLab Web site and creates a screen shot of your Web page using the last browser selected in Adobe BrowserLab (or the default browser if one has not been selected yet).

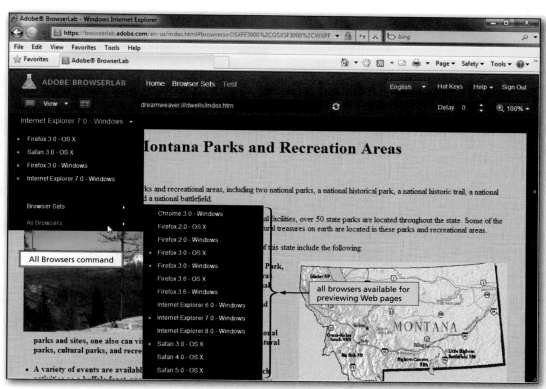

Figure 7

5

- Click a browser other than Internet Explorer or Firefox for Windows, such as Chrome or Safari, to preview the Web page using that browser (Figure 8).

Figure 8

• Click the View button on the Adobe BrowserLab Web page to display viewing options.

• Click 2-up View to display the index page in two browsers: the default browser, such as Internet Explorer, and the browser you selected, such as Safari (Figure 9).

How do the two browsers differ?

As shown in Figure 9, the font size and weight differ between Safari and Internet Explorer. Your results will differ depending on which browser you chose.

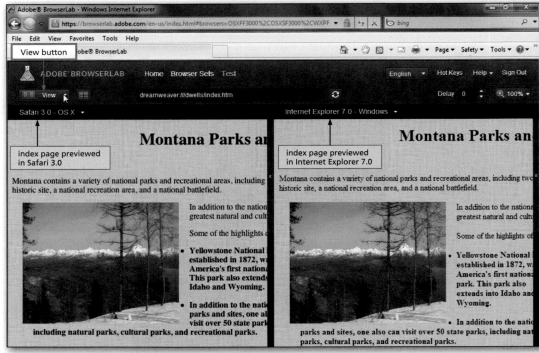

Figure 9

• Click the View button on the Adobe BrowserLab Web page to display viewing options.

• Click Onion Skin to place the two previews on top of each other (Figure 10).

What is the purpose of the Onion Skin option?

Placing one preview on top of another helps you identify subtle differences between the browsers.

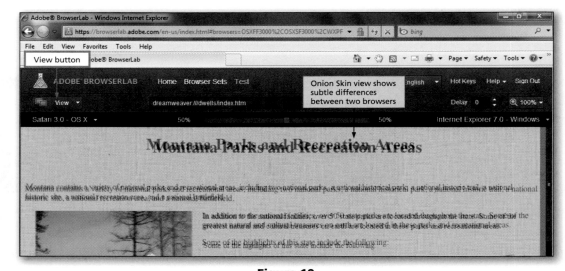

Figure 10

• Close the Adobe BrowserLab Web page.

• Close the index Web page.

Other Ways
1. On File menu, point to Preview in Browser, click Adobe BrowserLab

To Review BrowserLab Features

The following steps show how to learn more about BrowserLab key features.

1

- Use your browser to access the Adobe BrowserLab video Web page at http://tv.adobe.com/watch/adobe-browserlab-cs5-feature-tour/preview-your-web-designs (Figure 11).

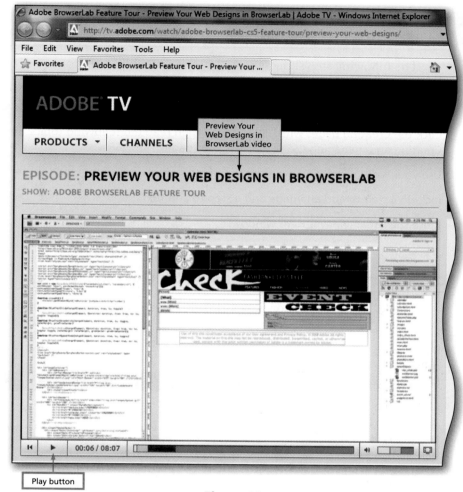

Figure 11

2

- If necessary, click the Play button to start the video and learn more about the key features in Adobe BrowserLab.

- After watching the video, close your browser.

BTW

Creating Custom Font Combinations
You can create custom font combinations such as verdana, arial, sans-serif to determine how a browser displays text in your Web page. Use the Edit Font List command in the CSS Property inspector to select the specific fonts you want in a single combination. Then select a generic font family such as sans-serif or serif to complete the combination.

CSS Starter Layouts

Dreamweaver CS5 includes updated and simplified CSS starter layouts. The complex descendent selectors from the CS5 layouts have been removed and replaced with simplified, easy-to-understand classes.

When you create a new HTML file, you can choose a CSS starter layout to create a page using a professionally designed layout that has been tested to be displayed correctly and consistently in various browsers.

To Learn How to Lay Out a Page with CSS

The following step shows how to learn the required steps for laying out a page with CSS.

- In Dreamweaver, click Help on the Application bar, and then click Dreamweaver Help.

- Click the Creating pages with CSS link, and then read the following topics: Understanding Cascading Style Sheets, Creating and managing CSS, and Laying out pages with CSS.

- Use your word processing program to write a summary diagramming the steps necessary to create a short CSS page.

- Include a step to add an image and a step to add text.

- Close the Dreamweaver Help window.

To Create a Web Page with a CSS Starter Layout

The following steps show how to create two pages using CSS starter layouts.

- If necessary, collapse the Adobe BrowserLab panel.

- Click File on the Application bar, and then click New to display the New Document dialog box (Figure 12).

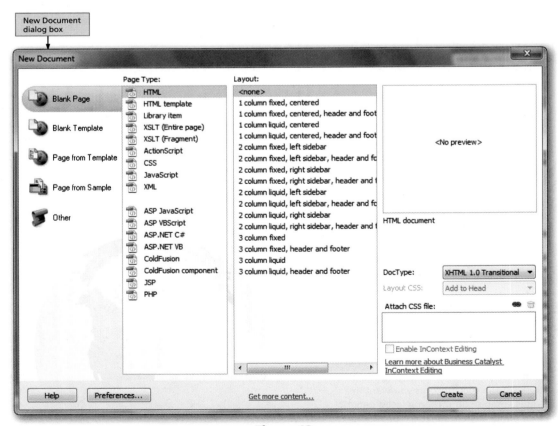

Figure 12

2

- If necessary, click Blank Page in the left pane and click HTML in the Page Type list to specify that you want to create a blank HTML document.

- Click 1 column fixed, centered in the Layout list to select the first CSS starter layout and display a preview in the right pane (Figure 13).

Q&A What is the difference between fixed layouts and liquid layouts?

A Web page with a liquid, or flexible, layout updates when users resize the width of the browser window. The Web page fills the window if users widen or narrow it. (Technically, liquid layouts are created with <div> tags that set the Web page content to a percentage of the browser window.) A Web page with a fixed layout does not change when users resize the browser window. (Technically, fixed layouts are set to a specific pixel dimension, such as 960 pixels.)

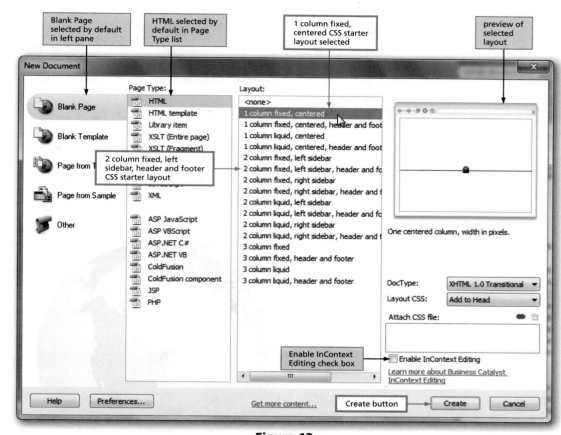

Figure 13

Q&A The New Document dialog box displays an option called Enable InContext Editing. What does that feature do?

When you create a Web page with InContext Editing enabled, you can specify which parts of the page can be edited using the InContext Editing tools. Users can then edit those areas of the page when they view the page in their browsers without needing to know HTML code or Web editing techniques.

Q&A When should I use CSS starter layouts?

Use CSS starter layouts to design the first page in a Web site, and then develop other pages for the site based on that page. CSS layouts also help you avoid page-design problems, so it's a good idea to use the starter layouts if you are new to laying out pages with CSS.

3

 Experiment

- Preview other layouts in the Layout list.

- Click 2 column fixed, left sidebar, header and footer in the Layout list to select the CSS starter layout.

- Click the Create button to create the page (Figure 14).

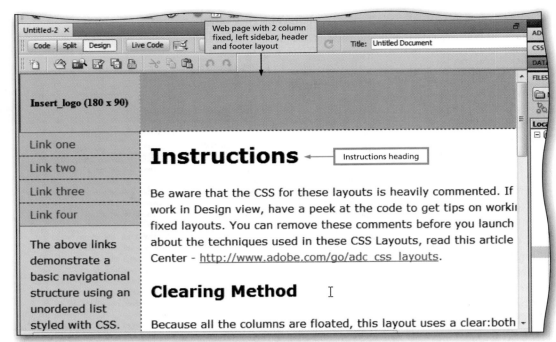

Figure 14

4

- Collapse the panel groups and Property inspector to provide more room to work.

- Save the page as `fixed_layout` in the parks folder.

- In the main document area of the page, select the word Instructions, and then type `Fixed Layout` to replace it.

- Click in the header, and then type `Header` to identify the header area.

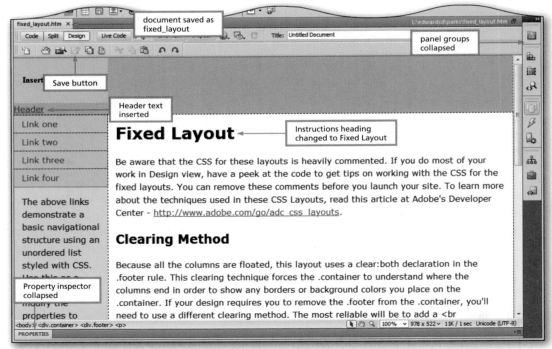

Figure 15

- Scroll down, select the text in the footer, and then type `Footer`.

- Scroll up to the top of the page.

- Click the Save button on the Standard toolbar to save the page (Figure 15).

5

- Click File on the Application bar, and then click New to display the New Document dialog box again.

- If necessary, click Blank Page in the left pane and click HTML in the Page Type list to specify that you want to create a blank HTML document.

- Click 2 column liquid, left sidebar, header and footer in the Layout list to select the CSS starter layout (Figure 16).

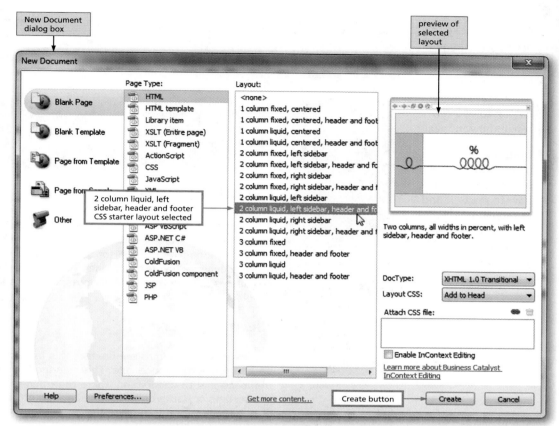

Figure 16

6

- Click the Create button to create the page.

- Save the page as **liquid_layout** in the parks folder.

- In the main document area of the page, select the word Instructions, and then type **Liquid Layout** to replace it.

- Click in the header, and then type **Header** to identify the header area.

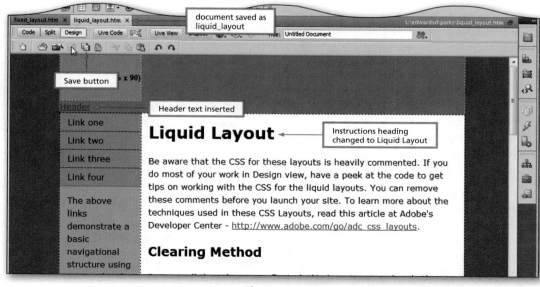

Liquid Layout

Be aware that the CSS for these layouts is heavily commented. If you do most of your work in Design view, have a peek at the code to get tips on working with the CSS for the liquid layouts. You can remove these comments before you launch your site. To learn more about the techniques used in these CSS Layouts, read this article at Adobe's Developer Center - http://www.adobe.com/go/adc_css_layouts.

Clearing Method

Figure 17

- Scroll as necessary to select the text in the footer, and then type **Footer**.

- Scroll up to the top of the page.

- Click the Save button on the Standard toolbar to save the page (Figure 17).

- Press the F12 key to preview the page in your browser.

- If necessary, click the Restore Down button so you can resize the window.

- Drag the lower-right corner of the browser window to resize it and observe how the liquid layout changes as the browser window is resized (Figure 18).

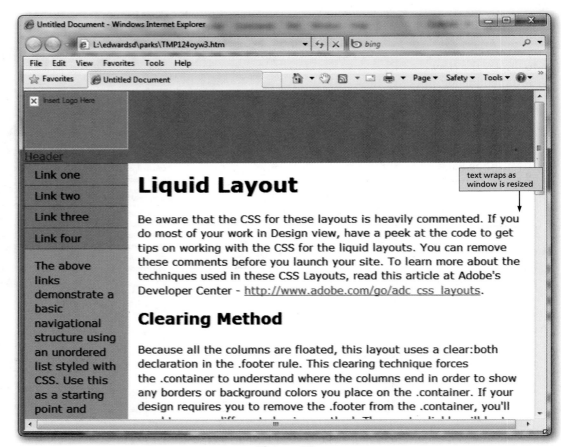

Figure 18

- Leave the browser window open and return to Dreamweaver.

- Display the fixed_layout page.

- Press the F12 key to preview the page in your browser.

- Drag the lower-right corner of the browser window to resize it and observe what happens to the fixed layout as the browser window is resized (Figure 19).

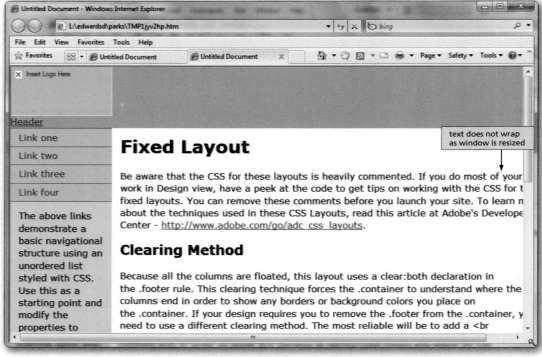

Figure 19

Q&A

Should I generally use a fixed or liquid layout for my Web pages?

The type of layout you choose depends on the type of site you are creating, the purpose of your site, and your audience. Liquid layouts are appropriate when you want to make sure a Web page fits the entire screen no matter what type of monitor or browser window size viewers are using. However, if the Web page contains a lot of text, consider that you cannot control the text wrapping with a liquid layout. A fixed layout gives you more control over the appearance of a Web page, though visitors with large monitors or high screen resolution might see extra blank space when they widen the browser window.

9

• Close the browser window, but leave the two documents open in Dreamweaver.

CSS Inspect

A new tool called CSS Inspect helps you identify HTML elements and their associated CSS styles on a Web page without having to hunt through code. You must first activate the CSS Inspect feature to use it.

To Use CSS Inspect

The following steps show how to activate and then use CSS Inspect.

1

• Click the Inspect button on the Document toolbar to display the Switch now command (Figure 20).

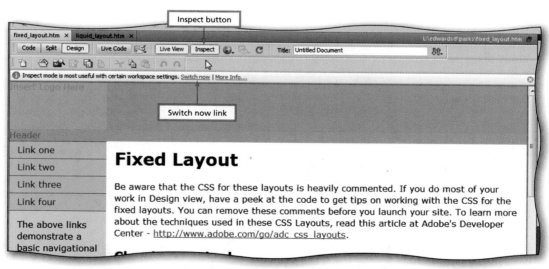

Figure 20

2

- Click Switch now to change the view to Inspect mode, with Code view displayed on the left and Live view displayed on the right.

- Point to the Header text to view the color-coded HTML elements and CSS styles associated with the text (Figure 21).

Q&A

Why does the CSS Styles panel appear?

The CSS Styles panel opens so you can change style rules. If necessary, double-click the CSS Styles tab to display the panel.

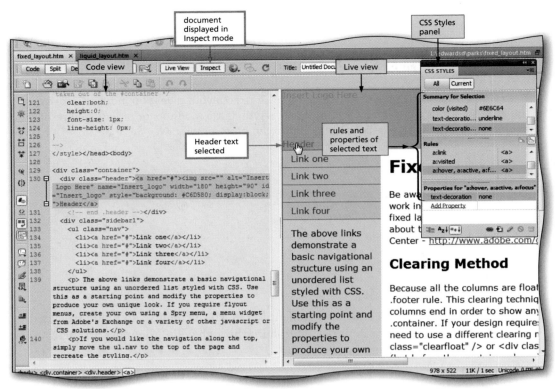

Figure 21

3

- Click "header" in the div class="header" element to display the rules for this element in the CSS Styles panel (Figure 22).

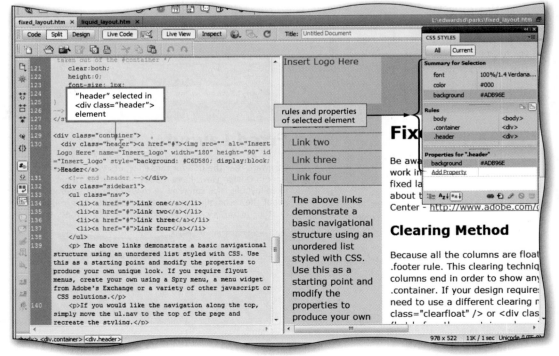

Figure 22

4

- Close the fixed_layout document.

- With the liquid_layout document open, click the Inspect button on the Document toolbar to display the Switch now command.

- Click Switch now to switch to Inspect mode and use the CSS Inspect feature.

- Point to the Liquid Layout heading to view the color-coded HTML elements and CSS styles associated with the heading (Figure 23).

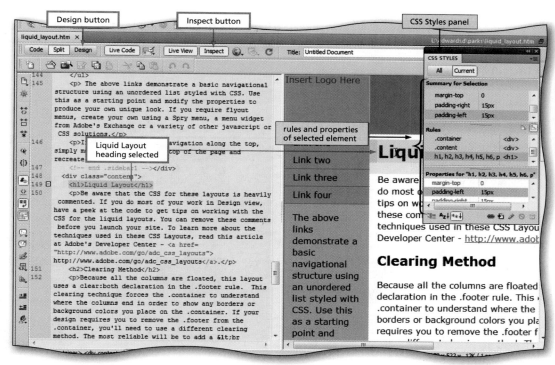

Figure 23

 Q&A

When should I use CSS Inspect?

If the Web page you are creating using CSS styles displays unexpected results, use CSS Inspect to find the names of styles to edit so you can update the properties in the CSS Styles panel.

5

- Click the Inspect button on the Document toolbar to turn off CSS Inspect.

- Click the Design button on the Document toolbar to return to Design view.

- Close the CSS Styles panel.

- Close the liquid_layout document.

Live View Navigation

Live view navigation, originally introduced in Dreamweaver CS5, allows the Web site developer to quickly and accurately check the code. In Live View, the links are active, and the page can be viewed as it would appear in a standards-compliant browser.

Adobe Widget Browser

A **software widget** is a standalone application that can be embedded and executed within a Web page. Two of the major types of widgets are Web widgets and desktop widgets. Web widgets are embedded in Web pages and desktop widgets are embedded on local computers. Recently released, the Adobe Widget Browser, an Adobe AIR application, lets the user configure and use widgets through a visual interface.

To Learn about the Widget Browser

The following steps show how to learn the basics of the Adobe Widget Browser.

- Use your browser to access the following site: http://tv.adobe .com/watch/learn-dreamweaver-cs5/ using-the-widget-browser.

- Review the video named Using the Widget Browser.

- Create a blank Dreamweaver Web page named **widget_browser**, and then title the page **Widget Browser.**

- Enter **Widget Browser** at the top of the page, apply Heading 1 to the text, press the ENTER key, and then type your name and class name and other information if required below the heading.

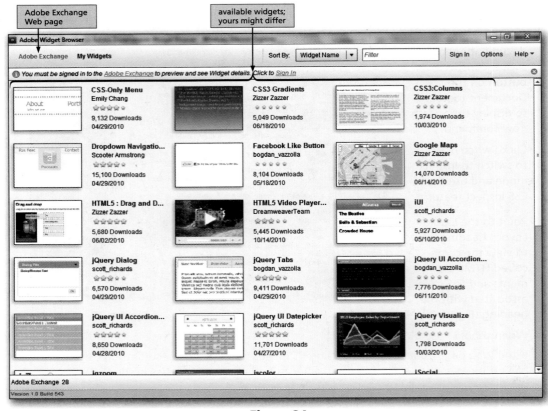

Figure 24

- Use your browser to search for, download, and install the Widget Browser, if necessary.

- Use your browser to locate a widget on the Adobe Exchange Web site (Figure 24).

- If necessary, sign into the Adobe Exchange Web site, and then download the widget you selected to My Widgets.

- Insert the widget into your Web page.

- Below the widget, enter a description of the widget and instructions on how to use the widget.

- Save and close the Web page.

Quitting Dreamweaver

After you have explored the new features in Dreamweaver CS5, your work in the Special Feature is complete.

To Close the Web Site and Quit Dreamweaver

To close the Web site, quit Dreamweaver CS5, and return control to Windows, complete the following step.

- Click the Close button on the upper-right corner of the Dreamweaver title bar.

Special Feature Summary

In this special feature, you learned about the new features in Dreamweaver CS5. You explored the options and settings in the Site Setup dialog box, previewed a Web page using Adobe BrowserLab, and reviewed the BrowserLab features. You also learned how to lay out a Web page with CSS, create a Web page using CSS starter layouts, and then inspect the page using CSS Inspect. Finally, you learned about the Widget Browser and downloaded a widget into a Web page.

1. Set up a practice Web site (DW 683)
2. Research advanced settings (DW 684)
3. Preview a Web page using BrowserLab (DW 685)
4. Review BrowserLab features (DW 689)
5. Learn how to lay out a page with CSS (DW 690)
6. Create a Web page with a CSS starter layout (DW 690)
7. Use CSS Inspect (DW 695)
8. Learn about the Widget Browser (DW 698)

Learn It Online

Test your knowledge of chapter content and key terms.

Instructions: To complete the Learn It Online exercises, start your browser, click the Address bar, and then enter the Web address `scsite.com/cs5dwcs5/learn`. When the Dreamweaver CS5 Learn It Online page is displayed, click the link for the exercise you want to complete and then read the instructions.

Chapter Reinforcement TF, MC, and SA

A series of true/false, multiple choice, and short answer questions that test your knowledge of the chapter content.

Flash Cards

An interactive learning environment where you identify chapter key terms associated with displayed definitions.

Practice Test

A series of multiple choice questions that test your knowledge of chapter content and key terms.

Who Wants To Be a Computer Genius?

An interactive game that challenges your knowledge of chapter content in the style of a television quiz show.

Wheel of Terms

An interactive game that challenges your knowledge of chapter key terms in the style of the television show *Wheel of Fortune*.

Crossword Puzzle Challenge

A crossword puzzle that challenges your knowledge of key terms presented in the chapter.

In the Lab

Create Web pages using the guidelines, concepts, and skills presented in this special feature. Labs are listed in order of increasing difficulty.

Lab 1: Creating a New Web Site and Learning about Site Setup

Problem: You need to create a new Web site using the new site setup process for Dreamweaver CS5. You will then create a new page, and define advanced site setup terms, as shown in Figure 25.

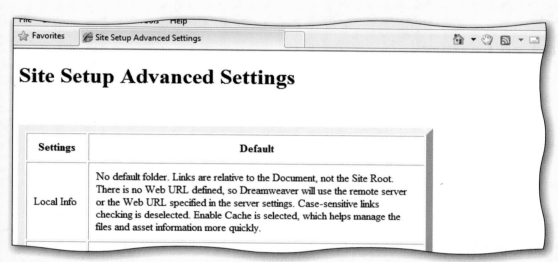

Settings	Default
Local Info	No default folder. Links are relative to the Document, not the Site Root. There is no Web URL defined, so Dreamweaver will use the remote server or the Web URL specified in the server settings. Case-sensitive links checking is deselected. Enable Cache is selected, which helps manage the files and asset information more quickly.

Figure 25

Perform the following tasks:

1. Create a folder on a USB or your computer's hard drive named `special`. If necessary, start Dreamweaver.

2. Click Site on the Application bar, and then click New Site to display the Site Setup for Unnamed Site dialog box.

3. Name the site `special_feature` and select the special folder.

4. Click Advanced Settings in the left pane of the dialog box. Click each setting to view its properties, and then write down on a piece of paper what the default settings are for four properties of your choice.

5. Save the Web site.

6. Create a new page in the site called `SFLab1`. Title the page `Site Setup Advanced Settings`.

7. Type `Site Setup Advanced Settings` at the top of the page, apply Heading 1, and then press ENTER twice.

8. Insert a table with five rows and two columns, 60% Table width, Border thickness of 10, and Cell padding of 10. Choose Top for the Heading setting.

9. In the first row, enter `Settings` in the left column and `Default` in the right column.

10. Complete the table by entering a setting type in the left column and the default settings in the right column.

11. Submit the document in the format specified by your instructor.

In the Lab

Lab 2: Using BrowserLab and Live View Navigation

Problem: You want to use BrowserLab to practice previewing local Web content from within Dreamweaver and create a page describing the four key features of BrowserLab. You also want to practice using Live View navigation. You will test a page using Live View, and then create a page describing the test as shown in Figure 26.

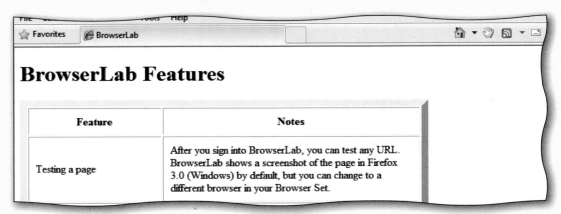

Figure 26a

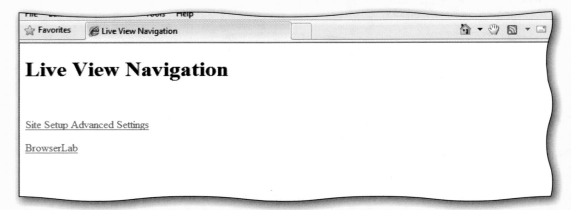

Figure 26b

Perform the following tasks:

1. If necessary, start Dreamweaver and open the Special Feature Web site you created in Lab 1.

2. Use your browser to navigate to www.adobe.com/go/lr_abl_en, and then read about BrowserLab. If a video showing BrowserLab in action is available, also view the video. *Note:* You will need to be able to hear audio in order to learn from a video. Use headphones if you are in a lab setting.

3. Take notes during your reading and the video on the following topics: testing a page, comparing a page, editing a browser set, and testing with a specific browser.

4. Create a new page with the file name **SFLab2a**. Title the page **BrowserLab**.

5. Type **BrowserLab Features** at the top of the page, apply Heading 1, and then press ENTER twice.

6. Insert a table with five rows and two columns.

7. Use your notes from Step 3 to complete the table.

8. Create a new page with the file name lab **SFLab2b**.

9. Title the page `Live View Navigation`.

10. Type `Live View Navigation` at the top of the page, press ENTER twice, and then apply Heading 1 to the text.

11. Below the heading, type `Site Setup Advanced Settings`, and then create a hyperlink to the SFLab1 file. Press ENTER.

12. Type `BrowserLab`, and then create a hyperlink to the SFLab2a file.

13. Click View on the Application bar, and then click Live View.

14. Press and hold Ctrl, and then click the Site Setup Advanced Settings link. Click the Back button (or click the Live View button twice). Press and hold Ctrl, click the BrowserLab link, and then click the Back button (or click the Live View button twice).

15. Save the page, and then submit the documents in the format specified by your instructor.

In the Lab

Lab 3: Using CSS Starter Layouts and Adding Widgets

Problem: You want to create a Cascading Style Sheet that you can use to create a new page. You will also install the Widget Browser and add a widget to the page (Figure 27).

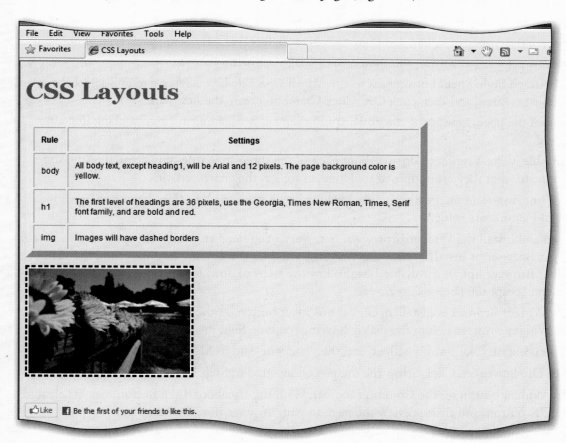

Figure 27

Perform the following tasks:

1. If necessary, start Dreamweaver and open the Special Feature Web site you created in Lab 1 and modified in Lab 2.

2. Click File on the Application bar, and then click New.

3. In the New Document dialog box, click CSS in the center pane, and then click Create.

4. Save the style sheet for the Special Feature Web site as **stylesheet.css**.

5. Type the following to create a body text style.

```
body {
font-family: Arial;
font-size: 12px;
background-color: #FF9;
}
```

6. Press ENTER after the last line. Type the following to create a style for heading 1.

```
h1 {
    font-size: 36px;
    font-family: Gweorgia, "Times New Roman", Times, serif;
    font-weight:bold; color:#C00
}
```

7. Press ENTER after the last line. Type the following to create a style for an image, and then save the style sheet.

```
img {
    border:dashed;
}
```

8. Click File on the Application bar, and then click New. Select HTML as the page type, if necessary.

9. Save the new page as **SFLab3** and then title the page **CSS Layouts.**

10. Click the Attach Style Sheet button next to the Attach CSS File box, navigate to and select the style sheet you just created, and then click OK. Click Create to create the new page.

11. At the top of the page, type **CSS Layouts**, and then apply Heading 1. Insert a blank line after the heading.

12. In a new table, write a sentence or two about each of the three style rules you created in the style guide. Indicate what they are supposed to define, as well as the characteristics.

13. On a new line, insert an image file you used from a previous exercise in this chapter and save it to the Special Feature site folder.

14. Download and install the Widget Browser, if necessary. (You need an Adobe ID to do so.) To access the Widget Browser or install it, click the Widget button on the Common toolbar, and then click the Widget Browser link in the dialog box. Follow the steps to download and install the Widget Browser and accept the license agreement.

15. Once the Widget Browser is installed, click the Widget button on the Common toolbar, and then click the Widget Browser link in the dialog box, if necessary. Sign in again if necessary.

16. Click the Facebook Like Button widget, and then click the Add to My Widgets button to install it.

17. Return to Dreamweaver. Click below the image you inserted in Step 13.

18. Click the Widget button on the Common toolbar. With the Facebook Like Button widget selected, click the OK button, and then preview the page in your browser to view the widget.

19. Submit the document in the format specified by your instructor.

Appendix A
Adobe Dreamweaver CS5 Help

Getting Help with Dreamweaver CS5

This appendix shows you how to use Dreamweaver Help. The Help system is a complete reference manual at your fingertips. You can access and use the Help system through the Help menu in Dreamweaver CS5, which connects you to up-to-date Help information online at the Adobe Web site. Or, if you prefer, you can download the Help topics to your computer in a single PDF file, which you can open and read with Adobe Reader. The Help system contains comprehensive information about all Dreamweaver features, including the following:

- A table of contents in which the information is organized by subject.
- A link to Popular resources, which includes a variety of examples, instructional tutorials, support articles, videos, and other instructional links.
- A search tool, which is used to locate specific topics.

Additional tutorials and online movies are available on the Adobe Dreamweaver resources Web site at *http://help.adobe.com*.

The Dreamweaver Help Menu

One way to access Dreamweaver's Help features is through the Help menu and function keys. Dreamweaver's Help menu provides an easy system to access the available Help options (see Figure A–1). Most of these commands open a Help window that displays the appropriate up-to-date Help information from the Adobe Web site. Table A–1 on the next page summarizes the commands available through the Help menu.

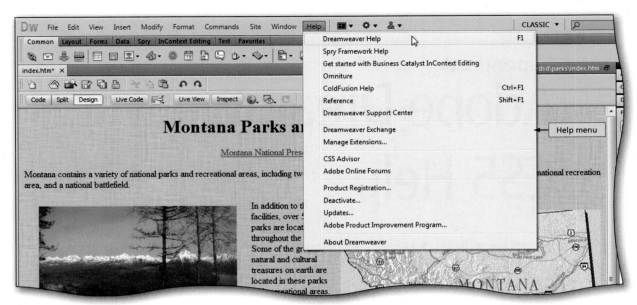

Figure A–1

Table A–1 Summary of Commands on the Help Menu	
Command on Help menu	**Description**
Dreamweaver Help	Starts your default Web browser and displays the Dreamweaver CS5 online help system at the Adobe Web site.
Spry Framework Help	Displays a complete Help document for the Spry framework for Ajax, a JavaScript library that provides the Web site developer with an option to incorporate XML data and other kinds of effects.
Get started with Business Catalyst InContext Editing	Provides information on how to make Web pages editable through any common browser so that content editors can revise Web page text while designers focus on design.
Omniture	Extensions that make it easier to measure the performance of online content.
ColdFusion Help	Displays the complete Help document for ColdFusion, a Web application server that lets you create applications that interact with databases.
Reference	Opens the Reference panel group, which is displayed below the Document window. The Reference panel group contains the complete text from several reference manuals, including references on HTML, Cascading Style Sheets, JavaScript, and other Web-related features.
Dreamweaver Support Center	Provides access to the online Adobe Dreamweaver support center.
Dreamweaver Exchange	Links to the Adobe Exchange Web site, where you can download for free and/or purchase a variety of Dreamweaver add-on features.
Manage Extensions	Displays the Adobe Extension Manager window where you can install, enable, and disable extensions. An extension is an add-on piece of software or a plug-in that enhances Dreamweaver's capabilities. Extensions provide the Dreamweaver developer with the capability to customize how Dreamweaver looks and works.
CSS Advisor	Connects to the online Adobe CSS Advisor Web site, which provides solutions to CSS and browser compatibility issues, and encourages you to share tips, hints, and best practices for working with CSS.

Table A–1 Summary of Commands on the Help Menu *(continued)*	
Command on Help menu	**Description**
Adobe Online Forums	Accesses the Adobe Online Forums Web page. The forums provide a place for developers of all experience levels to share ideas and techniques.
Product Registration	Displays your registration information and provides a print option.
Deactivate	Deactivates the installation of Dreamweaver CS5. If you have a single-user retail license, you can activate two computers. If you want to install Dreamweaver CS5 on a third computer, you need to deactivate it first on another computer.
Updates	Lets you check for updates to Adobe software online and then install the updates as necessary.
Adobe Product Improvement Program	Displays a dialog box that explains the Adobe Product Improvement Program and allows you to participate in the program.
About Dreamweaver	Opens a window that provides copyright information and the product license number.

Exploring the Dreamweaver CS5 Help System

The Dreamweaver Help command accesses Dreamweaver's primary Help system at the Adobe Web site and provides comprehensive information about all Dreamweaver features. Two categories of Help are available, as shown in Figure A–2: Adobe reference and Popular resources. In addition, you can view or download the Dreamweaver CS5 Help in a single PDF file.

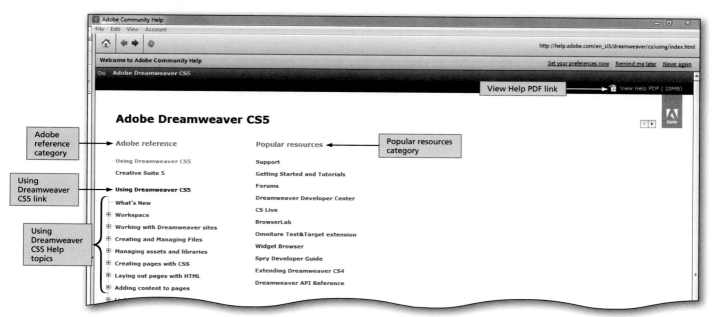

Figure A–2

BTW

Navigating to the Adobe Dreamweaver CS5 Page
If the Dreamweaver Help and Support Web page opens instead of the Adobe Dreamweaver CS5 page shown in Figure A–2 when you click Help on the Application bar and then click Dreamweaver Help (or press F1), click the Dreamweaver CS5 Help link on the Dreamweaver Help and Support page to navigate to the Adobe Dreamweaver CS5 page.

Adobe reference   This section provides extensive Help information, including links to the Using Dreamweaver CS5 Help topics. Using Dreamweaver CS5 is organized into a contents panel on the left and a panel displaying the Help information on the right.

Popular resources   This section provides access to several popular resources, including Support, Getting Started and Tutorials, Forums, Dreamweaver Developer Center, CS Live, BrowserLab, Omniture Test & Target extension, Widget Browser, Spry Developer Guide, Extending Dreamweaver CS4, and Dreamweaver API Reference.

View Help PDF   Click this link to download a Portable Document Format (PDF) file that contains Dreamweaver CS5 Help information. You then can open the PDF file using Adobe Acrobat and use Acrobat features to read, search, and print Help information.

Using the Contents Panel

The **contents** panel is useful for displaying Help when you know the general category of the topic in question, but not the specifics. You use the contents panel to navigate to the main topic, and then to the subtopic. When the information on the subtopic is displayed, you can read the information, click a link contained within the subtopic, or click the Previous or Next button to open the previous or next Help page in sequence. If a Comments link appears on the page, click it to view comments other users or experts have made about this topic.

To Find Help Using the Contents Panel

To find help using the contents panel, you click a plus icon to expand a Help category and display a list of specific topics. Click a link to display a list of specific subtopics. You then can click a link to open a page related to that subtopic. The following steps show how to use the contents panel to find information on displaying toolbars.

- In Dreamweaver, click Help on the Application bar, and then point to Dreamweaver Help (Figure A–3).

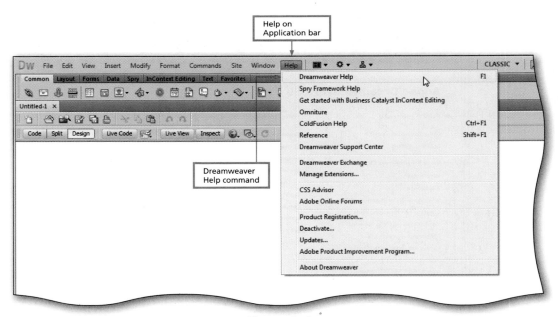

Figure A–3

2

- Click Dreamweaver Help to display the Welcome to Adobe Community Help site.

- If necessary, click the Using Dreamweaver CS5 icon to display the Adobe Dreamweaver CS5 page (shown in Figure A–2 on the previous page).

- If necessary, click the plus sign to the left of Workspace to expand that topic, and then click the Workspace link to display the Workspace page, including subtopics about the Dreamweaver workspace (Figure A–4).

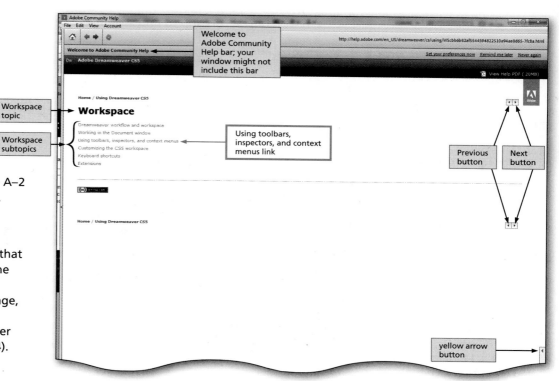

Figure A–4

 What is the purpose of the yellow arrow button in the lower-right corner of the window?

Clicking this button displays links to Using Dreamweaver CS4 and Dreamweaver CS3 Help files.

3

- Click 'Using toolbars, inspectors, and context menus' to display that Help page, including links to display toolbars, use the Property inspector, and use context menus.

- Click the Display toolbars link to review the page content, including links to related information (Figure A–5).

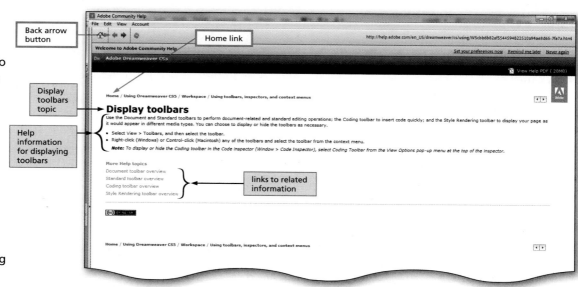

Figure A–5

4

- Click the Home link to return to the Adobe Dreamweaver CS5 page.

Using the Search Feature

The Search feature allows you to find any character string, anywhere in the text of the Help system.

To Use the Search Feature

The next steps show how to use the Search feature to obtain help about cropping images.

1

- On the Adobe Dreamweaver CS5 page, click View on the Application bar, and then click Show Search Panel to display the Search panel, including the Search Dreamweaver content text box.

- If necessary, click the Adobe reference only check box to indicate you want to search the Dreamweaver CS5 references only, not all of the Adobe Web site (Figure A–6).

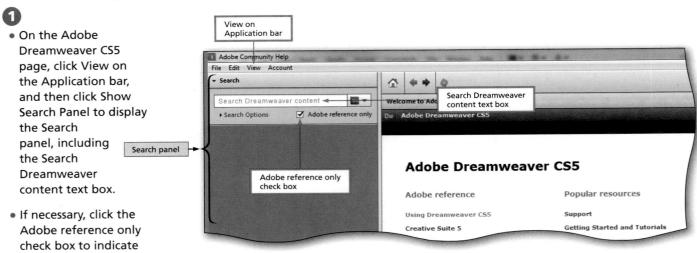

Figure A–6

2

- Click the Search Dreamweaver content text box, type **cropping**, and then press ENTER to display the results.

- Click the Search Options arrow to display additional search options, including Search Location and Filter Results (Figure A–7).

Q&A Why do the search results include topics related to Creative Suite CS5 products besides Dreamweaver?

Because Dreamweaver CS5 is part of Adobe Creative Suite CS5, help topics related to other Creative Suite CS5 products might provide helpful information.

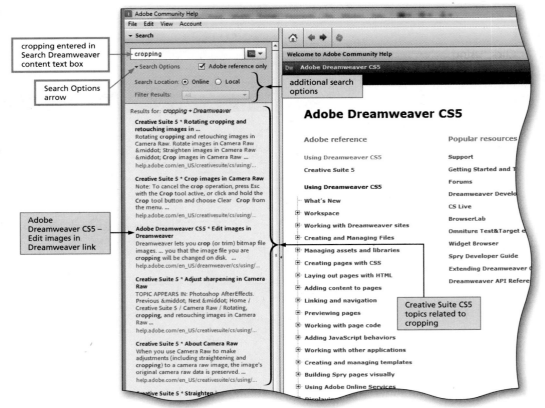

Figure A–7

3

- Click a result of your choice, such as the Adobe Dreamweaver CS5 – Edit images in Dreamweaver link to display the related Help topic (Figure A–8).

Figure A–8

4

- If necessary, click a link to a topic.

- Review the instructions and then close the window to return to Dreamweaver.

Context-Sensitive Help

Using **context-sensitive help**, you can open a relevant Help topic in panels, inspectors, and most dialog boxes. To view these Help features, you click a Help button in a dialog box, choose Help on the Options pop-up menu in a panel group, or click the question mark icon in a panel or inspector.

To Display Context-Sensitive Help on Text Using the Question Mark

Many of the panels and inspectors within Dreamweaver contain a question mark icon. Clicking this icon displays context-sensitive help. The following steps show how to use the question mark icon to view context-sensitive help through the Property inspector. In this example, the default Property inspector for text is displayed.

- Open a new document in Dreamweaver to prepare for using context-sensitive help.

Figure A–9

- Right-click the panel groups title bar and then click Close Tab Group to hide the panel groups, if necessary.

- Display the Property inspector, if necessary, to gain access to the question mark icon.

- Point to the question mark icon in the Property inspector (Figure A–9).

• Click the question mark icon to display an online Help page on setting text properties in the Property inspector (Figure A–10).

• Close the Adobe Community Help window.

Figure A–10

To Use the Options Menu to Display Context-Sensitive Help for the Files Panel

Panels and dialog boxes also contain context-sensitive help. The following steps show how to display context-sensitive help for the Files panel. In this example, the Files panel is open and displayed within the Dreamweaver window.

1

• Click Window on the Application bar to display the Window menu.

• If the Files command is not displayed with a check mark, click Files to display the Files panel.

Q&A What should I do if the Files command is displayed with a check mark?

Click outside the Window menu to close the menu.

• Click the Options button on the Files panel, and then point to Help (Figure A–11).

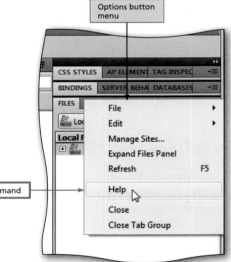

Figure A–11

2

• Click the Help command to display an online Help page about Using the Files panel (Figure A–12).

3

• Close the Adobe Community Help window.

Figure A–12

Using the Reference Panel

The Reference panel is another valuable Dreamweaver resource. This panel provides you with a quick reference tool for HTML tags, JavaScript objects, Cascading Style Sheets, and other Dreamweaver features.

To Use the Reference Panel

The following steps show how to access the Reference panel, review the various options, and select and display information on the <h1> tag.

1

• Click Help on the Application bar, and then point to Reference to highlight that command (Figure A–13).

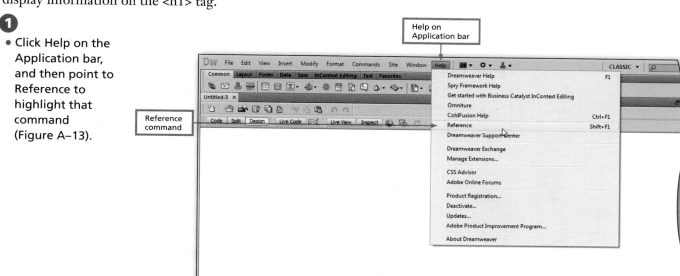

Figure A–13

2

• Click Reference to open the Reference panel.

• If necessary, click the Book pop-up menu button, and then click O'REILLY HTML Reference to display information about HTML tags (Figure A–14).

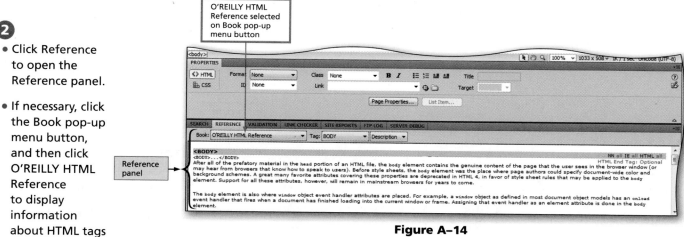

Figure A–14

3

• Click the Tag button and then point to H1 in the tag list to highlight the H1 tag (Figure A–15).

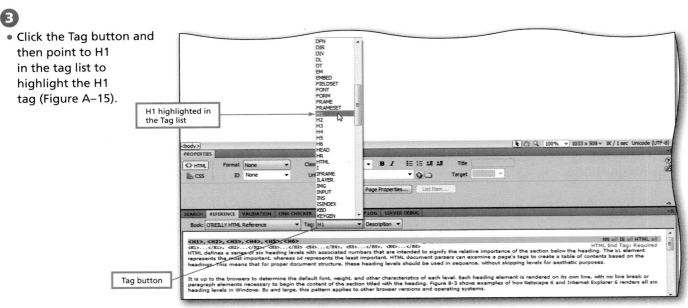

Figure A–15

4

• Click H1 to display information on the <H1> HTML tag (Figure A–16).

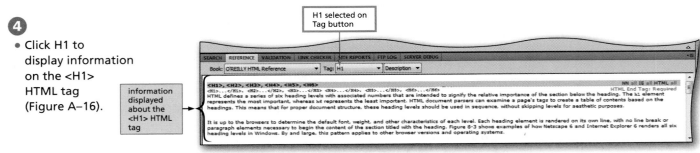

Figure A–16

5

• Click the Book button and then review the list of available reference books (Figure A–17).

6

• Right-click the horizontal bar on the Reference panel and then click Close Tab Group to close the panel.

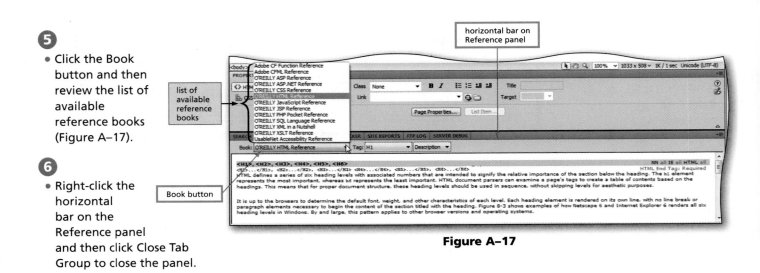

Figure A–17

Apply Your Knowledge

Reinforce the skills and apply the concepts you learned in this appendix.

Viewing the Dreamweaver Help Resources

Instructions: Start Dreamweaver. Perform the following tasks using the Dreamweaver Help command.

1. Click Help on the Application bar and then click Dreamweaver Help.
2. Click the plus sign to the left of Working with Dreamweaver sites, click the plus sign to the left of Setting up a Dreamweaver site, and then click the About Dreamweaver sites link.
3. Read the Help topic, and then use a word processing program to write a short overview of what you learned.
4. Submit your assignment in the format specified by your instructor.

Using the Search Box

Instructions: Start Dreamweaver. Perform the following tasks using the Search box in the Dreamweaver CS5 online Help system.

1. Press the F1 key to display the Using Dreamweaver CS5 Help page.
2. Click the Adobe reference only check box.
3. Click in the Search Dreamweaver content text box, type **adding sound**, and then press ENTER.
4. Click an appropriate link in the search results to open a Help page, click a link on the Help page about embedding a sound file, and then read the Help topic.
5. Use a word-processing program to write a short overview of what you learned.
6. Submit your assignment in the format specified by your instructor.

Using Community Help

Instructions: Start Dreamweaver. Perform the following tasks using the online Community Web page.

1. Click Help on the Application bar, and then click Dreamweaver Support Center.
2. Click the Getting Started and Tutorials link.
3. View the Getting started with Dreamweaver videos and tutorials list and then select the Designing for web publishing link.
4. Review the Designing for web publishing article.
5. Use your word-processing program to prepare a report on three new concepts.
6. Submit your assignment in the format specified by your instructor.

Appendix B
Dreamweaver and Accessibility

Web Accessibility

Tim Berners-Lee, World Wide Web Consortium (W3C) founder and instrumental in the invention of the World Wide Web, indicates that the power of the Web is in its universality. He says that access by everyone, regardless of disability, is an essential aspect of the Web. In 1997, the W3C launched the **Web Accessibility Initiative** and made a commitment to lead the Web to its full potential. The initiative includes promoting a high degree of usability for people with disabilities. The United States government established a second initiative addressing accessibility and the Web through Section 508 of the Federal Rehabilitation Act.

Dreamweaver includes features that assist you in creating accessible content. Designing accessible content requires that you understand accessibility requirements and make subjective decisions as you create a Web site. Dreamweaver supports three accessibility options: screen readers, keyboard navigation, and operating system accessibility features.

Using Screen Readers with Dreamweaver

Screen readers assist the blind and vision-impaired by reciting text that is displayed on the screen through a speaker or headphones. The screen reader starts at the upper-left corner of the page and reads the page content. If the Web site developer uses accessibility tags or attributes during the creation of the Web site, the screen reader also recites this information and reads nontextual information such as button labels and image descriptions. Dreamweaver makes it easy to add text equivalents for graphical elements and to add HTML elements to tables and forms through the accessibility dialog boxes. Dreamweaver supports two screen readers: JAWS and Window-Eyes.

Activating the Accessibility Dialog Boxes

To create accessible pages in Dreamweaver, you associate information, such as labels and descriptions, with your page objects. After you have created this association, the screen reader can recite the label and description information.

You create the association by activating the accessibility dialog boxes that request accessibility information such as labels and descriptions when you insert an object for which you have activated the corresponding Accessibility dialog box. You activate the Accessibility dialog boxes through the Preferences dialog box. You can activate Accessibility dialog boxes for form objects, frames, images, and media. Accessibility for tables is accomplished by adding Summary text to the Table dialog box and adding image IDs and Alt text through the Property inspector.

To Activate the Image Tag Accessibility Attributes Dialog Box

The following steps use the Montana Parks index page as an example to show how to display the Preferences dialog box and activate the Image Tag Accessibility Attributes dialog box.

1

- Start Dreamweaver and, if necessary, open the Montana Parks site.

- Double-click index.htm in the Files panel to open the index.htm page.

- Collapse all the panels, including the Property inspector, to provide additional workspace.

- Click Edit on the Application bar and then point to Preferences (Figure B–1).

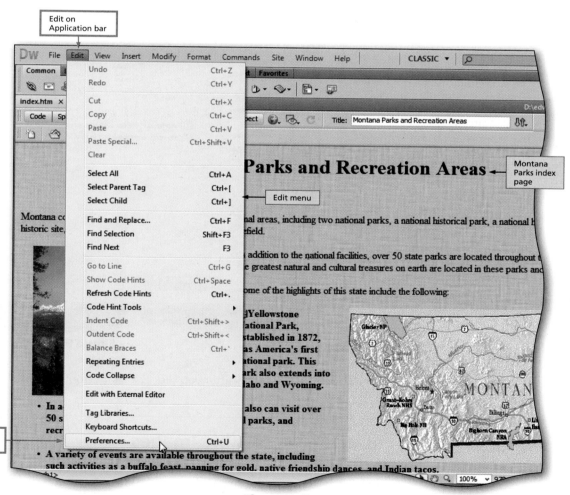

Figure B–1

• Click Preferences to display the Preferences dialog box (Figure B–2).

Q&A

When I open the Preferences dialog box, it displays different options. What should I do?

The Preferences dialog box displays the last category of options selected. Continue to Step 3.

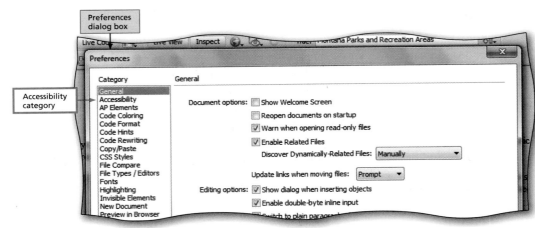

Figure B–2

• Click Accessibility in the Category list to display the accessibility options.

• If necessary, click the Images check box in the Accessibility area to select it.

• If necessary, deselect the other check boxes, and then point to the OK button (Figure B–3).

• Click the OK button to activate the Image Tag Accessibility Attributes dialog box for images and to close the Preferences dialog box.

Q&A

After clicking the OK button, should I notice a change in the Document window?

No. No change is apparent in the Document window after you click the OK button.

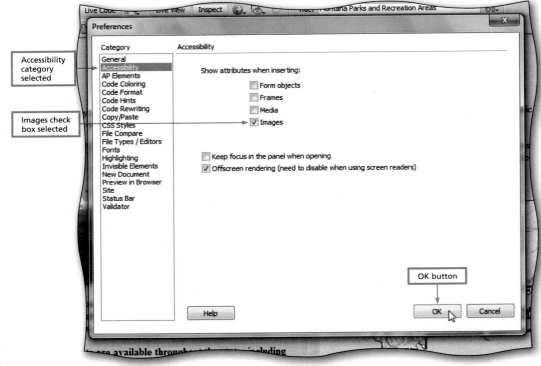

Figure B–3

Inserting Accessible Images

Selecting the Images check box in the Accessibility category of the Preferences dialog box activates the Image Tag Accessibility Attributes dialog box. Thus, any time you insert an image into a Web page, this dialog box will be displayed. This dialog box contains two text boxes: Alternate text and Long description. The screen reader reads the information you enter in both text boxes. You should limit your Alternate text entry to about 50 characters. For longer descriptions, provide a link in the Long description text box to a file that gives more information about the image. It is not required that you enter data into both text boxes.

To Insert Accessible Images

The following steps show how to use the Image Tag Accessibility Attributes dialog box when inserting an image.

- Position the insertion point in the Document window where you want to insert the image.

- Click Insert on the Application bar and then point to Image (Figure B–4).

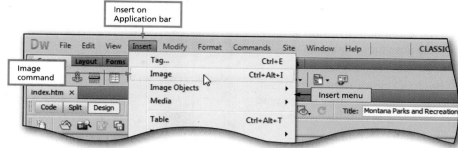

Figure B–4

- Click Image on the Insert menu to display the Select Image Source dialog box.

- If necessary, open the images folder in the parks folder, and then click an image file name of your choice.

- Point to the OK button (Figure B–5).

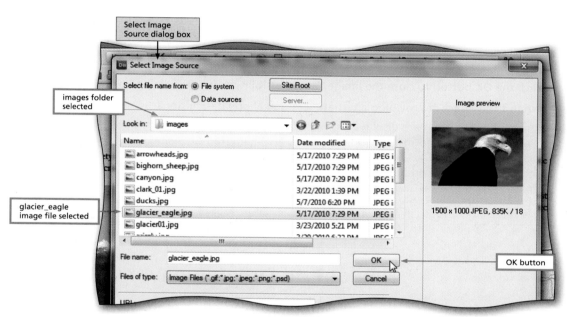

Figure B–5

3

- Click the OK button to display the Image Tag Accessibility Attributes dialog box (Figure B–6).

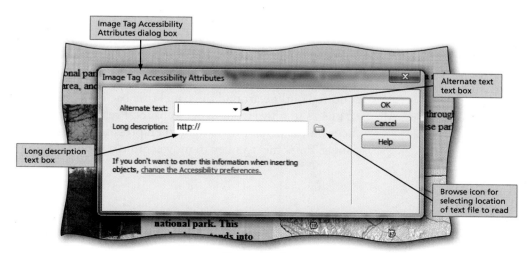

Figure B–6

4

- Type a brief description of the image in the Alternate text text box.

- Type a longer description in the Long description text box (Figure B–7).

Q&A How do I indicate that the screen reader should access a file instead of reading text in the Long description text box?

Click the Browse icon next to the Long description text box, and then use the Select File dialog box to select an .htm file that contains a long description of the image.

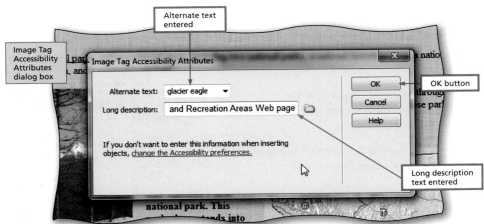

Figure B–7

5

- Click the OK button to close the Image Tag Accessibility Attributes dialog box.

Q&A What is the effect of providing alternate text and a long description?

Although no changes are displayed in the Document window, when the page is displayed in the browser, the screen reader recites the information you entered in the Image Tag Accessibility Attributes Alternate text text box. If you included a link to a file with additional information in the Long description text box, the screen reader accesses the file and recites the text contained within the file. If you typed additional information in the Long description text box, the screen reader accesses and recites the text.

Navigating Dreamweaver with the Keyboard

Keyboard navigation is a core aspect of accessibility. This feature also is of particular importance to users who have repetitive strain injuries (RSIs) or other disabilities, and to those users who would prefer to use the keyboard instead of a mouse. You can use the keyboard to navigate the following elements in Dreamweaver: panels, inspectors, dialog boxes, frames, and tables.

Using the Keyboard to Navigate Panels

When you are working in Dreamweaver, several panels may be open at one time. A dotted outline around the panel title bar indicates that the panel is selected. Press CTRL+F6 to move from panel to panel. Press the SPACEBAR to select a check box. Placing focus on the panel title bar and then pressing the SPACEBAR collapses and expands the panels. Press the TAB key to move within a panel. Use the arrow keys to scroll the panel.

To Use the Keyboard to Hide and Redisplay the Property Inspector

The following steps use the Montana Parks index page to show how to use the keyboard to hide and display the Property inspector and then change a setting.

1

- With the index.htm page for the Montana Parks Web site open in the Document window, click the first line (the "Montana Parks and Recreation Areas" heading) to place the insertion point in the heading.

- Press CTRL+F3 to redisplay the Property inspector (Figure B–8).

How do I hide the Property inspector?

Press the CTRL+F3 keys again to hide the Property inspector.

Figure B–8

2

- Press the TAB key three times to move to the Format button and the selected Heading 1 format.

- Press the UP ARROW key to select the Paragraph format (Figure B–9).

3

- Press the DOWN ARROW key to select the Heading 1 format again.

- Close Dreamweaver without saving any of the changes.

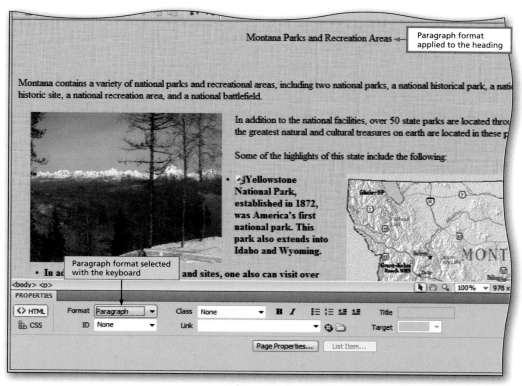

Figure B–9

Operating System Accessibility Features

The third method of accessibility support in Dreamweaver is through the Windows operating system's high contrast settings. **High contrast** changes the desktop color schemes for individuals who have vision impairment. The color schemes make the screen easier to view by heightening screen contrast with alternative color combinations. Some of the high contrast schemes also change font sizes.

You activate this option through the Windows Control Panel. The high contrast setting affects Dreamweaver in two ways:

- The dialog boxes and panels use system color settings.
- Code view syntax color is turned off.

Design view, however, continues to use the background and text colors you set in the Page Properties dialog box. The pages you design, therefore, continue to render colors as they will be displayed in a browser.

To Turn On High Contrast

The following steps show how to turn on high contrast and how to change the current high contrast settings in Windows 7.

1

- In Windows 7, click the Start button on the taskbar and then click Control Panel on the Start menu to open the Control Panel (Figure B–10).

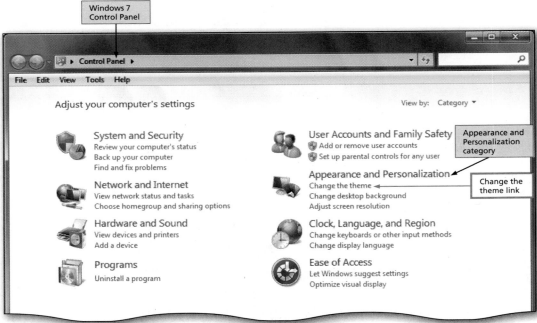

Figure B–10

2

- In the Appearance and Personalization category, click the 'Change the theme' link to display the Personalization window.

- Note your current theme, such as Windows 7.

- Scroll down, if necessary, to display the High Contrast themes (Figure B–11).

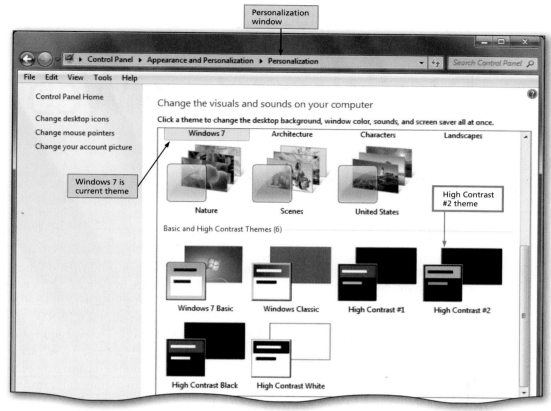

Figure B–11

3

- Click High Contrast #2 to display a preview of the theme on the desktop and in the Personalization window.

4

- Click your original theme to return the settings to their original values.

- Close the Personalization window to redisplay the Windows 7 desktop.

Q&A

What should I do if I want to retain the High Contrast #2 color scheme?

Select the theme, and then close the Personalization window.

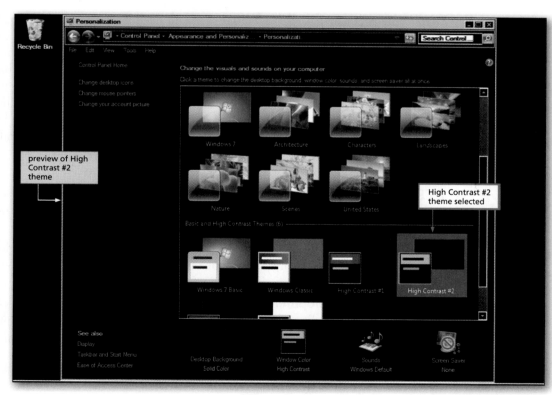

Figure B–12

Other Ways

1. Right-click desktop, click Personalize

Appendix C
Publishing to a Web Server

Publishing to a Remote Site

With Dreamweaver, Web designers usually define a local site and then do the majority of their designing using the local site. You defined a local site in Chapter 1. In creating the projects in this book, you have added Web pages to the local site, which resides on your computer's hard drive, a network drive, a USB drive, or possibly a CD-RW.

To prepare a Web site and make it available for others to view requires that you publish your site by uploading it to a Web server for public access. A Web server is an Internet- or intranet-connected computer that delivers the Web pages to online visitors. Dreamweaver includes built-in support that enables you to connect and transfer your local site to a Web server. Publishing to a Web server requires that you have access to a Web server. Your instructor will provide you with the location, user name, and password information for the Web server on which you will publish your site.

After you establish access to a Web server, you need a remote site folder. The remote folder will reside on the Web server and contain your Web site files. Generally, the remote folder is defined by the Web server administrator or your instructor. The name of the local root folder in this example is the author's first and last name. Most likely, the name of your remote folder also will be your last name and first initial or your first and last name. You upload your local site to the remote folder on the Web server. The remote site connection information must be defined in Dreamweaver through the Site Setup dialog box. You display the Site Setup dialog box, select the Servers category, and then enter the remote site information. Dreamweaver provides five different protocols for connecting to a remote site. These methods are as follows:

- **FTP (File Transfer Protocol)**: This protocol is used on the Internet for sending and receiving files. It is the most widely used method for uploading and downloading pages to and from a Web server.
- **Local/Network**: This option is used when the Web server is located on a local area network (LAN) or a company, school, or other organization intranet. Files on LANs generally are available for internal viewing only.
- **RDS (Remote Development Services) and WebDAV**: These protocols are systems that permit users to edit and manage files collaboratively on remote Web servers.

Most likely you will use the FTP option to upload your Web site to a remote server.

Defining a Remote Site

You define the remote site by changing some of the settings in the Site Setup dialog box. To allow you to create a remote site using FTP, your instructor will supply you with the following information:

- **Server name**: The name of the server where your remote site will be stored
- **FTP address**: The Web address for the remote host of your Web server
- **Username**: Your user name
- **Password**: The FTP password to authenticate and access your account
- **Web URL**: The URL for your remote site

To Define a Remote Site

Assume for the following steps that you are defining a remote site for the Montana Parks Web site.

- If necessary, start Dreamweaver, select the Montana Parks site, and then open the index.htm page.

- Click Site on the Application bar and then click Manage Sites to open the Manage Sites dialog box.

- If necessary, click Montana Parks to select the Montana Parks Web site (Figure C–1).

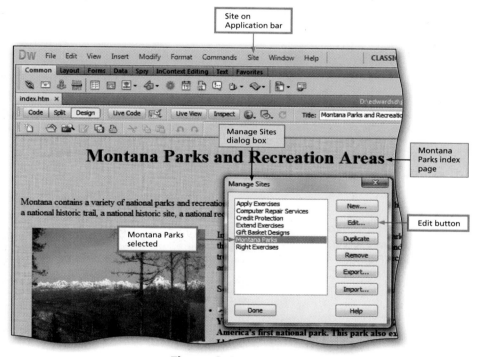

Figure C–1

- Click the Edit button to open the Site Setup for Montana Parks dialog box (Figure C–2).

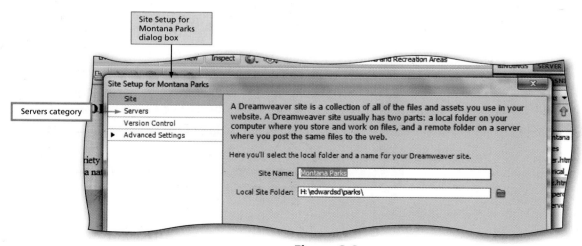

Figure C–2

● Click Servers to display
  an area for entering the
  server settings in the Site
  Setup for Montana Parks
  dialog box (Figure C–3).

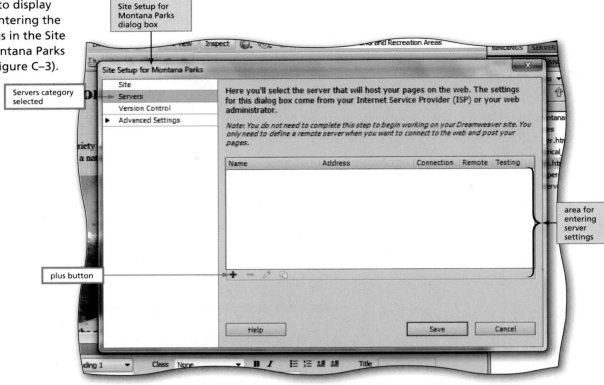

Figure C–3

● Click the plus button to
  display the Basic server
  information (Figure C–4).

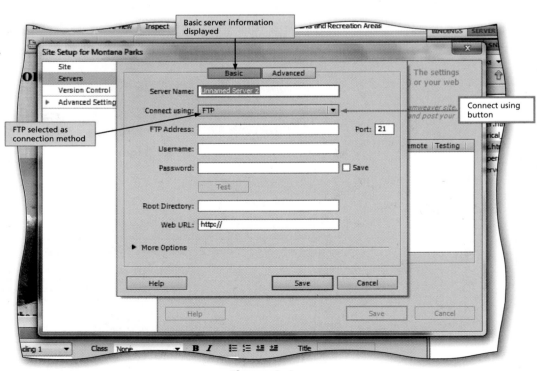

Figure C–4

5

- If necessary, click the Connect using button, and then click FTP to select FTP as the protocol for connecting to a remote site.

- In the appropriate text boxes, enter the Server Name, FTP Address, Username, Password, and Web URL information provided by your instructor (Figure C–5).

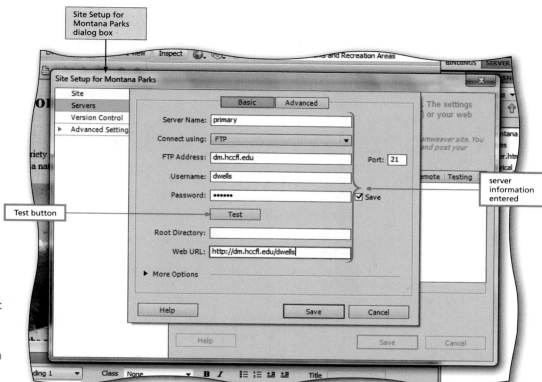

Q&A What if I am required to enter different information from that shown in Figure C–5?

Your information will most likely differ from that in Figure C–5.

Figure C–5

6

- Click the Test button to test the connection and to display the Dreamweaver dialog box (Figure C–6).

Q&A What should I do if a security dialog box is displayed?

If a Windows Security Alert dialog box is displayed, click the Allow access button.

Q&A What should I do if my connection is not successful?

If your connection is not successful, review your text box entries and make any necessary corrections. If all entries are correct, check with your instructor. The Site Setup dialog box should look similar to Figure C–5.

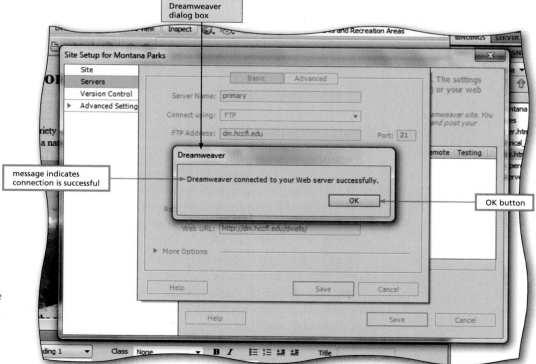

Figure C–6

7

- Click the OK button to close the Dreamweaver dialog box.

- Click the Save button in the Site Setup for Montana Parks dialog box to save the Basic server information and display the server information (Figure C–7).

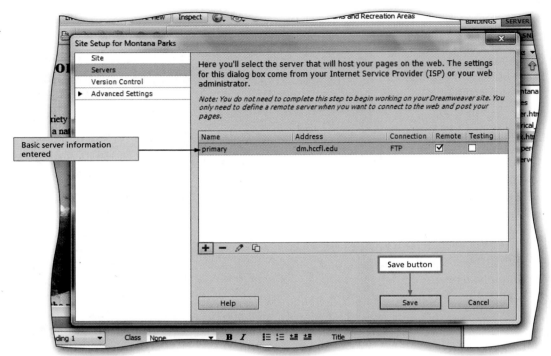

Figure C–7

8

- Click the Save button to save the site information for the Montana Parks Web site.

- Click the Done button to close the Manage Sites dialog box.

Q&A

What should I do if another Dreamweaver dialog box is displayed?

If another Dreamweaver dialog box is displayed, click the OK button.

Connecting to a Remote Site

Now that you have completed the remote site information and tested your connection, you can interact with the remote server. The remote site folder on the Web server for your Web site must be established before a connection can be made. This folder, called the **remote site root**, generally is created automatically by the Web server administrator of the hosting company or by your instructor. The naming convention generally is determined by the hosting company.

This book uses the last name and first initial of the author for the user name of the remote site folder. Naming conventions other than your last and first name may be used on the Web server to which you are connecting. Your instructor will supply you with this information. If all information is correct, connecting to the remote site is accomplished easily through the Files panel.

To Connect to a Remote Site

The following steps illustrate how to connect to the remote server and display your remote site folder.

1

- Click the 'Expand to show local and remote sites' button to expand the Site pane and show both a right (Local Files) and left (Remote Server) pane (Figure C–8).

Q&A What do the right and left expanded panes display?

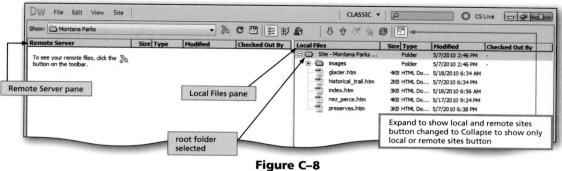

Figure C–8

The right pane contains the local site, and the left pane contains information for viewing your remote files by clicking the Connects to remote host button.

2

- Verify that the root folder for the site is selected in the Local Files pane.

- Click the 'Connects to remote host' button in the Remote Server pane to make the connection (Figure C–9).

Q&A What happens after I click the 'Connects to remote host' button?

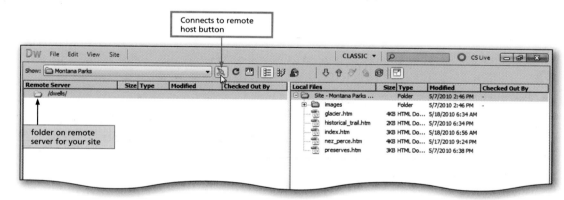

Figure C–9

The 'Connects to remote host/Disconnects from remote host' button changes to indicate that the connection has been made, and a default Home.html folder is created automatically.

Uploading Files to a Remote Server

Uploading is the process of transferring your files from your computer to the remote server. **Downloading** is the process of transferring files from the remote server to your computer. Dreamweaver uses the term **put** for uploading and **get** for downloading.

To Upload Files to a Remote Server

The following steps illustrate how to upload your files to the remote server.

- If necessary, click the Montana Parks root folder in the Local Files panel to select the root folder.

- Click the Put File(s) button on the Files panel toolbar to begin uploading the files and display a Dreamweaver dialog box.

- Point to the OK button in the Dreamweaver dialog box (Figure C–10).

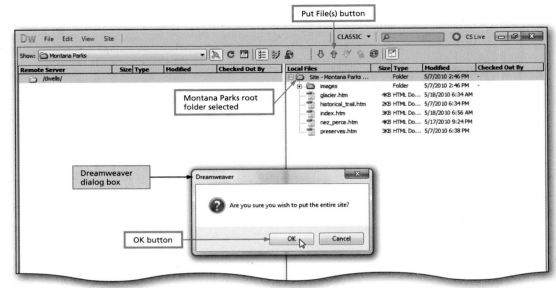

Figure C–10

- Click the OK button to begin uploading the files and to display a dialog box that shows progress information (Figure C–11).

Q&A

My files are uploaded, but they appear in a different order. Is that okay?

The files that are uploaded to the server may be displayed in a different order from that on the local site based on the server settings.

- Quit Dreamweaver.

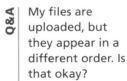 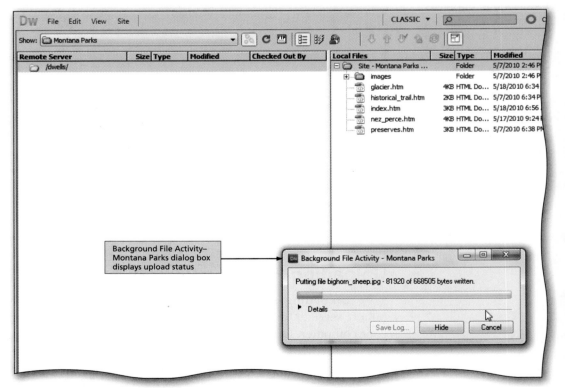

Figure C–11

Remote Site Maintenance and Site Synchronization

Now that your Web site is on a Web server, you will want to continue to maintain the site. When you are connected to the remote site, you can apply many of the same commands to a folder or file on the remote site as you do to a folder or file on the local site. You can create and delete folders; cut, copy, delete, duplicate, paste, and rename files; and so on. These commands are available through the context menu.

To mirror the local site on the remote site, Dreamweaver provides a synchronization feature. Synchronizing is the process of transferring files between the local and remote sites so both sites have an identical set of the most recent files. You can choose to synchronize the entire Web site or select only specific files. You also can specify Direction. Within Direction, you have three options: upload the newer files from the local site to the remote site (put), download newer files from the remote site to the local site (get), or upload and download files to and from the remote and local sites. Once you specify a direction, Dreamweaver automatically synchronizes files. If the files are already in sync, Dreamweaver lets you know that no synchronization is necessary. To access the Synchronize command, you first connect to the remote server and then select Synchronize on the Site menu (Figure C–12).

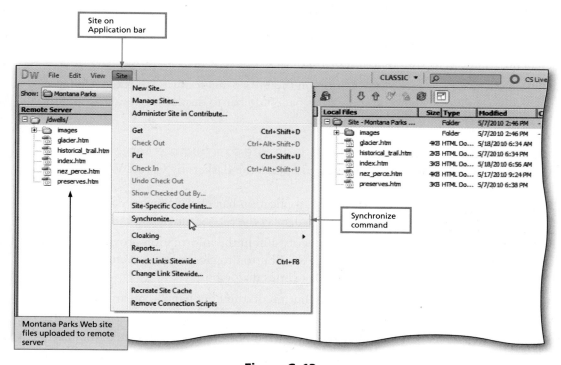

Figure C–12

To save the verification information to a local file, click the Save Log button at the completion of the synchronization process. Another feature within Dreamweaver allows you to verify which files are newer on the local site or the remote site; choose the Remote view by selecting Select Newer Local or Select Newer on Remote Server commands. These options are available through the Files panel Edit menu when the Remote site panel is displayed.

Apply Your Knowledge

Reinforce the skills and apply the concepts you learned in this appendix.

Defining and Uploading the Bryan's Computer Repair Services Web Site to a Remote Server

Instructions: Perform the following tasks to define and upload the Bryan's Computer Repair Services Web site to a remote server.

1. If necessary, start Dreamweaver. Click Site on the Application bar, click Manage Sites, and then click Computer Repair Services. Click the Edit button to display the Site Setup dialog box.

2. In the Site Setup dialog box, click the Servers category, fill in the information provided by your instructor, and then test the connection. Click the Save button to close the Site Setup dialog box, and then click the Done button to close the Manage Sites dialog box.

3. Click the 'Expand to show local and remote sites' button on the Files panel toolbar and then click the 'Connects to remote host button.'

4. Click the local file root folder and then click the Put File(s) button on the Site panel toolbar to upload your Web site. Click the OK button in response to the "Are you sure you wish to put the entire site?" dialog box.

5. Review your files to verify that they were uploaded. The files on the remote server may be displayed in a different order from those on the local site.

6. Click the 'Disconnects from remote host' button on the Files panel toolbar. Click the 'Collapse to show only local or remote site' button on the Files panel toolbar to display the local site and the Document window.

Defining and Uploading the Baskets by Carole Web Site to a Remote Server

Instructions: Perform the following tasks to define and upload the Baskets by Carole Web site to a remote server.

1. If necessary, start Dreamweaver. Click Site on the Application bar, click Manage Sites, and then click Gift Basket Designs. Click the Edit button to display the Site Setup dialog box.

2. In the Site Setup dialog box, click the Servers category. Fill in the information provided by your instructor, and then test the connection. Click the Save button to close the Site Setup dialog box, and then click the Done button to close the Manage Sites dialog box.

3. Click the 'Expand to show local and remote sites' button on the Files panel toolbar and then click the 'Connects to remote host' button.

4. Click the local file root folder and then click the Put File(s) button on the Files panel toolbar to upload your Web site. Click the OK button in response to the "Are you sure you wish to put the entire site?" dialog box.

5. Review your files to verify that they were uploaded. The files on the remote server may be displayed in a different order from those on the local site.

6. Click the 'Disconnects from remote host' button. Click the 'Collapse to show only local or remote site' button on the Files panel toolbar to display the local site and the Document window.

Defining and Uploading the Credit Protection Web Site to a Remote Server

Instructions: Perform the following tasks to define and upload the Credit Protection Web site to a remote server.

1. If necessary, start Dreamweaver. Click Site on the Application bar, click Manage Sites, and then click Credit Protection. Click the Edit button to display the Site Setup dialog box.

2. In the Site Setup dialog box, click the Servers category. Fill in the information provided by your instructor, and then test the connection. Click the Save button to close the Site Setup dialog box, and then click the Done button to close the Manage Sites dialog box.

3. Click the 'Expand to show local and remote sites' button on the Files panel toolbar and then click the 'Connects to remote host' button.

4. Click the local file root folder and then click the Put File(s) button on the Files panel toolbar to upload your Web site. Click the OK button in response to the "Are you sure you wish to put the entire site?" dialog box.

5. Review your files to verify that they were uploaded. The files on the remote server may display in a different order from those on the local site.

6. Click the 'Disconnects from remote host' button. Click the 'Collapse to show only local or remote site' button on the Files panel toolbar to display the local site and the Document window.

Appendix D

Customizing Adobe Dreamweaver CS5

This appendix explains how to change the screen resolution in Windows 7 to the resolution used in this book.

Changing Screen Resolution

Screen resolution indicates the number of pixels (dots) that the computer uses to display the letters, numbers, graphics, and background you see on the screen. When you increase the screen resolution, Windows displays more information on the screen, but the information decreases in size. The reverse also is true: as you decrease the screen resolution, Windows displays less information on the screen, but the information increases in size.

The screen resolution usually is stated as the product of two numbers, such as 1024×768 (pronounced "ten twenty-four by seven sixty-eight"). A 1024×768 screen resolution results in a display of 1,024 distinct pixels on each of 768 lines, or about 786,432 pixels. The figures in this book were created using a screen resolution of 1024×768.

This is the screen resolution most commonly used today, although some Web designers set their computers at a much higher screen resolution, such as 2048×1536.

To Change the Screen Resolution

The following steps change the screen resolution to 1024 × 768 to match the figures in this book.

1

- If necessary, minimize all programs so that the Windows 7 desktop appears.

- Right-click the Windows 7 desktop to display the Windows 7 desktop shortcut menu (Figure D–1).

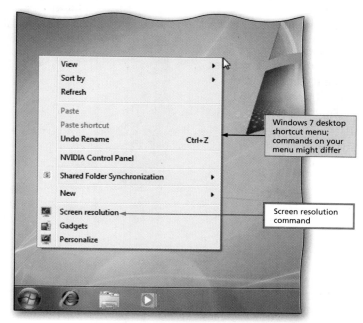

Figure D–1

2

- Click Screen resolution on the shortcut menu to open the Screen Resolution window (Figure D–2).

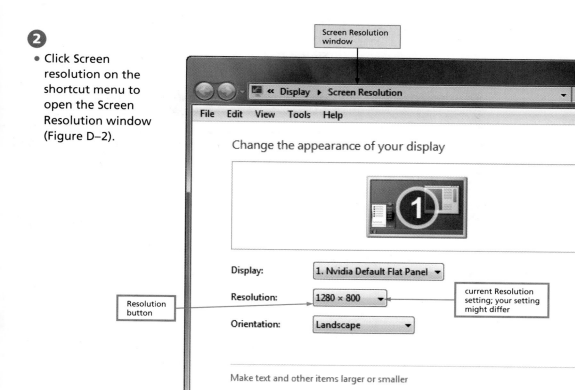

Figure D–2

- Click the Resolution button to display a list of resolution settings for your monitor.

- If necessary, drag the Resolution slider so that the screen resolution is set to 1024 × 768 (Figure D–3).

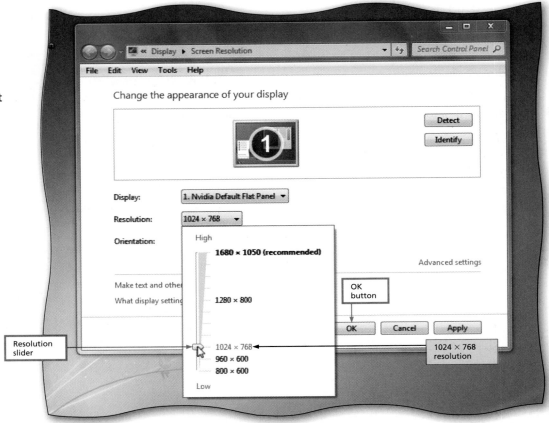

Figure D–3

- Click the OK button to set the screen resolution to 1024 × 768.

- Click the Keep changes button in the Display Settings dialog box to accept the new screen resolution (Figure D–4).

Figure D–4

Quick Reference Summary

In the Adobe Dreamweaver CS5 program, you can accomplish a task in a number of ways. The following table provides a quick reference to each task presented in this textbook. The first column identifies the task. The second column indicates the page number on which the task is discussed in the book. The subsequent four columns list the different ways the task in column one can be carried out.

Adobe Dreamweaver CS5 Quick Reference Summary

Task	Page Number	Mouse	Menu	Context Menu	Keyboard Shortcut
Absolute link, create	DW 155	Link text box in Property inspector	Insert | Hyperlink	Make Link	
Accordion widget, insert	DW 594	Click Spry Accordion button on Layout tab	Insert | Spry | Spry Accordion		
Accordion widget, set width	DW 601	In CSS Styles panel, expand style rule for widget, click .Accordion rule, click width, enter width in pixels			
Active X audio file, embed on Web page	DW 650	Click Media button arrow on Insert bar, click ActiveX, enter ClassID, click Embed check box, click Browse for File icon, select audio file	Insert | Media | ActiveX, enter ClassID, click Embed check box, click Browse for File icon, select audio file		
Add animated GIF to Web page	DW 664	Drag GIF file from Files panel or Assets panel to Web page			
Add Flash movie to Web page	DW 635	Drag SWF file from Files panel or Assets panel to Web page			
Add panel to Tabbed Panels widget	DW 573	Click widget, click Add panel button in Property inspector			
Add sound to Web page	DW 642	Click Media button arrow on Insert bar, click Plugin, select file	Insert | Media | Plugin		
Add video to Web page	DW 657	Click Media button arrow on Insert bar, click ActiveX, enter ClassID, click Embed check box, click Browse for File icon, select video file	Insert | Media | ActiveX, enter ClassID, click Embed check box, click Browse for File icon, select video file		

Adobe Dreamweaver CS5 Quick Reference Summary *(continued)*

Task	Page Number	Mouse	Menu	Context Menu	Keyboard Shortcut
Adobe BrowserLab, preview Web page with	DW 685		Window | Extensions | Adobe BrowserLab, click Preview button in Adobe BrowserLab panel *or* File | Preview in Browser | Adobe BrowserLab		
Align image	DW 128	Align button in Property inspector		Align	
Align table	DW 195	Align button in Property inspector	Format | Align	Align	
Alt text, specify for image	DW 125	Alt text box in Property inspector *or* drag image to page, enter Alt text (Image Tag Accessibility Attributes dialog box)			
Animated GIF, add to Web page	DW 664	Drag GIF file from Files panel or Assets panel to Web page			
AP Div, draw	DW 359	Click Draw AP Div button on Layout tab, draw AP element	Insert | Layout Objects | AP Div		
AP element, add image to	DW 363	Drag image to AP element			
AP element, insert	DW 359	Click Draw AP Div button on Layout tab, draw AP element	Insert | Layout Objects | AP Div		
AP element, name	DW 362	Click CSS-P Element text box, type name *or* Double-click element name in AP Elements panel			
AP Elements panel, display	DW 361	Click AP Elements tab in panel groups	Window | AP Elements		
AP elements, stack	DW 365	Draw AP elements so they overlap			
Apply background image to page	DW 60	Page Properties button in Property inspector	Modify | Page Properties	Page Properties	CTRL+J
Apply Spry effect to Web page element	DW 604	Click element, click Add behavior button in Behaviors panel, point to Effects, click effect			
Asset, add to Favorites List	DW 314	Select asset, click Add to Favorites button			
Assets panel, display	DW 124	Click Assets panel tab			
Assets panel, open or close	DW 124	Double-click Assets panel tab	Window | Assets		

Adobe Dreamweaver CS5 Quick Reference Summary *(continued)*

Task	Page Number	Mouse	Menu	Context Menu	Keyboard Shortcut
Audio file, embed on Web page	DW 650	Click Media button arrow on Insert bar, click ActiveX, enter ClassID, click Embed check box, click Browse for File icon, select audio file	Insert | Media | ActiveX, enter ClassID, click Embed check box, click Browse for File icon, select audio file		
Background, add to page	DW 60	Page Properties button in Property inspector	Modify | Page Properties	Page Properties	CTRL+J
Background color, change for Flash object	DW 632	Click Flash object, click Wmode button in Property inspector, click window, enter color value			
Background color, change for Menu Bar widget	DW 538	In CSS Styles panel, expand style rule for widget, click ul.MenuBarHorizontal a or ul.MenuBarVertical l a rule, change background-color property in CSS Styles panel			
Background color, change for Tabbed Panels widget	DW 586	In CSS Styles panel, expand style rule for widget, click .TabbedPanelsTab rule, click background-color box, select color			
Behavior, add for validating form	DW 476	Click Add behavior button in Behaviors panel, click Validate Form			
Behavior, add to hotspot	DW 378	Click Add behavior button in Behaviors panel, click behavior			
Behaviors panel, display	DW 377	Tag Inspector tab in panel groups, Behavior button	Window | Behaviors		
Block quote, create	DW 67	Remove Blockquote (Text Outdent) button in Property inspector	Format | Indent	List | Indent	CTRL+ALT+]
Block quote, remove	DW 67	Remove Blockquote (Text Outdent) button in Property inspector	Format | Outdent	List | Outdent	CTRL+ALT+[
Bold, apply to text	DW 67, DW 73	Bold button in Property inspector	Format | Style | Bold	Style	CTRL+B
Border, add or change for table	DW 235	Border text box in Property inspector			
Border, add to image	DW 235	Border text box in Property inspector			
Brightness and contrast, adjust for image	DW 144	Brightness and Contrast tool in Property inspector	Modify | Image | Brightness/Contrast		

Adobe Dreamweaver CS5 Quick Reference Summary (continued)

Task	Page Number	Mouse	Menu	Context Menu	Keyboard Shortcut
BrowserLab, preview Web page with	DW 685		Window | Extensions | Adobe BrowserLab, click Preview button in Adobe BrowserLab panel *or* File | Preview in Browser | Adobe BrowserLab		
Browsers, select	DW 81		Edit | Preferences | Preview in Browser		
Bulleted list, create	DW 67, DW 72	Unordered List button in Property inspector	Format | List | Unordered List	List | Unordered List	
Button, add to form	DW 459	Click Forms tab on Insert bar, click Button button	Insert | Form | Button		
Cell padding, set for table	DW 194	CellPad text box in Property inspector			
Cell spacing, set for table	DW 194	CellSpace text box in Property inspector			
Cell, change height in table	DW 197	H text box in Property inspector *or* drag cell border			
Cell, change horizontal alignment in table	DW 209	Horz button in Property inspector	Format | Align	Align	
Cell, change vertical alignment in table	DW 203	Vert button in Property inspector	Format | Align	Align	
Cell, change width in table	DW 197	W text box in Property inspector *or* drag cell border			
Center text	DW 70		Format | Align | Center	Align | Center	CTRL+ALT+SHIFT+C
Change background color for Menu Bar widget	DW 538	In CSS Styles panel, expand style rule for widget, click ul.MenuBarHorizontal a or ul.MenuBarVertical a rule, change background-color property in CSS Styles panel			
Change menu item names in Menu Bar widget	DW 528	Click Menu Bar widget, click Item *x* in Property inspector, change text in Text box *or* Select menu item name in Document window, change text			
Change menu names in Menu Bar widget	DW 524	Click Menu Bar widget, click menu name in Property inspector, change text in Text box *or* Select menu bar name in Document window, change text			

Adobe Dreamweaver CS5 Quick Reference Summary (continued)

Task	Page Number	Mouse	Menu	Context Menu	Keyboard Shortcut
Change order of panel in Tabbed Panels widget	DW 577	Click widget name tab, click panel in Panels list box, click 'Move panel down in list' button or 'Move panel up in list' button			
Check box, add to form	DW 438	Click Forms tab on Insert bar, click Checkbox button	Insert | Form | Checkbox		
Check links for Web site	DW 662		Window | Results | Link Checker, click Check Links button or File | Check Page | Links		SHIFT+F9
Check spelling	DW 79		Commands | Check Spelling		SHIFT+F7
Classic workspace, switch to	DW 37	Workspace switcher arrow on Application bar	Window | Workspace Layout		
Clear column widths for table	DW 204	Clear Column Widths button in Property inspector	Modify | Table | Clear Cell Widths	Clear All Widths	
Clear row heights for table	DW 204	Clear Row Heights button in Property inspector	Modify | Table | Clear Cell Heights	Clear All Heights	
Collapse Property inspector	DW 66	Double-click title bar	Window | Properties	Minimize	CTRL+F3
Collapsible Panel widget, add panel heading to	DW 511	Double-click placeholder text on tab, enter text			
Collapsible Panel widget, insert	DW 506	Click Spry Collapsible Panel button on Layout tab	Insert | Spry | Spry Collapsible Panel		
Column, change horizontal alignment in table	DW 209	Horz button in Property inspector	Format | Align	Align	
Column, change vertical alignment in table	DW 203	Vert button in Property inspector	Format | Align	Align	
Column, delete in table	DW 215	Modify | Table | Delete Column		Table | Delete Column	DEL
Column, insert in table	DW 215		Modify | Table | Insert Column	Table | Insert Column	TAB
Columns, set for table	DW 194	Table dialog box or Cols text box in Property inspector			
Contrast, adjust for image	DW 144	Brightness and Contrast tool in Property inspector	Modify | Image | Brightness/Contrast		
Convert table width	DW 196	Convert Table Widths to Pixels button or Convert Table Widths to Percent button in Property inspector	Modify | Table | Convert Width to Pixels or Convert Width to Percent		

Adobe Dreamweaver CS5 Quick Reference Summary (continued)

Task	Page Number	Mouse	Menu	Context Menu	Keyboard Shortcut
Create site	DW 47		Site | New Site		
Create page	DW 86	Options menu button on Files panel | File | New File	File | New	New File	CTRL+N
Create Web page with CSS Starter layout	DW 690	Click New button, click layout in Layout list	File | New, click layout in Layout list		
Crop image	DW 142	Crop tool in Property inspector	Modify | Image | Crop		
CSS Inspect, use to inspect Web page	DW 695	Click Inspect button, click Switch now			
CSS rule, create for new style	DW 299	Create new CSS style, click OK, click style category in CSS Rule definition dialog box			
CSS Starter layout, use to create Web page	DW 690	Click New button, click layout in Layout list	File | New, click layout in Layout list		
CSS Style, add to new external style sheet	DW 298	New CSS Rule button in CSS Styles panel, Rule Definition button, (New Style Sheet File)			
CSS Style, create	DW 297	New CSS Rule button in CSS Styles panel	Format | CSS Styles | New	Format | CSS Styles | New	
CSS style, display properties for	DW 307	Click 'Show information about selected property' button in About section of CSS Styles panel			
CSS style, remove	DW 311	Delete CSS Rule button in CSS Styles panel			
CSS Styles panel, display	DW 296	CSS Styles tab in panel groups	Window | CSS Styles		SHIFT+F11
Date object, insert	DW 392	Click Date button on Common tab of Insert bar	Insert | Date		
Default file name extension, set	DW 57	Edit | Preferences, New Document (Preferences dialog box)			
Definition list, create	DW 67	Format | List | Definition List	List | Definition List		
Delete page	DW 65			Edit | Delete	DEL
Description, add to page	DW 243		Insert | HTML | Head Tags | Keywords		
Design view, display	DW 38	Design button on Document toolbar	View | Design		
Disable Welcome screen	DW 85		Edit | Preferences | General		
Document, save	DW 58	Save button on Standard toolbar	File | Save or File | Save As	Save or Save As	CTRL+S CTRL+SHIFT+S
Dreamweaver, quit	DW 85	Close button	File | Exit		CTRL+Q
Dreamweaver, start	DW 37	Dreamweaver icon on desktop	Start | All Programs | Adobe Dreamweaver CS5		

Adobe Dreamweaver CS5 Quick Reference Summary *(continued)*

Task	Page Number	Mouse	Menu	Context Menu	Keyboard Shortcut
Edit site	DW 54	Sites pop-up menu button on Files panel, Manage Sites, site name, Edit button	Site | Manage Sites, *site name*, Edit button		
Editable region, create	DW 287	Click Templates button arrow on Common tab of Insert bar, click Editable Region	Insert | Template Objects | Editable Region	Templates | New Editable Region	CTRL+ALT+V
Effect, apply to Web page element	DW 604	Click element, click Add behavior button in Behaviors panel, point to Effects, click effect			
E-mail link, create	DW 156	Link text box in Property inspector	Insert | Email Link	Make Link	
Embed audio file on Web page	DW 650	Click Media button arrow on Insert bar, click ActiveX, enter ClassID, click Embed check box, click Browse for File icon, select audio file	Insert | Media | ActiveX, enter ClassID, click Embed check box, click Browse for File icon, select audio file		
Embed video on to Web page	DW 657	Click Media button arrow on Insert bar, click ActiveX, enter ClassID, click Embed check box, click Browse for File icon, select video file	Insert | Media | ActiveX, enter ClassID, click Embed check box, click Browse for File icon, select video file		
Expand Property inspector	DW 66	Double-click title bar	Window | Properties	Expand Panel	CTRL+F3
Favorites List, add asset to	DW 314	Select asset, click Add to Favorites button			
Files panel, collapse	DW 126	Collapse to Icons		Collapse to Icons	
Files panel, expand	DW 126	Expand Panels		Expand Panels	
Files panel, open or close	DW 147	Double-click Files panel tab	Window | Files	Close	F8
Flash movie, add to Web page	DW 635	Drag SWF file from Files panel or Assets panel to Web page			
Flash movie, play	DW 636	Click Flash movie object, click Play button in Property inspector			
Flash object, add to Web page	DW 628	Drag SWF file from Files panel or Assets panel to Web page			
Flash object, change background color	DW 632	Click Flash object, click Wmode button in Property inspector, click window, enter color value			

Adobe Dreamweaver CS5 Quick Reference Summary *(continued)*

Task	Page Number	Mouse	Menu	Context Menu	Keyboard Shortcut
Font, change for Menu Bar widget	DW 535	In CSS Styles panel, expand style rule for widget, click ul.MenuBarHorizontal li or ul.MenuBarVertical li rule, change background-color property in CSS Styles panel			
Form, insert	DW 419	Click Forms tab on Insert bar, click Form button	Insert | Form | Form		
Format, apply to paragraph	DW 66	Format button in Property inspector	Format | Paragraph Format	Paragraph Format	
Format Tabbed Panels widget text	DW 582	In CSS Styles panel, expand style rule for widget, click .TabbedPanelsContent rule, change font properties in CSS Styles panel			
Heading 1, create	DW 68	Format button in Property inspector	Format | Paragraph Format | Heading 1	Paragraph Format | Heading 1	CTRL+1
Height, change for image	DW 130	H text box in Property inspector *or* drag sizing handle			
Help	DW 84		Help | Dreamweaver Help		F1
History panel, display	DW 389	History tab in panel groups	Window | History		SHIFT+F10
Horizontal rule, insert	DW 416		Insert | HTML | Horizontal Rule		
Horizontal space, increase or decrease around image	DW 130	H Space text box in Property inspector			
Hotspot, add Show-Hide behavior to	DW 377	Click Add behavior button in Behaviors panel, click Show-Hide Elements			
Hotspot, create	DW 374	Click hotspot tool, draw hotspot			
Icon color, turn on or off	DW 44		View | Color Icons	Color Icons	
Image brightness or contrast, adjust	DW 142	Brightness and Contrast tool in Property inspector	Modify | Image | Brightness/Contrast		
Image height, change	DW 130	H text box in Property inspector *or* drag sizing handle			
Image placeholder, insert	DW 283		Insert | Image Objects | Image Placeholder		
Image width, change	DW 130	W text box in Property inspector *or* drag sizing handle			
Image, add to AP element	DW 363	Drag image to AP element			

Adobe Dreamweaver CS5 Quick Reference Summary *(continued)*

Task	Page Number	Mouse	Menu	Context Menu	Keyboard Shortcut
Image, align	DW 129	Align button in Property inspector		Align	
Image, crop	DW 142	Crop tool in Property inspector	Modify | Image | Crop		
Image, insert into page	DW 124	Drag image from Assets panel or Files panel	Insert | Image	Insert	CTRL+ALT+I
Image, specify Alt text image	DW 125	Alt text box in Property inspector *or* drag image to page, enter Alt text (Image Tag Accessibility Attributes dialog box)			
Indent text	DW 67	Blockquote (Text Indent) button in Property inspector	Format | Indent	List	CTRL+ALT+]
Insert Spry Accordion widget	DW 594	Click Spry Accordion button on Layout tab	Insert | Spry | Spry Accordion		
Insert Spry Collapsible Panel widget	DW 506	Click Spry Collapsible Panel button on Layout tab	Insert | Spry | Spry Collapsible Panel		
Insert Spry Menu Bar widget	DW 521	Click Spry Menu Bar button on Layout tab	Insert | Spry | Spry Menu Bar		
Insert Spry Tabbed Panels widget	DW 569	Click Spry Tabbed Panels button on Layout tab	Insert | Spry | Spry Tabbed Panels		
Insert Spry Tooltip widget	DW 560	Click Spry Tooltip button on Layout tab	Insert | Spry| Spry Tooltip		
Insert text using Paste Special command	DW 514		Edit | Paste Special		CTRL+SHIFT+V,
Inspect Web page with CSS Inspect	DW 695	Click Inspect button, click Switch now			
Insert bar, display	DW 38		Window | Insert		CTRL+F2
Insert bar, display as menu	DW 40			Show as Menu	
Invisible Element preferences, set	DW 119	Visual Aids button on Document toolbar, click Invisible Elements	Edit | Preferences | Invisible Elements		
Italic, apply to text	DW 67	Italic button in Property inspector	Format | Style	Style	CTRL+I
Jump menu, add to form	DW 451	Click Forms tab on Insert bar, click Jump Menu button	Insert | Form | Jump Menu		
Keywords, add to page	DW 242		Insert | HTML | Head Tags | Keywords		
Layout tab, display in Insert bar		Layout tab on Insert bar			
Line break, insert	DW 74		Insert | HTML | Special Characters | Line Break	Insert HTML | br	SHIFT+ENTER
Link target, specify	DW 322	Click link, click Target box arrow, click target type			

Adobe Dreamweaver CS5 Quick Reference Summary *(continued)*

Task	Page Number	Mouse	Menu	Context Menu	Keyboard Shortcut
Link text, format	DW 309	Page Properties button, Links (CSS) category			
Link, create	DW 67, DW 147	Link text box in Property inspector	Insert | Hyperlink	Make Link	
Link, delete	DW 159	Link text box in Property inspector		Remove Link	
Link, edit	DW 159	Link text box in Property inspector		Change Link	
Links, change color of	DW 159	Page Properties button in Property inspector	Modify | Page Properties	Page Properties	CTRL+J
Links, check for Web site	DW 662		Window | Results | Link Checker, click Check Links button *or* File | Check Page | Links		SHIFT+F9
List box, add to form	DW 443	Click Forms tab on Insert bar, click Select (List/Menu) button	Insert | Form | Select (List/Menu)		
List item, set properties for	DW 67	List Item button in Property inspector	Format | List | Properties	List | Properties	
Live view, display	DW 161	Live View button on Document toolbar	View | Live View		ALT+F11
Looping, turn off for Flash object	DW 632	Click Flash object, click Loop check box in Property inspector			
Menu, add to form	DW 443	Click Forms tab on Insert bar, click Select (List/Menu) button	Insert | Form | Select (List/Menu)		
Menu Bar widget, change background color	DW 538	In CSS Styles panel, expand style rule for widget, click ul.MenuBarHorizontal a or ul.MenuBarVertical a rule, change background-color property in CSS Styles panel			
Menu Bar widget, change menu item names	DW 528	Click Menu Bar widget, click Item *x* in Property inspector, change text in Text box *or* Select menu item name in Document window, change text			
Menu Bar widget, change menu names	DW 524	Click Menu Bar widget, click menu name in Property inspector, change text in Text box *or* Select menu bar name in Document window, change text			

Adobe Dreamweaver CS5 Quick Reference Summary (continued)

Task	Page Number	Mouse	Menu	Context Menu	Keyboard Shortcut
Menu Bar widget, customize font	DW 535	In CSS Styles panel, expand style rule for widget, click ul.Menu Bar Horizontal li or ul.MenuBarVertical li rule, change font properties in CSS Styles panel			
Menu Bar widget, insert	DW 521	Click Spry Menu Bar button on Layout tab	Insert | Spry | Spry Menu Bar		
Merge cells in table	DW 215	Merges selected cells using spans button in Property inspector	Modify | Table | Merge Cells	Table | Merge Cells	CTRL+ALT+M
Numbered list, create	DW 67	Ordered List button in Property inspector	Format | List | Ordered List	List | Ordered List	
Open page	DW 85	Double-click page in Files panel	File | Open *or* File | Open Recent	Open	CTRL+O
Ordered list, create	DW 67	Ordered List button in Property inspector	Format | List | Ordered List	List | Ordered List	
Outdent text	DW 67	Remove Blockquote (Text Outdent) button in Property inspector	Format | Outdent	List	CTRL+ALT+[
Page, create	DW 86	Options menu button on Files panel | File | New File	File | New	New File	CTRL+SHIFT+N
Page, delete	DW 65			Edit | Delete	DEL
Page, open	DW 85	Double-click page in Files panel	File | Open *or* File | Open Recent	Open	CTRL+O
Page title, enter	DW 77	Title text box on Document toolbar			
Panel, add to Tabbed Panels widget	DW 573	Click widget, click Add panel button in Property inspector			
Panel, change order of in Tabbed Panels widget	DW 577	Click widget name tab, click panel in Panels list box, click 'Move panel down in list' button or 'Move panel up in list' button			
Panel heading, add to Collapsible Panel widget	DW 511	Double-click placeholder text on tab, enter text			
Panel, set as default in Tabbed Panels widget	DW 578	Click widget name tab, click panel in Panels list box, click Default panel button			
Panels, open or close	DW 44		Window | Hide Panels	Close Tab Group	F4
Paragraph, center	DW 70		Format | Align | Center	Align | Center	CTRL+ALT+SHIFT+C
Paste Special command, use to insert text	DW 514		Edit | Paste Special		CTRL+SHIFT+V,
Placeholder, insert for image	DW 283		Insert | Image Objects | Image Placeholder		

Adobe Dreamweaver CS5 Quick Reference Summary (continued)

Task	Page Number	Mouse	Menu	Context Menu	Keyboard Shortcut
Play Flash movie	DW 636	Click Flash movie object, click Play button in Property inspector			
Plugin, add to Web page	DW 642	Click Media button arrow on Insert bar, click Plugin, select file	Insert	Media	Plugin		
Pop-up menu, add to form	DW 447	Click Forms tab on Insert bar, click Select (List/Menu) button	Insert	Form	Select (List/Menu)		
Preview Web page	DW 83		File	Preview in Browser	Preview in Browser	F12 CTRL+F12
Preview Web page with Adobe BrowserLab	DW 685		Window	Extensions	Adobe BrowserLab, click Preview button in Adobe BrowserLab panel *or* File	Preview in Browser	Adobe BrowserLab		
Primary browser, select	DW 81		Edit	Preferences	Preview in Browser		
Property inspector, collapse or expand	DW 66	Double-click title bar	Window	Properties	Minimize/Expand Panel	CTRL+F3
Property inspector, expand	DW 186	Property inspector expander arrow			
Quick Tag Editor, use	DW 159			Quick Tag Editor	CTRL+T
Quit Dreamweaver	DW 85	Close button	File	Exit		CTRL+Q
Radio group, add to form	DW 469	Click Forms tab on Insert bar, click Radio Group button	Insert	Form	Radio Group		
Relative link, create	DW 67, DW 147	Link text box in Property inspector *or* Point to File tool in Property inspector *or* Browse icon next to Link text box in Property inspector	Insert	Hyperlink	Make Link	SHIFT+drag to file
Remove site	DW 54	Sites pop-up menu button on Files panel, Manage Sites, *site name*, Remove button	Site	Manage Sites, site name, Remove button		
Reset button, add to form	DW 458	Click Forms tab on Insert bar, click Button button	Insert	Form	Button		
Row, change horizontal alignment in table	DW 209	Horz button in Property inspector	Format	Align	Align	
Row, change vertical alignment in table	DW 203	Vert button in Property inspector	Format	Align	Align	
Row, delete in table	DW 215		Modify	Table	Delete Row	Table	Delete Row	CTRL+SHIFT+M
Row, insert in table	DW 215		Modify	Table	Insert Row	Table	Insert Row	CTRL+M

Adobe Dreamweaver CS5 Quick Reference Summary *(continued)*

Task	Page Number	Mouse	Menu	Context Menu	Keyboard Shortcut
Rows, set for table	DW 194	Table dialog box *or* Rows text box in Property inspector			
Rule (line), insert horizontal	DW 416		Insert | HTML | Horizontal Rule		
Rule, create for new CSS style	DW 299	Create new CSS style, click OK, click style category in CSS Rule Definition dialog box			
Rulers, display	DW 354		View | Rulers | Show		
Rulers, show or hide	DW 56		View | Rulers | Show		CTRL+ALT+R
Save document	DW 58	Save button on Standard toolbar	File | Save *or* File | Save As	Save *or* Save As	CTRL+S CTRL+SHIFT+S
Secondary browser, select	DW 81		Edit | Preferences | Preview in Browser		
Select (List/Menu) object, add to form	DW 443	Click Forms tab on Insert bar, click Select (List/Menu) button	Insert | Form | Select (List/Menu)		
Set default panel in Tabbed Panels widget	DW 578	Click widget name tab, click panel in Panels list box, click Default panel button			
Shake effect, apply to Web page element	DW 604	Click element, click Add behavior button in Behaviors panel, point to Effects, click Shake			
Show-Hide Elements behavior, add to hotspot	DW 377	Click Add behavior button in Behaviors panel, click Show-Hide Elements			
Site, create	DW 47		Site | New Site		
Site, edit	DW 54	Sites pop-up menu button on Files panel, Manage Sites, site name, Edit button	Site | Manage Sites, site name, Edit button		
Site, remove	DW 54	Sites pop-up menu button on Files panel, Manage Sites, site name, Remove button	Site | Manage Sites, site name, Remove button		
Sound, add to Web page	DW 642	Click Media button arrow on Insert bar, click Plugin, select file	Insert | Media | Plugin		
Special character, insert	DW 78		Insert | HTML | Special Characters		
Spelling, check spelling	DW 79		Commands | Check Spelling		SHIFT+F7
Split cells in table	DW 215	Splits cell into rows or columns button in Property inspector	Modify | Table | Split Cell	Table | Split Cells	CTRL+ALT+S
Split view, display	DW 160	Split View button on Document toolbar	View | Code and Design		
Spry Accordion widget, insert	DW 594	Click Spry Accordion button on Layout tab	Insert | Spry | Spry Accordion		

Adobe Dreamweaver CS5 Quick Reference Summary *(continued)*

Task	Page Number	Mouse	Menu	Context Menu	Keyboard Shortcut
Spry Accordion widget, set width	DW 601	In CSS Styles panel, expand style rule for widget, click Accordion rule, click width, enter width in pixels			
Spry Collapsible Panel widget, insert	DW 506	Click Spry Collapsible Panel button on Layout tab	Insert | Spry | Spry Collapsible Panel		
Spry effect, apply to Web page element	DW 604	Click element, click Add behavior button in Behaviors panel, point to Effects, click effect			
Spry Menu Bar widget, insert	DW 521	Click Spry Menu Bar button on Layout tab	Insert | Spry | Spry Menu Bar		
Spry Tabbed Panels widget, insert	DW 569	Click Spry Tabbed Panels button on Layout tab	Insert | Spry | Spry Tabbed Panels		
Spry Tooltip widget, insert	DW 560	Click Spry Tooltip button on Layout tab	Insert | Spry | Spry Tooltip		
Squish effect, apply to Web page element	DW 606	Click element, click Add behavior button in Behaviors panel, point to Effects, click Squish			
Stacked AP elements, create	DW 365	Draw AP elements so they overlap			
Stacked AP elements, select	DW 369	Click element name in AP Elements panel *or* click AP element's selection handle			CTRL+SHIFT+click
Style, create	DW 297	New CSS Rule button in CSS Styles panel	Format | CSS Styles | New		
Style, remove	DW 311	Delete CSS Rule button in CSS Styles panel			
Submit button, add to form	DW 458	Click Forms tab on Insert bar, click Button button	Insert | Form | Button		
SWF Flash object, add to Web page	DW 628	Drag SWF file from Files panel or Assets panel to Web page			
Tabbed Panels, change order of panel in	DW 577	Click widget name tab, click panel in Panels list box, click 'Move panel down in list' button or 'Move panel up in list' button			
Tabbed Panels widget background color, change	DW 586	In CSS Styles panel, expand style rule for widget, click .TabbedPanelsTab rule, click background-color box, select color			
Tabbed Panels widget, add panel to	DW 573	Click widget, click Add panel button in Property inspector			
Tabbed Panels widget, insert	DW 569	Click Spry Tabbed Panels button on Layout tab	Insert | Spry | Spry Tabbed Panels		

Adobe Dreamweaver CS5 Quick Reference Summary *(continued)*

Task	Page Number	Mouse	Menu	Context Menu	Keyboard Shortcut
Tabbed Panels widget, set default panel in	DW 578	Click widget name tab, click panel in Panels list box, click Default panel button			
Tabbed Panels widget, set width	DW 592	In CSS Styles panel, expand style rule for widget, click .Tabbed Panels rule, click width, enter width in pixels			
Tabbed Panels widget text, format	DW 582	In CSS Styles panel, expand style rule for widget, click.Tabbed Panels Content rule, change font properties in CSS Styles panel			
Table cell, change height	DW 197	H text box in Property inspector			
Table cell, change width	DW 197	W text box in Property inspector			
Table ID, enter or change	DW 206	ID text box in Property inspector			
Table, delete	DW 216	Click table tag, press DEL			
Table, insert	DW 194	Table button on Layout tab or Common tab of Insert bar	Insert | Table		CTRL+ALT+T
Target, specify for link	DW 322	Click link, click Target box arrow, click target type			
Template, apply to Web page	DW 314	Click Templates icon in Assets panel, click template, click Apply button	Modify | Templates | Apply Template to Page | select template		
Template, create	DW 272		File | New | Blank Template		
Text area field, add to form	DW 456	Click Forms tab on Insert bar, click Text area button	Insert | Form | Text area		
Text, center	DW 70	Format | Align | Center	Align | Center		CTRL+ALT+SHIFT+C
Text field, add to form	DW 431	Click Forms tab on Insert bar, click Text Field button			
Text, format in Tabbed Panels widget	DW 582	In CSS Styles panel, expand style rule for widget, click .TabbedPanelsContent rule, change font properties in CSS Styles panel			
Title, enter for page	DW 77	Title text box on Document toolbar			
Toolbar, add or remove	DW 38		View | Toolbars	Toolbars	
Tooltip widget, insert	DW 560	Click Spry Tooltip button on Layout tab	Insert | Spry | Spry Tooltip		

Adobe Dreamweaver CS5 Quick Reference Summary (continued)

Task	Page Number	Mouse	Menu	Context Menu	Keyboard Shortcut
Turn off looping for Flash object	DW 632	Click Flash object, click Loop check box in Property inspector			
Unordered list, create	DW 67, DW 72	Unordered List button in Property inspector	Format | List | Unordered List	List | Unordered List	
Validate form behavior, add to form	DW 476	Click Add behavior button in Behaviors panel, click Validate Form			
Vertical space, increase or decrease around image	DW 135	V Space text box in Property inspector			
Video, add to Web page	DW 657	Click Media button arrow on Insert bar, click ActiveX, enter ClassID, click Embed check box, click Browse for File icon, select video file	Insert | Media | ActiveX, enter ClassID, click Embed check box, click Browse for File icon, select video file		
Visual Aids, show or hide	DW 119	Visual Aids button on Document toolbar	View | Visual Aids		CTRL+SHIFT+I
Web page, apply template to	DW 314	Click Templates icon in Assets panel, click template, click Apply button	Modify | Templates | Apply Template to Page | select template		
Web page, preview in browser	DW 83		File | Preview in Browser	Preview in Browser	F12 CTRL+F12
Welcome screen, disable	DW 85		Edit | Preferences | General		
Width, change for image	DW 130	W text box in Property inspector or drag sizing handle			
Width, set for Spry Accordion widget	DW 601	In CSS Styles panel, expand style rule for widget, click .Accordion rule, click width, enter width in pixels			
Width, set for Tabbed Panels widget	DW 592	In CSS Styles panel, expand style rule for widget, click .TabbedPanels rule, click width, enter width in pixels			
Width, set for table	DW 212	W text box in Property inspector			

Index